PC MAGAZINE
PROGRAMMER'S TECHNICAL REFERENCE:
THE PROCESSOR AND COPROCESSOR

PC MAGAZINE PROGRAMMER'S TECHNICAL REFERENCE: THE PROCESSOR AND COPROCESSOR

Robert L. Hummel

Ziff-Davis Press
Emeryville, California

Editor	Terry Somerson
Technical Reviewer	Jim Mack
Project Coordinator	Sheila McGill
Editorial Assistant	Noelle Graney
Proofreader	Jeff Barash
Cover Design	Tom Morgan/Blue Design, San Francisco
Book Design	Peter Tucker
Technical Illustration	Cherie Plumlee Computer Graphics & Illustration
Word Processing	Howard Blechman, Kim Haglund
Page Layout	Kevin Shafer & Associates, Bruce Lundquist, Sidney Davenport
Indexer	Ted Laux

This book was produced on a Macintosh IIfx, with the following applications: FrameMaker®, Microsoft® Word, MacLink®*Plus*, Aldus® FreeHand™, and Collage Plus™.

Ziff-Davis Press
5903 Christie Avenue
Emeryville, CA 94608

ISBN 1-56276-016-5
Manufactured in the United States of America
10 9 8 7 6 5 4 3 2 1

To my wife (my biggest supporter) who said,
"Who are you kidding? There's another thing
you're never gonna do."
And to Schaefer, Wendy, and Gwendolyn
who sustained me at the keyboard with love
and never complained.

CONTENTS AT A GLANCE

≡ TABLE OF CONTENTS

ᗕ ACKNOWLEDGMENTS

A WORK OF THIS SIZE AND COMPLEXITY IS THE RESULT OF DEDICATED, HARD work by a large number of people. In particular, I thank Cindy Hudson, Sheila McGill, and Cheryl Holzaepfel of Ziff-Davis Press. The result of their willingness to break the rules to produce a better product is obvious.

I have also been fortunate enough to know and work with some of the brightest and best in the personal computer industry. These gentlemen, who work on what is often called the "bleeding edge" of technology, were gracious enough to share their time, expertise, and quality hardware and software products with me. In particular, my gratitude goes to Frank van Gilluwe (V Communications), Frank Grossman (NuMega Technologies), Rob Larsen (Larsen Computing), Paul Passarelli (Crescent Software), Brett Salter (The Periscope Company), and Bob Smith (Qualitas). You'll find more information on their products in Appendix D.

I'm also indebted to the fine folks at WordPerfect Corporation in Orem, Utah. This manuscript was written and prepared using WordPerfect 5.1 running under DOS 5.0. Notwithstanding the alleged virtues of other products and environments, without WordPerfect 5.1's ability to create and edit tables and complex equations effortlessly, creating most of this book, and the appendices in particular, would have been nearly impossible.

⬛ INTRODUCTION

*I believe the gentleman is a computer
expert. Obviously he might have a
computer or two—who knows?*
Henry Darrow, Host of JackPot Bingo
Los Angeles, California 1986

MY OBJECTIVE FOR THIS BOOK WAS TO PROVIDE A COMPLETE, NO-NONSENSE
reference guide to the Intel series of processors and coprocessors. To that end
I've included information that ranges from descriptions of the internal architecture of the CPUs to lists of processor bugs to undocumented opcodes and
instructions. The theme of the book is simply, "Here's all the technical reference
material for programming the 80x86 and 80x87 you'll ever need."

My target audience is programmers of all languages and skill levels. Let's
face facts: eventually, *everyone* programs in assembly language. It's no coinci-
dence that almost all BASIC, Pascal, and C compilers provide some means of
calling assembly routines or using assembly mnemonics in-line. The latest and
greatest C++ compiler even includes an assembler in the package! Even so, the
popularity and usefulness of assembly is traditionally understated. Regardless of
their language of choice, all programmers need a good reference on the chip and
how it works.

In my role as senior technical editor of *PC Magazine,* I had to be familiar
with a vast assortment of hardware, software, and compatibility issues to ensure
that our assembly-language utilities would run successfully on our readers' computers. Often that meant poring through dozens of separate reference manuals,
hardware guides, OEM documentation, and underground bug lists. Having a
single reference like this one that listed chip-specific details and bugs would
have made that job a lot easier.

How to best use this book is up to you and will depend on your programming experience. Read it from beginning to end to get an overview of the workings, instruction set, and operation modes of the processor and coprocessor. Or
you may skip to a chapter that interests you or has a solution for a particular
problem you're trying to solve (formulas showing how to use the FPTAN function to derive the other trigonometric functions in Chapter 12, for example).

Fast access to reference material is essential for any programming book.
You'll find that this book contains comprehensive guides to the entire Intel

80x86 and 80x87 instruction set as well as the instructions provided by compatible chips by other manufacturers. I think you'll find that the design of Appendices A and B makes it easy to look up an instruction and find the information you need.

You'll need to understand, of course, what binary, hexadecimal, and decimal numbers are and be able to convert simple numbers between bases (for example, 1011 binary = 11 decimal = B hexadecimal). A short review of these principles, however, is included in this Introduction.

If possible, all information in this book was confirmed on a variety of computer systems, including a 80486DX, 80386DX (early and late steps), 80286, 8088, V20, 80387SX, 80287XL, and an 80287. The instruction timings, as mentioned, are from the latest versions of the Intel data sheets for the chips. Timings for other products were obtained from their manufacturers.

So who is this book for? It's for you—the person who wants to know the why of the processor as well as the how, who has a passion for creating, is willing to learn new techniques, and can hear the word "undocumented" whispered across a crowded room.

Conventions

Throughout this book, new terms and symbols are defined and explained as they are encountered in the text. The thorough index also serves as a quick reference. Finally, certain conventions were followed in presenting the details of processor operation, data structures, instruction encodings, and numeric procedures. These conventions are explained in this section.

Number Systems

When discussing the operation of the processor, explanations often required the use of three different number systems: binary, decimal, and hexadecimal. The following conventions are used for all numeric data presented in this book.

Decimal Numbers Unless otherwise indicated, all numbers shown in the text are decimal (base 10). For example, if the statement is made that there are 256 available interrupt vectors, the number 256 should be assumed to be a decimal number. Decimal numbers are found in the explanatory text and in program source code listings. Numbers shown as being entered into or displayed by DEBUG are never shown in decimal, always hexadecimal.

Hexadecimal (Hex) Numbers Numbers that have the letter h, in either uppercase or lowercase, as a suffix are to be interpreted as hexadecimal (base 16) numbers. For example, the number 21h in the instruction MOV AH,21h should be interpreted as a hexadecimal number equivalent to the decimal number 33.

If a hexadecimal number begins with one of the characters A-F, the syntax of most assemblers requires that a 0 be prepended. If not, the instruction MUL

BH, for example, would be ambiguous and could be interpreted either as a reference to the register BH or the hexadecimal number Bh.

The value for a byte is conveniently shown as two hexadecimal digits. Interrupt numbers, register values, and memory addresses are also typically shown in hexadecimal notation. Note that Intel, in its documentation, uses decimal numbers for its interrupts. So when Intel documentation mentions interrupt 13, the general protection exception, it should be interpreted as interrupt number Dh and not 13h.

There are two important exceptions to this convention for hexadecimal representation. The DEBUG program operates on the assumption that *all* numbers are hexadecimal, so no suffix will be shown in examples that use hexadecimal numbers entered into or displayed by DEBUG. Using the h suffix in an entry to DEBUG will, in fact, cause DEBUG to generate an error and ignore the input. (This is because the letter h is not a valid hexadecimal digit.) Program listing fragments that show instructions and the opcodes generated also omit the h suffix.

Memory addresses, shown in the segment:offset format, will only have an h suffix at the end of the offset portion of the address, but both numbers should always be assumed to be in hexadecimal. For example, the segmented address 0400:0048h should be interpreted as an address with a segment value of 0400h and an offset value of 0048h.

Binary Numbers Binary (base 2) numbers in the text will normally have the letter b as a suffix in either uppercase or lowercase. In many instances, using a binary number is more convenient than other notations. For example, specifying bit masks for logical operations is more naturally done with a binary number.

Note that a b suffix will not normally be included after the binary digits that are shown in instruction encodings, the FLAGS register, and processor data structures. These structures are typically shown as figures with bits numbered or grouped together.

Bit and Byte Order

The 80x86 family uses the *little endian* method of data storage (named for an obscure reference to Jonathan Swift's book *Gulliver's Travels*). This method places the highest-order byte at the highest address. The base address for the byte, word, or doubleword portion of an operand is always the same.

The graphic representations shown in this book, such as register layouts, structures, and bit fields, always show the lower memory address toward the right. In structures, addresses increase as you move toward the left and toward the top of the figure. Bit fields have the bit positions numbered from right to left in ascending order.

Bit numbers, structures, and memory addresses are identified using a 0-based numbering scheme. The least significant element in any structure is always numbered 0. Thus the bits in a byte would be numbered 0 through 7. The lowest segmented memory address the processor can generate is 0000:0000h using 16-bit displacements and 0000:00000000h using 32-bit displacements.

Reserved and Undefined Fields

In representations of processor structures, such as the FLAGS register, some bits or bit fields are not specifically defined by the processor as having known values. These fields are marked *reserved* and are typically shaded to indicate that they should not be used for any undocumented purpose, nor should their values be considered reliable. The value in a reserved field cannot be depended on to be consistent between different processors or even between processor revisions. (As each new chip is introduced, the masks that are used to make the chip are always being revised as bugs are found and corrected.) Using reserved fields for any purpose can cause incompatibility problems when moving your code to a different processor.

If a field is set to a value by an operation, but the returned value has no meaning in the context of the operation, that field is said to be *undefined*. After a DIV operation, for example, there is no correlation between the status of the zero flag and the result of the operation. So although the zero flag is altered by the DIV instruction, its value is said to be undefined.

Operand Order

The designers of Intel's assembler for the 80x86 chose to use an instruction syntax that mimicked the right-to-left order of normal arithmetic notation. The destination operand is always shown first, followed by the source operand. For example, consider the expression *A=5*. This is expressed in assembler syntax as *MOV A,5*. In both cases, the destination operand, A, appears first. This is the syntax used by most 80x86 assemblers, DEBUG, and this book.

FAMILY OVERVIEW

INTEL'S DEFINITION OF A MICROPROCESSOR IS "A SYSTEM OF ONE OR MORE integrated circuit devices that use semiconductor technology and digital logic to implement large computer functions on a smaller scale." So successful has Intel been in translating this definition from theory into reality that for millions of personal computer manufacturers and users, the definition of a microprocessor is "a chip made by Intel."

The era of the microprocessor is still relatively young. But in contrast to the majority of technological innovations, the rate of evolution of the personal computer has been extremely rapid. This chapter will present a brief history of the evolution of the Intel microprocessor family from its humble beginnings to the current state of the art. The major features and capabilities of each processor are compared and an overview of the related family of numeric coprocessors is provided.

Intel Microprocessor Evolution

Intel developed the first microprocessor "chip," the 4004, mainly for use in embedded applications. When they introduced the 4004 in 1971, they marketed it to manufacturers of industrial and commercial products. By including the chip in their designs, Intel claimed, the manufacturers could increase the efficiency and usefulness of their products.

By today's standards, the 4004 seems very primitive. It had, for example, an external data bus that was only 4 bits wide. This meant that data could only be transferred between the processor and external memory 4 bits at a time. As you might expect, this made it quite slow since most transfer operations had to be performed in multiple steps. To increase performance, Intel introduced the 8008 in 1972. The 8008 chip was simply an 8-bit version of the 4004, but it marked the dawn of the era of 8-bit microcomputing.

Two years later, in 1974, the now legendary 8080 chip was introduced. The 8080 was reminiscent of the architecture of the 8008, but had been designed to function as more of a general-purpose microprocessor. The introduction of this flexible chip proved to be very important to the industry. The success of Intel's 8080 stimulated development of competing 8-bit processors such as the Zilog Z80 and Motorola's 6800.

The 8086 and 8088

The next major milestone in microprocessor development was the introduction in 1978 of the 8086, Intel's first 16-bit microprocessor and the first member of what I'll call the 80x86 family. The chip, known officially as the iAPX 86, had full 16-bit registers, was able to transfer data to and from external memory 16 bits at a time, and could directly address up to one megabyte of physical memory. Coupled with an increase in processing speed, the 8086 promised tremendous performance increases. For system programmers, the similarity of the 8086 instruction set and architecture to that of the 8080 made conversion of source code less painful than it might have been.

Close on the heels of the 8086 was a version of the chip that maintained the 16-bit registers and data bus internally, but interfaced to the external world with an 8-bit bus. The 8088 allowed system designers to base their new designs around common, and consequently less expensive, 8-bit peripherals. The 8088 was, of course, the chip chosen by IBM for the original PC. Its widespread use has made it not only an industry-standard, but a world-standard architecture.

While discussing Intel's chips it's also appropriate to mention the NEC V20 and V30 chips, introduced as plug-in replacements for the 8088 and 8086 respectively. In addition to their transparent compatibility, the chips ran faster and cooler than their Intel counterparts. Everyday performance was increased somewhat by the inclusion of dedicated hardware on the chip itself to perform the effective address calculation used in many of the 8086's addressing modes. The two NEC chips also supported the extensions to the real-mode instruction set introduced with the 80186 and 80286. For all programming purposes, these chips may be treated as an 8086.

The 80186 and 80188

Intel development continued to support the embedded applications market that formed a large portion of its microprocessor sales. In 1982, the 16-bit 80186 (iAPX 186) and its 8-bit bus cousin, the 80188 (iAPX 188), were released. These chips contained not only the processor, but also most of the support chips required for the processor to perform useful work. They came close to being complete computers on a chip. The processor in these chips supported all the instructions of the 8086 as well as the additional real-mode instructions of the 80286, such as ENTER and LEAVE. Because of their infrequent appearance in personal computers, I won't mention specifics of these chips in this book.

The 80286

When the iAPX 286 was introduced in 1982, it caused quite a stir. First, the 80286 ran at a higher clock speed than the 8086 (even if it was only 6 MHz). This, coupled with dedicated hardware built into the chip to perform time-consuming internal calculations, boosted system performance. In addition, the chip would execute all code written for previous members of the iAPX 86 family without alteration. This upward compatibility allowed computer users to execute their existing 8086 applications more quickly simply by moving the code to a new machine. System programmers also began to look over the new architectural feature added to the 80286 known as Protected Virtual Address Mode, or more simply, protected mode.

The 80286's protected mode provided what seemed at the time to be very sophisticated mechanisms for implementing a bulletproof operating system that supported data protection, multitasking, memory management, and direct addressing of up to 16 megabytes of physical memory as well as virtual storage. It took years, however, before IBM and Microsoft eventually produced an operating system that used these mechanisms. And although the promised protected mode operating system finally arrived, it received a cold reception. The overwhelming majority of PC users continued to use their 80286-based machines simply as faster 8086s.

The 80386 and 80486

Intel dropped the iAPX designation with the introduction of the 80386DX, its first true 32-bit processor. Commonly known as simply the 80386, the chip was introduced in 1985 and rocked the PC industry. In addition to full upward compatibility with the 8086 and both the real and protected modes of the 80286, the 80386 provided full support for 32-bit operations and data types, memory paging, and an expanded instruction set. Other enhancements included built-in debugging support, a virtual 8086 mode, direct addressing of up to 4 gigabytes of physical memory, and a linear address mode that eliminated the 64k segment restriction.

Just as the 8086 beget the 8088, so the 80386DX beget the 80386SX, a version of the 80386 with a 32-bit internal and 16-bit external data bus. The 80386SX, announced in 1988, is identical to the 80386DX from a programmer's point of view and supports all the same modes of operation.

The 80386 had barely begun rolling off the production lines before rumors circulated concerning the next chip to be released by Intel. Many of us hoped that the 80486DX would be a full 64-bit processor that could be used to build a PC capable of outperforming a mainframe computer. When it became known that the 80486 would also be a 32-bit processor and quite similar to the 80386, speculation and interest in the chip dropped dramatically.

Announced in 1989, the 80486 is fully upward compatible, maintaining its ties with earlier 80x86 processors. The 80486's most obvious enhancement over the 80386 is the inclusion of floating-point hardware on the chip, eliminating the need for a separate math coprocessor. The 80486, in effect, comes with a built-in "80487." Also included on the chip is an 8k unified code and data cache that allows the 80486 to operate at high clock speeds without being hindered by relatively slow memory accesses.

In 1991, Intel introduced the 80486SX, an integer-only version of the 80486DX. The 80486SX was created from the same mask used to produce the 80486DX by severing the ties to the floating-point unit. The chip remains otherwise identical to the 80486DX. The later addition of floating-point hardware simply instructs the 8048SX to shut itself off; both integer and floating-point operations are handled by the new processor.

From a programming perspective, the 80486, 80486SX, 80386, and 80386SX can be grouped together. All four chips share the same operating modes and protection mechanisms. Where appropriate, any specific differences between the processors will be mentioned in the text.

Programmers need to be aware that the architecture of the 80486 has been reorganized in such a way that many common instructions, especially those that address memory operands, now execute significantly faster—many in a single clock cycle. Others, alas, will execute more slowly than on previous processors. This inconsistency can make it more difficult for an assembly language programmer to optimize code for execution speed across the entire 80x86 family.

Processor Capabilities

One major feature of each new member of the Intel processor family has been upwardly compatible object code. This simply means that each processor can execute programs that have been encoded for an earlier member of the family, but not necessarily the other way around. (A few minor operational differences exist, but these are well documented and are discussed in Chapter 14.) The 80286, for example, will run programs written for the 8086 without modification. And the 80486 will run programs written for any other member of the family.

Each processor, beginning with the 80286, has offered an upward-compatible superset of the instructions, registers, and operating modes that were available on earlier processors. Table 1.1 lists a few important features for each processor in the 80x86 family. The features themselves are explained below. Note that not all the features of a particular chip are necessarily implemented in the PC architecture nor are they necessarily available under MS-DOS.

TABLE 1.1

80x86 Family Processor Features

Processor Type	8088	8086	80286	80386SX	80386DX	80486
External data bus width (bits)	8	16	16	16	32	32
General register size (bits)	16	16	16	32	32	32
Memory address bus size (bits)	20	20	24	32	32	32
Maximum physical memory size	1Mb	1Mb	16Mb	16Mb	4Gb	4Gb
Instruction set size (excluding floating point)	90	90	113	141	141	147
Protected mode	No	No	Yes	Yes	Yes	Yes
Virtual 8086 mode	No	No	No	Yes	Yes	Yes
Processor clock speed (MHz)	5-10	5-10	6-16	16-20	16-33	25-50

External Data Bus Width

The central processing unit, or CPU, is connected to external memory and to the I/O ports by a set of parallel wires called the external data bus. All information passed between the CPU and system memory or I/O ports travels via this bus. The bus width—the number of parallel wires that carry data (as opposed to control signals)—puts a fixed upper limit on the amount of information that can be transmitted in one operation. One bit of information is transmitted per wire and, in somewhat overly general terms, one transfer is called a bus cycle.

The size of the external data bus has a significant and direct impact on the overall speed of data transfer in the computer system. Consulting Table 1.1, we see that the 8088 processor, used in the IBM PC, PC-XT, and many laptop computers, has an 8-bit external data bus. For the 8088 to transfer 16 bits of information, two bus cycles are required, each bus cycle transferring 8 bits of information.

The 80286 processor, which has a 16-bit external data bus, is able to transfer the same 16 bits of information that took the 8088 two bus cycles in only one bus cycle. The information transfer rate is therefore effectively doubled. Processors with a 32-bit bus, supported by the proper external hardware, are able to transfer 32 bits of information in a single bus cycle.

Register Size

Inside each processor, temporary storage locations called registers are used to manipulate program data and process the instructions that are being executed. And in the same way that the size of the external data bus limits the amount of information that can be transferred in a single bus cycle, the register size of a processor limits the amount of information that can be operated on in a single step. In general, larger registers are more efficient because they allow larger operands to be processed in a single step.

Inside the CPU there are several different types of register, but it is the size of the general-purpose registers that we refer to when specifying the type of processor. A processor's register size is specified in bits. The 80386, for example, has 32-bit general-purpose registers and is called a 32-bit processor. And although the 8088's external data bus is only 8 bits wide, its registers are 16 bits, qualifying it as a 16-bit processor. The registers available on each processor and their uses are discussed in detail in Chapter 3.

Memory Address Bus Size

As mentioned previously, the CPU uses the data bus to transfer data to and from system memory and I/O ports. In order to work with a specific memory area or specific I/O device, however, a unique address must be generated by the processor that causes the computer system to select that memory area or I/O device. The address is generated by the CPU and placed on another bus known as the address bus. (The same set of wires may be used as both the address and data bus if appropriate control signal wires are added.)

The maximum address size that can be transferred via the address bus determines the maximum amount of physical memory that can be addressed by the CPU. The 8086, for example, has a maximum address bus size of 20 bits. This means that the CPU can generate up to 2^{20} or 1,048,576 unique addresses. When used to interface with system memory, each of these addresses uniquely specifies a single byte. Thus the maximum amount of physical memory that the CPU can address is 1,048,576 bytes. (This is usually written more compactly as 1 megabyte or 1Mb.) Similarly, the 80486, with its 32-bit memory address size, is capable of generating up to 2^{32} or 4,294,967,296 addresses. So, if the computer system in which the CPU was installed provided the required hardware support, the 80486 could directly address up to 4096Mb or 4 gigabytes (4Gb) of memory. Memory and memory addressing are discussed in more detail in Chapter 4.

Instruction Set Size   Processors are usually divided into two categories according to the type of instructions that they provide for use by programmers. The first type is termed a Reduced Instruction Set Computer (RISC) processor and, as its name implies, is designed to execute a small set of basic instructions. Operations that are normally considered high-level, such as a single instruction to multiply two operands, must be programmed as a series of steps using the lower-level instruction primitives.

One reason that this approach has met with some success is that by simplifying the instruction set, the logic design of the RISC chip can be vastly simplified. Once simplified, the hardware design is optimized so that it executes the few available instructions extremely rapidly. So even though the processor must execute many low-level instructions in order to perform the same operation as a single high-level instruction, it should be able to do so in less time.

Fortunately (for programmers, not for the hardware designers), the 80x86 family of processors is Complex Instruction Set Computer (CISC) chips. In other words, the processor can accept a high-level instruction to perform an integer division, for example, and properly execute all the steps required to produce the answer with no further intervention by the programmer. The CPU interprets these complex instructions in a series of steps known as microcode.

A fair measure of the capability of a CISC chip is the number of instructions available. The instruction set of the 8086, known as the basic instruction set, is supported by all the members of the 80x86 family of processors. The more advanced processors have generally added new instructions to support their protected and virtual mode operations and additional registers. The instruction set is discussed in more detail in Chapter 6.

Operating Modes

As the processors evolved, more capabilities were added to keep pace with the developing needs of system designers. One such capability was the implementation of hardware support for protection mechanisms on the chip itself. Up to three modes of operation may be supported by the various members of the 80x86 family: real mode, protected mode, and Virtual-86 mode. Each of these modes, and the processors that support them, are described in this section.

Real Mode   The 8086 and 8088 operate in what is called real address mode, or simply real mode. In real mode, the 20-bit memory addresses that are generated by the CPU are sent directly to the address bus without any type of translation. In other words, the segmented address value generated by the processor corresponds directly to a physical memory location. If this seems obvious, it's because the term real mode was coined retroactively to distinguish it from the then-new protected mode of the 80286. The 80286 and later processors are also capable of running in real mode and when doing so, essentially act as if they were a fast 8086.

Protected Mode Protected Virtual Address Mode was the official name given to the mode of operation that was first available on the 80286 processor. When running in protected mode, the processor is able to use built-in hardware to become a super-processor. In protected mode, mechanisms are brought into play that can protect data from unauthorized access, support multitasking, and perform sophisticated memory management including automatic implementation of virtual storage.

Because these features are not present in the 8086 or 8088, programs written to take advantage of the protected mode require an 80286 or later processor. Conversely, programs written for the 8086 or 8088 will most likely violate the protection mechanisms implemented in protected mode. Because of this, they cannot run unmodified in a protected mode environment. Both the 80386 and the 80486 offer a protected mode operation that is upwardly compatible with the 80286. An overview of protected mode is presented in Chapter 15.

Virtual Mode The Virtual-86 mode of operation first appeared on the 80386 processor and was one of a series of major improvements that distinguished it from the 80286. This new form of protected mode operation allows the 80386 to provide multitasking, memory management, and full 8086 object code compatibility in the same operating system. The 80386 processor is fully upward compatible and (with the proper operating system) is capable of running simultaneously an 80386 protected mode program, an 80286 protected mode program, and an 8086 real mode program.

The virtual mode of the 80386 and 80486 was a valuable addition to the architecture. In effect, a simulated 8086 processor is produced by a combination of hardware support in the processor and operating system software. Imagine writing a processor simulator program that would read an executable file, interpret each instruction, and simulate access to memory, I/O space, and interrupts. This is analogous to what virtual mode provides, albeit with the assistance of specialized hardware support. An overview of virtual mode operation is presented in Chapter 15.

Processor Clock Speed

The processors in the 80x86 family are driven by an external clock. The clock frequency, also referred to as clock speed, is typically specified in megahertz (MHz) and determines how fast the processor will execute instructions. As the clock speed is increased, the processor is able to execute more instructions in the same time, or equivalently, the same number of instructions in less time. Ultimately, a speed is reached at which the operation of the solid-state circuitry that makes up the processor becomes unreliable.

The highest reliable speed at which a particular model of processor will operate varies from chip to chip and batch to batch. So, for example, two seemingly identical processors, produced on the same assembly line but made on different days, may have vastly different speed capabilities. Processors that can be run reliably at a higher clock speed can generally be sold for a higher price. To distinguish the chips, manufacturers "screen" their products, sorting them from those that are usable and have the highest reliable clock speed down to nonfunctional rejects.

The range of clock speeds shown in Table 1.1 is typical of the speeds available for each processor type. The IBM PC, for example, used an 8088 processor running at a clock speed of 4.77 MHz. The original IBM PC/AT ran its 80286 processor at what seems now to be a sluggardly 6 MHz clock speed.

The Math Coprocessor

The processors in the 80x86 family can operate directly on many data types, including integer, binary coded decimal (BCD), and packed BCD data. But none of the CPUs offers intrinsic support for floating-point data types. Special circuitry isn't necessary for the processor to handle floating-point data; given the correct series of instructions, the processors can perform operations on any numeric data type. But to perform complex mathematical operations efficiently and provide intrinsic support for floating-point data types, the 80x87 Numeric Processor Extension (NPX) is required.

Support for the NPX, commonly called the coprocessor, has been designed into each member of the 80x86 family. The processor works in tandem with the coprocessor, fetching and decoding instructions, calculating addresses of memory operands, and so on. In exchange, the coprocessor performs arithmetic and comparison operations on floating-point numbers. In addition, the coprocessor makes many trigonometric and transcendental functions available to the programmer as simple, single instructions. Because the processor and coprocessor have a well-defined hardware interface, no special setup or complicated data transfer is required. In practice, the instructions for the coprocessor may be treated simply as an addition to the basic instruction set of the processor.

Each processor in the 80x86 family has a corresponding coprocessor with which it is compatible. Table 1.2 shows the processor and coprocessor combinations that are compatible. The 80386 is unique in that it is able to function with either an 80387 or an 80287 coprocessor. The 80486 comes with both a processor and a coprocessor built into the same chip and requires no additional coprocessor. The 80486 CPU and floating-point unit (FPU) still act as if they were separate processors.

TABLE 1.2

Permissible Processor and Coprocessor Combinations

Processor	Coprocessor
8086, 8088	8087
80286	80287
80386DX	80287, 80387DX
80386SX	80387SX
80486DX	None required. Functions are built in.
80486SX	80487SX

The coprocessor provides very high-level instructions that perform complex tasks. Still, it is a simpler chip than the processor from a system programming point of view. For example, although there is minimal support for protected mode or multitasking operation, the coprocessor is able to function effectively in those environments. When a situation occurs that could corrupt the state of the coprocessor, such as switching between tasks, the processor saves the state of the coprocessor, including all intermediate calculations. Later, when the original task regains control of the processor, the state of the coprocessor can be restored and numeric processing can continue as if it had never been disturbed.

Another property of the coprocessor is that it is usually operated asynchronously with the main processor, using a different clock and clock speed. Once the coprocessor begins to execute an instruction, the processor is free to fetch and execute the next instruction. Of course, if the next instruction fetched is another coprocessor instruction the processor will have to wait until the coprocessor is finished. Or if the next instruction uses the result of the unfinished coprocessor instruction the processor must again wait until the coprocessor completes. More often than not, however, careful assembly language programming can allow the system to implement some level of parallel processing.

Data types are discussed in Chapter 2, while the coprocessor and its instruction set are discussed in more detail beginning in Chapter 10.

2. DATA TYPES

IN A COMPUTER SYSTEM, THE PRIMARY FUNCTION OF THE PROCESSOR IS TO fetch, manipulate, and store information. Before information can be processed, however, it must be converted into a form that is suitable for manipulation by the processor. Once converted, all information, regardless of source, purpose, or context, can be referred to simply as "data."

The terminology of data and data types varies among different languages and contexts and this inconsistency is often confusing. It's not uncommon to find very different terms used to represent the same thing. The data type known as a long integer in the BASIC language, for example, is called a short integer in 80x87 terms. To avoid confusion when mixing environments, always determine the size of the item in bits and refer to it as such. So the above data type could be referred to as a 32-bit integer in either context. Throughout this book, the terminology established by Intel will be used as the basis for naming data types.

In this chapter, data and the data types are defined from the point of view of the processor and for the information that they can be used to represent. Prior to that, a brief review of number systems and representations is presented.

Number Systems

The three number systems typically found in programming at the processor level are decimal (base 10), binary (base 2), and hexadecimal (base 16). Each of these systems uses a positional notation, where the position of each digit in the number relative to the radix determines the value of the digit. The radix (known as the decimal point in base 10 system) is always present, even if not explicitly shown, and separates the integer portion of a number from the fractional part.

In positional notation, the first digit position to the left of the radix represents the number of times the base raised to the 0 power (always 1, regardless of the base) is included in the number. Each digit farther from the radix increases the power of the base by 1. Digit positions to the right of the radix represent negative, or fractional, powers of the base. For example, the decimal number 13.56 can be expanded as follows:

```
1 * 10¹  = 10.
3 * 10⁰  =  3.
5 * 10⁻¹ =   .5
6 * 10⁻² =   .06

Total    = 13.56
```

Similarly, the binary number 1101.101b can be expanded and converted to decimal as follows:

```
1 * 2³  = 1000.    = 8.
1 * 2²  = 100.     = 4.
0 * 2¹  =  00.     = 0.
1 * 2⁰  =   1.     = 1.
1 * 2⁻¹ =    .1    = .5
0 * 2⁻² =    .00   = .0
1 * 2⁻³ =    .001  = .125


Total    = 1101.101 = 13.625
```

Table 2.1, which gives the powers of 2 from +64 to –64, can be used to convert to and from binary notation.

Not every decimal number can be converted to an equivalent binary number. The decimal number 1.0/10.0, for example, cannot be represented exactly in the binary number system. (Similarly, the number 1.0/11.0 cannot be expressed exactly in decimal.) For every base, there will be numbers that cannot be represented with a finite number of digits (repeating numbers).

Binary Numbers

Binary numbers are the foundation on which computer operations are based. Two separate systems for expressing binary, or base 2, numbers exist. They are known as the *one's complement* and *two's complement* systems. Both systems can represent positive and negative numbers, and both use a single bit to indicate the sign of the number. But the difference between the two systems lies in how negative numbers are formed.

In the one's complement system, the high-order bit of a binary number is used as the sign bit. The remaining bits represent the magnitude of the number. Changing a positive number to a negative number requires only that you reverse the value of each bit. Assume, for example, that we're using a byte for storage of a signed number and that the byte contains the binary number 00000001b. If we complement the value of each bit we will produce 11111110b, the one's complement notation for the decimal value –1. This notation allows numbers in the range from –127 (10000000b) to +127 (01111111b) to be represented. Note that two representations for zero, +0 (00000000b) and –0 (11111111b), are also available.

In two's complement notation, the high-order bit is also used to indicate the sign of the number. But to generate a number with an equivalent magnitude and opposite sign is a two-step process. First, the value of each bit in the original number is individually complemented. Then, 1 is added to the number as if it were an unsigned quantity. Any carry out of the word is ignored. This operation is called negation.

TABLE 2.1

The Powers of 2

Positive Powers of 2		Negative Powers of 2
2^{+n}	n	2^{-n}
1	0	1.
2	1	0.5
4	2	0.25
8	3	0.125
16	4	0.062,5
32	5	0.031,25
64	6	0.015,625
128	7	0.007,812,5
256	8	0.003,906,25
512	9	0.001,953,125
1,024	10	0.000,976,562,5
2,048	11	0.000,488,281,25
4,096	12	0.000,244,140,625
8,192	13	0.000,122,070,312,5
16,384	14	0.000,061,035,156,25
32,768	15	0.000,030,517,578,125
65,536	16	0.000,015,258,789,062,5
131,072	17	0.000,007,629,394,531,25
262,144	18	0.000,003,814,697,265,625
524,288	19	0.000,001,907,348,632,812,5
1,048,576	20	0.000,000,953,674,316,406,25
2,097,152	21	0.000,000,476,837,158,203,125
4,194,304	22	0.000,000,238,418,579,101,562,5
8,388,608	23	0.000,000,119,209,289,550,781,25
16,777,216	24	0.000,000,059,604,644,775,390,625
33,554,432	25	0.000,000,029,802,322,387,695,312,5
67,108,864	26	0.000,000,014,901,161,193,847,656,25
134,217,728	27	0.000,000,007,450,580,596,923,828,125
268,435,456	28	0.000,000,003,725,290,298,461,914,062,5
536,870,912	29	0.000,000,001,862,645,149,230,957,031,25
1,073,741,824	30	0.000,000,000,931,322,574,615,478,515,625
2,147,483,648	31	0.000,000,000,465,661,287,307,739,257,812,5
4,294,967,296	32	0.000,000,000,232,830,643,653,869,628,906,25
8,589,934,592	33	0.000,000,000,116,415,321,826,934,814,453,125
17,179,869,184	34	0.000,000,000,058,207,660,913,467,407,226,562,5
34,359,738,368	35	0.000,000,000,029,103,830,456,733,703,613,281,25
68,719,476,736	36	0.000,000,000,014,551,915,228,366,851,806,640,625
137,438,953,472	37	0.000,000,000,007,275,957,614,183,425,903,320,312,5
274,877,906,944	38	0.000,000,000,003,637,978,807,091,712,951,660,156,25
549,755,813,888	39	0.000,000,000,001,818,989,403,545,856,475,830,078,125
1,099,511,627,776	40	0.000,000,000,000,909,494,701,772,928,237,915,039,062,5
2,199,023,255,552	41	0.000,000,000,000,454,747,350,886,464,118,957,519,531,25
4,398,046,511,104	42	0.000,000,000,000,227,373,675,443,232,059,478,759,765,625
8,796,093,022,208	43	0.000,000,000,000,113,686,837,721,616,029,739,379,882,812,5
17,592,186,044,416	44	0.000,000,000,000,056,843,418,860,808,014,869,689,941,406,25
35,184,372,088,832	45	0.000,000,000,000,028,421,709,430,404,007,434,844,970,703,125
70,368,744,177,664	46	0.000,000,000,000,014,210,854,715,202,003,717,422,485,351,562,5
140,737,488,355,328	47	0.000,000,000,000,007,105,427,357,601,001,858,711,242,675,781,25

Continued

Positive Powers of 2		Negative Powers of 2
2^{+n}	n	2^{-n}
281,474,976,710,656	48	0.000,000,000,000,003,552,713,678,800,500,929,355,621,337,890,625
562,949,953,421,312	49	0.000,000,000,000,001,776,356,839,400,250,464,677,810,668,945,312,5
1,125,899,906,842,624	50	0.000,000,000,000,000,888,178,419,700,125,232,338,905,334,472,656,25
2,251,799,813,685,248	51	0.000,000,000,000,000,444,089,209,850,062,616,169,452,667,236,328,125
4,503,599,627,370,496	52	0.000,000,000,000,000,222,044,604,925,031,308,084,726,333,618,164,062,5
9,007,199,254,740,992	53	0.000,000,000,000,000,111,022,302,462,515,654,042,363,166,809,082,031,25
18,014,398,509,481,984	54	0.000,000,000,000,000,055,511,151,231,257,827,021,181,583,404,541,015,625
36,028,797,018,963,968	55	0.000,000,000,000,000,027,755,575,615,628,913,510,590,791,702,270,507,812,5
72,057,594,037,927,936	56	0.000,000,000,000,000,013,877,787,807,814,456,755,295,395,851,135,253,906,25
144,115,188,075,855,872	57	0.000,000,000,000,000,006,938,893,903,907,228,337,647,697,925,567,626,953,125
288,230,376,151,711,744	58	0.000,000,000,000,000,003,469,446,951,953,614,188,823,848,962,783,813,476,562,5
576,460,752,303,423,488	59	0.000,000,000,000,000,001,734,723,475,976,807,094,411,924,481,391,906,738,281,25
1,152,921,504,606,846,976	60	0.000,000,000,000,000,000,867,361,737,988,403,547,205,962,240,695,953,369,140,625
2,305,843,009,213,693,952	61	0.000,000,000,000,000,000,433,680,868,994,201,773,602,981,120,347,976,684,570,312,5
4,611,686,018,427,387,904	62	0.000,000,000,000,000,000,216,840,434,497,100,868,801,490,560,173,988,342,285,156,25
9,223,372,036,854,775,808	63	0.000,000,000,000,000,000,108,420,217,248,550,443,400,745,280,086,994,171,142,578,125
18,446,744,073,709,551,616	64	0.000,000,000,000,000,000,054,210,108,624,275,221,700,372,640,043,497,085,571,289,062,5

Assume again that we're using a signed byte format for storage and calculate the two's complement of the number +15. The two's complement representation of +15 is 00001111b. The steps below show how the negation is performed:

00001111b	original number
11110000b	complement each bit (NOT operation)
11110001b	add 1

The final result doesn't bear much resemblance to the original number. Recognizing negative numbers in the two's complement system can take quite a bit of practice. Unlike the one's complement system, the two's complement system has only one representation for 0. This example shows how the complement of 0 is formed:

00000000b	"positive" 0
11111111b	bit-wise complement
00000000b	add 1 (carry out of high bit is discarded)

The Intel family of processors uses two's complement notation for negative numbers. The NEG (negate) instruction is provided to change the sign of numbers.

Hexadecimal Numbers

The processor accepts, processes, and produces only binary values. But hexadecimal (hex) notation is often used as a shorthand representation of binary by programmers. In the hex system, there are 16 possible values for each digit. The values 0 through 9 are represented by the digits 0 through 9 and the values 10 through 15 are represented by the characters A, B, C, D, E, and F. For example, the hex number 13Ah, expressed in decimal, would be converted as shown:

```
1 * 16² = 256
3 * 16¹ =  48
A * 16⁰ =  10


Total   = 314
```

Changing a number from binary to hex or hex to binary is considerably easier. Each hex digit represents exactly four binary digits. To form a hex number from a binary number, start at the radix (the right-most digit for an integer value) and group four digits at a time. Then convert the groups of four binary digits into a single hex digit. This operation is shown below:

```
101011010100011010101111011101111b         binary number

101 0110 1010 0011 0101 0111 0110 1111      group the digits

 5    6    A    3    5    7    6    F        translate to hex

        56A3576Fh                           final hex number
```

Converting from hex to binary works the same way. Each hex digit is simply expanded into its binary equivalent.

Several tables are provided here for working with hex numbers. Table 2.2 lists the hex digits and their binary equivalents. Table 2.3 is a hex addition table, and Table 2.4 gives a multiplication table for single hex digits.

Data Access and Alignment

For the processor to be able to transfer data to and from system memory or the I/O ports, two criteria must be satisfied. First, the processor must be able to generate an address that uniquely identifies the location of the data. Second, the size of the data must be one of the processor's fundamental units of data transfer: the byte, word, or doubleword.

All data operations performed by the processor use either one or a combination of the fundamental data transfer types. While some instructions seem to specify different data types, these instructions simply combine movements of the three fundamental types. The LDS EBX mem instruction, for example, specifies a 48-bit area of memory as its source operand. The 48-bit operand, however, is not a new fundamental data type, but a combination of a word that is moved into the DS register, and a doubleword that is moved into the EBX register.

TABLE 2.2	

Hex Digits and Their Binary Equivalents

Hex	Binary
0	0000
1	0001
2	0010
3	0011
4	0100
5	0101
6	0110
7	0111
8	1000
9	1001
A	1010
B	1011
C	1100
D	1101
E	1110
F	1111

TABLE 2.3	

Single-Digit Hex Addition Table

+	1	2	3	4	5	6	7	8	9	A	B	C	D	E	F
1	2	3	4	5	6	7	8	9	A	B	C	D	E	F	10
2	3	4	5	6	7	8	9	A	B	C	D	E	F	10	11
3	4	5	6	7	8	9	A	B	C	D	E	F	10	11	12
4	5	6	7	8	9	A	B	C	D	E	F	10	11	12	13
5	6	7	8	9	A	B	C	D	E	F	10	11	12	13	14
6	7	8	9	A	B	C	D	E	F	10	11	12	13	14	15
7	8	9	A	B	C	D	E	F	10	11	12	13	14	15	16
8	9	A	B	C	D	E	F	10	11	12	13	14	15	16	17
9	A	B	C	D	E	F	10	11	12	13	14	15	16	17	18
A	B	C	D	E	F	10	11	12	13	14	15	16	17	18	19
B	C	D	E	F	10	11	12	13	14	15	16	17	18	19	1A
C	D	E	F	10	11	12	13	14	15	16	17	18	19	1A	1B
D	E	F	10	11	12	13	14	15	16	17	18	19	1A	1B	1C
E	F	10	11	12	13	14	15	16	17	18	19	1A	1B	1C	1D
F	10	11	12	13	14	15	16	17	18	19	1A	1B	1C	1D	1E

The Byte

The address and I/O space of the processor are divided into units of 8 bits called bytes. The byte is the smallest unit of data that the processor can uniquely address and is one of the fundamental units of data. The entire 1 megabyte physical memory space of the 8086, for example, can be thought of as a linear string of bytes at addresses numbered 0 through 1,048,575 (2^{20}–1). Operations on individual bits in memory are possible, but they require the address of the byte in which the target bit is located. The byte is a fundamental unit of data for all of the processors in the 80x86 family.

TABLE 2.4

Single-Digit Hex Multiplication Table

*	1	2	3	4	5	6	7	8	9	A	B	C	D	E	F
1	1	2	3	4	5	6	7	8	9	A	B	C	D	E	F
2	2	4	6	8	A	C	E	10	12	14	16	18	1A	1C	1E
3	3	6	9	C	F	12	15	18	1B	1E	21	24	27	2A	2D
4	4	8	C	10	14	18	1C	20	24	28	2C	30	34	38	3C
5	5	A	F	14	19	1E	23	28	2D	32	37	3C	41	46	4B
6	6	C	12	18	1E	24	2A	30	36	3C	42	48	4E	54	5A
7	7	E	15	1C	23	2A	31	38	3F	46	4D	54	5B	62	69
8	8	10	18	20	28	30	38	40	48	50	58	60	68	70	78
9	9	12	1B	24	2D	36	3F	48	51	5A	63	6C	75	7E	87
A	A	14	1E	28	32	3C	46	50	5A	64	6E	78	82	8C	96
B	B	16	21	2C	37	42	4D	58	63	6E	79	84	8F	9A	A5
C	C	18	24	30	3C	48	54	60	6C	78	84	90	9C	A8	B4
D	D	1A	27	34	41	4E	5B	68	75	82	8F	9C	A9	B6	C3
E	E	1C	2A	38	46	54	62	70	7E	8C	9A	A8	B6	C4	D2
F	F	1E	2D	3C	4B	5A	69	78	87	96	A5	B4	C3	D2	E1

The bits in a byte are numbered from 0, the low-order bit, to 7, the high-order bit. In a diagram of a byte, the high-order bit is always shown toward the left. In memory, byte addresses increase as you move toward the top of the page. Figure 2.1 shows the numbering of the individual bits in a byte and Figure 2.2 shows the addressing of individual bytes in memory.

FIGURE 2.1

The fundamental data units

Byte at address m

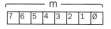

Word at address m

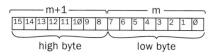

high byte   low byte

Doubleword at address m

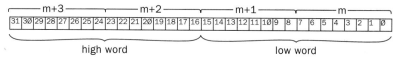

high word   low word

FIGURE 2.2

Bytes, words, and doublewords in memory

Doubleword at 14h
= 1652A3ØFh

Word at 11h = A54Bh

17h	16	} Byte at 17h = 16h
16h	52	
15h	A3	} Word at 14h = A3ØFh
14h	ØF	} Word at 13h = ØF6Ch
13h	6C	
12h	A5	Doubleword at 1Øh = 6CA54B7Eh
11h	4B	
10h	7E	

The Word

The second fundamental unit of data is the word. A word is two bytes, or 16 bits, long and any two consecutive bytes in memory may be addressed as a word. Of the two bytes that form a word, the byte containing bit 0 of the word is called the low byte and the byte containing bit 15 of the word is called the high byte. If the word is stored at address m, then the low byte is stored at address m and the high byte is stored at address m+1. The word is considered a fundamental unit of data for all the processors in the 80x86 family.

The bits in a word are numbered from 0 to 15, with 0 being the low-order bit and 15 being the high-order bit. As with the byte, the high-order bit is always shown toward the left in a diagram. Figure 2.1 shows how the bits within a word are numbered and how each byte that makes up the word is addressed. Examples of addressing words in memory are shown in Figure 2.2. Note that words in memory may overlap each other or other data types.

The Doubleword

The design of the 32-bit processors, the 80386 and 80486, allows the use of a third fundamental data type: the doubleword. The doubleword, as its name implies, is two words, or 32 bits, in length. A doubleword, sometimes abbreviated to dword, is formed by any two consecutive words or, equivalently, by any four consecutive bytes. The word containing the low-order bit, bit 0, of the doubleword is called the low word. The word containing the high-order bit, bit 31, is called the high word. If the address of the doubleword is m, then the address of the low word is also m and the address of the high word is m+2.

The bits in a doubleword are numbered from 0 to 31, with 0 being the low-order bit and 31 being the high-order bit. In a doubleword diagram, the low-order bit is always shown toward the right and the high-order bit is shown toward the left. Figure 2.1 shows the layout of a doubleword and how the individual bytes would be addressed. Figure 2.2 shows how doublewords would appear in memory. Note that doublewords in memory may overlap each other or other data types.

Data Alignment

When data is aligned, a word is stored at an address that is a multiple of 2 and a doubleword is stored at an address that is evenly divisible by 4. The 80x86 processors are able to retrieve any data type from any valid address and do not require that data be aligned. This is not the case with all microprocessors. This flexibility provides for the most efficient use of memory by allowing data structures to be packed without regard for the address of individual items.

When accessing memory, the processor will still retrieve data in fundamental units from aligned addresses. To address an unaligned data item, the processor will perform as many memory accesses as required. For example, assume that an 80386 is to read a doubleword from memory at address 2013h. Two bus operations will be required, as shown in Figure 2.3. The first will access the four bytes beginning at address 2010h. Three of these bytes will be ignored, but the byte at 2013h is part of the desired doubleword. The next bus operation will again fetch four bytes, this time starting at 2014h. The byte at 2017h will be ignored, leaving the three remaining bytes of the desired doubleword.

FIGURE 2.3

Unaligned memory accesses

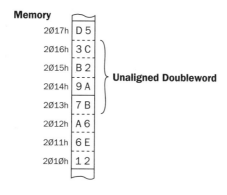

Unaligned memory operands can cause a performance penalty by requiring an extra bus cycle for each affected memory access. In the case of the stack, frequent word or doubleword access is made to memory. To avoid a significant performance degradation, it is important to ensure that the stack is always aligned so that word operands are located at even addresses and doubleword operands are located at addresses that are evenly divisible by 4.

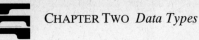

Processor Data Types

The byte, word, and doubleword are the fundamental units of data access used by the processor. These data units can be manipulated by the processor regardless of the information that is contained within them—to the processor, they're just groups of bits. For certain types of information, however, the processor provides a higher level of support in the form of specialized instructions designed to manipulate the data based on the information it contains. The definitions of these data types, both numeric and nonnumeric, are illustrated in Figure 2.4 and discussed below.

The numeric data formats supported by the processor include signed and unsigned binary and decimal. With the addition of a coprocessor, intrinsic support is provided for several floating-point formats. Numeric formats may contain sign, magnitude, and exponent fields. The nonnumeric data formats include string and ASCII formats.

Unsigned Numbers

Unsigned numbers, also known as ordinal numbers, contain only a magnitude field. Unlike other data types, no sign information is stored in the number; the high-order bit is the most significant bit of the magnitude. An unsigned number will hold a value in the range from 0 to 2^n-1, where n is the number of bits in the data unit. An unsigned byte will hold a value in the range from 0 to 255, an unsigned word will hold a value from 0 to 65,535, and an unsigned dword will hold a value in the range of 0 to 4,294,967,295.

Unsigned numbers are used as iteration counters for the repeat, shift, rotate, and loop instructions. Unsigned numbers are also used to represent the offset from the start of a segment in memory address calculations.

Integers

Integers, or signed numbers, contain both a sign and magnitude field. The high-order bit of the data unit is used as the sign bit. A sign bit of 0 indicates a positive number while a sign bit of 1 indicates a negative number. The remaining bits in the data unit are used to hold the magnitude of the number.

Because the Intel processors use two's complement notation, the range of permissible values for an integer will always contain one more negative number than positive number. An integer data type can store a value from -2^{n-1} to $+2^{n-1}-1$. An integer byte will hold values in the range –128 to +127, an integer word will hold values from –32,768 to +32,767 and an integer doubleword can represent a value from –2,147,483,648 to +2,147,483,647.

Decimal Numbers

Computers are designed to work with binary numbers. Humans, on the other hand, are decimal machines. At some point between ourselves and the computer, therefore, the number systems have to be converted. Unfortunately, because the processor is limited by design to a fixed number of digits (precision), many decimal numbers cannot be converted to binary and back again without suffering some loss of accuracy. To eliminate the conversion as a source of error, the binary coded decimal system was introduced.

FIGURE 2.4	

The processor data types

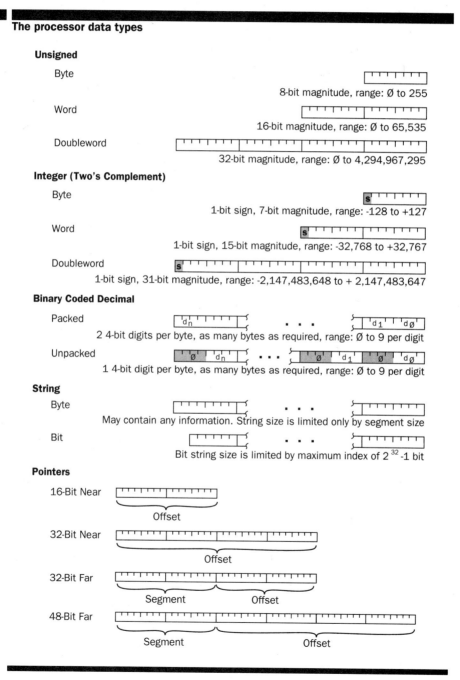

The binary coded decimal (BCD) system is an arbitrary but standardized data storage format. The rules used to manipulate BCD numbers are dictated by a few special instructions supported in the processor. In the BCD format, 4 bits (a nibble) in the data unit are used to represent a single decimal digit in the range of 0 through 9. If the decimal digit is stored in the low nibble of the byte and the upper nibble is not used, the format is known as unpacked BCD. If two decimal digits are stored in each byte (one in the high 4 bits, one in the low 4 bits), the format is known as packed BCD. Neither format makes any provision for a sign bit. Sign information, therefore, must be stored and manipulated separately.

For most purposes, the processor treats BCD numbers as a series of unsigned bytes. As many BCD digits as are required can be used to represent a single number, up to the limit of available memory. Operations on BCD digits are supported by the processor, but BCD numbers are not an intrinsic data type, and all manipulation of BCD numbers is performed by the programmer.

The BCD data type is used in financial programming, where small inaccuracies in conversion to binary would create problems during repeated calculations, such as in determining compound interest. COBOL, a popular business high-level language, offers a high-level interface to the BCD data type.

Strings

A string is a contiguous sequence of data units. The data unit may be a bit, byte, word, or doubleword. The term string, as applied to this data type, is more descriptive of the method of storage than of the type of data being stored. A string may be thought of as a one-dimensional array of identically sized elements. To access any item in the string, we must know the address of the first element, the number of the desired element, and the length of an element. Given this information, we can calculate (or let the processor calculate) the address of the desired element. A special case of the string data type is the ASCII string. In this case, the elements of the string are treated as ASCII characters and used to hold messages, help text, and so on.

Beginning with the 80386 processor, several instructions were introduced to manipulate individual bits in memory and bit fields in operands. Because of this, Intel has formalized the bit string data type. The bit test instructions available on the 80386 and 80486 provide intrinsic support for addressing memory at the bit level by using a signed bit displacement to address the bit and the carry flag to manipulate its value.

A string with byte, word, or doubleword elements is limited in size only by the amount of memory that can be addressed by the processor. In real mode, string size is limited to 64k, the maximum memory addressable in a single segment. In protected mode, the 80386 and 80486 can have a string size of up to 4 gigabytes. The size of a bit string is limited by the number of bits available in the displacement argument. This displacement is 32 bits on the 80386 and 80486, giving a maximum string size of 4 gigabits (2^{32}-1 bits).

Pointers

A pointer is a logical, rather than a mathematical data type. When we say that an area of memory or a register contains a pointer, we are using a shorthand method for specifying how the data is to be interpreted. Pointers are used in address calculations and specify either an offset alone or both a segment (selector) and an offset value.

Because a pointer contains an offset value, the size of the pointer is dependent on the size of the offset used by the processor. On the 80386 and 80486, the addressing mode in which the processor is operating determines the offset size.

A near pointer is an unsigned value that specifies a displacement from the beginning of a segment. On the 8086, 8088, 80286, and the 80386 and 80486 when running in 16-bit addressing mode, a near pointer is 16 bits. If the processor is an 80386 or an 80486 and is operating in 32-bit address mode, the near pointer is a 32-bit value.

A far pointer is made up of two separate unsigned values that specify a 16-bit segment value (called a segment selector in protected mode) as well as an offset value. On the 8086, 8088, 80286, and the 80386 and 80486 when running in 16-bit addressing mode, a far pointer is 32 bits: 16 bits for the segment and 16 bits for the offset. If the processor is an 80386 or an 80486 and is operating in 32-bit address mode, the far pointer is a 48-bit value: a 16-bit segment value and a 32-bit offset.

Coprocessor Data Types

The 80x87 math coprocessor is more specialized than its companion processor. The processor, for example, is basically designed to manipulate generic data, independent of the meaning of that data. Of course, a few specialized instructions that are able to manipulate the basic data formats are within each processor's instruction set, but these are the exception rather than the rule. The coprocessor, on the other hand, is very specialized. All data is assumed to be numeric, and all instructions are designed to manipulate that data mathematically. The coprocessor is dedicated entirely to performing floating-point calculations. Figure 2.5 illustrates the data formats that are supported intrinsically by the coprocessor.

Some of the data formats that are supported by the processor are duplicated on the coprocessor. The reason for this duplication is two-fold. First, regardless of the type of processor, all systems with a coprocessor installed will support the same data types. Second, by supporting the integer data types, all calculations can be performed on the coprocessor, eliminating the need to transfer data back and forth when manipulating integers.

It should be noted that each of the data formats shown here is used only when the coprocessor is loading or storing data. Internally, all data operands are converted to the 80-bit temporary real format.

FIGURE 2.5

The coprocessor data types

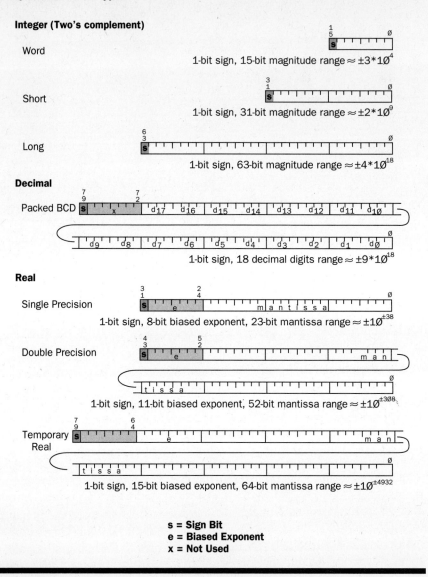

Integer (Two's complement)

Word

1-bit sign, 15-bit magnitude range $\approx \pm 3*10^{4}$

Short

1-bit sign, 31-bit magnitude range $\approx \pm 2*10^{9}$

Long

1-bit sign, 63-bit magnitude range $\approx \pm 4*10^{18}$

Decimal

Packed BCD

1-bit sign, 18 decimal digits range $\approx \pm 9*10^{18}$

Real

Single Precision

1-bit sign, 8-bit biased exponent, 23-bit mantissa range $\approx \pm 10^{\pm 38}$

Double Precision

1-bit sign, 11-bit biased exponent, 52-bit mantissa range $\approx \pm 10^{\pm 308}$

Temporary Real

1-bit sign, 15-bit biased exponent, 64-bit mantissa range $\approx \pm 10^{\pm 4932}$

s = Sign Bit
e = Biased Exponent
x = Not Used

Integers

The integer formats available on the coprocessor are consistent in format with those available on the processor and are shown in Figure 2.5. The high-order bit of the data unit in which the integer is stored is used to indicate the sign of the number. A 0 in the sign bit indicates a positive number, while a 1 indicates a negative number. Two's complement notation is used for all integer formats.

The byte integer format that is available on the processor is not supported on the 80x87. Byte integers may be converted to word integers using the CBW (convert byte to word) instruction. The word integer (16 bits) format is identical to that of the processor.

The 32-bit integer format that was introduced on the 80386 and 80486 processors is supported on all coprocessors as the short integer format. And, an additional 64-bit integer format, called the long integer, has been added. The long integer format can represent an integer value in the range from -2^{63} to $+2^{63}-1$. (2^{63} in decimal is 9,223,372,036,854,775,808—a significant improvement in range compared to even a 32-bit integer.)

Packed BCD

Although the processor provides some instructions for manipulating the packed BCD format, the coprocessor can be said to truly support this format. As shown in Figure 2.5, the packed BCD data type is treated as a single unit that is 80 bits in length. Eighteen 4-bit wide fields are defined to hold the digits of the decimal number. To be considered valid, each digit field must contain a value that is in the range from 0 to 9. Bit 79, the high-order bit, is used as the sign bit; two's complement notation is not used for BCD operands. Bits 72 through 78 of the format are unused; they are ignored when loading and cleared to 0 when storing BCD operands.

The packed BCD data type is frequently used in financial and accounting software. The packed BCD format supported by the 80x87 is compatible with the COBOL language standard. All packed BCD operands are converted to temporary real when loaded. When stored, the temporary real number will be rounded if necessary and converted back to BCD.

Real Numbers

Real numbers are the system of numbers that we use in everyday calculations. Mathematically, the system of real numbers is classified as infinite and continuous. This means that for any real number, there is an infinite quantity of real numbers that is larger and an infinite quantity that is smaller. Between any two real numbers there is also an infinite quantity of numbers. For example, between 2. and 3. is 2.5. Between 2. and 2.5 is 2.25. Between 2.5 and 2.25 is 2.125, and so on. By adding significant digits (more precision), a new number can be found between any two real numbers.

On a computer system, the number of digits available to represent real numbers is limited. Because of this, only a fixed subset of real numbers can be represented. For example, if you were to define a number storage format that provided room for only two digits to the right of the decimal point (radix), the number 1.135 could not be represented exactly. You would be forced to choose either 1.13 or 1.14 as the best approximation. In the coprocessor, the number of representable numbers is still quite large and forms, in most cases, an acceptable approximation to the entire set of real numbers.

Floating-Point Format The data formats for representing real numbers on the 80x87 are normalized floating-point binary representations that are divided into sign, exponent, and mantissa fields. These formats are shown in Figure 2.5 and a summary of their key parameters is given in Table 2.5. The floating-point format that is used is analogous to the scientific notation format used to represent decimal numbers. For example, the decimal number –95.345 would be written as $-9.5345*10^1$ in scientific notation: the sign is negative, the exponent is +1, and the mantissa is 9.5345. As a notational convenience, the letter E or D is often substituted for the number 10 in the exponent. The number would then be written as –9.5345E+1.

TABLE 2.5

Floating-Point Format Parameters

Parameter	Short Real	Long Real	Temporary Real
Data unit size (bits)	32	64P	80
Sign field size (bits)	1	1	1
Mantissa field size (bits)	23	52	64
Implied integer bit in mantissa?	Yes	Yes	No
Exponent field size (bits)	8	11	15
Exponent range	–126 to +127	–1022 to +1023	–16382 to +16383
Exponent bias	+127 (7Fh)	+1023 (3FFh)	+16383 (3FFFh)

Binary floating-point numbers are formed in exactly the same fashion. For example, the binary number +1101.011b could be written as $+1.101011b*2^3$. In this case, the sign is positive, the exponent is +3, and the mantissa is 1.101011b. The binary number 0.0001b can be written as $1.0b*2^{-4}$. When written in this format, with a single 1 digit to the left of the radix, the number is normalized.

One result, then, of using a normalized number format is that each binary number has only one digit to the left of the radix (the integer portion of the number) and that digit will be a 1. (The exception to this rule, of course, is the value 0, which is treated as a special case.) Because the integer digit is invariably a 1, there isn't any reason to actually store it. Instead, its presence can be assumed and the freed bit be used to store an additional bit of mantissa. In the short and long normalized binary real formats, the leading 1 bit is implicit and is not actually stored. Of course, the bit is inserted into the number by the processor before any calculations are performed. The value of the exponent is not affected by this storage convention.

The exponent portion of the floating-point number is stored as a biased exponent. This means that a predetermined constant (the bias value) is added to the true exponent of the number and the resulting value is then stored as part of the floating-point representation of the original number. The bias value for each format has been chosen so that the result of the addition of the true exponent and the bias is always a positive number. This simplifies numeric comparisons (during sorts, for example) by allowing two real numbers of the same format and sign to be compared as if they were unsigned binary numbers. The true exponent of a number is determined by subtracting the bias value from the stored exponent.

Short Real   The short real format (also called the single precision real format) is a 32-bit data item. The sign field is 1 bit long, the mantissa field is 23 bits long, and the exponent field is 8 bits long. The mantissa field is normalized and uses one implicit bit for the integer portion of the number giving 24 significant binary digits. The stored exponent is the sum of the true exponent and the bias value, +127.

The short real format can represent numbers in the order of $\pm 10^{\pm 38}$. The short real format is used by the coprocessor only when transferring data to or from memory. Internally, all short real numbers are converted to the temporary real format. Figure 2.5 displays the layout of the short real format. Table 2.5 summarizes the key parameters of the format.

Long Real   The long real format (also called double precision real) is 64 bits long. The sign field is 1 bit, the mantissa field is 52 bits, and the exponent field is 11 bits. As with the short real format, the mantissa field is normalized and uses an implicit bit for the integer portion of the number. This gives the long real format up to 53 significant binary digits. The stored exponent is biased and is the sum of the true exponent and the bias value, +1023.

The long real format extends the range of representable numbers considerably. Values on the order of $\pm 10^{\pm 308}$ can be stored. The long real format is used by the coprocessor only when reading data from or writing data to memory. Internally, all long real numbers are converted to the temporary real format. Figure 2.5 displays the layout of the long real format. Table 2.5 summarizes the key parameters of the format.

Temporary Real   The temporary real format (recently renamed the extended precision real by Intel) is an 80-bit format that is divided up into a 1-bit sign field, a 15-bit biased exponent field, and a 64-bit mantissa. Unlike the other real number formats, the integer portion of the normalized number is present in the format, not implied. There is no implicit bit in the temporary real format. The stored exponent is biased and is the sum of the true exponent and +16383.

The temporary real format is used by the coprocessor internally for all calculations. All data types read from memory are converted to temporary real automatically. Because the precision and range of the temporary real format are so much greater than the other formats, errors introduced by the calculations on the final result will probably occur outside the range of a short real or long real format.

PROCESSOR ARCHITECTURE

MOST HIGH-LEVEL LANGUAGES ARE DESIGNED TO CONCEAL THE INTERNAL workings of the processor from the programmer—the rationale being that doing so will make the program portable across processors. Assembly language programmers take the opposite approach, eschewing portability to obtain exceptional performance on a single platform. A basic familiarity with the processor and its internal operation is required to write assembly language programs; writing the most effective assembly language programs possible requires a thorough understanding of the processor and computer hardware. At the assembly code level, the more you know about the hardware, the better the software you can write.

This chapter will present an overview of the internal architecture of the 80x86 processor family. Beginning at the hardware level, we'll examine how the processors go about their work and explain the theory of operation of some of their sub-CPU level units and internal structures. Next, a discussion of the register set available on each processor is presented along with an explanation of the addressing modes used by the processor when accessing memory. Finally, the stack implementation used in the 80x86 family is examined, including 16-bit and 32-bit stack operation.

Architectural Overview

The processor is a very complex array of logic circuits that is executing a series of tasks dictated by a built-in "hardware program." The tasks are to fetch, decode, and execute instructions; to fetch operands; and to store results. A processor must have the capability to perform these tasks if it is to accomplish useful work.

The first task is for the processor to fetch instructions from memory, for it is only by this operation that it can determine what to do. A processor without the ability to receive instructions is of little value. Once an instruction has been fetched, it must be decoded. Although the instructions that are fetched from memory are already in machine code—the lowest level of programming information external to the CPU—they still represent complex operations and the CPU must decode them into simpler steps. The information that results from decoding the instruction is used to specify any operands that need to be accessed, what operation is to be performed, and where the result of the operation is to be stored.

As a result of the decoding operation, additional memory or I/O access may be required. For example, if one of the operands of an instruction is located in memory, its address will have to be calculated and then the operand itself will have to be retrieved before the instruction can be executed. Once the instruction has been decoded and the operands located and retrieved, the processor must perform the logic associated with executing the instruction. If a result is generated by the operation, it must be stored as directed by the instruction. This may involve another memory address calculation and access.

These fundamental steps of the processor's operation are simply repeated for as long as the processor is turned on. Note that these same steps form the basis for almost any software program: read data in, act on it, write it back out. The difference is, of course, that the operation of the processor is controlled by hardware, rather than by software.

In this section, we'll take a processor-by-processor look at the basic hardware blocks that make up the CPU. In addition, some of the physical parameters that influence the operation of the processor, such as bus size and internal caches, will be discussed.

The 8086/8088 CPU

Internally, the 8086 and 8088 CPUs are divided into two separate processing units called the *execution unit* and the *bus interface unit* (BIU). This division of the instruction execution logic from the bus control logic marked the distinction between Intel's second and third generations of microprocessors. The execution unit and the BIU are independent processing units that operate asynchronously with each other to maximize overall performance of the CPU.

The execution unit executes instructions while the BIU assumes the burden of fetching instructions from memory, reading operands from memory or I/O, and transferring results back to memory or I/O. Figure 3.1 gives a simplified block diagram of the processing units in the CPU, their relationship to each other, and some of the signals and data that typically pass back and forth.

The Execution Unit The execution unit executes all instructions as well as manipulating the general registers and the status and control flags. The execution unit also sends data and addresses to the BIU when bus activity is required. The execution units used in the 8086 and 8088 are identical.

Instructions are fed to the execution unit over the prefetch queue bus, which is 8 bits wide. The instruction bytes are then processed by the control system, which contains the logic required to decode the instructions and translate them into microcode and control signals. As required by the specific instruction, control signals are directed to the other sections of the execution unit.

The *arithmetic and logic unit* (ALU), as its name implies, performs the arithmetic and logical operations represented in the instruction set. The ALU temporary registers and internal data paths are 16 bits wide in both the 8086 and 8088 processors. The ALU also maintains the CPU status and control flags (flags register). The general registers block represents the programmer-accessible general registers provided in the execution unit. The execution unit is responsible for moving data to and from the registers as required by the instruction.

FIGURE 3.1

8086/8088 CPU block diagram

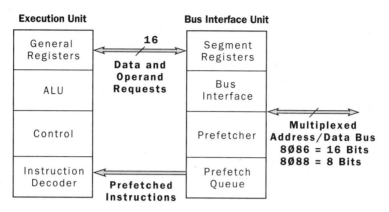

The execution unit has no direct connection to the system bus. Instead, the execution unit receives its instructions from the BIU via the prefetch queue bus. If data is required from memory or an I/O device, the request is passed to the BIU, which locates and retrieves the data, then makes it available to the execution unit. Data that must be written to memory or sent to an I/O device is passed to the BIU by the execution unit, then the BIU is requested to perform the transfer.

The Bus Interface Unit The BIU processes all requests from the execution unit to read data from or write data to memory or I/O devices. The BIU is responsible for all interaction with the system bus, as shown in Figure 3.1. Instructions are prefetched by the BIU and placed in the *instruction prefetch queue*, a small FIFO (first-in, first-out) RAM array, for the execution unit. The BIU interacts with the segment and instruction pointer registers to produce 20-bit addresses for routing to the system bus. The BIUs in the 8086 and 8088 are functionally identical, but are configured differently to accommodate the size difference in the external data buses on the two processors.

All requests for access to memory and I/O devices pass through the BIU and it is the BIU that combines the segment and offset portions of an address, using a dedicated hardware adder, to determine the 20-bit address to be routed to the system bus. All system (external) bus cycles are initiated by the BIU.

During periods when it is not performing other actions, one of the functions of the BIU is to prefetch instructions from memory. The instructions read are those that follow the currently executing instruction in memory. The instructions are stored in the instruction prefetch queue.

Pipelining The separation of the execution and control (BIU) functions of the processor enables it to use a technique called *pipelining* to increase performance. Pipelining, as implemented on the 8086 and 8088, is simply an overlapping of the instruction execution and fetch operations. This is possible because the execution unit and the BIU can operate asynchronously and in parallel.

A simple processor, configured as a single unit, operates serially. First, an instruction is fetched and decoded. If the decoding reveals that a memory operand is required, a bus cycle is initiated to read the operand. Next, the instruction is executed. Finally, the result of the operation, if any, is stored. The top half of Figure 3.2 illustrates schematically what this process might look like.

FIGURE 3.2

Serial and pipelined processing

Serial Processing

| Fetch 1 | Decode 1 | Get Data 1 | Execute 1 | Store Result 1 | Fetch 2 | Decode 2 | Execute 2 | . . . |

Time ⟶

Pipelined Processing

BIU

| Fetch 1 | Fetch 2 | Get Data 1 | Fetch 3 | Store Result 1 | Fetch 4 |

Execution Unit

| Decode 1 | Execute 1 | Decode 2 | Execute 2 |

On the 8086 and 8088, the functions of the execution unit and the BIU are decoupled. An executing instruction that is not fetching operands or storing results leaves the BIU free to perform instruction prefetching. This parallel operation is called pipelining and is illustrated in the bottom half of Figure 3.2. As shown, the execution and fetch cycles are effectively overlapped and the execution unit and the BIU operate in parallel. Compared to serial processing, pipelining has two advantages: the execution unit will almost always find an instruction waiting in the prefetch queue and, since the execution unit does not spend its time performing bus operations, more instructions can be executed in the same amount of time.

The Instruction Prefetch Queue   When not busy accessing memory or I/O devices, the BIU will prefetch instructions for the execution unit. The prefetch logic instructs the BIU to load bytes (for the 8088) or words (for the 8086) from memory addresses that follow the currently executing instruction—that is, the next logical instruction as long as execution proceeds serially. As each byte or word is read, it is placed into the instruction prefetch queue in the BIU where it can be accessed by the execution unit with little or no delay. Because the execution unit must wait for data operands to be read from memory by the BIU, an execution unit request will be processed first if both an execution unit request and a prefetch request are received.

The prefetch queue in the 8088 holds four bytes and the BIU will begin a fetch cycle whenever there is one or more bytes empty in the queue. The 8088, because of its 8-bit system bus, always prefetches a byte at a time. In the 8086, the prefetch queue is six bytes long and the BIU will begin a prefetch cycle whenever there are two or more bytes empty in the queue. Because the 8086 uses a 16-bit system bus, two instruction bytes can be prefetched in each cycle. Table 3.1 lists the size of the prefetch queue and other parameters for each of the processors.

TABLE 3.1

Prefetch Queue Parameters

Processor	88	86	286	386SX	386DX	486SX	486DX
Size of prefetch queue (bytes)	4	6	6	16	16	32	32
Number of empty bytes required to initiate prefetch cycle	1	2	2	2	4	16 (burst)	16 (burst)
Decoded instruction queue length (instructions)	none	none	3	3	3	none	none

When an instruction that causes program control to be transferred to a non-sequential location (a jump, call, interrupt, or return instruction, for example) is executed, the instructions that have been prefetched will no longer be valid. In this case, the BIU flushes (empties) the prefetch queue and immediately starts an instruction prefetch cycle at the target address. If control is transferred to an odd numbered address, the 8086 BIU will fetch a byte from the target address, then resume prefetching a word at a time.

After the prefetch queue is flushed, a delay in execution will occur until the BIU is able to execute a bus cycle and place an instruction in the queue for the execution unit. This side effect of flushing the prefetch queue is often used to generate a small delay between two operations, such as back-to-back I/O on the same device. By executing a jump to the next instruction (coded as JMP $+2), the queue will be flushed and a delay introduced before the next instruction is processed.

Self-Modifying Code Another interesting property of the operation of the prefetch queue becomes evident when executing instructions that modify the instruction stream. These instructions, usually called self-modifying code, act directly on the area of system memory from which the processor is retrieving and executing instructions. If an instruction that has already been prefetched is then modified in memory, the copy of the original form of the instruction that is in the prefetch queue will be executed, not the modified version that is in system memory. A direct examination of system memory would, however, display the modified code. To avoid this situation, the displacement of the instruction to be modified from the modifying instruction must be greater than the length of the prefetch queue. Equivalently, the prefetch queue could be flushed with a control transfer instruction as described above.

The interaction of self-modifying mode and the prefetch queue has frequently been exploited by wiley programmers in schemes to frustrate code disassemblers. The technique is simple, but very effective until you realize what is happening. Briefly, here's how it works.

Assume that somewhere in the initialization code for your program you are about to move the address of a callable routine from a particular memory location to the BX register. Just before the instruction that performs the load, you add an instruction that modifies the move instruction, rendering it meaningless. When your program executes normally, the unmodified version of the move instruction will already be in the prefetch queue when the modification is performed. The modification will therefore have no effect on the program's normal execution. The assembler listing for these instructions would look something like that shown here:

```
Offset Encoding  Source Code

0000  FE 06 0004 R  INC BYTE PTR [$+4]   ;Modify next instruction
0004  8B 1E 0100    MOV BX,DS:[100H]    ;Already in queue
```

Now assume that our junior disassembler comes along and is single-stepping through your code with DEBUG. Because the debugger is using interrupts and other control transfer operations to step through your program, the prefetch queue will be flushed after each instruction and reloaded before execution of the next one. The result is that the modified version of the instruction will be loaded and executed. The opcode 8Bh will be patched to 8Ch and in place of the original instruction MOV BX,DS:[100h], will be the phony instruction MOV DS:[100h],DS. Your program will try to call a routine using an incorrect address and fail. And our would-be code breaker is left wondering why your program executes differently depending on how it's executed. Scatter a few of these modifications throughout your code and tracing through it becomes more trouble than it's worth.

The 80286 CPU

The concept of pipelined architecture, which enhanced the efficiency of the 8086, was logically expanded in the design of the 80286 processor. The operation of the 80286 is divided into four independent processing units, each of which operates asynchronously and in parallel with the others. The four processing units of the 80286 are the *execution unit, address unit instruction unit*, and the *bus interface unit* (BIU). A simplified block diagram of the four processing units and their interconnection is shown in Figure 3.3. As in the 8086, the parallel operation of these units allows the 80286 to make effective use of the system bus while minimizing the time spent waiting for information.

The operation of the execution unit of the 80286 is similar to that of the 8086 and is responsible for executing instructions. The 80286 BIU is comparable to the BIU of the 8086, but lacks the address generation function. The BIU handles all memory and I/O read, write, and fetch operations and is the CPU's interface to the system bus. Responsibility for address generation, however, has been moved to a separate unit, the address unit. Finally, the instruction unit is responsible for decoding instructions from the prefetch queue in preparation for the execution unit.

FIGURE 3.3

80286 CPU block diagram

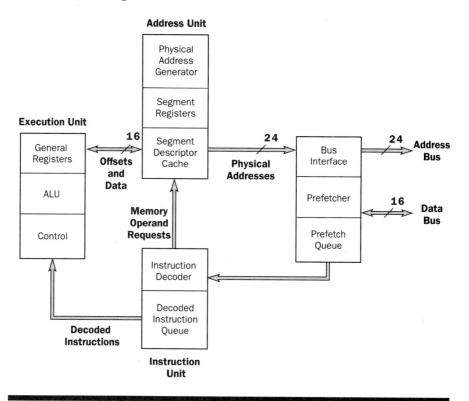

The Execution Unit   The execution unit manipulates the general registers as well as the status and control flags and executes all instructions. In the 80286, the execution unit does not have to decode instructions, but fetches them from a decoded instruction queue that holds three fully decoded instructions. As required by the instruction, control signals are sent to other units within the execution unit. The execution unit will also, when necessary, send requests to the BIU to perform data transfers to and from memory and I/O devices.

The arithmetic and logic unit performs the arithmetic and logical operations that are required by the instruction set. The ALU also maintains the CPU status and control flags. The general registers also form part of the execution unit, and it is the execution unit that moves data to and from the registers as required.

The Bus Interface Unit   The bus interface unit (BIU) handles all communication and data transfer between the CPU and the system bus. The BIU handles bus operation details including generating the address, command, and data signals required to access memory and I/O devices. Unlike the 8086, the address and data lines of the 80286 are not multiplexed and use dedicated signal lines. The BIU communicates directly with the other processor units within the CPU to receive requests for bus activity.

Because the execution unit must wait for data when executing instructions, data request operations have priority use of the BIU. When not otherwise occupied, however, the BIU uses idle bus cycles to prefetch instructions. The prefetch queue in the 80286 is six bytes long, the same size as in the 8086. A prefetch cycle will be attempted whenever two or more bytes in the prefetch queue are empty. Instead of sending the instructions directly to the execution unit, as in the 8086, the BIU of the 80286 sends them to the instruction unit, which decodes them before passing them to the execution unit.

A control transfer instruction causes the BIU to flush the prefetch queue and immediately begin loading instructions from the new execution address. The 80286 prefetches a word at a time. If, however, control is transferred to an odd numbered address, the word from the nearest lower word address is fetched and the low byte is ignored. Further prefetching then retrieves words from even addresses.

When executing instructions in real mode that are near the end of a code segment, the internal logic of the prefetch operation may fetch up to six bytes past the end of the code segment. Note that any attempt to execute these instructions (in other words, execution past the end of the code segment) will cause the processor to generate an exception (interrupt 0Dh). In protected mode, the prefetch operation itself will never cause the processor to generate a segment overrun error; prefetching stops at the last physical word in the code segment.

The Instruction Unit   The instruction unit was introduced in the 80286 architecture and decodes prefetched instruction bytes for use by the execution unit. As bytes are prefetched from the code segment by the BIU, the instruction unit retrieves them from the prefetch queue and decodes them. Up to three fully decoded instructions are available in the queue provided by the instruction unit. Immediate data operands and operand offsets associated with the prefetched instructions are also taken directly from the prefetch queue.

The Address Unit   Memory management, protection, and virtual addressing make address generation on the 80286 much more complex than on the 8086. The address unit was introduced to handle the additional workload. In real mode, the address unit works much the same as in the 8086. Segment and offset values are summed together by a dedicated adder to produce a physical memory address. When running in protected mode, however, every memory reference, including code prefetches, must be checked against the permissions and segment limits of the current task to detect memory protection violations. Once permission for the memory access is granted, the logical address still must be translated to a physical address for use by the BIU.

As you can imagine, if not performed separately by the address unit, the address verification and translation process would require substantial CPU resources. To prevent performance from being affected too greatly, a cache has been designed into the address unit. One *segment descriptor cache register* is provided for each of the four segment registers. Whenever a segment register is loaded with a new value, the segment descriptor associated with that value (and which specifies the access rights, segment base address, and segment size) is automatically loaded into the appropriate segment descriptor cache register. Once loaded, all references to that segment will use the segment information in the cache instead of accessing memory. The descriptor cache is not accessible outside the address unit.

The 80386 CPU

The architecture of the 80386 is reminiscent of the 80286, but has again been greatly enhanced. The CPU has been divided into six independent processing units: the *bus interface unit* (BIU), *code prefetch unit*, *instruction decode unit*, *execution unit*, *segmentation unit*, and *paging unit*. Because each of these units operates independently and in parallel, the CPU will typically be performing prefetch, decode, execution, memory management, and bus access services for several different instructions at the same time. This six-level pipelining gives the 80386 a large performance advantage. A simplified block diagram of the layout of the processing units of the 80386 is given in Figure 3.4. Note that all of these units are capable of direct communication with the BIU, allowing instructions, immediate data, and memory offsets to be retrieved at different stages of execution. The overall performance of the 80386 has also been improved by the addition of specialized hardware such as a 64-bit barrel shifter, a three-input adder dedicated to effective address processing, and an early-out multiplier.

The principle architectural difference between the two types of 80386 (the 80386DX and the 80386SX) is the width of the external address and data buses; internally, both chips use 32-bit data pathways. The address bus of the 386DX is 32 bits wide, giving it the potential to directly address 4 gigabytes (2^{32} bytes) of physical memory. The address bus of the 386SX is only 24 bits wide, providing access to 16Mb (2^{24} bytes) of physical memory.

The Bus Interface Unit   As in the 80286, the bus interface unit (BIU) is the connection between the CPU and the outside world of the processor bus. Without exception, all requests for access to the bus that come from the other on-chip processing units pass through the BIU. Because of the parallel operation of the processing units, the possibility exists that more than one bus request may be received by the BIU at the same time. In addition to performing the bus interface, the BIU must queue and prioritize these requests. To avoid delaying program execution, requests from the execution unit for data transfers have priority over code prefetch requests from the code unit.

FIGURE 3.4

80386DX/80386SX CPU block diagram

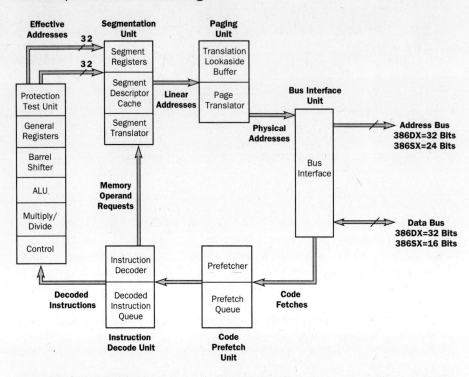

The Code Prefetch Unit The responsibility for prefetching instructions, which fell on the BIU in the 80286, has been split into a separate processing unit on the 80386. When the BIU is not performing bus cycles that are part of an instruction execution, the code prefetch unit will request instruction prefetches. Because the execution unit must wait while data is being retrieved, code prefetches are given a lower priority by the BIU. The 80386 can store up to 16 bytes of prefetched instructions in the prefetch queue, a substantial improvement over the 6-byte queue of the 80286. Once prefetched, the instructions are ready for decoding by the instruction unit.

The Instruction Decode Unit The instruction decode unit reads prefetched instruction bytes from the prefetch queue, decodes them, and places them in a three-deep decoded instruction queue for use by the execution unit. The instruction unit will start to decode an instruction whenever there is a free slot in the decoded instruction queue and there are bytes available in the prefetch queue. When an instruction is decoded, the machine code bytes are translated into microcode entry points and control signals used by the other processing units. If immediate data or opcodes are specified by the instruction, these are also taken from the prefetch queue. Opcodes can be decoded at the rate of one byte per clock cycle. Immediate data and address offsets, regardless of their length, are decoded in one clock cycle.

The Execution Unit   The execution unit of the 80386 retrieves instructions that have been decoded by the instruction unit and executes them. During the execution of an instruction, the execution unit may have to communicate with each of the other processing units that make up the CPU. The functions of the 80386 execution unit can be divided into three major units: the control unit, the data unit, and the protection test unit.

The function of the control unit is to speed up certain types of operations including multiplies, divides, and effective address calculations. This speed-up is accomplished with a combination of microcode and parallel hardware. In effect, the control unit contains hard-coded software designed to perform these tasks quickly and efficiently.

The data unit contains the arithmetic and logic unit and the eight 32-bit general registers of the 80386. Both the ALU and the general registers have been associated with the execution unit since the 8086. In addition, however, the 80386 data unit includes a 64-bit barrel shifter, specialized hardware that performs multiple bit shifts in a single clock cycle. An early-out multiplier, implemented in microcode, terminates the multiply algorithm when no significant digits remain to be processed.

The protection test unit monitors memory access to detect segmentation violations. Access to memory for any reason, including execution, is strictly controlled when the processor is running in protected mode. This unit implements protection violation checks in microcode.

The Segmentation Unit   The segmentation unit performs the first stage of address translation, converting logical addresses into linear addresses. As in the 80286, segment descriptor caches are employed both to speed up the translation and to allow protection violations to be detected without affecting performance unacceptably. A dedicated three-input adder, implemented in microcode, also speeds the address calculation. The address translation is performed at the request of the execution unit. Note that the protection violation checks performed by the segmentation unit are separate from the static segmentation violation checks performed by the protection test unit on the execution unit. Once translated, the linear addresses are passed to the paging unit.

The Paging Unit   The paging unit translates the linear addresses generated by the segmentation unit into physical memory addresses. If paging is not enabled, the physical address is the same as the linear address and no translation is performed. When paging is enabled, the translation from linear to physical address must be performed continuously for every memory reference. Once the translation is complete, the physical address is passed to the BIU.

The paging unit contains a cache called the *translation lookaside buffer* (TLB), which holds the 32 most recently used page table entries. The TLB is configured as a *four-way set associative* cache with 32 page table entries. The structure of the TLB for both the 386DX and 386SX is shown in Figure 3.5.

The 386DX/386SX translation lookaside buffer (TLB) structure

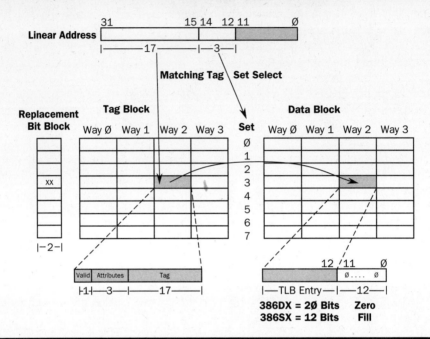

In the four-way set associative structure, there are four possible cache locations in which to store data from a particular area of memory. As seen in Figure 3.6, the cache comprises three blocks: the *replacement block*, the *tag block*, and the *data block*.

The tag block is divided into four arrays, or *ways*. Each way has space for eight *sets* of four entries. Each entry in the tag block is 21 bits wide and is divided into a 17-bit *tag field*, a 3-bit *attribute field*, and a 1-bit *valid field*. The three attributes bits are the user/supervisor (U/S), read/write (R/W), and dirty (D) bits.

The data block is divided into four ways. Each way has space for eight sets of four entries. In the 386DX, each entry in the data block contains the high-order 20 bits of a physical address field. The TLB entry is zero-extended on the right with 12 zero bits to form a 32-bit address. Because the lower 12 bits are zero, each entry uniquely identifies a 4k page in memory. In the 386SX, the 12 high-order bits of the physical address are stored in the TLB. When zero-extended on the right, a 24-bit physical address is formed.

The replacement block contains 2 bits that are used to determine where the next entry is to be written to the TLB. A pseudorandom replacement algorithm is implemented, but details of its operation are proprietary and have not been published by Intel.

FIGURE 3.6

80486 CPU block diagram

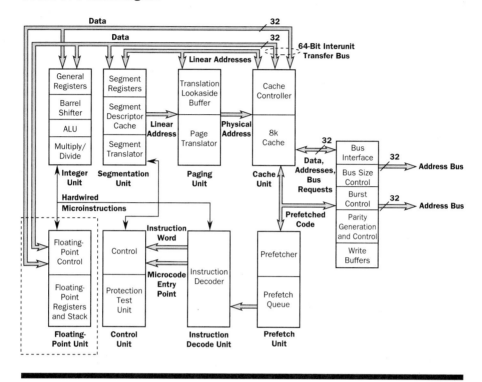

A TLB lookup operation on the 386DX, for example, would operate as follows (see Figure 3.5).

1. Bits 12, 13, and 14 of the linear address are used to select one of the eight TLB sets.

2. The high-order 17 bits of the linear address are compared to the tag field in each of the four entries in the selected set in the tag block.

3. If no match is found, a TLB miss is reported. If a match is found, and the valid bit is set, a TLB hit is reported.

4. The set and way of the matching tag entry are used as indexes into the data block to select the high-order 20 bits of the physical address.

5. The TLB entry is zero-extended on the right to form a 32-bit physical address.

The 80486 CPU

The 80486 processor combines an integer processing unit (the CPU), a floating-point processing unit (the math coprocessor), and a unified code/data cache in a single chip. Because these units are included in a single package, the signals that pass between them run at fast "on-chip" speeds rather than at the slower speeds of external circuitry. The impact of the external bus and device speeds on overall processing time is reduced even more by the use of the on-chip cache.

The architecture of the 80486 bus is similar to that of the 80386 in that the address and data buses are 32 bits wide. The 80486 bus also provides support for parity checking, burst cycles, cacheable cycles, and cache invalidation cycles, and can be configured dynamically for 8-, 16-, or 32-bit data operations.

Data transfers from memory can now be performed with burst transfers, a technique that allows a doubleword to be read in a single clock cycle. This capability allows the processor to quickly fill the internal cache and prefetch queue without monopolizing the bus. The 80486 also implements write buffering, allowing the processor to begin a write operation, then continue other operations internally while waiting for the bus to complete execution of the write.

In addition to the internal cache, support is provided for write-back and flush controls over an external cache. This control is especially necessary in a multiprocessor environment so that the contents of the external cache are appropriate to the processor it is serving at any instant.

Internally, the 80486 is divided into nine processing units, as shown in Figure 3.6, and is similar in architecture to the 80386. The *cache unit* is new, as is the inclusion of the floating-point unit (FPU). Each of the nine units can operate in parallel, allowing pipelined operation of the 80486 to provide a continuous execution rate of one clock cycle per instruction for most instructions.

The pipelining method used in the 80486 incurs an additional clock of execution time when certain back-to-back operations on an addressing register are performed. If an instruction that alters a register is immediately followed by an instruction that uses the altered register to address memory, three clocks instead of two are required for execution. If an unrelated instruction is placed between the two references to the register, the penalty clock is not incurred. The following code illustrates this situation:

```
ADD   EBX,6              ;Back-to-back
NOT   DWORD PTR [EBX]    ; takes 3 clocks


ADD   EBX,6              ;Separate with un-
INC   ECX                ; related instruction
NOT   DWORD PTR [EBX]    ; takes 2 clocks
```

Most high-level languages perform addressing via the stack or base pointer and will not normally incur this penalty. The processor also includes special hardware to perform stack increment and decrement operations and an extra register port to execute back-to-back stack push/pop instructions in a single clock.

The Bus Interface Unit   As in the other processors, the bus interface unit (BIU) of the 80486 is solely responsible for the interface to the external processor bus. Unlike the other processors, however, the BIU exchanges data internally only with the cache unit and instruction prefetch unit; requests from all other processing units pass through the cache unit first. All requests for access to the bus, including instruction prefetch, memory reads, and cache fills, are prioritized and executed by the BIU.

The BIU reads data from the external bus 16 bytes at a time for transfer to the cache unit. If the cache contents are updated by an internal processor operation, the contents of the cache are written to external memory by the BIU. If a read request cannot be cached, it is simply passed directly to the requesting unit.

When an instruction prefetch is requested by the code prefetch unit, the BIU returns the information to both the code prefetch unit and the cache. Although this may seem redundant, further prefetches of the same code, such as in tightly coded loops, may then be satisfied by access to the cache.

The BIU can buffer up to four 32-bit write transfers to memory. Once a write operation has been buffered, the unit that initiated the operation can resume processing. Addresses, data, or control information can be buffered. Single writes into I/O space are not buffered, but multiple I/O writes may be. The buffers can accept writes as fast as one per clock cycle. If no higher-priority bus request is pending and the bus is available, the write will be performed immediately and no delay is incurred. If all four buffers are full, additional write requests will not be accepted and the requesting unit will be forced to wait.

The BIU can reprioritize bus requests. A read request received while a write request is pending will be executed first. This is because the processing unit will most likely be delayed while waiting for a read to complete, but a delayed write has less likelihood of holding up the operation of the processor. I/O reads are never reordered before buffered writes to memory. In this way, a device status will not be read before all memory writes are completed.

To prevent the reordering from creating a situation where invalid data is read, reordering takes place only if all buffered writes are cache hits. In that case, the data in the cache will have been updated by the buffered write and the data simply needs to be copied to memory. A read of that same data (hence a cache hit) will be satisfied from the updated value in the cache and not the unupdated value in memory.

All reordered writes are reflagged as cache misses when a read is put in front of them. This allows them to be usurped only once. Invalidating the internal cache causes all pending writes to be reflagged as misses. Disabling the cache unit disables the write buffers.

The Cache Unit   The 80486 CPU contains 8k of high-speed RAM configured as an on-chip cache and managed by the cache unit. When caching is enabled, all requests for bus access issued by the other processing units in the CPU pass through the cache unit first before going to the BIU. If a bus access request can be satisfied by the cache, the request is immediately satisfied and no bus cycle is initiated by the BIU. This condition is called a *cache hit*. If the request cannot be satisfied by the cache, a condition called a *cache miss*, the requested memory area is read into the cache by the BIU in 16-byte transfers called *cache line fills*. The read request is then satisfied by the cache unit.

Write operations are likewise screened through the cache. If the target of a write operation is found in the cache, the cache is updated immediately and a bus write operation is initiated to write the change to memory. This operation is called *cache write-through*. The cache unit uses only physical memory addresses and is unaware of their logical or linear counterparts. This strategy minimizes the number of times the cache data must be replaced when the same physical memory is addressed by a different logical or virtual address.

The cache unit and the code prefetch unit are closely coupled and receive instruction prefetches simultaneously. An instruction prefetch request that is a cache miss will cause a cache line fill. The data will be transferred both to the cache unit and the code prefetch unit simultaneously.

Inside the CPU, the cache unit shares two 32-bit internal data buses with the segmentation, integer, and floating-point units. When 64-bit segment descriptors are moved from the cache to the segmentation unit, 32 bits are passed on each bus, giving a 64-bit internal transfer bus.

The 80486 cache is organized as a *four-way set associative* cache. This organization is not optimal under all conditions and the algorithm represents a performance trade-off by Intel. A direct-mapped cache, for example, operates much more quickly when the memory request is a cache hit. A fully associative cache, on the other hand, has a high cache hit-to-miss ratio. In the four-way set associative structure, there are four possible cache locations in which to store data from a particular area of memory.

As can be seen in Figure 3.7, the 8k of cache memory in the data block is divided into four 2k ways. Each way is again divided up as 128 sets of four 16-byte cache lines. Also associated with each set are four 21-bit tag fields in the tag block, and a 3-bit LRU field and a 4-bit valid field in the Valid/LRU block. Each cache line is used to hold a copy of 16 contiguous bytes of memory. The first byte in each cache line corresponds to a memory address that is evenly divisible by 16 (a paragraph boundary).

The cache unit determines if a physical address is a cache hit as follows. First, the 32-bit physical address is divided into three fields, the index, tag, and byte fields, as shown in Figure 3.7. The 7 bits of the index field specify the set number, from 0 to 127, that will be used as an index into both the data and tag blocks. The tag, the 21 high-order bits of the address, is then compared to the contents of the four tag fields associated with the selected set. If a match is found, it indicates that a 16-byte cache line is present for that physical address. The number of the way in which the matching tag was found indicates the number of the way in which the cache line is located. The low-order 4 bits of the physical address are then used to select the desired byte within the cache line. A 4-bit valid field is associated with each set. One bit is used for each cache line in the set and indicates whether the data that is cached is valid.

As memory accesses are requested, data will be read from memory into the cache. The cache unit decides where the new data will be written by examining the bits in the VALID and LRU fields to implement a pseudo-LRU (least recently used) algorithm as shown in Figure 3.8. All cache writes update the LRU bits.

FIGURE 3.7

80486 cache organization

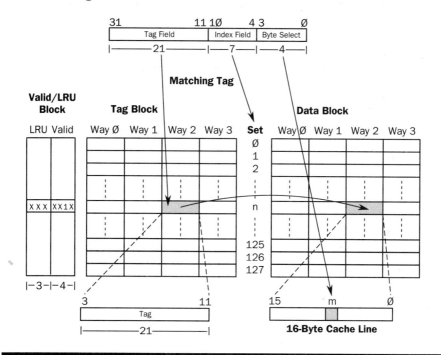

The index field of the physical address is used to select the appropriate set number. First, the valid bits in the Valid/LRU block entry associated with the selected set are checked for any invalid bits. If a bit is found that indicates an invalid line is present, the cache line associated with that bit is marked for replacement. If no invalid lines are found, the pseudo-LRU algorithm is used as shown in Figure 3.8. When the processor is reset or the cache is flushed, all lines in all sets are flagged as invalid. Cache lines can also be invalidated by a *cache line invalidation* operation on the processor bus.

The cache configuration is controlled by two bits in the processor control register CR0, the machine status register of the processor. These bits are the *Cache Disable* (CD) bit and the *Not Write-through* (NW) bit. When caching is enabled (CD=0), memory reads and instruction prefetches are cacheable. (A cache write miss does not update the cache under any circumstances.) If caching is disabled (CD=1), a cache miss will not cause a cache line fill. Note, however, that valid data already present in the cache when caching is disabled will still be used to satisfy read requests if a cache hit occurs. Only when all data in the cache is marked invalid, such as after a cache flush or when the processor has been reset, will all read requests be forwarded to the BIU.

When cache write-throughs are enabled (NW=0), all writes, including those that hit in the cache, are written through to memory. If cache write-throughs are disabled (NW=1), a write request that hits in the cache will not be written to memory. Neither will cache invalidation operations be recognized.

FIGURE 3.8

The 80486 cache unit pseudo-LRU replacement algorithm

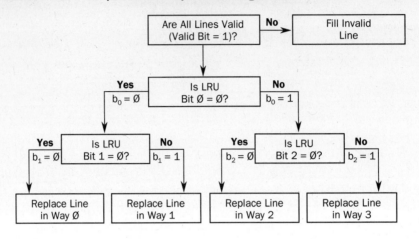

LRU Bits Before Replacement				LRU Bits After Replacement		
b_0	b_1	b_2	Replace Line	b_0	b_1	b_2
0	0	X	0	1	1	X
0	1	X	1	1	0	X
1	X	0	2	0	X	1
1	X	1	3	0	X	0

When both CD and NW are set to 1 and the cache is flushed, the cache will be completely disabled. This mode is used for special debugging situations that require bus memory cycles to appear at the processor pins. It is also possible to use the 8k cache as fast static RAM in this mode. The contents of the cache may be preloaded by controlling memory references or by using the test functions provided by the processor to load the cache. When the cache is disabled, the cache memory is static.

The Code Prefetch Unit The code prefetch unit sends requests to the BIU to read bytes from the instruction stream during what would otherwise be idle bus cycles. The code prefetch unit is closely coupled with the cache unit, and prefetched data is read into both the cache and the prefetch queue simultaneously. An instruction prefetch cycle reads a 16-byte block of memory. The memory address of the prefetch is generated by the prefetch unit itself, which has a direct connection to the segmentation unit. If a prefetch request can be satisfied from the cache, no bus cycle will be initiated.

The prefetch queue in the 80486 holds 32 bytes and accepts prefetches in 16-byte transfers. As with the other processors, the prefetch queue is flushed whenever a control transfer instruction, such as a jump, interrupt, task switch, and so on, is executed. The prefetch unit will never access beyond the end of a code segment nor will it access a page that is not present.

The Instruction Decode Unit   The instruction decode unit reads prefetched instructions from the prefetch queue and translates the machine code bytes into control signals for the other processing units and microcode entry points for execution. Instructions are decoded in a two-step process. During the first decode step, the instruction unit determines if the instruction requires a memory access. If so, a bus cycle request is initiated immediately so that the memory operand will be available by the time the instruction is fully decoded and ready to execute.

Note that unlike the 80286 and 80386, the 80486 has no decoded instruction queue. Most instructions can be decoded at the rate of one per clock. This, coupled with the two-step decode process, makes the queue unnecessary. The instruction decode unit is flushed whenever the prefetch queue is flushed.

Control Unit   The control unit executes the instructions that have been decoded and exerts control over the integer, floating-point, and segmentation units. The control unit of the 80486 contains the processor's microcode, the instructions that control the operation of the processor. In previous processors, the function of the control unit was integrated in the execution unit.

Integer Unit   The integer (datapath) unit of the 80486 contains the processor's eight 32-bit general registers, the arithmetic and logic unit, and a 64-bit barrel shifter that performs multiple bit shifts in one clock cycle. Single load, store, addition, subtraction, and logic instructions are also executed in one clock cycle.

The two 32-bit data buses connecting the integer, cache, and floating-point unit are used together for transferring 64-bit operands in a single operation. The integer unit has a separate 32-bit connection to the segmentation unit that is used to transfer data to generate effective addresses.

Segmentation and Paging Units   Taken together, the segmentation unit and the paging unit constitute the memory management unit (MMU) of the 80486 and are used to implement both memory protection and virtual memory management. The segmentation unit translates a logical (segmented) address into a linear (unsegmented) address. The location of a segment in the linear address space is provided by a processor data structure known as a *segment descriptor*. The linear address of the segment is then combined with an offset to form the complete linear address.

Whenever a segment register is loaded with a new value, the segment descriptor associated with that value (and that specifies the access rights, segment base address, and segment size) is automatically loaded into a special register in the segment descriptor cache located in the segmentation unit. Once loaded, all references to that segment will use the segment information in the cache instead of accessing memory.

The paging unit performs the management of virtual memory. Virtual memory allows the processor to work with data structures that are larger than available physical memory by keeping them partly in memory and partly on disk. The linear address space of the processor is divided into 4k blocks called *pages*. To implement paging, page tables are used to map a linear address to a physical address. The physical address is then passed to the BIU (via the cache) for memory access.

The paging unit is able to raise *page faults* when it identifies a situation that demands attention. For example, if access is requested to a page that is not currently in memory, a page fault will be generated, giving the operating system an opportunity to load the required page from disk. If paging is not enabled, no translation is performed and the physical address generated is identical to the linear address input.

The paging unit contains its own cache called the translation lookaside buffer (TLB), which holds the 32 most recently used page table entries. The TLB is configured as a four-way set associative cache with 32 page table entries, a Valid/Attributed/Tag block, and a LRU block. The structure of the TLB is shown in Figure 3.9.

FIGURE 3.9

The 80486 translation lookaside buffer (TLB) structure

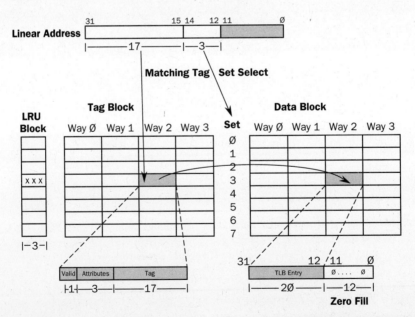

There are two main differences between the TLBs of the 80486 and 80386 processors. First, the TLB in the 80486 can be accessed without disabling paging. Also, while the 80386 TLB uses a proprietary pseudorandom replacement algorithm, the TLB in the 80486 uses the same pseudo-LRU algorithm as implemented in the cache unit. (For an explanation of the algorithm, see the description of the cache unit earlier in this chapter.)

Floating-Point Unit   The 486DX chip includes an integrated math coprocessor that is referred to as the floating-point unit (FPU). From the programmer's point of view, the FPU operates identically to an external math coprocessor. In hardware terms, however, execution speed is significantly improved when all operands are in registers or accessible in the cache. When data is read from or written to external memory, burst transfers are used to minimize execution time.

The 486SX chip is a special version of the 486DX in which the internal floating-point unit and signal output pins have been mechanically disabled. All other operations of the processor (integer instructions, caching, virtual memory, etc.) are unchanged. The 487SX chip, nominally identified as the math coprocessor for the 486SX, is in reality a 486DX with some additional control signals. When the 486SX and 487SX are installed in the same system, the 487SX asserts the MP# (math present) signal causing the 486SX to float its outputs and get off the bus. The 487SX, having disabled the 486SX, then handles all processing in the system. From a programming perspective, the 486SX/487SX combination is identical to a 486DX.

The 80x86 Registers

It was customary in the early days of microprocessor development for the designers of the chip to impose strict limitations on how the processor's registers could be used. Designers were not overly concerned with the plight of programmers. Because of the architecture of the chip, all arithmetic and logical operations, for example, might have had to be performed using a register called the Accumulator. Much of the programmer's time was spent writing instructions to move data from memory to the Accumulator and back again. A great deal of effort was required to perform anything more than the simplest tasks.

Fortunately, the 8086 chip provides an instruction set rich in possibilities, an adequate quantity of registers, and far fewer restrictions than other processors. Restrictions in the chip architecture still mean that some 8086 operations execute faster when certain registers are used as operands. There are still restrictions on certain register/operation combinations as well, but the result is far greater freedom for the programmer.

The 8086 has 14 16-bit registers whose contents completely define the current state of the processor. These registers include four general-purpose registers, two pointer registers, two index registers, four segment registers, the instruction pointer register, and the flags register. The 8086 registers and their organization and layout are illustrated in Figure 3.10.

The descriptions that follow outline the properties of the 8086 register set. Programs written using this information will execute correctly on all 80x86 processors.

The more advanced processors in the 80x86 family have enhanced and expanded the register set. These differences are described later in this chapter.

FIGURE 3.10

The 8086 register set

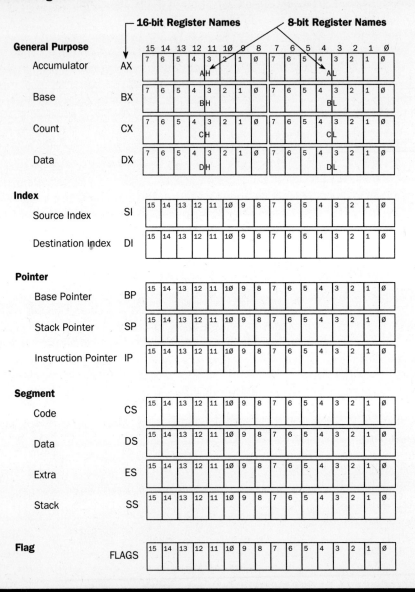

The General-Purpose Registers

The four general-purpose registers are designated AX, BX, CX, and DX. Any of these registers may be used as an operand in both 8- or 16-bit arithmetic or logical instruction. They possess the useful property that each may be referenced as either a single 16-bit register or as two separate 8-bit registers. This aliasing allows programmers to save both time and space, as 8-bit instructions often occupy fewer bytes of memory and execute faster than their 16-bit forms. Many instructions, such as the string and bit-shift functions, for example, make extensive use of the 8-bit registers.

The AX register is known mnemonically as the Accumulator or Arithmetic register. The AX register is unique in that all I/O instructions and some string operations must be performed using this register. To reduce code size, some instructions assume the AX register as a default operand. The DIV BL instruction, for example, will divide the 16-bit AX register by the 8-bit BL register. The 8-bit quotient will be stored in the AL register and the 8-bit remainder in the AH register. Instructions that reference immediate data also require fewer bytes when they reference the AX register.

The BX register, called the Base register, is the only general-purpose register that may be used as the base (starting memory offset) in address calculations when accessing memory. This, coupled with the fact that it may be aliased as BH and BL, makes it one of the most versatile and overtaxed registers in the 8086 instruction set.

The CX, or Count register, is used by the 8086 as the variable in loop and repeated string operations. It is also used as the count in bit-manipulation instructions. As you can imagine, nested loops must often save and restore the CX register, requiring the programmer to juggle registers. The JCXZ instruction is the only conditional jump instruction that both tests a register (instead of the status flags) and jumps in a single instruction.

The DX register is commonly called the Data register and is the designated register for holding the port address in some I/O instructions. It is also combined semantically with the AX register (and written as DX:AX) to represent a single 32-bit quantity in some arithmetic instructions. The instruction MUL AX,BX will multiply the two 16-bit quantities in AX and BX and put the 32-bit result in the register combination DX:AX. The most significant part of the value is stored in DX and the least significant part is stored in AX.

The Index Registers

The Source Index (SI) register and Destination Index (DI) register derive their names from their use in the 8086 string operations. For example, the 8086 move-string instruction MOVSB will copy consecutive bytes of memory from an address specified by SI (the source) to the address specified by DI (the destination).

SI and DI may be used as operands in all arithmetic and logical operations, just as the general-purpose registers. In addition, SI and DI may be used in 8086 address calculations for indexed addressing, hence the term index register. As index registers, they specify an additional offset from a memory base or base register, a convenience when operating on tables and arrays. Some high-level languages preempt SI and DI for internal use and require that values of these registers be preserved by subprograms.

The Pointer Registers

The 16-bit Base Pointer (BP) register is the workhorse register of stack data manipulation. It is most often used as a base to address the area of memory used for the stack. (Both the segment registers and the stack are discussed in detail later in this chapter.) BP is often used by high-level languages to create a stack frame in subroutines to allocate temporary storage and access parameters that have been passed on the stack. BP can be addressed only as a 16-bit register, not as two separate 8-bit quantities.

The Stack Pointer (SP) register, in conjunction with the stack segment register, is used to implement the program stack in the 8086. This is explained fully in the discussion of the stack later in this chapter. The 8086 depends on having a valid stack at all times, so you must be careful when switching or setting a program's stack to avoid crashing the machine. All operations that use SP as a memory operand, such as PUSH and POP, invariably use the stack segment for address calculations.

The Instruction Pointer

The Instruction Pointer (IP) register is a special case of pointer register. It is used by the processor, along with the CS register, to point to the area of memory where the next instruction to be executed is stored. The term Program Counter (PC register) may be used interchangeably with Instruction Pointer and refers to the identical register.

The 8086 processor was designed to maintain control of execution, so the instruction set contains no 8086 instructions that will set the IP register directly. Instead, IP is changed as a consequence of any control transfer instruction, such as CALL or JMP. By using these instructions creatively, however, you can set the IP register to any desired value quite simply.

The Segment Registers

The 8086 has four 16-bit registers that are collectively referred to as the segment registers. These are the Code Segment (CS), Data Segment (DS), Extra Segment (ES), and Stack Segment (SS) registers. These segment registers are a key ingredient in the implementation of the 20-bit addressing scheme inherent in the architecture of the 8086. One or more segment registers are always referenced, either implicitly or explicitly, by operations that access memory.

Each segment register selects a single contiguous 64k block of memory, known as a segment. When combined with an operand that provides an offset from the beginning of this segment, any byte within that block can be uniquely specified. By properly setting the values of a segment register and an index register, for example, the two registers can point to any memory location in the 8086 memory space. The mechanics of memory segmentation and address calculation are discussed more fully later in this chapter.

During memory operations, many 8086 registers are associated implicitly with a particular segment register. This association is designed to reduce instruction length and execution time and must be taken into account by the programmer when using them. The Instruction Pointer, for example, is always associated with the CS register. Other default associations are shown in Table 3.2.

TABLE 3.2

Default Segment Register Associations

Register	Associated Segment	Situation
IP	CS	Always
BX	DS	When used as a base register
SI	DS	When used as an index register
DI	DS	When used as an index register
	ES	When used as the destination during string operations
SP	SS	All stack operations
BP	SS	When used as a base register

The CS register, in combination with the IP register, points to the segment and offset of the next instruction to be fetched and executed by the processor.

The DS register holds the segment of memory that is used by default to calculate the 20-bit address for most memory accesses (with the exceptions noted in Table 3.2).

The ES register is used in conjunction with the DI register to specify the destination segment for string operations. It is frequently used to augment DS by allowing access to a second data segment.

The SS register is used for all memory accesses that involve the SS and BP registers in the address calculation. Instructions that reference the stack, such as PUSH and POP, also implicitly use the SS register.

The Flags Register

The 8086 Flags register is a 16-bit register that is used to report and control the status of the processor. The Flags register is also referred to as the Status register or the program status word (PSW). Each bit in the Flags register is also called a flag. To avoid confusion, I'll use the word FLAGS, capitalized, when referring to the entire Flags register.

Each flag is either set (bit=1) or cleared (bit=0). To make discussions of the flags more succinct, individual flags in the FLAGS register are often referred to by several short abbreviations that identify either just the flag or the flag and its current state. If the carry flag (CF) is set (turned on), its condition is Carry (CY). If the carry flag is cleared (turned off), its condition is No Carry (NC). Figure 3.11 illustrates the conditions that the bits in the FLAGS register indicate.

The flags are updated as a result of most arithmetic and logical operations. There are also many instructions that update the flags directly. Complete information on how each 8086 instruction affects the flags and how these flags are interpreted by the conditional jump instructions is presented later in the next chapter.

FIGURE 3.11

The 8086 FLAGS register

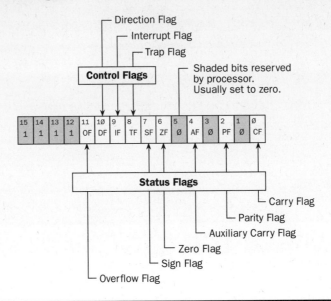

Processor Status Flags The *carry flag* (CF) indicates whether an arithmetic operation caused a carry (or borrow) out of the high-order bit. It is used to implement arithmetic operations on data items larger than register size and as an overflow indicator for unsigned arithmetic. For example, adding the bytes 55h and B1h gives a result of 106h. Because the number 106h will not fit into a byte, this operation would produce a result of 06h and set the carry flag to indicate an unsigned overflow has occurred. Figure 3.12 shows an example of how a carry is used to add two 32-bit numbers using 16-bit registers.

FIGURE 3.12

Using the carry flag in multiword math

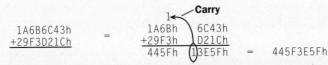

The example above shows how two 32-bit unsigned integers can be added using 16-bit operations with carry. This is the assembly code to perform the operation:

```
MOV AX, 1A6Bh ;Load most significant word of
              ;  first number
MOV BX, 6C43h ;Load least significant word

ADD BX,0D21Ch ;This sets CF=1
ADC AX,29F3h  ;Add number & carry to AX
```

Some shift and rotate instructions also affect the carry flag. The status of the carry flag is represented as CY, when the carry bit = 1, and NC, when the carry bit = 0.

Because of the importance of the carry flag when performing arithmetic operations, the 8086 has more instructions designed to directly manipulate and test the carry flag than any other flag. This versatility was probably responsible for the common use of the carry flag as an error signal between different program units. Many BIOS and DOS routines, for example, use the carry flag to return an indication of whether their operation has been successful.

The *parity flag* (PF) indicates the parity of the lower 8 bits of the result of an arithmetic or logical operation. If there are an even number of bits set to 1 in the lower 8 bits of the result, the parity is said to be even. For even parity, PF will be set to 1, which is represented as PE, for Parity Even. If, however, there are an odd number of bits set to 1 in the lower 8 bits of the result, the parity is said to be odd. PF is cleared to 0 for odd parity, and the flag state is represented as PO, for Parity Odd.

The *auxiliary carry flag* (AF) performs a function analogous to the carry flag, but operates on the lower 4 bits of the result only. The auxiliary carry flag is set to 1 if there is a carry or borrow out of bit 3 and is represented as AC (auxiliary carry). If no carry is generated, the flag is cleared to 0 and represented as NA (no auxiliary). This flag is used when performing arithmetic operations with BCD numbers that occupy only the lower 4 bits of a byte.

The *zero flag* (ZF) indicates if the result of an arithmetic or logical operation is zero. When ZF is set to 1, it is represented as ZR (zero). If the result is not zero, ZF is cleared to 0 and represented as NZ (not zero).

When performing comparisons, the operands are subtracted inside the processor and the result used to set the flags. In this case, a zero result indicates a match. Hence instructions that test for the state of the zero flag have aliases that use the term "equal" in place of "zero." The instructions JZ (jump if zero) and JE (jump if equal), for example, generate the identical opcode.

The *sign flag* (SF) is always set to the same value as the most significant bit of the result of any arithmetic or logical operation. The sign flag will only be meaningful, of course, if signed arithmetic is being performed. SF is represented as NG (negative) when set to 1 and as PL (plus) when cleared to 0.

The *overflow flag* (OF) is used to indicate a magnitude overflow or underflow in signed binary arithmetic similar to the way the carry flag is used in unsigned arithmetic. In this case, the carry flag isn't meaningful because it represents a carry out of the high-order bit. For signed numbers, the high-order bit (leftmost bit in the number) is not the same as the most significant bit (leftmost bit in the magnitude portion of the number).

The overflow flag is made equal to the logical exclusive-or of the carries into and out of the high-order bit. For example, adding two bytes that contain the value +127 (7Fh) will give a result of FEh and set the overflow flag. A carry was generated into bit 7 when the lower 7 bits of the byte were added. But because bit 7 is reserved for the sign of the number, the result is invalid and OF is set.

When OF is set to 1, it is represented as OV (overflow). When OF is cleared to 0, it is represented as NV (no overflow or number valid).

Processor Control Flags   When the *trap flag* (TF) is set to 1, it places the processor in single-step mode. This mode is generally initiated by a debugger to cause the processor to generate the single-step exception (interrupt 1) at the end of each instruction. An exception handler in the debugger then can regain control of the machine.

The trap flag can be modified only by copying FLAGS to the stack (using the PUSHF instruction), setting the trap flag bit, and then returning the new flags to FLAGS (using POPF). No common abbreviations exist for the states of the trap flag since it is rarely displayed during debugging.

The *interrupt enable flag* (IF), if set to 1, tells the processor to acknowledge the presence of external interrupts. These interrupts are input to the processor via an external connection. If the interrupt flag is cleared to 0, the interrupts are ignored. Interrupts and the interrupt process are discussed in detail later in Chapter 4.

When IF is set to 1, it is represented as EI (enable interrupts). When IF is cleared to 0, it is represented as DI (disable interrupts).

The *direction flag* (DF) determines if string operations will increment or decrement the string index registers after each iteration of the instruction. If the direction flag is cleared to 0, the flag is said to be in the "up" direction and the string index registers will be incremented (DF=UP). If the direction flag is set to 1, the flag is "down" and the string index registers will be decremented (DF=DN).

Most high-level language compilers generate code to clear the direction flag to UP in their initialization or start-up code. The remainder of the code is designed to operate on the assumption that the flag is changed only by compiler-generated code. An easy way to bring a high-level language program to a rapid crash is to change the direction flag in an assembly procedure and not restore it.

80286 Register Enhancements

So far, I've discussed registers only in the context of the 8086. All of these registers are, of course, present in the entire 80x86 family. The 80286 processor, however, enhanced the register set to accommodate its increased functionality. Most of these enhancements were designed to support the protected mode of the processor and will not normally be of any concern when programming in the chip's real mode, under DOS for example.

80286 FLAGS Register   The 80286 chip, for all its seeming difference from the 8086, is still just a 16-bit processor and as such, uses the same register set as the 8086. The FLAGS register, however, has had two additional fields defined, as shown in Figure 3.13. These fields are the I/O Privilege Level (IOPL) flag and the Nested Task (NT) flag. These flags are not used when the processor is running in 8086 emulation mode (real mode) and have an effect only when the processor is in protected mode. Consequently, real-mode programs can generally ignore these bits. A practical exception might be a virtual disk device driver that has to switch into protected mode to access extended memory.

FIGURE 3.13

The 80286 FLAGS register

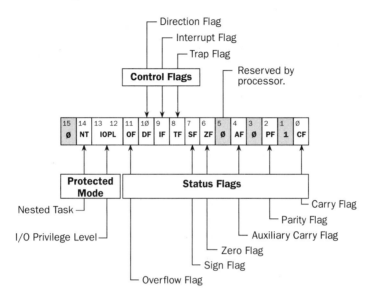

The *I/O privilege level flag* is 2 bits wide and is used to support protected mode. It specifies the privilege level required to perform I/O operations. If the current privilege level is less than or equal to IOPL, the instruction can be executed. If not, a protection exception will be generated. An IOPL of 00 is the most privileged and 11b is the least privileged. Real-mode programs run at IOPL=00.

The *nested task flag* controls the function of the IRET instruction. If NT is 0, then the IRET functions normally by restoring the FLAGS, CS, and IP registers from the stack. If NT is 1, however, the return is performed by executing a task switch that returns control to the calling task. For real-mode programs, NT=0.

80286 Protected Mode Management Registers   The *machine status word* (MSW) is a special-purpose processor control register and is not used for data storage or manipulation. The MSW indicates the processor configuration and status and is used more or less exclusively for systems programming. The machine status word is a 16-bit register that indicates the current configuration and status of the 80286. Only the lower 4 bits are used by the 80286; the remaining bits are reserved for compatibility with more advanced processors. Figure 3.14 shows the machine status word bits and their functions.

The *Protected Mode Enable flag* (PE) is set to 1 to switch the 80286 into its protected mode. The flag remains set as long as the processor is in protected mode. Once set, however, the PE flag cannot be cleared except by restarting the processor via a system reset, which returns the processor to real mode. This is the technique used by the VDISK.SYS device driver when using extended memory and is one of the worst "kludges" ever forced on programmers.

FIGURE 3.14

The 80286 machine status word

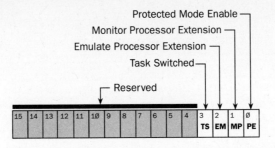

The ability to switch from real mode to protected mode is essential, as the processor is always initialized in real mode when power is applied. But the inability to make a smooth transition from protected mode to real mode on demand is a major failing of the 80286.

The *monitor processor extension flag* (MP) indicates whether a math coprocessor is present. This flag, also called the *math present flag,* is set if a math coprocessor is available and cleared otherwise.

The *emulate processor extension flag* (EM) indicates that the functions of the math coprocessor will be emulated in software.

The *task switched flag* (TS) is set by hardware and reset by software. Once the TS flag is set, the next instruction that attempts to use the math coprocessor will generate a "math coprocessor not present" exception (interrupt 7). This gives the system software the opportunity to save the state of the math coprocessor before allowing another task to use it.

Three additional special-purpose registers are used to manage memory access when implementing the virtual addressing and memory protection functions on the 80286. The three descriptor tables that control memory access are located at addresses stored in the global descriptor table register (GDTR), the local descriptor table register (LDTR), and the interrupt descriptor table register (IDTR).

The GDTR is a 40-bit register that is divided into two fields. The first field is a 24-bit base field that is used to give the real memory address of the beginning the system's global descriptor table (GDT). The second field is a 16-bit limit field that specifies the maximum offset permitted in accessing the table.

The LDTR is similar to the GDTR but refers to the currently executing task. In addition, the LDTR contains a third field, a 16-bit selector field that identifies the descriptor for that table.

The IDTR's 24-bit base and 16-bit limit fields define the extent of the interrupt descriptor table (IDT). The IDT is located in physical memory and defines the interrupt handlers for up to 256 different interrupts.

The Task Register (TR) is used to hold a selector that points to the Task State Segment descriptor. This register points to the information that defines a particular task and is used during an operating system task switch.

80386 Register Enhancements

The 80386 chip (including the 80386SX) has expanded the basic register set considerably to accommodate its 32-bit operations and new operating modes. The general purpose, base, index, flags, and instruction pointer registers may now be accessed as full 32-bit registers. The segment registers remain at 16 bits, but two new 16-bit segment registers, FS and GS, have been added for general program use. The 80386 register set remains an upward compatible superset of that on the 8086. Thus programs written for an 8086 or 80286 will run without modification on the 80836. Where an 8086 register has been extended to 32 bits, the prefix E, for Extended, has been added. The new and extended registers are shown in Figure 3.15.

The low-order word of the EAX, EBX, ECX, EDX, EBP, ESI, EDI, ESP, and EBP registers is named separately and may be treated as a normal operand in instructions. This flexibility provides compatibility with the 8086 and 80286 register sets. The high-order 16 bits of a register cannot be referenced separately.

For example, if the EAX register contains 12AE34C1h, AX would contain 34C1h, AH would contain 34h, and AL would contain C1h. Just as an operation on the AL register does not affect the AH register, so operations on the lower half of the extended registers leave the upper 16 bits untouched.

The two new segment registers, FS and GS, function as general purpose segment registers. Having these extra registers available allows an 80836 real mode program to access up to six 64k memory segments simultaneously when executing under DOS.

80386 FLAGS Register The 80386 supports the IOPL and NT flags as described earlier for the 80286. Two additional flags have been added to support the new features built into the chip as shown in Figure 3.16. These are the resume flag (bit 16) and the virtual 8086 mode flag (bit 17).

The *resume flag* (RF), also called the restart flag, controls whether debug exceptions are recognized (RF=0) or ignored (RF=1). The use of the 80386 debug registers to generate these exceptions is discussed later in this chapter. When the EFLAGS register is pushed on the stack, a 0 is always used for the RF flag.

The *virtual 8086 mode flag* (VM) indicates what type of protected mode the processor is operating in. When set (VM=1), the flag indicates that the processor is executing an 8086 task in virtual mode. If clear, the processor will operate in normal protected mode.

FIGURE 3.15

The 80386/80486 register set

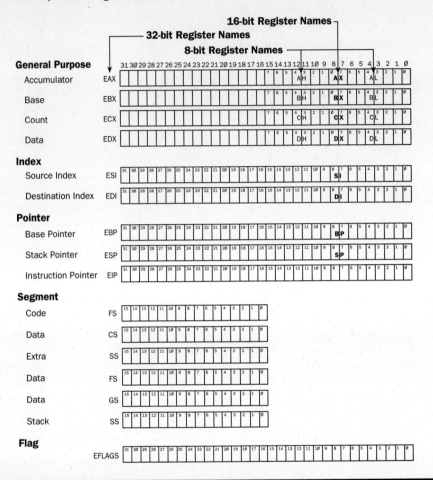

80386 Protected Mode Management Registers   The 80386 processor contains the GDTR, LDTR, IDTR, and TR registers as described earlier for the 80286 except that the base field is 32 bits to accommodate the memory space of the 80386. While the machine status word (MSW) is emulated to provide compatibility with 80286 software, its functionality has been replaced by the special control registers of the 80386. Figure 3.17 shows the format of the 80386 control registers CR0 through CR3. CR1 is reserved for future processors and is undefined for the 80386.

The CR0 register contains system flags that are used to indicate and control the state of the system as a whole, rather than the state of an individual task. CR0 is an extension of the MSW on the 80286. The definitions of the emulation flag (EM), math present flag (MP), protection enable flag (PE), and task switched flag (TS) are the same as for the 80286 MSW.

FIGURE 3.16

The 80386/80486 EFLAGS register

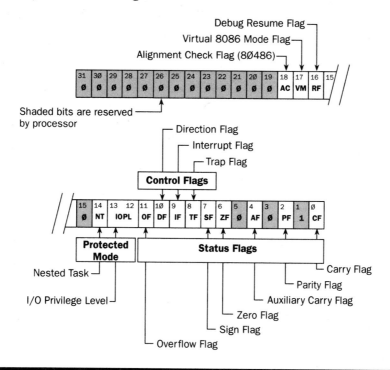

The *extension type flag* (ET) is new in the 80386, and indicates the type of math coprocessor installed in the system. This flag is required since the 80386DX can support either an 80287 or 80387DX. ET=1 if an 80387 is present and ET=0 if an 80287 or no coprocessor is present. This bit is ignored if EM=1 .

The *paging flag* (PG) indicates whether the processor will use page tables to translate linear addresses into physical addresses. If PG=0, paging is disabled and linear addresses are passed through as physical addresses. If PG=1, paging is enabled.

CR2 and CR3 are used by the paging mechanism. CR2 is used to report error information when a page exception occurs. The high-order 20 bits of CR3 are called the Page Directory Base Register (PDBR) and contains the physical address of the page that contains the page table directory.

80386 Debug Registers   Considerably enhanced support for debugging has been built into the 80386. In addition to the single-step execution exception (enabled via the trap flag) and the breakpoint exception (INT 3), eight dedicated debug registers, DR0 through DR7, have been added. These debug registers can support both instruction breakpoints and data breakpoints, allowing software-only debugging programs to provide the same support that previously required additional hardware. The eight debug registers are shown in Figure 3.18.

FIGURE 3.17

The 80386/80486 control registers

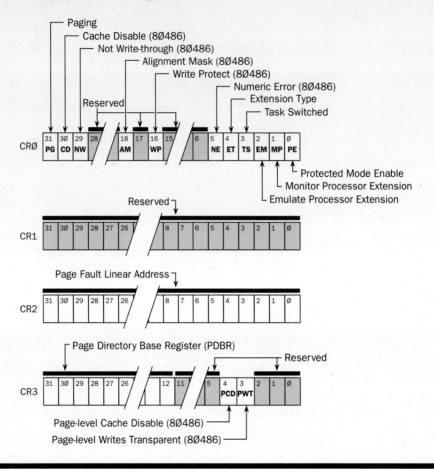

Debug registers DR0 through DR3 are used to hold the linear address that is associated with one of the four breakpoint conditions defined in DR7. The DR4 and DR5 registers do nothing on the 80386 and are reserved by Intel for future processors.

DR6 is the debug status register. It permits the controlling debug program to determine the condition that caused it to get control. When the processor detects an enabled debug exception, it sets the 4 low-order bits of this register. By interpreting the bits, the control program can determine which condition caused the exception. B0 is set, for example, if the condition specified by R/W 0 and LEN 0 had occurred at DR0. Each Bn bit will be set regardless of the status of the corresponding Gn bit or Ln bit in DR7.

If a task switch has occurred, and the debug trap bit in the new task is enabled, the BT bit is set before passing control to the debug handler. This condition is simply reported, and is not controlled by DR7.

FIGURE 3.18

The 80386/80486 debug registers

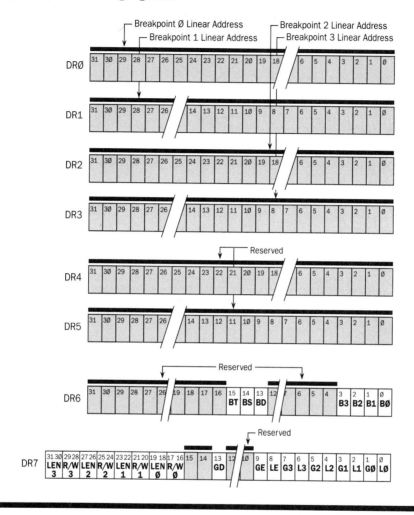

The BS bit is set if the debug handler was entered due to the occurrence of a single-step exception (interrupt 1). This condition will occur if the trap flag is set in the EFLAGS register.

The BD bit is set if the next instruction to be executed will read or write one of the eight debug registers. This flag is used to coordinate use of the debug registers by more than one debugger.

The DR6 register is never cleared by the processor. After each exception, the programmer must clear the register to avoid ambiguous results.

DR7 is the debug control register and it both defines and selectively enables each breakpoint register. For each address in registers DR0 through DR3, the correspondingly numbered LEN and R/W fields in DR7 specify the type of action that should cause a breakpoint. The LEN and R/W bits are interpreted as shown in Table 3.3.

TABLE 3.3

Debug Control Register R/W and LEN Fields

R/W Field Bits	Action
ØØ	Break on instruction execution only (LEN must = ØØ also)
Ø1	Break on data write only
1Ø	Undefined—do not use
11	Break on data read or write, but not instruction fetches

LEN Field Bits	Action
ØØ	One byte length
Ø1	Two byte length
1Ø	Undefined—do not use
11	Four byte length

The low-order 8 bits of the DR7 register can be set selectively to enable any combination of the four breakpoint conditions. The L0 through L3 bits enable the breakpoints at the local, or task, level. These bits are automatically reset at every task switch to avoid unwanted debugging in the new task. The global bits (G0 through G3) are not reset by a task switch.

The LE and GE bits control whether or not the processor will slow its execution to be able to report data breakpoints on exactly the instruction that caused them. If these bits are not set, the possibility exists that the processor execution may get ahead of the breakpoint. Intel recommends that these bits be enabled whenever data breakpoints are active. The LE bit controls this action for the local task, while GE performs the same action globally.

80386 Test Registers   The 80386 provides two 32-bit test registers, TR6 and TR7, as a mechanism for programmers to verify proper operation of the Translation Lookaside Buffer (TLB) when power is applied to the chip. The TLB is a cache used internally by the 80386 to translate linear addresses to physical addresses. Figure 3.19 shows the layout of the test registers.

In the 80386, nine fields are defined in test register TR6. The C field, bit 0 of TR6, contains the command bit. If C is cleared to 0, an entry will be written to the TLB. If C is set to 1, a TLB lookup will be performed.

The linear address field of TR6 is used as the key into the TLB. During a write, the TLB entry that is written is allocated to the linear address specified in this field. During a TLB lookup, this value is used to find a matching TLB entry.

FIGURE 3.19

The 80386/80486 test registers

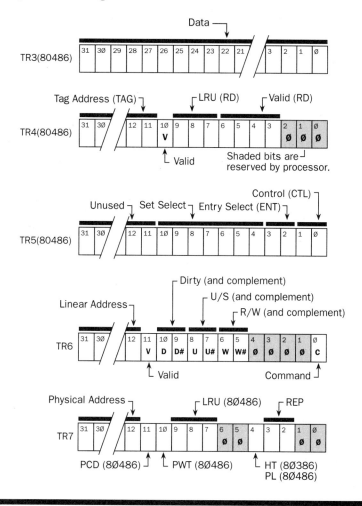

The V (valid) bit in TR6 indicates that the TLB entry being referenced is valid. Entries that have not been written are marked invalid (V=0). The valid bits for all entries can be cleared by writing to CR3.

The D and D# (Dirty), U and U# (user/supervisor), and W and W# (read/ write) bits are used in combination to control the TLB lookup or report status. The bits are reported in both normal and one's complement form to provide flexibility in programming the TLB. Table 3.4 shows the effect on a TLB lookup and the value of the bit after a TLB write for each of the four value combinations each bit pair may have. Bit refers to the normal bit, such as D, and Bit# refers to the bit complement, such as D#.

The physical address field in TR7 is the data field of the TLB. When writing to the TLB, the TLB entry is set to this value (which corresponds to the linear address specified in TR6). During a TLB lookup, the physical address in the TLB entry is written to this field if HT=1. If HT=0, this field is undefined.

The TR6 Translation Lookaside Buffer Bit-Pairs

Bit	Bit#	Effect During TLB Lookup	Bit Value After TLB Write
Ø	Ø	8Ø386: Undefined	Undefined
		8Ø486: Do not match	
Ø	1	Match if the bit is clear	Bit cleared to Ø
1	Ø	Match if the bit is set	Bit set to 1
1	1	8Ø386: Undefined	Undefined
		8Ø486: Match if the bit is set or clear	

The hit (HT) bit is set to 1 to indicate that a TLB lookup was successful. If the lookup was a miss, HT is cleared to 0. For a TLB write, HT must always be set to 1.

The REP field is used to specify which of the four associative blocks in the TLB is to be written. For a TLB read, with HT set to 1, REP indicates in which block the match was found. If HT is 0, REP is undefined.

80486 Register Enhancements

The 80486 implements the same register sets the 80386 as shown in Figure 3.15. Most of the enhancements to the 80486 register set have been in the form of additional bit definitions for protected mode operating conditions.

80486 EFLAGS Register   The 80486 supports all the flags described for the 80386 and defines one additional flag as shown in Figure 3.16. Bit 18 of the EFLAGS register has been defined as the *alignment check flag* (AC). When both the AC flag and the AM bit of the CR0 register are set, the processor will generate an alignment-check exception when an instruction references an unaligned operand. An example of an unaligned operand would be a word starting on an odd address. This capability was added to support system designs in which the 80486 must exchange data with another processor that requires that all data be aligned.

80486 Protected Mode Management Registers   The GDTR, LDTR, IDTR, and TR registers in the 80486 are identical to those in the 80386 as described earlier. Control register CR0, on the other hand, had five additional system flags defined to handle the 80486's built-in cached and floating-point hardware and provide some additional operating system support. These flags are shown in Figure 3.17.

The *numeric error flag* (NE), also called the numeric exception flag, is used to enable the 80486 to report floating-point numeric errors. If NE=0 and the

IGNNE# processor control input signal is active, numeric errors will be ignored. If NE=0 and IGNEE# is inactive, a numeric error will halt the processor and signal the interrupt controller to generate an interrupt. This latter method provides compatibility with earlier processors when used in PC implementations.

The *write protect flag* (WP) has been added specifically to support the copy-on-write method of creating new processes used in UNIX-style operating systems. If WP=1, user-level pages are treated as write-only, and are protected against supervisor-mode access.

The *alignment mask flag* (AM) is used in conjunction with the AC flag (in the EFLAGS register) to enable and disable alignment checking. Alignment checking is performed only when AM=1, AC=1, and the current privilege level (CPL) is 3.

The *not write-through flag* (NW) and *cache disable flag* (CD) are used to manage the 80486's instruction and data cache. If NW=0, cache write-throughs and cache invalidation cycles are enabled. If NW=1, invalidation cycles as well as write-throughs that hit in the cache are disabled. The CD flag is set to 1 to disable the cache and cleared to 0 to enable the cache.

The initial design for the 80486 defined these two bits in the opposite sense. Bit 30 was defined as the cache enable flag and bit 29 was defined as the write-through flag. Intel changed the way these bits are interpreted to address a problem with existing software. Software that had been written for the 80386 processor, on which these two bits are undefined, was writing zeroes into these bits. (This was according to Intel guidelines which stated that only zeros should be written into undefined bits.) As a result, the cache and all write-throughs were disabled. If the cache was later disabled improperly, both the cache and external memory could become stale. Any DMA writes into external memory would not invalidate the corresponding cache entries and the cache data would be invalid. Further, writes that hit in the cache would not be written to external memory. With the bit definitions reversed, the problem is avoided. Nonetheless, early versions of the chip still have this problem.

The 80486 also defines two additional fields in control register CR3. The *page-level writes transparent flag* (PWT), bit 3 of CR3, is used to communicate with the memory management hardware and is driven on the PWT pin of the processor during bus cycles which are not paged. The PWT pin is used to control write-through in an external cache on a cycle-by-cycle basis.

The *page-level cache disable flag* (PCD), bit 4 of CR3, is driven on the PCD bin during bus cycles which are not paged. This pin is used to control caching in an external cache on a cycle-by-cycle basis.

Beginning with the C-step of the 80486DX, the definition of the PWT and PCD bits has been changed. Prior to the change, the bits were used to determine cacheability of pages even when paging was disabled. Beginning with the C-step, however, these bits are ignored during the caching process when paging is disabled. (The 80486DX assumes PCD=0 and PWT=0.)

Early versifons of the 80486DX also initialized the ET bit in CR0 to 0 at reset. The bit could be set or cleared by software. In a later version of the processor, the ET bit was "hardwired" to 1 to force the use of 80387 coprocessor protocol.

80486 Debug Registers

The debug registers in the 80486 are identical in layout and operation to those in the 80386 and are shown in Figure 3.18.

80486 Test Registers

The test registers on the 80486 support power-up testing of the Translation Lookaside Buffer (TLB) just as they do on the 80386. In addition, three additional registers, TR3, TR4, and TR5, have been defined to support diagnostic testing of the 80486 cache when power is applied to the chip. The layout of the test registers is shown in Figure 3.19.

The TR3 register, called the cache test data register, holds a doubleword that is to be written to the cache fill buffer or is read from the cache read buffer. The fill and read buffers each have storage for four doublewords, which pass through this register one at a time.

TR4 is called the cache test status register and has four fields defined. The Valid field (bits 3-6) holds the four Valid bits of the set that was accessed on a cache lookup. The V-bit (bit 10) field contains the valid bit for the particular entry that is accessed. The V-bit contains a copy of one of the bits in the Valid field if a cache lookup is performed and contains the new V-bit for the entry and set selected during a cache write. The Tag Address (TAG) field is the address that becomes the tag during a cache write. After a cache read, the LRU field is ignored during a cache write.

The cache test control register, TR5, contains three fields. The entry select (ENT) selects one of the four entries in the set addressed by the set select field during a cache read or write. During cache fill buffer writes or cache read buffer reads, the ENT field selects one of the four doublewords in a cache line. The set select field selects one of the 128 sets. The control field (CTL) determines the function performed as shown in Table 3.5.

Addressing Modes

The 8086 provides several methods of calculating memory addresses not only when accessing data, but also when determining the next instruction to execute. A short discussion of these addressing modes, and the conventions used to indicate them, follows.

Program Memory Addressing

The CS:IP register pair holds the segment and offset, respectively, of the next instruction that will be executed by the processor. After each instruction has been executed, the IP register is then incremented to point to the beginning of the next instruction in memory. The use of the CALL or JMP instructions, however, may modify the CS:IP register pair in such a way as to transfer the control of the program to a different area of memory.

TABLE 3.5

The TR5 Control Field Bit Definitions

CTL	Function Performed
ØØb	Write to cache fill buffer or read from cache read buffer
Ø1b	Perform cache write
1Øb	Perform cache read
11b	Flush the cache (mark all entries as invalid)

Relative Addressing   In this form, an 8-bit or 16-bit program relative displacement forms part of the instruction. In other words, the displacement, a signed number, added to the contents of the IP register, indicates the area in memory where execution is to resume. Because the contents of CS are not affected by this addressing, this is termed an intrasegment displacement.

Direct Addressing   New 16-bit values for both the CS and IP registers form part of the instruction. On execution, CS and IP are loaded with the new values. Execution then resumes from that point in memory. Because the segment may be changed with this instruction, it is known as an intersegment displacement.

Indirect Addressing   A 16-bit value forms part of the instruction and is interpreted as a memory address. For an intrasegment displacement, the 16-bit value stored in memory at this address is loaded into the IP register. Two 16-bit values are similarly loaded as the new values for the CS and IP registers for an intersegment displacement.

Data Memory Address Modes

The 8086 provides several different methods for addressing the contents of memory as data. These methods include both direct and indirect address. In general, memory-to-memory data transfers are not supported by 8086 instructions and a register must be used as temporary storage. Some string and stack operations, however, do perform direct memory-to-memory transfers without using one of the registers as an intermediary.

Immediate Operands   In immediate mode, the operand is included in the code segment as part of the instruction. The instruction ADD AX,1234h will cause the processor to add the numeric value 1234h to the current contents of the AX register. No additional memory access is performed. Immediate mode instructions generally execute faster than instructions that require an additional memory access but may require more bytes. Not all instructions can accept immediate operands.

Direct Memory Address A 16-bit value forms part of the instruction and is interpreted as a memory address. The contents of that address then become the operand for the instruction. The size of the operand is determined by the instruction coding. The instruction MOV AX,[100h] will move the 16-bit value stored at offset 100h into the AX register. Contrast this to the instruction MOV AX,100h, which moves the value 100h into the register AX. The brackets are used to indicate a memory reference.

Indirect Indexed Address The value contained in one of the SI or DI index registers is interpreted as an offset and is used to calculate a memory address. You may optionally include an immediate operand that is added to the offset before the memory address is calculated. For example, assume that SI contains the value 3A40h. Then instruction MOV AX,[SI] would be equivalent to MOV AX,[3A40h]. And the instruction MOV AX,[SI-30h] would be equivalent to MOV AX,[3A10h].

By convention, at least one of the operands in the address field of the instruction must be enclosed in brackets to indicate to the assembler that indirect addressing is being used. The following are examples of this addressing form:

```
MOV   AX,[SI]
MOV   BX,[DI][6]
MOV   [SI-4],CX
```

All offsets used in indirect indexing are normally taken relative to the DS register. A segment override may be used to change this. During certain string operations, the DI register is used as an offset relative to the ES register and cannot be overridden. Overrides and string instructions are discussed in Chapter 6.

Base Relative Address The value contained in the BX or BP register is interpreted as an offset and is used to calculate a memory address. By default, the processor will interpret the BX register as an offset relative to the DS register, and the BP as an offset relative to the SS register.

You may combine the use of a base register with an immediate operand, an index register, or both. The value of the register and/or immediate operand is then added to the offset before the memory address is calculated. When using base relative addressing with the BP register, a second operand, an index register, or an immediate operand (even if it is 0) must always be specified. The instruction MOV AX,[BP] will be assembled as MOV AX,[BP+0].

For example, assume that BX contains the value 4010h. Then the instruction MOV AX,[BX] would be equivalent to MOV AX,[4010h]. And the instruction MOV AX,[BX+110h] would be equivalent to MOV AX,[4120h]. At least one of the operands must be enclosed in brackets to indicate to the assembler that indirect addressing is being used. In this book, all operands in the address field are enclosed in brackets when using this addressing form as shown here:

```
MOV   AX,[BX]
MOV   CX,[BP][SI]
MOV   [BX+DI+9],DX
```

Additional 80386 Addressing Modes

The 80386 removes some of the limitations on register usage imposed by previous processors. With other 80x86 processors, only the BX, BP, DI, and SI registers can be used in indirect indexed memory addressing. With the 80386, any general purpose 32-bit register can be used as a base or index. The same register can be used as both the base and the index. These examples are instructions that execute correctly on the 80386:

```
MOV   EBX,[EAX]       ;Move Dword from memory
ADD   BX,[ESP][-6]   ;Add word from stack
```

Note that the relaxed restrictions on the use of registers applies only to the 32-bit forms. AX, CX, DX, and SP *cannot* be used as index registers in their 16-bit forms, as these examples show:

```
MOV   EAX,[BX]  ;Legal - BX is index
MOV   EBX,[AX]  ;Illegal - AX is not index
MOV   EBX,[EAX] ;Legal - EAX is index
```

To enhance performance when dealing with arrays and tables, a scaling factor may be used with the index register. The value in the index register is first multiplied by the scaling factor, which can be 1, 2, 4, or 8, before being used to calculate the effective address. Instruction execution time is not increased by the use of a scale factor, but code complexity is significantly reduced. For example, assume that SI contains the number of the element you wish to access in the word array TABLE. To load that value into AX, while preserving SI, you might use the following code on an 8086:

```
PUSH  SI                 ;Save SI
SHL   SI,1               ;Offset *2 for word access
MOV   EAX,[TABLE][SI]    ;Load correct word
POP   SI                 ;Restore SI
```

But on the 80386, the same effect can be had with the single instruction below.

```
MOV   AX,[TABLE][ESI*2] ;Load word from table
```

Segment selection for memory addresses is consistent with that of the 8086. If the base register is ESP or EBP, then the default segment will be SS. If any other general register is used as the base, the default segment is DS. Normally, the base register is defined to be the one that appears first in the address field of the instruction. The exception to this rule occurs when scaling is used. If two registers are referenced, the register that is scaled is automatically the index register, and the other is the base, regardless of the order. Note that if two registers are used, only one can have a scaling factor. The following examples illustrate how to determine the base register:

```
MOV    EAX,[EDX][EBP]    ;EDX first, use DS
MOV    EAX,[EBP][EDX]    ;EBP first, use SS
MOV    EAX,[EDX*4][EBP]  ;EDX is scaled = Index
                         ;so EBP = Base, use SS
MOV    EAX,[EDX][EBP*4]  ;EBP is scaled = Index
                         ;so EDX = Base, use DS
```

One further advantage that can be gained using the 80386's enhanced registers is in accessing the stack. Since ESP can be used as a base register, there may be no need to use BP to establish a stack frame before accessing passed parameters in procedures.

The Stack

The 8086 processor design requires that a stack be available to it at all times during normal operation. Even if you wrote your software so that it never needed a stack, the processor would still require that one be provided to preserve its state while it handles exceptions and interrupts. For programming purposes, a stack is a natural mechanism for implementing nested procedure calls and returns as well as interrupts.

Instructions such as PUSH, POP, and their variations are available to allow you to manipulate a stack directly. In addition, some instructions, such as CALL, RET, and INT, make use of the stack implicitly.

On the 8086, stacks are implemented in the normal memory space of the processor. In other words, the memory used for a stack is part of conventional memory and is indistinguishable from the memory used for instructions or data storage. (Contrast this to the math coprocessor, which uses a register stack implemented on the chip itself.)

A system may have an unlimited number of stacks. Only one stack, however, can be the "current" stack. The current stack is defined as the area of memory that is pointed to by the SS:SP register pair. The SS register defines which 64k segment of memory, known as the stack segment, contains the stack. The SP register contains the offset of the current stack top from the start of the stack segment. Figure 3.20 shows a schematic of the stack and stack nomenclature.

The size of your stack is defined more by a programming decision than by any physical limitation. There is no lower limit on the size of a stack, although too small a stack will not hold enough information to be useful. The maximum size for a stack is, of course, 64k, limited by the amount of memory addressable by the SS register. The stack bottom (initial stack pointer value) may be located anywhere within the stack segment. By convention, the initial stack pointer is made an even number to optimize fetches of word data for chips with a 16-bit data bus.

FIGURE 3.20

The 8086 stack model

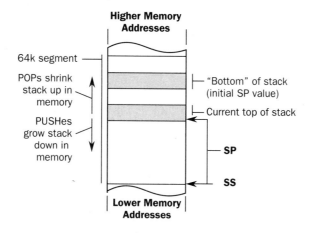

Stack Operation

The 8086 stack grows down. That is, as data is added to the stack, the value contained in the stack pointer register decreases. Conversely, as data is removed from the stack, the stack pointer value increases. The SP register always points to the current stack top.

On the 8086 and 80286, stack operations move 16-bit operands. On the 80386, doubleword operations are available, such as pushing a 32-bit register. Stack operations with byte operands are not allowed on any processor.

The stack operates by adding or removing one word at a time. The last word to be added to the stack is always the first one to be removed. This type of stack operation is known as last-in-first-out (LIFO), or equivalently, first-in-last-out (FILO). Both terms are used interchangeably in the literature.

Stack operations available on the 8086 never move or erase stack entries, they only update the stack pointer. Entries may be written over, however, as a consequence of stack operations. Figure 3.21 illustrates how PUSH and POP change the stack pointer and how data is written to and read from the stack.

FIGURE 3.21

Operation of the 8086 stack model

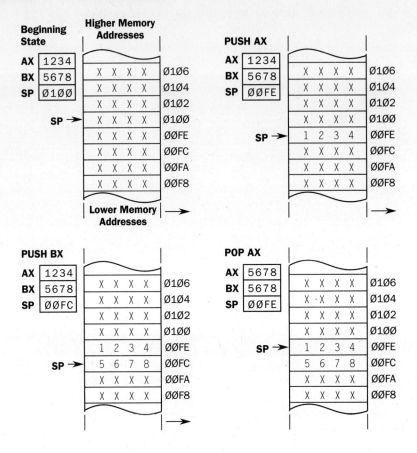

Differences Among Processors

On the 8086 and 8088, an operand is pushed onto the stack by first writing the operand to the new stack top address, then decreasing the SP register by 2. So, for example, the instruction PUSH AX could be represented as:

```
MOV   SS:[SP-2],AX
SUB   SP,2
```

On the 80286 and later processors, however, first the stack pointer is decreased, then the value to be added to the stack is written. The instruction PUSH AX would then be implemented as:

```
SUB   SP,2
MOV   SS:[SP],AX
```

By exploiting this difference in operation between processors, it can be determined if an 80286 or more advanced processor is installed in a particular computer. The following code fragment shows how this is done:

```
PUSH   SP
POP    AX
CMP    AX,SP
JNE    CHIP_IS_88_86
JE     CHIP_IS_286_386
```

On the 8086 and 8088, the value of SP pushed is the value that SP will have after the PUSH is complete. On the other processors, PUSH SP will put the value of SP before the PUSH onto the stack.

Utility: Identifying the CPU via Software

Sometimes a program needs to know what type of processor it is running on or if a math coprocessor is installed. This may be necessary in order to determine at execution time if advanced instructions, such as those that manipulate the 32-bit registers of the 80386, can be used. The decision as to whether to use a software-based floating-point emulator or a numeric coprocessor can also be made at execution time if the presence of the math chip can be determined.

Although the members of the 80x86 family are upwardly compatible, there are documented differences in their behavior that can be used to distinguish one generation of processor from the next. The utility CPUID, the assembly language source code for which is given in Listing 3.1, will identify the processor type on which it is being executed and the type of numeric coprocessor, if any, that is installed in the system.

LISTING 3.1

```
;==============================================================================
; CPUID.ASM - Identify the installed processor and coprocessor.
;
; From: PC Magazine Programmer's Technical Reference
;       The Processor and Coprocessor
;       Robert L. Hummel
;
; To create an executable version of this program, use the following
; commands:
;       MASM CPUID;
;       LINK CPUID;
;       EXE2BIN CPUID.EXE CPUID.COM
;       DEL CPUID.EXE
;------------------------------------------------------------------------------
; The identification techniques used here are those that have been
; recommended by Intel and do not depend on the use of undocumented
; features of the chips.
;------------------------------------------------------------------------------
```

```
CSEG     SEGMENT PARA    PUBLIC 'CODE'
         ASSUME          CS:CSEG,DS:CSEG,ES:CSEG,SS:CSEG ;Set by DOS Loader

         ORG     100H                    ;COM file format

;========================================================================
; This routine calls the CPUID proc to determine the CPU and NDP type.
; An explanation is then displayed on the console.
;------------------------------------------------------------------------
MAIN           PROC    NEAR
               ASSUME  CS:CSEG,DS:CSEG,ES:CSEG,SS:CSEG

               MOV     DX,OFFSET PROGID        ;Display program info
               CALL    PRINT$

;------------------------------------------------------------------------
; CPUID returns the CPU and NDP code in AX. Note that the case AX=0400h
; indicates a 486SX chip without the accompanying 487SX.
;------------------------------------------------------------------------
               CALL    CPUID                   ;Returns ID in AX

               CMP     AX,0400H                ;Test special case
               JE      MAIN_2


               MOV     BX,AX                   ;Save the ID



               OR      AX,3030H                ;Make into ASCII

               MOV     BYTE PTR [CPU+2],AH     ;Place into strings in

               MOV     BYTE PTR [NDP+5],AL     ; case they're needed


               MOV     DX,OFFSET CPUIS         ;Start CPU message
               CALL    PRINT$

               MOV     DX,OFFSET CPU86         ;Assume 8086/88

               CMP     BH,1                    ;If <> 1, use other msg
               JE      MAIN_1

               MOV     DX,OFFSET CPU           ;Use general message

               CMP     BH,04                   ;If 80486, we're done
               JE      MAIN_2
MAIN_1:
               CALL    PRINT$

;------------------------------------------------------------------------
; Report the type of coprocessor.
;------------------------------------------------------------------------
               MOV     DX,OFFSET NDPIS         ;Start NDP message
               CALL    PRINT$
```

```
                  MOV       DX,OFFSET NDPNONE      ;Assume no NDP

                  CMP       BL,1                   ;If 0 (below 1) no NDP
                  JB        MAIN_2

                  MOV       DX,OFFSET NDP87        ;Assume 8087

                  JE        MAIN_2                 ;If=1, is 8087

                  MOV       DX,OFFSET NDP          ;Use general message
MAIN_2:
                  CALL      PRINT$

                  MOV       AX,4C00H               ;Terminate program
                  INT       21H                    ; thru DOS

MAIN              ENDP

;========================================================================
; All program data appears here.
;------------------------------------------------------------------------
PROGID            DB        "CPUID 1.0 ",254," Robert L. Hummel",13,10
                  DB        "PC Magazine Programmers' Technical Reference"
                  DB        13,10,"The Processor and Coprocessor",13,10,10
                  DB        "$"

CPUIS             DB        "The CPU is an $"
CPU86             DB        "8086/8088.",13,10,"$"
CPU               DB        "80X86.",13,10,"$"

NDPIS             DB        "The math coprocessor is $"
NDPNONE           DB        "not present.",13,10,"$"
NDP87             DB        "an 8087.",13,10,"$"
NDP               DB        "an 80x87.",13,10,"$"

SX486ONLY         DB        "The CPU is an 80486SX.",13,10
                  DB        "No 80487SX is installed.",13,10,"$"

NDP_STATUS        DW        -1
;========================================================================
; This procedure returns a code in the AX register to indicate the type
; of processor and coprocessor that are installed in the system. The
; return is interpreted as follows.
;
; AH    CPU Type
;
; 01    8086 or 8088
; 02    80286
; 03    80386DX or 80386SX
; 04    80486DX or 80486SX
;
; AL    NDP Type
;
; 00    None installed
; 01    8087
```

```
;  02      80287
;  03      80387DX or 80387SX
;  04      80486DX or 80487SX
;
; Note: A return code of 0400 indicates an 80486SX without an 80487SX.
;-------------------------------------------------------------------------
CPUID          PROC    NEAR
        ASSUME  CS:CSEG,DS:CSEG,ES:CSEG,SS:CSEG

               MOV     DX,0100H
               MOV     WORD PTR [NDP_STATUS],-1 ;Make non-zero


;-------------------------------------------------------------------------
; On the 8088 and 8086, bits 12-15 of the FLAGS register are always set
; to 1 when transferred to the stack. This section tries to clear the
; bits. If they can be cleared, it's not an 8086/88.
;-------------------------------------------------------------------------
               PUSHF                           ;Load FLAGS
               POP     AX                      ; into AX register

               AND     AH,0FH                  ;Clear high 4 bits

               PUSH    AX                      ; and put back into
               POPF                            ; FLAGS

               PUSHF                           ;Load FLAGS
               POP     AX                      ; into AX register

               AND     AH,0F0H                 ;Isolate 4 high bits

               CMP     AH,0F0H                 ;If set, CPU is
                                               ; an 8086 or 8088

               JE      CPUID_2


;-------------------------------------------------------------------------
; On the 80286, bits 12-15 of the FLAGS register are always cleared to
; 0 when transferred to the stack.
;-------------------------------------------------------------------------
               INC     DH

               PUSHF                           ;Load FLAGS
               POP     AX                      ; into AX register

               OR      AH,0F0H                 ;Set high 4 bits

               PUSH    AX                      ; and put back into
               POPF                            ; FLAGS

               PUSHF                           ;Load FLAGS
               POP     AX                      ; into AX register

               AND     AH,0F0H                 ;If all clear, must
                                               ; be an 80286

               JZ      CPUID_2


;-------------------------------------------------------------------------
```

```
; The CPU must now be an 80386 or 80486. To test for an 386, we try to
; set the alignment check bit that was defined only for the 80486. If
; we can't use it, the CPU must be a 386.
;
; 1. Save the current stack pointer because we may change it.
; 2. Round the stack pointer DOWN so that it is aligned on a dword
;    boundary. This prevents the stack from causing an alignment fault.
; 3. Try to change the setting of the AC (alignment check) bit in the
;    EFLAGS register.
; 4. Restore the original EFLAGS and stack pointer.
;-------------------------------------------------------------------
.386     ;ENABLE 32-BIT INSTRUCTION MODE

              INC     DH

              MOV     ECX,ESP              ;Save current stack ptr
              AND     ESP,NOT 3            ;Align it to doubleword

              PUSHFD                       ;Load EFLAGS
              POP     EAX                  ; into EAX register

              MOV     EBX,EAX              ;Save for restoration

              XOR     EAX,00040000H        ;Complement AC bit

              PUSH    EAX                  ; and put back into
              POPFD                        ; EFLAGS

              PUSHFD                       ;Load EFLAGS
              POP     EAX                  ; into EAX register

              XOR     EAX,EBX              ;If bit not changed
                                           ; must be 386
              JZ      CPUID_1


;-------------------------------------------------------------------
; By default, CPU is 80486 or later. Restore the state of the AC bit in
; EFLAGS.
;-------------------------------------------------------------------
              INC     DH

              PUSH    EBX
              POPFD


;-------------------------------------------------------------------
; Restore the original stack pointer.
;-------------------------------------------------------------------
CPUID_1:
              MOV     ESP,ECX


;-------------------------------------------------------------------
; This section checks for the presence of a Coprocessor (NDP).
;
; At first, we must use the no-wait form of the instructions until we
; definitely know that there is a coprocessor present. Otherwise the CPU
; will WAIT for us to go buy one.
```

```
;
; 1. Initialize the coprocessor = reset the NDP status word.
; 2. Ask the NDP to write the status word to an area of memory we know
;    is non-zero.
; 3. If status word not Ø, no NDP present.
;------------------------------------------------------------------------
.8086   ;GENERATE 16-BIT CODE AGAIN

CPUID_2:
                FNINIT                              ;Reset the status word

                FNSTSW  WORD PTR [NDP_STATUS]   ;Write status word

                CMP     BYTE PTR [NDP_STATUS],Ø ;If not Ø, no NDP
                JNE     CPUID_3


;------------------------------------------------------------------------
; Next, we check to see if a valid control word can be written. If not,
; no NDP is present. Do not use a WAIT or the wait form of the FSTCW
; instruction.
;------------------------------------------------------------------------
                FNSTCW  WORD PTR [NDP_STATUS]        ;Write ctrl word
                AND     WORD PTR [NDP_STATUS],1Ø3FH ;Mask bits
                CMP     WORD PTR [NDP_STATUS],3FH    ;Correct value?
                JNE     CPUID_3


;------------------------------------------------------------------------
; Assume that the coprocessor type matches the CPU type. The only time
; this is not true is when an 80386 is paired with an 80287. If the CPU
; type indicated is an 80386, then test explicitly for the NDP type.
;------------------------------------------------------------------------
                MOV     DL,DH                   ;Set NDP type

                CMP     DH,3                    ;If not 386, we're done
                JNE     CPUID_3


;------------------------------------------------------------------------
; An 80386 can have either an 80287 or an 80387 installed. It is only
; necessary to know this if 387-specific instructions will be used or
; if a denormal exception handler is to be used.
; Remember that the NDP has been initialized to its default values.
; 1. Generate +infinity
; 2. Generate -infinity
; 3. The 80287 says that +infinity = -infinity. The 80387 says they
;    are different.
;------------------------------------------------------------------------
                FLD1                            ;Put a 1 on the stack
                FLDZ                            ;Now put a Ø on stack
                FDIV                            ;Divide 1/Ø, leave
                                                ; infinity on stack

                FLD     ST                      ;Duplicate infinity
                FCHS                            ;Make negative
                FCOMPP                          ;Compare & discard them

                FSTSW   [NDP_STATUS]            ;Write the NDP flags
```

```
                MOV       AX,WORD PTR [NDP_STATUS] ;Place in AX and...
                SAHF                               ; then into FLAGS

                JNE       CPUID_3                 ;If not equal,NDP=387

                DEC       DL                      ;Otherwise, 287

;-----------------------------------------------------------------------
; Return to caller with AX set.
;-----------------------------------------------------------------------
CPUID_3:
                MOV       AX,DX
                RET

CPUID           ENDP

;=======================================================================
; This routine simply uses the DOS "Print String" function to display a
; message on the console and is included only to clarify the appearance
; of the MAIN proc. It is assumed that the string offset is passed in
; the DX register.
;-----------------------------------------------------------------------
PRINT$                    PROC    NEAR
        ASSUME            CS:CSEG,DS:CSEG,ES:CSEG,SS:CSEG

                MOV       AH,9
                INT       21H

                RET

PRINT$          ENDP

CSEG            ENDS
                END     MAIN
```

CPUID does not attempt to distinguish between the 8086 and 8088, the 80386DX and 80386SX, or the 80486DX and 80486SX/80487SX combination. This is simply because these processors differ only in areas that do not affect the programmatic interface. Because floating-point instructions cannot be used, the case of the 80486SX processor *without* the companion 80487SX installed is identified.

The CPUID program contains three procedures. The MAIN procedure simply calls the identification procedure and is responsible for formatting the data for display. The CPUID procedure contains all the code to perform the identification. This procedure can easily be adapted for use in your own programs. Finally, the PRINT$ procedure displays the program's output on the display and is used principally to make MAIN more readable.

Identifying the CPU

Identification of the CPU is accomplished by using the known values of certain bits in the Flags register. Some of these bits are undocumented, but only in the sense that they are not normally referenced during programming. The following explanations describe what is happening in the CPUID procedure.

8086 Check The four high-order bits of the 8086/8088 Flags register are always set to 1 when the value of FLAGS is placed on the stack. This is not true for other members of the 80x86 family. To test for this condition, the following steps are used.

First, a copy of the current flags is moved to the AX register via the stack. The four high-order flag bits are cleared by ANDing them with zeros. The remainder of the flag bits are untouched. The modified flags are put back into the Flags register via the stack. Then, the flags are again transferred to AX. If the cleared bits have been set to 1s, the processor is an 8088 or an 8086.

80286 Check The 80286 processor acts just the opposite of the 8086: it always clears the four high-order bits of its Flags register to 0s when transferring them to the stack. This property doesn't hold true for any other processor.

The identification procedure for the 80286 is very similar to that for the 8086. The difference, however, is that an attempt is made to set the upper 4 bits of the Flags register. If the bits are returned as cleared, the CPU is an 80286. The 80386 and later processors will always set at least one of the high-order 4 bits.

80386/80486 Check As noted in the code, the 80386 is identified by the process of elimination. If the CPU is not an 8086 or 80286, but doesn't have the properties of an 80486, it must be an 80386. The 80486 is identified by the ability to set the Alignment Check (AC) bit, which was undefined before this processor.

When testing for the availability of the AC bit, we must be careful not to execute any instructions that would cause an alignment check while we have the bit set. If an alignment check (interrupt 11h) is generated, no appropriate interrupt handler may be in place. This is the reason the stack pointer is aligned to a doubleword boundary.

80x87 Check Knowing whether a math coprocessor is installed or not is perhaps more important than knowing its type. Programs that have been linked with software-based coprocessor emulators, for example, must determine at execution time whether to use the math chip or the emulator. And a program that executes the WAIT instruction, telling the processor to wait for a ready signal from the coprocessor, when no coprocessor is installed, will hang the computer.

An attempt is made to initialize the coprocessor and have it write a copy of its status word over a known non-zero area of memory. If the upper 8 bits of memory are still non-zero, then we can assume that the status word was never written and there is no coprocessor.

Next, the coprocessor control word is written to memory. When initialized, certain bits of the control word are consistently set to either 1 or 0 across the 80x87 family. These bits are masked off and tested. If the proper settings are not detected, it is assumed that no coprocessor is present.

Having thus satisfied ourselves that a coprocessor is present, we can assume, with one exception, that its type is a match to the CPU. The 80386DX has the ability to function with either the 80287 or the 80387DX. If the CPU has been previously identified as an 80386, the coprocessor is tested to distinguish between the two possible types.

Because of the changes that have occurred over time in the international standard for floating-point math (the standard to which Intel designs its coprocessors), the 80287 and 80387 handle the case of positive and negative infinity differently. After a reset, the 80287 defaults to projective closure, where $+\infty$ is equal to $-\infty$. The 80387, on the other hand, supports only affine closure, where $-\infty<+\infty$. Positive and negative infinity are generated, then compared to distinguish the two chips.

MEMORY STRUCTURE AND MANAGEMENT

MEMORY MANAGEMENT IS THE STRATEGY BY WHICH A PROCESSOR MAKES SYStem memory resources available to software programs. The characteristics of a memory management system originate in the hardware. Simple processors provide correspondingly simple memory management. More advanced processors provide hardware support for sophisticated memory management techniques that include dividing memory among multiple tasks and handling structures that are larger than physical memory by keeping them partially in memory and partially on a mass storage device such as a hard disk.

In previous chapters, memory was introduced as a contiguous string of bytes. The format of the various data types and how they are stored and addressed were also covered. This chapter will discuss memory management from the point of view of both the processor and the programmer. The management mechanisms implemented by the Intel 80x86 family of processors will be presented. Specific topics that are covered include segmentation, paging, virtual memory, and reserved and dedicated memory areas. The strategies used to protect memory during program execution are covered separately in Chapter 15.

Terminology

The terminology of memory models can be confusing. Often there is more than one common term that refers to a particular type of addressing mechanism or memory addressing scheme. To make reading and explaining a little easier, let's review the terms that will be used in this chapter.

Logical Address When software refers to memory, regardless of operating mode, memory model, or any other architectural concerns, the address it uses is called a logical address. Software depends on the memory management mechanisms of the processor to translate the logical addresses it uses into valid memory read and write operations. When the processor is operating in real mode, a logical address is called a segmented address. In protected mode, the logical address is called a virtual address.

Segmented Address In real mode, memory references are made using a two-part logical address called a segmented address. A segmented address is written in the form *segment:offset* where both terms refer to physical locations in the system memory.

Virtual Address   When operating in protected mode, programs reference memory using a two-part logical address called a virtual address. Like the segmented address, a virtual address is written in the form *segment:offset*. The segment term, however, does not necessarily have a fixed correspondence with a particular address in physical memory. Data in memory may be relocated, changing its physical address, while retaining the same logical address.

Linear Address   Each two-part segmented or virtual address will eventually be translated into a one-part linear address. The linear address is an unsigned number that specifies the offset of the desired memory location into the linear address space of the processor. On the 8086, 8088, and 80286 processors, the linear address will be the same as the physical address of the memory operand. On the 80386 and 80486, a further translation may be required if memory paging is in effect.

Physical Address   The physical address of a memory operand is the numerical equivalent of the signals that are ultimately placed on the pins of the processor's address bus. The physical address is the end result of the translation of a logical address. To be considered a valid address, there must be a device capable of decoding the address and completing the memory access bus cycle. Typical memory devices include RAM, ROM, and memory-mapped I/O devices.

The term *memory space* represents the set of all valid addresses that can be used to access memory. Different types of memory space exist depending on the type of address being used. A processor has only one *physical* memory space, but may have many *logical* address spaces, for example.

Segmentation

How a processor looks at memory is, in many ways, dependent on the sophistication of the chip itself. A simple processor is apt to employ a simple memory architecture. Intel's 8080, for example, is a relatively simple 8-bit processor and uses a straightforward memory addressing scheme: all memory addresses refer to the same memory space.

In other words, a memory location's logical address (the memory address seen by software programs) is exactly the same as its physical address (that seen by the hardware). There is no mapping or translation that takes place in the processor. This type of memory architecture is known as a *flat* memory model.

The 8086 processor was designed to support a different type of memory architecture, known as a *segmented* model. In contrast to the flat memory model, where all logical memory is visualized as one contiguous address space, the segmented memory model divides memory into units called *segments*. Each segment represents an address space that can be treated as if it were an independent flat memory space. Segments may range from small to as large as permitted by the particular processor implementation.

Segmentation is a logical way to divide a processor's memory space and relieves the computer system designer from having to implement a rigid memory structure. Unlike systems that are restricted to the use of memory units of a fixed size, a system of segments can be relatively unorganized and each segment can vary in size to suit the particular application. Another benefit of the segmented architecture is support for dynamically relocatable code. Programs that are written to use segment-relative addressing make all memory references relative to the start of a segment. The programs can then be moved about in memory, as might be done by an operating system, without affecting their addressing operations.

Likewise, segments are convenient for implementing protection mechanisms. Each segment can be a separate, protected memory area with a definite beginning and an equally definite end. Access to each segment can be checked and either allowed or disallowed according to the privilege level of the accessing program, the type of access (read, write, instruction fetch, etc.) and whether the segment is present in physical memory.

A Flat Memory Model

Although the memory architecture of all members of the 80x86 family is based on segmentation, it is possible to implement a flat memory model by setting all segments to point to the same area of memory. In this way, the explicit use of segments is removed. This technique was used to great advantage when programs written for the 8080 were recoded for the 8086. (This is also reflected in the structure of the .COM file format.) The 8080 had only a 64k memory space and implemented a flat memory architecture. When all the segments in an 80x86 processor are set to the same value, 64k of memory is accessible and the environment is very similar to that provided by the 8080. In addition, the program doesn't lose any of the relocation ability granted by segmentation. If relocated, all segment values are changed at the same time to the same value.

Support for the flat model is expanded on the 80386 and 80486, which have the ability to form virtual addresses that use a 32-bit offset. By setting all segments to the same value, the 80386 and 80486 provide a flat address space of four gigabytes of memory.

Real Mode Memory Management

The native memory architecture and address space model of the 8086 and 8088 processors are based on segmented addressing. This is the only model supported by the 8086 and 8088, which operate only in real mode. The more advanced members of the 80x86 family default to emulation of 8086 real mode when initialized. No protection mechanisms are enforced by the processor when it is operating in real mode and the applications programs (acting through the operating system) must coordinate memory use to avoid overwriting each other. Any area in the memory space may be addressed, read, written, or executed by any program that is running on the processor.

The 8086 uses 20 bits to represent physical memory addresses, giving it access to 1Mb of physical memory. (Note that physical memory never includes enhancements such as expanded memory that are not directly addressable by the processor.) External to the 8086, physical memory appears as a linear string of bytes numbered from 0 to $2^{20}-1$. But internally, an immediate problem occurs since a 20-bit address will not fit into the 16-bit registers used in the 8086. To solve this problem, the chip designers used the technique of segmented memory architecture.

Segmentation in Real Mode

In real mode, programs running on the processor access memory via a two-part segmented address. The segmented address consists of a segment value and an effective address offset value. A segmented address is written as two 16-bit values in the form *segment:offset* and is usually expressed in hexadecimal with the *h* suffix omitted. The value given for the segment portion of a segmented address specifies the location in physical memory from which displacements are measured. This physical memory address is called the *base address* or the *segment address*.

A segment's base address is constrained to begin at a byte address in physical memory that is an integer multiple of 16 (10h). Because of this, the last digit of the base address of a segment will always be 0. A segment base of 2D4Eh, for example, would refer to the physical memory address 2D4E0h. The programmer must view memory as a collection of overlapping blocks that start at physical memory addresses 0, 16 (10h), 32 (20h), and so on in multiples of 16 (10h) bytes that are called *paragraphs*.

The second portion of a segmented address is called the *effective address offset* and specifies an unsigned displacement from the segment's base address. The offset is used to address a specific byte within a segment. In real mode, the offset value is limited to 16 bits, providing access to up to 64k (2^{16}) bytes per segment. Figure 4.1 shows how an offset value is used in conjunction with a segment address to locate a specific byte within a segment.

Segmented to Physical Address Translation

When the processor accesses physical memory it must use a physical address. In the 1Mb physical memory space available in real mode, each byte has a unique physical address that ranges from 0 to FFFFFh. Programs, however, refer to memory using a segmented address where both the segment and offset are 16-bit values. It is the responsibility of the address generation logic in the processor to perform the translation from the segmented address to a physical address. This is done by shifting the segment value left 4 bit positions (that is, shifting it by one hex digit, which is the same as multiplying it by 10h) and then adding the value of the offset. This operation is illustrated in Figure 4.2.

In the example shown in Figure 4.2, the address would be shown in segmented form as 1BA4:204E. (By convention, the two parts of a segmented address always represent hexadecimal values even though the "h" suffix is omitted.)

An important property of segmented memory is that each memory location is pointed to by 2^{12} different segment:offset combinations. Although potentially confusing, this property can often be exploited to make some programming tasks easier. Figure 4.3 illustrates three segment:offset addresses that all refer to the same byte in memory.

Segment Wraparound

The address that results from the addition of the segment and offset values of a segmented address provides the starting physical address for a memory access.

Regardless of the starting address or the size of the data type, memory access is restricted to the 64k block of memory that begins at the segment base address. This address restriction becomes significant only when accessing a data type at an address that would cross a segment boundary.

FIGURE 4.1

Combining segments and offsets in segmented addressing

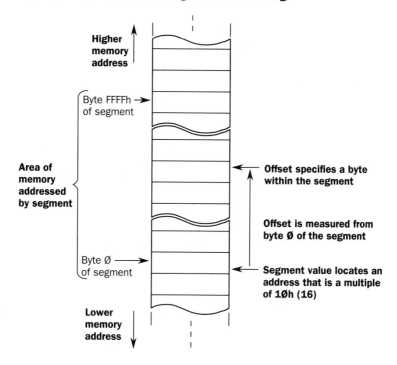

FIGURE 4.2

Real mode physical address generation

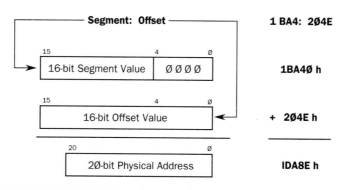

FIGURE 4.3

Correlating segmented and physical addresses

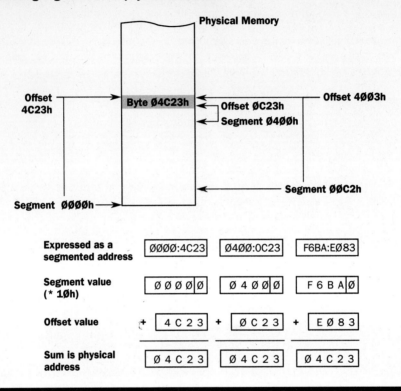

For example, consider the situation where an attempt is made to read the word at a segmented address of 4000:FFFF. First, the segmented address is translated to the physical address 4FFFFh by multiplying the segment value by 10h and adding it to the offset value. Next, the bus interface unit of the processor will attempt to read two consecutive bytes beginning at physical address 4FFFFh. The two bytes at physical address 4FFFFh can (for the purpose of this example) be represented as a low byte located at the logical address 4000:FFFF and a high byte located at the next contiguous byte, segmented address 4000:10000. The 17-bit offset value shown for the second byte is too large and specifies an address that is outside the 64k addressing range of the specified segment value.

In reality, this situation does not occur because the 8086 and 8088 implement *segment wraparound*. The offset addresses required to access the bytes in a word or larger data type are taken modulo 64k, which causes an attempt to read beyond the end of a segment to be wrapped back to the beginning. So in the previous example, the two bytes returned would be located at 4000:FFFF and 4000:0000.

Segment wraparound occurs without incident only on the 8086 and 8088 processors. On the 80286 and later processors, any attempt to access a word or larger data type that crosses a segment boundary will cause the processor to generate exception 0Dh. This condition is called *segment overrun*.

Protected Mode Memory Management

Protected mode memory management differs from real mode memory management in several important ways. Protected mode provides the programmer with additional tools to expand the limitations on segment size and use in order to implement protection mechanisms. While segments are still used, their meaning and interpretation in determining physical memory addresses are vastly different. Finally, protected mode addressing introduces the concepts of virtual memory, whereby a large physical memory space can be simulated using a combination of memory and mass storage.

Protected mode operation is available only on the 80286 and later processors; the 8086 and 8088 processors operate only in real mode. There are also important differences in capability between the protected mode memory management of the 80286 and that of the 80386 and later processors. The 32-bit effective offset of the 80386 and 80486, for example, provides a significantly larger segment limit compared to the 80286. Fields in control structures that were marked as reserved on the 80286 have been defined for the 80386 and 80846. Finally, the 80386 and later processors add the optional step of page translation (discussed in a later section of this chapter) to the process of logical-to-physical address translation.

Segmentation and Virtual Addressing

In protected mode, as in real mode, programs deal exclusively with logical addresses. Accessing memory is a matter of loading a segment register with an appropriate value and then specifying a displacement from that base address. In real mode, a program's logical addresses could be easily converted to equivalent physical addresses using straightforward mathematics. In protected mode, however, no such mathematical relationship exists between a logical address and a physical address. For this reason, a protected mode logical address is referred to as a *virtual address*.

A virtual address is used by a program running in protected mode in much the same way as a segmented address is used when running in real mode. Virtual addresses are specified in two parts: an effective address offset and a *segment selector* that indirectly provides the segment base address. On the 80286, the offset is a 16-bit value. On the 80386 and later processors, the offset may be either a 16-bit or a 32-bit value. The segment selector is always 16 bits.

The processor is responsible for translating a virtual address into a *linear address*. On the 80386 and later processors, the linear address is then passed to the paging unit for translation into a physical address. If paging is disabled, the linear address is identical to the physical address. On the 80286, which does not implement paging, the linear address is always the same as the physical address. To maintain a consistent terminology throughout this discussion, the term linear address will be used to represent the result of the virtual address translation step.

Segment Selectors A virtual address is composed of two parts: a 16-bit segment selector and a 16-bit or 32-bit effective address offset. The function of the offset portion of the address is identical to its counterpart in real mode: it specifies the displacement of the desired address, in bytes, from the segment base address. The segment selector, however, has a completely different format and meaning than the segment value in real mode. Rather than containing a physical address, the segment selector is a pointer to the information the operating system needs to define the segment. The format of a protected mode segment selector is shown in Figure 4.4.

FIGURE 4.4

Protected mode segment selector format

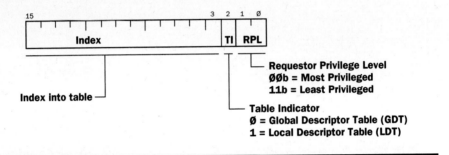

The two low-order bits of the segment selector specify the *requestor privilege level* (RPL) of the selector. The RPL field is used to prevent a less-privileged program from using a more-privileged program to access protected data. The RPL field is not related to memory address selection. (Protection is discussed in Chapter 15.)

The *table indicator* (TI) bit specifies whether the segment selector points to a segment that is part of the system's global address space (TI=0) or part of the local address space that belongs to a specific program or task (TI=1). Global address space refers to data and code segments that are designed to be available to all tasks running on the system. Examples of global code and data include operating system service routines, common libraries, and run-time support modules.

In a system, there is only one global address space and any segment selector that has the TI bit cleared points to that space. All tasks running on the system share the same global address space; two different tasks using the same values for the TI and index fields will point to the same segment.

A segment that is located in a task's local address space is distinguished by having the TI bit of its segment selector set to 1. Unlike global address space, which is common to all tasks, a completely separate local address space may be created for each task. The code and data that a task places in its local address space are private to that task.

The remaining 13 bits of the segment selector are referred to as the *index* field, which uniquely specifies which of the 8,192 (2^{13}) possible segments is being referenced by the virtual address. The index field is used as a pointer to a segment in either the global or local address space depending on the value of the TI bit. The index points into a list of linear segment base addresses, called a descriptor table, that is used by the operating system to manage segments. The descriptor tables and their use are discussed in the sections that follow.

Overall, the high-order 14 bits of the segment selector are used to specify a segment in memory. Thus a protected mode program has access to up to 16,384 (2^{14}) segments. On the 80286, each segment can be as large as 64k, providing a total virtual address space of one gigabyte (2^{30} bytes). On the 80386 and 80486, which support a 32-bit offset value, each segment can be up to four gigabytes, providing a virtual address size of 64 terabytes (2^{46} bytes).

Segment Descriptor Tables   The index field of the selector points to an entry in either the task's *local descriptor table* (LDT) or the system's *global descriptor table* (GDT), depending on the value of the TI bit in the segment selector. These descriptor tables are data structures, stored in system memory, that dictate how virtual addresses are translated to linear addresses.

A descriptor table is a variable length data structure containing at least one but not more than 8,192 separate entries. Each entry is exactly eight bytes long. The relationship between a segment selector, the descriptor table registers, and the descriptor tables is shown in Figure 4.5.

Segment selectors and descriptor tables

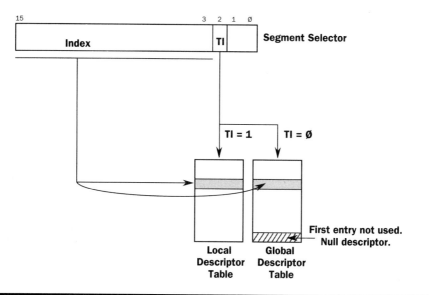

One GDT is used for all tasks and one LDT is present for each task that is being run. The first descriptor in the GDT is not used by the processor but may be used by programs as a *null descriptor*. Even though it is not a valid descriptor, no exception is generated if this descriptor is loaded into a segment register. An exception will be generated, however, if any attempt is made to access memory using the null descriptor. This property is useful for debugging. If the segment registers are set to this value, for example, any unplanned access to an uninitialized segment will generate an exception.

When the segment selector TI field is used to select the appropriate table, a valid index field will point at an entry in the descriptor table. Each entry contains a system structure called a *segment descriptor*. The information stored in these segment descriptors is used by the processor to translate virtual addresses into linear addresses. Figure 4.5 shows how a segment descriptor might be selected from either the LDT or the GDT, depending on which table is indicated by the value of the TI bit.

The Descriptor Table Registers   The processor locates the GDT using the *global descriptor table register* (GDTR). This register, shown in Figure 4.6, holds the linear base memory address and the limit of the GDT. The base address given is 24 bits wide on the 80286 and 32 bits wide on the 80386 and later processors. The limit field is always 16 bits and represents the length of the GDT in bytes. The LGDT and SGDT instructions are provided to read and write the contents of the GDTR.

The *local descriptor table register* (LDTR), also shown in Figure 4.6, holds information that identifies the linear base memory address and the limit of an LDT. The LDT is specified by a 16-bit segment selector that is loaded into the LDTR. The processor implicitly loads the base and limit values. To the processor, an LDT is simply a data structure. Each LDT is stored in a separate segment in memory. A segment descriptor for each LDT segment in the system is stored in the GDT. The LLDT and SLDT instructions are provided to read and write the contents of the LDTR.

FIGURE 4.6	

Descriptor table registers

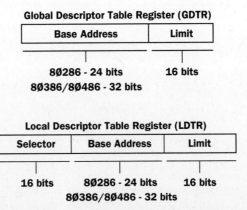

Segment Descriptors

The descriptor tables contain another system structure called a *segment descriptor*. Two general segment descriptor formats are available for the different classes of segment being described. Both descriptor formats are eight bytes long. The segment descriptor contains the information the processor needs to coordinate access to the segment. It describes the base address and limit of the segment in linear memory as well as status and control information about the segment. The descriptor forms a link between a segment in memory and a task. If no descriptor for a segment is available, either in the GDT or the LDT, the segment is invisible to the task and there is no mechanism by which it can be accessed.

The first type of descriptor is called a memory segment descriptor or simply a segment descriptor. Illustrated in Figure 4.7, it holds information that describes a segment included in the address space (either global or local) available to a task. Note that the high-order two bytes of the descriptor are not defined for use with the 80286. To ensure upward compatibility with the 80386 and 80486, programs written for the 80286 must set these fields to 0. The fields of the segment descriptor are defined below.

FIGURE 4.7

Segment descriptor format

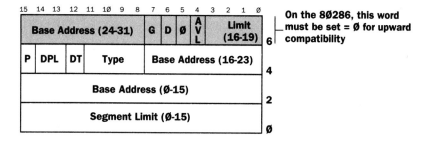

Field	Description
G	Granularity
D	Default
AVL	Available
P	Present
DPL	Descriptor Privilege Level
DT	Descriptor Type

Segment Base: This field specifies the base address of the segment within the processor's linear address space. On the 80286, this field is 24 bits wide; thus the segment may start at any *byte* within the 16Mb address space.

On the 80386 and 80486, the field is broken into two parts that are combined by the processor to give one 32-bit value; the segment may start at any *byte* within the processors' four gigabyte address space. (Contrast this to real mode, where a segment's base is constrained to be at an address evenly divisible by 10h.)

Segment Limit: This field specifies the size of the segment. On the 80286, this field is a 16-bit unsigned number that represents the number of *bytes* that are in the segment—a maximum of 64k.

On the 80386 and 80486, the limit field is broken into two parts that are combined by the processor to give one 20-bit unsigned value. The limit is interpreted according to the setting of the granularity bit in the segment descriptor. If the granularity bit is set for byte granular, the segment limit is in bytes and the maximum segment size is 1Mb (2^{20} bytes). If set for page granular, the limit is in units of 4k pages, giving a maximum segment size of four gigabytes ($2^{20} * 2^{12} = 2^{32}$ bytes).

If a page granular limit is used, the lower 12 bits of an effective address offset are not checked. Setting granularity to page (G=1) and a limit of 00000h will provide a range of valid offsets from 0 to FFFh (4095).

Type: This 4-bit field is used to distinguish the different segment descriptor formats and specify the intended use of a segment. This field is used to implement protection and is not used for address generation. The field is subdivided into four 1-bit fields whose interpretation depends on the setting on the high-order bit in the field. Figure 4.8 gives the interpretation of the type field.

FIGURE 4.8

Type field definitions for segment descriptors

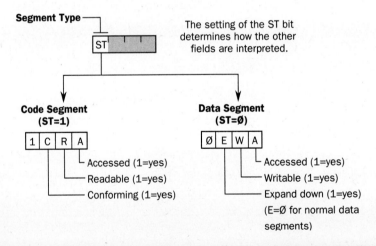

DT (descriptor type): This bit (also named the S field) distinguishes the two types of segment descriptors. The bit will always be set (DT=1) for a segment descriptor. If cleared (DT=0), the descriptor is not a segment descriptor and is either a special or system segment descriptor (described below).

DPL (descriptor privilege level): Specifies the privilege level of the segment. This field is used to implement protection and is not used for address generation.

P (present): This bit indicates whether the descriptor is valid (P=1) or not valid (P=0) for use in address generation. If invalid, the processor will generate a segment-not-present exception if an attempt is made to load a segment register with a segment selector that points to the descriptor.

A segment that is swapped out of memory (onto a hard disk, for example) will have this bit cleared to indicate that it is not available for use. If an attempt is made to access the segment, an exception handler in the system software can intercept the processor exception and reload the segment into memory. This bit gives the operating system the power to implement virtual memory that is invisible to application programs.

Figure 4.9 shows how a segment descriptor with P=0 (not present) is interpreted by the processor. The fields marked *available* are not used by the processor and may be used by system software for any purpose. One use of this available area would be to store information that could be used to locate and reload the segment.

FIGURE 4.9

Not-present segment descriptor format

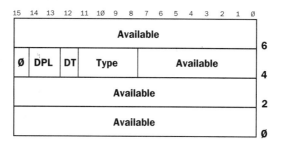

DPL - Descriptor Privilege Level
DT - Descriptor Type

AVL (available): (80386/80486 only) This bit is provided to allow systems programmers to expand the protection mechanisms of the processor. It is typically used to implement protection for memory-mapped I/O. If set (AVL=1), the field indicates that the descriptor is available for use by system software. If AVL=0, the segment is essentially declared unrelocatable and unswappable.

D (default operation size): (80386/80486 only) This bit is recognized only in code segment descriptors and specifies whether the default size for operands and effective addresses is 16-bit (D=0) or 32-bit (D=1). This bit is not used for address generation. The setting of this bit can be overridden for single instructions using the override prefixes described in Chapter 6.

G (granularity): (80386/80486 only) Specifies the units that are used to specify the segment limit. If the bit is cleared to 0, the limit is interpreted in bytes. If the bit is set to 1, the limit is interpreted in units of 4k pages. (See the description of the limit field, above.)

The general layout of the system descriptor is the same as the segment descriptor shown in Figure 4.7. This format is used for special purpose control descriptors, such as call gates and task descriptors, that are used to implement protection. Segment descriptors point to system data segments, including the descriptor tables themselves. Most of the fields in the system descriptor format are identical to those in the segment descriptor format as well. The fields that are the same include the segment base, limit, DT, DPL, P, AVL, D, and G fields. The type field, however, is defined quite differently. The correlation between the values for the type field and the system segments they define is given in Table 4.1.

TABLE 4.1

Type Field Definitions for System Segments

Type Field Value		Bit Settings			Description
0	0	0	0	0	Reserved
1	0	0	0	1	Available 16-bit TSS
2	0	0	1	0	LDT
3	0	0	1	1	Busy 16-bit TSS
4	0	1	0	0	16-bit Call Gate
5	0	1	0	1	16-bit Task Gate
6	0	1	1	0	16-bit Interrupt Gate
7	0	1	1	1	16-bit Trap Gate
8	1	0	0	0	Reserved
9	1	0	0	1	Available 32-bit TSS
Ah	1	0	1	0	Reserved
Bh	1	0	1	1	Busy 32-bit TSS
Ch	1	1	0	0	32-bit Call Gate
Dh	1	1	0	1	Reserved
Eh	1	1	1	0	32-bit Interrupt Gate
Fh	1	1	1	1	32-bit Task Gate

Segment Registers In real mode, the segment registers of the processor hold a 16-bit value that can be mathematically translated to the base memory address of a segment. In protected mode, the segment registers are still loaded with a value that will give the program access to the segment, but their operation is quite different.

In protected mode, each segment register has a 16-bit *visible* portion, which corresponds to the format of the register in real mode. In addition, there is an *invisible* portion that is inaccessible to programs. The invisible portions of the segment registers are called the *segment descriptor cache registers*, and hold the information that is used to implement protection and determine the mapping of segment selectors to a linear address. The segment descriptor cache register area is 48 bits wide on the 80286 and 88 bits wide for the 80386 and later processors.

The full formats of the segment registers for an 80286 are shown in Figure 4.10. The segment register format for the 80386 and later processors is shown in Figure 4.11.

FIGURE 4.10

80286 segment register format

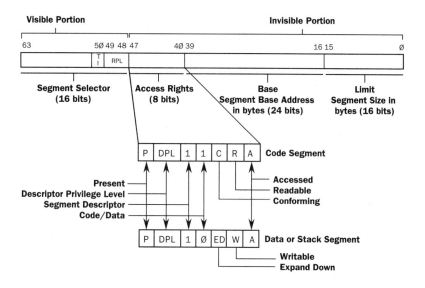

FIGURE 4.11

80386 and 80486 segment register format

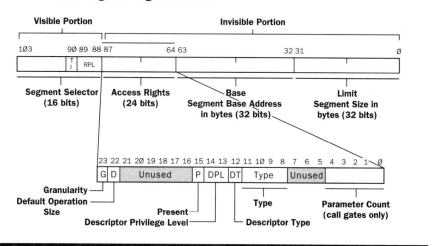

A segment selector is loaded into a segment register using the processor instructions provided for that purpose. Explicit loads are performed by instructions such as MOV, POP, LDS, LES, LFS, LGS, and LSS. An implicit segment selector load operation is performed by control transfer instructions, such as far JMPs or CALLs that change the value of the CS register. When any of these instructions are used, the processor automatically loads the invisible portion of the segment register.

Paged Memory Operation

The 80386 and 80486 processors provide hardware support for another memory management technique called *paging*. Paging is different from segmentation in that it uses small blocks of memory of a fixed size; a segment's size is variable. If paging is disabled, then the linear address that was produced by the segment translation phase of address generation is passed directly to the system bus as a physical address. If paging is enabled, the page translation mechanism of the processor performs the mapping of linear address space to physical address space.

Paging must be enabled if the operating system is to implement page-level protection checks, create virtual pages of memory, or use the processor's Virtual-86 mode. Paging operation is invisible to applications programs as well as to the segmentation mechanism of the processor. Paging is not available on the 80286, 8086, or 8088 processors.

Pages and Page Frames   A *page* is a contiguous 4k area in *linear* memory. A page always starts at a linear address that has the lower 12 bits set to 0 (is evenly divisible by 1000h). A *page frame* is a contiguous 4k block of *physical* memory. Like the page, a page frame is located at an address that is evenly divisible by 1000h.

The Page Directory and Page Tables   A linear address is produced when a virtual address is translated by the segmentation unit. This linear address is then further translated to a physical address when paging is enabled. The translation process locates the correct page using a two-step process involving table lookups based on the value of the linear address.

Page translation begins with the CR3 control register of the processor. (Refer to Chapter 3 for a description of the processor control registers.) The high-order 20 bits of CR3 hold the page frame address of a system data structure called the *page directory*. CR3 is sometimes referred to as the page directory base register (PDBR) for this reason. The page directory structure itself is always exactly one page (4k) in size and is always located in physical memory at an address that is evenly divisible by 1000h. Because of this, only 20 bits are needed to uniquely locate the page directory anywhere in the processor's four gigabyte address space.

On the 80386SX processor, which uses a 24-bit physical address, only the lower 12 bits of the 20-bit page frame address are used. When zero-extended 12 bits on the right, a 24-bit address that lies within the 16Mb physical address space of the processor is created.

The page directory is made up of 1,024 32-bit entries. Each entry is a pointer to another similar data structure called a *page table*, which contains pointers to pages in physical memory. The format of these pointers, called simply page table entries, is illustrated in Figure 4.12. The page frame address field has already been discussed. The remaining fields are defined below.

FIGURE 4.12

Page table entry format

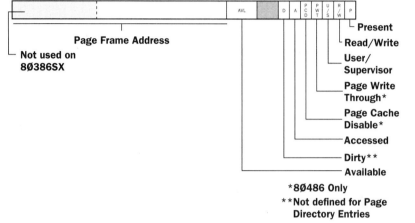

P (present): This bit indicates whether the page address in the entry maps to a page frame in physical memory (P=1) or is not valid (P=0) for use in address generation. If marked not-present, the page is not in physical memory and the processor will generate a page-fault exception if an attempt is made to use the entry for address translation. Note that page tables themselves may be swapped out of memory as indicated by the clearing of the P bit in their entry in the page directory.

An entry for a page table that is swapped out of memory (onto a hard disk, for example) will have this bit cleared to indicate that it is not available for address translation. If an attempt is made to access the page, an exception handler in the system software can intercept the processor exception and reload the page into memory. This bit gives the operating system the power to implement demand-paged virtual memory that is invisible to application programs.

Figure 4.13 shows how a table entry with P=0 (not present) is interpreted by the processor. With the exception of the P bit field, the entire entry may be used by system software for any purpose. One use of this available area would be to store information that could be used to locate and reload the page.

R/W (read/write): The read/write bit is used to implement page-level protection and is not involved in address translation.

U/S (user/supervisor): The user/supervisor bit is used to implement page-level protection and is not involved in address translation.

PWT (page write-through): (80486 only) This bit is provided to allow software to control the operation of an external memory cache when handling pages or page tables. When a page table entry has the PWT bit set to 1, the cache is directed to use write-through caching. If the bit is clear, write-back cache operation may be possible. The operation of the on-chip cache is not affected by the setting of this bit.

FIGURE 4.13

Not-present page entry format

31 30 29 28 27 26 25 24 23 22 21 20 19 18 17 16 15 14 13 12 11 10 9 8 7 6 5 4 3 2 1 0

Available	0

Available for operating system use

PCD (page cache disable): (80486 only) When this bit is set to 1 in an entry, caching of the corresponding page is disabled, even if hardware requests that it be cached by asserting the KEN# signal input. Caching must be disabled for addresses that are used as memory-mapped I/O ports. Other pages that will not benefit from caching may also have their PCD bit set.

The 80486 will force the PCD output signal to high whenever the cache disable (CD) bit in control register CR0 is set regardless of the value of this bit in a page table entry.

A (accessed): This bit provides information on whether the page pointed to by the entry has been read or written. If the bit is set (A=1) in an entry in the page directory, it indicates that the corresponding page table has been accessed. If the bit is set in an entry in the page table, it indicates that the indicated page in memory has been accessed. The bit is set by the processor and is provided to allow operating system memory management software to test different pages for frequency of use.

D (dirty): The dirty bit is defined only for page table entries, not for entries in the page directory. The dirty bit is set in a page table entry by the processor when the corresponding memory page is written to. This bit is also used by operating system memory management software to determine if a page in memory has been changed since the last time it was copied to disk.

AVL (available): These 3 bits are provided for use by systems software programmers for whatever purpose they wish. Information related to page use, for example, could be stored here to help decide which pages to swap out to memory.

Linear-to-Physical Address Translation   The paging mechanism of the processor begins the linear-address-to-physical-address translation process by dividing the linear address into three fields as shown in Figure 4.14. The 10-bit *directory index* field is used as an index into the page directory. (See Figure 4.15.) The index is multiplied by 4 (the number of bytes in an entry) to give the offset of the desired entry in the page directory table. Because the low 12 bits of the page directory base address are always zero, the physical address of the entry is formed by concatenating the two values.

FIGURE 4.14

Linear address format

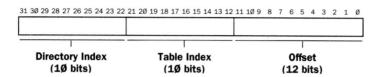

FIGURE 4.15

Linear-to-physical address translation

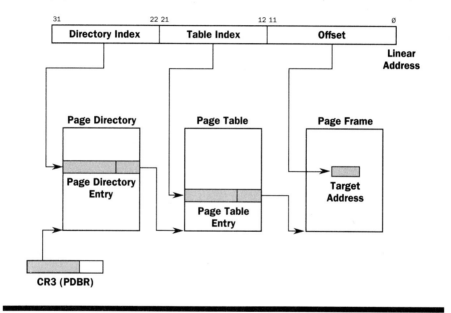

The page directory entry selected by the directory index field contains the base page frame address of a page table. (We'll assume that the page holding the page table is either already in physical memory or is placed there by the virtual memory management software as we try to access it.) The *table index* field of the linear address, bits 12 through 21, are now used as an index into the page table. Because page table entries are 4 bytes long, the table index is multiplied by 4 and concatenated onto the page frame address retrieved from its entry in the page directory.

The selected page table entry now contains the base page frame address of the page that contains the addressed area of memory. The low-order 12 bits of the linear address are added, without translation, to the base address of the page to produce the final physical address.

The Page Translation Cache (TLB)   Because the page translation process requires two table look-ups and possibly swapping pages into memory, an on-chip page translation cache has been built into the 80386 and 80486 processors. This cache is called the *translation lookaside buffer* (TLB) and stores the most recently used page table entries.

The TLB is typically invisible to applications software, but is accessible to operating system software to support page cache management in multiple-processor environments. The TLB can be flushed by either reloading the CR3 (PDBR) register with a MOV instruction or by performing a task switch to a task state segment (TSS) that has a different CR3 value than the current TSS. The hardware aspect of TLB operation is discussed in Chapter 3.

Dedicated and Reserved Memory Areas

Intel preempts the use of some physical memory addressable by their processors at the extreme high and low memory addresses. These areas are dedicated to specific processor functions or reserved for the operation of Intel's own hardware and software products. The reserved physical memory addresses are 0h through 7Fh and the last 16 bytes of physical memory.

The addresses from 0h to 7Fh (128 bytes) are used to hold the interrupt vector table for interrupts 0h through 1Fh. These interrupts are typically generated by the processor to signal the occurrence of some event, usually an error. The segmented addresses of the interrupt handling routines for these interrupts are stored at these addresses. (Note that when IBM wrote the BIOS for the PC, it used many of these interrupts for its own purposes in violation of Intel's warning.)

The 16-byte memory area at the end of physical memory is reserved for system initialization code. When the processor is powered up or reset, the first instruction executed will be at that address. System initialization and initial register values are discussed in Chapter 13.

Segment Math

Segments are treated completely differently by a processor operating in protected mode. The values in the segment registers don't indicate the actual address of a segment of memory, but act as pointers to a table that contains the real location of the segment. This allows a protected mode operating system to move the program around in memory at will—which is required to implement program swapping, for example.

In protected mode, then, the processor is allowed to figure that loading a segment register with an improper value might enable a program to corrupt another program or the operating system itself. This isn't allowed. (That's why they call it protected mode.) But in real mode, this restriction doesn't exist and allows us to use the DS and ES segment registers as general-purpose registers and to perform the heinous (but useful) crime of segment math. Consider the following example.

Let's assume you are programming a mathematical procedure that will be executed a large number of times inside a loop, and therefore minimizing execution time is important. At some point in the code, you must free up a register that has a predefined function, such as using CX for a loop counter. If all your other register values must be preserved, your two choices would normally be to store CX temporarily on the stack or in local memory. But if the ES register is not being used, it can be employed to hold the value of CX. A comparison of the execution time and code size for the three options is shown in Table 4.2.

TABLE 4.2

Misusing Segment Registers

Bytes	Clock Cycles	Instructions
2	19	PUSH CX
		:
		POP CX
8	29	MOV WORD PTR [TEMP],CX
		:
		MOV CX,WORD PTR [TEMP]
4	4	MOV ES,CX
		:
		MOV CX,ES

Register-to-register operations are by far the fastest way to get things done on the 8086. Keep in mind, however, that segment registers cannot be manipulated with arithmetic or logical instructions and that CS and SS must always contain valid values. Be warned that using segment registers in this way may make your code harder to convert should you choose to move to a protected mode operating system. Used judiciously, however, segment math can help you through an otherwise sticky spot in your code.

INPUT/OUTPUT

EACH MEMBER OF THE 80X86 PROCESSOR FAMILY HAS AN ADDRESS SPACE, SEP-
arate and different from its memory space, that is used for communication with
peripheral devices. To the programmer, the architecture of this *input/output
(I/O)* address space is seen as a contiguous block of 64k 8-bit registers located at
addresses in the range from 0 to 65535 (FFFFh). Each of these addresses corresponds to a special register, called a *port*, that is external to the processor and
may be connected to a peripheral device.

This chapter will present the structure and organization of the processor's
I/O address space, the instructions used to access it, and how I/O operation is
controlled when operating in protected mode. Data transfer size, reserved locations, and memory-mapped I/O will also be discussed.

The I/O Address Space

The I/O address space of the processor is completely distinct from its memory
space; memory and the I/O space do not intersect. The processor addresses I/O
space by placing a valid address on the address bus and sending or receiving data
on the data bus, just as when accessing memory. To distinguish the two operations, the processor uses its M/IO (memory-I/O) signal as an additional address
line to indicate to the external hardware which address space it is addressing.
(Note that keeping the address spaces separate is a system design decision and
not a requirement of the processor. A system that is designed so that the memory and I/O address spaces do overlap will not decode the M/IO signal as part of
the address.)

I/O space is treated differently by the processor than memory space because
its use is different. I/O ports are typically used to exchange commands and data
with external devices. An I/O device, such as a disk controller or serial communications interface, usually requires relatively few control ports. As a result, a
typical device uses only a few port addresses. This contrasts sharply to memory
usage, where memory is usually allocated in large blocks of thousands or millions of bytes. For the same reason, the protection mechanisms used for I/O are
designed to work at the port level, rather than at the segment or page level,
which is the case with memory.

The characteristics of an I/O port are completely determined by the external
hardware that responds to the port address. For example, whether a port is read-
only, write-only, or bidirectional depends only on the ability of the addressed
device to accept or produce data. The processor itself makes no distinction and

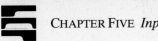

will happily read a write-only port or write to a read-only port. A read from an invalid or nonexistent port will return the value of the data lines at the time of the read. Because no data is being forced on the bus by a device, the bus is floating, and the values of the data lines are undefined.

I/O ports appear as a consecutive series of 64k addresses and a specific I/O port is accessed by its unique address. Unlike system memory, I/O space is not segmented and no segment registers are used when addressing I/O ports. All I/O ports can be thought of as residing in a single 64k segment. I/O space cannot be remapped and port addresses cannot be relocated.

I/O Port Organization

As with memory, the I/O address space of the processor is byte-granular and any port can be addressed individually as a byte. Any consecutive pair of I/O addresses may be treated as a single 16-bit I/O port. The address of the 16-bit port will be the lower of the two 8-bit ports addressed. An instruction to output a word to a 16-bit port will send the least significant byte of the operand to the lower-addressed 8-bit port and the most significant byte to the higher-addressed port. On the 80386 and 80486, any four consecutive ports may be addressed as a single 32-bit I/O port. Transfer of a doubleword to a 32-bit port will result in the low-order word going to the 16-bit port at the specified address, and the high-order byte going to the 16-bit port at the specified address + 2.

The addresses of 16-bit and 32-bit I/O ports do not need to be aligned on word or doubleword boundaries, respectively. A word port may begin at an I/O address in the range from 0 to 65534 (FFFEh). A doubleword port may begin at any I/O address in the range from 0 to 65532 (FFFCh). Figure 5.1 gives some examples of how I/O ports may be addressed.

The first 256 ports in I/O space, numbered 0 through 255, may be addressed directly by specifying the port number as immediate data. Any port in the I/O space may be addressed by using the DX register to hold the port number. The I/O instructions are detailed later in this chapter.

Intel reserves I/O ports F8h through FFh (248 through 255) for its own use. Typically these ports are used by Intel hardware and software products such as debuggers and hardware diagnostic tools and for interchip communication. Ports FFFEh and FFFFh are also indicated as reserved on the 8086 and 8088 processors.

As part of its normal operation, for example, the 80386SX processor may perform I/O at addresses 8000F8h and 8000FCh as part of its coprocessor interface. These I/O addresses are beyond the normal range of I/O space, but if decoded by a device, would fall within the Intel reserved area.

Memory-Mapped I/O

The use of the processor's I/O space and I/O instructions is not mandatory. A system designer may, instead, choose to locate I/O devices in the processor's memory space. When this is done, the devices are said to use *memory-mapped I/O*. Memory-mapped I/O operates somewhat differently and has both advantages and disadvantages when compared to standard I/O.

FIGURE 5.1

Addressing ports in I/O space

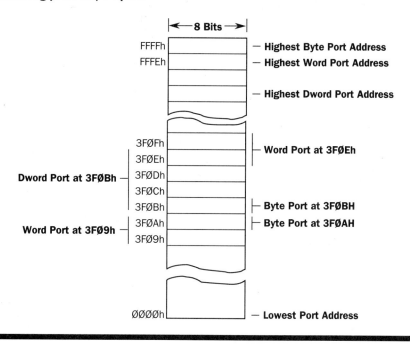

A memory-mapped device uses an area of system memory to communicate with the processor in much the same way as two subroutines might use a common data area to exchange information. To transmit data to the I/O device, for example, the processor would put the address of the memory area that corresponds to the device on the address bus and place the data on the data bus. When the device's address-decode logic recognizes the address as belonging to it, it will latch the data from the data bus. The data is then interpreted according to the design of the device. To read data from the device, the processor reverses the procedure, reading the data as if it were coming from RAM or ROM.

A memory-mapped device may be designed to send and receive data at any address or range of addresses in the memory space of the processor. Any processor instruction that references memory, such as MOV, XCHG, TEST, MOVS, and so on, may be used to address the device. Unlike traditional I/O, where the data must always pass through the Accumulator register, memory-mapped I/O allows memory-to-I/O, I/O-to-memory, and I/O-to-I/O data transfers. The full range of memory addressing modes available to the processor may be employed in memory-mapped I/O. In addition, the string instructions and repeat prefixes may be used to transfer blocks of data quickly and with relatively few instructions. From a programmer's point of view, memory-mapped I/O devices are extremely flexible.

For an example, consider the case of a printer with a memory-mapped interface. Our printer might be designed to respond to the 256 contiguous memory addresses in the range from E0000h to E00FFh. Rather than build a circuit to recognize each of these addresses individually, we would design the address-decode logic to ignore the low-order 8 bits of the address bus. Thus the interface would respond equally to any address of the form E00*xx*h, where *x* represents a don't-care condition of the bits. Assuming the DS:[SI] register pair points to a 256-byte buffer and the ES register contains the value E000h, we could transfer the entire block to the printer with these instructions:

```
MOV    CX,256    ;Length of buffer
XOR    DI,DI     ;DI=0 (starting offset)
REP    MOVSB     ;Transfer data
```

Memory-Mapped I/O in Protected Mode

By design, a memory-mapped I/O device responds to a specific address or range of addresses located in the processor's physical memory area. As such, the system must ensure that the area of memory used by the device is not swapped out by a virtual memory system or relocated. This is not a problem in real mode, where the logical addresses used in a program have a one-to-one correspondence with physical memory addresses. In protected mode, however, the same correspondence does not hold true and the operating system is ultimately responsible for controlling how logical addresses are translated into physical addresses. (See Chapter 4 for an explanation of this translation process.)

In addition, because memory-mapped I/O devices reside in the processor's memory space, they are subject to the same protection mechanisms as ordinary memory—the I/O protection mechanisms are not used. Hence, protection is implemented by the processor at the segment and page level, giving the programmer more flexibility in implementing protection of memory-mapped I/O devices. Using standard protection mechanisms, individual devices may be designated invisible, accessible but protected, or fully accessible on a task-by-task basis.

The memory area corresponding to the memory-mapped I/O device must not be virtualized, relocated, or cached. To see why, imagine a very simple I/O device whose function is to accept a byte at address 10000h and return the complement of that byte at address 10001h. Figure 5.2 shows what might happen for a sequence of two read/writes to the device when caching is enabled.

In the first panel, the byte 00h is written to memory location 10000h. The value is stored in the cache and then written through to memory. Our I/O device immediately performs the complement and places the value FFh at memory location 10001h.

Next, the processor reads a byte from location 10001h. The address is not found in the cache, so the processor initiates a bus cycle that accesses the I/O device and retrieves the value into the cache.

In the third panel, the byte F0h is again written to address 10000h. As before, the cache is written through and the byte is sent to the device, which immediately complements it and places the result at address 10001h.

FIGURE 5.2

Memory-mapped I/O errors caused by caching

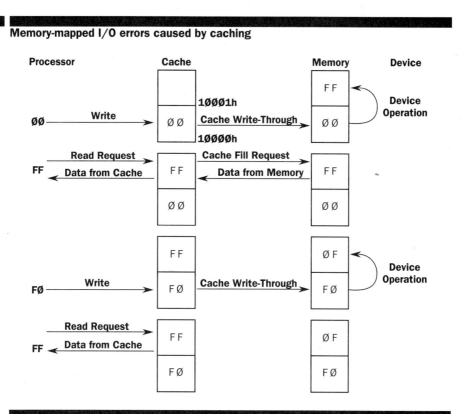

Finally, the processor attempts to read the resulting value. But this time the address *is* found in the cache. The processor has not processed any instructions that would indicate that the value in the cache does not reflect the value at the target memory address. As a result, the value in the cache, FFh, and not the correct value, 0Fh, is returned.

The ability of the 80486 to reorder memory reads and writes can cause additional problems with using memory-mapped I/O on that processor. Under certain well-established circumstances, the 80486 will change the order of read and write requests to memory, placing a newer read request ahead of pending write requests. (See Chapter 4 for a discussion of this process.) Because of this, a read-write instruction sequence to a memory-mapped I/O area can be reversed. Traditional I/O instructions do not suffer from this rearrangement as all pending memory operations are completed before an I/O operation is initiated.

I/O Instructions

Special instructions are provided to access the I/O space of the processor. These I/O instructions provide programs a method of exchanging data between the accumulator and the I/O ports or memory and the I/O ports. I/O instructions are provided to transfer either a single data item or a block of data. I/O-specific instructions are not used to communicate with memory-mapped devices.

Register I/O Instructions

The first group of I/O instructions transfers a single data item at a time using the Accumulator register. Data may be transferred to an 8-bit I/O device using the AL register or to a 16-bit device using the AX register. On the 80386 and 80486, 32-bit I/O is supported using the EAX register as the source or destination. The IN (input from port) instruction moves data from the I/O device to the accumulator. The OUT (output to port) instruction performs the complementary action, moving data from the accumulator to the I/O device.

Access to the entire I/O space of the processor is provided by the long form of the I/O instructions. These instructions use the DX register to specify the device address as a 16-bit value. If, however, the address of the target I/O device is within the range from 0 to 255 (00h to FFh) it may be specified as 8-bit immediate data in the short form of the I/O instructions. Here are examples of these instructions:

```
IN    AL,DX      ;Input byte 8-bit port, address in DX
IN    EAX,FFh    ;Input dword from port at FFh
OUT   14h,AX     ;Output word to 16-bit I/O port at 14h
OUT   DX,AL      ;Output byte to 8-bit port, address in DX
```

Block I/O Instructions

The second group of I/O instructions transfers data directly from an I/O port to memory and from memory to an I/O port. As with the register instructions, data may be transferred in 8-bit, 16-bit, or 32-bit (if supported by the processor) quantities, but the accumulator is not used for the data transfer. The operation of these instructions is analogous to the string manipulation instructions provided by the processor and so they are also referred to as string I/O instructions. Of all the 80x86 processors, only the 8088 and 8086 do not support the block I/O instructions.

The INS (input string from port) instruction copies the value from the I/O address specified in the DX register to the memory area pointed to by the ES:[DI] (or ES:[EDI]) register combination. The OUTS (output string to port) instruction copies the data unit in memory pointed to by the DS:[SI] (or DS:[ESI]) register pair to the I/O address specified in the DX register. After the transfer, the DI/EDI or SI/ESI register is automatically incremented or decremented by the size of the data unit in bytes, depending on the setting of the direction flag. As with the other string instructions, the INS and OUTS instructions may be combined with the REP prefix to perform their operation repeatedly. The CX/ECX register is used to hold the desired number of iterations.

Unlike the register I/O instructions, there is no short address form of the block I/O instructions; all port addresses must be specified in the DX register. Programmers must ensure that the target I/O devices can handle the speed at which the processor will transfer the data using the block I/O instructions.

I/O and Bus Operation

Occasionally, a data item must be transferred to an I/O port using more than one bus cycle. This situation occurs when the data item is larger than the processor bus or when the port address is unaligned. A word transfer on the 8088, for example, will take two bus cycles and an unaligned doubleword transfer on the 80386SX will require three bus cycles. *When more than one bus cycle is performed by an I/O instruction, the exact order of the bus cycles used to transfer the operand is undefined.* For example, executing the instruction OUT 2,EAX on the 80486DX will first transfer the high-order 16 bits of EAX to the 16-bit port at address 4, then transfer the low-order 16 bits of EAX to the 16-bit port at I/O address 2. Intel makes no guarantee that this order of operation will remain constant across processors or even across revisions of the 80486DX. If the order in which I/O bus cycles are performed is important, the order of the I/O operations should be coded explicitly.

In general, parity errors are not automatically masked on bus cycles to I/O space. This operation may be a source of spurious parity errors that need to be handled by the system software or ROM code.

I/O instructions on the 80486 are synchronized with the I/O device. Before an I/O instruction is executed, all previously executed instructions are allowed to complete and the write buffers are cleared. In addition, execution of new instructions will be delayed until the last ready signal from the last bus cycle to the I/O device has been returned. This usually is not a problem on processors that do not buffer memory reads and writes.

Protection and I/O

When the processor is operating in real mode, the I/O ports are always accessible and any program may read data from or write data to them. In protected mode, however, two mechanisms may be employed to limit a task's access to the I/O space of the processor. Use of the I/O instructions is controlled by the setting of the IOPL (I/O Privilege Level) field in the FLAGS register and access to individual ports in the I/O space is controlled by the I/O permission bit map of a task's TSS segment. These mechanisms are used only for I/O space. Protection for memory-mapped I/O does not use these mechanisms, but is implemented using segmentation or page-level control.

This discussion is applicable only to the 80286 and later processors that support protected mode operation. In addition, the I/O permission bit map mechanism is implemented only on the 80386 and later processors.

I/O Privilege Level

System hardware, support processors, and mass storage subsystems, for example, are typically controlled via I/O ports. As such, most protected mode operating system software will try to restrict program access to the I/O instructions to itself and a small number of "trusted" device drivers. In the ring protection model used by Intel, these tasks would be executing in privilege levels 0 and 1, respectively. An arrangement of this sort almost guarantees that all devices will

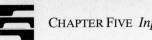

be virtualized through device drivers and reduces the likelihood of fast (that is, direct) device I/O being performed by an individual application.

Protected Mode   In protected mode, the IN, INS, OUT, OUTS, CLI, and STI instructions are classified as *IOPL-sensitive* instructions. The use of these instructions by a particular task is controlled by the setting of the IOPL field in the FLAGS register. To use the IOPL-sensitive instructions, a task must be running at a privilege level at least as privileged as (numerically equal to or less than) the current level specified by the IOPL field. Use of these instructions by a less privileged task results in the generation of a general protection exception by the processor.

Each task maintains its own copy of the FLAGS register. The IOPL field, therefore, can be set separately for each task. The value of the IOPL field may be changed only by using the POPF instruction. The POPF instruction, however, is privileged and may be executed only if the task is running at privilege level 0 (most privileged). An illegal attempt to change IOPL does not result in an exception, but the attempt is ignored and the current IOPL remains the same. Thus a task is prevented from changing its IOPL at will.

An attempt to change the setting of the interrupt flag using the POPF instruction is treated the same as if the STI or CLI instruction were issued: the POPF is interpreted as an IOPL-sensitive instruction. A change to the status of the Interrupt flag will be allowed only if the current privilege level is at least as privileged as (numerically equal to or less than) the current privilege level specified by the IOPL field. An attempt to use POPF to change IOPL without proper privilege level does not result in an exception, but the attempt is ignored and the status of the interrupt flag remains unchanged.

Virtual-86 Mode   The operation of the I/O protection mechanisms when the 80386 and 80486 processors are executing a Virtual-86 task is different than when executing in protected mode. First, the STI, CLI, PUSHF, POPF, LOCK, INT, and IRET instructions are classified as IOPL-sensitive. Although the INT instruction is IOPL-sensitive, the INT 3 (CCh), INTO, and BOUND instructions are not. (Neither are they IOPL-sensitive in protected mode.) Notably, the I/O instructions—IN, OUT, INS, and OUTS—are *not* IOPL-sensitive in V-86 mode; the IOPL field is ignored for I/O instructions. Instead, the I/O permission bit map is consulted to determine if addressing the specified port is allowed. The I/O permission bit map is explained in the section that follows.

The I/O Permission Bit Map

The IOPL check, used alone, provides a crude all-or-nothing I/O protection philosophy. And on the 80286, this is the only mechanism allowed. The 80386 and 80486 processors, however, provide a new mechanism that implements protection at the level of individual I/O ports. The data structure that manages this protection is called the *I/O permission bit map* and is available only on the 80386 and 80486 processors.

An I/O instruction, executed in protected mode, will first cause the processor to check the IOPL field of the task. If the task's current privilege level is at least as privileged as (numerically equal to or less than) the value of the IOPL field, no further checking is performed and the I/O operation is allowed to proceed. If not, however, the processor will then proceed to check the I/O permission bit map in the task's TSS segment. If the processor is operating in V-86 mode, the IOPL field is ignored and all I/O requests are immediately checked against the I/O permission bit map.

Each task maintains an I/O permission bit map in its task state segment (TSS), as shown in Figure 5.3. The beginning of the map is specified by a pointer, called the *I/O map base*, that is located in the fixed portion of the table. The starting position of the table within the TSS is then able to vary, depending on the structure of the remainder of the table. The I/O map base field in the TSS is 16 bits wide and contains the offset of the beginning of the bit map, in bytes, from the start of the segment. The length of the map is also variable, although it must always be a multiple of 8 bits.

FIGURE 5.3

Locating the I/O permission bit map in the TSS

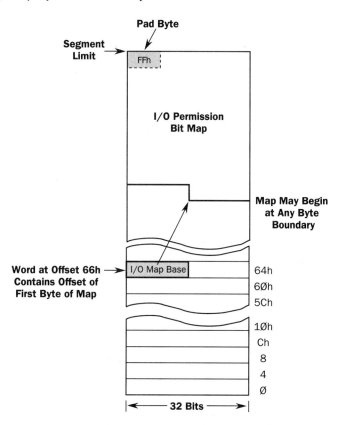

Each bit in the I/O permission bit map corresponds to a byte address in I/O space. The first bit represents the 8-bit port at address 0, the second bit represents the 8-bit port at address 1, and so on. If the bit in the I/O permission bit map corresponding to the port being accessed is cleared to 0, the I/O operation is allowed to proceed. If the bit is set to 1, the processor generates a general protection exception. When word or doubleword ports are being accessed, the bits representing the two or four adjacent byte ports, respectively, must all be 0 for the operation to proceed. For I/O to the 32-bit port at 4 to be allowed, for example, bits 4 through 7 in the I/O permission bit map would have to be 0.

A bit map that represented each of the 64k I/O addresses would require 8k of memory. Because I/O space is usually sparsely populated, allocating 8k for each task would be a waste of resources. Fortunately, the bit map for a task does not have to represent the entire I/O space. Ports with addresses that extend beyond the end of the map are treated as if their corresponding bits in the map were set to 1.

When required to check an I/O permission bit map, the 80386DX will read a single byte from the table based on the address of the port. Because ports may be unaligned, however, the permission bits corresponding to a word or doubleword port may extend past the end of the original permission byte read. A word port located at I/O address 7, for example, would use permission bit 7 in the first byte of the map and bit 0 in the second byte of the map. In this case, the 80386DX would then have to read the additional byte in the map to finish the check.

The 80386DX determines the highest port address represented in the table from the value of the I/O map base pointer and from the TSS segment limit value. Subtracting the two values gives the number of bytes in the I/O permission bit map. Each byte represents eight ports and the first bit is always port 0.

To improve processor efficiency in the case of unaligned ports, the logic of the 80386SX and 80486 processors was redesigned to always fetch two bytes from the I/O permission bit map: the byte containing the bit that corresponds to the base address of the port and the succeeding byte. In doing so, however, the designers created a new problem. To illustrate, assume that the bit corresponding to the I/O port address being checked by an 80386SX is in the last byte of an I/O permission bit map. The new logic in the 80386SX will automatically try to fetch the next contiguous byte in the table. But there isn't one! Instead, the fetch will be interpreted as an attempt to access memory beyond the limit of the TSS segment—a protection violation. In response, the processor will generate an exception.

To prevent an exception from being generated erroneously, the end of the I/O permission bit map must be padded with an additional byte. The byte must have the value FFh to provide compatibility with the 80386DX.

The 80386SX and 80486 processors ignore the value of the pad byte and do not include it when calculating the limit of the I/O permission bit map. The 80386DX, however, *does* consider the byte significant. By setting the byte to

FFh, access to the additional eight ports will be denied. The effect is the same (to the 80386DX) as if the byte had not been included in the table.

For example, if we want to allow a task access to I/O ports 0 through 3FFh (1023), the I/O permission bit map would have to be 129 bytes long. This includes 128 bytes to represent each I/O port with its own bit (1024/8) and the one extra byte of padding. The first 128 bytes of the table would contain the value 00h, to indicate I/O to those addresses was allowed. The pad byte would contain FFh by definition. The length of the TSS segment would then be set equal to the offset of the last byte in the bit map: I/O map base + 128.

To indicate that no I/O permission bit map is present in the TSS, simply use a value for the map base that is greater than or equal to the TSS limit value but no greater than DFFFh. In that case, all I/O will cause an exception. The maximum value for the I/O map base is DFFFh, which is determined by subtracting the maximum table size (2000h) from the highest possible 16-bit offset in the TSS segment (FFFFh).

6 INSTRUCTION ENCODING AND TIMING

THE 80X86 MICROPROCESSORS ARE COMPLEX INSTRUCTION SET COMPUTER (CISC) chips. They provide instructions that allow you to manipulate data in their registers, memory, and I/O ports. The 8086 processor has just 70 instructions. Incredibly, all software, ranging from the simplest text editor to an intricate and complex database, can be written using just those 70 primitive assembly language instructions. These instructions include logical and arithmetic operations on unsigned, integer, and binary-coded-decimal (BCD) numbers; string primitives; compare and transfer; bit manipulation; and I/O. The more advanced processors add instructions that support 32-bit operands, virtual memory access, and multitasking.

In this chapter I'll discuss the types of instructions that are available on the 80x86 processors, how instructions are encoded, effective address generation, and the factors that influence instruction execution time. Complete encodings, timings, and detailed explanations of operation are given in Appendix A for all the processor instructions. The coprocessor instruction set is discussed in Chapter 12 and a complete list of the coprocessor instructions is given in Appendix B.

Introduction to Instruction Encoding

It's appropriate to start this chapter with a bit of friendly advice: the information presented here gets quite technical. Instruction encodings are complex and operate at the machine code level. Further, the rules and exceptions of instruction timing are terribly convoluted. If you feel that the depth of information isn't improving your understanding of the instructions, just skip to the instruction reference in Appendix A. *Memorizing the detailed information in this chapter isn't necessary for you to program in assembly language.* A sound approach is to learn enough about what each of the instructions does so that you'll know when it's appropriate to use it. Then, go back to the reference when you need more information.

Many of you, on the other hand, may be looking for a way to shave a few more bytes or clock cycles out of a sort routine to speed it up from adequately fast to blazingly fast. Or, you may just be trying to understand how to use 32-bit registers and instructions in your real mode programs. If so, you'll find that the comprehensive details on instruction encoding, timing, and processor operation presented here will help you achieve your goal.

Opcode Usage

When we view the processor as a unit, it appears to be a very flexible device with many capabilities. The 8086 can be commanded to perform addition, subtraction, multiplication, or division, for example, with just a single instruction. But it is more descriptive to think of processor instructions as subroutines that are performed within the chip.

Inside the processor, a special "program" is always running. Invisible to us, its purpose is to fetch and decode our stored instructions from memory, identifying the operands and the operation to be performed. Once identified, the processor control program makes the necessary data available to the internal hardware, causes the correct action to occur, and produces the desired result. The processor is, after all, simply a very large collection of digital circuits that transform inputs to outputs according to the rules of Boolean logic.

Before the processor can act on our instructions, we must transform them from the mnemonic form that we understand into the machine code form that the processor is able to accept. The process of this transformation, whether performed with an assembler, debugger, or manually, is called *instruction encoding*.

Ultimately, every program for the PC, whether written in assembly language or in a high-level language, ends up in memory as a collection of opcodes and data. Assembly language programmers in particular need to be familiar with reading opcodes and deciphering instructions at this level. Although you won't need to be able to recognize every instruction on sight, memorizing a few of the most common—such as NOP (90h), INT (CDh), and MOV AH (B4h)—will prove to be extremely valuable. The following example will demonstrate why knowing opcodes is important.

Suppose you have a commercial utility that refuses to run under any version of DOS newer than version 3.1. You'd like to change that by patching the executable code with DEBUG. Having a program check the DOS version is a fairly common practice and DOS INT 21h function 30h is usually used for this purpose. But to patch the code, you must find where in the program it is being executed.

To call this function, the following assembly code would typically be used:

```
MOV   AH,30H
INT   21H
```

Unfortunately, DEBUG doesn't allow you to search for the mnemonics of these instructions. DEBUG does, however, allow you to search memory for a string of bytes. To do so, you look up the opcodes for the desired instructions (in Appendix A) and determine the following:

```
MOV   AH,30H   ;Encoded as:  B4 30
INT   21H      ;Encoded as:  CD 21
```

You can now locate the instruction using DEBUG's S (search) command. Once found, the logic that tests the version returned can be altered to suit your needs.

Instruction, Mnemonic, and Opcode Defined

Assembly language programmers (and authors) often use the terms instruction, mnemonic, and opcode as if they were interchangeable. This is not the case, however, and can lead to confusion or at least imprecise expression. The three terms express different implementations of the same idea and, for the purpose of this book, I'll define the terms here.

Instruction An instruction is a request for action, issued by a programmer, that is interpreted by the processor. An instruction is indivisible; that is, one cannot issue part of an instruction and receive part of an action. The set of possible instructions is defined by the internal construction of the processor and is not expandable.

More completely, an instruction comprises not only the action desired, but also any operands on which the action will be performed. Operands may be explicit or implicit, or an instruction may take no operands at all. For example, while it is acceptable to say that you have instructed the processor to perform the arithmetic function addition, the more complete expression of that instruction might be "Add the contents of register BX to the contents of register AX, leave the result in AX and update the FLAGS register according to the result." This later form clearly expresses the action you wish the processor to perform, but if you had to write it that way, it wouldn't make for compact source code. For the sake of convenience (both the programmer's and the assembler's), instructions are represented by mnemonics.

Mnemonic A mnemonic is a short word or abbreviation that is used as a convenient representation of the action portion of an instruction. The mnemonic ADD, for example, represents the addition instruction. Mnemonics are simply symbols used to represent instructions. As such, they need bear no direct relationship to the instruction set of a processor as defined by the chip maker. Each writer of an assembler or debugger program may choose to use a different mnemonic to represent the same instruction.

Although the effects of this freedom may at first seem an invitation to mass confusion, the ability to alias a single instruction with more than one mnemonic can be useful. The mnemonics JL (jump if less than) and JNGE (jump if not greater than or equal to), for example, both express the same relationship between two operands and represent the same instruction. But chances are that one of them will allow you to express the action in a fashion that is more intuitive and consistent with your algorithm.

Intel defines a general set of mnemonics to be used to represent their instructions, but some mnemonics are dependent on the particular implementation of the assembler writer. All mnemonics and syntax used in this book are based on those defined by Intel and those used in Microsoft's MASM version 5.0 and later.

Opcode   The word opcode, a contraction of operation code, is the term given to the exact bit sequence that is sent to the processor to command it to perform a specific instruction. It is the opcode we refer to when we speak of "machine code." The opcode is a packet of information that is loaded and analyzed by the processor. The processor does not make the same distinction between instruction and data that we do. Opcodes are simply a form of data that the processor uses to determine which predetermined function it should perform as defined by its design.

The term opcode properly specifies the action in combination with operands. In most cases, an opcode doesn't make sense without specifying operands. The opcode that instructs the processor to push the AX register onto the stack, for example, is 01010000b. The 5 high-order bits, 01010b, represent the instruction to push a register onto the stack. The low-order 3 bits, 000b, specify the AX register as the operand. (This representation is known as instruction encoding and is covered in detail later in this chapter.)

Some instructions have several forms, each of which uses a distinct opcode. One opcode, for example, may be required when the operands are registers and another for when the operands are in memory. Many instructions have an alternate form that is used when the AX register is one of the operands. In general, the 8086 designers attempted to provide shorter or faster forms of many instructions to allow programmers to build compact and efficient programs. Different forms of an instruction appear as separate entries in the instruction set reference in Appendix A.

Three other terms, machine code, executable code, and object code, are synonyms for opcode and may be used interchangeably. Don't, however, confuse object code with an object file (with an .OBJ extension). An object file is an intermediate translation of instructions that must undergo an additional step (linking) before it becomes executable machine code.

8086/8088/80286 Instruction Encoding

The process of translating an assembly code program written in mnemonics into object code is called assembly. The reverse process, converting object code back into assembly source code, is called disassembly. (Note that because the letter d was already used for the *dump* command, DEBUG uses the letter u, for *unassembly*, to perform disassembly.) Both processes make good use of the fact that there is a one-to-one correspondence between object code and assembly code. Given any valid instruction, the object code can be created. And given any sequence of bytes that represents a valid opcode, the mnemonic instruction can be recreated.

In general, the opcodes have been designed to compress the most information into the least space. This is simply because shorter instructions require less memory to store and less time to read from memory. Opcodes in the 80x86 instruction set vary from one to seven or more bytes long depending on the complexity of the instruction, operands specified, and whether or not any prefixes have been selected. As a result, it isn't possible to state a simple rule that describes how instructions are encoded. Some bit fields within the encoding, for example, have different interpretations depending on the contents of other bit fields. Certain fields may not even be present depending on the setting of a flag in the opcode. The general rules for encoding and decoding instructions are given here, but the specific encoding for any particular instruction can be found in the detailed description of that instruction in Appendix A.

The instruction encoding scheme for the 8086, 8088, and 80286 processors is identical. The 80386 and 80486, however, have more instructions and addressing modes than can be accommodated within the framework of the 8086's encoding scheme. Because of this, encoding for the 80386 and 80486 will be discussed separately.

Encoding Format

The general format of an encoded instruction consists of a one-byte opcode, an optional addressing mode byte, an optional displacement field of one or two bytes, and an optional immediate operand field of one or two bytes. Figure 6.1 shows how this encoding will be presented in this book. Each box of the encoding represents one or more bytes of object code and the elements are shown in byte order, with the low address byte on the left.

FIGURE 6.1

General form for instruction encoding for the 8086, 8088, and 80286 processors

opcode	mod	reg	r/m	disp	immed

Instruction encodings will always be shown as bit fields. Each box is a symbol, representing a byte or bytes that make up the instruction. Inside each box, each digit shown represents one bit in the encoding. Entries should therefore be interpreted as binary notation even though the b suffix is omitted in the box. One digit will be shown for each bit required in the field, including leading zeros.

The 80286 sets a maximum length for an instruction of ten bytes. The 80386 and 80486 both set an instruction length limit of 15 bytes. The only way these limits can be exceeded is by using redundant and reduplicated prefixes—no legitimate instruction exceeds these lengths. The 8086/8088 and 80186/80188 have no instruction length limit.

The Instruction Prefixes

The default operation of some instructions can be modified by the use of a *prefix*. A prefix is an instruction that, when executed, does not result in an immediate action by the processor. Instead, the execution of the prefix instructs the processor to modify its execution of the following instruction. Technically, the prefix is not considered part of the opcode of the instruction it modifies. It is, however, part of the instruction that the prefix-opcode pair is intended to execute.

All prefixes are one byte in length and one or more prefixes may be combined in a single instruction. The prefix instructions available on the 80286 and earlier processors are REP*cond* (repeat on condition) and LOCK.

The Repeat Prefixes   The REP (repeat) prefix is used in conjunction with the string instructions MOVS (move string) and STOS (store string) to cause the processor to execute these instructions multiple times. The REP prefix will cause the processor to execute the subsequent instruction the number of times specified by the CX register.

The REPE (repeat while equal) prefix, also aliased as REPZ (repeat while zero), is used with the string instructions CMPS (compare strings) and SCAS (scan string) and will make these instructions repeat the number of times specified by the CX register as long as the Zero flag (ZF) is set to 1. The action of the string instruction itself sets or clears the Zero flag before performing the test that determines if another repetition will occur.

The REPNE (repeat while not equal) prefix, equivalently expressed as REPNZ (repeat while not zero), operates similarly to REPE, but terminates the repetition unless ZF is cleared to 0 by each execution of the string instruction.

Note that insofar as the encoding goes, the REP and REPE/REPZ prefixes are identical. By convention, the REP mnemonic is used to prefix the STOS and MOVS string instructions. The Zero flag is set by the processor before the instruction begins and, since no comparison is being made by the instructions, is not reset by the instruction. The result is that the prefix will continue the repetition until CX is 0.

The encodings for the three prefixes are shown in Table 6.1. More details on the operation and use of REP are given in the descriptions of each instruction in Appendix A.

TABLE 6.1

The Instruction Prefixes

Instruction Prefix	Encoding
REP	F3h
REPE/REPZ	F3h
REPNE/REPNZ	F2h
LOCK	FØh

The Lock Prefix   The LOCK prefix asserts control over the data bus when operating in a multiprocessor environment. The primary reason for using this instruction is to prevent other processors in the system from modifying an area of memory while the processor executing the locked instruction is accessing it. More details on the operation and use of LOCK are given in the instruction reference in Appendix A.

The Segment Override Prefixes

All instructions that reference memory use an implied segment register to calculate the absolute address. The default segment register is chosen according to the rules described in Chapter 3. One-byte opcodes exist, however, to override the default selection of a prefix for most memory references. The opcodes for the segment override prefixes are shown in Table 6.2.

TABLE 6.2

Opcodes for the Segment Override Prefixes

Segment	Opcode
CS	ØØ1Ø111Øb (2Eh)
DS	ØØ11111Øb (3Eh)
ES	ØØ1ØØ11Øb (26h)
SS	ØØ11Ø11Øb (36h)

Avoid using a prefix that restates the default, such as the reference to DS in the instruction MOV AX,DS:[BX]. Encoding redundant prefixes simply wastes space. Sometimes, however, using a redundant prefix can help clarify an assembly source code listing. Most assemblers will detect and ignore the redundant prefix without generating any code.

Not all instructions will accept a segment override. Instructions such as PUSH and POP, that implicitly access the stack segment (SS), for example, cannot be overridden.

The Opcode

The next field in the encoding sequence is the opcode. The opcode always occupies at least one byte and specifies the instruction to be executed. In some compact instruction forms, the 3 low-order bits of the opcode byte specify a register operand. In other cases, the opcode uses additional bits in the addressing mode byte (in place of the *reg* field) to specify a complete encoding. For most instructions, however, the opcode itself uses fewer than the full 8 bits in the opcode byte. The remaining bits are then used to specify other details of the instruction. Typically, the additional fields that are encoded in the opcode byte are the *d*, *w*, and *s* fields. (The *reg* field may also be encoded in this byte, but a complete treatment of this field appears in the section on the addressing mode byte.)

The *d* (direction) field indicates the direction of data flow in the instruction. Since general memory-to-memory transfers aren't permitted on the 80x86 processors, at least one of the operands will always be a register. The *d* field determines whether the register specified by the *reg* field is the source (op_2) or the destination (op_1) of the operation.

If *d*=0, then the *reg* field specifies the register that is used as the source operand. In this case, the destination will always be memory. Otherwise, if *d*=1, the destination is a register specified by *reg* and the source may be either memory or another register. For example, in the instruction SUB [HEIGHT],AX, the destination is memory, so *d* will be 0 and *reg* will be used to specify AX. In the instruction ADD BX,[WIDTH], the BX register is the destination, so *d* will be 1 and *reg* will specify BX.

The *w* (word/byte or width) field indicates whether the operands should be treated as 8-bit or 16-bit quantities. In most cases, the instruction will make sense only if both operands are the same size. The four general-purpose registers AX, BX, CX, and DX, as well as memory, can be addressed as either byte- or word-sized operands. The *w* field, therefore, controls how memory is accessed and, in combination with the *reg* field, determines the register that is being addressed.

If *w* is 0, both operands are treated as 8-bit quantities. Alternately, 16-bit operands are specified when *w* is 1. The instruction MOV DL,2 would clear *w* to 0 and the instruction MOV DX,1234H would encode *w* as 1. Note that the instruction MOV CH,1234H cannot be encoded since the operands are different sizes.

The *s* (sign extend) field is set to 1 to indicate that a single byte of immediate data is included in the encoding and should be sign-extended to a 16-bit operand before use. This simply means that eight copies of bit 7 (the sign bit) of the 8-bit operand are placed to the left of the byte operand, to become bits 8 through 15 of a new 16-bit operand. If the *s* field is 0, no action is taken on the immediate data. Unfortunately, not all instructions support this encoding option.

By providing this field, the chip designers have allowed us to eliminate a useless byte from an encoding. If a word operand has a value that is in the range −128 to +127, then bits 7 through 15 will all have the same value (0 for positive numbers, 1 for negative numbers). The high-order 8 bits are eliminated from the instruction encoding and generated in the processor (by replicating bit 7 of the immediate data byte) when the instruction is executed.

The Addressing Mode Bit

The next and by far the most complex byte in the encoding sequence is the addressing mode byte. Into this byte is placed information on operand types, specifics of registers used in the instruction, as well as memory addressing modes. (The one-byte instructions that use implied operands or no operands, such as CWD and HLT, do not use this byte. Other one-byte instructions, when used with a single register argument, encode their register reference into the lower 3 bits of the opcode byte.)

The addressing byte is divided into three fields designated *mod* (mode), *reg* (register), and *r/m* (register/memory) as shown in Figure 6.2. These three fields and their definitions are discussed below.

The *mod* Field Bits 7 and 6 of the addressing mode byte are referred to as the *mod* field. The contents of the *mod* field determine how the *r/m* field and any optional *disp* (displacement) field are to be interpreted. The possible values for the *mod* field and their interpretations are shown in Table 6.3.

The *reg* Field The *reg* (register) field occupies bits 5 through 3 of the addressing mode byte and is used either to specify a register operand or to hold additional opcode bits. The *w* field in the opcode byte determines whether the *reg* field is interpreted as a reference to an 8-bit or 16-bit register. The interpretation of the *reg* field for the two values of *w* is shown in Table 6.4. While the *r/m* field can specify either a memory or register operand, the *reg* field can only be used to specify a register operand.

FIGURE 6.2

Addressing mode byte format

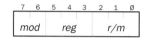

Field	Size	Description
mod	2	mode
reg	3	register
r/m	3	register/memory

TABLE 6.3

Definitions of the Encoding for the *mod* Field of the Addressing Mode Byte

mod	Interpretation
ØØb	If *r/m*≠11Øb, then *mod*=ØØb indicates that a register operand is specified by the *r/m* field. The register must be a base register (BP or BX), index register (SI or DI), or a combination of base and index registers. If, however, *r/m*=11Øb, the operand is not a register. It is a 16-bit memory displacement from the beginning of the segment and is encoded as part of the instruction.
Ø1b	An 8-bit signed displacement (*disp8*) is included in the encoding. The byte will be sign-extended and added to the register operand specified by the *r/m* field.
1Øb	A 16-bit signed displacement (*disp16*) is included in the encoding that will be added to the register operand specified by the *r/m* field.
11b	The instruction references two registers. The *reg* field specifies the destination operand and the *r/m* field specifies the source operand. The *w* field in the opcode specifies the size of the operands. No memory reference is included in the instruction.

TABLE 6.4

Interpretation of the *reg* Field

reg	w=Ø	w=1
ØØØb	AL	AX
ØØ1b	CL	CX
Ø1Øb	DL	DX
Ø11b	BL	BX
1ØØb	AH	SP
1Ø1b	CH	BP
11Øb	DH	SI
111b	BH	DI

Many instructions are able to reference a segment register as one of their operands. These forms of the instructions use a unique opcode and usually the reference to the *reg* field is replaced with a reference to the *sreg* field. When specified, the *sreg* field is interpreted according to the information shown in Table 6.5.

TABLE 6.5

Interpretation of the *sreg* Field

sreg	Register
000b	ES
001b	CS
010b	SS
011b	DS

The *r/m* Field The *r/m* (register/memory) field occupies bits 2 through 0 in the addressing mode byte. It is, as its name implies, a dual-purpose field whose interpretation is governed by the *mod* field. If *mod*=11b, then *r/m* specifies a register operand and is encoded using the same values as the *reg* field. If *mod*≠11b, then the operand is a memory reference as defined in Table 6.6. The segment registers shown are the default segments invoked by the memory reference listed according to the rules presented in Chapter 3. The segment register references are not encoded explicitly into the addressing mode byte.

TABLE 6.6

Interpretation of the *r/m* Field

r/m	mod=00b	mod=01b	mod=10b	mod=11b w=0	w=1
000b	DS:[BX+SI]	DS:[BX+SI+*disp8*]	DS:[BX+SI+*disp16*]	AL	AX
001b	DS:[BX+DI]	DS:[BX+DI+*disp8*]	DS:[BX+DI+*disp16*]	CL	CX
010b	SS:[BP+SI]	SS:[BP+SI+*disp8*]	SS:[BP+SI+*disp16*]	DL	DX
011b	SS:[BP+DI]	SS:[BP+DI+*disp8*]	SS:[BP+DI+*disp16*]	BL	BX
100b	DS:[SI]	DS:[SI+*disp8*]	DS:[SI+*disp16*]	AH	SP
101b	DS:[DI]	DS:[DI+*disp8*]	DS:[DI+*disp16*]	CH	BP
110b	DS:[*disp16*]	SS:[BP+*disp8*]	SS:[BP+*disp16*]	DH	SI
111b	DS:[BX]	DS:[BX+*disp8*]	DS:[BX+*disp16*]	BH	DI

The symbols *disp8* and *disp16* used in the table represent an 8-bit or 16-bit signed number, respectively, that is interpreted as a relative displacement and added to the register reference shown to generate the complete effective address offset. The displacements are included as data in the encoding and are explained in the section on the *disp* field below.

A quick study of Table 6.6 shows that the references generated for each value of the *r/m* field for *mod*=00b, 01b, or 10b are quite consistent. The register argument shown under the *mod*=00b case is simply augmented with an 8-bit displacement for *mod*=01b and a 16-bit displacement for *mod*=10b. The one important exception, however, is the case when *mod*=00b and *r/m*=110b. The logic of the table would indicate that this combination should generate an indirect memory reference using the BP register with no additional displacement field specified. But, as shown, this is not the case. This combination was used by the chip designers to allow the encoding of a direct reference to a memory address. The address encoded into the instruction for direct addressing will be interpreted as an unsigned displacement from the beginning of the data segment (DS). (The segment referenced can be changed with a segment override prefix.)

As a side effect of this special addressing mode, the BP register cannot be used to access memory without specifying a displacement, even if that displacement is 0. For example, you cannot encode the instruction MOV AX,[BP] because there is no *mod* and *r/m* combination that will generate an indirect memory reference using only BP. Most assemblers, when they encounter an indirect reference to BP, will simply encode the equivalent form MOV AX,[BP+0].

The Displacement Field

The next portion of the instruction encoding is called the displacement field. If present in the encoding, this field contains a constant that will be used to calculate an effective address or program relative address. In the encoding diagrams that appear in the instruction reference in Appendix A, the displacement is represented by the symbol *disp* and may range in size from zero bytes (that is, no displacement is present) to four bytes (80286 and earlier chips) to six bytes (80386 and 80486). The *disp* field is interpreted according to its usage, which varies between instructions and between forms of the same instruction. The three forms of *disp*, explained below, are signed relative displacement, unsigned segment-relative displacement, and absolute displacement.

Signed Relative Displacement   The *disp* field is interpreted as a signed number (an integer). During the effective address calculation, *disp* is combined arithmetically with other address components to arrive at the final memory address. If necessary, the encoded value of *disp* will be sign-extended to the required operand size before being combined. Signed relative displacement is used for both memory address and program address calculations.

In memory address calculations, *disp* is usually combined with a register reference such as in the instruction MOV AX,[BX–2]. Here, the *disp* field will have the value –2 and be encoded as a byte. During the effective address calculation, it will be sign-extended to a word and added to the contents of the BX register to yield the effective memory address.

The conditional jump instructions use signed relative displacement in program address calculations. The encoding for the instruction JC *label*, for example, will contain a 1-byte displacement field. If the Carry flag is set, the *disp* field will be sign-extended to a word and added to the contents of the IP register (the offset of the following instruction) to determine the new IP address at which to resume execution.

Unsigned Segment-Relative Displacement The *disp* field is interpreted as an unsigned number that specifies an offset relative to a segment register. The contents of the displacement field are used as the effective address or new program address without modification. Because no sign-extension is possible, this form of the *disp* field will always occupies two bytes. (On the 80386 and 80486, four bytes will be used for a 32-bit displacement.) Unsigned segment-relative displacement is used for both memory address and program address calculations.

In memory address calculations, the *disp* is interpreted as an offset from the beginning of the DS segment register. (The choice of DS may be altered with a segment override prefix.) No other register is used in the address calculation. The instruction MOV AX,[5h], for example, will move the contents of the word at DS:0005h into the AX register. This form of the encoding is typically used when accessing memory operands whose addresses are known before execution time and can be encoded directly.

A program address can also be encoded as a segment-relative displacement. The segment referenced is the code segment (CS) and cannot be overridden. The intrasegment near direct form of the JMP instruction uses this program addressing mode. For example, the instruction JMP *near_label*, where *near_label* is an offset in the same code segment as the address of the jump instruction, will be encoded with an opcode byte of E9h and a two-byte displacement field that represents the offset of *near_label* from the beginning of the code segment. Note that the current contents of the CS register are irrelevant—the offset is relative to the base address of the segment.

Absolute Displacement The *disp* field is interpreted as two unsigned numbers that specify the segment and offset values of a specific memory location. Because both the segment and offset are specified, no registers (including segment registers) are used in the address calculation. This form of the displacement field always occupies four bytes and no sign extension is used. (On the 80386 and 80486, six bytes are required to specify a 16-bit segment and 32-bit displacement.)

The two instructions that use absolute displacement are the far direct forms of JMP and CALL. For either instruction, the address of the next instruction to execute, both segment and offset, is included in the encoding. The absolute displacement specifies two constants that are to be loaded into the CS and IP registers when the instruction is executed.

Note that this form of displacement is not available for memory addressing. You cannot instruct the processor to access an arbitrary memory location that is not currently addressed by one of the segment registers.

The Immediate Data Field

The final portion of the instruction encoding is called the immediate data field. If present in the encoding, this field contains a constant that will be used as either an operand or an argument to the instruction. In the encoding diagrams that appear in the instruction reference in Appendix A, immediate data is represented by the symbol *immed* and may range in size from zero bytes (that is, no immediate data is present) to four bytes. The *immed* field is interpreted according to its usage, which varies between instructions and between forms of the same instruction. If required, immediate data is placed at the end of the encoding.

When one of the operands of an instruction is a constant that is known at assembly time, many instructions allow this constant to be encoded into the instruction as immediate data. The *immed* field may contain data that will be used as one of the operands to an instruction. In the instruction ADD AX,5, for example, the constant 5 will be encoded into the instruction as immediate data. This particular form of the ADD instruction would be shown as ADD *accum,immed* in the instruction reference.

On the 80286 and later processors, immediate data may also be used as an argument to some instructions. In the shift and rotate instructions, for example, a byte of immediate data (shown as *immed8*) can be used to specify the number of times the instruction is to operate. The instruction SHL BX,6, for example, would be encoded using the form SHL *reg,immed8*.

Encoding Examples

While the details of instruction encoding are critical, you don't have to memorize them for everyday use. Normally, we delegate instruction encoding to an assembler or debugger. After all, putting a friendlier layer between the programmer and the processor is one major reason why assemblers were developed. Periodically, however, a situation arises when you may wish to encode an instruction manually.

For example, perhaps you cannot get the assembler to generate a specific instruction or form of an instruction without convoluted programming. A common example is trying to specify an intersegment jump to an absolute address. You cannot simply write JMP FAR 1234:5678h, which is what you want to do. Instead you must write code that is the same functionally, but not cosmetically. This problem can be neatly avoided by simply encoding the jump yourself.

Example 1: *Determine the encoding for JMP FAR 1234:5678H.*

First, look up the JMP instruction in the detailed instruction descriptions in Appendix A. There you will see that the opcode for the far (intersegment) direct form of the JMP instruction is EAh. The opcode is followed by a four-byte absolute displacement that specifies the segment and offset that are the target of the jump. You know that the 80x86 processors always store the most significant part of an operand at the highest memory address, so you write the following code:

```
DB   0EAH         ;JMP FAR

DW   5678H,1234H  ;1234:5678H
```

Example 2: *Determine the machine language encoding for the instruction MOV [BX+DI-6],CL.* (Assume 16-bit operation on the 80386/80486.)

The instruction can be written symbolically as MOV *mem,reg*. The encoding form for this instruction is found in Appendix A as follows:

100010*dw*	*mod*	*reg*	*r/m*	*disp*

Since the destination of the operation is memory, $d=0$ and the *reg* field specifies the source register. The *reg* encoding for the CL register is 001b with $w=0$ to indicate an 8-bit operand. The encoding so far looks like this:

10001000	*mod*	001	*r/m*	*disp*

An *r/m* value of 001b will generate a reference to [BX+DI+*disp*]. The displacement is in the range −128 to +127, and can thus be encoded as *disp8* and sign-extended by the processor. A 8-bit displacement is specified when *mod*=01b. The complete encoding for the instruction is shown below:

10001000	01	001	001	11111010	= 88h 49h FAh

You can confirm this encoding by using DEBUG to assemble the instruction and then display the object code as shown in the following example. First, start up DEBUG. (It is assumed that DEBUG.COM is in the current directory or in a directory included in your PATH statement.) Next, tell DEBUG to begin assembling instructions starting at CS:100h with the A 100 command. (Remember, in DEBUG, all numbers are assumed to be hex by default. Don't add an "h" suffix.) Now enter the instruction to be assembled and press the Enter key. DEBUG will encode the instruction into memory and prompt you for the next instruction. Exit assembly mode by entering a blank line. The U 100 L 1 command tells debug to unassemble one instruction beginning at CS:100. The three bytes of the encoded instruction are shown. Exit DEBUG with the Q (Quit) command. Note that the segment displayed by DEBUG will probably be different on your computer.

```
DEBUG
-A 100
854D:0100 MOV [BX+DI-6],CL
854D:0103
-U 100 L 1
854D:0100 8849FA        MOV [BX+DI-06],CL
-Q
```

Example 3: *Decoding instructions.*
While browsing through the object code of an executable program, you encounter the following string of bytes (shown in hex):

```
26 81 0E 65 10 FC FE 4E 5A
```

What instruction or instructions, if any, does this object code represent?

To answer this question, you must perform the same decoding process that the processor does when it loads and executes object code. The only difficult part is finding the instruction to which the opcode corresponds. This can be a tedious process unless you have an opcode matrix such as that given in Appendix C at the end of this book.

To use the matrix, use the first digit of the opcode byte to find the row and the second to find the column. The entry in that cell will give the instruction as well as other information you might need to identify the instruction. These are the decoded instructions:

```
OR   WORD PTR ES:[1065h],FEFCh
DEC  SI
POP  DX
```

80386/80486 Instruction Encoding

The instruction encoding scheme for the 8086, 8088, and 80286 processors is also used for the 80386 and 80486 processors. Programs written to use the basic, upwardly compatible subset of the register and instruction sets of the 80386 and 80486 are encoded identically to those for the 8086. The 32-bit processors, however, have added many new instructions, registers, and addressing modes. As a result, these processors have more potential instructions than can be accommodated by the limited permutations of the 8086's encoding fields. The 80386 and 80486 processors define rules for an expanded encoding scheme, typically used to encode instructions that take advantage of some of their unique properties such as scaling or 32-bit addressing and operands. Only the expanded encoding scheme of the 80386 and 80486 is explained in this section. To determine the encoding of a 16-bit instruction, see the previous section on encoding instructions for the 8086.

When executing in 16-bit real mode (8086 emulation mode), the 80386 and 80486 will interpret and execute 16-bit instructions exactly the same as the 8086 (subject to the documented differences in the actions of the chips described in Chapter 14). In other words, the two bytes B4h 10h can be expected to represent the instruction MOV AH,10h when executed on either an 80486 or an 8088. Programs developed to run under DOS, for example, that use only the 16-bit subset of instructions and registers available on the 8086, will not use the new encodings.

On the other hand, any program that references a 32-bit memory or register operand, uses a 32-bit effective address, or uses scaling will require the new encodings. Note that all of these features are available on the 80386 and 80486 even when the chips are running in real mode. To access these, however, you must use the new encodings explained in this section. Finally, all references to 16- or 32-bit mode refer to the end result of the combination of the segment type and override prefixes as explained later in this section.

The Encoding Format

All instruction encodings on the 80386 and 80486 can be described using the format shown in Figure 6.3. The general format of an encoded instruction for these processors is similar to that for the 8086 but has several additional elements. For example, the instruction prefixes are the same as previously described in the 8086 encoding but two new prefixes, unique to the 80386 and 80486, may also be present in the encoding and switch the processor between modes of using 16-bit or 32-bit address and operand sizes. In addition, some fields have different interpretations depending on whether the chip is operating in 32-bit or 16-bit mode. A complete description of each of the fields is given in the following section.

FIGURE 6.3

General form for instruction encoding for the 80386 and 80486 processors

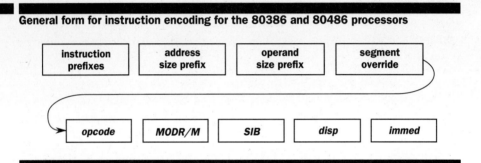

The general encoding format consists of one or more instruction prefixes, an address size byte, an operand size byte, a segment override byte, a one- or two-byte opcode, an addressing mode byte, a scale-index-base byte, a displacement field of zero, one, two, or four bytes, and an immediate operand field of zero, one, two, or four bytes. Figure 6.2 shows how this encoding will be presented in this book. Each box of the encoding represents one or more bytes of object code and the elements are shown in the order in which the bytes would appear in memory.

The Instruction Prefixes

No new instruction prefixes have been defined for the 80386 and 80486, but all those valid for the 8086 may be used. These include the string operation prefixes REP, REPE (REPZ), and REPNE (REPNZ), as well as the LOCK prefix. A short explanation of these prefixes was given previously in the section on 8086 encoding. More detailed explanations are given in the instruction reference in Appendix A. The encodings for these prefixes are given in Table 6.1.

The Address Size Prefix

All logical addresses for the 8086 are comprised of a 16-bit segment and a 16-bit offset (called the effective address) that are combined in the processor to give a 20-bit physical address. All references to memory operands on the 8086 eventually result in an effective address offset that is a 16-bit unsigned number in the range from 0 to 65535 (64k). This effective address configuration is the limit that gives the 8086 the 64k segment size limit.

An effective address represents the offset of the memory operand from the base address of a segment pointed to by one of the segment registers. For example, if the BX register contains 13A4h, the instruction MOV AX,[BX+4] will generate an effective address of 13A4h+4, or 13A8h. The word of memory at DS:13A8h would be copied into the AX register.

When operating in real (8086-emulation) mode, the 80386 and 80486 calculate effective addresses exactly as does the 8086. By default, all effective address calculations are made using 16-bit quantities and result in a 16-bit unsigned number in the range from 0 to FFFFh (65535).

The 80386 and 80486, however, are 32-bit processors. And one of the capabilities built into them is the ability to use 32-bit operands in their effective address calculations. A new one-byte prefix has been defined to instruct the processor to treat all the components of an effective address as 32-bit quantities, *even when operating in real mode*. This prefix, called the *address size prefix*, has the value 67h and changes the addressing mode for only the one instruction that immediately follows it.

For example, if the EBX register contains 3EF7h, the instruction MOV AX,[EBX] would copy the word of memory at DS:3EF7h into AX. There's nothing too outstanding about the use of EBX as the effective address operand until you consider that EBX could have just as easily contained the 32-bit value FFFFFFFEh. In this case, using the full 32-bits of the EBX register in the effective address calculation, the instruction would be addressing a word in memory that is four gigabytes (4096Mb) from the start of the segment! Using 32 bits, valid effective addresses can be generated in the range from 0 to FFFFFFFFh (4,294,967,296).

There is an additional restriction placed by the processor on programs that are executing in real mode: all effective addresses, regardless of size, must be in the range from 0 to FFFFh. The ability to address larger segments is only available when the processor is operating in protected mode. So even when using a 32-bit effective address, real mode programs are still limited to addressing within a 64k segment.

The restriction on the value of the effective address in real mode applies only to the final result of the effective address calculation. One or all of the operands involved may be out of the valid range, but if the final result is within the specified range, the instruction will be considered valid. For example, assume that the EBX register contains 000133D8h and that the ECX register contains FFFF0000h. The instruction MOV AX,[EBX] will be invalid because the effective address (the value in EBX) is greater than FFFFh (65535). Likewise, the instruction MOV AX,[ECX] will be invalid for the same reason. But the instruction MOV AX,[EBX][ECX] will be valid since the effective address (EA = EBX+ECX = 000033D8h) falls within the valid range. Because the effective address will most likely not be known until execution time, the processor is responsible for detecting and reporting an invalid effective address.

The processor does this by issuing either the INT Ch or INT Dh exception to indicate an illegal instruction, as described in Chapter 5.

Default Address Size Selection   In protected mode, the 80386 and 80486 rely on the D (default) bit in the code segment descriptor that describes the current code segment to establish the default addressing mode: either 16-bit or 32-bit. If cleared to 0, an effective address will default to 16-bit operands. If set to 1, all effective addresses will be calculated using 32-bit operands. It doesn't make sense to specify the addressing size for a noncode segment since no effective address calculations are performed except when executing code.

The processor will calculate all addresses according to the default size specified in the descriptor. If the processor encounters an address size prefix byte, it will reverse the default address size for the next instruction only.

The 80386 and 80486 addressing modes are too complex to fit into the encoding scheme of the 8086. In addition, many of the new encodings redefine the field encodings. *Placing an address size override prefix before an 8086 instruction that uses 16-bit addressing will not necessarily produce the equivalent 32-bit instruction.* For example, the instruction MOV AX,[BX] is encoded as 8Bh 07h. But prefixing this with 67h (the address size prefix) does not produce the instruction MOV AX,[EBX] as you might expect. Instead, the bytes 67h 8bh 07h result in the instruction MOV AX,[EDI]. A complete description of the addressing modes of the 80386 and 80486 is given later in this chapter.

The address prefix byte overrides the default effective address size for the single instruction that follows. The real and Virtual-86 modes of the 80386 and 80486 do not use segment selectors, so there is no default and therefore no method for setting the default address size to 32 bits. To use 32-bit operands in an effective address calculation, each instruction must be prefixed individually and the result must still be less than 64k.

Stack Address Size   Instructions that use the stack pointer register and stack segment register for addressing, such as PUSH and POP, also provide an address size of 16 or 32 bits. If the stack addressing size is 16 bits, stack instructions will use the 16-bit SP register. If the stack addressing size is 32 bits, the ESP register will be used.

The stack addressing size for real mode is 16 bits. In protected mode, the B bit in the segment descriptor for the data segment defines the default stack addressing size. If the bit is cleared to 0, the stack will be addressed using SP. If B is set to 1, ESP will be used to address the top of the stack.

The Operand Size Prefix

Most instructions for the 8086 generally allow operation with two sizes of operand: either an 8-bit byte or a 16-bit word. The operand may be in memory or it may be a register. A single bit in the encoding is all that is required to indicate to the processor which of the two possible operand sizes is to be used. This bit, the *w* bit, is cleared to 0 to indicate an 8-bit operand and set to 1 when a 16-bit operand is to be used.

When operating in real (8086-emulation) mode, the 80386 and 80486 behave just as the 8086 does. Operands are either byte- or word-sized depending on the setting of the *w*-bit in the instruction encoding. This being the case, it would seem that there is no way to take advantage of the 32-bit operands available on these processors without defining additional bits in the encoding. The designers of the chips, however, chose to implement a different scheme. A one-byte prefix instruction called the *operand size override prefix* has been added to the instruction set. The operand size prefix byte, which has the value 66h, tells the processor to interpret a reference to a word-size operand as a reference to a doubleword-size operand for the next instruction only. As for a word operand, the double-word operand can be either an extended register or a memory reference.

For example, consider the instruction MOV AX,BX, which tells the processor to perform a 16-bit data move from the BX register to the AX register. The encoding for this instruction (shown as hexadecimal bytes) is as follows:

```
89h D8h        ;MOV AX,BX
```

If, however, you prefix this instruction with the operand size prefix, it will be interpreted as a 32-bit data move by the processor. The encoding would appear as follows:

```
66h 89h D8h   ;MOV EAX,EBX
```

Access to the full set of 32-bit registers and all of their power and ease of use is available in real mode with the simple use of this prefix. Fortunately, most assemblers provide a method for automatically generating this prefix when needed, so you don't have to encode it manually. Unfortunately, simple debuggers, including the copy of DEBUG that comes with DOS, don't recognize the operand size prefix and aren't equipped to deal with 32-bit operands. DEBUG, faced with a byte it cannot decode, will simply display the operand size prefix as DB 66.

Default Operand Size Selection   In protected mode, the 80386 and 80486 use segment descriptors to manage memory. A single bit is used in a code descriptor to specify what the default operand size will be when executing code in that segment. If this bit, called the default (D) bit, is cleared to 0, the default operand size will be a word. If the bit is set to 1, the default operand size will be a doubleword. It doesn't make sense to specify the operand size for a noncode segment—since no instructions will be executed, there won't be any operands.

When executing in a code segment, the processor will interpret all operand references according to the default size specified in the descriptor. If the processor encounters an operand size prefix byte, it will reverse the default operand size for the next instruction only. So, using our previous example, the bytes 89h

D8h, with and without the operand size prefix, would be interpreted as shown here for a segment with a 16-bit default and a segment with a 32-bit default.

Encoding	Meaning When Executed in a 16-Bit Segment (D=0)	Meaning When Executed in a 32-Bit Segment(D=1)
89h D8h	MOV AX,BX	MOV EAX,EBXP
66h 89h D8h	MOV EAX,EBX	MOV AX,BX

Simply, then, the effect of the operand prefix byte is to reverse the default operand size for the single instruction that follows. Because the real and Virtual-86 modes of the 80386 and 80486 do not use segment selectors, there is no default and therefore no method for setting the default operand size to double-word. To access 32-bit operands in real or Virtual-86 mode, each instruction must be prefixed individually.

The Segment Override Prefix

All instructions that reference memory use an implied segment register to calculate the absolute address. The default segment register is chosen according to the rules described in Chapter 3. One-byte opcodes exist, however, to override the default selection of a prefix for most memory references. Two new opcodes for the segment override prefix have been defined to accommodate the two new segment registers available, and they are shown in Table 6.7.

TABLE 6.7

Opcodes for the Segment Override Prefixes for the 80386 and 80486

Segment Override Prefix	Opcode
CS	00101110b (2Eh)
DS	00111110b (3Eh)
ES	00100110b (26h)
FS	01100100b (64h)
GS	01100101b (65h)
SS	00110110b (36h)

Note that encoding redundant prefixes simply wastes space. So actually encoding a prefix that restates the default, such as DS in the instruction MOV AX,DS:[BX], should be avoided. Because most assemblers will detect and ignore the redundant prefix without generating any code, this technique is often used to help clarify an assembly source code listing.

On the 8086 and 8088, which have no instruction length limit, redundant prefixes waste space without affecting instruction actions. Redundant prefixes, however, can cause an instruction to exceed the instruction size limit of 15 bytes on the 80386 and 80486, rendering the instruction invalid and causing the processor to generate an exception. Not all instructions will accept a segment override, as was explained in Chapter 3.

The Opcode

The *opcode* field is next in the encoding sequence, and occupies from one to two bytes. As on the 8086, the opcode specifies the instruction that is to be executed. Often subfields are defined within the opcode byte or bytes to specify the direction of the data flow, the size of the operands, a register operand, or whether sign-extension is to be performed. Typically, the additional fields that are encoded in the opcode byte are the *d*, *w*, and *s* fields. These fields are defined below.

The *d* (direction) field indicates the direction of data flow in the instruction and operates identically in 16-bit and 32-bit mode. Since memory-to-memory transfers aren't permitted, at least one of the operands must be a register. The *d* field determines whether the register specified by the *reg* field is the source (op_2) or the destination (op_1) of the operation.

If *d*=0, then the *reg* field specifies the register that is used as the source operand. In this case, the destination will always be memory. Otherwise, if *d*=1, the destination is a register specified by *reg* and the source may be either memory or another register. For example, in the instruction SUB [HEIGHT],EAX, the destination is memory, so *d* will be 0 and *reg* will be used to specify EAX. In the instruction ADD EBX,[WIDTH], the EBX register is the destination, so *d* will be 1 and *reg* will specify EBX.

The *w* (width) field indicates whether the operands should be treated as 8-bit, 16-bit (in 16-bit mode), or 32-bit (in 32-bit mode) quantities. In most cases, the instruction will make sense only if both operands are the same size. The four general-purpose registers EAX, EBX, ECX, and EDX, as well as memory operands, can be addressed as byte operands as well as word or doubleword depending on the mode. The other registers, except for the segment registers, can be addressed as word or doubleword operands. The *w* field, therefore, controls how memory is accessed and, in combination with the *reg* field, determines the register that is being addressed.

If *w* is 0, both operands are treated as 8-bit quantities. Alternately, 16-bit operands are specified when *w* is 1 and the processor is in 16-bit mode. If 32-bit mode is being used, *w*=1 will specify a 32-bit operand. The instruction MOV DL,2 would clear *w* to 0 and the instruction MOV EDX,1234H would encode *w* as 1.

The *s* (sign) field is set to 1 to indicate that a byte or word of immediate data is included in the encoding and should be sign-extended to full operand length before use. If the *s* field is 0, no action is taken on the immediate data. By providing this field, the chip designers have allowed us to eliminate a byte of useless information from an encoding. If an operand has a value that is in the range −128 to +127, then all the bits from bit 7 through the high order bit will have the same value (0 for positive numbers, 1 for negative numbers). The high-order bits are eliminated from the instruction encoding and generated in the processor (by replicating bit 7 of the immediate data byte) when the instruction is executed.

The Addressing Mode Byte

Instructions that use effective addressing will have an addressing mode byte and possibly a *scale-index-base* (SIB) byte following the opcode. These bytes contain information on operand types and specifics of the registers used in the instruction, as well as the memory addressing mode being invoked.

When the 80386 and 80486 are operating in 16-bit mode, the encodings for the addressing mode byte are identical to those for the 8086. But when operating in 32-bit mode, the encodings for the addressing mode byte are *completely* different. Consequently, adding an address size override prefix to a 16-bit instruction that generates an effective address will *not* produce an equivalent 32-bit instruction. This encoding difference is the reason why most general-purpose programming tools, such as DEBUG, do not recognize 32-bit mode instructions.

For example, the encoding for the instruction MOV AX,[BX] in 16-bit mode is 8Bh 07h. You wish to change the addressing mode to use a 32-bit effective address given by EBX. But simply adding the address size prefix byte to give the encoding 67h 8Bh 07h, generates the instruction MOV AX,[EDI]. The desired instruction, MOV AX,[EBX], is properly encoded as 67h 8Bh 03h.

The addressing mode byte is divided into three fields designated *mod* (mode), *reg* (register), and *r/m* (register/memory). The SIB byte is likewise divided into three fields designated *ss* (scale), *index*, and *base*. The format of these bytes is shown in Figure 6.4 and their definitions are discussed below.

FIGURE 6.4

Addressing mode and SIB byte format

Addressing Mode Byte

```
 7  6  5  4  3  2  1  0
┌──────┬────────┬────────┐
│ mod  │  reg   │  r/m   │
└──────┴────────┴────────┘
```

Field	Size	Description
mod	2	mode
reg	3	register
r/m	3	register/memory

Scale-Index-Base (SIB) Byte

```
 7  6  5  4  3  2  1  0
┌──────┬────────┬────────┐
│scale │ index  │  base  │
└──────┴────────┴────────┘
```

Field	Size	Description
scale	2	scale factor
index	3	index register
base	3	base register

The *mod* Field   Bits 7 and 6 of the addressing mode byte are referred to as the *mod* field. The contents of the *mod* field determine how the *r/m* field is to be interpreted and whether an SIB byte or *disp* (displacement) field is included in the encoding. With the additional options presented on the 80386 and 80486, the addressing mode byte has become even more convoluted than it was previously.

In 16-bit mode, only the addressing mode byte is present in the encoding and the interpretation is the same as presented for the 8086 earlier in this chapter. Table 6.8 gives the interpretations of the four possible values for *mod* when operating in 32-bit mode.

TABLE 6.8

Definitions of the Encoding for the *mod* Field of the Addressing Mode Byte in 32-bit Mode

mod	Interpretation
ØØb	If r/m≠1ØØb, and r/m≠1Ø1b, then a 32-bit register operand is specified by the r/m field. The register may be a single general-purpose register (EAX, EBX, ECX, or EDX) or an index register (ESI or EDI) without scaling. If r/m=1ØØb, then the SIB byte is present and indicates the addressing format. If r/m=1Ø1b, then a memory operand is specified by a 32-bit unsigned displacement encoded as part of the instruction.
Ø1b	If r/m=1ØØb, then the SIB byte is present and indicates the addressing format. If r/m≠1Ø1b, an 8-bit signed displacement (*disp8*) is included in the encoding. The byte will be sign-extended and added to the register operand specified by the r/m field.
1Øb	If r/m=1ØØb, then the SIB byte is present and indicates the addressing format. If r/m≠1Ø1b, a 32-bit signed displacement (*disp16*) is included in the encoding that will be added to the register operand specified by the r/m field.
11b	The instruction references two registers (the size is determined by the w field in the opcode). The *reg* field specifies the destination operand and the r/m field specifies the source operand. No memory reference is included in the instruction.

The *reg* Field   The *reg* (register) field occupies bits 5 through 3 of the addressing mode byte and is used either to specify a register operand or to hold additional opcode bits. Unlike the *r/m* field, which can specify an effective address, the *reg* field always specifies a register operand whose size is determined by the *w* field in the opcode byte. The register referenced by *reg* is determined by the value of *w* and the mode the chip is in. Table 6.9 gives the interpretation of *reg* for both values of *w* and both 16-bit and 32-bit modes.

Instructions that reference a segment register as one of their operands use a different encoding. These forms usually replace the reference to the *reg* field with a reference to the *sreg* field. When specified, the *sreg* field is interpreted according to the Table 6.10.

The *r/m* Field   The *r/m* (register/memory) field occupies bits 2 through 0 in the addressing mode byte. It is a multipurpose field whose interpretation is governed by the *mod* field and whether the instruction is being executed in 16-bit or 32-bit mode. When the *r/m* field is interpreted in 16-bit mode, no SIB byte is present and the interpretation is the same as for the 8086. A complete explanation of the interpretation of the *r/m* field is given in the section on 8086 encoding earlier in this chapter. When the *r/m* field is interpreted in 32-bit mode, however, the result may specify either a register or a memory operand, or indicate that the SIB byte follows to complete the encoding.

TABLE 6.9

Interpretation of the *reg* Field in 16-bit and 32-bit Modes

reg	w=Ø	w=1	
	Both Modes	16-bit Mode	32-bit Mode
ØØØb	AL	AX	EAX
ØØ1b	CL	CX	ECX
Ø1Øb	DL	DX	EDX
Ø11b	BL	BX	EBX
1ØØb	AH	SP	ESP
1Ø1b	CH	BP	EBP
11Øb	DH	SI	ESI
111b	BH	DI	EDI

TABLE 6.10

Interpretation of the *sreg* Field on the 80386 and 80486

sreg	Register
ØØØb	ES
ØØ1b	CS
Ø1Øb	SS
Ø11b	DS
1ØØb	FS
1Ø1b	GS

If *mod*=11b, then *r/m* specifies a register operand and is encoded using the same values as the *reg* field. If *mod*≠11b and *r/m*=100b, then the SIB byte follows in the encoding and specifies the operand. (An explanation of the SIB byte follows this section.) If *mod*≠11b and *r/m*=101b, then the operand is a 32-bit unsigned number that is interpreted as an offset from the start of a segment. Otherwise, the result is an effective address as defined in Table 6.11. The segment registers shown are the default segments invoked by the memory reference listed according to the rules presented in Chapter 3. The segment register references are not encoded explicitly into the addressing mode byte and can be changed using a segment override prefix.

The symbols *disp8* and *disp32* in the table represent an 8-bit or 32-bit signed number, respectively, that is interpreted as a relative displacement and is added to the register reference shown to generate the complete address. The displacements are included as data in the encoding and are explained in the section on the *disp* field that follows. The *off32* symbol represents a 32-bit unsigned number that is interpreted as an offset from the start of a segment. For the case *r/m*=100b, the default segment will be determined by the SIB byte.

TABLE 6.11

Interpretation of the *r/m* Field in 32-bit Mode

r/m	mod=00b	mod=01b	mod=10b	mod=11b w=0	w=1
000b	DS:[EAX]	DS:[EAX+*disp8*]	DS:[EAX+*disp32*]	AL	EAX
001b	DS:[ECX]	DS:[ECX+*disp8*]	DS:[ECX+*disp32*]	CL	ECX
010b	DS:[EDX]	DS:[EDX+*disp8*]	DS:[EDX+*disp32*]	DL	EDX
011b	DS:[EBX]	DS:[EBX+*disp8*]	DS:[EBX+*disp32*]	BL	EBX
100b[1]	[SIB]	[SIB+*disp8*]	[SIB+*disp32*]	AH	ESP
101b	DS:[*off32*]	DS:[EBP+*disp8*]	DS:[EPB+*disp32*]	CH	EBP
110b	DS:[ESI]	DS:[ESI+*disp8*]	DS:[ESI+*disp32*]	DH	ESI
111b	DS:[EDI]	DS:[EDI+*disp8*]	DS:[EDI+*disp32*]	BH	EDI

[1] An *r/m* value of 100b implies that the SIB byte is present and represents an addressing mode of the form [base + *scale*·*index*].

As in 16-bit mode, the effective addresses generated for each value of the *r/m* field for *mod*=00b, 01b, or 10b are consistent. The register argument shown under the *mod*=00b case is simply augmented with an 8-bit displacement for *mod*=01b and a 32-bit displacement for *mod*=10b with the exceptions noted earlier.

The Scale-Index-Base Byte

The encoding of the scale-index-base (SIB) byte is very similar to the addressing mode byte but is used only in 32-bit [base+scale*index+*disp*] mode addressing. The byte is divided into three fields called, appropriately enough, the *scale*, *index,* and *base* fields, which are shown in Figure 6.4. When this byte is specified by the addressing mode byte, it is interpreted to give a complete effective address for the operand. Each of the fields is described below.

The *scale* Field   The scale field occupies bits 7 and 6 of the SIB byte. This field, in combination with the *index* field, specifies the scaled index register portion of the 32-bit effective address. The base register is specified by the *base* field. (Refer to Chapter 3 for an explanation of this 32-bit addressing mode.)

In all cases, *scale* specifies the positive power of 2 by which the contents of the *index* will be multiplied before being used in the effective address calculation. If *scale*=10b, for example, the index register will be multiplied by 4. Table 6.12 gives the scaling value used for each of the possible values of *scale*.

The *index* Field   The *index* field occupies bits 5 through 3 of the SIB byte and specifies the register operand that will be multiplied by the scaling factor specified by the *scale* field before being added to the effective address. The *index* field always specifies a 32-bit register. Table 6.13 gives the interpretation of the *index* field. Note that the ESP register cannot be used as an index.

An *index* value of 100b indicates that no index register is given. In that case, Intel documentation indicates that the *scale* field should be set to 00b as well. Officially, the resulting effective address is undefined. Unofficially, encodings with *index*=100b will not normally be generated, do not perform useful work and, on occasion, cause the processor to crash. Presumably, this encoding is being reserved to indicate the presence of another addressing mode byte for future 64-bit processors.

TABLE 6.12

The *scale* Field and Scaling Values

scale	Scaling Value
ØØb	1
Ø1b	2
1Øb	4
11b	8

TABLE 6.13

Interpretation of the *index* Field

index	Register Operand
ØØØb	[EAX]
ØØ1b	[ECX]
Ø1Øb	[EDX]
Ø11b	[EBX]
1ØØb	no index
1Ø1b	[EBP]
11Øb	[ESI]
111b	[EDI]

The *base* Field   The *base* field occupies bits 2 through 0 in the SIB byte and specifies the register operand that will be taken as the base for the effective address. The base register also selects the default segment register that will be used to locate the memory operand. Table 6.14 gives the possible values for *base* and their interpretations. A *base* of 101b is used to address a 32-bit displacement in combination with a scaled index as well as the EBP register in combination with a displacement and a scaled index.

The Displacement Field

The next portion of the instruction encoding is called the displacement field. If present in the encoding, this field contains a constant that will be used in the calculation of an effective address or program relative address. In the encoding diagrams that appear in the instruction reference in Appendix A, the displacement is represented by the symbol *disp* and may range in size from zero bytes (that is, no displacement is present) to six bytes (a two-byte segment and a four-byte offset). The *disp* field is interpreted according to its usage, which varies between instructions and between forms of the same instruction. The three forms of *disp* are signed relative displacement, unsigned segment-relative displacement, and absolute displacement. These three types of displacement are defined earlier in this chapter in the section on 8086 addressing.

TABLE 6.14

Interpretation of the *base* Operand Field

base	Interpretation
ØØØb	DS:[EAX]
ØØ1b	DS:[ECX]
Ø1Øb	DS:[EDX]
Ø11b	DS:[EBX]
1ØØb	SS:[ESP]
1Ø1b	if *mod*=ØØb, then DS:[*disp32*] if *mod*≠ØØb, then SS:[EBP]
11Øb	DS:[ESI]
111b	DS:[EDI]

The Immediate Data Field

The immediate data field is always placed at the end of the encoding. If present in the encoding, this field contains a constant that will be used as either an operand or an argument to the instruction. In the encoding diagrams that appear in the instruction reference, immediate data is represented by the symbol *immed* and may range in size from 0 bytes (that is, no immediate data is present) to four bytes. The *immed* field is interpreted according to its usage, which varies between instructions and between forms of the same instruction. Immediate data is explained earlier in this chapter in the section on 8086 addressing.

Encoding Examples

Example 1: *Assume that an 80386 is running in 8086-emulation mode and determine which instruction is represented by the following byte sequence*:

```
67h 8Bh 44h ØBh Ø5h
```

The first byte is the address size override prefix that will reverse the default size for the effective address calculation. Since the processor is in real mode, the default is to a 16-bit effective address. This instruction, therefore, reverses that and uses a 32-bit effective address.

The next byte, 8Bh, is the opcode for MOV *reg16,mem16*. This can be found by using the opcode matrix in Appendix C to find the general instruction and then looking up the instruction in the instruction reference in Appendix A. Because the *d* bit in the opcode is 1, the direction of data flow is into the operand specified by the *reg* field in the addressing mode byte and *w*=1 means that the operand size is 16 bits (the default).

The next byte is the addressing mode byte and can be broken down into its three fields. Since 44h = 01000100b, the fields are: *mod*=01b, *reg*=000b, and *r/m*=100b. The *mod*=01b value indicates that a *disp8* byte is included in the encoding and should be sign-extended and added to the effective address. The displacement field is always the last field in the encoding, so *disp8*=05h. The *reg*=000b value selects the AX register as the destination of the MOV instruction. The *r/m* field has the value 100b, which means that the SIB byte is included in the encoding and will specify the effective address.

The next byte is the SIB byte (0Bh = 00001011b) and can be broken down as follows. The *scale* field is 00, which means that the index register will not be multiplied before use. The *index* field value of 001b selects the ECX register as the index register. Finally, the *base* field value of 011b indicates that the EBX register will be used as the base and selects the DS register for memory access. The resultant effective address is DS:[EBX+ECX+5].

The instruction represented by this series of bytes is therefore MOV AX,WORD PTR DS:[EBX][ECX*1][5]. You can verify this by assembling the instruction and looking at the resulting listing.

Example 2: *Assume that an 80486 is running in 8086-emulation mode and determine the encoding for the instruction*

```
MOV [ESI*4][ESP],EAX.
```

Since the processor is in real mode, the defaults will be 16-bit effective addresses and 16-bit operands. This instruction uses a 32-bit effective address and is moving 32 bits of data. Therefore both the address size (67h) and operand size (66h) override prefixes will be required.

The form of the instruction is MOV *mem,reg*. The instruction listing gives the encoding for this form as 100010*dw*. The direction of data flow is to memory from a register, so *d*=0. The operand size is 32 bits, so *w*=1. The opcode byte is therefore 89h.

The next byte to encode will be the addressing mode byte. The *mod* field must be set to 00b to indicate that no displacement field is present. The *r/m* field must be set to 100b to indicate that the SIB byte is being used to generate the effective address. (This is required because, among other reasons, the effective address uses scaling.) The *reg* field is used to specify the source operand, EAX, and is set to 000b. The addressing mode byte is 00000100b=04h.

The base register for the effective address will be ESP. (Even though ESI is first, it cannot be the base because it is scaled.) This sets the *base* field to 100b. The index register is scaled by 4, which indicates that *scale*=10b. Finally, the *index* field is set to 110b to select ESI. The SIB byte is then 10110100b=B4h.

The final encoding for the instruction MOV [ESI*4][ESP],EAX is 67h 66h 8Ah 04h B5h. You can verify this by assembling the instruction and looking at the resulting listing or by entering the bytes into a debugger that supports the 80386.

Instruction Execution Time

Assembly code is the realm of the small and the fast, and the best programmers will spend inordinate amounts of time crafting their routines to remove one more byte or reduce execution time by a few more clocks. Optimization efforts should be concentrated in the sections of the code that are executed repeatedly such as loops, sorts, and searches.

The execution time for each instruction is given in the instruction reference in Appendix A. The timings represent the number of clock cycles required to execute each particular form of an instruction. The duration of each clock period is determined from the system clock speed by this formula:

1 clock = 1000/(system speed in MHz) nanoseconds (nS)

Determining the execution time for a series of instructions is not as straightforward as simply adding up the timings for the individual instructions. A number of variables regarding the instructions themselves can influence execution time significantly. In addition, events that occur outside of the system (including interrupts, exceptions, memory refresh, and so on) will also affect the real-world elapsed time. This section explains the adjustments that must be made to the timings shown in Appendix A to arrive at a better estimate of execution time.

Many instructions have multiple timings. For example, the timing for conditional jumps will vary depending on whether control is transferred (the jump is taken) or the jump falls through (not taken). Other instructions will list different times for execution in real mode and in protected mode. The timing for these two conditions is listed separately in the instruction reference in Appendix A.

If an effective address has to be calculated, this may also add to execution time. The 8086 and 8088 (and to a lesser extent the more advanced processors) will all show increased execution time when accessing memory operands. Execution time for repeating instructions (such as the shift and rotate instructions) can vary as a function of the repeat factor. And finally, the alignment of data operands will affect the time required to fetch them. The effect of all these factors on timing is explained in detail later in this section.

Instruction Timing Assumptions and Penalties

The timings for individual instructions, for all the processors, assume the following conditions. Additional assumptions for particular processors are provided later in this section.

- The instruction is prefetched and waiting in the instruction queue.

- Control transfer statement timings include any additional clocks needed to reinitialize the instruction queue.

- All memory operands are aligned. (See the processor-specific assumptions below.)

- Bus cycles do not require wait states.

- No other processors contend for bus access.

- Internal components of the processor do not contend for bus access.

- No exceptions are detected during execution of the instruction.

During normal program operation, the instruction to be executed has already been prefetched. This assumption is generally valid during normal program execution. A series of instructions that take fewer than two clocks per byte to execute, however, can deplete the queue and the processor will idle until more instructions can be prefetched.

Wait states increase the time between a processor request for data and the receipt of that data. Wait states do not necessarily add to execution time, unless the instruction queue becomes depleted, since bus access and instruction execution can take place simultaneously.

As shown, certain assumptions about the external environment are necessary as well. Most PC configurations use a single processor, and the assumption that there are no local bus HOLD requests delaying processor access to the bus is valid. The listed timings cannot account for external interrupts that occur during execution. It must also be assumed that no exceptions are detected during execution of the instruction. For example, the timing for the DIV instruction will not be valid if the division error exception is generated.

The internal components of the processor may compete for access to the bus. For example, if part of the processor (the execution unit) is executing an instruction that accesses memory, another part of the processor (the bus interface unit) will have to wait to fetch an instruction and vice versa.

Due to all the factors that cannot be predicted with certainty, an average program will take approximately 5-10 percent longer to execute than would be indicated by the timings. This error can be significant for programmers working in real-time environments where the timing and response speed of the processor are critical. In that case, special hardware must be used to determine the exact execution time.

8086 and 8088   On the 8086 and 8088, the timings presented are subject to the following additional assumption:

- Memory operands are aligned. On the 8086, a four-clock penalty is assigned for each reference to a 16-bit operand located at an odd memory address. Since all 8088 accesses are 8-bit, no alignment is required, but four additional clocks must be added for each access to a word memory operand.

The 80286   On the 80286, the timings presented are subject to the following additional assumptions.

- Memory operands are aligned. A two-clock penalty is assigned for accessing a 16-bit memory operand at an odd physical address.

- Effective address calculations do not use the base + index + displacement form. If the base + index + displacement form is used add a one-clock penalty.

- No task switch is required. The clock penalty required for a task switch is given later in this section.

The 80386 On the 80386, the following assumptions apply when using the timings listed in the instruction set reference:

- Memory operands are aligned.

  80386DX: A two-clock penalty is assigned for accessing a 32-bit memory operand at a physical address that is not evenly divisible by 4.

  80386SX: A two-clock penalty is assigned for accessing a 16-bit memory operand at an odd physical address.

  80386SX: A two-clock penalty is assigned for accessing a 32-bit memory operand at an even physical address.

  80386SX: A four-clock penalty is assigned for accessing a 32-bit memory operand at an odd physical address.

- Effective address calculations do not use two general register components. One register, scaling and a displacement can be used with the indicated timing. If the effective address calculation uses two general register components, add a one-clock penalty.

- No task switch is required. The clock penalty required for a task switch is described in detail later in this section.

- Some timings are dependent on the subsequent instruction. The clock penalty required is described in detail later in this section.

The 80486 On the 80486, assumptions must be made about the state of each of the internal components of the processor in order to specify timings. These additional assumptions and the penalties incurred when they are invalid are listed below.

- Both data and instruction accesses "hit" in the cache. The 80486 timings assume that memory fetches of both data and instructions can be found in the cache. Intel claims a combined instruction and data cache hit rate of over 90 percent. If a cache miss occurs, the 80486 will be required to use an external bus cycle to transfer the required code or data into the cache. The additional clocks required for a cache miss are noted in the instruction reference in Appendix A. The cache miss penalty bytes are based on the 80486 using the fastest bus it can support. The processor 32-bit burst speed is defined as r-b-w, where r, b, and w are defined as:

  r The number of clocks in the first cycle of a burst read or the number of clocks per data cycle in a nonburst read.
  b The number of clocks for the second and subsequent cycles in a burst read.
  w The number of clocks for a write.

  The fastest bus supported is 2-1-2 with zero wait states. The cache miss clocks assume this bus. For slower buses, r-2 clocks should be added for the first doubleword accessed.

- Instructions that read multiple consecutive data items and miss the cache are assumed to start their first access on a 16-byte (paragraph) boundary. If not, an extra cache fill may be required, which will add up to r+3*b clocks to the cache miss penalty.

- The cache is filled before subsequent access to the line is allowed. If a read operation misses in the cache while a cache fill is already in progress, due to a previous read or prefetch, the read must wait for the cache to fill. A read or write must also wait for a cache line to fill completely before it can be accessed.

- Memory operands are aligned. For each access to an unaligned operand, add three clocks. The number of memory accesses for each instruction is listed in the instruction reference in Appendix A.

- The target of a jump instruction is assumed to be in the cache. If not, add r clocks to allow time for accessing the target instruction of a jump. If the target instruction is not completely contained in the first double-word read, add a maximum of 3*b clocks. If the target instruction is not completely contained in the first 16-byte burst (due to misalignment), add a maximum of r+3*b clocks.

- Page translations "hit" in the TLB. A TLB miss will add 13, 21, or 28 clocks to the timing depending on whether the accessed and/or dirty bits in neither, one, or both of the page entries needs to be set in memory. This penalty assumes that neither page table entry is in the data cache and that a page fault does not occur on the address translation.

- No invalidate cycles contend with the instruction for use of the cache. A one-clock penalty is imposed for each invalidate cycle that contends with the CPU for the internal cache/external bus.

- Effective address calculations use a base and no index register. If the effective address calculation uses both a base and index register, a one-clock penalty *may* be added to the timing.

- A base register used in an effective address calculation is not the destination of the preceding instruction. A one-clock penalty is imposed for back-to-back operations on the same register. Note that specialized on-chip hardware is used to ensure that the PUSH and POP instructions do not incur this penalty.

- A displacement field and immediate field are not used in the same instruction. If used together, an additional one clock *may* be required.

- There are no write-buffer delays. If there is no write-buffer delay but all the write buffers are full, then a w clock penalty is added. Intel documentation specifies that this case rarely occurs.

The Effective Address Calculation

The effective address calculation must be performed whenever a memory operand is used. On the 8086 and 8088, this calculation adds a specified number of clocks to the instruction's execution time depending on the components used in the effective address. Table 6.15 shows the possible addressing combinations and the number of clocks required to calculate the resulting effective address.

TABLE 6.15

Additional Clocks Required for Effective Address Calculations

Effective	Address Components	Additional Clocks Required			
		86/88	286	386	486
Displacement	[disp]	6	Ø	Ø	Ø
Base or Index	[BX] [BP] [SI] [DI]	5	Ø	Ø	Ø
Base + disp Index + disp	[BX + disp] [BP + disp] [SI + disp] [DI + disp]	9	Ø	Ø	Ø
Base + Index	[BX + SI] [BP + DI]	7	Ø	Ø	Ø
	[BX + DI] [BP + SI]	8	Ø	Ø	Ø
Base + Index + disp	[BX + SI + disp] [BP + DI + disp]	11	1	Ø	Ø
	[BX + DI + disp] [BP + SI + disp]	12	1	Ø	Ø
Segment Override	sreg:[]	2			
Base + scale * index (32-bit mode)	[reg32 + scale * reg32]	–	–	1	1*

* One clock may be added to the 80486 execution time depending on the state of the processor.

On the 80286 and later processors, the effective address calculation is performed by dedicated hardware and generally does not add to the execution time. The exception to this rule is that [base+index+displacement] addressing adds one clock to the 80286 and 80386 timings listed in Appendix A. The additional clock *may* be required on the 80486, depending on the internal state of the processor.

Other Timing Factors

There are several additional factors that influence the timing of an instruction. These factors generally represent different modes of operation and must be taken into account when determining timings.

Control Transfer Instructions The timings shown for the control transfer instructions, including JMP, CALL, and INT, include any additional clocks required to reinitialize the instruction queue starting at the target of the transfer. In addition, the time required to fetch the target instruction is also included.

The conditional transfer instructions will show two timings. The unlabeled timing is the clock count to be used when control is transferred to the target instruction. The label NJ (no jump) indicates the timing when the jump is not taken.

Repeating Instructions   Many instructions, such as the bit shift and rotate instructions, repeat their operation a specified number of times. The timings for these instructions are presented as a formula in the form $x+(y*n)$. Here, x is the initial number of clocks required to start the instruction, y is the number of clocks required to execute each iteration specified, and n is the number of repetitions.

When accessing memory operands that are misaligned, or for 16-bit memory operands on the 8088, the appropriate clock penalty should be added to the value for y so that it is multiplied by the number of repetitions.

Next Instruction Dependency   On the 80286 and 80386, the number of clocks required to execute some instructions is influenced by the instruction that follows them. In this case, the symbol m is used in the timing formula and represents the number of components in the following instruction.

The number of components in an instruction is determined as follows. The entire displacement, if present, counts as a single component. The entire immediate data, if present, counts as a single component. Every other byte of the instruction, including any prefixes, counts as one component.

Task Switching Between Different TSS Types   If, on the 80386 or 80486, an exception occurs during the execution of an instruction and a task switch is required to pass control to the exception handler, the instruction time of the instruction should be increased by the number of clocks required to perform the task switch. The number of clocks is dependent on the Task State Segment (TSS) type of both the current task and the exception handler and whether either task is executing in Virtual-86 mode. Table 6.16 summarizes the possible task switch times for exceptions.

TABLE 6.16

Clocks Required to Switch Tasks Between TSS Types for Exceptions

80386

Old Task	New Task 386-Type TSS VM=0	286-Type TSS	
386-Type TSS VM=0	309	282	
386-Type TSS VM=1	314	231	
286-Type TSS	307	282	

80486

Old Task	New Task 486-Type TSS	286-Type TSS	VM-Type TSS
486-type TSS or 286-type TSS	199	180	177

7

INTERRUPTS AND EXCEPTIONS

IN PREVIOUS CHAPTERS, WE ESTABLISHED THAT THE 80X86 PROCESSORS ARE able to execute complex instructions and communicate with external devices. In this chapter, we'll review the processor's method of recognizing requests for service from external devices: the interrupt. In addition, we'll cover the related topic of processor-generated exceptions and software interrupts.

This chapter will present the mechanisms used to service external interrupts, software interrupts, and exceptions in both the real and protected modes of the processor. The details of the interrupt transfer mechanisms are provided along with the processor data structures that enable interrupt handling. In addition, a comprehensive list of reserved interrupts and processor-generated exceptions is presented for each of the processors.

Interrupt or Exception?

An interrupt is a control transfer mechanism that causes the processor to stop execution of the current program, transfer control to an interrupt service routine (or handler), and resume program execution when the interrupt is complete. Other control transfers, such as those taken as a result of the JMP, CALL, and RET instructions, are always initiated under program control. An interrupt transfer, however, may be *forced* by an event that is not a part of a program's normal execution, such as a request for service from an external device. In this case, the processor treats the interrupt service routine as if it had a higher priority than the application. The handling of an interrupt is usually transparent to the underlying application program and typically leaves the processor in the same state that it was in when the interrupt occurred.

The term interrupt is loosely used to describe three related but different control transfer mechanisms. The mechanisms are distinguished based primarily on their origin. Specifically, an *interrupt* is a condition that has as its origin an *external* event, such as a device signaling for attention. An interrupt may occur at any time during execution of a program. By definition, interrupts are asynchronous with the operation of the processor: simply reproducing the internal state the processor had when an interrupt occurred is not sufficient to cause an interrupt to be reproduced. To avoid confusion, these interrupts are called *external interrupts* and are further classified as maskable and nonmaskable depending on how they are signaled to the processor.

The second type of control transfer is the *exception*. As with an interrupt, an exception represents a high-priority request for service. The distinction between the two, however, is that the conditions that cause an exception are internal—they originate within the processor—generally in response to a situation detected while executing an instruction. As such, exceptions are always synchronous with the operation of the processor. By definition, an exception may be reproduced by restoring the state of the processor and executing the same series of instructions.

The third category is called *software interrupts* which are generated by processor instructions such as INTO and INT *n*. Although they are called interrupts, they are handled by the processor as if they were exceptions. Software interrupts are a direct result of the execution of an instruction and thus are synchronous and repeatable.

External Interrupts

External interrupts are caused by physical events that occur outside the boundaries of the processor. External interrupts are typically routed through a programmable interrupt controller, prioritized, and signaled to the processor via the INTR, or maskable interrupt line. Another interrupt path is provided to the processor that bypasses INTR. This line is called the nonmaskable interrupt (NMI) line, and is used to signal catastrophic events or regain control of the processor when it is in a shutdown state. The processor's handling of these external interrupts is explained in detail in this section.

Maskable Interrupts

The interrupts that arrive at the processor via the INTR (interrupt request) signal line are called *maskable interrupts*. The INTR line is usually driven by a programmable interrupt controller (PIC), which manages interrupts under software control of the processor. The PIC accepts interrupt requests from devices, prioritizes them, and activates the INTR line of the processor as required. Although the INTR line is activated as soon as the interrupt request is accepted by the PIC, the processor will always complete the currently executing instruction before reacting to the signal. Even then, the action taken by the processor is dependent on the setting of the Interrupt flag (IF) and other pending interrupts.

If the Interrupt flag is cleared (with the CLI instruction, for example), interrupts signaled on INTR are *masked*, or disabled. The processor will simply ignore the interrupt request and proceed on to execute the next instruction. To allow the processor to service the interrupts, the IF flag must be set to 1 (such as with the STI instruction). Specific interrupts may be enabled or disabled (selectively masked) by programming the PIC directly. Interrupt requests that are terminated by the external device before they are recognized by the processor are lost.

Temporary Masking In some cases, interrupts will not be immediately acknowledged by the processor even though interrupts are enabled. If interrupts are masked (IF=0) and the STI (set interrupt flag) instruction is executed, pending interrupts will not be recognized until *after* the instruction that follows STI has been executed. This operation helps prevent excessive stack usage by allowing a procedure to enable interrupts, then immediately execute a RET instruction. Similarly, if interrupts are disabled and the restoration of the FLAGS register by the IRET instruction enables them, interrupts will not be recognized until after the next instruction has completed.

Another case where interrupts will not be recognized is when instruction prefixes are used. Prefixes are considered to be part of the instruction that they precede. No interrupts are allowed between the LOCK prefix, for example, and the locked instruction. On the 8086 and 8088, however, multiple prefixes will not be properly recognized after a repeated string instruction has been interrupted and then restarted; only the prefix immediately preceding the string primitive is restored. To avoid this situation, interrupts should be disabled before the operation and enabled afterward. If a large count is being used for the repetition or disabling interrupts is not desired, this technique should be used:

```
Move:
    LOCK                        ;Prefix 1
    REP                         ;Prefix 2
    MOVSB [DEST],CS:[SRC]       ;CS override is prefix 3
    OR    CX,CX                 ;If not 0, was interrupted
    JNZ   Move                  ;Restart with correct prefixes
```

On the 8086 and 8088, a MOV to any segment register or a POP with any segment register as the operand will also disable interrupts until after the following instruction. This allows a far pointer to be loaded without interruption. On the 80286 and later processors, this is only true when the SS segment register is specified. This property is especially important when setting or swapping stacks. If an interrupt occurred after loading the SS register but before loading the SP register, the interrupt would attempt to save the FLAGS, CS, and IP registers on the stack, writing over the wrong area of memory.

An early version of the 8088 contained a hardware bug that did not correctly disable interrupts after a MOV or POP to a segment register. Subsequent revisions of the chip were fixed, but if you suspect that your code may be executed on one of the defective processors, you must make allowances for the problem. For example, assuming interrupts are enabled and AX contains the new value for SS, the stack could be safely swapped, as shown here:

```
CLI                 ;Disable interrupts
MOV   SS,AX         ;Point to new stack
MOV   SP,SPOINTER
STI                 ;Enable interrupts
```

On the 80386 and later processors, an interrupt may still occur between the instructions that set SS and SP. While NMI, INTR, debug, and single-step interrupts are temporarily masked, a page fault or general protection exception can still occur before a valid SS:SP combination has been set. To avoid this, use the LSS SP,*mem* instruction to set both registers at once.

In two cases, interrupts are properly recognized in the middle of an instruction. The processor will recognize a pending interrupt between iterations of a repeated string instruction. Each time one iteration of the string instruction has completed, interrupts will be allowed. If program logic requires that interrupts be disabled during repeated string operations, they must be disabled and enabled manually. If the count is high, repeated string operations may keep interrupts disabled for an unacceptable length of time. The processor also recognizes interrupts when executing instructions that include WAIT or FWAIT.

Interrupt Acknowledge Bus Cycles   The processor acknowledges an interrupt request and begins servicing the interrupt by performing two consecutive interrupt acknowledge (INTA) bus cycles. A bus hold request that arrives during the INTA cycles is not recognized until the cycles have completed. The first INTA cycle signals the PIC that the interrupt request has been acknowledged. The PIC responds during the second INTA cycle by placing a byte on the data bus that indicates the interrupt number (0 to 255) associated with the requesting device. The processor reads this byte and uses it as an index into the interrupt vector table. (The interrupt vector table is explained later in this chapter.)

The Nonmaskable Interrupt

An external interrupt does not necessarily have to be routed through an interrupt controller or use the INTR line. The nonmaskable interrupt (NMI) line, mentioned earlier, is available to signal the processor. The NMI line is edge-triggered and asynchronous (the INTR is level-triggered and synchronous) and, in theory, is to be used to inform the processor that some catastrophic event has occurred or is about to occur. For a computer, such events would include a bus parity error, failure of some critical hardware component such as the timer, or an imminent loss of power.

The NMI is the highest-priority external interrupt and cannot be disabled by the processor. If, however, the NMI is received while the processor is executing an instruction that changes the SS (stack segment) register, the interrupt will not be recognized until after the following instruction has executed. The NMI is hard-wired as interrupt 2, so no interrupt acknowledge (INTA) bus cycles are required or generated by the processor to retrieve the interrupt type as with INTR. Although NMI cannot be disabled by the processor, it can be disabled externally under program control if appropriate hardware is installed into the system.

On the 8088 and 8086 processors, an NMI that occurs during the handling of a previous NMI can interrupt the NMI handler. On the 80286 and later processors, however, additional NMIs will not be serviced by the processor until an IRET is executed or the CPU is reset. If an NMI request occurs while a previous NMI is being serviced, the second request is saved and will be serviced after an IRET is executed. Only one NMI request can be saved by the processor.

Software Interrupts

Although called an interrupt, a software interrupt is treated as if it were an exception generated by the processor. Software interrupts are a direct result of the execution of an instruction and thus are synchronous and repeatable. Unlike hardware interrupts, software interrupts cannot be masked.

In real mode, software interrupts are used as a convenient form of interprogram communication. The implementation of the interrupt calling convention on the 80x86 processors provides an address-independent mechanism for supplying operating system services to applications programs. Both the BIOS and DOS use the interrupt mechanism to provide system services to applications.

Any interrupt, including those assigned to exceptions reserved by the processor, may be generated with a software interrupt using the INT *n* (opcode CDh *n*) instruction. In addition, certain processor instructions are explicitly linked with interrupt types. The breakpoint instruction (opcode CCh) generates interrupt 3. The INTO instruction generates interrupt 4 if the overflow flag is set. And the BOUND instruction will generate interrupt 5 if the supplied index violates an array's boundaries. Each of these instructions is discussed in more detail in the instruction reference in Appendix A; the interrupts they generate are discussed in the section on exceptions that follows.

Exceptions

An exception is the processor's normal, documented, and predictable response to a situation, detected during the execution of an instruction, that requires special handling. Exceptions may be reproduced by reexecuting the same series of instructions that produced the exception the first time. Exceptions are similar to interrupts in that they force a transfer of control to occur. Unlike interrupts, exceptions are completely internal to the processor, do not pass through the interrupt controller, and cannot be masked. Exceptions always have a higher priority than signals arriving over the INTR or NMI lines.

Exception Classes

The category of processor exceptions is further divided into three classes of exception: *faults*, *traps*, or *aborts*. How an exception is classified depends on when the exception is detected and whether the instruction that caused the instruction is restartable.

Fault   A fault is an exception that is reported *before* the instruction causing the exception is executed. The fault is detected either before the actual instruction execution or the processor is restored to its state before the instruction was executed. In either case, if the cause of the fault is remedied, the instruction may be restarted. The values of CS and IP saved on the stack point to the instruction that caused the fault.

Trap   A trap is an exception that is detected *during* the execution of an instruction and is reported at the boundary of the next instruction. Note that the instruction that caused the exception may still be executing when the exception is detected and generated. If the trap is detected during a control transfer instruction, the values of CS and IP saved on the stack point to the instruction to which control would have been transferred.

Abort   An abort is an exception that is generated by the processor when it is faced with a severe error. Aborts may be caused by hardware errors and by inconsistent or illegal values in system tables. Because of the nature of these errors, the operation that caused the error cannot be identified nor can the program be restarted. For example, if during normal processor operation the global descriptor table was suddenly discovered to be corrupted, it would be impossible for the processor to determine in retrospect how that happened.

Exception Error Codes

One of the key factors behind implementing faults and traps is the possibility of error recovery. If the problem that caused the trap or fault can be fixed, the interrupted program can be restarted transparently. This principle is put to work when virtual memory and paging systems are implemented.

To aid in the analysis of problems, the processor pushes an error code onto the stack of the exception handler for exceptions that are localized to a specific segment. The format of the error code is shown in Figure 7.1. Some exceptions will push an error code of 0 when there is no error information.

FIGURE 7.1

Exception error code format

15		3	2	1	0	**8Ø286**
Selector Index			T I	I D T	E X T	**Error Code Format**

31		16	15		3	2	1	0
Reserved			Selector Index			T I	I D T	E X T

8Ø386/8Ø486 Error Code Format

Field	Value	Description
EXT	= Ø	Interrupted program caused the exception
	= 1	External event caused the exception
IDT	= Ø	TI bit determines table
	= 1	Selector is for gate descriptor
TI	= Ø	Selector is for GDT
	= 1	Selector is for LDT

The error code format is similar to a segment selector, but the RPL field has been replaced with two 1-bit fields. The interpretation of the fields is as follows.

EXT Field Bit 0 is defined as the EXT (external) field and is set to 1 by the processor if the error can be determined to have been caused by an event external to the program, such as a hardware interrupt. If clear, the program caused the exception.

IDT Field The IDT (interrupt descriptor table) field (I bit) will be set if the index field of the error code refers to a gate descriptor in the interrupt descriptor table. If the I bit is clear, the meaning of the index field is determined by the TI field.

TI Field If the IDT field is 0, the TI (table index) field indicates whether the error code refers to the global descriptor table (GDT) or the local descriptor table (LDT). If TI=0, the index field points to the GDT. If TI=1, the index field points to the LDT.

Index Field The index field combined with the TI field forms a 14-bit pointer to the table entry that is associated with the exception. The IDT and TI fields are used to determine if the index points into the IDT, LDT, or GDT structures as described above.

On the 80386 and later processors, page faults may occur. These faults use a different format for the error code as indicated in the exception description later in this chapter.

Processor-Defined Exceptions

Intel processors reserve interrupts 0 through 1Fh for their own use. To date, only some of these interrupts have been defined by the 80x86 processors; the remainder are reserved for future processors. Table 7.1 describes the identified interrupts, shows the processors for which they are valid, and gives other pertinent information about them.

Interrupt 0: Divide Error This exception is generated during a division operation using the DIV or IDIV instructions if the quotient is too large to fit in the destination register or if an attempt is made to divide by zero.

On the 8086 and 8088 processors, this exception is a trap, and the values of CS and IP saved on the stack point to the first byte of the instruction following the DIV or IDIV instruction that caused the exception. The contents of the quotient and remainder registers (AL and AH or AX and DX) are left in an undefined state.

On the 80286 and later processors, this exception is a fault, and the values of CS and IP saved on the stack point to the first byte of the failing instruction, including any prefixes. The AX and DX registers contain the values they had before the operation, allowing the operation to be restarted. The 80286 and later processors can also generate the largest negative value as a quotient from the IDIV instruction without generating an exception. The 8086 and 8088 cannot.

For more details on the conditions that will cause this exception, see the listings for DIV and IDIV in the instruction reference in Appendix A.

TABLE 7.1

Processor-Defined Exceptions

Interrupt Number	Description	Type	CS:IP Points to Instruction That Caused Exception	Pushes Error Code on Stack	Processor 8088/ 8086	80286	80386	80486
Ø	Divide error	F [1]	Yes [1]	No	•	•	•	•
1	Single-step	T	No	No	•	•	•	•
	Debug exceptions	T,F	[2]	No			•	•
2	Nonmaskable interrupt (NMI)	T	No [3]	No	•	•	•	•
3	Breakpoint interrupt	S,T	No [4]	No	•	•	•	•
4	INTO Overflow	S,T	No [5]	No	•	•	•	•
5	BOUND range exceeded	S,F	Yes	No		•	•	•
6	Invalid opcode	F	Yes	No		•	•	•
7	Coprocessor not available	F	Yes	No		•	•	•
8	Double-fault	A	Yes	Yes [6]		•	•	•
9	Coprocessor segment overrun	A	No	No		•	•	[7]
Ah	Invalid task segment	F	Yes	Yes			•	•
Bh	Segment not present	F	Yes	Yes			•	•
Ch	Stack fault	F	Yes	Yes			•	•
Dh	General protection	F,A	Yes	Yes		•	•	•
Eh	Page fault	F	Yes	Yes			•	•
Fh	Reserved by Intel	–	–	–	–	–	–	–
1Øh	Coprocessor error	F	Yes [8]	No		•	•	•
11h	Alignment check	F	Yes	Yes				•
12h-1Fh	Reserved by Intel	–	–	–	–	–	–	–

F	Fault
T	Trap
A	Abort
S	Software generated
[1]	On the 8Ø86 and 8Ø88 only, interrupt Ø is a trap, not a fault. The CS:IP saved on the stack points to the instruction that follows the trapped instruction.
[2]	Some debug exceptions are traps and others are faults. Refer to Chapter 9 for more details.
[3]	The NMI is generated by an external signal.
[4]	The saved CS:IP points to the byte after the breakpoint instruction.
[5]	The INTO instruction may be executed at any time, regardless of when the overflow occurred.
[6]	The error code pushed is always Ø.
[7]	This exception is not used by the 8Ø486. Interrupt Dh occurs instead.
[8]	The saved CS:IP value points to the instruction that caused the exception to be detected, not the instruction that caused the error.

Interrupt 1: Single-Step   When the single-step Trap flag (TF) in the FLAGS register is set, the processor is said to be in single-step mode. In this condition, an exception will occur after the execution of most instructions. The single-step trap exception is not generated after prefix instructions, instructions that modify segment registers, or after the WAIT or FWAIT instructions. The values of CS and IP saved on the stack point to the next instruction that would have been executed had the exception not been generated.

The Trap flag is cleared automatically as part of the interrupt transfer mechanism. Thus, the processor is not in single-step mode when it enters the single-step exception handler. This allows the exception handler to execute without being single-stepped itself. When the handler returns control to the underlying application, the FLAGS register is restored from the stack. If the Trap flag was set on entry to the handler, it will be restored by the IRET and another single-step interrupt will be generated after the execution of the instruction following the IRET. Single-step is not masked by the Interrupt flag (IF).

Beginning with the 80386, this exception is used to support the built-in debugging features of the processor. Whether the interrupt is issued as a trap or as a fault is dependent on the condition that caused it. The exception is a fault for an instruction address breakpoint or a general detect. A trap is issued for a data address, a single-step, or a task-switch breakpoint. The RF flag in the EFLAGS register can be used to mask debug faults. Chapter 9 discusses the debugging capabilities of the 80386 and 80486.

The priority of the single-step interrupt is dependent on the context and varies across processors. This priority determines the order in which multiple pending interrupts are services. An explanation of priorities is given later in this chapter.

Interrupt 2: Nonmaskable   The nonmaskable interrupt (NMI) is actually a hardware-generated interrupt, not an exception. It is distinguished from other hardware interrupts that are signaled on the INTR line because it cannot be masked by clearing the Interrupt flag (IF) in the FLAGS register. This interrupt is generated when an external signal is received on the processor's NMI line. The nonmaskable interrupt is discussed in the section on external interrupts earlier in this chapter.

Interrupt 3: Breakpoint   Interrupt type 3 is a software interrupt that is treated by the processor as if it were a trap exception. The breakpoint interrupt is hard-wired to the breakpoint instruction (opcode CCh) and is generated whenever that instruction is executed. Typically, the breakpoint will be inserted into a program that is being debugged to transfer control to the debugger. Because the breakpoint is only one byte long (as opposed to INT *n*, which requires two bytes), the instruction can be substituted for any processor instruction without affecting adjacent code.

The values of CS and IP saved on the stack point to the byte after the breakpoint instruction. A debugger would normally replace the original byte that had been displaced by the breakpoint opcode and then perform whatever diagnostics it wanted to. The breakpoint exception is not maskable.

The priority of the breakpoint interrupt varies across processors. This affects when it will get control. See the section on priorities later in this chapter.

Interrupt 4: INTO Overflow   Interrupt type 4 is a software interrupt that is treated as a trap exception by the processor. An overflow interrupt is generated if the Overflow flag (OF) is set and the INTO instruction is executed. The same processor instructions are used to manipulate both signed and unsigned numbers. Because of this, the processor cannot implicitly determine if the overflow condition is an error. The Overflow flag is set and applications can test the flag directly or with this instruction, as appropriate. Details on the INTO instruction are given in the instruction reference in Appendix A.

Interrupt 5: BOUND Range Exceeded   Interrupt type 5 is a software interrupt that is treated as a fault exception by the processor. The BOUND interrupt is generated if the operands passed to the BOUND instruction indicate that the index given will fall outside the permissible bounds of the array. Presumably, the application executing the BOUND instruction will have set up an interrupt handler for this interrupt. Details on the INTO instruction are given in the instruction reference in Appendix A.

Interrupt 6: Invalid Opcode   This exception is generated by the 80286 and later processors when an attempt is made to execute an unreserved invalid opcode. An opcode may be classified as invalid for a number of reasons. For example, the opcode may not be defined for the particular processor or may not be permitted in the current operating mode. The invalid opcode exception will also be generated if an attempt is made to execute an instruction with an incorrect type of operand, even if it is possible to encode the instruction. For example, the BOUND, LDS, LES, and LIDT instructions encoded to address a register instead of memory will generate this exception. Finally, the use of the LOCK prefix with an instruction that may not be locked will cause this exception. (See the entry for LOCK in the instruction reference in Appendix A for details.)

Note that attempting to execute the POP *mem* or PUSH *mem* instructions using undefined bit encodings for bits 3-5 of the second opcode byte will generate the general protection exception Dh (13), not exception 6. Exceeding the instruction length limit of the processor will also generate the general protection exception and not the invalid opcode exception.

To be detected as an invalid opcode, the processor must actually attempt to execute the opcode. Prefetching an invalid opcode, for example, will not cause this exception. The CS:IP saved on the stack points to the first byte of instruction causing the exception, including prefixes. No error code is pushed onto the stack and the exception may be handled within the same task.

Table 7.2 lists the opcodes that are reserved by Intel for its processors. These opcodes are undefined, but will not generate an invalid opcode exception.

Generally, these opcodes perform the same action as other, smaller instructions. The opcode 0Fh 12h 00h, for example, corresponds to the instruction MOV AL,[BX+SI], which is normally encoded as 8Ah 00h.

TABLE 7.2

Reserved Undefined Opcodes

Single-Byte Opcodes
82
D6
F1

Two-Byte Opcodes
0F 07
0F 10
0F 11
0F 12
0F 13

F6 xx
F7 xx

C0 xx
C1 xx
D0 xx
D1 xx
D2 xx
D3 xx

Notes: All opcodes shown in hexadecimal.
xx indicates any hex value.

Interrupt 7: Coprocessor Not Available   If the status bits in the 80286's machine status word (MSW) indicate that the functions of the math coprocessor are to be emulated in software, the execution of an ESC or WAIT (floating-point) instruction will generate this exception. The values of CS and IP saved on the stack point to the first byte of the ESC or WAIT instruction that generated this exception.

On the 80386 and later processors, this exception will occur for either of two conditions. The exception will be generated during the execution of an ESC instruction if the emulate (EM) bit of control register CR0 is set. Interrupt 7 will also be issued if the processor encounters either a WAIT or an ESC instruction and either the monitor processor extension (MP) or task switched (TS) bits of CR0 are set.

Interrupt 8: Double-Fault   Normally, if an exception occurs while processing a previous exception, the two exceptions will be handled in series. If this cannot be done, however, exception 8 is generated indicating that two separate protection violations have occurred during the execution of a single instruction.

To ensure that a usable task state exists to handle the exception, a task gate must be used for this exception. The back link field in the TSS will identify the TSS of the task that caused the exception. The saved address will point at the instruction that was about to execute or was being executed when the error was detected. An error code of 0 is always pushed onto the stack by this exception. The instruction causing the fault cannot be restarted.

If, while handling this exception, another protection violation occurs, the processor will enter shutdown state, and no further interrupts or exceptions are recognized. A signal on either the RESET or NMI lines can bring the processor out of shutdown if no errors occur while handling the NMI. If an error does occur while handling the NMI, only RESET can exit shutdown. An NMI input will not bring the processor out of protected mode, while RESET will. (This property is used deliberately to switch the 80826 from protected mode to real mode.) The shutdown state is signaled on the processor bus to allow external hardware to take appropriate action.

The 80386 and 80486 processors divide faults into three categories in order to determine which combinations should be signaled as a double-fault. Exceptions are classed as either benign faults, contributory faults, or page faults. Table 7.3 gives the category for each of the processor faults and indicates the combinations that will produce a double-fault on the 80386 and 80486 processors.

TABLE 7.3

Fault Categories and Double-Fault Combinations

Fault Categories

Fault Category	Interrupt Type
Benign Exceptions	1 Debug exceptions
	2 NMI
	3 Breakpoint
	4 Overflow
	5 Bound
	6 Invalid opcode
	7 Coprocessor not available
	10h Coprocessor error
Contributory Exceptions	Ø Divide error
	9 Coprocessor segment overrun
	Ah Invalid TSS
	Bh Segment not present
	Ch Stack exception
	Dh General protection
Page Faults	Eh Page fault

Double-Fault Combinations

First Exception Category	Second Exception Produces a Double-Fault?		
	Benign	**Contributory**	**Page Fault**
Benign	No	No	No
Contributory	No	Yes	No
Page Fault	No	Yes	Yes

This exception may also be generated in real mode on the 80286 and later processors if the interrupt table limit is too small. An interrupt that occurs in real mode causes the processor to consult the interrupt vector table. In real mode, the base and upper limit of the table are set to 0 and 3FFh, respectively, at initialization. If the LIDT instruction has been used to change the limit, however, and an interrupt occurs which would access a vector beyond the limit, this exception is generated. The values of CS and IP saved on the stack point to the first byte of either the instruction that caused the exception or to the instruction that was ready to execute when an external interrupt occurred. No error code is placed on the stack.

Interrupt 9: Coprocessor Segment Overrun If the middle portion of an operand in an instruction being processed by the math coprocessor causes a page or segment violation, this exception will be generated. This exception is detected during the test performed on each data transfer between the coprocessor and memory. The values of CS and IP saved on the stack point to the first byte of the instruction that caused the exception.

On the 80386 processor, this exception is not normally issued. This exception is not used by the 80486 processor; interrupt Dh occurs instead.

Interrupt Ah (10): Invalid Task State Segment This exception is generated if, during a task switch, the task gate points to an invalid task state segment (TSS). A TSS is considered invalid for the cases given in Table 7.4. An error code is pushed onto the stack as indicated to identify the cause of the fault. The EXT (external) bit indicates whether the exception was caused by a condition that was not under the control of the program. An external interrupt being handled via a task gate, for example, may have caused a task switch to an invalid TSS.

TABLE 7.4

Invalid TSS Conditions and Error Codes

Condition	Error Code
TSS descriptor limit < 43 (80286)	TSS id + EXT
TSS descriptor limit < 103 (80386/80486)	
Invalid LDT or LDT not present	LDT id + EXT
Stack segment selector outside table limit	SS id + EXT
Stack segment is not writable	SS id + EXT
Stack segment DPL ≠ CPL	SS id + EXT
Stack segment RPL ≠ CPL	SS id + EXT
Code segment is outside table limit	CS id + EXT
Code segment selector does not refer to code segment	CS id + EXT
Nonconforming code segment DPL ≠ new CPL	CS id + EXT
Conforming code segment DPL > new CPL	CS id + EXT
DS or ES segment selector outside table limit	DS or ES id + EXT
FS or GS segment selector outside table limit (80386/80486)	FS or GS id + EXT
DS or ES segments are not readable	DS or ES id + EXT
FS or GS segments are not readable (80386/80486)	FS or GS id + EXT

The fault can occur in the context of either the original or the new task. If the processor has not completely verified the presence of the new TSS, the error will be in the context of the old task. As soon as the existence of the new TSS is established, however, the task switch is considered complete: the task register (TR) is updated and, if the switch occurred because of a call or interrupt, the backlink will be set to point to the old task. Any errors detected after the task switch are handled in the context of the new task. This exception should be handled using a task gate to ensure that a valid TSS exists to process it.

Interrupt Bh (11): Segment Not Present When an attempt is made to access a segment that has the present bit of its descriptor cleared to zero, exception Bh will be generated. A segment load instruction with the CS, DS, ES, FS, or GS segment register as the target will cause this error. A load with the SS registers as the target, however, will cause a stack fault (interrupt Ch). An attempt to use a gate descriptor that is marked not-present or an attempt to load the local descriptor table register (LDTR) with the LLDT instruction will also generate this exception. Loading the LDTR during a task switch, however, will generate the invalid TSS exception (interrupt Ah) instead. To restart the instruction that caused the fault, the handler must make the segment present and return. The interrupted program will then resume execution.

If the segment not-present exception occurs during a task switch, the task switch will not be completed. The processor implements a task switch by first loading all the segment registers, then checking for valid values. If the exception occurs during one of these checks, the registers that have not been checked may not be valid for referencing memory. The handler for this exception, therefore, should not depend on being able to use the values found in any of the segment registers without causing another exception.

Before trying to resume the interrupted task, all segment registers should be checked for validity. If the fault is handled with a task switch, the switch back to the interrupted task will cause the processor to check all the registers as they are loaded from the TSS. Alternately, the handler may PUSH, then POP all the segment registers. The processor will check the validity of each segment register that is loaded with a POP. The TSS of the interrupted task may also be examined directly by the handler and the contents verified.

An error code is pushed onto the stack by this exception. If the exception was caused by an external event, the EXT bit in the error code will be set. If the code refers to an interrupt descriptor table (IDT) entry, the I-bit will be set.

Typically, this exception is used by operating system code to drive a virtual memory system at the segment level. Because gates do not have any definite association with segments, however, a not-present indicator in a gate descriptor does not indicate a swapped-out segment. Not-present gates may be used by an operating system to trigger exceptions.

Interrupt Ch (12): Stack Fault A stack fault exception is caused by two general conditions: a stack overflow or underflow or a reference to a stack segment that has its not-present bit set during an intertask or interlevel transition. Any operation that either implicitly or explicitly references the stack can cause this exception, for example, the stack-specific instructions such as PUSH, POP, ENTER, and LEAVE. References to memory that are resolved using the SS register, such as MOV SI,[BP+6], will also cause this exception. When the SS register is loaded with a segment selector that points to a descriptor that is valid and has its not-present bit set, the stack fault is issued, not the segment not-present exception (interrupt Bh).

When a stack fault is detected, an error code is always pushed onto the stack of the exception handler. The error code will contain a selector to the segment that caused the fault if the exception was due to a not-present segment or an overflow of the new stack during an interlevel call. (The two cases can be distinguished by checking the present bit in the descriptor.) All other error sources result in an error code of 0.

The return address pushed onto the exception handler's stack points to the instruction that needs to be restarted to resume execution. If the stack fault was caused by a task switch's attempt to load the stack segment, the pointer indicates the first instruction in the new task. Otherwise, the return address points to the instruction that caused the fault.

If the stack fault exception occurs during a task switch, the task switch will not be completed. The processor implements a task switch by first loading all the segment registers, then checking for valid values. If the exception occurs during one of these checks, the registers that have not been checked may not be valid for referencing memory. The handler for this exception, therefore, should not depend on being able to use the values found in any of the segment registers.

Before trying to resume the interrupted task, all segment registers should be checked for validity. If the fault is handled with a task switch, the switch back to the interrupted task will cause the processor to check all the registers as they are loaded from the TSS. Alternately, the handler may PUSH, then POP all the segment registers. The processor will check the validity of each segment register that is loaded with a POP. The TSS of the interrupted task may also be examined directly by the handler and the contents verified.

Interrupt Dh (13): General Protection　The general protection fault is issued for all protection violations that do not otherwise generate an exception. Examples of the types of errors that are covered by this umbrella exception are as follows:

- Exceeding segment limits using the CS, DS, ES, FS, or GS segment registers or when referencing a descriptor table.

- Memory accesses with the DS, ES, FS, or GS segment registers when the register contains a null selector. (This property is often used to detect such accesses.)

- Loading the DS, ES, FS, or GS segment registers with the descriptor of a system segment or a segment that is executable but not readable.

- Loading SS with the descriptor of a read-only, executable, or system segment. (If the faulty selector comes from a TSS during a task switch, however, interrupt Ah is generated.)

- Attempting to write into a read-only code or data segment, read from an execute-only segment, or execute a nonexecutable segment.

- Memory accesses with the DS, ES, FS, or GS segment registers when the register refers to a segment at a more trusted privilege level than the current privilege level.

- Switching to a busy task.

- Loading CR0 with PG=1 (paging enabled) and PE=0 (protection disabled). (80386/80486 only.)

- An interrupt or exception transferring control via a trap or interrupt gate to a privilege level other than 0 when operating in Virtual-86 mode. (80386/80486 only.)

- Exceeding the instruction length limit for the processor.

A general protection fault will always push an error code onto the stack of the exception handler. If the fault was detected when loading a descriptor, the error code will indicate the descriptor. The source of the descriptor may be an operand in the instruction, a selector from a gate that is the operand of the instruction, or a selector from a TSS involved in a task switch. For all other faults, an error code of 0 will be pushed.

In real mode, the 80286 and later processors will generate this exception if a memory operand does not fit within a segment. In real mode, this exception can occur only if a word operand is addressed at offset FFFFh. The values of CS and IP saved on the stack point to the first byte of the instruction causing the exception. No error code is pushed onto the stack.

Interrupt Eh (14): Page Fault   This fault is generated by the 80386 and later processors if an error is detected during linear to physical address translation. If paging is enabled (the PG bit in CR0 is set to 1), the page fault exception will be generated if either a page directory or page table entry that is needed for the address translation has its present bit cleared to 0 or if the privilege level of the current tasks is insufficient to access the indicated page.

The format of the error code pushed onto the stack of the exception handler is shown in Figure 7.2. The three fields defined in the error code are interpreted as follows:

P (present): The P field (bit 0) indicates whether the fault was caused by a not-present page (P=0) or by a page-level protection violation (P=1).

R/W (read/write): The R/W field (bit 1) indicates the type of access that caused the fault. A read fault is indicated by R/W=0 and a write fault by R/W=1.

U/S (user/supervisor): The U/S field (bit 2) indicates the mode the processor was operating in at the time of the exception. If U/S=0, the processor was in supervisor mode. If U/S=1, the processor was operating in user mode.

Page fault error code

Field	Value	Description
P	Ø	Fault caused by not-present page
	1	Fault caused by page-level protection violation
R/W	Ø	Fault caused by a read
	1	Fault caused by a write
U/S	Ø	Fault occurred in supervisor mode
	1	Fault occurred in user mode

The 32-bit linear address that was used for the access that caused the fault is stored by the processor in control register CR2. The exception handler will typically use this address to find the page directory and page table entries for the page. If another page fault could occur during exception handling, the value of CR2 should be saved on the stack.

During a task switch, the processor may access up to four segments. Any of these segments may cause a page fault. If the fault occurs when saving the state of the original task in the task's TSS or when reading the GDT to locate the TSS descriptor for the new task, the exception is generated in the context of the old task. If the fault occurs while reading the TSS or LDT of the new task, the exception is generated in the context of the new task and the saved values of CS and EIP point to the next instruction of the new task and *not* to the instruction that caused the task switch. An operating system that allows page faults during a task switch should invoke the page fault exception handler via a task gate.

A page fault is *not* temporarily masked by a move to the SS register as performed, for example, in the code fragment here:

```
MOV    AX,Stack_Segment
MOV    SS,AX
MOV    SP,Stack_Top
```

On the 80286 and earlier processors, all interrupts and exceptions are inhibited until after the instruction following the MOV SS,AX instruction has executed. (The defective version of the 8088 mentioned earlier in this chapter is the exception.) On the 80386 and later processors, however, this is not the case. If the MOV SP,Stack_Top instruction accesses memory, a page fault can be generated after SS has been set but before SP is set. The result is that SS:SP does not point to a valid stack. If the exception handler is invoked by a task gate or is a more privileged procedure, the invalid stack will not be used. If the handler is invoked by a trap or interrupt gate and the page fault occurs at the same privilege level as the handler, the invalid stack will be used.

Systems that implement paging and handle page faults *within* the faulting task with a trap or interrupt gate should ensure that code that executes at the same privilege level as the handler should use the LSS instruction to set a new stack. Normally, this situation will only be of concern within the operating system kernel.

Interrupt 10h (16): Coprocessor Error   The processor reports this exception when it detects a signal from the coprocessor that an error has occurred during the execution of a floating-point instruction. The exception is not generated until the execution of a subsequent WAIT or ESC coprocessor instruction. This exception will be generated only if the EM (emulate) bit in the machine status word (on the 80286) or control register CR0 (on the 80386 and later) is cleared to zero. The values of CS and IP saved on the stack point to the first byte of the ESC or WAIT instruction that caused the error to be recognized. The address of the failed instruction is saved by the coprocessor. (This error is covered in greater detail in Chapter 11.)

Interrupt 11h (17): Alignment Check   The alignment check fault is generated by the 80486 when an attempt is made to access unaligned operands. Alignment checking must be specifically enabled by setting both the AM bit in control register CR0 and the AC flag in the EFLAGS register. In addition, the processor must be operating with a current privilege level (CPL) of 3 (user level) in order for this fault to occur. (In real mode, CPL=0 and this fault cannot occur.) Table 7.5 gives the alignment requirements for the various data types.

TABLE 7.5

Data Alignment Check Requirements

Data Type	Operand Address Must Be a Multiple of *n* Bytes
Word	2
Doubleword	4
Short real	4
Long real	8
Temporary real	8
Segment selector	2
48-bit segmented pointer (mem32:16)	4
32-bit flat pointer (mem32)	4
32-bit segmented pointer (mem16:16)	2
48-bit pseudo descriptor (mem16:32)	4*
FSTENV/FLDENV save area	2 or 4, depending on operand size
FSAVE/FRSTOR save area	2 or 4, depending on operand size
Bit string	4

* In user mode, a 48-bit pseudo descriptor should be aligned at an odd word address (4x+2) to avoid generating an alignment-check fault.

Interrupts in Real Mode

In real mode, the processor transfers control to interrupt and exception handlers using a jump table. This table, known as the interrupt vector table (IVT), is 400h bytes long and begins at physical memory address 0. The table contains a four-byte entry for each possible interrupt type (0 through FFh). The table entries are far pointers to the entry points of the handlers. The layout of the IVT and its entries is shown in Figure 7.3.

FIGURE 7.3

The real mode interrupt vector table

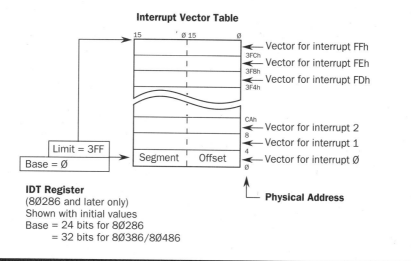

Beginning with the 80286 processor, the location and size of the IVT are determined from the contents of the interrupt descriptor table register (IDTR). When initialized, the processor is operating in real mode and the IDTR register is set to describe an IVT located at address 0 with a length of 400h bytes—compatible with the 8086. The LIDT (load interrupt descriptor table register) instruction is valid in real mode, however, and can be used to change these default values. This is usually done as part of the setup for protected mode. If the size of the IVT has been reduced and an interrupt occurs that is beyond the limit of the IDT, a double-fault exception (interrupt 8) is generated.

When an INTR interrupt is recognized, the processor will issue two INTA bus cycles to retrieve the type (number) of the interrupt. For processor exceptions, software interrupts, and the NMI, the interrupt number is already known, so no bus cycles are initiated. The processor scales the interrupt type by 4 to form an index into the table.

As part of the transfer mechanism, the processor pushes, in order, values for the FLAGS, CS, and IP registers onto the stack. (In 32-bit mode, the EFLAGS, CS, and EIP registers are pushed.) The values pushed for these registers depend on the type of interrupt being processed. Traps will push the CS:IP of the instruction following the one that caused the trap. Faults push the CS:IP of the instruction that caused the fault, allowing the problem to be diagnosed and the instruction possibly restarted. Next, the single-step Trap flag (TF) and Interrupt flag (IF) in the FLAGS register are cleared. Finally, the CS and IP registers are loaded with values taken from the IVT. Exceptions in real mode do not push error codes onto the stack.

The values of the CS, IP, and FLAGS registers are automatically saved by the interrupt mechanism. The interrupt handler is responsible for not altering any other registers or otherwise corrupting the state of the processor. If done so, the interrupt will be transparent to the underlying application and executing an IRET (return from interrupt) instruction will allow the application to resume execution.

Interrupts in Protected Mode

Interrupt handling in protected mode is very similar to interrupt handling in real mode. External interrupts, exceptions, and software interrupts occur and must be handled by service routines. In protected mode, there are more possible processor exceptions—those generated by protection violations, virtual memory implementations, or paging systems, for example. Interrupts may also invoke a task switch. This section describes interrupts and interrupt handling in protected mode.

The Interrupt Descriptor Table

The interrupt descriptor table (IDT) structure has a function that is analogous to the interrupt vector table used when the processor is operating in real mode. The interrupt type is scaled appropriately and used as an index into the table. The entry for each interrupt specifies where the handler for that interrupt is located. The IDT is an array of eight-byte interrupt descriptors, called gates, and may contain up to 256 entries, one for each interrupt type. (The IDT may actually contain more entries, but these will never be accessed by the interrupt mechanism.) The structure of the IDT is illustrated in Figure 7.4.

FIGURE 7.4

Protected mode interrupt descriptor table

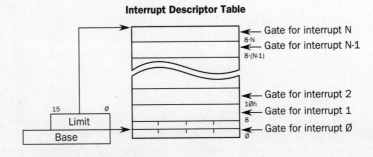

IDT Register

Base = 24 bits for 80286
     = 32 bits for 80386/80486

The processor locates the IDT using the contents of the interrupt descriptor table register (IDTR). The register holds both the base address of the start of the table and its limit; both values are specified in bytes. If the processor were capable of swapping the IDT segment out of memory, it would not then be able to determine where to direct the segment not-present exception in order to reload it! The IDT, therefore, *must* be located in physical memory, although the address contained in the IDTR may point anywhere within the physical memory space of the processor.

The IDT does not need to contain an entry for all 256 interrupts. The first entry in the table will always correspond to interrupt type 0, but the upper entry may be set using the limit field of the IDTR. Entries that are present in the table but are unused may be identified by placing a 0 in the access rights byte of the descriptor. If an attempt is made to access a descriptor that would be past the limit of the table or has a 0 in its access rights byte, a general protection fault is generated and an error code is pushed onto the stack. Bit 1 of the error code will be set to 1, bit 2 will be 0. The 14 high-order bits will contain the index into the IDT for the gate that caused the exception.

The IDTR is accessed using the LIDT (load IDT register) and SIDT (store IDT register) processor instructions. Both instructions take one operand, the effective address of six contiguous bytes of memory. If the processor is an 80286 the base address is specified using the low-order 24 bits of the base address memory operand. The high-order 8 bits are ignored by the LIDT instruction and are stored as 1s by the SIDT instruction.

On the 80386 and later processors, the operation of SIDT and LIDT is dependent on the current operand size. If the operand size is 16 bits, then the LIDT loads only the low-order 24 bits of the base address memory operand; the upper 8 bits of the base address field in the IDTR are cleared to zero. Similarly, SIDT will copy the values of the low-order 24 bits of the base address field to the low-order 24 bits of the base address memory operand and write zeros in the high-order 8 bits. If the operand size is 32 bits, then all 32 bits of the memory operand will be loaded or written.

An interrupt that references a descriptor beyond the limit of the IDT will cause the processor to enter shutdown state, and no further interrupts or exceptions will be processed. A signal on either the RESET or NMI lines can bring the processor out of shutdown if no errors occur while handling the NMI. If errors occur, only RESET can exit shutdown. An NMI input will not bring the processor out of protected mode, while RESET will. The shutdown is signaled by the processor with a special bus operation. External hardware can use this signal to generate an NMI or take other appropriate action.

Each descriptor entry in the IDT may contain one of three special types of descriptors called the interrupt, trap, and task gates. Figure 7.5 shows the format of these gates, which are described in detail below.

Interrupt Gates and Trap Gates

Interrupt gates and trap gates both invoke interrupt procedures and are distinguished by whether the Interrupt flag (IF) will be cleared upon entry to the handler. (In real mode, IF is always cleared, disabling maskable interrupts.) An interrupt gate points to a procedure that will be entered with interrupts disabled (IF=0). A trap gate points to a procedure that will be entered with the Interrupt flag *unchanged*.

FIGURE 7.5

Interrupt descriptor formats

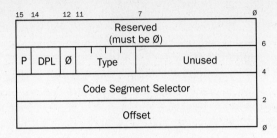

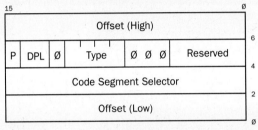

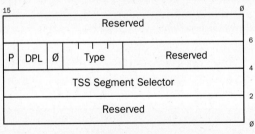

Field	Description
P	Present
DPL	Descriptor privilege level
Type	Value of the Type field determines the gate type as follows:

Value	Gate type
Ø1Ø1b	Task gate
Ø11Øb	16-bit (8Ø286) interrupt gate
Ø111b	16-bit (8Ø286) trap gate
111Øb	16-bit (8Ø386/8Ø486) interrupt gate
1111b	16-bit (8Ø386/8Ø486) trap gate

When either of these gates is used, the single-step Trap flag (TF) will also be cleared to prevent debugging from delaying interrupt response. The old nested task (NT) state is also saved on the stack (when the FLAGS register is pushed) and the NT flag is cleared. Procedures pointed to by either an interrupt or trap gate are processed in the context of the current task.

The transfer mechanism of an interrupt or trap gate is similar to the processing of interrupts in real mode and the FLAGS register and the return address are pushed onto the stack of the interrupt handler. When the handler is finished, control is returned to the interrupted program using an IRET (return from interrupt) instruction. If an error code was pushed, the interrupt handler is responsible for removing it. If an interrupt gate is used, it must have a current privilege level that is more privileged than the current I/O privilege level (CPL < IOPL) in order for IRET to be able to change the value of IF and reenable interrupts. TF is also restored by IRET.

Interrupt and trap gates have the same structure as call gates. (Call gates are discussed in more detail in Chapter 15.) The gate contains a segment selector and offset that point to the code segment of an interrupt handler. On the 80286, the offset is 16 bits. On the 80386 and later processors, the offset is 32 bits. The access right byte contains the present (P) bit, the descriptor privilege level (DPL), and the type identifier that distinguishes interrupt gates from trap gates. The fifth byte of the descriptor is not used by interrupt or trap gates and corresponds to the parameter word count field of the call gate.

Protection Considerations   A privilege level transition may occur when passing control to a nonconforming code segment. The DPL of the target code segment determines the new current privilege level (CPL). The DPL of the new nonconforming code segment must be numerically less than or equal to (have the same or greater privilege as) the CPL. If the new segment is conforming, no privilege transition occurs and a general protection exception (Dh) will be generated if DPL > CPL.

If an increase in privilege level is required to handle the interrupt, a stack switch will take place, with the new stack being loaded from the task state segment (TSS) and the old stack pointer (SP or ESP) saved on the new stack. Figure 7.6 shows what the stack of the exception handler would look like on the 80286 processor. It is assumed that the exception pushes an error code. Examples are shown for cases with and without a change in privilege level. Note that both the error code and the return address are pushed onto the stack of the handler. (This is not the case if a task gate is used as discussed later in this section.) Figure 7.7 shows the same information for a 32-bit stack, such as might be used on the 80386 and later processors.

The DPL in the gates in the IDT controls access to interrupts made with the INT *n* and INT 3 (opcode CCh) instructions. The CPL must be at least as privileged as the DPL to access these interrupts. If not, a general protection exception (interrupt Dh) is issued with an error code that identifies the gate that generated the exception. Gates corresponding to exceptions (generated by the processor) and external interrupts are accessed without regard to the CPL of the underlying application.

FIGURE 7.6

16-bit stack contents after an exception with error code for interrupt or trap gates

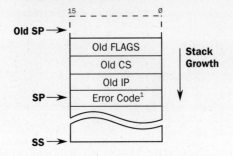

Stack Without Privilege Transition

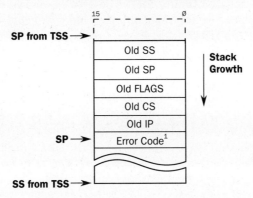

Stack with Privilege Transition

[1] Not pushed if no error code is generated

Task Gates

In some situations, it may be advantageous to have an interrupt or exception provoke a task switch. If the IDT entry for the interrupt contains a task gate descriptor, a task switch will be performed by the processor when the interrupt is recognized. The format of a task gate is shown in Figure 7.5.

Interrupt handling by a task gate differs significantly from using either a trap or interrupt gate. All of the processor's registers are saved as part of the task switch mechanism. Only the FLAGS (or EFLAGS), CS, and IP (or EIP) registers are saved by an interrupt or trap gate. The new task is also completely isolated from the task that was interrupted. The handler is not limited by the privilege level of the interrupted task and executes in a separate address space. Once the task state segment (TSS) selector is retrieved from the descriptor in the IDT corresponding to the interrupt, the task switch proceeds normally. (Task switches are described in more detail in Chapter 15.) Task gates are subject to the same scrutiny regarding privilege and presence as other gates.

FIGURE 7.7

32-bit stack contents after an exception with error code for interrupt or trap gates

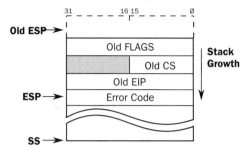

Stack Without Privilege Transition

| 31 | 16 15 | Ø |

Old ESP →

Old FLAGS

Old CS

Old EIP

ESP → Error Code

Stack Growth

SS →

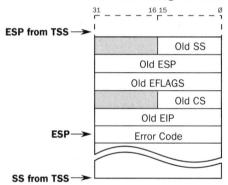

Stack with Privilege Transition

| 31 | 16 15 | Ø |

ESP from TSS →

Old SS

Old ESP

Old EFLAGS

Old CS

Old EIP

ESP → Error Code

SS from TSS →

When the task switch is performed, the nested task (NT) bit is set in the FLAGS register of the new task and the TSS selector of the interrupted task is saved in the backlink field of the new TSS. To return to the interrupted task, the handler executes an IRET. Because NT is set, the IRET instruction will cause another task switch—this time back to the original task.

When the handler executes an IRET, its task state is saved in its TSS. Because the state of the handler is saved, a subsequent task switch to the handler will *restart* the handler and control will be transferred to the first instruction that follows IRET. An interrupt task thus resumes execution each time it is called, while an interrupt procedure (invoked with an interrupt or task gate) starts executing at the beginning of the procedure when it is called. In either case the interrupted task is resumed where it was interrupted. Once an interrupt task gets control, its TSS is marked busy. If another of the same interrupt type occurs, a general protection exception (Dh) will occur if the task gate is accessed.

Some exceptions, by the nature of the errors they are reporting, require the use of a task gate to ensure that a valid task is available to handle the exception. The invalid TSS exception (interrupt Ah), for example, can be generated by an error in either the original or new TSS during a task switch. A task gate should also be used to ensure a valid task exists to handle the double-fault interrupt (interrupt 8).

Interrupt Priorities

When simultaneous external interrupts occur, the programmable interrupt controller is responsible for selecting the highest priority interrupt and passing it on to the processor via the INTR line. Internally, the processor must perform a similar action when multiple simultaneous interrupt requests are received. The internal priorities of the various interrupt types have changed between processors, most noticeably between the 8086 and later processors.

Note that in the explanations that follow, the term interrupt is used in the general sense to refer to all processor generated exceptions and software interrupts. An interrupt generated by a request on either the NMI or INTR lines is called an external interrupt. The NMI, processor exceptions, and software interrupts are collectively called *unmaskable* interrupts.

8086/8088

On the 8086 and 8088 processors, the prioritization of multiple, simultaneous interrupts and exceptions is dynamic and context sensitive. The same interrupt will be handled differently depending on the setting of the Trap flag (TF) and Interrupt flag (IF) and which other interrupt or interrupts are pending at the time. Because no general rules can be formulated, the interrupt handling sequences can, at best, be presented as a series of special cases in this section.

In general, when simultaneous interrupt requests are received and well-behaved interrupt handlers are in place, the interrupt with the highest priority is *recognized* first and *serviced* last. The processor will transfer control first to the handler for the higher-priority interrupt. Once the handler has control, it will allow the lower-priority interrupt to be recognized by the processor and control will be transferred to the second handler. The service routine for the lower-priority interrupt will thus execute first, then return control (via IRET) to the handler of the higher-priority interrupt. This general behavior will not hold for certain combinations of interrupts or if the IF flag is left disabled by the interrupt handlers.

Because a processor fault occurs *within* the instruction being executed, it is always recognized first, regardless of what other interrupt requests may be pending. Thus if a single-step trap is pending and a request is received over either or both of the NMI and INTR lines during the execution of an instruction that causes a processor exception (such as the divide error), the exception will be processed first.

Any unmaskable interrupt (which includes the NMI, software interrupts, and processor exceptions) has a higher priority than an external interrupt received over the INTR line. If an unmaskable interrupt request is received simultaneously with an INTR request, control will be transferred to the unmaskable interrupt handler with the IF flag cleared and INTR interrupts disabled. The INTR request will not be recognized until the unmaskable interrupt handler sets IF=1 or executes an IRET instruction (assuming that IF was set in the interrupted task).

If an INTR (maskable) interrupt request is detected simultaneously with an unmaskable interrupt (NMI, single-step, exceptions, and software interrupts), the clearing of the IF by the interrupt transfer mechanism will mask INTR. This makes INTR effectively the lowest-priority interrupt and it will be serviced only after all other interrupts have been serviced. To avoid this situation, other interrupt handlers must reenable interrupts when they get control.

The unmaskable interrupts may be further divided into four categories: the single-step trap, the NMI, processor faults, and other processor traps. If the single-step trap and one of either the NMI or another trap is pending, the single-step trap will have the higher priority. If the NMI and a trap other than single-step is pending, the NMI will have higher priority. If, however, an NMI, single-step, and another trap are pending, the NMI will have the highest priority, followed by processor traps except single-step, with the single-step trap having the lowest priority.

A program that is being debugged using the single-step trap usually will be run with interrupts disabled. Upon entry to the single-step handler, interrupts will be enabled, allowing any pending INTR requests to be serviced. This procedure allows external interrupts to be serviced quickly despite single-stepping.

If an NMI is received while single-stepping a program, however, the debugger should return immediately to allow the NMI to be serviced. The debugger will then regain control after the next program instruction is executed. The net effect is that single-step is disabled for one instruction. To check that control has been passed to the single-step handler from the NMI handler, examine the code at the CS:IP saved on the stack by the single-step trap.

Figure 7.8 shows the sequence of events that occurs when a program is single-stepped. Figure 7.9 illustrates what happens when single-stepping is enabled and either an NMI or INTR (with interrupts enabled) is received during the execution of an instruction. Finally, Figure 7.10 shows what happens when single-stepping is enabled and an NMI, INTR, and processor fault occur simultaneously.

80286 and Later Processors

The priority of the single-step trap exception is different on the 80286 and later processors. The change was made to prevent an external interrupt (INTR or NMI) from being single-stepped if it occurred while single-stepping through a program. The 80286 and later processors will still single-step through an interrupt handler invoked with a software interrupt or by a processor exception.

When operating in real mode, any interrupt or exception will automatically clear the Interrupt flag (IF), masking any further INTR requests until set by an IRET or manually. This is the same procedure as for the 8086. In protected mode, however, the task gate assigned to the interrupt service routine specifies whether INTR requests are to be masked or enabled during the handler.

FIGURE 7.8

Single-stepping on the 8086 and 8088

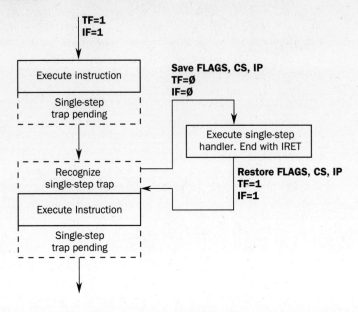

FIGURE 7.9

Simultaneous single-step and NMI on the 8086 and 8088

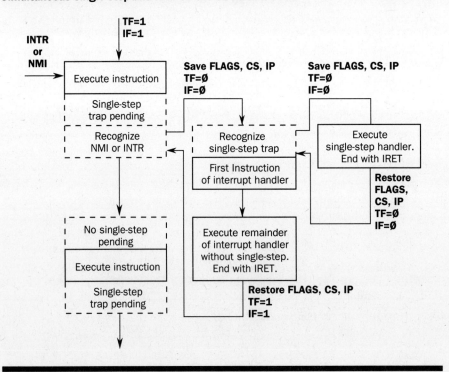

FIGURE 7.10

Simultaneous single-step, INTR, fault, and NMI on the 8086 and 8088

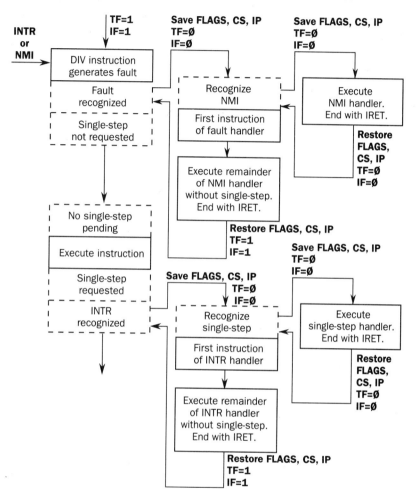

If more than one exception or interrupt is pending at an interrupt boundary, the processor will dispatch them in a well-defined order. The priority of interrupts varies somewhat among processors and they will be recognized in the order shown in Table 7.6. The interrupts are shown with the first recognized at the top of the list (number 1) and last recognized at the bottom of the list.

The processor will first recognize a pending exception or interrupt from the class with the highest priority. Execution is then transferred to the first instruction of the interrupt handler. Lower-priority exceptions are discarded, but lower-priority interrupts are held pending. When the interrupt handler restarts the failed instruction, any discarded exceptions will be reissued if appropriate.

TABLE 7.6	

Interrupt Priorities for the 80286 and Later Processors

80286

1	Processor faults and aborts (other than listed below)
2	Processor traps (other than listed below)
3	Single-step trap (interrupt 1)
4	NMI (interrupt 2)
5	Coprocessor segment overrun (interrupt 9)
6	INTR (all)

80386

1	Processor fault or abort (other than listed below)
2	Processor trap (other than listed below)
3	Single-step trap (interrupt 1)
4	Debug trap from the previous instruction
5	Debug fault for the next instruction
6	NMI (interrupt 2)
7	INTR (all)

80486

1	Debug trap from the previous instruction
2	Debug fault for the next instruction
3	NMI (interrupt 2)
4	INTR (all)
5	Processor fault from fetching next instruction (interrupt Bh or Dh)
6	Processor fault from instruction decoding (interrupt 6, 7, or Dh)
7	Exception if ESC instruction and TS and MP bits in CRØ set (interrupt 10h)
8	Exception if WAIT or ESC and EM or TS bits of CRØ set (interrupt 10h)
9	Exception (asserted on ERROR# line)
10	Processor fault for memory operands (interrupt Bh, Ch, or Dh)
11	Alignment fault for memory operands (interrupt 11h)
12	Page fault for memory operands (interrupt Eh)

Once inside the service routine for the NMI, the coprocessor segment over-run exception and additional NMIs are masked by the processor until an IRET instruction has been executed or the CPU is reset. An additional NMI received while NMIs are masked will be latched by the processor and services after the execution of an IRET. Only one additional NMI can be saved. In real mode, all INTR requests are also masked when IF is cleared to 0 during the transfer.

COMBINING 16-BIT AND 32-BIT CODE

THE 80386 AND 80486 PROCESSORS HAVE BEEN DESIGNED AS FULL 32-BIT PROCESsors. They implement a 32-bit internal architecture, have 32-bit general registers, and support operations on 32-bit data types. Their native mode of operation is 32-bit protected mode. When initialized, however, the processors emulate the 16-bit architecture of the 8086 and 8088 and support real mode operation. Applications written for the 16-bit protected mode architecture of the 80286 can also be accommodated without change. If code written for the older 16-bit processors is to be run in a system designed to support 32-bit operation, the potential interface problems must be addressed.

In this chapter, the mechanics of control transfer that must be considered when interfacing 16-bit and 32-bit code on the 80386 and 80486 processors will be discussed. The information presented here is applicable only to the 80386 and 80486, the members of the 80x86 family that support 32-bit operations. Although some of the techniques and properties discussed are applicable to real mode operation, they are primarily aimed at protected mode operations.

Although this is a short chapter, the context in which this material is applicable (mixed 16-bit and 32-bit segments) is quite complex. The concepts involved are straightforward, but mixing code size remains an advanced problem that is typically encountered only by systems programmers. A thorough working knowledge of other processor topics is a prerequisite for the material in this chapter.

16-bit and 32-bit Processor Architecture

In real mode, the processor's operation is an emulation of the 16-bit architecture and operation of the 8086. In protected mode, however, the full 32-bit architecture of the processor is available. The 80386 and 80486 processors both support execution of protected mode software that has been designed to use either a 16-bit or a 32-bit architecture. In addition, they provide several mechanisms that allow programs written for either segment size type to use a mixed architectural model as described below.

The eight general-purpose registers may be addressed as both 16-bit and 32-bit operands. In addition, any general-purpose register may hold a 16-bit or 32-bit effective address, allowing access to up to four gigabytes of memory per segment. To improve efficiency, default typing for code and stack segments allows the dominant address and operand size to be selected automatically during program execution and stack access. The register and effective address size are not fixed, however, and prefix instructions are provided that allow 16-bit or 32-bit operands or effective addresses to be generated, regardless of the mode. The operand size for control transfers is specified by the gate, not the default type of the segment, allowing transfers to be made among different segment sizes. This support includes call gates, interrupt gates, and trap gates.

Each of these mechanisms is discussed in this section as it pertains to combining both 16-bit and 32-bit code in a single environment.

Establishing Segment Type

In protected mode, segments are distinguished by the type of information they contain. Classifying a segment as 16-bit or 32-bit, therefore, may be seen as adding another characteristic to a segment that is already strictly typed. A segment is identified as being either 16-bit or 32-bit by the value of its attribute bit in its segment descriptor. If either the D (default) bit or B (big) bit is set, the segment is interpreted as a 32-bit segment. If neither bit is set, the processor interprets the segment as 16-bit. (Segment descriptors are discussed in detail in Chapter 15.)

(Strictly speaking, the segment size bits are not applicable in real mode or Virtual-86 mode because those modes do not use segment descriptors. When switching the processor from protected mode to real mode, Intel documentation notes that segments should be created that contain values *appropriate* to real mode execution. In other words, they should be byte granular and have a limit of FFFFh (64k). The documentation also notes that if the segment registers are not reloaded before switching to real mode, execution will continue after the switch using the last descriptors that were loaded in protected mode. Thus the segments created for the real mode transition could be page granular and have a limit greater than 64k. If this is done, the real mode program would be able to directly address up to four gigabytes of memory using the address size prefix to generate 32-bit effective addresses.)

The D bit is used to identify the default operand and address sizes that are used within a code segment. A code segment with D=0 is a 16-bit segment and, by default, all operands and effective addresses will be 16 bits. (This is the default size for full-size operands and addresses. It does not affect the use of byte operands and special data types such as pointers, which are specified in the instruction encoding and are addressable in either mode.) A code segment with its D bit set to 1 will be a 32-bit segment and the default size for both operands and effective addresses will be 32 bits.

Stack segments represent a subset of the more general class of data segments. While a data segment may be read-only, a stack segment must be both readable and writable. For stack segments, the B bit determines the default address size for instructions that use the stack implicitly. If B=0, the stack will be a 16-bit stack and the SP register will be used for stack addressing. If B=1, the stack will be a 32-bit stack and use the ESP register for addressing.

Code Segments

A code segment contains instructions that direct the operation of the processor. The vast majority of processor instructions access either memory, the general registers, or both. The interpretation of these instructions is dependent on whether the code segment is a 16-bit or a 32-bit segment.

In code segments, the default type of the segment establishes the rules by which the processor calculates the size of operands and the size of effective address offsets. In effect, the segment type is used as an additional encoding field for certain instructions, and the segment type directly modifies their functions. Ideally, the segment size should be chosen so it represents the default size for most of the operations in the code, minimizing the number of override prefixes generated. The operand size prefix and address size prefix may be employed to reverse the default for either condition for a single instruction. (Instruction encoding and instruction prefixes are discussed in Chapter 6.)

By default, when executing in a 16-bit code segment, the processor interprets addresses and operands as if it were running in real mode. The size of all general register and data references is controlled by the *s* bit in the instruction encoding and will be either 8 bits or 16 bits. The effective address offset is calculated as a 16-bit quantity for all memory references using the same procedure as in real mode and allowing up to 64k of data to be addressed. The maximum size of the code segment is limited to 64k, but unlike real mode, the length of the segment may be less than 64k.

When executing in a 32-bit code segment, the processor will use its 32-bit extended encoding scheme. The size of all general register and data references is either 8 bits or 32 bits as controlled by the *s* bit in the instruction encoding. All memory references will be performed with a 32-bit effective address offset, allowing addressing of up to four gigabytes per segment. The size of the code segment itself may also be up to four gigabytes.

Operand and Address Size   Table 8.1 shows how both 16-bit and 32-bit code segments interpret the instruction MOV *accumulator,[source_index]*. In this example, the accumulator will be either the AX or EAX register and the source is a memory operand indirectly addressed through the SI or ESI register. Note that the instructions must be encoded according to the rules presented in Chapter 6.

TABLE 8.1

Operand and Address Interpretation in 16-bit and 32-bit Code Segments

	Code Segment Type	
	16-bit (D=Ø)	32-bit (D=1)
Default operation	MOV AX,[SI]	MOV EAX,[ESI]
With operand size prefix	MOV EAX,[SI]	MOV AX,[ESI]
With address size prefix	MOV AX,[ESI]	MOV EAX,[SI]
Address size and operand size prefixes	MOV EAX,[ESI]	MOV AX,[SI]

In 16-bit mode, the default operation is to form a 16-bit effective address using the contents of the SI register as a pointer, then retrieve a 16-bit operand from that address and place it in the AX register as shown. The second column shows that the same instruction, interpreted in a 32-bit segment, would move a 32-bit operand located at the 32-bit effective address, specified by the contents of the ESI register, to the EAX register. The remaining rows of the table show how the operand and address size prefixes can be used to change the interpretation of the instruction.

Pointer Size The size of the address used by near and far pointers is also dependent on the type of the code segment in which they are generated. Table 8.2 shows the size and format that will be used for near and far pointers in the two segment types. The 8-bit signed relative displacement used in the short form of the JMP instruction is available in either segment type.

TABLE 8.2

Pointer Types in 16-bit and 32-bit Code Segments

	Code Segment Type	
Pointer Type	16-bit (D=Ø)	32-bit (D=1)
Near	16-bit unsigned offset *off16*	32-bit unsigned offset *off32*
Far	32-bit segmented *seg16:off16*	48-bit segmented *seg16:off32*

Stack Segments

Stack segments may also be classified as 16-bit or 32-bit segments. Stack segments, however, are not executable and do not contain instructions. Consequently, they do not contain any references to effective addresses or operand size. The stack segment type comes into play, however, when executing instructions that make *implicit* use of the stack and is the *only* factor that determines whether the SP or ESP register will be used as the stack pointer. Examples of implicit stack instructions include PUSH, POP, CALL, RET, INT, and IRET. Processor exceptions and external interrupts will also reference the stack using the default pointer.

Explicit references to memory using the SP or ESP register, on the other hand, are resolved relative to the stack segment and are interpreted as any other memory address operation. The SP or ESP register is treated simply as an effective address offset relative to the stack segment. Whether SP or ESP is used in the effective address calculation is independent of the stack segment type and is dependent only on the code segment type and whether the address size prefix is used. *An operand or address size prefix used before an implicit stack operation has no influence on the stack pointer used for stack addressing.*

16-bit Stack Segments A 16-bit stack segment type implies the use of the 16-bit SP register as the stack pointer by all stack instructions. The smallest data type that can be pushed onto or popped from the stack is a word, just as when the processor is operating in real mode. A 16-bit stack type limits stack operations only in that the pointer is 16 bits and the segment size cannot exceed 64k.

Note that a 16-bit stack is fully compatible with 32-bit operands. When a 32-bit operand is pushed onto a 16-bit stack, for example, the high-order 16 bits of the operand are pushed, then the low-order 16 bits of the operand are pushed. The effect is that the high-order word of the operand is at the higher stack address. Popping a 32-bit operand off the stack reverses the procedure.

A 16-bit stack can be shared by both 16-bit and 32-bit code segments. As the code in each segment requires, implicit stack operations will push or pop 16-bit or 32-bit operands. The stack pointer will be the SP register for all implicit stack operations. The stack address size of implicit stack references is controlled by the type of the stack segment, not the code segment type.

32-bit Stack Segments A stack segment may also be created with a default address size of 32 bits and will use the ESP extended stack pointer register for all implicit operations. Like other 32-bit segments, a 32-bit stack segment can be up to four gigabytes in length. Both word and doubleword operands may be pushed onto or popped from a 32-bit stack. A 32-bit stack operation with a 16-bit operand will change the value of the ESP register by 2. A stack operation with a 32-bit operand will change ESP by 4.

Although a 32-bit stack may be shared by both 16-bit and 32-bit code segments, the stack pointer is determined by the type of the stack segment and not the type of the code segment using the stack. Both the 16-bit and the newer 32-bit code segments will use the ESP pointer for implicit stack references. If the 16-bit code was written without knowledge of the 32-bit registers, however, problems may occur because the code is not aware of the 32-bit ESP pointer that will be used for stack addressing.

Using a 32-bit stack, the PUSH AX instruction, executing in a 16-bit code segment, could write to the stack anywhere within its possible four gigabyte limit. This would seem to indicate that code that was written for a pure 16-bit environment could access more than 64k of data. This, however, is not the case. All explicit references to the stack by the 16-bit code segment would use the SP register; data would be pushed and popped using ESP, but would only be addressed using SP. For example, examine the following code fragment, assuming that the stack is a 32-bit segment and ESP=18148h.

```
PUSH    AX          ;Save AX on the stack
                    ; [ESP-2]=AX
                    ; ESP=ESP-2 (=18146h)
PUSH    BP          ;Save BP on the stack
                    ; [ESP-2]=BP
                    ; ESP=ESP-2 (=18144h)
MOV     BP,SP       ;Create a stack frame with
                    ; the wrong pointer
                    ; BP=SP=8144h (ESP MOD 64k)
MOV     CX,[BP+2]   ;Try to address AX we pushed earlier
                    ; but it's not at 8146h
```

In this example, the implicit references to the stack use ESP, but the explicit references use SP. Simply, if a stack is to be shared by a 16-bit and 32-bit segment, the stack pointer must point to the lower 64k of the segment or any explicit reference to the stack segment by the 16-bit code will be incorrect. (The explicit reference could, of course, be made into a 32-bit reference using the address size prefix. Older 16-bit code will not contain the prefix, and if the code could be modified to include the prefix, it would be worthwhile to rewrite it as a full 32-bit procedure.)

Data Segments

Data segments hold data. Since data types vary from a single byte to ten-byte reals to bit strings up to four gigabits long, it makes no sense to speak of a 16-bit or 32-bit data segment. A data segment, then, cannot strictly be said to have a type. Access to data is a function of the instruction doing the addressing, not the segment in which the data resides.

Stack segments, as previously discussed, are a special class of data segments. Stack segments must allow reading and writing and the type (specified by the B bit in the descriptor) is used to determine the default pointer (SP or ESP) used by implicit stack operations.

Control Transfer Between Segment Types

The programming considerations of the mechanics that govern the operation of 16-bit and 32-bit procedures must also be extended to control transfer operations. In particular, programmers must be concerned with return addresses larger than 16 bits, use of the stack, and matching of the operand type used by CALL/RET and INT/IRET instruction pairs. Each of these problems and possible solutions are discussed below.

Direct Transfers

Control transfers that do not use gates use a pointer to identify the next instruction to be executed. When transferring control between code segments of a different default size, the size of the pointer is established by the code segment that *executes* the transfer. The D bit, combined with an operand size prefix if present, determines whether the pointer uses a 16-bit or a 32-bit offset.

A JMP, CALL, or RET instruction that is executed in a 32-bit code segment can always transfer control to an address in either a 16-bit or a 32-bit code segment. If control is transferred to another 32-bit procedure, the EIP register will be loaded with the new 32-bit offset value. If control is transferred to a 16-bit procedure, the 16-bit offset will be ANDed with 0000FFFFh, and then loaded into the EIP register.

If a control transfer to a 32-bit code segment originates in a 16-bit segment, the target of the transfer must be within the first 64k of the new segment; an unmodified 16-bit procedure cannot transfer control to an offset greater than FFFFh because it is not addressable using the IP register. The transfer can be performed, however, if an operand size prefix is used before the instruction, creating a 32-bit pointer.

Stack Management   The CALL and RET instructions assume the use of the stack as part of their control transfer mechanism. These instructions, however, manage the stack differently depending on whether they are executed in a 16-bit or a 32-bit mode. The operand size used for a matching CALL and RET must be the same, or the transfer will not be performed correctly.

A CALL instruction, executed with a 16-bit operand size, will push only 16-bit register values onto the stack. If executed with a 32-bit operand size, the CALL instruction will push 32-bit register values onto the stack. The corresponding RET instruction must use the same operand size or incorrect values will be restored to the IP/EIP register and, for far returns, the CS register. Note that calls between privilege levels will also push the SP or ESP register, as determined by the operand size attribute used by the instruction. Figure 8.1 illustrates the contents of the stack after a 16-bit call and a 32-bit call with no parameters. The SS and SP/ESP registers are pushed only for interlevel calls.

FIGURE 8.1

Stack contents after 16-bit and 32-bit far calls

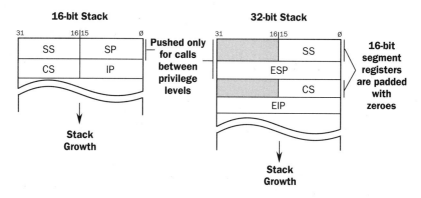

Control Transfers Through Gates

The operand size in effect for a CALL instruction is specified by the D bit and modified by an operand size prefix, if present. This operand size normally determines the size of the operands that are pushed onto the stack. If, however, the segment selector provided as part of the target address points to a gate descriptor, the type of the call is determined solely by the type of the gate. A CALL through a 16-bit gate (i.e., an 80286 gate) will always use a 16-bit operand size. A CALL through a 32-bit gate will use a 32-bit operand size. The gate itself contains the offset of the target procedure. A 32-bit gate, for example, will contain a 32-bit offset. Consequently, a 16-bit procedure can transfer control to any 32-bit offset—even one greater than 64k—by using a call gate.

When a 32-bit gate is created with the intention of having it called from 16-bit procedures, the difference in how parameters are handled must be considered. For a 16-bit gate, the count field of the gate descriptor specifies the number of 16-bit words that are to be copied to the new stack frame. For a 32-bit gate, the count specifies the number of doublewords to be copied. For a 16-bit call to operate properly with a 32-bit gate, the number of words to be copied must be even so that it can be specified as the equivalent number of doublewords.

A control transfer initiated by an interrupt or exception will always use a gate. As with other gate transfers, the operand size used is determined by the gate descriptor. Interrupt gate descriptors are located in the interrupt descriptor table (IDT) and may be either 16-bit or 32-bit gates.

An interrupt that transfers control to an interrupt handler via a 32-bit gate can be used to interrupt either 16-bit or 32-bit procedures. In either case, the correct values for CS and IP/EIP will be saved. A 16-bit gate may be successfully used to handle an interrupt that occurs while executing a 16-bit procedure. If, however, a 32-bit procedure is executing with an EIP greater than FFFFh and an interrupt transfers control to a 16-bit handler, the handler will not be able to properly save the return address to the 32-bit procedure.

9 DEBUGGING

DEBUGGING IS THE PROCESS OF ANALYZING AND REMOVING BUGS FROM A program or from a hardware design—a familiar practice for many of us. The tools we use to accomplish this are called debuggers, and vary greatly in complexity. At the high end of the scale are sophisticated debuggers that rely on special hardware to control execution of the processor, monitoring its signals and controlling its operation directly. They are able to analyze system problems that may keep the processor from executing any software at all. Simple software-based debuggers, on the other hand, are used when the hardware system is stable, but a program may not be. Software debuggers rely on the support built into the processor for their operation.

This chapter does not teach how to debug or how to design and write a debugger. Instead, it discusses the features built into the 80x86 family specifically to support software debugging. This chapter will cover the features available family-wide as well as the new registers, exceptions, and flags built into the 80386 and 80486 processors that give them true hardware support for debuggers and in-program debugging.

Debugging Terminology

In many cases, the terminology used for particular aspects of computer operation has evolved or been borrowed. This is especially true in the case of debugging. (It sometimes seems as if the first step in designing a debugger is to create a new term for everything.) To keep things straightforward, we'll review the terms used for 80x86 debugging as applied to the operation of the processor.

An *exception* is the processor's normal, documented, and predictable response to a situation—detected during the course of program execution—that requires special handling. All the possible processor exceptions and their causes and handling are covered in detail in Chapter 7. In this chapter, we'll be discussing the subset of those exceptions that are used to execute programs under the control of a debugger and are called, naturally enough, debug exceptions.

Simply, an exception forces a transfer of control to occur. In the case of a debug exception, control is usually transferred to a control program, or debugger. Debug exceptions are reported in two classes: faults and traps.

If the processor is able to detect that an instruction is going to cause an exception *before* the instruction itself is executed, the exception issued is called a *fault*. If the processor detects the exception after beginning to execute the instruction, but restores the state of all registers and internal processing units to

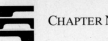

the state they had prior to execution, then issues the exception, it is also called a fault. After the situation that caused the exception is handled, the instruction that has faulted may be restarted. The values of CS and IP saved on the stack point to the instruction that caused the fault.

A *trap* is an exception that is detected *during* the execution of an instruction and is recognized at the boundary of the next instruction. Note that the instruction that caused the exception either will have completed or will still be executing when the exception is generated. If the trap is generated during a control transfer instruction, the values of CS and IP saved on the stack point to the instruction to which control would have been transferred.

A *handler* is the routine to which control is passed when an exception is detected. An exception handler is a more-specialized case of the general category of interrupt service routines (ISRs). The actions of a handler differ according to the purpose of the exception. Typical handlers for debug exceptions may save the state of the program being debugged, display the contents of the registers, and accept commands from the console.

A *breakpoint* is an area of memory that, when accessed, will transfer control (break) to the debugging control program. The logic required to detect and react to a breakpoint may be implemented in hardware, software, or a combination of the two. All processors in the 80x86 family support software breakpoints. The 80386 and later processors support hardware breakpoints as well.

Two of the flags in the FLAGS register are important to debugging operations: the single-step Trap flag (TF) and the Resume flag (RF). The Trap flag is used to switch the processor into and out of single-step operation. The Resume flag, available on the 80386 and later processors, is used to control the generation of repeated debug faults from a single instruction. Both of these flags are discussed in more detail later in this chapter.

80x86 Debugging Support

Although advanced for its day, it's easy to see the 8086 as primitive and underpowered compared to the more advanced members of the 80x86 family. Even so, the 8086 processor was designed with on-chip hardware and instruction set extensions that provided direct support for debugging. The upward compatibility of the chips has ensured that the capabilities of the 8086 have been preserved faithfully through the 80486.

Two interrupt vectors are dedicated to debugging support: the single-step interrupt and the breakpoint interrupt. Both of these interrupts are supported directly by the processor and require no cooperation from the program being debugged.

Single-Stepping

A good computer system executes the instructions we give it very quickly. When something goes wrong, however, it is useful to be able to slow down the computer to a speed at which we can examine its operation. While changing the clock speed may not be practical, all the processors in the 80x86 family support a mode of operation in which one instruction is executed at a time under the control of a supervisory program. This is called *single-step* operation.

Single-stepping is a convenient means for debuggers to execute a program slowly. The code being debugged requires no changes to the source code, nor does the executable code have to be patched at run time. The code is executed one instruction at a time, and then control is passed back to the debugger. In many cases, a status display is provided by the debugger and may include a dump of the contents of the registers, status of the flags, or the contents of certain memory locations. The capabilities of the debugger may also allow checking the number of times an instruction has executed and stopping when a variable reaches a certain value. The only contribution of the processor to this process is the generation of the single-step exception that transfers control to the debugger.

The single-step capability of the processor is controlled by the setting of the single-step Trap flag (TF) in the FLAGS register. When TF=1, the processor is said to be in single-step mode and an exception (interrupt 1) will occur after the execution of most instructions. Specifically, the execution of an instruction will cause the processor to *generate* the single-step exception if the TF flag was set when the execution of the instruction began. The exception is not *recognized* until the boundary of the next instruction. The single-step trap is not generated after prefix instructions, after instructions that modify the SS register, or after the WAIT instruction. The values of CS and IP saved on the stack point to the next instruction that would have been executed had the exception not been generated.

The Trap flag is automatically cleared as part of the interrupt transfer mechanism. Thus, the processor is not in single-step mode when it enters the single-step exception handler. This allows the exception handler to execute without being single-stepped itself. When the handler returns control to the underlying application (usually via an IRET instruction), the FLAGS register is restored from the stack. If the Trap flag was set on entry to the handler, it will be restored by the IRET and another single-step interrupt will be generated after the execution of the instruction following the IRET. The single-step exception is not masked by the Interrupt flag (IF).

On the 8086 and 8088 processors, the exact order in which the single-step exception is handled when it occurs simultaneously with other interrupts depends on the context in which it occurs. The priority of the interrupt also varies across processors. This priority determines the order in which multiple pending interrupts are serviced and affects the operation of single-step mode. A complete explanation of the priorities of the single-step exception and other exceptions is given in Chapter 7. The execution of an instruction when the processor is in single-step mode is shown in Figure 9.1 and explained below.

Assuming that no interrupts are pending and that the Trap flag is set (TF=1), the single-step exception will be generated by the execution of the MOV AX,BX instruction. Single-step is a trap, and is generated only at the successful completion of an instruction. Execution continues to the next instruction. Before the ADD CX,DX instruction is executed, the pending single-step trap is recognized. The current values of the FLAGS, CS, and IP registers are pushed onto the stack, and the Interrupt and single-step Trap flags are cleared.

Control is then transferred to the location specified by the doubleword at address 0000:0004h (the vector for interrupt 1) where the single-step handler performs its operation. Upon completion, the handler executes an IRET instruction, restoring FLAGS, CS, and IP to the values they had before the exception. Because TF is set, the execution of the ADD CX,DX instruction will generate a single-step exception and the process will be repeated.

FIGURE 9.1

Single-step operation

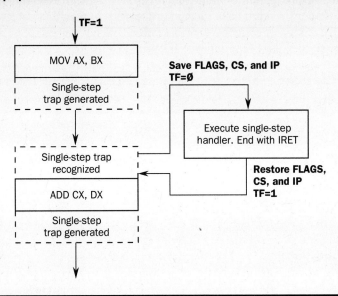

Breakpoint Interrupt

Single-stepping through object code may not always be desired or required. In many cases, the major portion of the program may have already been debugged and only a small portion may need to be examined in detail. If that portion of the code is executed at the end of the program, single-stepping to the point of execution would be extremely tedious. The same reasoning applies if the program executes loops that repeat for a large number of iterations. Tracing through a loop for 999 repetitions, for example, would not be a prudent use of time. In these cases, we want to execute the program at full speed up to a certain point, then get control and single-step through it. This facility is provided by the breakpoint interrupt instruction.

The breakpoint interrupt instruction allows execution of a program to be controlled by placing a special opcode (CCh) into the object code being debugged. When executed, the opcode causes the processor to generate an exception (interrupt 3) that transfers control to the debugger. The breakpoint instruction can be used for code breakpoints only; the opcode must be executed to pass control to the debugger. If placed in a data area, it will have no effect (except to corrupt the data). Because using the breakpoint instruction requires that the code being debugged be modified, breakpoints cannot be set in ROM (read-only memory) or in other nonwritable memory. If the breakpoint instruction is to be used in protected mode, a data segment with read/write access must be created to overlay the code segment that is to be modified. This implies that the debugger must have sufficient privilege to do so.

Even with its limitations, the breakpoint instruction is a powerful and versatile tool. An unlimited number of breakpoint instructions may be used, subject only to the ability of the debugger to keep track of them. When setting a breakpoint at a multibyte instruction, the first byte of the opcode is replaced by the breakpoint opcode. Normal program execution will then execute the breakpoint instruction and ignore the remaining bytes of the original instruction opcode. The necessity of having a breakpoint instruction that is only one byte in length becomes clear when replacing single-byte opcodes in a program. Consider the following code fragment, for which is shown a memory offset and the instruction opcodes.

```
Offset Opcode            Assembly Code
  0000  83 FE 00          CMP  SI,0
  0003  74 01             JE   LABEL1
  0005  46                INC  SI
  0006          LABEL1:
  0006  2B FE             SUB  DI,SI
```

Assume that a breakpoint is to be set at offset 5. Using the breakpoint opcode, CCh, only the byte at offset 5 would be changed. This would replace the INC SI opcode, but leave the remainder of the code unchanged. If, however, the two-byte form of the interrupt instruction (CDh 03h) had to be used for the breakpoint instruction, the two bytes at offsets 5 and 6 would be patched, giving the following code. Assuming that the jump at offset 3 is *not* taken, the following code would be executed:

```
  0000  83 FE 00          C12MP  SI,0
  0003  74 01             JE     LABEL1
  0005  CD 03             INT    3      ; patched code
```

When the debugger got control, it would restore the two bytes at offset 5 and 6, and continue the execution of the program. So far, so good. If, however, the jump at offset 5 *is* taken, the following code would be executed.

```
  0000  83 FE 00          CMP  SI,0
  0003  74 01             JE   LABEL1 ;Assume jump is taken
  0005  CD                           ;Part of patch - not executed
  0006          LABEL1:
  0006  03 FE             ADD  DI,SI ;Unintentionally modified!
                                     ; plus NO breakpoint generated
```

In this case, the JE LABEL1 instruction still transfers control to offset 6. But the byte at offset 6 has been patched while installing the two-byte interrupt opcode. Because the instruction INT 3 is not executed, the code will not be back-patched to its original state. Instead, only a portion of the opcode is executed, not stopping execution and unintentionally changing the operation of the program.

Note that a similar problem will occur if the single-byte breakpoint opcode is not placed at an instruction boundary. If the intention had been to break at offset 0000, but the breakpoint opcode was placed at offset 1 by mistake, no breakpoint interrupt would be generated and the instruction OR SP,0 (opcode 83h, *CCh*, 00h) would be executed instead.

Debugging with the 80386 and 80486

As processors grow more complex, so do the programming problems involving them. It may have been that the complexity of the systems being written for the 80286 prompted the designers at Intel to add a new level of hardware debugging support to the 80386 processor. Whatever the reason, the new registers, instructions, and debugging power of the 80386 tremendously advanced the level of debugging support provided by the processor.

Beginning with the 80386, the processor contains hardware to set and detect breakpoints without altering the object code being debugged. Breakpoints can be set to detect not only an instruction execution, but memory reads and writes as well. The breakpoints are supported by on-chip hardware that provides full support without slowing down execution. Because the target code can be monitored without being modified, breakpoints can be set in protected mode code segments without creating overlaying read/write data segments. For the same reason, breakpoints can also be set in ROM.

The additional support for debugging allows a software debugger unprecedented control of the processor by implementing hardware breakpoints for a wide range of conditions. The new debugging facilities described in this section are available only on the 80386 and later processors.

Debug Registers

Eight dedicated debug registers, DR0 through DR7, have been added to the architecture of the processor. These debug registers can support both instruction (code) breakpoints and data breakpoints, allowing software-only debugging programs to provide the same support that previously required dedicated hardware. Direct access to the debug registers is restricted to a task operating in real mode or at privilege level 0 (most privileged). The debug address control registers may be read or written using the special MOV DR*n,reg32* or MOV *reg32*,DR*n* form of the MOV instruction.

The DR4 and DR5 debug registers are not accessible outside the processor and are reserved by Intel for future processors. The remainder of the debug registers are grouped by function: address control (DR0 through DR3), control (DR7), and status (DR6). The format and control fields of the eight debug registers are shown in Figure 9.2 and are discussed in the following paragraphs.

FIGURE 9.2

The 80386/80486 debug registers

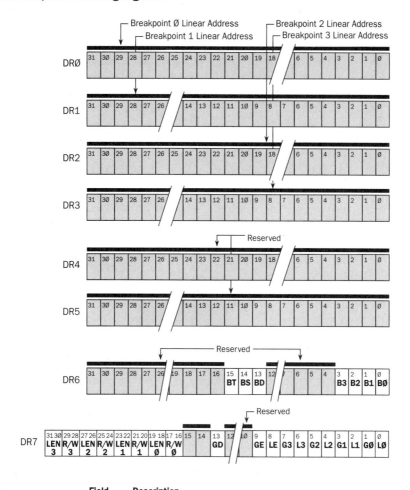

Field	Description
BT	Break on task switch
BS	Break on single-step
BD	Break on debug contention
B*n*	Break on address in DR*n*
GD	Delete access to any debug register
GE	Enable exact matching for data breakpoints globally
LE	Enable exact matching for data breakpoints locally
G*n*	Enable breakpoint *n* globally
L*n*	Enable breakpoint *n* locally
LEN*n*	Length of breakpoint at address in DR*n*
R/W*n*	Type of breakpoint at address in DR*n*

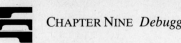

Debug Address Control Registers DR0-DR3   Debug registers DR0 through DR3 are used to hold the 32-bit linear address that is associated with one of the four breakpoint conditions defined in DR7. If paging is enabled, the addresses in these registers will be further translated to physical addresses by the paging unit. If not, the register address will be the same as the physical address. (For a discussion of paging and logical-to-physical address translation, see Chapter 4.)

When paging is enabled and pages are swapped in and out of memory, different tasks will most likely have different linear-to-physical address relationships. Thus an address (and the corresponding breakpoint) specified by a register may be applicable to one task, but not another. The control register, DR7, provides bits to enable the breakpoints either globally (in effect for all tasks) or locally (effective for only the current task).

Debug Control Register DR7   The overall operation of the debug hardware is governed by the settings in DR7, the debug control register. Eighteen separate fields are defined in the register, allowing the breakpoint conditions to be defined for each of the linear addresses specified in registers DR0 through DR3. Breakpoints may also be enabled or disabled on either a local or a global basis. For each address specified in register DRn (where n represents a number from 0 to 3), there are four corresponding fields in DR7: R/Wn, LENn, Ln, and Gn as explained below.

The *R/W* (read/write) field is 2 bits wide and specifies the type of breakpoint that will be implemented at the corresponding linear address. Of the four possible values for R/W, only three have been defined as shown here:

R/W Field	Breakpoint Action
00b	Break on instruction execution only (corresponding LEN must = 00)
01b	Break on data write only
10b	Undefined—do not use
11b	Break on data read or write, but not instruction fetches

The *LEN* (length) field is also 2 bits wide and specifies the length of the area of memory that is to be monitored. Values have been defined for LEN that specify lengths of one, two, or four bytes as shown here:

LEN Field	Memory Size Monitored
00b	One byte
01b	Two bytes (word)
10b	Undefined—do not use
11b	Four bytes (doubleword)

The value of the LEN field must be considered when setting the corresponding address for a breakpoint. The processor requires that the address specified be aligned on a boundary that corresponds to the defined value of the LEN field. If LEN=11b, for example, the address must be aligned on a doubleword boundary. If not, the breakpoint may not perform as expected. (This requirement is explained in more detail in the section on data breakpoints later in this chapter.)

The low-order 8 bits of the DR7 register can be set selectively to enable any combination of the four breakpoint conditions. The Ln (local) bits enable the breakpoints at the level of the current task. These bits are automatically cleared at every task switch to avoid unwanted debugging in the new task. The Gn (global) bits enabling the breakpoints are not reset by a task switch.

The actual read or write operation to an area of memory may not always occur at the same time as the instruction that requested the read or write is executed. The normal pipelined operation of the processor will overlap memory read and write operations with the execution of previous and subsequent instructions. (Pipelining is discussed in Chapter 3.) As a result, data breakpoints that monitor memory may not be reported at the appropriate instruction or may be missed entirely. To account for these conditions during debugging, the *LE* (local exact) and *GE* (global exact) bits are provided.

Applicable only to the 80386, these bits control whether the processor will slow its execution in order to be able to report data breakpoints on exactly the instruction that caused them. These bits should be enabled whenever data breakpoints are active. The LE bit controls this action when the current task is executing, while GE performs the same action for all tasks.

The 80486 processor always uses exact data breakpoint matching when debugging; the settings of the LE and GE bits are ignored. If any of the Ln or Gn bits are set to enable debugging, the processor automatically slows execution as if the LE or GE bit were set. If a breakpoint is enabled, exact matching will cause instructions that access memory and normally execute in one clock to require two clocks.

The GD (global debug register access detect) bit, when set, causes a debug exception to occur if an instruction attempts to read or write to any of the debug registers. Normally, the debug registers may be accessed by a task operating in real mode or at privilege level 0 in protected mode. By setting this bit, a software debugger can ensure that it has complete control over the on-chip debug hardware. The GD bit is automatically cleared when interrupt 1 is generated, allowing the handler to access the debug registers without generating another exception.

Debug Status Register DR6   If any one of the debug breakpoint conditions is satisfied, a debug exception (interrupt 1) will be generated. To determine which condition caused the exception, the controlling debug program examines DR6, the debug status register.

When the processor determines that one of the four possible debug exception conditions has been met, it sets the corresponding status bit of this register.

By interpreting the setting of the bits, the control program can determine which condition caused the exception. The Bn (break at address n) bit is set to 1 if the condition specified by R/Wn and LENn has occurred at the address specified in register DRn.

The Bn bit for a breakpoint condition will be set regardless of the status of the corresponding Gn or Ln bit in DR7. Bn may also be set, even if neither Gn nor Ln is set, if more than one breakpoint condition occurs at the same time and if the breakpoint occurs due to a condition other than that described by n.

The BS (break on single-step) bit is set if the debug handler was entered due to the occurrence of a single-step exception (interrupt 1). This condition will occur if the Trap flag is set in the EFLAGS register. The mechanics of single-stepping, discussed earlier in this chapter, are not affected. Single-stepping is reported, but not controlled, by the debug registers.

The BD (break on debug contention) bit is set if the next instruction to be executed will read or write one of the eight debug registers. This flag is used by one debugger to protect the debug registers from manipulation by another debugger.

If a task switch has occurred, and the debug trap bit (T-bit) in the new task's TSS is set, the BT (break on task switch) bit is set before passing control to the debug handler. This condition is simply reported, but not controlled, by DR7. Reporting of task switches is discussed later in this chapter.

The status bits in the DR6 register are only set by the processor, never cleared. Thus, each time the debug program gets control, it must clear the register to avoid ambiguous results when the next exception is generated.

Breakpoints

The hardware breakpoints provided by the debug registers are powerful tools for debugging. Breakpoints can be set on memory reads, writes, and instruction execution. The use and limitations of each of the different breakpoint types are discussed in the following section.

Data Breakpoints Data breakpoints are used to monitor an area of memory and report whether a read or write occurs as determined by the setting of the LENn fields. The combination of a linear address, specified by one of the registers DR0 through DR3, and its corresponding LEN field specifies a small range of memory addresses for a data breakpoint. As mentioned earlier, the LEN field specifies a range of one, two, or four bytes.

When testing to see if a data breakpoint has been satisfied, the processor uses the value of the LEN field to mask the address specified in the debug address register. If LEN≠00b, the starting breakpoint address is then effectively rounded down to the nearest word (LEN=01b) or doubleword (LEN=11b) boundary. A doubleword data breakpoint (LEN=11b) set at an address of 1A33h, for example, will *not* break at the four bytes 1A33h-1A36h as might be expected. Instead, the starting byte will be determined as 1A33h AND (NOT LEN)=1A30h, and the four bytes 1A30h-1A33h will be used for the breakpoint. Two or more adjacent breakpoints, set for smaller data sizes, can be used to cover an unaligned operand. A breakpoint for an unaligned word operand, for example, can be set using two adjacent byte breakpoints.

If R/W=11b, the breakpoint will be triggered if any byte within the specified range of memory is either read or written. Instruction fetches performed by the processor to fill the prefetch queue will *not* trigger this breakpoint. A data write breakpoint (R/W=01b) will be triggered only if a byte within the specified memory range is written to.

Data breakpoints are traps—the debug exception is generated only *after* the address has been accessed. (On the 80386, the LE or GE bit must be set if the trap is to be reported accurately or at all, as described earlier.) If the operation that triggered the exception was a write, the location at the breakpoint address will have already been changed when the debugger gets control. If required, the debugger can save the contents of the location before the breakpoint is enabled and restore it when the debugger gets control.

Code Breakpoints   Code execution breakpoints monitor attempts made to execute the instruction at a specified memory address. The value of the LEN field must be 00b for a code breakpoint and the operation of the breakpoint for any other value of LEN is undefined. The breakpoint must point to the first byte of the instruction opcode. If any prefixes are used, the breakpoint must point to the first prefix of the instruction. Code breakpoints are faults, and the debug exception is generated *before* the instruction is executed. Code breakpoints are reported accurately, independent of the setting of the LE or GE bits.

When a code breakpoint fault is detected, the stack is set up such that an IRET will restart the faulted instruction. If this were done, however, the attempt to execute the instruction would immediately generate another debug fault—an endless loop. To defeat this behavior, the processor automatically sets the debug Restart flag (RF) in the copy of the EFLAGS register that is pushed onto the stack by the code breakpoint fault. When RF is set, debug faults are masked. (Note that debug traps, aborts, and non-debug faults are not affected by the value of RF.) When an IRET is executed, the image of EFLAGS loaded into the register will have RF set to 1, and the instruction will be restarted without generating another debug code breakpoint for the same instruction. The RF flag is automatically cleared after the successful completion of the next instruction, except for IRET or POPF and JMP, CALL, or INT instructions that cause a task switch.

It is possible that an instruction that is restarted could cause other faults. If so, additional retries of the instruction will all be performed with RF=1, continuing to inhibit the debug code breakpoint fault. The RF flag is cleared by the processor only after the instruction execution has been completed.

Debuggers executing in real mode must use the 32-bit form of the IRET instruction to control the RF flag, which is located in the high-order 16 bits of the EFLAGS register. The debugger must remove the 16-bit information that has been placed on the stack by the fault and push appropriate values for the 32-bit EIP register, the 16-bit CS register, and the 32-bit EFLAGS register. Executing an IRET instruction, prefixed with an operand size override prefix, will execute a 32-bit interrupt return, popping a 32-bit value into the EFLAGS register.

Task Switch Breakpoint

If a task switch has occurred, and the debug trap bit (T-bit) in the TSS of the new task is enabled, the BT bit is set in DR6 before a debug exception is generated. (The trap bit is not defined for an 80286-type [16-bit] TSS.) This condition is only reported, but not controlled, by any bits in the DR7 register.

If the handler for the debug exception is a task, the TSS for the handler should *not* have its T-bit set. Doing so will cause each invocation of the debug fault handler to execute a debug fault and the processor will enter an endless loop.

THE MATH COPROCESSOR

The processors of the 80x86 family are fundamentally integer processing units and are designed to operate directly on a variety of integer data types. None of the CPUs, however, offers intrinsic support for operations on floating-point data types. Of course, specialized hardware isn't a prerequisite for performing floating-point math. An integer CPU, given the correct series of instructions, can perform any operation on any numeric data type; floating-point emulators are a practical example of this principle. A dedicated floating-point processor, however, will reduce the amount of time required to perform complex mathematical operations and provide intrinsic programming support for floating-point data types.

This chapter presents a brief overview of the history, capabilities, and architecture of the math coprocessor. The formats, fields, and interpretation of the coprocessor's numerical register set and control and status registers are also examined in detail. The hardware mechanisms used to implement emulation of coprocessor functions in software are reviewed as well.

Throughout this chapter and this book, the term *processor* is used to refer to a member of the 80x86 family. The term *coprocessor* will refer exclusively to the numeric processor extension. In the case of the 80486, the term processor refers only to the integer data unit and associated support units; the term coprocessor refers to the floating-point unit.

Overview

Each processor in the 80x86 family has a corresponding coprocessor with which it is compatible. Table 10.1 shows the compatible processor and coprocessor combinations. The 80386DX is unique in that it is able to function equally well with either an 80387DX or an 80287 coprocessor. The 80486DX contains both a processor and a coprocessor on the same chip and requires no additional floating-point hardware. The 80486SX CPU is an 80486DX with the floating-point unit disabled. If an 80487SX is later installed, it will disconnect the 80486SX chip and provide both floating-point and integer functions.

The math coprocessor is known by a variety of labels including the numeric processor extension (NPX), the numeric data processor (NDP), and the floating-point unit (FPU). The terms are equivalent and may be used interchangeably.

TABLE 10.1

Compatible Processors and Coprocessors

Processor	Compatible Coprocessor
8086 and 8088	8087
80286	80287
	80287XL
80386DX	80287
	80387DX
80386SX	80387SX
80486DX	None required. Math functions are built in.
80486SX	80487SX

History and Evolution

Toward the end of the 1970s, small computer systems were pushing hard against their performance limitations. As more sophisticated applications were ported to and written for mini- and microcomputers, the need for greater storage capacity, I/O speed, and floating-point operation became more pressing.

In 1977, Intel adopted a standard for expressing real numbers in a binary floating-point format and introduced the Floating Point Arithmetic Library (FPAL), its first commercial software product based on the standard. FPAL was a set of single-precision arithmetic subroutines designed to run on the 8080 and 8085 microprocessors. Using FPAL, a single-precision multiply could be performed in about 1.5 milliseconds running on a 1.6 MHz 8080A CPU.

Intel continued to work for improvements in floating-point processing. Its next step was the introduction of the 8232 chip, a single-chip arithmetic processor for the 8080/8085 family. The chip could work with both single- and double-precision numbers and performed a single-precision multiply in about 100 μs and a double-precision multiply in about 875 μs when running at a 2 MHz clock speed.

In 1979, the Institute of Electrical and Electronic Engineers (IEEE) began work on an industry standard for representation of binary floating-point numbers. The formats proposed by the IEEE were identical to those that had been pioneered by Intel.

In 1980, the 8087 NPX was introduced. Giving an average of about ten times the performance of the 8232, the 5 MHz 8087 was able to perform a single-precision multiply in about 19 μs and a double-precision multiply in about 27 μs. Compared to Intel's floating-point emulator (highly optimized 8086 assembly code written to perform the equivalent numeric functions), the 8087 performed the same floating-point operations typically 65 to 170 times as fast.

The 80287 NPX followed in 1983, and maintained good compatibility with the 8087 while also providing a close implementation of the developing IEEE standard for floating-point arithmetic. The small differences between the draft standard and the 80287 hardware implementation were easily bridged with software interface routines. Performance was up again, with the time required for an 8 MHz 80287 to perform a single-precision multiply dropping to just 11.9 µs and a double-precision multiply taking only 16.9 µs.

The 80387DX coprocessor provided both upward compatibility with the 8087 and 80287 as well as an expanded instruction set. The 80387DX was introduced in 1986 and implemented the final IEEE floating-point math standard (standard 754). In addition to the standard instructions, new complex trigonometric functions were added to improve ease of use. Performance continued to improve, with a 33 MHz 80387 performing a single-precision multiply in 0.8 µs and a double-precision multiply in 1.4 µs.

The 1989 introduction of the 80486DX processor was the first of the 80x86 family to include floating-point math hardware on the same chip with the CPU. The FPU on the 80486 is equivalent to the 387DX, conforming to both IEEE 754 and the newer IEEE 854 standard. Times for single-precision and double-precision multiplies average 0.33 µs and 0.42 µs respectively on a 33 MHz 80486 system.

Interface and Capabilities

The processor and coprocessor work in tandem. The processor fetches and decodes instructions, calculates addresses of memory operands, and so on. In exchange, the coprocessor performs arithmetic and comparison operations on floating-point numbers. In addition, the coprocessor makes many trigonometric and transcendental functions available to the programmer as simple, single instructions.

Many devices in a computer system, such as a video display controller or an interrupt controller, must be programmed using nonintuitive I/O instructions. Without the programming information that is specific to the device, writing programs for these devices or trying to understand existing object code is nearly impossible. Because the processor and coprocessor share a well-defined hardware interface, there's no need for special setup or complicated data transfer. In practice, the instructions for the coprocessor may be treated simply as an extension to the basic instruction set of the processor.

The instruction set of the coprocessor is designed to complement the encoding form of normal processor instructions. Operands, for example, may be located either in memory or in the coprocessor registers. Memory addressing is performed using the same operand and addressing modes available to the processor. These properties make integrating floating-point operations into an application a relatively simple matter.

The basic (8087-compatible) coprocessor instruction set provides a full range of load and store instructions that move real, integer, and BCD data operands between the numeric registers of the coprocessor and system memory. The arithmetic instructions provide the basic four-function math operations of addition, subtraction, multiplication, and division. More advanced complex instructions are available to perform square root, scaling, remaindering, modulo, rounding, and absolute value functions. Transcendental functions, including tangent, logarithms, and exponentiation are also provided. The 80x87 instruction set is discussed in detail in Chapter 12 and in Appendix B.

Applications

One goal in creating the NPX was to bring the power of easy numeric programming within the grasp of application programmers. Coprocessor operation and the floating-point instruction set were designed to make the conversion of algorithms from human-readable forms to assembly code as straightforward as possible, minimizing the chance for errors to occur. As such, a large proportion of programs that use the coprocessor are popular scientific and business applications.

Typical applications that require the high precision and fast processing capability of the NPX include business data processing, scientific data reduction, graphics processing, and financial operations. Embedded applications can also make good use of the coprocessor in real time programming including process and machine control, navigation, robotics, and data acquisition.

Data Types

Compared to the processor, the functions of the coprocessor are very specialized. All data that is transferred to or from the numeric registers, for example, is assumed to be numeric. The coprocessor instructions are designed to manipulate that data mathematically. The entire architecture of the coprocessor is dedicated to performing floating-point calculations.

The coprocessor data formats were introduced in Chapter 2. The format and meaning of the numeric encodings are discussed in the context of numeric operations in Chapter 11. For completeness, a brief review of coprocessor data types is presented here. Figure 10.1 illustrates the data formats that are supported intrinsically by the coprocessor. Each of the data formats shown may be used when the coprocessor is loading or storing data. Internally, however, all data operands are converted to the 80-bit temporary real format.

Integers   The signed integer formats available on the coprocessor are identical to those intrinsic to the processor. The high-order bit of the data unit in which the integer is stored indicates the sign of the number. A number with a 0 in the sign bit is a positive number, while a 1 indicates a negative number. Two's complement notation is used for all integer formats.

Packed BCD   The packed BCD data type is treated as a single numeric unit that is 80 bits in length. Eighteen 4-bit wide fields are defined to hold individual decimal digits. To be considered valid, each digit field must contain a value that is in the range from 0 to 9. Bit 79, the high-order bit, is used as the sign bit; two's complement notation is not used for BCD operands. Bits 72 through 78 of the format are unused; they are ignored when loading a value from memory and cleared to 0 when storing BCD operands to memory.

Short Real   The short real format (also called the single-precision real format) is a 32-bit data item. The sign field is 1 bit long, the mantissa field is 23 bits long, and the exponent field is 8 bits long. The mantissa field is normalized and uses one implicit bit for the integer portion of the number giving 24 significant binary digits. The stored exponent is the sum of the true exponent and the bias value, +127 (7Fh).

FIGURE 10.1

The coprocessor data types

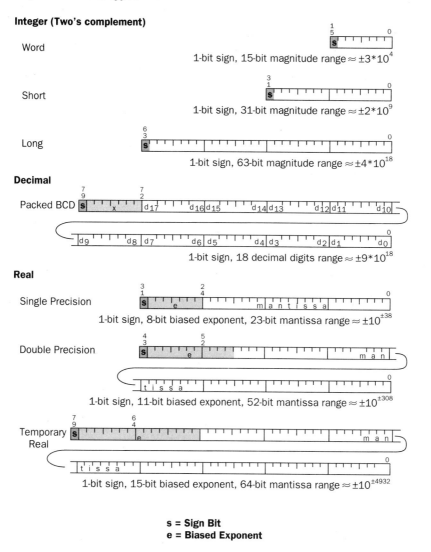

Integer (Two's complement)

Word

1-bit sign, 15-bit magnitude range $\approx \pm 3*10^{4}$

Short

1-bit sign, 31-bit magnitude range $\approx \pm 2*10^{9}$

Long

1-bit sign, 63-bit magnitude range $\approx \pm 4*10^{18}$

Decimal

Packed BCD

1-bit sign, 18 decimal digits range $\approx \pm 9*10^{18}$

Real

Single Precision

1-bit sign, 8-bit biased exponent, 23-bit mantissa range $\approx \pm 10^{\pm 38}$

Double Precision

1-bit sign, 11-bit biased exponent, 52-bit mantissa range $\approx \pm 10^{\pm 308}$

Temporary Real

1-bit sign, 15-bit biased exponent, 64-bit mantissa range $\approx \pm 10^{\pm 4932}$

s = Sign Bit
e = Biased Exponent

Long Real The long real format (also called double-precision real) is 64 bits long. The sign field is 1 bit, the mantissa field is 52 bits, and the exponent field is 11 bits. As with the short real format, the mantissa field is normalized and uses an implicit bit for the integer portion of the number. This gives the long real format up to 53 significant binary digits. The stored exponent is biased and is the sum of the true exponent and the bias value, +1023 (3FFh).

Temporary Real   The temporary real format (recently renamed the extended precision real by Intel) is an 80-bit format that is divided into a 1-bit sign field, a 15-bit biased exponent field, and a 64-bit mantissa. Unlike the other real number formats, the integer portion of the normalized number is present in the format, not implied. There is no implicit bit in the temporary real format. The stored exponent is biased and is the sum of the true exponent and +16383 (3FFFh).

The temporary real format is used by the coprocessor internally for all calculations. All data types read from memory are converted to temporary real automatically. Because the precision and range of the temporary real format are so much greater than the other formats, errors introduced by the calculations on the final result will probably occur outside the range of a short real or long real format.

Architecture

Like the processor, the coprocessor is a complex array of microcircuits designed to implement complex functions. The processor and coprocessor have a complementary relationship and are designed to work in tandem. The processor fetches and decodes instructions and calculates addresses of memory operands while the coprocessor works in parallel to siphon off specially coded floating-point instructions called *escape* (ESC) instructions. As a result, despite its seemingly complex performance, the coprocessor is a simpler device architecturally than the processor.

Because the processor and coprocessor are both physically and programmatically separate microprocessors, the coprocessor is able to operate asynchronously with respect to the main processor, often using an entirely different clock generator and clock speed. When the processor encounters an ESC instruction (that is, an instruction bound for the NPX), it calculates the memory address if an operand is referenced and then immediately proceeds to decode and execute the next instruction. Unless the next instruction is another ESC instruction or uses the result of the unfinished ESC instruction, operation of both processors can proceed in parallel. Because many floating-point operations can take up to several hundred clocks to complete, careful assembly language coding to allow parallel operation can often improve application performance.

The basic architecture of the coprocessor is shown as a simplified block diagram in Figure 10.2. The NPX is divided into the *control unit* (CU) and the *numeric execution unit* (NEU). The control unit performs both the bus interface and instruction decoding functions of the NPX. The control unit accesses and buffers the operands and opcodes that are passed to the NEU. It also executes the control instructions for the coprocessor. The NEU executes the decoded numeric instructions, performs the calculations on the data, and passes the results back to the control unit as required. The operation of each of these units is explained in more detail below.

Control Unit

One of the responsibilities of the control unit is to synchronize the operation of the coprocessor and the processor. Synchronization is necessary when the two processors must exchange information, access the results of each other's operations, or decode instructions. Instructions destined for the NPX, for example, are usually intermixed in an applications object code with ordinary processor instructions. Only the processor performs instruction fetches. The NPX control unit, however, is hard wired to the status lines of the processor, and is able to read the instructions as they are fetched in parallel with the processor.

FIGURE 10.2

Coprocessor internal architecture

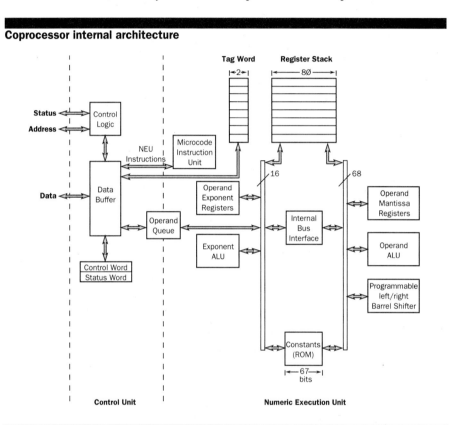

The NPX must read and decode the same instructions as the main processor if the processor/coprocessor pair is to operate correctly. The coprocessor must, therefore, emulate the instruction fetch and decode characteristics of its host processor. The NPX must maintain, for example, a prefetch queue that is identical in size to that of the processor. When required, the coprocessor identifies its companion processor at reset and matches the length of the queue automatically. The NPX then monitors the instruction queue so that instructions are removed from the queue and decoded simultaneously with the CPU.

Both the processor and the coprocessor decode a special class of instructions, known as floating-point or ESC instructions, that are bound for the NPX. (Complete details on the encoding of coprocessor ESC instructions are given in Chapter 12.) For all practical purposes, the processor ignores these instructions and the control unit of the NPX decodes them. The processor decodes the ESC instructions sufficiently, however, to differentiate between those that reference memory and those that don't. If an ESC instruction references memory, the processor calculates the effective address of the memory operand and initiates a memory read bus cycle. The processor ignores the data that is placed on the bus as the result of the read cycle. If the ESC instruction does not contain a memory reference, the CPU immediately begins to decode and execute the next instruction.

The NPX control unit is ultimately responsible for performing the details of the bus operations that are required for coprocessor operations even though the processor performs the effective address calculation. If memory is being accessed, the NPX saves the effective address of the operand. If a register operand is specified, the value of the operand is saved. If the operand requires more than one bus cycle to access, due to size or alignment, for example, the NPX control unit will take control of the system bus and transfer the remainder of the operand. If an operand is being written to memory, the processor calculates the effective address and initiates a read bus cycle. The NPX control unit saves the effective address, but ignores the data on the bus. The NPX control unit then becomes the local bus master and initiates write cycles as required to transfer the operand to memory. ESC instructions that do not require the participation of the NEU are executed by the control unit independently of the NEU. These instructions typically set or report the state of the NPX and include FINIT, FCLEX, FSTSW, FSTSW AX, and FSTCW.

Numeric Execution Unit

The second major processing unit of the coprocessor is called the numeric execution unit (NEU), and is also shown in Figure 10.2. The NEU is the actual floating-point processor within the NPX and performs all operations that access and manipulate the numeric data in the coprocessor's registers. The NEU is able to perform arithmetic, logical, and transcendental operations as well as supply a small number of mathematical constants from its on-chip ROM.

The numeric registers in the NEU are 80 bits wide and are configured to match the format of the 80-bit temporary real data type. (The register stack and its operation are discussed later in this chapter.) Internally, the numeric data is routed into two pathways for processing: a 64-bit mantissa bus and a 16-bit sign/exponent bus. Outside the register stack, an additional 4 bits are added to the mantissa bus for a total of 68 bits. Specialized hardware inside the NEU, including dedicated exponent and mantissa adders and a programmable left/right barrel shifter, is invoked as needed to perform specific mathematical functions.

As ESC instructions are decoded they are passed to the microinstruction sequencer, a small computer in itself, that then programs the on-chip hardware units to perform the specific tasks required by each instruction. When the execution of an ESC instruction begins, the NEU drives its BUSY signal active. The BUSY status of the NEU is reported in the NPX's control word as well as driven to an external pin where it can be monitored by the processor. This signal is used in conjunction with the processor's WAIT instruction to resynchronize the processor and coprocessor when required.

Synchronization

Synchronization must be established between the processor and coprocessor in two situations. In the first case, the execution of an ESC instruction that requires the participation of the NEU must not be initiated if the NEU has not completed the execution of a previous instruction. With the exception of a few instructions that control or report the state of the NPX, most ESC instructions use the NEU. Instructions that do not use the NEU and consequently do not require synchronization include the FSTSW, FSTCW, FLDCW, FSTENV, and FLDENV instructions.

The second case that requires processor/coprocessor synchronization is when a processor instruction accesses a memory location that is an operand of a previous coprocessor instruction. In this case, the CPU must synchronize with the NPX to ensure that the NPX instruction has completed its execution. If not, the processor could alter a value before the NPX has read it or read a value from memory before the NPX has written to it. As mentioned previously, once the CPU has decoded an instruction bound for the coprocessor, it can continue to fetch and execute instructions. NPX instructions typically require more time to execute than CPU instructions, so the ESC instruction will probably not have completed by the time the CPU attempts to access the common memory location.

The processor WAIT instruction (or the equivalent FWAIT instruction) is provided for the purpose of establishing synchronization. When it encounters a WAIT instruction the processor will monitor its TEST line, which is typically connected to the BUSY# signal of the coprocessor. A WAIT instruction will cause the processor to stop execution as long as TEST is active. As soon as the TEST line becomes inactive, the processor will proceed to execute the next instruction.

The encoding of a WAIT instruction prior to all numeric ESC instructions is mandatory only for the 8087 coprocessor. Before the execution of any ESC instruction is started, the programmer must ensure that the 8087 has completed all activity from the previous ESC instructions. Because typical floating-point instructions may require execution times on the order of hundreds of clocks, the CPU will most likely have finished its processing of the original ESC instruction long before the NPX has. The 80286 and later processors automatically test their TEST line before executing an NPX instruction and do not require that the WAIT be explicitly coded.

(Most assemblers will automatically insert the WAIT instruction before ESC instructions, eliminating the need to code them explicitly. If the target coprocessor is an 80287 or later, an assembler directive can usually be specified to eliminate the generation of WAIT instructions except when required.)

Many coprocessor instructions have extremely long execution times. To prevent a WAIT instruction from delaying interrupt processing for the entire duration of the ESC instruction execution, the CPU can be interrupted at five-clock intervals while it is waiting on the TEST line. When the TEST line becomes inactive, pending interrupts will be ignored while the CPU immediately executes the next instruction.

Whenever an unmasked floating-point exception occurs, the NPX signals the error condition to the processor. (Exceptions are discussed in more detail later in this chapter.) If the processor and coprocessor are operating in parallel, the processor may have already changed data needed by the exception handler to correct and restart the ESC instruction. Encoding a WAIT or FWAIT instruction after the ESC instruction allows the processor to acknowledge any pending floating-point exceptions and is required if the exceptions are to be processed accurately.

Coprocessor Specifics

In general, the members of the 80x87 math coprocessor family are compatible. But because the processors that they are designed to operate with vary so widely in capability and operation, minor differences in the operation and hardware characteristics of the coprocessor are inevitable. This section briefly outlines some of the important operational differences between coprocessor types and specifics of their operation. Compatibility between coprocessors is covered in detail in Chapter 14.

The 8087   At RESET, the 8087 monitors the BHE#/S7 line of the processor to determine if the CPU is an 8086 or an 8088. The 8087 then sets its own prefetch queue length to match the processor's: four bytes for an 8088 and six bytes for an 8086. The control unit of the coprocessor maintains synchronization with the CPU by monitoring the status signals S0#, S1#, S2#, and S6 to determine when an instruction is being fetched. The CPU's QS0 and QS1 queue status lines are monitored as well so that instructions are decoded from the instruction queue synchronously with the CPU.

The 80287   Before executing most ESC instructions, the 80286 CPU examines the NPX's BUSY# line and delays execution until the NPX indicates that it is able to accept the instruction. Unlike the 8086 and 8088 processors, which required that explicit WAIT instructions be coded and executed to test the BUSY# signal before each ESC instruction, the 80286 does not require them and they are treated effectively as NOPs by the processor.

The 80286 processor uses I/O addresses F8h, FAh, and FCh to communicate with the 80287. These I/O operations are performed automatically by the CPU and are not related to I/O instructions performed by tasks. Any task may use ESC instructions (and consequently the I/O instructions invoked by these ESC instructions) regardless of its current IOPL. To guarantee correct operation, applications must not perform explicit I/O to any of the reserved ports (F8h-FFh). The I/O privilege level of the task should be set to protect the integrity of the 80287 in multitasking environments by preventing accidental tampering.

Like the 80286, the 80287 can operate in both real mode and protected mode if required to match the operating mode of the processor. Following a

RESET, the 80287 is initialized to real-mode operation. The FSETPM instruction is provided to switch the coprocessor into protected mode if required to match the operating mode of the processor. The 80287 is the only coprocessor that requires this instruction. When operating in protected mode, the NPX can access any area of memory available to the current task. All memory references are automatically verified by the 80286's memory management and protection mechanisms and protection violations cause a processor exception.

The operating mode of the coprocessor affects only the format in which instructions and data pointers are stored in memory by an FSAVE or FSTENV instruction. When operating in real mode, the 20-bit physical addresses of the instruction and data pointers are saved. In protected mode, the 16-bit selector and 16-bit offset for both pointers are saved. (The instruction and data pointer registers are discussed later in this chapter.)

The 80387 and 80486   The 80386 processor and its corresponding coprocessor, the 80387, exchange both instructions and operands using I/O bus cycles. To the processor, the 80387 NPX looks like a special peripheral. Whenever the processor encounters an instruction bound for the NPX, it initiates I/O bus cycles automatically using reserved I/O addresses. These I/O operations are performed using 32-bit I/O addresses with the high-order bit set (that is, port addresses greater than 80000000h) and are invisible to software. Programs running on the processor are not able to access these locations since the instruction set will not accommodate a 32-bit I/O address.

Because the CPU initiates all memory access, the coprocessor can use any memory that is currently accessible to the processor. If the processor is operating in protected mode, the full memory protection mechanisms of the processor are in effect for all coprocessor operations. Protection violations that result from the operation of the NPX are reported as exceptions.

Unlike the 80287, the operating mode of the 80387 does not have to be set explicitly to match the operating mode of the processor. The FSETPM instruction is implemented as an NOP for compatibility reasons. The operating mode does affect how instruction and data pointers are stored in memory following an FSAVE or FSTENV instruction. Four saved-data formats are possible depending on the operating mode and the operand size attribute in effect when the instruction is executed. These formats are presented later in this chapter.

The floating-point unit (FPU) of the 80486DX is the on-chip equivalent of the 387DX. Because the FPU is on the same chip as the CPU, opcodes and data are exchanged directly between the two units. A computer system that is built around the 80486SX processor will not be able to execute ESC instructions without an 80487SX chip installed. Once installed, however, the 80487SX processor disables the 80486SX and operates identically to the 80486DX.

The Registers

From a programmer's point of view, installing an 80x87 coprocessor into a computer system simply expands the existing instruction and register sets of the processor. The register set of the 80x87 coprocessors is, for most purposes, identical across the entire family. All coprocessors have eight 80-bit numeric registers that can be addressed individually or used in a classical stack format. Three additional 16-bit registers are used to hold status, control, and floating-point stack information. The 80x87 also has access to two data and instruction pointers that are physically located in the CPU. Each type of register is explained in detail in this section.

The Register Stack The coprocessor contains eight 80-bit floating-point numeric registers that are functionally divided into three fields: a 1-bit sign field, a 15-bit exponent field, and a 64-bit mantissa field as shown in Figure 10.3. The format of the registers corresponds to the 80-bit temporary real data type used for floating-point calculations.

FIGURE 10.3

NPX register stack

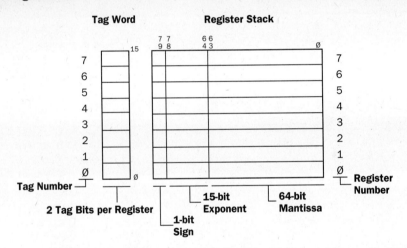

Tag	Meaning
ØØ	Valid
Ø1	Zero
1Ø	Special (NaN, ∞, Denormal, or unsupported)
11	Empty

The numeric registers of the coprocessor are organized in an eight-element *classical stack* architecture. Don't confuse the 80x87 *register* stack with the 80x86 *program* stack. The program stack is implemented in memory using the SS and SP registers as pointers. The 80x87 stack is implemented using physical registers as elements. The registers that make up the stack are located within the coprocessor itself. The coprocessor stack does not reside in memory and the registers do not point to memory.

The register stack operates by adding or removing one data entry at a time. The most recent entry is added at the top of the stack and will be the first one to be removed. This type of stack operation is known as last-in-first-out (LIFO), or equivalently, first-in-last-out (FILO). The terms may be used interchangeably.

In a classical stack machine, the operation of the processor does not depend on the use of addressable registers, as is the case with the 80x86 processor, for example. Instead, the stack machine is designed to use the stack for *all* data manipulation. The processor instructions do not take explicit operands, but implicitly use the value at the top of the stack for unary operations or the top two values on the stack for binary operations. For example, to evaluate the formula 159+(5+(101+2)) on a hypothetical stack machine (using a hypothetical instruction set), this sequence could be used:

```
PUSH 101    ;Load operand
PUSH  22    ;Load operand
ADD         ;Add top two stack elements
PUSH   5    ;Load operand
ADD         ;Add top two stack elements
PUSH 159    ;Load operand
ADD         ;Add top two stack elements
POP         ;Clear the stack
```

The first two instructions shown in this example place operands on the stack. In this case, we've use the two constants 101 and 22 for operands. The third instruction, ADD, will remove the top two operands from the stack, add them together, and push the result back onto the stack. When the ADD operation is complete, the stack will have one less entry than when we began, and the original two operands will have been destroyed. Figure 10.4 shows how the stack machine would execute these and the subsequent instructions given in the example. Note that this type of operation may require the presence of temporary registers internal to the stack machine that are used during the calculation; operands are not moved into processor general registers for the operations.

(This type of expression evaluation may be familiar to many of you as postfix or reverse-Polish notation [RPN]. A popular line of pocket calculators use postfix notation and are examples of classical stack machines. To perform addition, both operands are placed on the stack using the ENTER key, then operated on by using the + key. The display always shows the contents of the top entry on the stack. The FORTH programming language is also designed to emulate the operation of a classical stack machine for programming purposes.)

Although the picture of the floating-point stack shown in Figure 10.4 is operationally correct, the mechanical implementation is somewhat different. Floating-point stack operations never physically move or erase entries on the stack. Instead, 3 bits of the status register hold a pointer that indicates which of the eight registers is current at the top of the stack. As operands are added to the stack or removed from the stack, the pointer is updated so that one of the eight floating-point registers is always designated as the top element of the stack. This element is referred to as the stack top (ST), or equivalently ST(0), meaning the 0th element of the stack. Figure 10.5 shows an example of the actual operation of the NPX floating-point stack during the same series of operations given in the previous example. In this example, register 4 has arbitrarily been designated as the stack top when execution begins. Note that operands that are popped as part of an instruction execution are not erased or removed from the stack. The tag word is updated to show them as empty, however, and attempts to use them in calculations will result in an exception.

FIGURE 10.4

Operation of a classical stack machine

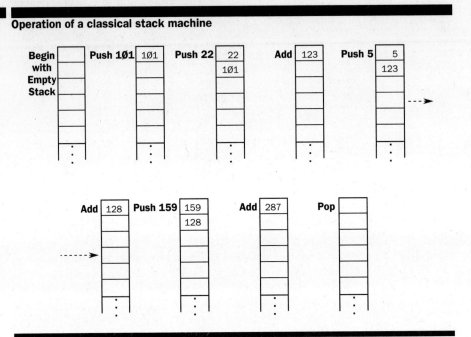

A major disadvantage of the classical stack machine architecture is that only the top register is visible to the programmer. To access a register that is farther down on the stack, the operands above it must be removed. To avoid this shortcoming, the numeric registers of the coprocessor are also addressable individually. Most floating-point instructions permit registers to be addressed by number and explicitly encoded into instruction opcode. An instruction would specify the second stack element as ST(1), the third as ST(2), and so on.

Because they can be addressed individually, the numeric registers may be used as general-purpose floating-point registers to hold constants, temporary values, counters, and so on. The register stack could be loaded by pushing the operands, then addressed individually as required. This flexibility makes design of numerical programs easier and allows for increased efficiency in coding. The dual addressing modes of the register stack are discussed more fully in Chapters 11 and 12.

FIGURE 10.5

NPX stack machine implementation

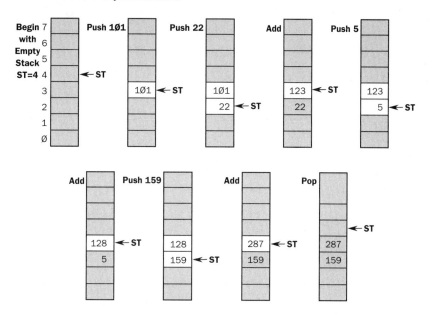

Stack entries marked as empty are shown shaded.

Status Word   The coprocessor maintains a 16-bit register, called the *status word*, that is divided into 14 fields whose values report the state of the coprocessor. The individual flags in the status register are analogous to the status flags in the CPU's FLAGS register. The fields of the status word are shown in Figure 10.6 and described below.

If, during the execution of an ESC instruction, the NEU encounters an exception, it reports it by setting one of the lower 6 bits of the status register. (The situations that generate these six exceptions are discussed in Chapter 11.) A separate bit is dedicated to provided reporting for each of these error conditions: invalid operation exception (IE bit), denormalized operand exception (DE bit), zero divide exception (ZE bit), overflow exception (OE bit), underflow exception (UE bit), and precision exception (PE bit). These exception bits are "sticky," and are cleared only by the FINIT, FCLEX, FLDENV, FSAVE, and FRSTOR instructions.

Bit 6, the *Stack Fault* flag (SF), is defined only for the 80386 and later processors and distinguishes an invalid operation that occurs due to a stack overflow (attempting to load an operand into a register that is not empty) or underflow (attempting to pop an operand from an empty register) from other types of invalid operations. When SF is set, the C_1 field (bit 9) indicates whether the condition was a stack overflow ($C_1=1$) or underflow ($C_1=0$).

FIGURE 10.6

The NPX status word

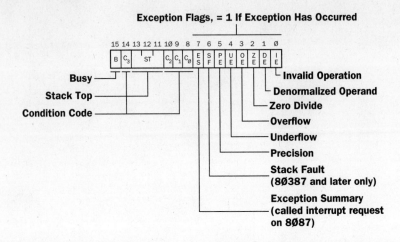

Bit 7 is designated the *Interrupt Request* (IR) flag on the 8087 and the *Exception Summary Status* (ES) flag on the 80287 and later coprocessors. The ES flag is set by the coprocessor if one or more of the exception bits are unmasked and set. If not, the ES flag is cleared. If ES is set, the NPX's ERROR# signal is asserted. The ES flag provides a simple method of checking for a pending floating-point interrupt.

The condition code flags of the NPX are located in bits 8, 9, 10, and 14 (designated C_0, C_1, C_2, and C_3, respectively) of the status register. The NEU updates the values of these flags to reflect the status of arithmetic operations. The test and compare functions also use these flags to report the result of their operations. Table 10.2 shows the interpretation of the condition code flags after the examine, compare, test, and remainder operations.

The condition code flags can be examined by storing the contents of the status register, using the FSTSW AX instruction, for example, then copying them into the FLAGS register using the SAHF instruction. If this is done, the C_0 bit corresponds to the Carry flag, C_2 to the Parity flag, and C_3 to the Zero flag. C_1 has no corresponding bit in the FLAGS register. Once loaded into FLAGS, the result of the numeric operation can be tested with a conditional jump or set instruction.

The number of the register stack element that is the current stack top is reported in bits 11, 12, and 13 of the status register. These three bits are referred to collectively as the *stack top* (ST) field. If ST=101b, for example, numeric register 5 is the current stack top. Note that an operation that loads (pushes) an element onto the register stack, decrements the value in the ST field, then copies the operand to the new stack top register. If ST=000b, a load operation leaves ST=111b. Conversely, popping the stack when ST=111b will leave ST=000b.

TABLE 10.2

The NPX Condition Codes

Instruction Type	C_3	C_2	C_1	C_0	Meaning
Examine	0	0	0	0	Valid, positive unnormalized (+Unnormal)
	0	0	0	1	Invalid, positive, exponent=0 (+NaN)
	0	0	1	0	Valid, negative, unnormalized (–Unnormal)
	0	0	1	1	Invalid, negative, exponent=0 (–NaN)
	0	1	0	0	Valid, positive, normalized (+Normal)
	0	1	0	1	Infinity, positive (+∞)
	0	1	1	0	Valid, negative, normalized (–Normal)
	0	1	1	1	Infinity, negative (–∞)
	1	0	0	0	Zero, positive (+0)
	1	0	0	1	Empty
	1	0	1	0	Zero, negative (–0)
	1	0	1	1	Empty
	1	1	0	0	Invalid, positive, exponent=0 (+Denormal)
	1	1	0	1	Empty
	1	1	1	0	Invalid, negative, exponent=0 (–Denormal)
	1	1	1	1	Empty
FCOM or FTST	0	0	x	0	ST > source operand (FCOM) ST > 0 (FTST)
	0	0	x	1	ST < source operand (FCOM) ST < 0 (FTST)
	1	0	x	0	ST = source operand (FCOM) ST = 0 (FTST)
	1	1	x	1	ST is not comparable
Remainder	q_1	0	q_0	q_2	Complete reduction. The three low bits of the quotient stored in C_0, C_3, and C_1
	u	1	u	u	Incomplete reduction

ST = Stack top
x = Don't care; bit is not affected by instruction
u = Bit is undefined following instruction

Bit 15 of the status register is designated the *busy* (B) bit. On the 8087 and 80287, the busy bit reflects the status of the coprocessor's BUSY# signal. The busy bit is cleared to 0 when the NEU is idle and set to 1 if the NEU is currently executing an ESC instruction. The busy bit will also be set if the NPX is signaling an exception. This allows the exception condition to be handled before an attempt is made to execute another ESC instruction.

On the 80387 and later coprocessors, the busy bit does not reflect the status of the NPX's BUSY# signal. Instead, it is set to the same value as the ES bit to maintain compatibility with the 8087 and 80287.

Control Word The coprocessor maintains another 16-bit register, called the *control word*, which is divided into 12 fields. Different types of numeric processing require different types of handling. To accommodate this, the NPX provides several operational options that are selectable by programming the control word. By setting or clearing these fields, the programmer can exercise control over the operation of certain aspects of the coprocessor. The individual flags that make up the control word are analogous to the processor control flags in the CPU's FLAGS register. The fields of the control word are shown in Figure 10.7 and described below.

FIGURE 10.7

The NPX control word

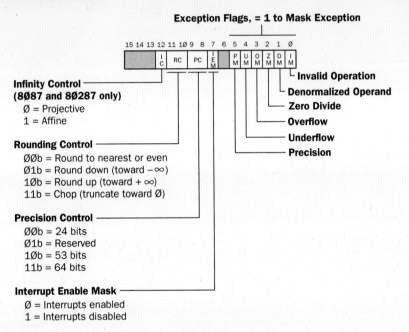

Shaded bits are reserved.

The low-order 8 bits (bits 0 through 7) of the control word are used to control the NPX's exception and error masking. The lower 6 bits individually mask the six possible numerical error exceptions detected by the NEU. The position of each masking bit is the same as the position of the corresponding reporting flag in the status register. If the masking bit is set to 1 (exception masked), the NPX will handle the exception internally using its on-chip *masked response*. If a masking bit is cleared to 0 (exception unmasked), the NPX will issue an interrupt request to invoke an external handler; this is called the *unmasked response*.

On the 8087 only, the behavior of an unmasked exception is dependent on the value of bit 7 of the control word, the *interrupt enable mask* (IEM) field. An unmasked interrupt will set the interrupt request bit in the status register, but will not generate an interrupt if the IEM bit is set to 1. This bit is not defined for later processors and is ignored.

The setting of the *precision control* (PC) field (bits 8 and 9) controls the internal operating precision of the NEU. Normally, the NEU uses a 64-bit mantissa for all internal calculations. Different settings of the precision control field, however, can be used to reduce this precision to 53 or 24 bits for compatibility with earlier-generation math processors. This feature is provided for compatibility with the IEEE 754 standard and affects the operation of only the FADD, FSUB, FSUBR, FMUL, FDIV, FDIVR, and FSQRT instructions. (Note that lowering the precision will not decrease the execution time of floating-point instructions.)

The setting of the *rounding control* (RC) field (bits 10 and 11) controls the type of rounding that is used in numeric calculations. Options are provided for rounding in a specific direction, chopping (truncation), and the round-to-nearest-or-even mode specified by the IEEE 754 standard. Rounding control affects only arithmetic instructions.

The *infinity control* (IC) field (bit 12) controls whether infinity is treated as affine or projective. Affine closure treats positive infinity as a separate and distinct quantity from negative infinity; when compared, positive infinity is reported as having a greater value than negative infinity. Projective closure treats both cases of infinity as a single unsigned quantity. This bit is effective only on the 8087 and 80287. To conform to the IEEE standard, the 80387 and later coprocessors support only affine closure and the setting of this bit is ignored.

Tag Word   The coprocessor monitors the operands in each of the registers of the floating-point stack with a 16-bit register called the *tag word*. The format of the tag word was shown earlier in Figure 10.3. Each of the eight floating-point registers is described by 2 bits in the tag word that reflect the type of entry that is in the register. The NEU uses the information in the tag word to optimize its performance by quickly distinguishing between empty and nonempty registers.

The eight fields of the tag word correspond to the *physical* numbers of the floating-point registers. The ST field in the status register must be used to determine the relationship between a tag field entry and the ST-relative stack registers ST(0) through ST(7).

Normally, the tag word is not used directly by applications. Programmers may, however, examine the values in the tag word to quickly interpret the contents of the floating-point registers without extensive decoding. The NPX updates the tag word when the FSTENV and FSAVE instructions are executed to accurately reflect the contents of the floating-point stack. During the execution of other instructions, the tag word is updated only to indicate whether a stack location is empty or nonempty.

Exception Pointers   When the processor decodes an ESC instruction, it saves the address of the instruction and the instruction opcode in a set of registers called the *exception pointers*. If a reference to a memory operand is encoded in the instruction, the address of the operand is saved in the data pointer. If no memory operand was specified by the instruction, the value stored in the data pointer is undefined. The following instructions, however, do not affect the value stored in the data pointer: FCLEX, FLDCW, FLDENV, FRSTOR, FSTCW, FSTENV, FSTSW, and FSAVE. The FINIT instruction will clear the pointers only on an 80486 or 80487SX.

The instruction, opcode, and data pointers are physically located in the CPU—not in the NPX—but appear to be part of the coprocessor. They can be accessed only by using the FSTENV, FSAVE, FLDENV, and FRSTOR instructions. The FSTENV and FSAVE instructions copy the contents of the exception pointers into memory, where they may be examined. If an exception occurs, the handler can use this information to determine the exact cause of the exception.

When stored into memory, the format of the exception pointers is dependent on both the processor type and on the current operating mode. The formats of the saved data for 16-bit real mode, 16-bit protected mode, 32-bit real mode, and 32-bit protected mode are shown in Figures 10.8 through 10.11.

FIGURE 10.8

16-bit real-mode exception pointer memory format

15 12 11 10 0	
Data Pointer (bits 16-19) Ø Ø Ø Ø Ø Ø Ø Ø Ø Ø Ø Ø	
Data Pointer (bits Ø-15)	
Instruction Pointer (bits 16-31) Ø Opcode (11 bits)	
Instruction Pointer (bits Ø-15)	
Tag Word	
Status Word	
Control Word	

On the 80287 and later coprocessors, the instruction address saved includes any prefixes that preceded the floating-point instruction. On the 8087, however, the saved address does not include prefixes. Exception handlers must account for this difference.

System Interface Considerations

During initialization, system software must assess the installed hardware and configure itself appropriately to allocate and monitor the available physical resources—including the math coprocessor. In a typical personal computer system, this responsibility falls to the ROM initialization code. In a protected-mode system, the operating system usually performs this task.

FIGURE 10.9

32-bit real-mode exception pointer memory format

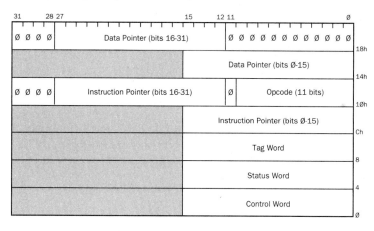

Shaded areas are reserved.

FIGURE 10.10

16-bit protected-mode exception pointer memory format

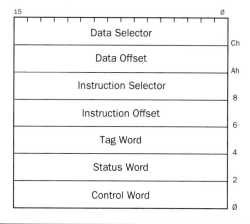

In this section, an overview of the system control issues related to the coprocessor, including emulation and exception handling, is presented. Note that assembly language routines that can recognize the presence of a math coprocessor have been given in the CPUID program presented in Chapter 3.

System Configuration

Once the system has determined whether a coprocessor is present in the system, it must configure itself accordingly. Configuration requires that the MP (Monitor Processor Extension) and EM (Emulate Coprocessor) flags be set correctly in the processor's machine status word (on an 80286) or processor control register CR0 (80386 and later). The MP flag indicates to the processor that a coprocessor is present in the system. If ESC instructions are to be executed directly by the coprocessor, the MP flag must be set to 1 and the EM flag must be cleared to 0.

FIGURE 10.11

32-bit protected-mode exception pointer memory format

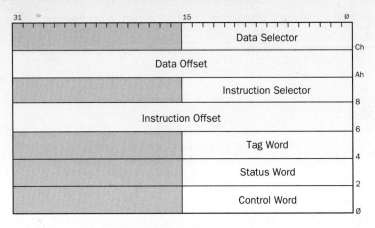

Shaded areas are reserved.

The MP flag also determines how the processor handles execution of the WAIT instruction. If MP=1 and the processor encounters a WAIT instruction, it will test the task switched (TS) bit in the current task state segment (TSS). If TS=1 under these conditions, the context of the current task is different from that of the coprocessor and the processor will generate interrupt 7 (coprocessor not available). This operation gives the exception handler the opportunity to save and restore the state of the coprocessor in a multitasking environment. (The coprocessor state is not automatically saved by a task switch.)

On the 80286 and 80386 processors, the MP flag supported the use of a WAIT instruction to force the processor to wait on a device other than a numeric coprocessor. The device would report its status on the processor's BUSY# signal pin. The 80486DX processor has no BUSY# pin. In this case, the MP flag is not relevant and should be set to 1 for normal operation of the on-chip FPU. An 80486SX-based system should set this bit only if an 80487SX is present.

If ESC instructions are to be emulated in software, the EM flag must be set to 1 and the MP flag must be cleared to 0. If the processor encounters an ESC instruction and finds EM=1, it immediately generates interrupt 7. This passes control to an exception handler, which can then emulate the floating-point instruction in software. If EM=1, the WAIT instruction does not cause the processor to check the status of its ERROR# pin.

On the 80286, the EM flag can be changed only by using the LMSW (load machine status word) instruction, which is executable only when the task is running in either real mode or in protected mode at privilege level 0 (most privileged). The setting of the EM flag can be examined, regardless of privilege level, using the SMSW (store machine status word) instruction.

Table 10.3 summarizes the system response to execution of ESC and WAIT instructions for each combination of the EM, TS, and MP flags.

TABLE 10.3

System Response for Coprocessor Configuration Flag Settings

CPU CR0 Bit			Instruction Type	
EM	TS	MP	ESC	WAIT
0	0	0	Execute	Execute
0	0	1	Execute	Execute
0	1	0	Interrupt 7	Execute
0	1	1	Interrupt 7	Interrupt 7
1	0	0	Interrupt 7	Execute
1	0	1	Interrupt 7	Execute
1	1	0	Interrupt 7	Execute
1	1	1	Interrupt 7	Interrupt 7

On the 80386DX, the ET (Coprocessor Extension Type) flag in control register CR0 should be set to indicate the type of coprocessor that is present in the system, if any. If an 80387DX is present, ET should be set to 1. If an 80287 is present or no coprocessor is installed, ET should be cleared to 0.

The NE (Numeric Exception) flag is defined only for the 80486 processor and determines whether unmasked floating-point exceptions are handled through interrupt vector 10h (NE=1) or through an external interrupt (NE=0). Systems using an external interrupt controller to invoke numeric exceptions (such a system is used on the IBM AT and compatible computers running under DOS) should ensure that NE is cleared to 0 (the default value at RESET). When configured this way, coprocessor errors are reported via interrupt 0Dh.

When NE=0, the 80486 works in conjunction with the IGNNE# input and the FERR# output pins. If an unmasked floating-point error occurs while the IGNNE# line is inactive, the processor will halt before executing the next non-control ESC or WAIT instruction. When FERR# is driven active, the external interrupt controller supplies an interrupt vector to handle the error. If IGNNE# is active, unmasked floating-point errors are ignored and floating-point execution continues.

If NE=1, an unmasked floating-point exception causes a software interrupt 10h to be invoked immediately before executing the next non-control or WAIT instruction. The IGNNE# signal is ignored.

Emulation

A computer system without a math coprocessor is still capable of performing floating-point math if the operating system chooses to emulate the execution of ESC instructions transparent to the application. The hardware-assisted emulation described here is available only on the 80287 and later coprocessors.

If the MP (Monitor Coprocessor Extension) flag is cleared to 0 and the EM (Emulate Math Coprocessor) flag is set to 1, an attempt to execute an ESC instruction will automatically cause the processor to generate interrupt 7 (coprocessor not available). An exception handler may then determine the address of the instruction causing the exception by examining the address saved by the interrupt. The address will point to the first byte of the ESC instruction that caused the fault, including any prefixes. The instruction may then be decoded and emulated in software. Before control is returned to the original task, the saved address must be adjusted to point past the original ESC instruction.

In order to use the emulator successfully, applications that are executing in protected mode must use code segments that are readable as well as executable. The emulator must read the code in order to decode and emulate the ESC instruction. If this is not the case, the emulator will not be able to read the instruction that caused the exception.

Operating systems that use software floating-point emulators must also account for a slight difference in how floating-point exceptions may be reported. If an ESC instruction results in an exception, the coprocessor will not report the exception until it encounters the next WAIT or ESC instruction. The address saved by the exception, therefore, points to this second instruction. If a software emulator is in use, exception handlers may be invoked from within the emulator itself (as is the case with Intel's floating-point emulators). Thus the address saved by the exception may point to the code being executed inside the emulator and not to an ESC instruction. In either case, the instruction that caused the exception can be identified by examining the exception pointers.

The emulation scheme described here is based on properties of the processor and coprocessor hardware. It is not the same as the software-based emulation mechanism used in many programming languages when operating under DOS in real mode. These software-based schemes use software interrupts instead of ESC instructions in the application object code and will work equally well for all systems, including those based on the 8086 and 8088.

Under this scheme, if a coprocessor is present in the system, the software interrupt handlers (installed by the system or by an application) will patch the executable code to execute an ESC instruction directly. If no coprocessor is present, the interrupt handlers provide floating-point emulation of the instruction. Note that an explicitly coded WAIT instruction will not be modified. If no coprocessor is present, the 8086 and 8088 will wait forever. The FWAIT instruction should always be used when the CPU is to wait for an 8087. Note also that the software interrupt versions of the floating-point instructions will *not* cause the exception pointers in the CPU to be loaded.

Initialization (FINIT)

The FINIT (floating-point initialization) instruction is designed to place the coprocessor in a known state. When executed, all numeric errors are masked, the tag word is set to indicate that all registers are empty, the ST (stack top) field in the status register is cleared to 000b, and the default values for the rounding, precision, and infinity controls are loaded. Table 10.4 shows the values that the fields in each of the coprocessor registers hold after an FINIT instruction has executed.

TABLE 10.4

Coprocessor State After FINIT

Field	Value	Interpretation
Control Word		
Infinity Control[1]	0	Projective (8087 and 80287) Affine (80287XL and later)
Rounding Control	00b	Round to nearest
Precision Control	11b	64 bits
Interrupt-Enable Mask	1	Interrupts masked
Exception Masks	111111b	All exceptions masked
Status Word		
Busy	0	Not busy
Condition Code	????b	Indeterminate
Stack Top	000b	Register 0 is stack top
Exception Summary[2]	0	No interrupt pending
Stack Flag[3]	0	–
Exception Flags	000000b	No exceptions
Tag Word		
Tags	1111111111111111b	All registers empty
Registers		
Registers 0–7	–	Not changed
Exception Pointers		
Instruction Opcode	–	Not changed[4]
Instruction Address	–	Not changed[4]
Operand Address	–	Not changed[4]

[1]The infinity control bit is not meaningful for the 80287XL, 80387, 80486 FPU, or the 80487SX. These coprocessors support only affine closure regardless of the setting of this bit.
[2]This bit is called the interrupt request bit on the 8087.
[3]Defined for the 80287XL and later coprocessors only.
[4]The 80486DX and 80487SX clear this register.

Following a RESET signal, the 80287 is initialized in real mode. Once the 80287 has been switched into protected mode (using the FSETPM instruction), only another hardware RESET will switch it back to real mode. (The situation is the same for the 80286.) The FINIT instruction will not change the operating mode of the 80287. This is not an issue for other coprocessors as the 8087 operates only in real mode, and the 80387 and later processors operate identically independent of operating mode.

The FINIT instruction does not initialize the 80387 coprocessor to the same state it has following RESET. After a RESET, the ERROR# output is asserted to indicate to the external hardware that an 80387 is present. This is done by setting the IE and ES bits in the status word and clearing the IEM bit in the control word. To clear this condition, a FINIT instruction with no proceeding WAIT instruction (FNINIT) must be executed, leaving the status word and control word with the same values as an 80287 after RESET.

Unlike previous coprocessors, the FPU of the 80486 and the 80487SX clears the exception pointers during a FINIT. System software should not count on the values in these registers after a FINIT instruction has executed.

Exceptions

The NPX checks for six different classes of exception conditions that can occur during instruction execution. Table 10.5 lists the exceptions, the cause of each exception, and the masked and unmasked response of the NPX in each case. Note that the execution of a single instruction may generate more than one exception. The causes of floating-point exceptions and errors are discussed in more detail in Chapter 11.

An exception that is not masked in the control word will set the corresponding exception flag in the status word and assert the ERROR# signal. When the processor attempts to execute another ESC or WAIT instruction, an exception will occur. The exception condition must be resolved by the exception handler. The return address pushed onto the stack does not point to the failing instruction. The address of the failing instruction is saved in the CPU's exception pointer registers described previously.

Note that an exception condition does not necessarily indicate a numerical error has occurred. The stack overflow and underflow exceptions, for example, could be used to provide "virtual registers" to extend the size of the floating-point register stack.

On the 80486DX and the 80487SX, the exception that is generated is dependent on the setting of the NE (Numeric Exception) flag. When NE=0, IBM AT-type hardware error handling is used and the external interrupt controller supplies an interrupt vector to handle the error. If NE=1, an unmasked floating-point exception causes a software interrupt 10h to be invoked immediately before executing the next non-control or WAIT instruction.

TABLE 10.5

Masked and Unmasked Exception Responses

Exception	Masked Response	Unmasked Response
Invalid Operation	If one operand is a NaN, return it. If both operands are NaNs, return the NaN with the larger absolute value. If neither operand is a NaN, return *indefinite*.	Request interrupt.
Zero Divide	Return ∞ signed with the exclusive-OR of the two operand signs.	Request interrupt.
Denormal	If a memory operand, continue. If a register operand, convert to a valid unnormal, then reevaluate for additional exceptions.	Request interrupt.
Overflow	Return properly signed ∞	If the destination is a register, adjust the exponent, store the result, and request interrupt. If the destination is memory, request interrupt.
Underflow	Denormalize result.	If the destination is a register, adjust the exponent, store the result, and request interrupt. If the destination is memory, request interrupt.
Precision	Return rounded result.	Return rounded result, request interrupt.

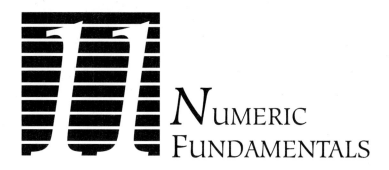

Numeric Fundamentals

THE PROCESSOR AND COPROCESSOR ARE BOTH ABLE TO DETECT ERRORS THAT occur during normal execution. Unlike the processor, however, the coprocessor is empowered to alter data in an attempt to fix these errors and bring its calculations to a successful conclusion. Numeric processing is an exacting process and can generate many errors and warnings. In giving the coprocessor more authority over handling errors, its designers have simplified the task of programming, but have complicated the task of understanding the coprocessor.

In this chapter, the NPX's treatment and interpretation of numeric values and operations are presented. Topics covered include the operation of the rounding, precision, and infinity controls. The response of the NPX to errors, both masked and unmasked, is also discussed. In addition, complete maps of the encodings for real, integer, and BCD data types are presented along with a discussion of the supported and unsupported formats.

Numeric Basics

Basic to all numeric applications are the concepts of number systems, accuracy, precision, and error handling. Number systems and the coprocessor data types have been discussed earlier in Chapters 2 and 10. In this section, the capability to control the actions of the coprocessor and influence the result of numeric processing is presented.

Rounding Control

A realizable representation of a binary floating-point number will have a fixed number of digits and therefore a limited precision. A number can be represented exactly if its required precision is not greater than the available precision. If, however, the destination for a number has fewer bits (less precision) than is needed to represent the number exactly, the FPU will *round* the value during arithmetic and store operations. A temporary real value in an FPU register, for example, may be rounded when written to an integer memory operand.

The FPU has four possible rounding modes, one of which is selected depending on the value of the rounding control (RC) field in the NPX control word as shown in Table 11.1. (The fields and format of the control word are discussed in Chapter 10.)

The *round to nearest or even* mode is the default, and is selected automatically whenever the coprocessor is initialized. Typically, this mode works best for most applications, and provides the most accurate and statistically unbiased estimate of the true result.

TABLE 11.1

The RC Field and Rounding Modes

RC	Mode	Action, where $a<b<c$
00b	Round to nearest or even	Closer to b of a or c. If equally close, select the even number (least significant bit=0). (Default)
01b	Round down (toward $-\infty$)	a
10b	Round up (toward $+\infty$)	c
11b	Chop (toward 0)	Smaller in magnitude of a or c

The *chop* mode is typically used in integer arithmetic. A number is always chopped to the nearest integer that is smaller in magnitude. The number 6.7 will be chopped to 6, for example, and –4.5 will be chopped to –4. Chopping is also referred to as truncation or rounding toward zero.

The remaining two modes, *round up* and *round down,* provide what is collectively referred to as directed rounding and are used to implement interval arithmetic. Interval arithmetic generates two results, one calculated with all operations rounding up and the other with all operations rounding down. The two results form the upper and lower error bounds of the calculation and give a result that is independent of individual rounding errors.

Precision Control

The FPU is able to calculate results with 24, 53, or 64 bits of precision as selected by the precision control (PC) field of the control word. Normally, PC=11b, selecting the default 64-bit mantissa for all internal calculations. Different settings of the precision control field, however, can be used to reduce this precision to 53 or 24 mantissa bits as shown in Table 11.2.

TABLE 11.2

The PC Field and Precision Modes

PC	Precision (bits)
00b	24
01b	*reserved*
10b	53
11b	64

The alternate precision settings are provided for compatibility with earlier-generation math processors as required by the IEEE 754 standard. The precision control affects the operation of only the FADD, FSUB, FSUBR, FMUL, FDIV, FDIVR, and FSQRT instructions. Lowering the precision nullifies the advantages of the temporary precision internal format and does not generally decrease the execution time of floating-point instructions.

Infinity Control

When the 8087 was engineered, no independent standard for floating-point calculations was in existence. When the 80287 was designed, IEEE standard 754 was still in a draft form. By the time the 80387 was produced, the standard had been finalized. One subject covered by the standard was the closure of real number systems. The 8087 and 80287 implement both projective and affine closure while the 80387 and 80486 implement affine closure only. The 80287XL, Intel's replacement revision of the 80287, brings it into conformance with the IEEE standard; it, too, supports affine closure exclusively.

In the projective closure mode, negative infinity ($-\infty$) and positive infinity ($+\infty$) are treated in operations as a single, unsigned quantity. (This is analogous to the way the processor treats the values -0 and $+0$.) In the affine mode, the sign of the infinity is respected and propagated throughout calculations.

The 8087 and 80287 select projective closure as their default state when initialized, clearing the infinity control (IC) bit in the NPX control word to 0. They may both be switched to affine closure by setting IC=1. The later coprocessors support only affine closure, regardless of the setting of IC.

Special Numeric Values

This section covers the NPX's generation and handling of special numeric values: nonnormalized reals, zeros, infinities, and NaNs. The average numeric program, based on computations that involve valid operands, will not require special programming to accommodate these numeric types. In most cases, these values will not appear at all. If they do, the default NPX operation will likely provide suitable responses and results. Most programmers, therefore, will not require the detailed knowledge of these special numeric values presented here. If you anticipate that your numeric programming will have to accommodate these values or if you are trying to increase your understanding of the numeric processor, then the information in this section will be of interest.

The first part of this section discusses the NPX's generation and handling of each type of special numeric value. Following this is a tabular listing of the bit encodings allocated to each type. Note that many of the values supported on early coprocessors and defined here were reclassified as unsupported in the final revision of the IEEE 754 standard. Where appropriate, the particular chips that do or do not support a particular format are noted.

Nonnormal Real Numbers

Binary floating-point numbers are usually stored in normalized form. When normalized, the leftmost (integer) bit of the mantissa is always a 1. In the short real and long real formats, this 1 digit is not actually stored, but is implied in the format. In the temporary real format, all digits of the mantissa, including the integer 1, are stored explicitly. Normalizing allows the greatest number of significant digits to be stored in a fixed-length format. (See Chapter 3 for more information on real number formats.)

Although a great quantity of numbers can be represented as binary real numbers, there exists a set of real numbers that are too small in magnitude (too close to zero) to be represented accurately in one of the standard normalized formats. A number, r, that meets these conditions is termed *tiny,* and is defined by the following formulas:

$$-2^{Emin} < r < 0$$

or

$$0 < r < +2^{Emin}$$

Here, Emin is defined to be –126 for short real, –1022 for long real, and –16382 for temporary real.

To accommodate these tiny values, the NPX supports nonnormalized formats. In a nonnormal number, the first stored digit of the mantissa is *not* 1. Consequently, the nonnormal holds fewer significant digits than the maximum allowed and some precision is lost. Nonnormals formed from the short real and long real formats are classified as denormals. Nonnormals encoded in the temporary real format may be either denormals or unnormals.

Denormals The NPX's masked response to an underflow is to produce a *denormal*. Underflow occurs when the exponent of the true result is too small (too negative) to be represented in the desired format. For example, assume that the destination is a short real, and the exponent of the true result is –200. An underflow will occur because the minimum exponent that can be represented by a short real is –126. (Remember that these exponents represent powers of 2, not powers of 10.)

The unmasked response of the NPX is to signal an underflow exception and request an interrupt if the destination is memory. If the destination is a register, the NPX adds 24576 (6000h) to the exponent, forcing it into the available range for a temporary real, returns the result, then requests the interrupt. The exception handler simply subtracts 6000h to recover the original exponent. In either case, program execution stops when an unmasked underflow occurs.

In contrast, the masked response of the NPX is to denormalize the operand, a response designed to allow program execution to continue without external intervention. The process of denormalization, however, introduces an error into the calculations. This error results in a precision loss and is similar in impact to the error induced by a rounding operation. As with rounding errors, the final result must be examined to determine if the error introduced by denormalization has had a significant effect on the result. (A serious error introduced by denormalization will probably produce an invalid operation as calculations continue.)

The response of an unsophisticated floating-point processor (such as a pocket calculator) to an underflow situation is to underflow "abruptly" and return a zero result. If this zero is propagated through a series of calculations, it will most likely lead to an incorrect result. When the underflow exception is masked, the 80x87 coprocessors are designed to underflow gradually, losing precision, but retaining an operand that is valid. Gradual underflow is implemented by denormalizing the operand.

The process of denormalization is very straightforward. When the exponent of the true result is smaller (more negative) than can be accommodated by the desired format, the base 2 exponent of the value is incremented and the digits in the mantissa (including the integer 1 bit, whether explicit or implicit) are shifted one place to the right. Any digits shifted out of the right side of the mantissa are lost. This process is repeated until the exponent is within range or all significant digits have been lost. Because the most significant bit of the number is now zero, the representation is no longer normalized. The denormalization process for a short real is illustrated here:

Operation	Exponent	Mantissa (1+23 bits)
True Result	–129	1.011010101001......00
Denormalize	–128	0.1011010101001.....00
Denormalize	–127	0.01011010101001....00
Denormalize	–126	0.001011010101001...00

Before the result produced in the example is stored, the mantissa will be rounded to 24 bits and the exponent will be biased by adding +126. Denormalization will always produce a denormal or, if all nonzero bits are shifted out, a true zero.

Because the short real and long real formats do not store the integer bit of the mantissa explicitly, the processor and programmer must identify a denormal by its exponent, which is always the minimum allowable for its format. In biased form, the minimum exponent will always be 0. While this same exponent is assigned to the various representations of zero, a denormal will always have a nonzero mantissa. The tag value used for a denormal is 10b (special). If *all* the nonzero bits are shifted out of the mantissa, the result will be a true zero and, if in a floating-point register, will be tagged as such (tag=01b).

On the 8087 and 80287, accessing a denormal, such as during a floating-point load operation, or using a denormal as an operand may produce an exception as shown in Table 11.3. If the 80287XL and later coprocessors encounter a denormal during an arithmetic operation, they will raise the denormal exception, then attempt to normalize the operand and continue the operation.

Unnormals A denormal with a biased exponent greater than zero is called an *unnormal*. Unnormals are generated and supported by only the 8087 and 80287 coprocessors, and the discussion below applies only to their handling of unnormals. The 80287XL and later coprocessors will automatically normalize operands if needed, so the encoding of a denormal with a nonzero biased exponent is never created by the coprocessor. If an unnormal is encountered during an arithmetic operation, the 80287XL and later coprocessors will raise the invalid operation exception.

TABLE 11.3

8087 and 80287 Response to Denormal Operands

Operation	Exception	Masked Response
FLD *short_real* FLD *long_real*	Denormal (DE)	Load as an equivalent unnormal
Compare and test	Denormal (DE)	Convert internally to an equivalent unnormal and continue
Division or FPREM with denormal divisor	Invalid (IE)	Return real indefinite
All other arithmetic	Denormal (DE)	Convert internally to an equivalent unnormal and continue

---

An unnormal is created by the NPX only as a "descendent" of a denormal and therefore as an unmasked response to an underflow. By supporting unnormals, the NPX allows computations to continue following an underflow while still indicating that a loss of precision (and a potential loss of accuracy) has occurred. A register that contains an unnormal is tagged as valid (tag=00b).

Unnormalcy is propagated through calculations: unnormal operands generate unnormal results as long as their unnormality has a significant affect on the result. If the affect of an unnormal on the result is insignificant, a normal result will be produced.

The results of operations involving unnormals are summarized in Table 11.4. The source of the unnormal is irrelevant; it may be the original operand or a transient value created internally from a denormal. Unnormals can be converted to normals using the FPREM instruction.

Pseudo-denormals   A special case of denormal occurs when a temporary real is encoded with an exponent of 00...00b and has the most significant bit of its mantissa set to 1. In this case, the number generated is called a *pseudo-denormal*. Pseudo-denormals are supported by the 8087 and 80287 and treated no differently than other denormals.

The 80287XL and later processors do not generate pseudo-denormals, but will use them as operands if they are encountered. Internally, the exponent is changed to 00...01b, the mantissa is unchanged, and the denormal exception is raised.

Zeros

The signed integer data formats support only a single signed representation for zero (+0). The real formats, on the other hand, support both a positive and negative representation for zero. In computations, both signed zeros behave as if they were a single unsigned quantity. If desired, the FXAM instruction can be employed to determine the sign of a zero.

TABLE 11.4

Operations with Unnormal Operands

Operation	Result
Addition and subtraction	Normalization of operand with larger magnitude determines normalization of result
Multiplication	If either operand is unnormal, the result is unnormal
Division with an unnormal dividend	Result is unnormal
FPREM with an unnormal dividend	Result is normalized
Division or FPREM with an unnormal divisor	Signal invalid operation
Compare or FTST	Normalize as much as possible before making comparison
FRNDINT	Normalize as much as possible before rounding
FSQRT	Signal invalid operation
FST or FSTP to short real or long real	If value is above destination's underflow boundary, then signal invalid operation, else signal underflow
FSTP to extended real	Store as usual
FIST, FISTP, or FSBTP	Signal invalid operation
FLD	Load as usual
FXCH	Exchange as usual
All transcendental instructions	Undefined. Operands are not checked, but must be normals

Zeros come in two types, the first of which is called a *true zero* and is supported on all 80x87 coprocessors. If a true zero is placed in a floating-point register either by a load operation or as a result of a calculation, the tag is set to 01b. The results of operations involving true zeros are summarized in Table 11.5.

TABLE 11.5

Operations with True Zeros

Operation Type	Operands	Result
FBLD	+0	+0
FBSTP		
FLD		
FPTAN		
FSIN	−0	−0
FSINCOS[1]		
FSQRT		
F2XM1		
FABS	±0	+0
FCHS	+0	−0

TABLE 11.5

(continued)

Operation Type	Operands	Result
FCHS (cont.)	-0	$+0$
FCOS	±0	$+1$
FILD	$+0$	$+0$
FPATAN	$+0 / +x$ $+0 / +0$ $+0 / +\infty$	$+0$
	$-0 / +x$ $-0 / +0$ $-0 / +\infty$	-0
	$+0 / -x$ $+0 / -0$ $+0 / -\infty$	$-\pi$
	$-0 / -x$ $-0 / -0$ $-0 / -\infty$	$+\pi$
	$-x / \pm0$ $+\infty / \pm0$	$+\pi/2$
	$+x / \pm0$ $-\infty / \pm0$	$-\pi/2$
FPREM FPREM1	0 rem ±0 x rem ±0	Invalid operation
	$+0$ rem $\pm x$	$+0$
	-0 rem $\pm x$	-0
	$+x$ rem $\pm y$	$+0^2$
	$-x$ rem $\pm y$	-0^2
FSCALE	$+0$ by $-\infty$ $+0$ by $+x$	$+0$
	-0 by $-\infty$ -0 by $+x$	-0
	±0 by $+\infty$	Invalid operation
FST FSTP FRNDINT	$+0$ $+x^3$	$+0$
	-0 $-x^3$	-0
FIST FISTP	±0 $\pm x^4$	$+0$

TABLE 11.5

(continued)

Operation Type	Operands	Result
FTST	± 0	Zero
FXAM	$+0$	$C_3=1, C_2=C_1=C_0=0$
	-0	$C_3=C_1=1, C_2=C_0=0$
FXTRACT	$+0$	Both $+0$
	-0	Both -0
FYL2X	$\pm x * \log(\pm 0)$	Zero-divide
	$\pm 0 * \log(\pm 0)$	Invalid operation
FYL2XP1	$+x * \log(+0+1)$ $-x * \log(-0+1)$	$+0$
	$+x * \log(-0+1)$ $-x * \log(+0+1)$	-0
Addition	$(+0) + (+0)$	$+0$
	$(-0) + (-0)$	-0
	$(+0) + (-0)$ $(+x) + (-x)$	0^5
	$(\pm 0) + (+x)$	$+x$
	$(\pm 0) + (-x)$	$-x$
Subtraction	$(+0) - (-0)$	$+0$
	$(-0) - (+0)$	-0
	$(+0) - (+0)$ $(-0) - (-0)$ $(+x) - (+x)$ $(-x) - (-x)$	0^5
	$(\pm 0) - (-x)$ $(+x) - (\pm 0)$	$+x$
	$(\pm 0) - (+x)$ $(-x) - (\pm 0)$	$-x$
Multiplication	$+0 * +0$ $-0 * -0$ $+0 * +x$ $-0 * -x$	$+0$
	$+0 * -0$ $+0 * -x$ $-0 * +x$	-0
	$x * +y$ $-x * -y$	$+0^3$
	$+x * -y$ $-x * +y$	-0^3

TABLE 11.5

(continued)

Operation Type	Operands	Result
Division	±0 / ±0	Invalid operation
	±x / ±0	Zero-divide
	+0 / +x −0 / −x	+0
	+0 / −x −0 / +x	−0
	+x / +y −x / −y	+0[3]
	+x / −y −x / +y	−0[3]
Compare	±0 to +x	±0 < +x
	±0 to ±0	±0 = ±0
	±0 to −x	±0 > −x

Note: x and y denote non-zero positive finite operands.
[1]SIN result.
[2]When y divides into x exactly.
[3]When extreme underflow denormalizes the result to zero.
[4]When the magnitude of x < 1 and is not rounded up.
[5]Sign is + if rounding is nearest, up, or chop. Sign is − if rounding is down.

Pseudo-zeros A second type of zero, called a *pseudo-zero*, is encodable only in the temporary real format. Pseudo-zeros are supported on the 8087 and 80287 coprocessors only. The 80287XL and later coprocessors treat pseudo-zeros as an unsupported format as described later in this chapter.

A pseudo-zero is an unnormal with an all-zero mantissa and a biased exponent that is neither all zeros nor all ones. True zeros have an all-zero exponent, and an all-ones exponent is reserved for indefinites and NaNs. A pseudo-zero will be produced by the multiplication of two unnormals that each contains more than 64 leading zeros in its mantissa. (An unlikely but possible occurrence.)

Pseudo-zeros are handled no differently than other unnormals by the 8087 and 80287 except in the following cases, when they produce the same result as true zeros:

- Compare and test instructions

- FRNDINT

- Division, when the dividend is a true zero or pseudo-zero (the divisor is a pseudo-zero)

The pseudo-zero is treated as an unnormal by the NPX during addition or subtraction with a true zero or another pseudo-zero proceeds. The sign of the result, however, is determined as if the operands were both true zeros, as shown in Table 11.5.

Infinities

The real data formats of the NPX support both a positive and a negative signed representation of infinity. These values are encoded with a biased exponent of all ones and a mantissa of 1▲00...00b. Infinities are distinguished from other NaNs by this special value of their mantissa. If an infinity is stored in a floating-point register, a tag of 10b (special) is used. An infinity may be coded explicitly or it may be created by the NPX as its masked response to an overflow or zero-divide exception. If directed rounding (round up or round down) is in use, the masked response may be to create the largest valid magnitude representable in the destination format rather than infinity.

On the 8087 and 80287 only, infinities behave differently depending on the setting of the infinity control (IC) bit in the control word. When the projective model of infinity (available only on the 8087 and 80287) is selected, the infinities behave as a single value and the sign is disregarded. Under the projective model, infinity cannot be compared to any other value other than infinity. When the affine model of infinity is used, the signs of infinities are respected and normal comparisons are possible. (The affine mode of infinity is available on all coprocessors, and is the only model available on the 80287XL, 80387, and 80846.) Table 11.6 gives the results of operations that involve infinities for both the projective and affine models of infinity.

TABLE 11.6

Operations with Infinities

Operation Type	Operands	Projective Result[1]	Affine Result
FBLD FLD FRNDINT FST FSTP	$+\infty$	$+\infty$	$+\infty$
	$-\infty$	$-\infty$	$-\infty$
FABS	$\pm\infty$	$+\infty$	$+\infty$
FCHS	$+\infty$	$-\infty$	$-\infty$
	$-\infty$	$+\infty$	$+\infty$
FPATAN	$+x \,/\, +\infty$ $+0 \,/\, +\infty$	$+0$	$+0$
	$-x \,/\, +\infty$ $-0 \,/\, +\infty$	-0	-0
	$+\infty \,/\, +\infty$	$+\pi/4$	$+\pi/4$
	$-\infty \,/\, +\infty$	$-\pi/4$	$-\pi/4$

TABLE 11.6

(continued)

Operation Type	Operands	Projective Result[1]	Affine Result
FPATAN (cont.)	$+\infty / \pm x$ $+\infty / \pm 0$	$+\pi/2$	$+\pi/2$
	$-\infty / \pm x$ $-\infty / \pm 0$	$-\pi/2$	$-\pi/2$
	$+\infty / -\infty$	$+3\pi/4$	$+3\pi/4$
	$-\infty / -\infty$	$-3\pi/4$	$-3\pi/4$
	$+x / -\infty$ $+0 / -\infty$	$+\pi$	$+\pi$
	$-x / -\infty$ $-0 / -\infty$	$-\pi$	$-\pi$
FPREM FPREM1	$\pm\infty$ rem $\pm\infty$ $\pm\infty$ rem $\pm x$ $\pm\infty$ rem ± 0	IE	IE
	$+x$ rem $\pm\infty$	$+x$	$+x$
	$-x$ rem $\pm\infty$	$-x$	$-x$
	$+0$ rem $\pm\infty$	$+0$	$+0$
	-0 rem $\pm\infty$	-0	-0
FRNDINT	$+\infty$	$+\infty$	$+\infty$
	$-\infty$	$-\infty$	$-\infty$
FSCALE	$\pm\infty$ by $\pm\infty$ $\pm x$ by $\pm\infty$	IE	IE
	$+\infty$ by ± 0 $+\infty$ by $\pm x$	$+\infty$	$+\infty$
	$-\infty$ by ± 0 $-\infty$ by $\pm x$	$-\infty$	$-\infty$
	$+0$ by $\pm\infty$	$+0$	$+0$
	-0 by $\pm\infty$	-0	-0
FSQRT	$+\infty$	IE	$+\infty$
	$-\infty$	IE	IE
FTST	$+\infty$	IE	$+\infty > 0$
	$-\infty$	IE	$-\infty < 0$
FXAM	$+\infty$		$C_0=C_2=1$ $C_1=C_3=0$

TABLE 11.6 (continued)

Operation Type	Operands	Projective Result[1]	Affine Result
FXAM (cont.)	$-\infty$		$C_0=C_1=C_2=1$ $C_3=0$
FXTRACT	$+\infty$	IE	IE[1]
			$ST(0)=+\infty$ $ST(1)=+\infty$ [2]
	$-\infty$	IE	IE[1]
			$ST(0)=-\infty$ $ST(1)=+\infty$ [2]
F2XM1	$+\infty$	Undefined	$+\infty$
	$-\infty$	Undefined	-1
FYL2X	$\pm\infty * \log(1)$ $\pm 0 * \log(+\infty)$ $+x * \log(-\infty)$	Undefined	IE
	$+\infty * \log(x>1)$ $-\infty * \log(0<x<1)$ $+x * \log(+\infty)$	Undefined	$+\infty$
	$-\infty * \log(x>1)$ $+\infty * \log(0<x<1)$ $-x * \log(+\infty)$	Undefined	$-\infty$
FYL2XP1	$\pm\infty * \log(1)$ $\pm 0 * \log(+\infty)$ $+x * \log(-\infty)$	Undefined	IE
	$+\infty * \log(x>0)$ $-\infty * \log(-1<x<0)$ $+x * \log(+\infty)$	Undefined	$+\infty$
	$-\infty * \log(x>0)$ $+\infty * \log(-1<x<0)$ $-x * \log(+\infty)$	Undefined	$-\infty$
Addition	$(+\infty) + (+\infty)$	IE	$+\infty$
	$(-\infty) + (-\infty)$	IE	$-\infty$
	$(+\infty) + (-\infty)$	IE	IE
	$(+\infty) + (\pm 0)$ $(+\infty) + (\pm x)$	$+\infty$	$+\infty$
	$(-\infty) + (\pm 0)$ $(-\infty) + (\pm x)$	$-\infty$	$-\infty$
Subtraction	$(+\infty) - (+\infty)$ $(-\infty) - (-\infty)$	IE	IE

TABLE 11.6

(continued)

Operation Type	Operands	Projective Result[1]	Affine Result
Subtraction (cont.)	$(+\infty) - (-\infty)$	IE	$+\infty$
	$(-\infty) - (+\infty)$	IE	$-\infty$
	$(+\infty) - (\pm 0)$ $(+\infty) - (\pm x)$ $(\pm 0) - (-\infty)$ $(\pm x) - (-\infty)$	$+\infty$	$+\infty$
	$(-\infty) - (\pm 0)$ $(-\infty) - (\pm x)$ $(\pm 0) - (+\infty)$ $(\pm x) - (+\infty)$	$-\infty$	$-\infty$
Multiplication	$(+\infty) * (+\infty)$ $(-\infty) * (-\infty)$ $(+\infty) * (+x)$ $(-\infty) * (-x)$	$+\infty$	$+\infty$
	$(+\infty) * (-\infty)$ $(+\infty) * (-x)$ $(-\infty) * (+x)$	$-\infty$	$-\infty$
	$(\pm\infty) * (\pm 0)$	IE	IE
Division	$\pm\infty / \pm\infty$	IE	IE
	$+\infty / +x$ $-\infty / -x$	$+\infty$	$+\infty$
	$+\infty / -x$ $-\infty / +x$	$-\infty$	$-\infty$
	$+x / +\infty$ $-x / -\infty$	$+0$	$+0$
	$+x / -\infty$ $-x / +\infty$	-0	-0
Compare	$+\infty$ to $+\infty$	$+\infty = +\infty$	$+\infty = +\infty$
	$-\infty$ to $-\infty$	$-\infty = -\infty$	$-\infty = -\infty$
	$+\infty$ to $-\infty$	$+\infty = -\infty$	$+\infty > -\infty$
	$-\infty$ to $+\infty$	$-\infty = +\infty$	$-\infty < +\infty$
	$+\infty$ to $\pm x$	IE	$+\infty > \pm x$
	$-\infty$ to $\pm x$	IE	$-\infty < \pm x$

Note: IE - invalid operation exception.
[1] Not supported on the 80287XL, 80387, or 80846.
[2] FXTRACT signals IE on the 8087 and 80287 for all operand combinations.

Pseudo-infinities A second pair of infinities, called *pseudo-infinities,* are encodable only in the temporary real format. Pseudo-infinities are supported by the 8087 and 80287 coprocessors only. The pseudo-infinities are handled by the

80287XL and later coprocessors as an unsupported format as discussed later in this chapter.

A pseudo-infinity has a biased exponent of all ones and a mantissa of 0▲00...00. (True infinities have a mantissa of 1▲00...00.) The 8087 and 80287 will never generate a pseudo-infinity, but otherwise make no distinction between a pseudo-infinity and a true infinity.

NaNs

The real number formats provide for bit combinations that do not correspond to any of the previously defined number types. A member of this set of values is called a *NaN* (not-a-number) and has an exponent that is all ones (11...11b) and any mantissa value except 1▲00...00b, which is reserved for the infinities. The 8087 and 80287 treat NaNs differently than the 80287XL and later processors as explained in this section.

8087 and 80287   When the NPX encounters a NaN, it signals the invalid operation exception. The NPX's masked response is to return a NaN as a result of the operation. If both operands are NaNs, the result will be the NaN with the larger magnitude. This property assures that a NaN will propagate through a series of calculations and will eventually appear in the final result.

If the invalid operation exception is unmasked, the use of a NaN can trap to an error handler. Because a wide range of NaN values is available, a program can direct error handling by checking the magnitude of the NaN detected. By uniquely encoding the NaNs to indicate where they occurred or what type of operation was being performed, the NaN will serve as an error code to identify the faulty operation.

80287XL, 80387, and 80486   The 80287XL, 80387, and 80486 divide NaNs into two categories: signaling NaNs (*SNaN*s) and quiet NaNs (*QNaN*s). A NaN that has a 0 as the most significant (integer) bit of its mantissa is an SNaN; the remaining bits of the mantissa may be set to any value. The NPX does not generate a SNaN as the result of an operation. If, however, an SNaN is used as an operand to an arithmetic operation, the invalid operation exception will be raised. (Note that load operations from the stack, FXCH, FCHS, and FABS with SNaN operands will not cause an exception to be raised.)

A quiet NaN is similar to a signaling NaN except that it has a 1 as the most significant digit of its mantissa. The 80287XL and later processors generate only one QNaN, the real indefinite (described below), as their masked response to an invalid operation exception or as the result of an operation in which at least one of the operands is a QNaN. The NPX will create a QNaN from an SNaN by setting the most significant bit of its mantissa to 1; the remaining bits of the operand are not changed.

Both quiet and signaling NaNs are supported in all operations. Table 11.7 gives the rules applied by the NPX when generating QNaNs.

TABLE 11.7

Rules for Generating Quiet NaNs

Operation	Result
Real operation on an SNaN and a QNaN	The QNaN operand
Real operation on two SNaNs	The QNaN that results from converting the SNaN that has the larger mantissa
Real operation on two QNaNs	The QNaN that has the larger mantissa
Real operation on an SNaN and another number	The QNaN that results from converting the SNaN
Real operation on an SNaN and another number	The QNaN operand
Invalid operation with no NaN operands	The QNaN real infinitive

Real Indefinite One special NaN, *real indefinite,* is generated by the NPX as its masked response to an invalid operation exception. Indefinite is signed negative, has an exponent of all ones (11...11b), and a mantissa of 1▴100...00b. (In the short real and long real formats, the integer 1 bit is implied and not stored explicitly.) On the 80287XL and later coprocessors, indefinite is treated as a QNaN.

Unsupported Formats

The real number formats provide an opportunity to encode many bit patterns that do not necessarily correspond to defined formats. Many of these encodings, known as pseudo-NaNs, pseudo-infinities, pseudo-zeros, and unnormals are supported on the 8087 and 80287, meaning that they could be used as operands and in most cases were treated in the same fashion as were the more standard types from which they were derived. In some cases, these formats would be generated by the coprocessor.

After the 80287 was in production, but before the 80387, 80486, and 80287XL were designed, the final version of the IEEE 754 standard was issued. The final version of the standard eliminated support for many data types. In this case, conformance to the standard was deemed more important than upward compatibility. On the 80287XL, 80387, and 80486, the pseudo-NaN, pseudo-infinity, pseudo-zero, and unnormal formats are unsupported. These coprocessors do not generate them, and will raise an invalid operation exception if they encounter them in an arithmetic operation. The tag for these unsupported formats is 10b (special).

Real Data Type Encodings

The complete encoding maps for the real, integer, and BCD number formats are presented in Tables 11.8 through 11.11. In all tables, the most significant bits are on the left and all numbers are in binary notation. Field width for different formats is identified where appropriate.

Note that for each data type *one* encoding is reserved for the special type indefinite. A real indefinite can be loaded and stored like any other NaN. A BCD indefinite will be written by the NPX, but an attempt to load an indefinite will produce an undefined result. The integer indefinite is the same as the largest negative number supported by the format. The NPX will write this same result for either an indefinite or when the value in the source register represents or rounds to the largest negative integer representation. In situations where the source is ambiguous, the IE flag can be examined to determine if the operation was the result of an invalid operation. When this encoding is loaded, it is always interpreted as a negative number.

TABLE 11.8

Short Real and Long Real Encodings

Class			Sign	Biased Exponent (Long-11 Bits) (Short-8 Bits)	Mantissa[1] (Long-52 Bits) (Short-23 Bits)
Positive	NaNs	Quiet	0	11...11	▲11...11 ▲10...00
		Signaling	0	11...11	▲01...11 ▲00...01
	Infinity		0	11...11	▲00...00
	Reals	Normals	0	11...10 00...01	▲11...11 ▲00...00
		Denormals	0	00...00	▲11...11 ▲00...01
	Zero		0	00...00	▲00...00
Negative	Zero		1	00...00	▲00...00
	Reals	Denormals	1	00...00	▲00...01 ▲11...11
		Normals	1	00...01 11...10	▲00...00 ▲11...11
	Infinity		1	11...11	▲00...00
	NaNs	Signaling	1	11...11	▲00...01 ▲01...11
		Indefinite	1	11...11	▲10...00
		Quiet	1	11...11	▲10...01 ▲11...11

[1] 1▲ implied except for denormals

TABLE 11.9

Extended Real Encodings

Class			Sign	Biased Exponent (15 Bits)	Mantissa (64 Bits)
Positive	NaNs	Quiet	0	11...11	1▲11...11 1▲10...00
		Signaling	0	11...11	1▲01...11 1▲00...01
	Infinity		0	11...11	1▲00...00
	Pseudo-NaNs	Quiet	0	11...11	0▲11...11 0▲10...00
		Signaling	0	11...11	0▲01...11 0▲00...01
	Pseudo-infinity		0	11...11	0▲00...00
	Reals	Normals	0	11...10	1▲11...11 1▲00...00
		Unnormals			0▲11...11 0▲00...01
		Pseudo-zeros		00...01	0▲00...00
		Pseudo-denormals		00...00	1▲11...11 1▲00...00
		Denormals			0▲11...11 0▲00...01
	Zero		0	00...00	0▲00...00
Negative	Zero		1	00...00	0▲00...00
	Reals	Denormals	1	00...00	0▲00...01 0▲11...11
		Pseudo-denormals	1		1▲00...00 1▲11...11
		Pseudo-zeros	1	00...01	0▲00...00
		Unnormals	1		0▲00...01 0▲11...11
		Normals	1	11...10	1▲00...00 1▲11...11
	Pseudo-infinity		1	11...11	0▲00...00
	Pseudo-NaNs	Signaling	1	11...11	0▲00...01 0▲01...11
		Quiet	1	11...11	0▲10...00 0▲11...11

TABLE 11.9

(continued)

Class			Sign	Biased Exponent (15 Bits)	Mantissa (64 Bits)
Negative (cont.)	Infinity		1	11...11	1▲00...00
	NaNs	Signaling	1	11...11	1▲00...01 1▲01...11
		Indefinite	1	11...11	1▲10...00
		Quiet	1	11...11	1▲10...01 1▲11...11

TABLE 11.10

Integer Encodings

Class		Sign	Magnitude (Word-15 Bits) (Short-31 Bits) (Long-63 Bits)
Positive	(Largest)	0	11...11
	(Smallest)		00...01
Zero		0	00...00
Negative	(Smallest)	1	11...11
	(Largest/Indefinite)		00...00

Numeric Exceptions

When the NPX attempts a numeric operation with invalid operands or produces a result it cannot represent, it signals a numeric exception. All together, the NPX checks for six different classes of exception conditions as shown below:

- Invalid operation
- Divide by zero
- Denormalized operand
- Numeric overflow
- Numeric underflow
- Inexact result (precision loss)

TABLE 11.11

Packed BCD Encodings

Class		Sign	Unused	BCD Digit 17	BCD Digit 16	BCD Digit 15	...	BCD Digit 0
Positive	Largest	0	000000	1001	1001	1001	...	1001
	Smallest			0000	0000	0000		0000
	Zero	0	000000	0000	0000	0000	...	0000
Negative	Zero	1	000000	0000	0000	0000	...	0000
	Smallest	1	000000	0000	0000	0000	...	0000
	Largest			1001	1001	1001		1001
Indefinite		1	111111	1111	1111	uuuu	...	uuuu

u - Bit is undefined and may contain either value.

The invalid operation, zero-divide, and denormal exceptions are detected before the operation that would have generated them is executed. This allows an exception handler to analyze the problem and possibly restart the instruction. The underflow, overflow, and precision exceptions, however, are not signaled until a result has been calculated. Each of these exceptions is discussed in more detail below.

Invalid Operation The invalid operation exception generally indicates that a program error has occurred. The exception may occur in response to either a floating-point stack error or an arithmetic error. The conditions under which an invalid operation exception will be signaled are presented in three groups below. The first group of conditions applies to all coprocessors. The second group is specific to the 8087 and 80287. The third group is specific to the 80287XL and later coprocessors.

Group 1: All Coprocessors

- Stack overflow: attempting to load an operand into a register that is not empty. (See the discussion of stack exceptions below.)

- Stack underflow: attempting to pop an operand from an empty register. (See the discussion of stack exceptions below.)

- FPREM, FPREM1: divisor is zero or dividend is infinity.

- FSCALE: scale is nonzero or infinity.

- FSQRT: operand is negative and nonzero or closure is affine and operand is $-\infty$.

- FXCH: one or both registers is tagged empty.

- Addition: closure is affine and operands are opposite-signed infinities.

- Subtraction: closure is affine and operands are same-signed infinities.

- Multiplication: operands are infinity and 0.

- Division: both operands are infinity or zero.

Group 2: 8087 and 80287 only

- FBSTP, FIST, FISTP: source register is empty (stack underflow); a NaN, denormal, unnormal, infinity, or exceeds representable range of destination.

- FPREM: divisor is unnormal or denormal.

- FSQRT: operand is denormal or unnormal or closure is projective and operand is infinity.

- FST, FSTP: destination is short real or long real and source register is unnormal with exponent in range.

- FTST: closure is projective and operand is infinity.

- FXTRACT: operand is infinity.

- Arithmetic: one or both operands is a NaN.

- Addition: closure is projective and both operands are infinity.

- Subtraction: closure is projective and both operands are infinity.

- Division: the divisor is denormal or unnormal; the dividend is 0 and the divisor is a pseudo-zero.

- Compare: closure is projective and infinity is being compared with 0 or a normal.

Group 3: 80287XL, 80387, 80486

- FBSTP, FIST, FISTP: source register is empty (stack underflow), a NaN, infinity, or exceeds representable range of destination.

- FCOS, FPTAN, FSIN, FSINCOS: operand is infinity.

- FYL2X: operand is negative and nonzero.

- FYL2XP1: operand < -1.

- Arithmetic: one or both operands is an unsupported format or a signaling NaN.

- Compare: one or both operands is a NaN.

On the 8087 and 80287, stack exceptions are not distinguished from other conditions that raise the invalid operation exception. The reporting of stack exceptions on the 80287XL, 80387, and 80486, however, has been enhanced by the addition of the stack flag (SF) in the NPX status word. If an invalid operation exception is signaled, and SF=1, the exception was due to a stack error. The

O/U# (overflow/not underflow) bit of the condition code (C_1) is set to 1 for an overflow and cleared to zero for an underflow.

When the invalid operation exception is masked, the NPX will store the value indefinite into the destination register, destroying its original contents. When the invalid operation exception is unmasked, an error is generated, the top of stack pointer is not changed, and the source operands are unaltered.

Numeric Overflow and Underflow Typically, the range of the temporary precision real format (used internally by the NPX for all calculations) makes an overflow condition during calculations rare. Overflow will more likely occur when a result is being written to a short real or long real memory operand, each of which has a more limited range.

The *overflow* exception is signaled by the NPX if the exponent of the true result is too large (too positive) for the destination format. If the overflow exception is masked, the value returned depends on the rounding mode in effect as shown in Table 11.12.

TABLE 11.12

Masked Overflow Responses for Directed Rounding

Rounding Mode	True Result		Result
	Normalization	Sign	
Nearest or even	Normal or unnormal	+	$+\infty$
		−	$-\infty$
Chop (toward zero)	Normal or unnormal	+	Largest finite positive number
		−	Largest finite negative number
Up	Normal	+	$+\infty$
		−	Largest finite negative number
	Unnormal	+	$+\infty$
		−	Largest exponent, result's mantissa
Down	Normal	+	Largest finite positive number
		−	$-\infty$
	Unnormal	+	Largest exponent, result's mantissa
		−	$-\infty$

If the true exponent of a number is too small (too negative) to be represented in the destination format, the result is an *underflow* exception. The masked response of the NPX to this situation is to denormalize the operand as explained previously. In cases of severe underflow (and hence severe denormalization), the resulting value will be 0.

The NPX's unmasked response to an overflow or underflow exception depends on whether the destination is a floating-point register or memory. If an overflow is detected and the destination is the floating-point stack, the NPX subtracts 24576 (6000h) from the exponent, forcing it to near the middle of the available range for a temporary real. If an underflow is detected and the destination is the floating-point stack, the NPX adds 24576 (6000h) to the exponent, forcing it to near the middle of the available range for a temporary real. In both cases, the mantissa is then rounded if required by the setting of the PC field and the operation type. The roundup bit (C_1) in the status word is set if the mantissa was rounded upward.

If an unmasked overflow or underflow exception occurs and the destination is memory (such as with the store instructions), no value is stored and the original operand is left unchanged on the floating-point stack.

Zero-Divide   The *zero-divide* exception is signaled if an attempt is made to divide a valid nonzero operand by zero. This is possible not only for the explicit division instructions, but also for operations that perform division internally, such as FYL2X and FXTRACT.

Denormal   If the operand to an instruction is a denormal, the *denormal* exception is signaled. This exception was built into the 8087 and 80287 to allow an external software handler to implement the provision of the then-proposed IEEE standard that called for all operands to be normalized prior to use. The 80287XL, 80387, and 80486 will automatically normalize denormal operands before use. This exception is still issued, however, to retain compatibility with handlers that perform functions other than normalization.

Precision   The *precision* exception is signaled by the NPX if the result of an operation will lose significant digits when stored in the destination format. The NPX will round the number (according to the rounding mode in effect) and signal this exception. The precision exception indicates that some precision has been lost, and occurs frequently in a typical series of calculations. (The transcendental instructions in particular are prone to generate this exception.)

For the most part, the loss in precision is minimal and occurs in the extra precision bits of the temporary real format. These bits are truncated when the value is written to the short or long real formats. The precision exception will also be raised during an underflow if significant bits in the mantissa are lost during denormalization. This exception is provided to support systems that must perform exact arithmetic.

12 THE COPROCESSOR INSTRUCTION SET

THE INSTRUCTION SET OF THE COPROCESSOR IS SMALLER AND MORE FOCUSED than that of the processor. Because of this, and the fact that the same addressing modes are used to access memory, the coprocessor instruction set is easier to understand. A brief review of principles and operations common to the instruction set is presented here. Details on individual instructions are presented in the coprocessor instruction reference in Appendix B.

In this chapter, the instructions available on the coprocessor are reviewed according to their type. Syntax, encoding, and execution time for the instructions is also discussed. Common transcendental identities are presented to assist you in coding your own advanced mathematical functions. Finally, a special section on the software emulation mechanism of the coprocessor is presented.

Throughout this chapter, the term *stack* refers to the NPX's floating-point register stack, not the program stack pointed to by the SS:SP register pair.

Instruction Syntax

Most NPX instructions (excluding those used to control the coprocessor) take one or two arguments as inputs and produce one or two results as outputs. The inputs may be taken from the register stack or from memory, but the operation of the NPX is most efficient when the inputs are from the register stack. Some instructions operate implicitly on the top floating-point stack element (ST), either alone or in combination with another operand. Other instructions allow, or require, the programmer to specify the operand or operands.

As with the processor instructions, the arguments to an NPX instruction specify (implicitly or explicitly) a source operand and a destination operand. The source operand supplies one of the inputs to the operation and the destination receives the result. The destination may also supply an additional input. For example, the processor instruction ADD AX,CX implements the function AX=AX+CX. In this case, the CX register is the source and the AX register is the destination. Both AX and CX provide inputs and AX receives the result of the operation.

Floating-point instruction syntax isn't as straightforward. The same basic mnemonic has different interpretations depending on whether the classical stack or conventional operand mode of the instruction is used. The difference in syntax is used by the assembler or debugger to determine the instruction form. For example, the FMUL instruction may be written with no operands, a source operand only, or both a source and destination operand as shown below. Each instruction performs a completely different operation:

```
FMUL            ;ST(1)=ST(1)*ST, FPOP
FMUL ST(1)      ;ST(1)=ST(1)*ST
FMUL ST,ST(1)   ;ST=ST*ST(1)
```

Depending on the form of the instruction, assemblers make assumptions as to which opcode variant of the instruction is being specified. The encoding for the instruction FMUL, with no explicit operands, is equivalent to the fully specified instruction FMULP ST(1),ST. In this chapter, only the explicit instruction forms that specify all operands will be used. The entries in Appendix B specify all valid forms for an instruction accepted by the assembler and describe the operation of the resulting instruction.

Instruction Encoding

The coprocessor instructions are a subset of the more general ESC (escape) instruction format. The ESC instruction is provided to allow the CPU to communicate with other external devices in the computer system. In this case, the external device is the numeric coprocessor. The encoding for all ESC instructions starts with the high-order 5 bits of the first opcode byte set to 11011b. Coprocessor instructions are divided into two categories depending on whether or not they access memory.

The format of a nonmemory ESC instruction is shown in Figure 12.1, and always occupies two bytes. The high-order 5 bits of the first opcode byte are set to 11011b, as mentioned, and bits 7 and 6 of the second byte are set to 11b. The remaining 9 bits of the encoding are used to specify the particular floating point instruction. Instructions that specify a floating-point register use bits 0-2 of the second opcode byte to specify the register number.

The format of coprocessor instructions that reference memory is also shown in Figure 12.1. These instructions may specify a memory address anywhere within the address space of the processor using any addressing mode available to the processor *at the time the instruction is executed.* The interpretation of the *mod, r/m, disp,* and SIB (if present) fields is exactly the same as for a processor instruction. (A complete explanation of these addressing modes is given in Chapter 6.) Note that coprocessor instructions do not support immediate data operands. As with processor instructions, the segment and address size prefixes may be used to change the default for an instruction.

Instruction Types

For the purpose of discussion, the NPX instructions can be divided into six categories. Each of these categories, and the instructions that they comprise, is discussed in this section. A complete description, encoding, and algorithm for each instruction is given in the coprocessor instruction reference in Appendix B.

FIGURE 12.1

Coprocessor instruction formats

Nonmemory Instructions

11011	eee		11	eeeeee

11011	eee		11	eee	rrr

operand is ST(i), where i=*rrr*b

Memory Instructions

11011	eee		mod	eee	r/m		disp

11011	eee		mod	eee	r/m		SIB	disp

Symbol	Definition
e	Opcode bit
rrr	Floating-point register number 0-7
mod	Mode field (2 bits)
r/m	Register/memory field (3 bits)
disp	Displacement field (zero, two, or four bytes)
SIB	Scale-index-base addressing byte

Data Transfer

The data transfer instructions shown in Table 12.1 move operands among elements of the register stack and between the stack top and memory. All NPX data types can be loaded from system memory, converted to temporary real, and pushed onto the register stack in a single operation. Similarly, the temporary real in the stack top register can be converted to one of the supported formats and written to memory in a single operation.

TABLE 12.1

NPX Data Transfer Instructions

Real Transfer

FLD	Load real
FST	Store real
FSTP	Store real and pop
FXCH	Exchange registers

Integer Transfer

FILD	Load integer
FIST	Store integer
FISTP	Store integer and pop

BCD Transfer

FBLD	Load BCD
FBSTP	Store BCD and pop

On the 8087 and 80287, the execution of a data load instruction updates the tag register corresponding to the destination register to accurately reflect the contents of the register. The 80287XL, 80387, and 80486/7 update the tag word only to indicate whether a stack register is empty or nonempty.

Arithmetic

The NPX instruction set provides the four basic arithmetic functions: addition, subtraction, multiplication, and division. These functions are available both in classical stack form as well as in register-oriented forms that eliminate most operand shuffling before an instruction can be used. The advanced arithmetic functions provided include absolute value, square root, and modulo arithmetic. A list of the arithmetic instructions available on the NPX is shown in Table 12.2.

Each of the basic four functions have instruction forms that are designed to make efficient use of the NPX's register stack by combining the operation of the function with a register pop. By eliminating unwanted operands in a single step, programming effort is reduced. Subtraction and division are not commutative operations, but the reversed forms of those instructions eliminate the necessity

TABLE 12.2

NPX Arithmetic Instructions

Addition

FADD	Add real
FADDP	Add real and pop
FIADD	Add integer

Subtraction

FSUB	Subtract real
FSUBP	Subtract real and pop
FISUB	Subtract integer
FSUBR	Subtract real reversed
FSUBRP	Subtract real reversed and pop
FISUBR	Subtract integer reversed

Multiplication

FMUL	Multiply real
FMULP	Multiply real and pop
FIMUL	Multiply integer

Division

FDIV	Division real
FDIVP	Division real and pop
FIDIV	Division integer
FDIVR	Division real reversed
FDIVRP	Division real reversed and pop
FIDIVR	Division integer reversed

Advanced

FABS	Absolute value
FCHS	Change sign
FPREM	Partial remainder
FPREM1[1]	Partial remainder
FRNDINT	Round to integer
FSCALE	Scale
FSQRT	Square root
FXTRACT	Extract exponent and mantissa

[1] 80287XL, 80387, and 80486 only

to swap operands. Addition and multiplication are commutative operations, so the order of the operands is irrelevant and no reversed operation is required.

The basic four arithmetic functions are each available in the six forms shown in Table 12.3. The classical stack forms are used when the NPX is being programmed as a classical stack machine. In the classical stack mode, the operands are not coded explicit, but are always assumed to be the stack top (the source) and the next stack element (the destination). After the operation, the result is returned to ST(1), and the stack is popped, leaving the result in what is then ST.

TABLE 12.3

Basic Arithmetic Instruction Forms

Instruction Form	Mnemonic	Operands	Operation
Classical stack (automatic POP)	F*op*[1]	ST,ST(1)	ST(1)=ST(1) *op* ST POP
Register	F*op* ST,ST(i)	ST,ST(i)	ST=ST *op* ST(1)
	F*op* ST(i),ST	ST(i),ST	ST(i)=ST(i) *op* ST
Register with POP	F*op*P ST,ST(i)	ST,ST(i)	ST=ST *op* ST(1) POP
	F*op*P ST(i),ST	ST(i),ST	ST(i)=ST(i) *op* ST POP
Real memory	F*op* DWORD PTR [*mem*]	ST,[*real32*]	ST=ST *op* [*real32*]
	F*op* QWORD PTR [*mem*]	ST,[*real64*]	ST=ST *op* [*real64*]
Integer memory	F*op* WORD PTR [*mem*]	ST,[*int16*]	ST=ST *op* [*int16*]
	F*op* DWORD PTR [*mem*]	st,[*int32*]	ST=ST *op* [*int32*]

[1]F*op* is any addition, subtraction, multiplication, or division function.

The register form is a generalization of the classical form and gives the NPX programmer a great deal of flexibility to implement counters, multiple accumulators, and other short-cut operations. The stack top is always one of the operands, although it doesn't necessarily have to be used as the source operand. The other operand can be any floating-point stack register. The instruction FADD ST(4),ST, for example, will add the contents of ST to the contents of ST(4) and return the result to ST(4). The register pop form is equivalent to the classical stack form, but the explicit operands tend to make it easier to understand at the source code level.

The memory forms increase the flexibility of the basic arithmetic instructions. A real or integer number in memory may be used as the source operand without the additional step of loading it into a floating-point register. This property is useful when the stack is full or an operand is used too infrequently to justify loading it onto the stack. Any memory addressing mode available to the processor at the time the instruction is executed may be used.

Comparison

The NPX provides a variety of comparison instructions for testing operands and the results of calculations. Each of the instructions listed in Table 12.4 analyzes the element at the top of the stack, either in relation to another operand or to an internal constant, and returns the result in the condition code bits of the coprocessor status word.

TABLE 12.4

The NPX Comparison Instructions

FCOM	Compare real
FCOMP	Compare real and pop
FCOMPP	Compare real and pop twice
FICOM	Compare integer
FICOMP	Compare integer and pop
FTST	Test ST against +0.0
FUCOM[1]	Unordered compare real
FUCOMP[1]	Unordered compare real and pop
FUCOMPP[1]	Unordered compare real and pop twice
FXAM	Examine ST

[1] 80287XL, 80387, and 80486 only.

To examine the condition code bits after a comparison, the status word must be copied to memory (using the FSTSW instruction) or the AX register (using the FSTSW AX instruction). Note that instructions other than those listed here also modify the condition code bits. To ensure the correct condition is preserved, the status word should be stored immediately after a comparison.

If loaded into the FLAGS register, the comparison codes can be used to direct the J*cond* and SET*cond* processor instructions. The interpretation of the condition code bits for each type of comparison instruction is given in the entry for that instruction in Appendix B.

Constant

Internally, the coprocessor contains a small ROM that holds the values of some commonly used constants listed in Table 12.5. The constants are loaded onto the stack with full temporary real (80 bit) precision and are accurate to approximately 19 decimal digits. The load constant instructions occupy only two bytes as opposed to the four bytes a load from memory instruction would use plus the ten bytes of memory required to store the constant.

TABLE 12.5	
The NPX Load Constant Instructions	
FLDZ	Load +0.0
FLD1	Load +1.0
FLDPI	Load π
FLDL2T	Load $\log_2 10$
FLDL2E	Load $\log_2 e$
FLDLG2	Load $\log_{10} 2$
FLDLN2	Load $\log_e 2$

Transcendental

The basic transcendental instructions available on all 80x87 coprocessors (shown in Table 12.6) perform the core calculations from which all common trigonometric, inverse trigonometric, hyperbolic, inverse hyperbolic, logarithmic, and exponential functions may be derived. Note that the 80287XL and later coprocessor provide the SIN and COS functions directly.

TABLE 12.6	
The NPX Transcendental Instructions	
FCOS[1]	Cosine
FPTAN	Partial tangent
FPATAN	Partial arctangent
FSIN[1]	Sine
FSINCOS[1]	Sine and Cosine
F2XM1	$2^x - 1$
FYL2X	$Y \log_2 X$
FYL2XP1	$Y \log_2(X+1)$

[1] 80287XL, 80387, 80486 only.

The transcendentals always operate on ST or ST and the next stack element. They return their results to the stack. The arguments to the trigonometric functions are expressed in radians. The logarithmic and exponential functions work from a base of 2.

The transcendental instructions perform no argument checking. On the 8087 and 80287, all arguments to the transcendental functions must be reduced manually until they are within the specified range of the function. The trigonometric functions on the 80287XL and later coprocessors will automatically reduce an operand until it is in range. External code must be provided to perform this operation for the other transcendental functions, however.

It is the responsibility of the programmer to ensure that all operands are valid and in range. All operands must be normals; denormals, unnormals, infinities, and NaNs are always invalid arguments. *A transcendental operation with an invalid argument will produce an undefined result without signaling an exception.* For functions that are periodic, the FPREM or FPREM1 instructions may be used to bring an argument in range. The valid ranges for the instructions are specified in the individual entries in the coprocessor instruction reference in Appendix B.

To aid you in developing algorithms for the more advanced transcendental instructions, the identities given in Table 12.7 present the trigonometric, inverse trigonometric, hyperbolic, inverse hyperbolic, logarithmic, and exponential functions in terms of the core functions. In addition, some useful equivalences are also presented. (All arguments are assumed to be valid and in range.)

TABLE 12.7

Identities for Deriving Advanced Functions

Trigonometric

$$\sin x = \sqrt{\frac{\tan^2 x}{1 + \tan^2 x}}$$

$$\cos x = \sqrt{\frac{1}{1 + \tan^2 x}}$$

$$\cot x = \frac{\cos x}{\sin x} = \frac{1}{\tan x}$$

$$\csc x = \frac{1}{\sin x} = \sqrt{1 + \cot^2 x} = \sqrt{1 + \frac{1}{\tan^2 x}}$$

$$\sec x = \frac{1}{\cos x} = \sqrt{1 + \tan^2 x}$$

$$\tan x = \frac{\sin x}{\cos x}$$

$$\sin^2 x + \cos^2 x = 1$$

Inverse Trigonometric

$$\sin^{-1} x = \tan^{-1}\left(\sqrt{\frac{x^2}{1 - x^2}}\right)$$

TABLE 12.7

(Continued)

Inverse Trigonometric (continued)

$$\cos^{-1}x = \tan^{-1}\left(\sqrt{\frac{1-x^2}{x^2}}\right)$$

$$\cot^{-1}x = \tan^{-1}\left(\frac{1}{x}\right)$$

$$\csc^{-1}x = \tan^{-1}\left(\sqrt{\frac{1}{x^2-1}}\right)$$

$$\sec^{-1}x = \tan^{-1}\left(\sqrt{x^2-1}\right)$$

$$\sin^{-1}x + \cos^{-1}x = \frac{\pi}{2}$$

$$\tan^{-1}x + \cot^{-1}x = \frac{\pi}{2}$$

Hyperbolic

$$\cosh^2 x - \sinh^2 x = 1$$

$$\tanh x = \frac{\sinh x}{\cosh x}$$

$$\sinh(x) = \frac{e^x - e^{-x}}{2}$$

$$\cosh x = \frac{e^x - e^{-x}}{2}$$

$$\tanh x = \frac{\sinh x}{\cosh x} = \frac{e^2 - 1}{e^{2x} + 1}$$

$$\csch x = \frac{1}{\sinh x} = \frac{2}{e^x - e^{-x}}$$

$$\sech x = \frac{1}{\cosh x} = \frac{2}{e^x - e^{-x}}$$

$$\coth x = \frac{\cosh x}{\sinh x} = \frac{e^{2x} + 1}{e^{2x} - 1}$$

TABLE 12.7

(Continued)

Inverse Hyperbolic

$$\sinh^{-1}x = 1n\,(x + \sqrt{x^2 + 1})$$

$$\cosh^{-1}x = 1n\,(x + \sqrt{x^2 - 1})$$

$$\tanh^{-1}x = \frac{1}{2}1n\,(\frac{1+x}{1-x})$$

$$\operatorname{csch}^{-1}x = 1n\left(\frac{1 \pm \sqrt{1+x^2}}{x}\right)$$

$$\operatorname{sech}^{-1}x = 1n\left(\frac{1 \pm \sqrt{1-x^2}}{x}\right)$$

$$\coth^{-1}x = \frac{1}{2}1n\,(\frac{x+1}{x-1})$$

Exponentiation

$$10^x = 2^{x \bullet \log_2 10}$$

$$e^x = 2^{x \bullet \log_2 e^*}$$

$$Y^x = 2^{x \bullet \log_2 Y^*}$$

Logarithms

$$\log_{10}x = \frac{\log_2 x}{\log_2 10}$$

$$1nx = \frac{\log_2 x}{\log_2 e}$$

$$\log_y x = \frac{\log_2 x}{\log_2 y}$$

$$\log_y x = \log_y 2^* \log_2 x$$

Coprocessor Control

Typically, the coprocessor control instructions are not used during calculations, but are used for system-level activities such as initialization, exception handling, and task switching. Table 12.8 lists the control instructions available on the 80x87 coprocessors.

TABLE 12.8

NPX Control Instructions

FINIT/FNINIT	FDISI/FNDISI[1]
FENI/FNENI[1]	FLDCW
FRSTPM[2]	FSTCW/FNSTCW
FSTSW/FNSTSW	FCLEX/FNCLEX
FSETPM[3]	FSTENV/FNSTENV
FLDENV	FSAVE/FNSAVE
FRSTOR	FINCSTP
FDECSTP	FFREE
FNOP	FWAIT

[1] These instructions have no affect on the 80287 and later coprocessors.
[2] 80287XL only.
[3] 80287 and 80287XL only. No affect on 80387 and 80486.

As discussed in Chapter 10, the NPX control instructions that do not access the numeric execution unit of the NPX do not need to wait for the current NPX instruction to complete before they begin execution. Instead, they can be executed immediately by the control unit of the NPX. For 8087 programs, this means that the WAIT instruction that is automatically inserted before each ESC instruction by the assembler can be omitted. To indicate to the assembler that no WAIT should be encoded, these instructions have an alternate "no-wait" mnemonic form with an "N" as the second letter.

The no-wait instruction form is intended for use in critical portions of code when processor interrupts are normally disabled and a WAIT is not desirable. Only the 8087 requires explicit WAIT instructions to synchronize the CPU and NPX. If the code is targeted exclusively at 80287 or later coprocessors, most assemblers provide an option to eliminate generation of most WAIT instructions.

The wait and no-wait forms of the floating-point instructions assemble to the identical floating-point opcode. The two instruction forms are an assembler convention—not a coprocessor convention.

Instruction Execution Time

The execution of an NPX instruction involves three major steps: instruction fetch, execution, and operand transfer. Each of these steps contributes to the total execution time as described below.

The processor and coprocessor fetch and decode instruction in parallel as discussed earlier in Chapter 10. If pipelining is in effect, instruction prefetch is performed using otherwise unoccupied bus cycles. Because NPX instructions usually take much longer to execute than to fetch, the processor will typically have adequate time to maintain a full prefetch queue. As a result, instruction fetch does not add appreciably to execution time unless a control transfer instruction has been executed, flushing the prefetch queue.

The execution times given in the coprocessor instruction reference in Appendix B encompass times for best-case and worst-case operand values that may be found in extreme cases. The typical specification represents a value for the operand values that characterize most applications. Where appropriate, the figures include a value for overhead operations, including CPU execution, local bus operation, and overhead for the WAIT instruction when used.

The execution times shown assume that no exceptions are detected. Because they tend to terminate execution prematurely, the invalid operation, unmasked denormal, and zero-divide exceptions will usually decrease execution time, but still fall within the given range. The precision exception has no affect on execution time. Unmasked overflow, unmasked underflow, and masked denormal exceptions impose the additional penalty clock shown in Table 12.9.

TABLE 12.9

Penalty Clocks Imposed by NPX Exceptions

Exception	Penalty Clocks
Overflow (unmasked)	14
Underflow (unmasked)	16
Denormal (masked)	33

Software Emulator Encoding

Most assemblers and high-level programming languages support an option that will convert ESC instructions to software interrupts to allow software emulation of a coprocessor. (This type of emulation is different from the hardware-supported technique, discussed in Chapter 10, that generates an exception if an instruction attempts to access the NPX.) This type of emulation is not dependent on the processor architecture, but I have included it here because an adequate description of the mechanics of the process does not normally appear in most programming references. The process is described for Microsoft's MASM, but applies to most other assemblers and high-level languages as well.

The assembler supports a command line switch (/E) that tells it to assemble floating-point instructions in such a way as to prepare them to be linked with a floating-point emulator. In preparation for software emulation, the assembler inserts one or two *segment fixup* requests for each coprocessor instruction as it writes the .OBJ module. Simply, the fixup mechanism marks a place in the machine code where a value is to go that cannot be determined from the source code. These values include references to externals, segment addresses, and group addresses.

For example, a direct CALL NEAR instruction can reference a procedure that is not in the same .OBJ file if the name of the procedure is specified by an EXTRN declaration. Because the address of the procedure is not known as assembly, zeros are placed where the two-byte offset would go and the instruction is marked as the target of a fixup. When the final program is linked, the linker will match the fixup request to the address of the procedure by *adding* the true offset of the procedure to the stored offset in the .OBJ file. Because the stored offset is 0, the result will be a properly encoded CALL instruction.

To emulate the coprocessor in software, the fixup mechanism of the linker is pressed into service to transform ESC instructions into software interrupts. To make the process work, MASM must be operating in the 8087 (default) or 80287 mode. In these modes, WAIT instructions (opcode 9Bh) are automatically generated *by the assembler* and placed before each coprocessor instruction that is not a "no-wait" form. The no-wait forms will bypass the emulator. The 80387 mode of MASM does not generate WAIT instructions, making floating-point instructions unemulatable by this method.

If you wish to encode explicit WAIT instructions (not those generated automatically by MASM) and your code might be linked with an emulator, they *must* be coded as FWAIT instructions. The FWAIT instruction will be converted into a software interrupt and handled by the emulator. A WAIT instruction will not be changed by the assembler. If a WAIT instruction is executed when no coprocessor is present, the computer will wait forever.

The next step is to assemble the source file with the /E switch. Using this switch instructs MASM to write one or two fixup requests into the .OBJ file for each MASM-generated WAIT instruction. The offset of the WAIT preceding each ESC in the .OBJ file is marked as a fixup target as if it contained an external reference. The fixup, however, is pointed to the WAIT instruction, not a memory reference. The object code generated is exactly the same as if the /E switch had not been used. Only the fixup requests are added.

The name of the external reference that will satisfy the fixup varies, depending on the type of instruction and whether a segment override prefix is specified for a memory operand. (We'll cover this in a moment.) When linked, the external reference resolves to a 16-bit constant value. (The fixup is 16 bits because it is masquerading as a segment address fixup.) The fixup value is added to the object code of the WAIT instruction and one or more bytes of the following ESC instruction, creating a new instruction. Each difference external reference resolves to a different fixup value, commonly called the *magic number*.

For example, if we assume that MASM is operating in the 8087 or 80287 mode, assembling the instruction FLD DWORD PTR [SI] produces the following:

```
9B      WAIT                 ;Generated by MASM
D9 04   FLD DWORD PTR [SI]   ;Coded by programmer
```

The values shown to the left of each instruction represent the object code generated and are shown in hexadecimal. (This information is written to the .LST file.) The assembler also writes a fixup request into the object code. The target of the fixup is a word operand located at the offset of the WAIT instruction.

When the code above is linked, the external reference written into the .OBJ file for the fixup will be satisfied by the software emulator library. The two consecutive bytes at the target location (the WAIT opcode), addressed as a word, give the word value D99Bh. (The byte at the lower memory address is stored in the low-order byte of the word.)

In this case, the value provided for the fixup will be 5C32h. (We'll discover where this value comes from in a moment.) The value of the reference is *added* to the original value at the target location. The resulting addition (D99Bh+5C32h) yields 35CDh. (Any carry is ignored.) As a result of this fixup, the object code at the target location is now 35CDh—the encoding for the software interrupt instruction INT 35h!

When the program is executed, presumably the emulator library will have installed a handler for interrupt 35h. When what was coded as a floating-point instruction is executed, the handler will get control and emulate the original instruction.

If desired, the original instruction can be restored by simply subtracting the same magic number (5C32h) from 35CDh. This is the method used by programs that come linked with an emulator, but will use a real coprocessor if installed. If a coprocessor is detected, the emulation interrupt handler will simply "backpatch" the code in the main program to its original floating-point instruction. If an 80287 or later processor is detected, the unneeded WAIT instruction is usually patched to a NOP.

Floating-point instructions that use a segment override prefix are patched in two steps. The first operation patches the WAIT instruction and the prefix, the second patches the prefix and the first byte of the ESC instruction. Two fixup requests are written into the .OBJ file with their targets one byte apart. For example, consider the following code.

```
9B         WAIT                    ;Generated by MASM
2E D9 04   FLD DWORD PTR CS:[SI]   ;Coded by programmer
```

In memory, the four opcode bytes appear as follows:

```
9B 2E D9 04
```

The first fixup adds the magic number 0E32h to the two consecutive bytes at the first target location (the WAIT opcode). So, 0E32h added to 2E9Bh gives 3CCDh. The bytes now look like this:

```
CD 3C D9 04
```

Now the second fixup adds the magic number C000h to the second target location (one byte past the WAIT instruction). C000h added to D93Ch yields 993Ch. (Ignore the carry.) The conversion is now complete, and the bytes in memory look like this:

```
CD 3C 99 04
```

The result is software interrupt 3Ch. As with the previous example, reversing the process will restore the original instruction.

The external names and corresponding magic numbers used by Microsoft products are shown in Table 12.10. If no segment override prefix is specified, the WAIT/ESC instruction combination fixup is FIDRQQ. If a segment override prefix is encoded, the FI*x*RQQ fixup is targeted at the WAIT instruction and the FJ*x*RQQ fixup is targeted at one byte past the WAIT instruction.

TABLE 12.10

Fixups and Magic Numbers Used for NPX Emulation

Instruction Type	External Symbol	Fixup Value
No segment override	FIDRQQ	5C32h
DS: (3Eh)	FIARQQ	FE32h
	FJARQQ	4000h
CS: (2Eh)	FICRQQ	0E32h
	FJCRQQ	C000h
ES: (26h)	FIERQQ	1632h
	FJERQQ	0000h
SS: (36h)	FISRQQ	0632h
	FJSRQQ	8000h
FWAIT	FIWRQQ	A23Dh

The FWAIT instruction is treated differently by the assembler when the /E switch is used. A NOP is encoded, followed by a WAIT instruction. This two-byte combination is then written to the .OBJ file with its own fixup that converts it into an INT 3Dh instruction.

The decision to emulate is made at link-time. If a dummy file that defines all the external symbols shown in Table 12.10 as zeros is linked with the object code, the fixup operation will leave the original ESC instructions unchanged and will pass directly to the physical coprocessor. The source code does not have to be altered in any way.

Processor Initialization

EACH TIME YOU TURN ON THE POWER TO YOUR PC OR SEND THE PROCESSOR a RESET signal, you begin the complex process of system initialization. Before DOS loads, before the memory count, and even before the BIOS takes over, the first step in this sometimes lengthy bootstrap process begins: the initialization of the processor and coprocessor. Processor initialization is nothing more than ensuring that the chip is in a known state and can be put to work.

As soon as the system board is energized with the proper voltage levels and clock signals, it applies a signal to the RESET pin of the processor. This pin is supplied specifically to gain control over the chip when it is in an unknown state (such as when power is first applied) or an undesirable state (such as halted with interrupts disabled).

The RESET function regains control by forcing the processor to a predetermined state, loading known values into specific registers. This action gives system designers a method to force the chip to execute a bootstrap program.

8086/8088 Initialization

On the 8086 and 8088, the initialization process is quite simple. The positive-going edge of a pulse on the processor's RESET pin causes the CPU to cease all activity until the signal again goes low. When that occurs, the prefetch queue is guaranteed to be empty and the registers are set to the values listed in Table 13.1. The FLAGS register is set so that maskable interrupts are disabled. The CS register contains FFFFh and the IP register contains 0000h, so the processor will immediately begin an instruction fetch at physical address FFFF0h.

The address pointed to by CS:IP is 16 bytes below the top of the processor's physical memory space—one megabyte in the case of the 8086 and 8088. In PC-compatible systems, this address points to the BIOS ROM and a FAR JMP is typically encoded at this location, which transfers control to the ROM Power-On Self Test (POST) and system initialization code.

To see this for yourself, load DEBUG and use the U command to unassemble the starting bootstrap code as follows. Note that the target of the jump instruction will probably be different for your computer.

```
DEBUG
-U FFFF:0000 L 1
FFFF:0000 EA5BE000F0     JMP F000:E05B
-Q
```

In this case, after initialization the 8086 will perform an intersegment jump to the initialization ROM code at the address shown.

TABLE 13.1

8086/8088 Processor State After RESET

Register	Value
IP	0000h
FLAGS	F000h
CS	FFFFh
DS	0000h
ES	0000h
SS	0000h

Note. Values of other registers are undefined.

80286 Initialization

The 80286 is initialized by driving the RESET pin high, forcing the processor to halt all execution and local bus activity. As long as RESET is asserted, no processor activity occurs. When RESET becomes inactive, the processor will initialize internally (this takes 3-4 clocks), then begin execution in real mode with the registers set to the state shown in Table 13.2.

TABLE 13.2

80286 Processor State After RESET

Register	Value	
IP	FFF0h	
FLAGS	0002h	
MSW	FFF0h	
CS	F000h	base=FF0000h limit=FFFFh
DS	0000h	base=000000h limit=FFFFh
ES	0000h	base=000000h limit=FFFFh
SS	0000h	base=000000h limit=FFFFh
IDTR		base=000000h limit=03FFh

Note. Values of other registers are undefined.

When initialized, the FLAGS register is set so that interrupts are disabled. System initialization routines should enable interrupts as soon as the system has installed handlers for them. The interrupt descriptor table register (IDTR) is set to accommodate vectors for interrupts 0-FFh. The machine status word (MSW) is set to FFF0h, indicating that the processor will begin executing in real mode, not protected mode (PE=0). Maskable interrupts are disabled and no math processor (MP=0) or emulation (EM=0) is assumed.

When the 80286 is reset, the physical base address of CS is set to FF0000h in the invisible portion of the descriptor. When CS is combined with the initial IP value of FFF0h, it establishes a starting execution address of FFFFF0h, 16 bytes below the top of the processor's maximum 16Mb physical memory address. Normally, in a PC-compatible system, the system directs this instruction fetch to the first instruction from physical address FFFF0h. A control transfer instruction that reloads CS will reset the high-order 4 bits of the CS base to 0.

The interrupt descriptor table register is initialized to define the interrupt vector table as beginning at physical address 000000h, the bottom of physical memory. The remaining segment registers are initialized to allow access to the first 64k of memory. Initialization then proceeds as with the 8086.

8087, 80287, and 80287XL Initialization

Following RESET, the 8087, 80287, and 80287XL are initialized to the same state they have following a FINIT instruction. Table 13.3 shows the initial values of the NPX registers following reset. All error masks are set, the tag word is set to indicate that all registers in the floating-point stack are empty, the stack top (ST) field is reset to 0, and the default rounding, precision, and infinity controls are set. Although infinity control is initialized to 0, the 80287XL supports only affine closure and ignores the setting of this bit. The 80287 and 80287XL are initialized in real mode and may be switched into protected mode using the FSETPM instruction if desired.

80386 Initialization

The 80836 is equipped to return diagnostic information in its registers as part of its response to RESET. To enable the chip's built-in self-test (BIST), external hardware must enable the BUSY# signal during the trailing edge of the RESET signal. If the chip passes the test, EAX will contain zero. A nonzero result indicates a faulty chip. If the proper interpretation routine is written into the BIOS, this information can be preserved and used to configure or check the system each time the chip is reset. If the test hasn't been requested, the contents of EAX are random and may be nonzero.

After initialization, the processor registers will have the value shown in Table 13.4. The EDX register will always hold a component identifier and revision number. For the 80386, DH will contain 3 and DL will contain a revision number. (See Chapter 14 for more information on processor signatures.) The bits of the FLAGS register are set so that interrupts are disabled. System initialization routines should enable interrupts as soon as the system can handle them. The interrupt descriptor table register is set to accommodate vectors for interrupts 0-FFh. The processor begins execution in real mode, and the initial value of control register CR0 will reflect the presence of an 80387 chip, which is detected automatically by the processor. (The processor cannot detect an 80287.)

TABLE 13.3		
8087, 80287, and 80287XL Coprocessor State After RESET		

Register	Value	Meaning
Control word	037Fh	
Infinity control	0	Projective[1]
Rounding control	00b	Round to nearest
Precision control	11b	64 bits
Interrupt enable mask	0	Interrupts enabled
Exception masks	111111b	All exceptions masked
Status word	0000h	
Busy	0	Not busy
Condition code bits	—	Undefined
Stack top (TOP)	000b	TOP=0
Interrupt request	0	No interrupt pending
Exception flags	000000b	No exceptions
Tag word	FFFFh	All empty
Registers	—	Not changed
Exception pointers		
Opcode	—	Not changed
Instruction address	—	Not changed
Operand address	—	Not changed

[1] Although reset to 0, only affine infinity control is supported on the 80287XL.

The physical base address of CS is set to FFFF0000h internally. When combined with the initial IP value of FFF0h, execution begins at FFFFFFF0h, 16 bytes below the top of the processor's maximum 4Gb physical memory address. Normally, in a PC-compatible system, this address is mapped to the system ROM and the processor fetches the first instruction from physical address FFFF0h. A control transfer instruction that reloads CS will reset the high-order 12 bits of the CS base to 0.

The IDTR is initialized to define the interrupt vector table as beginning at physical address 00000000h, the bottom of physical memory. The remaining segment registers are initialized to allow access to the first 64k of memory. Initialization then proceeds as with the 8086.

80387 Initialization

Following a reset, the 80387 is initialized to a state that is slightly different from the state it has following a FINIT instruction. Table 13.5 shows the initial values of the 80387 registers following reset. All error masks are set, the tag word is set to indicate that all registers in the floating-point stack are empty, the stack top

(ST) field is reset to 0, and the default rounding, precision, and infinity controls are set. Although the infinity control bit is cleared to 0, it is meaningless for the 80387, which supports only affine closure. The condition code bits are also reset to 0. After a hardware reset, the 80387 asserts the ERROR# signal to indicate its presence to the 80386. This is accomplished by setting the IE and ES bits in the status word and clearing the IEM bit in the control word. After a FINIT, the state of the 80387 is the same as the 8087 after reset.

TABLE 13.4

80386 Processor State After RESET

Register	Value	
EIP	0000FFF0h	
EFLAGS	00000002h	
CR0	00000000h - no coprocessor or 80287[1] present	
	00000010h - 80387 present	
EAX	(Self-test result if self-test requested)	
EDX	(Component/revision ID)	
DR7	00000000h	
CS	F000h	base=FFFF0000h limit=FFFFh
DS	0000h	base=00000000h limit=FFFFh
ES	0000h	base=00000000h limit=FFFFh
FS	0000h	base=00000000h limit=FFFFh
GS	0000h	base=00000000h limit=FFFFh
SS	0000h	base=00000000h limit=FFFFh
IDTR		base=00000000h limit=03FFh

[1]Only the 80386DX supports the 80287.

80486 Initialization

Like the 80386, the 80486 is equipped to return diagnostic information in its registers after reset. To enable the chip's built-in self-test (BIST), external hardware must assert the AHOLD signal during the falling edge of the RESET signal. If the chip passes the test, EAX contains zero. A nonzero result indicates a faulty chip. If the proper interpretation routine is written into the BIOS, this information can be preserved and used to configure or check the system each time the chip is reset. Note that the 80486 BIST takes approximately 2^{20} clock periods to execute. If the test hasn't been requested, the contents of EAX are random.

After initialization, the processor registers will have the value shown in Table 13.6. The EDX register will always hold a component identifier and revision number. For the 80486, DH will contain 4 and DL will contain a revision number. (See Chapter 14 for more information on processor signatures.) The FLAGS register is set so that interrupts are disabled. System initialization routines should enable interrupts as soon as the system can handle them. The interrupt descriptor table register is set to accommodate vectors for interrupts 0-FFh. The processor begins execution in real mode with paging and the internal cache disabled.

TABLE 13.5

80387 Coprocessor State After RESET

Register	Value	Meaning
Control word	037Fh	
Infinity control	0	Affine
Rounding control	00b	Round to nearest
Precision control	11b	64 bits
Interrupt enable mask	0	Interrupts enabled
Exception masks	111111b	All exceptions masked
Status word	8081h	
Busy	1	Exception pending
Condition code bits	0	Cleared
Stack top (TOP)	000b	TOP=0
Exception summary	1	Exception pending
Stack flag	0	No error
Exception flags	000001b	Invalid operation
Tag word	FFFFh	All empty
Registers	—	Not changed
Exception pointers		
Opcode	—	Not changed
Instruction address	—	Not changed
Operand address	—	Not changed

The physical base address of CS is set to FFFF0000h internally. When combined with the initial IP value of FFF0h, execution begins at FFFFFFF0h, 16 bytes below the top of the processor's maximum 4Gb physical memory address. Normally, in a PC-compatible system, this address is mapped to the system ROM and the processor fetches the first instruction from physical address FFF0h. A control transfer instruction that reloads CS will reset the high-order 12 bits of the CS base to 0.

TABLE 13.6

80486 Processor State After RESET

Register	Value	
EIP	0000FFF0h	
EFLAGS	00000002h[1]	
CR0	60000010h[1]	
EAX	(Self-test result if self-test requested)	
EDX	(Component/revision ID)	
DR7	00000000h	
CS	F000h	base=FFFF0000h limit=FFFFh
DS	0000h	base=00000000h limit=FFFFh
ES	0000h	base=00000000h limit=FFFFh
FS	0000h	base=00000000h limit=FFFFh
GS	0000h	base=00000000h limit=FFFFh
SS	0000h	base=00000000h limit=FFFFh
IDTR		base=00000000h limit=03FFh

[1]Undefined bits may have any value.

The IDTR is initialized to define the interrupt vector table as beginning at physical address 00000000h, the bottom of physical memory. The remaining segment registers are initialized to allow access to the first 64k of memory. Initialization then proceeds as with the 8086.

On an 80486DX system or an 80486SX system with an 80487SX installed, the registers of the floating-point unit are *unchanged* after reset unless the BIST is invoked. If the BIST is performed, the registers will have the values shown in Table 13.7.

TABLE 13.7

80486DX FPU and 80487SX Coprocessor State After RESET

Register	Value	Meaning
Control word	037Fh	
Infinity control	0	Affine
Rounding control	00b	Round to nearest
Precision control	11b	64 bits
Interrupt enable mask	0	Interrupts enabled
Exception masks	111111b	All exceptions masked
Status word	0000h	
Busy	0	Not busy
Condition code bits	0	Cleared
Stack top (TOP)	000b	TOP=0
Exception summary	0	No exception pending
Stack flag	0	No error
Exception flags	000000b	No exceptions
Tag word	FFFFh	All empty
Registers	—	Undefined
Exception pointers		
Opcode	0	Cleared
Instruction address	0	Cleared
Operand address	0	Cleared

14. INCOMPATIBILITIES AND BUGS

A MAJOR FEATURE OF EACH NEW MEMBER OF THE 80X86 FAMILY IS THAT IT provides, according to Intel, full upward compatibility with earlier members of the family. By upward compatibility, Intel means that code written for an earlier processor, an 8088, for example, will produce the same result when executed on a more advanced processor such as the 80486—but not the other way around. And, for the most part, this claim is true. Nevertheless, there are a number of situations in which different members of the 80x86 family or even different versions of the same processor just do *not* work the same way.

This chapter discusses the instructions and situations that produce different results on different processors when operating in real mode (RM), protected mode (PM), and Virtual-86 mode (VM). In some cases, the incompatibilities are intentional or consequential changes to the operation of the processors. In other cases, changes have occurred in the side effects associated with an instruction. And finally, some differences are due to outright bugs that appear and disappear over the lifetime of a processor.

Processor Incompatibilities

Most of the incompatibilities listed here don't have a major impact on existing software or on the process of writing software. They may, however, require application programmers to include code specifically designed to work around the incompatibilities. Sometimes you get lucky, and the code workaround that is required for a later processor will also work on previous processors. But if not, the application will have to include code to identify the processor at execution time, such as the CPUID program in Chapter 3, and modify its behavior accordingly.

In this section, the operational differences among the members of the 80x86 family are presented. If you're writing software designed to operate across the entire family, you'll have to take into account the distinctions of each processor, from the 8088 up to the 80486 and possibly include processor-specific workarounds to accommodate them.

8086 to 80286 Real Mode

A working 8086 program, when executed on an 80286 processor, operating in real mode, will see the following differences in environment and operation:

Instruction timing is different. In general, instructions require fewer clocks to execute on the 80286 than on the 8086. This difference will affect code that depends on delays caused by instruction execution. Timing loops, for example, that depend on the repetition of an instruction to create a fixed delay will not produce the same results on the 80286. (Instruction execution times are given in the instruction reference in Appendix A.)

Because of the reduced instruction execution time, back-to-back I/O operations on the same I/O port will not give the I/O hardware sufficient time to recover. A jump to the next instruction (JMP $+2), placed between the I/O operations, will flush the prefetch queue and cause a delay while the processor refills the queue. Note that the instruction MOV AL,AH does not produce a long enough delay for the I/O port to recover.

New instructions available. An 8086 program executing on the 80286 can access the following new instructions available in real mode:

- PUSH immediate data

- PUSHA and POPA

- Shift and rotate by immediate count

- Multiply immediate data

- String I/O

- ENTER, LEAVE, and BOUND

For more information on these instructions, see the instruction reference in Appendix A.

IDIV maximum quotient. If the quotient from an IDIV instruction was 80h or 8000h, for byte or word operations, respectively, the 8086 would generate the divide error exception (interrupt 0). The 80286 will return the result and will not generate the exception. (See the entry for IDIV in the instruction reference in Appendix A for more information.)

Shift and rotate counts are masked. On the 80286, the count argument for the shift and rotate instructions is taken MOD 32 (masked to 5 bits), limiting the count to a maximum value of 31. This operation limits the maximum time the shift and rotate instructions can execute. No masking is performed on the 8086.

PUSH SP instruction saves a different value. On the 8086, a PUSH SP operation saves the value that SP had *before* the PUSH operation. On the 80286, PUSH SP saves the value SP will have *after* the PUSH operation. If the value saved by the PUSH SP instruction is important, the following code, executed on an 80286, will produce the same result as PUSH SP on an 8086:

```
PUSH    BP
MOV     BP,SP
XCHG    BP,[BP]
```

FLAGS image is different. The image of the FLAGS register that is saved on the stack by interrupts, exceptions, and the PUSHF instruction is different on the 80286. On the 8086, bits 12-15 are always set to 1s. On the 80286, operating in real mode, these bits are always cleared to 0s.

New exceptions. In real mode, the 80286 can produce the following exceptions that were undefined for the 8086:

5	Bound exception
6	Invalid opcode
7	Coprocessor not available
8	Interrupt table limit too small
9	Coprocessor segment overrun
Dh	Segment overrun
10h	Coprocessor error

A program that executes correctly on an 8086 may contain a bug that causes it to produce one of these exceptions when run on an 80286. (See Chapter 7 for further information on processor exceptions.)

Undefined opcode exception. Attempting to execute illegal or undefined opcodes that executed on the 8086 will generate the undefined opcode exception (interrupt 6) on the 80286. In other cases, such as for the POP CS instruction, the opcode has been redefined on the 80286 to perform a protected-mode instruction.

Instruction length limit of ten bytes. This limit can only be exceeded if duplicate and redundant prefixes are encoded in the instruction. If the instruction contains more than ten bytes, the 80286 will generate the invalid opcode exception (interrupt 6). The 8086 has no instruction length limit.

Segment wraparound. On the 8086, accessing a word operand or executing a multibyte instruction located at offset FFFFh will cause the address to be wrapped back to offset 0. On the 80286, these situations will cause the processor to generate the segment wraparound (general protection) exception, interrupt Dh.

Stack wraparound. On the 8086, a PUSH operation with SP=1 will wrap up to offset FFFFh. On the 80286, this situation causes the processor to enter shutdown mode. The 8086 has no shutdown mode.

Address space wraparound. On the 8086, addresses that exceed 1Mb automatically wrap back to the beginning of the address space. For example, on the 8086 the address FF00:8000 is the same as 0000:7000. This behavior is not emulated on the 80286, but may be forced by external hardware (as it is on PC-compatible systems).

Bus LOCK restricted. On the 80286, use of the LOCK instruction, and the corresponding bus signal, is restricted. See the entry for the LOCK instruction in the instruction reference in Appendix A for details.

Divide exception is a fault. The value of CS:IP saved on the stack by the divide error exception (interrupt 0) is different. On the 8086, the divide error exception is a trap and leaves the saved CS:IP pointing to the instruction that follows the trapped instruction. On the 80286, the exception is a fault, and the saved CS:IP points to the faulting instruction, including any prefixes.

Interrupt vector table limit. The LIDT instruction can be used to set a limit on the size of the interrupt vector table while the 80286 is operating in real mode. If an interrupt or exception attempts to read a vector beyond the limit, the 80286 enters shutdown mode. The 8086 has no LIDT instruction and no shutdown mode.

Single-step interrupt priority is different. The priority of the single-step interrupt has been changed to prevent an INTR interrupt handler from being single-stepped if it occurs while single-stepping through a program. (See Chapter 7 for further information on interrupt priorities.)

NMI does not interrupt NMI. After an NMI is recognized, further NMIs are masked until an IRET is executed. One masked NMI will be queued by the processor. (See Chapter 7 for further information on the NMI.)

Initial CS:IP is different. After reset, the 80286 initializes CS:IP to F000:FFF0; the 8086 initializes CS:IP to FFFF:0000h. The same physical address (FFFF0h) is specified in both cases. This change provides more code space without having to reload CS. Normally, an intersegment jump to the initialization routine is placed at this address. (Processor initialization is discussed in Chapter 13.)

Prefetch queue. The prefetch queue on the 80286 is six bytes, the same size as the 8086 and two bytes longer than the 8088. Self-modifying code must be sure to flush the queue after modifications.

Initial register values differ after RESET. The 80286 initializes some registers differently than the 8086 after a hardware reset. See Chapter 13 for a discussion of reset operation.

Reserved I/O ports. On the 80286/80287 system, I/O ports F8h-FFh are reserved for communication between the CPU and the NPX.

8086 to 80386 Real Mode/Virtual-86 Mode

A working 8086 program, when executed on an 80386 processor operating in either real mode or Virtual-86 mode, will see the same differences in environment and operation as listed for transition to the 80286, in addition to the amplifications and corrections described below:

New instructions available. An 8086 program executing on the 80386 can access the following new instructions:

- LFS, LGS, and LSS
- Bit test and scan
- Double-shift
- Conditional byte set
- Conditional near jumps
- Move data with zero or sign extension
- Generalized multiply

32-bit registers available. An 8086 program has complete access to the expanded and extended register set of the 80386 as well as the new real-mode instructions.

The register set available to an 8086 program includes all the registers available on the 8086 plus the two new segment registers, FS and GS, as well as the test, control, and debug registers. Instructions also have access to 32-bit operands using the operand size override prefix (66h).

Although these facilities are available, a program written for the 8086 will not invoke them unintentionally unless it has a hidden bug or uses a previously undocumented or unsupported opcode. No changes to a working 8086 program are required to run in V86 mode.

32-bit effective addresses restricted. On the 80386, a 32-bit effective address can be specified by an 8086 program running in V86 mode by using the address size override prefix (67h). If the value of the 32-bit offset exceeds FFFFh, however, the processor will generate a pseudo-protection fault (interrupt 12 or 13 with no error code) to maintain compatibility with 80286 real-mode operation.

FLAGS image is different. The image of the FLAGS register saved on the stack by interrupts, exceptions, and the PUSHF instruction is different. On the 8086, bits 12-15 are always set to 1s. On the 80386, operating in real mode, bit 15 is always 0, while bits 12-14 reflect the last value loaded into them.

Instruction length limit of 15 bytes. This limit can be exceeded only if duplicate and redundant prefixes are encoded in the instruction. If the instruction contains more than 15 bytes, the 80386 will generate the invalid opcode exception (interrupt 6). The 8086 has no instruction length limit.

Segment wraparound. On the 8086, accessing a word operand or executing a multibyte instruction located at offset FFFFh will cause the address to be wrapped back to offset 0. On the 80386, these situations will cause the processor to generate an exception. If the segment involved in the access is addressed via the CS, DS, ES, FS, or GS segment registers, the processor will generate the segment wraparound exception, interrupt Dh, also called the general protection exception. If the segment is addressed via the SS register, the processor will raise the stack fault exception, interrupt Ch.

Stack wraparound. On the 8086, a PUSH operation with SP=1 will wrap up to offset FFFFh. On the 80386, this situation causes the processor to enter shutdown mode.

Bus LOCK restricted. On the 80386, use of the LOCK instruction, and the corresponding bus signal, is further restricted. See the entry for the LOCK instruction in the instruction reference in Appendix A for details.

Response to bus hold. The 80386 responds to requests for control of the bus from other bus masters between transfers of parts of an unaligned operand.

Prefetch queue. The prefetch queue on the 80386 is 16 bytes, while the queue is six bytes on an 8086 and four bytes on an 8088. Self-modifying code must be sure to flush the queue after modifications.

Initial register values differ after RESET. The 80386 initializes some registers differently after a hardware reset. See Chapter 13 for a discussion of reset operation.

8086 to 80486 Real Mode/Virtual-86 Mode

A working 8086 program, when executed on an 80486 processor operating in either real mode or V86 mode, will see the same differences in environment and operation as listed for transition to both the 80286 and 80386, in addition to the amplifications and corrections described below:

New instructions available. An 8086 program executing on the 80486 can access the following new instructions available in real mode:

- Application: BSWAP, CMPXCHG, and XADD

- System: INVD, INVLPG, and WPINVD

Bus LOCK restricted. On the 80486, use of the LOCK instruction and the corresponding bus signal is further restricted. See the entry for the LOCK instruction in the instruction reference in Appendix A for details.

Response to bus hold. The 80486 responds to requests for control of the bus from other bus masters between transfers of parts of an unaligned operand. The 80486 also responds to a bus hold signal during reset initialization.

Prefetch queue. The prefetch queue on the 80486 is 32 bytes, while the queue is six bytes on an 8086 and four bytes on an 8088. Self-modifying code must be sure to flush the queue after modifications.

Initial register values differ after RESET. The 80486 initializes some registers differently after a hardware reset. See Chapter 13 for a discussion of reset operation.

80286 Real Mode to 80386 Real Mode/Virtual-86 Mode

A working 80286 real-mode program, when executed on an 80386 processor operating in either real mode or Virtual-86 mode, will see the following differences in environment and operation:

Instruction timing is different. In general, instructions take less time to execute on the 80386 than on the 80286. This can affect code that depends on delays caused by instruction execution. Timing loops, which depend on the repetition of an instruction to create a fixed delay, will not operate the same on the 80286. (Instruction execution times are given in the instruction reference in Appendix A.)

New instructions available. An 80286 program executing on the 80386 operating in real or V86 mode can access the following new instructions:

- LFS, LGS, and LSS

- Bit test and scan

- Double-shift

- Conditional byte set

- Conditional near jumps

- Move data with zero or sign extension

- Generalized multiply

For more information on these instructions, see the instruction reference in Appendix A.

32-bit registers available. An 80286 program has complete access to the expanded and extended register set of the 80386 as well as the new real-mode instructions.

The register set available to an 80286 program includes all the registers available on the 80286 plus the two new segment registers, FS and GS, as well as the test, control, and debug registers. Instructions also have access to 32-bit operands using the operand size override prefix (66h).

Although these facilities are available, a program written for the 80286 will not invoke them unintentionally as the previously undefined opcodes would have generated an invalid opcode exception (interrupt 6). No changes to a working 80286 program are required to run in V86 mode.

32-bit effective addresses restricted. On the 80386, a 32-bit effective address may be specified by an 80286 program running in V86 mode by using the address size override prefix (67h). If the value of the 32-bit offset exceeds FFFFh, however, the processor will generate a pseudo-protection fault (interrupt 12 or 13 with no error code) to maintain compatibility with 80286 real-mode operation.

Bus LOCK restricted. On the 80386, use of the LOCK instruction and the corresponding bus signal is further restricted. Specifically, the 80286 string move instructions cannot be locked. (For further information, see the entry for LOCK in the instruction reference in Appendix A.)

Instruction length limit of 15 bytes. This limit can be exceeded only if duplicate and redundant prefixes are encoded in the instruction. If the instruction contains more than 15 bytes, the 80386 will generate the invalid opcode exception (interrupt 6). This should not be a problem, as the instruction length limit of the 80286 is ten bytes.

Prefetch queue. The prefetch queue on the 80386 is 16 bytes, while the queue in the 80286 is six bytes. Self-modifying code must be sure to flush the queue after modifications.

Initial register values differ after RESET. The 80386 initializes some registers differently after a hardware reset. See Chapter 13 for a discussion of reset operation.

Machine status word. Some of the 12 high-order bits of the MSW, which are reserved on the 80286, are defined on the 80386. 80286 software should ignore these bits and change the MSW by reading the old value, changing bits 0-3 only, then writing the value to the MSW.

80286 Real Mode to 80486 Real Mode/Virtual-86 Mode

A working 80286 real-mode program, when executed on an 80486 processor operating in either real mode or Virtual-86 mode, will see the same differences in environment and operation as listed for transition to the 80386, in addition to the amplifications and corrections described below:

New instructions available. An 80286 program, executing on the 80486, can access the following new instructions available in real mode:

- Application: BSWAP, CMPXCHG, and XADD

- System: INVD, INVLPG, and WPINVD

Exception 9 cannot occur. The coprocessor segment overrun error is not generated by the 80486. Instead, the general protection exception (interrupt Dh) occurs. (See Chapter 7 for further information on processor exceptions.)

Bus LOCK restricted. On the 80486, use of the LOCK instruction and the corresponding bus signal is further restricted. Specifically, the 80286 string move instructions cannot be locked. (For further information, see the entry for LOCK in the instruction reference in Appendix A.)

Response to bus hold. The 80486 responds to requests for control of the bus from other bus masters between transfers of parts of an unaligned operand. The 80486 also responds to a bus hold signal during reset initialization.

Prefetch queue. The prefetch queue on the 80486 is 32 bytes, while the queue in the 80286 is six bytes. Self-modifying code must be sure to flush the queue after modifications.

Initial register values differ after RESET. The 80486 initializes some registers differently after a hardware reset. See Chapter 13 for a discussion of reset operation.

Machine status word. Some of the 12 high-order bits of the MSW, which are reserved on the 80286, are defined on the 80486. 80286 software should ignore these bits and change the MSW by reading the old value, changing bits 0-3 only, then writing the value to the MSW.

80286 Protected Mode to 80386 Protected Mode

A working 80286 protected-mode program, when executed on an 80386 processor operating in protected mode, will see the following differences in environment and operation:

Initialization code. 80286 protected-mode code cannot be run on an 80386 unless initialization code is executed to configure the 80386 to an 80286-compatible state.

Instruction timing is different. In general, instructions take less time to execute on the 80386 than on the 80286. This can affect code that depends on delays caused by instruction execution. Timing loops, which depend on the repetition of an instruction to create a fixed delay, will not operate the same on the 80286. (Instruction execution times are given in the instruction reference in Appendix A.)

New instructions available. An 80286 program executing on the 80386 can access the following new instructions:

- LFS, LGS, and LSS

- Bit test and scan

- Double-shift

- Conditional byte set

- Conditional near jumps

- Move data with zero or sign extension

- Generalized multiply

For more information on these instructions, see the instruction reference in Appendix A.

32-bit registers available. An 80286 program has complete access to the expanded and extended register set of the 80386 as well as the new real-mode instructions.

The register set available to an 80286 program includes all the registers available on the 80286 plus the two new segment registers, FS and GS, as well as the test, control, and debug registers. Instructions also have access to 32-bit operands using the operand size override prefix (66h).

Although these facilities are available, a program written for the 80286 will not invoke them unintentionally as the previously undefined opcodes would have generated an invalid opcode exception (interrupt 6). No changes to a working 80286 program are required to run in V86 mode.

32-bit effective addresses. On the 80386, a 32-bit effective address may be specified by an 80286 program running in V86 mode by using the address size override prefix (67h).

Bus LOCK restricted. On the 80386, use of the LOCK instruction, and the corresponding bus signal, is further restricted. Specifically, the 80286 string move instructions cannot be locked. (For further information, see the entry for LOCK in the instruction reference in Appendix A.)

Instruction length limit of 15 bytes. This limit can be exceeded only if duplicate and redundant prefixes are encoded in the instruction. If the instruction contains more than 15 bytes, the 80386 will generate the invalid opcode exception (interrupt 6). This should not be a problem, as the instruction length limit of the 80286 is ten bytes.

Prefetch queue. The prefetch queue on the 80386 is 16 bytes, while the queue in the 80286 is six bytes. Self-modifying code must be sure to flush the queue after modifications.

Initial register values differ after RESET. The 80386 initializes some registers differently after a hardware reset. See Chapter 13 for a discussion of reset operation.

Machine status word. Some of the 12 high-order bits of the MSW, which are reserved on the 80286, are defined on the 80386. 80286 software should ignore these bits and change the MSW by reading the old value, changing bits 0-3 only, then writing the value to the MSW.

Address space wraparound. On the 80286, addresses that exceed 16Mb automatically wrap back to the beginning of the address space. This behavior is not emulated on the 80386. No expand-down segments should have a base address in the range FF0001h-FFFFFFh. No expand-up segments should wrap around the 80286 address space.

Descriptor reserved fields. The 80386 uses the high-order word of segment descriptors to hold an extension of the base and limit fields. For compatibility with the 80286, a task must place zeros in this word.

New descriptor types. The 80386 defines more descriptor types than were used on the 80286. Descriptors with the type field set to values 8-15 will cause a protection exception on the 80286, but may be defined for 80386 segment types. Only type values 00h and 80h should be used for 80286 undefined descriptors.

New exceptions. In protected mode, the 80386 can produce the following exceptions that were undefined or defined differently for the 80286:

6   Invalid opcode

Eh   Page fault

Because there is no place to store the Page Descriptor Base Register (PDBR) in an 80286 TSS, a task switch to an 80286 task does not update the PDBR. All 80286 tasks must therefore use the same page directory.

80286 Protected Mode to 80486 Protected Mode

A working 80286 protected-mode program, when executed on an 80486 processor operating in protected mode, will see the same differences in environment and operation as listed for transition to the 80386, in addition to the amplifications and corrections described below:

New instructions available. An 80286 program, executing on the 80486, can access the following new instructions available in real mode:

- Application: BSWAP, CMPXCHG, and XADD

- System: INVD, INVLPG, and WPINVD

Prefetch queue. The prefetch queue on the 80486 is 32 bytes, while the queue in the 80286 is six bytes. Self-modifying code must be sure to flush the queue after modifications.

80386 to 80486 (All Modes)

A working 80386 program, when executed on an 80486 processor, will see the following differences in environment and operation:

New instructions available. An 80386 program, executing on the 80486, can access the following new instructions available in real mode:

- Application: BSWAP, CMPXCHG, and XADD

- System: INVD, INVLPG, and WPINVD

New Flag. The Alignment Check (AC) flag has been defined in the EFLAGS register. In conjunction with the alignment mask (AM) bit, it controls the generation of the alignment check exception (interrupt 11h).

New exception. In protected mode, the 80486 can produce the following exception, which previously was undefined:

11h Alignment check

The alignment check error cannot occur unless previously reserved bits are set. (See Chapter 7 for further information on processor exceptions.)

New test registers. New test registers have been defined for testing of the cache.

New control register bits. Five new bits have been defined in CR0 as shown below:

NE Numeric error

WP Write protect

AM Alignment mask

NW Not write-through

CD Cache disable

Two new bits have been defined in CR3:

PCD Page-level cache disable

PWT Page-level write transparent

New page table entry bits. Two new bits have been defined in page table entries to control the caching of pages:

PCD Page-level cache disable

PWT Page-level write transparent

ET bit in MSW. On the 80486, the processor extension type (ET) bit in CR0 should always be set to 1 to indicate compatibility with 80387 protocols.

Segment descriptor loads. On the 80386, a locked read and write would be initiated to set the accessed bit of a segment descriptor during a load. On the 80486, the locked read and write are generated only if the accessed bit is not already set.

Initial register values differ after RESET. The 80486 initializes some registers differently after a hardware reset. See Chapter 13 for a discussion of reset operation.

Prefetch queue. The prefetch queue on the 80486 is 32 bytes, while the queue in the 80386 is 16 bytes. Self-modifying code must be sure to flush the queue after modifications.

Coprocessor Incompatibilities

In this section, the operational differences between different members of the 80x87 family, including the built-in floating-point unit of the 80486DX, are presented. If you're writing software designed to operate on every processor/ coprocessor combination, you'll have to take into account the differences between each member of the family from the 8087 up to the 80486 and possibly include coprocessor-specific workarounds for these differences. Code for identifying the coprocessor at execution time is presented in Chapter 3.

The 80287XL

The 80287XL, introduced by Intel as a replacement for its standard 80287 coprocessor, is different enough from the standard 80287 that it deserves comment. Physically, the 80287XL is a pin-compatible replacement for the 80287. From a programming perspective, the 80286XL is an 80387 in an 80287 package.

The 80287XL implements the instructions and operating procedures of the 80387, including affine-only infinity, nonsupport of special data types, and automatic normalization of denormal operands. The only practical differences between the 80287XL and the 80387 are the inclusion of the FSETPM instruction, which is used on 80286-based systems to turn on coprocessor support for protected mode, and the fact that the 80287XL does not support 32-bit operations. Interestingly enough, the 80287XL also includes an FRSTPM instruction (to return the chip to real mode) that was not present on the 80287.

The standard software method used to distinguish an 80287 from an 80387 (testing for projective or affine treatment of infinity) will misidentify an 80287XL as an 80387. But an 80287XL, for all practical purposes, acts just like an 80387, so the error has no consequence from a software perspective unless the software attempts 32-bit operations, which will fail. For incompatibility reasons, treat the 80287XL as though it were a 16-bit 80387.

8087 to 80287 Real Mode

The 8087 was designed before work on the IEEE standard 754 for floating-point operations was even begun. When the 80287 was manufactured, the standard was still in an early draft. Because the chips were developed without a final standard, and because the hardware itself was in a period of rapid evolution, the 8087 and 80287 differ from each other in a number of ways. A working program written for an 8087 will see the following changes in environment and operation when run on an 80287:

Disabled instructions. The 8087 instructions FENI/FNENI and FDISI/ FNDISI perform no function on the 80287. If encountered by the 80287, these instructions will be treated as NOPs, and the internal state of the 80287 will not be affected. 8087 error handlers may have to be rewritten to account for this difference.

Error signal not routed through the PIC. The coprocessor error signal does not pass through a programmable interrupt controller (PIC) on an 80286-based system as it does on an 8086/8087 system. Instead, errors are signaled on a dedicated ERROR# line. NPX error handlers may have to delete PIC-specific code.

Segment overrun. If the second or subsequent words of a floating-point operand cross a segment limit, the coprocessor segment overrun exception (interrupt 9) will be generated. An attempt to execute a coprocessor instruction located beyond the limit of a segment will generate the segment wraparound (general protection) exception, interrupt Dh.

Task switch support. ESC, FWAIT, and WAIT instructions executed on the 80287 may generate the coprocessor not available exception (interrupt 7) dependent on the values of the ET and MP bits in CR0 and the T bit in the new task's TSS. This allows the state of the 80287 to be saved when switching tasks. (See Chapter 10 for more details of these bits and coprocessor operation.)

Exceptions use interrupt 10h. All coprocessor errors in an 80286-based system are reported using interrupt 10h. An 8086/8087 system may use another exception vector. If so, both exception vectors should point to the coprocessor error handler.

Exception pointers include prefixes. The value of CS:IP saved by the 80286 for coprocessor exceptions points to any prefixes that precede the ESC instruction causing the error. On the 8086, the CS:IP saved points to the ESC instruction.

NPX saved pointer format. The format in which instructions and data pointers are stored in memory by an FSAVE or FSTENV instruction is different for the 80287, operating in protected mode, than for the 8087. (Save formats are discussed in detail in Chapter 10.)

Synchronization. Except for NPX control instructions, the 80286 automatically synchronizes all 80287 instructions by testing the BUSY# line. No explicit WAIT instructions are required as on the 8087.

Reserved I/O ports. On the 80286/80287 system, I/O ports F8h-FFh are reserved for communication between the CPU and the NPX.

8087 to 80387/80486DX Real Mode/Virtual-86 Mode

A working 8087 program, when executed on an 80387 or 80486, will see the same differences in environment and operation as listed previously for transition to the 80287, in addition to the amplifications and corrections described below and in the next section:

Exceptions use interrupt 10h. All real-mode coprocessor errors in 80386/80486-based systems are reported using interrupt 10h. An 8086/8087 system may use another exception vector. If so, both exception vectors should point to the coprocessor error handler. In V86 mode, the V86 monitor can redirect the coprocessor error to another vector if desired.

Denormals. The 80387 automatically normalizes denormal numbers when possible. Software written for the 8087 that uses the denormal exception solely to normalize denormal operands can be run faster on an 80387 system by masking the denormal exception.

8087/80287 to 80387/80486DX

A working 80287 program, when executed on an 80387 or 80486, will see the differences in environment and operation listed below. An 8087 program must take into account the differences listed previously for a transition to the 80287.

NPX state after RESET/FINIT. The 8087 and 80287 state after reset is the same as after executing the FINIT instruction. On the 80387, the ERROR#

signal is asserted to indicate that an 80387 is present. A FINIT must be executed to clear the error and place the NPX in the same state as an 8087 or 80287 after reset. (See Chapter 10 for more information on coprocessor initialization.)

NaN types. The 8087 and 80287 generate only one type of NaN (equivalent to a quiet NaN), but encountering any NaN will raise an invalid operation exception. The 80387 and 80486 generate only quiet NaNs and make a distinction between signaling and quiet NaNs. An invalid operation exception is raised any time a signaling NaN is encountered or if a quiet NaN is encountered by the FCOM, FIST, and FBSTP instructions.

Unsupported types. The 8087 and 80287 define and support the following special types: pseudo-zeros, pseudo-NaNs, pseudo-infinities, and unnormals. The tag word encoding is 00b (valid) for the pseudo-zero and pseudo-NaN types, and 10b (special) for the pseudo-infinity and unnormal types.

The 80387 and 80486 neither generate nor support these formats and will raise an invalid operation exception if they are encountered in an arithmetic operation. The tag word encoding is 10b (special) for all the unsupported types.

Invalid operation exception. The 8087 and 80287 will raise an invalid operation exception if a denormal is encountered in the FSQRT, FDIV, or FPREM instructions, or during conversion to BCD or integer. The 80387 and 80486 do not raise this exception. Instead, the number is automatically normalized, then the operation proceeds.

Denormal exception. The denormal exception is not raised by the 8087 and 80287 in transcendental functions or FXTRACT. It is raised by the 80387 and 80486 in the same situations.

Overflow exception. If the overflow exception is masked, and the masked response to an overflow is infinity, then the 8087 and 80287 will signal overflow; overflow is only signaled when the rounding is not set to round to zero. If rounding is set to chop, for example, the result will be positive or negative infinity. On the 80387 and 80486, if the rounding mode is chop, the result will not be infinity, but will be the most positive or most negative number.

If the overflow exception is not masked, the 8087 and 80287 will not raise the precision exception or round the mantissa. The 80387 and 80486 will raise the precision exception in this case and if the result is stored in the stack, the mantissa will be rounded according to the setting of the precision control bits or as specified by the opcode.

Underflow exception. When the underflow exception is masked, the 80387 and 80486 will signal underflow if the result is both tiny and denormalization results in a loss of accuracy. The 8087 and 80287 signal underflow on tininess, regardless of loss of accuracy, if rounding is toward zero.

If the underflow exception is not masked, the 8087 and 80287 do not round the mantissa if the destination is the stack. The 80387 and 80486 round a result bound for the stack according to the precision control (for instructions controlled by precision control) or to extended precision.

Exception precedence. When the denormal exception is unmasked, it has the highest precedence on the 8087 and 80287. The denormal precedence is not affected by exception masking on the 80387 and 80486.

Status word initialization. The 80387 and 80486 clear bits C_0-C_3 after FINIT, incomplete FPREM, and RESET. On the 8087 and 80287, these bits retain their previous value.

Condition bit C_2. On the 80387 and 80486, this bit serves as a incomplete bit for the FPTAN instruction. It is undefined for the 8087 and 80287.

Infinity control. The 8087 and 80287 support both affine and projective infinity. After reset, the default value is projective. The 80387 and 80486 support only affine closure. The infinity control bit remains programmable, but has no effect.

Stack fault. A stack overflow or underflow signals the invalid operation exception on the 8087 and 80287. On the 80387 and 80486, a stack overflow or underflow not only signals the invalid operation exception, but also sets the stack fault bit in the control word and sets bit C_1 to distinguish between an overflow or underflow condition.

Tag word. The 8087 and 80287 determine the class of a register operand by checking the tag before each access and update the tag after every change to a register; the tag always reflects the most recent status of the register. If the tag word is loaded with a class that is discrepant with the register contents, the 8087 and 80287 will give precedence to the tag description.

When the 80387 and 80486 load the tag word with the FLDENV or FRSTOR instructions, the tag values are interpreted only as empty (11b) or nonempty (00b, 01b, or 10b). Subsequent register accesses always examine the register to determine the class, ignoring the tag. The tag word is updated to reflect the nonempty register contents before a FSTENV or FSAVE instruction.

FSETPM instruction. The FSETPM instruction is required to switch the 80287 into protected-mode operation. This instruction is not available on the 8087 and is treated as a NOP by the 80387 and 80486. The FSETPM instruction is supported by the 80287XL.

Instructions. The instructions listed below and all transcendental instructions operate differently on the 8087 and 80287 than they do on the 80387 and 80486. Details of operation differences are given in the entries for the instructions in the coprocessor instruction reference in Appendix B.

F2XM1	FPATAN	FSINCOS
FBSTP	FPREM	FSQRT
FCOS	FPREM1	FUCOM
FDIV	FPTAN	FUCOMP
FIST	FSCALE	FUCOMPP
FISTP	FSETPM	FXAM
FLD	FSIN	FXTRACT

Bugs

The difference between a bug and an incompatibility is largely in the eye of the beholder. A bug is an unintentional and generally undocumented change in processor operation that affects either a large installed base of software or causes software developers to test for many different cases. Most bugs are fixed when the next revision of the chip is released. A bug that is never fixed eventually becomes a documented incompatibility.

Some bugs, for example, are introduced and repaired as chips are revised, so chip operation varies depending on the version of the chip you get. Some bugs can only be addressed in hardware. Early 80386DX chips, for example, had a bug that required the processor to be run with pipelining turned off. These systems will never perform as they were intended. Other problems are software related and place a tremendous burden on the software manufacturer to test for every possible combination and chip revision in existence—and are even more troublesome because they cannot be anticipated. They are subject to change as new and better bugs are introduced.

Fortunately, some bugs occur only under the most improbable circumstances (not at all relevant to PC-compatible operation) that need concern only hardware system designers. The bugs listed here are those that you may have to write code to work around. Most of these bugs apply only to early versions of the chips and were fixed in later revisions. Unless you can specify that everyone running your program must have the latest chip revision, however, you'll have to include the code workarounds anyway. Most will only concern programmers writing operating systems and other large projects that encompass system issues.

A bug that keeps you from performing a useless task should be considered a feature. Purposefully writing irrational sequences of code just to prove that a processor does or does not have a bug is futile. If you find yourself tempted, the advice given below in a gag from an old vaudeville routine may be appropriate:

Patient: Doctor, it hurts when I do this.

Doctor: Don't do that.

Chip Steps

Microprocessors go through a development cycle that leads them from design to breadboard to prototype and finally to production. Even after they reach production, the designs are continually being modified and enhanced. The different versions of the processor are called *steps* or *steppings,* and manufacturers usually, but not always, give them a unique alphanumeric designation which they stamp on the chip package. Unfortunately, software cannot read the chip step identifier to determine what version of a processor it is running on. To aid developers somewhat, the 80386 and 80486 chips are designed to place a signature, a *component identifier*, and *revision identifier,* in their DX register after a reset operation. (The 8086, 8088, and 80286 do not generate a signature.)

After reset, the DH register of the processor holds the component identifier that differentiates between processor families. The DL register holds the revision level of the chip, which typically begins with 0 and is incremented with component steppings. Note, however, that the revision level does not usually change with each chip step, nor does it follow a uniform pattern.

The component and revision identifiers for the most common steps of the 80386 and 80486 processors are given in Table 14.1. Note that the step IDs don't follow a rigid pattern, and some steps are produced for OEMs and not sold through general distribution channels. Other step IDs include a code that identifies the particular plant or line on which they were manufactured.

TABLE 14.1

Common Processor Steps and Signatures

Processor	Step	Component ID (DH)	Revision (DL)
80386DX	B0-10	03h0	03h
	D0	03h	05h
	D1-2	03h	08h
80386SX	A0	23h	04h
	B	23h	05h
	C	23h	08h
80486DX	A1	0	0
	B2-6	4	1
	C0	3	2
	D0	4	4
	cA2-3	4	10h
	cB0	4	11h

8086 and 8088 Bugs

The following bugs involving certain instructions and operations are known to occur on some steps of the 8086 and 8088:

Interrupts not cleared after MOV to SS. An early version of the 8088 contained a hardware bug that did not correctly disable interrupts after a MOV or POP to the stack segment register. Subsequent steps of the chip fixed this problem. To work around this bug, interrupts should be cleared and then reenabled manually as shown here:

```
CLI                 ;Disable interrupts
MOV   SS,AX         ;Point to new stack
MOV   SP,SPOINTER
STI                 ;Enable interrupts
```

Repeated instruction not restarted properly. On the 8086 and 8088 multiple prefixes will not be properly recognized after a repeated string instruction has been interrupted and then restarted; only the prefix immediately preceding the string primitive is restored. (The NEC V20 and V30 do not have this bug.) To avoid this situation, the following workaround should be used:

```
Move:
        LOCK                            ;Prefix 1
        REP                             ;Prefix 2
        MOVSB [DEST],CS:[SRC]           ;CS override is prefix 3
        OR    CX,CX                     ;If not 0, was interrupted
        JNZ   Move                      ;Restart with correct prefixes
```

80286 Bugs

The following instructions and operations are known to behave other than as documented on some steps of the 80286 (see the listings in Appendix A for additional details and workarounds):

AAA	PUSH
CMPS	REP CMPS
INS	REP INS
LODALL	REP MOVS
MOVS	REP OUTS
POP	REP SCAS
POPF	REP STOS

Interrupts not masked properly. When operating in real mode or in protected mode with CPL≤IOPL, the processor may improperly recognize a pending INTR interrupt after executing POPF, even if interrupts were disabled prior to the POPF and the value popped into the FLAGS register had IF=0. Note that even if improperly recognized, the interrupt is executed correctly. A workaround is given in the POPF entry in Appendix A.

80287 Bugs

The following instructions are known to behave other than as documented on some steps of the 80287 (see the listings in Appendix B for additional details and workarounds):

FSTSW

FSTCW

80386 Bugs

The following instructions and operations are known to behave other than as documented on some steps of the 80386DX and 80386SX (see the listings in Appendix A for additional details and workarounds):

AAA	POPA
INS	POPAD
LAR	REP INS
LOCK	REP MOVS
LSL	STOS
MOV	VERR
MOVS	VERW

IRET to TSS with limit too small. If an IRET causes a task switch to a TSS with a valid descriptor type but an invalid (too small) limit, a double fault exception (interrupt 8) will be incorrectly generated instead of the proper invalid TSS fault (interrupt Ah). Further, if the double fault entry in the IDT is a trap gate, a processor shutdown results.

Double fault error. If the IDT entry for the invalid TSS fault (interrupt Ah) is invalid for any reasons, a processor shutdown results instead of the proper double fault abort (interrupt 8).

REP MOVS during single step. If a repeated MOVS instruction is executed while single-stepping is enabled, the single-step trap is generated every two iterations instead of every iteration. If a data breakpoint is satisfied during an odd iteration of REP MOVS, the breakpoint trap is not taken until after a subsequent even iteration. If the REP MOVS instruction ends with an odd number of iterations, then the single-step or breakpoint trap will occur properly after the final iteration. (No workaround.)

Task switch to V86 mode. The prefetch limit is not updated to FFFFh by a task switch to V86 mode. An IRET should be used to transfer control to a V86 task.

A second bug occurs if a task switch is performed to a V86 task that has a not-present LDT descriptor. The segment not present fault (interrupt Bh) will be generated instead of the proper invalid TSS fault (interrupt Ah). This situation can be avoided by using a null selector for the LDT of a V86 task.

FAR jump near page boundary. If, while executing in V86 mode, an intersegment direct jump (opcode EAh) is located within 16 bytes of the end of a page, and the next page is not cached in the TLB, the jump instruction does not set the prefetch limit to the end of the new code segment; instead, the limit is left at the end of the old segment. If the old limit is greater than the new limit, this can allow fetching past the end of the new segment without causing a segment limit violation. If the old limit is less than the new limit, a spurious general protection fault can occur.

Normal 8086 programs should not encounter this problem. The general protection fault handler must test to determine if the fault is real or caused by this bug. If caused by this bug, an IRET back to the task will set the prefetch limit to the proper value.

Page fault error code unreliable. If a certain sequence of prefetch operations is happening when a page fault (interrupt Eh) occurs, the three defined bits in the error code are unreliable. The page fault linear address stored in CR2, however, will always be correct and should be used to determine the corresponding page table entry.

Double page faults. If a second page fault occurs while the processor is attempting to enter the page fault exception handler for the first time, the processor will generate the page fault exception (interrupt Eh) instead of the double fault (interrupt 8) as it should.

I/O addresses incorrect. Accessing I/O addresses in the range from 1000h to FFFFh or accessing coprocessor ports (800000F8h to 800000FFh) as a result of executing ESC instructions can generate incorrect I/O addresses if paging is enabled and the corresponding linear memory address is marked present and dirty.

Direct access to I/O ports is not a problem on most PC-compatible computers, for which all I/O ports are typically restricted to addresses below 1000h. To prevent problems with the coprocessor, the memory page at linear address 80000xxxh should be marked either not present or mapped such that bit 31 of the page's physical address is a 1.

Breakpoints malfunction. Breakpoints associated with the debug registers DR0-DR3 do not work correctly after a MOV from CR3, TR5, or TR7 has been executed. The contents of the debug registers are not altered, but spurious breakpoints may result until the next jump instruction is executed. Breakpoints should be disabled before a MOV from one of the indicated registers, and then reenabled after executing a jump instruction. (See the MOV entry in Appendix A for more details.)

Breakpoints missed. Breakpoints will be missed under the following conditions:

- A data breakpoint is set to a *mem16* operand of a VERR, VERW, LSL, or LAR instruction and the segment with the selector at *mem16* is not accessible.

- A data breakpoint is set to the operand of the write cycle of a REP MOVS instruction, and the read cycle of the next iteration generates a fault.

- A code or data breakpoint is set on the instruction following a MOV or POP to SS and the instruction requires more than two clocks.

I/O to masked ports. When executing in protected or V86 mode, the processor will allow doubleword I/O to certain ports that have been masked in the I/O permission bit map. If the bit corresponding to the last byte of a doubleword is set to 1 in the bit map and the remaining bits are 0, then a doubleword access to that port does not generate the general protection exception (interrupt Dh).

TSS limit check. The processor microcode checks the TSS limit to ensure it is at least 101 bytes. In fact, the minimum size for the TSS is 103 bytes. TSS limits of 101 and 102 bytes should, but will not, generate an invalid TSS fault (interrupt Ah).

Fault occurring during task switch with single-step enabled. If a fault occurs during a task switch when single-stepping is enabled, the new task will be entered with single-step enabled if TF=1 when the task switch occurs, the fault occurs while the processor is saving the state of the current task, and a task gate is used to handle the fault.

80387 Bugs

The following instructions and operations are known to behave other than as documented on some steps of the 80387DX and 80387SX (see the listings in Appendix B for additional details and workarounds):

FINIT

FSAVE

FSTENV

Paging anomalies with FSAVE, FRESTOR, FSTENV, and FLDENV. If either of the last two bytes of an FSAVE or FSTENV operand is not writable, or either of the last two bytes of an FRESTOR or FLDENV is not readable, then the instruction cannot be restarted. This problem arises in demand-paged systems or demand-segment systems, which increase segment length on demand. This situation can be avoided by aligning these operands on any 128-byte boundary.

Operand wraparound. If, in protected mode, an instruction accesses an operand that overruns a segment limit but starts and ends in pages of a segment that are both valid and present (spans through an invalid or inaccessible page), the coprocessor may be put into an indeterminate state. To avoid this, ensure that coprocessor operands do not wrap around the end of a segment.

Opcode overrun. If an ESC instruction has its first byte in the last byte of a page or segment and the second byte located in a page or segment that will cause a fault, the processor will hang when it tries to signal the fault. The processor remains stopped until an INTR, NMI, or RESET occurs. A hardware watchdog timer will usually provide a timer interrupt and allow the system to recover. (No workaround.)

80486 Bugs

The following instructions and operations are known to behave other than as documented on some steps of the 80486DX and 80486SX/80487SX (see the listings in Appendices A and B for additional details and workaround):

AAA	FDIVR
CMPXCHG	FPTAN
INS	FSCALE
INVD	FSINCOS
FDIV	WBINVD

CMPXCHG opcode. The encoding shown for this instruction was changed beginning with the B step of the 80486. See Appendix A for more details.

TSS limit check. The processor microcode checks the TSS limit to ensure it is at least 101 bytes. In fact, the minimum size for the TSS is 103 bytes. TSS limits of 101 and 102 bytes should, but will not, generate an invalid TSS fault (interrupt Ah).

Code breakpoint errors. A code breakpoint that is set on a branch instruction (JMP, CALL, etc.) will clear the lower 4 bits of DR6 when satisfied.

Another bug occurs if a code breakpoint is set on an instruction that immediately follows a RETN, JCXZ, intrasegment indirect CALL, or intrasegment indirect JMP. In this case, the breakpoint is taken even when the control transfer instruction is executed. A code breakpoint set at the target instruction will not be taken because the erroneous breakpoint will set the RF flag. (No workaround.)

Write to TR5 may hang CPU. If a prefetch is pending while performing a write to TR5 with the control bits set to 01b, 10b, or 11b, the CPU may hang. This situation can be avoided by ensuring that no prefetches are pending. A workaround is given in the notes for the MOV instruction in Appendix A.

Write to CR0 may corrupt cache. If the MOV CR0,*reg32* instruction is used to disable the cache, a line in the cache may be corrupted. Since this instruction is not typically used by applications, this problem should not normally be encountered. A workaround is given in the MOV entry in Appendix A.

General protect fault error. If a segment violation occurs on the target of a short jump and an external interrupt (NMI or INTR) occurs on the same CLK as the GP fault, the 80486 will not correctly handle the GP fault. (No workaround.)

FPU error not reported after WAIT. A bug in the FPU creates three cases when the FERR# error is generated by a floating-point operation, but not reported correctly. Although most PC-compatible systems probably contain hardware to correct the error, the following software workarounds will avoid the problem: replace all FWAIT instructions with FNOP instructions or follow them with NOP instructions and mask all floating-point errors (the normal condition).

Floating-point performance degradation. Although not a bug, if an unmasked exception occurs when the numeric exception (NE) bit in CR0 is clear and the IGNNE# pin is active, the performance of the FPU will be retarded as long as the exception remains pending. Prior to executing each floating-point instruction, the processor must classify the exception and determine the action to be taken dependent on the values of the NE bit and IGNNE#. This microcode requires 22 clock cycles and is added to the execution time of every floating-point instruction while the exception is pending. Continued execution with the exception pending risks data integrity.

To avoid this situation, all unmasked floating-point exceptions should be cleared (using FCLEX or FINIT) before returning from the interrupt handler or unmasked exceptions should not be ignored by not asserting IGNNE#.

15 PROTECTION, TASK SWITCHING, AND VIRTUAL-86 MODE

THE 80286 AND LATER PROCESSORS USE A MECHANISM TO PROVIDE AN ENVIronment in which multiple programs or tasks can be prevented form interfering with each other. This mechanism is called *protection,* and different operating systems—UNIX and OS/2, for example—use the hardware protection mechanism of the processor as the basis on which their protection rules are formed.

Properly applied, protection prevents an application from corrupting the operating system or another application. The protection provided is from *unauthorized* access, of course; a misbehaved program can still do all the damage it is allowed to. Protection is also a convenient method for enforcing resource management in a multitasking or multiuser system.

In this chapter, we'll present a discussion of the protection and multitasking mechanisms available on the 80286 and later processors. Details of both segment-level protection and, for the 80386 and 80486, page-level protection mechanisms will be presented. Hardware support for task switching is also discussed. Finally, a section on the Virtual-86 mode of the 80386 and 80486 processors is presented.

Details of the processor's segmentation and protected-mode memory management mechanisms, covered in detail in Chapter 4, are not repeated here. Unless you are already familiar with these topics, it is suggested that you review the appropriate part of Chapter 4 before reading this chapter.

Protection

The Intel processors implement protection in three fundamental forms, each of which contributes to the overall stability of the system and restricts the amount of interference one program can cause another. The hardware protection mechanisms of the processor isolate system software from applications, applications from each other, and enforce data type-checking.

Protection is implemented as a four-level privilege model that isolates user-level applications (typically running as least-privileged) from various levels of system software (running as privileged to most-privileged). The privilege model restricts the addressability, or visibility, of software modules. A module that is not visible to an application cannot be accessed or executed.

Segment-Level Protection

When the processor is running in protected mode, every memory reference is subject to protection checks beginning at the segment level. A segment is the smallest region of memory that can be assigned unique protection attributes.

A modular program is usually divided into segments reflecting the structure of the program. For example, a code segment may be created for each module in the program. Each code module may have a private data segment as well as share a common data segment with other code modules. A program may also have one or more stack segments. Each byte in a segment is protected in the same way by the processor.

Application development tools that are part of a protected-mode development system will usually create segments and the appropriate protection attributes as an application is developed. As such, the protection rules enforced by the operating system are automatically selected.

Each segment in a system is described and defined by a segment descriptor. The format of the descriptor depends on the type of segment it describes. Different descriptor formats are used for data, code, and system (special purpose) segments as described in Chapter 4. Access to a segment is subject to three types of check: type, limit, and privilege. Each of these access checks is explained below.

Type Checking   Each time a segment selector is loaded into a segment register, the processor verifies that the segment descriptor (and hence the segment described by the descriptor) is compatible with its intended use. If an attempt is made to load an inappropriate segment type, a protection exception is generated. The format of a segment descriptor and the fields it comprises are shown in Figure 15.1. (See Chapter 4 for a complete field-by-field description of a segment descriptor.)

When the DT (descriptor type) bit is 1, the descriptor describes either a code or data segment, and the purpose of the segment is encoded in the type field as shown in Figure 15.2. The parameters defined by the type field serve as a first protection check on the segment. By controlling access based on type, the processor can detect programming errors such as an errant attempt to write over code or read-only data.

The processor verifies that the type information in a descriptor is appropriate to its use whenever the selector for that descriptor is loaded into a segment register. The CS register, for example, can be loaded only with a selector that describes an executable segment. Similarly, a selector that points to the descriptor for an executable segment that is not also marked readable cannot be loaded into a data segment register. And only selectors for writable data segments can be loaded into the SS register. Table 15.1 shows the segment types that will satisfy the type check when their selectors are loaded into the various segment registers.

Even if the segment load passes the type check, an exception may still be generated if an instruction attempts to access the segment in a manner that is inconsistent with its type. No data segment, for example, can be written to unless its type field indicates that it is writable. Attempting to read from the code segment will also fail unless the segment is marked readable. And no instruction may write to an executable segment. (If it is necessary to write to a code segment, a data descriptor can be created to describe the same segment and used to access the code.)

FIGURE 15.1

Segment descriptor format

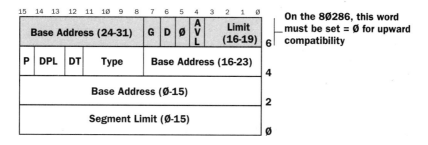

Field	Description
G	Granularity
D	Default
AVL	Available
P	Present
DPL	Descriptor Privilege Level
DT	Descriptor Type

FIGURE 15.2

Descriptor type field

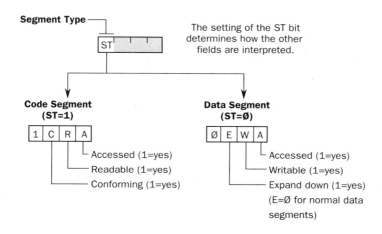

TABLE 15.1

Compatible Segment Registers and Types

Register	Segment Types			
	Read Only	Read-Write	Execute Only	Execute-Read
DS, ES, FS, GS	Yes	Yes	No	Yes
SS	No	Yes	No	No
CS	No	No	Yes	Yes

Limit Checking   Unlike real mode, the length of a protected-mode segment is not fixed. The limit field of a segment descriptor indicates its length and is used by the processor to prevent programs from addressing memory beyond the segment boundary.

On the 80286 processor, the limit is always expressed in bytes, and the maximum size of a segment is 64k. On the 80386 and 80486, however, the G (granularity) bit in the segment descriptor determines whether the limit field is specified in bytes (G=0) or pages (G=1). If page granularity is selected, the limit is given as a multiple of 4k pages. (Note that when G=1, a limit of 0 pages gives access to the bytes at offset 0 to 4095 in the segment.)

For all segments (except expand down), the number in the limit field represents the maximum offset from the start of the segment. As such, the numeric value of the limit is always one less than the segment size in bytes. [If page granular, the limit is (limit*4096)+4095 bytes].

The processor will signal a general protection exception if an attempt is made to access a memory operand, any portion of which falls beyond the limit. Addressing a word operand, for example, located at the limit will cause an exception. A doubleword operand, accessed at address limit-2, for example, will also cause this exception.

The interpretation of the limit field is modified dependent on the setting of the E (expand down) bit in the type field. E=0 for normal data segments and E=1 for stack (expand down) segments. For expand down segments, the limit field is interpreted not as the maximum permissible offset, but as the *minimum* permissible offset. The range of valid offsets is from the value of the limit in bytes + 1 up to 2^{20}-1 bytes (for 16-bit segments) or 2^{32}-1 bytes (for 32-bit segments). An expand down segment will have its maximum size when limit=0.

Common programming errors that may attempt to modify memory beyond the end of the segment, such as a subscript out of range or an invalid pointer, are detected by the limit check when they occur. The cause of the problem can then be immediately identified during application development and corrected. Without limit checking, the errors caused by these problems may overwrite critical portions of the application or operation system or go undetected until other modules or programs are run.

Limit checking is also applied to the segment descriptor tables. (These tables are described in detail in Chapter 4.) Both the interrupt descriptor table (IDT) and global descriptor table (GDT) have 16-bit limits. Access to the tables is limit-checked to prevent a program from addressing memory that is beyond the end of the table and consequently loading an invalid descriptor. Because each descriptor is eight bytes, a descriptor table will have a limit of $8n$-1, where n is the maximum number of descriptors in the table.

Privilege Checking   Another protection attribute that is assigned to each segment is *privilege level*. The processor checks the privilege level of a segment to determine which procedures are allowed to access the segment. Like type and limit checking, privilege checking is performed automatically by the processor hardware.

Protection is hierarchical; the processor protection mechanism defines four levels of privilege, numbered from 0 to 3. In most Intel literature, these levels are pictured as rings of privilege, as shown in Figure 15.3. In this model, level 0, the most privileged level, is called the *kernel*. The kernel is usually the domain of the operating system and has direct access to all system resources. Typical services provided by code executing at this level of privilege include memory management (including virtualizing memory), multitasking, device I/O, and intertask communication.

The next ring, privilege level 1, is less privileged than the kernel, and is typically allocated to system services including file sharing, display management, and data communications. This system service ring relies on the services of the kernel.

Level 2, the next ring outward from the kernel, is dedicated to custom extensions that may allow a generic operating system to be tailored to a specific application. This level might contain a database manager or logical file access system, for example. In theory, different front-end systems for different applications could be built on the same base of kernel and system services. Device drivers would typically reside in either or both levels 2 and 1.

The outermost, and least privileged ring, level 3, is often called the *user level* or applications level. Tasks executing at this level of privilege must rely on the more privileged levels to perform all system functions. In theory, programs executing at this level are isolated from each other and from the operating system and are unable to adversely affect their operation.

The four-ring model provides possibilities for the construction of very sophisticated operating systems and applications. Unless you are writing a stand-alone application or an operating system, however, your choice of privilege levels will likely have been predetermined by the operating system designers. (Operating system-specific details will be found among the development tools and documentation for that specific system.)

Privilege levels are checked when a segment selector is loaded into a segment register. The processor is concerned with three different privilege levels: the current, descriptor, and requestor privilege levels.

FIGURE 15.3

Intel's ring model of privilege

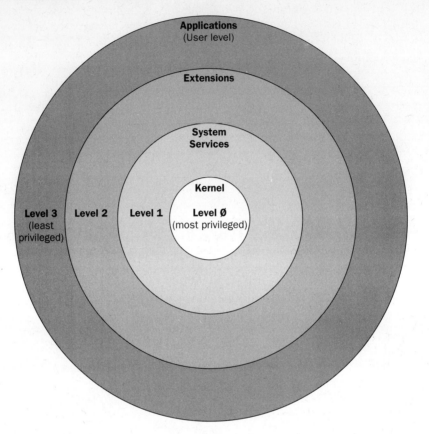

Assuming that the selector is valid, the low-order two bits of the CS register will hold the *current privilege level* (CPL) of the task being executed. The emphasis in the term CPL is on the word *current*. A task's CPL is dynamic and changes as the value held by CS changes. As control is transferred between modules and rings during normal program execution, the CPL will always be determined by the *current* CS value, that is, the segment from which instructions are being fetched. A segment in a program has a fixed privilege level. A task, on the other hand, has a privilege level that depends on where in the application or system code it is currently executing. The lower two bits of the SS register always hold a copy of the CPL.

Segment descriptors contain the *descriptor privilege level* (DPL) field. This field contains the privilege level that is defined for the segment. The descriptor privilege, including code segment privilege, is assigned when the descriptor (and the associated segment) is created.

A segment selector contains the *requestor privilege level* (RPL) field. The RPL field represents the privilege level of the procedure that created the selector. If the RPL is less privileged than the CPL, the CPL is downgraded to match the RPL. If a segment selector is passed from a less privileged program to a more privileged program, the memory access takes place at the less privileged level.

Privilege checking is applied both to tasks and to descriptors for main memory segments, gates, and task state segments. (Gates and task state segment are discussed later in this chapter.)

Data Access

Data may be accessed in either data segments or readable code segments. When the DS, ES, FS, GS, or SS segment register is loaded with a selector, for example, the CPL, DPL, and RPL are checked. The CPL is taken from the lower two bits of the CS register, the DPL is taken from the descriptor, and the RPL is taken from the lower two bits of the segment selector.

Data access to data segments and nonconforming code segments is allowed to proceed only if the CPL is more privileged (numerically less) than the DPL. If an attempt is made to load a segment register with a DPL that is more privileged than the CPL, a general protection exception (interrupt Dh) will be generated by the processor.

Note that while checking the CPL and DPL provides some protection from unauthorized access for code and data segments, it is not sufficient to prevent all errors. Consider the situation where a task with a CPL of 3 (least privileged) passes a selector for a descriptor with a DPL of 0 (most privileged) to a procedure that has a CPL of 0. Although the level 0 procedure can access the level 0 data without problem, if the selector passed to the called routine is incorrect, the original routine is simply using the more privileged routine to corrupt data. This situation clearly cannot be allowed to exist and is prevented by use of the RPL value.

The RPL field in the selector is used for pointer validation. The RPL is intended to indicate the privilege of the originator of a selector. Although a selector may be successively passed to routines of more privilege, the RPL always reflects the privilege level of the original supplier of the selector, not the most recent supplier. The load instruction is allowed to proceed only if the DPL has no more privilege than the selector's RPL. If not, a general protection exception occurs. Access to a segment will be denied if the originator of the pointer did not have access to the segment, regardless of the CPL at the time of access.

Accessing Code Segments as Data   Code segments are addressed using the CS register. An execute-only code segment cannot be loaded into another segment register or read from using a CS segment override prefix. A segment marked as executable (code/data bit in the descriptor type field = 1) may be addressed using another segment register only if it is also marked as readable (readable bit in the descriptor type field = 1).

An execute-only type attribute maintains the privacy of a code segment, and any attempt to read the code (using the CS selector) will result in a general protection fault. Note that a legitimate attempt to read the code, by an error handler, for example, will also be prohibited. A code segment cannot be loaded into SS and is never writable.

It may be desirable to read from a code segment. For example, when data is stored in the code segment, as might be the case in a ROM-based embedded system, the ability to read from the code segment is crucial. While a code segment can be read from (by setting the readable bit in the type field), it can never be written. To write to a code segment, a data segment must be created and mapped to the same memory space as the code segment. In other words, an aliased descriptor that allows writing is created.

A code segment may be read by loading a data segment register with a selector for a readable, executable code segment. If the code segment is nonconforming, the same privilege rules apply as for access to a data segment. If the code segment is conforming, the access is always valid because the privilege level of a conforming code segment is effectively the same as the CPL, regardless of its DPL. If a CS override is used to access a readable, executable code segment whose selector is already in CS, the access is always valid because the DPL of the code segment selected by CS is the CPL.

Control Transfer

Three types of control transfers can take place within a protected-mode task. Transfers *within* a segment (a near jump, call, or return) cause no change in privilege level, do not reload the CS register, and are subject only to limit checking. The processor verifies only that the instruction does not attempt to transfer control to a location outside the segment. To speed the check, the limit value is cached in the invisible portion of the segment descriptor.

Control transfers *between* segments (a far jump, call, or return) reload the CS register and cause the processor to perform a privilege check. Control may be transferred in either of two ways: via a gate (discussed later in this section) or by specifying the descriptor of another executable segment.

If the DPL of the target code segment is equal to the CPL of the source segment, no privilege level change is required and the transfer proceeds without further privilege checks. If, however, the CPL is numerically greater (less privileged) than the DPL of the target segment, the processor will complete the transfer only if the type field of the target segment indicates that it is a *conforming* code segment. A conforming code segment runs at the (lesser or equal) privilege level of the calling procedure, regardless of the conforming segment's DPL. The processor keeps the calling procedure's CPL in the invisible portion of the CS register and uses this value in place of the DPL of the conforming code segment. Execution in a conforming code segment is the only condition in which the CPL may be different from the DPL of the current code segment.

Conforming code segments are normally used for libraries or exception handlers that may provide a service to the calling program but require no access to protected system facilities. These routines may be safely run by any caller with at least as much privilege as the conforming code segment.

All other code segments are termed *nonconforming*. Transfers to both non-conforming code segments of different privilege levels (via a far call or return) or conforming segments of more privilege require additional privilege checks to ensure system integrity. Note that a jump to a nonconforming segment with a DPL that differs from the CPL is *never* allowed.

When completing the control transfer involves a change of privilege, the processor must verify that the current task is allowed to access the destination address and that the correct entry address for the destination procedure is used. To implement this type of transfer, a special descriptor is used, called a *gate*. Control transfer instructions reference the gate instead of specifying the target code segment directly. From the viewpoint of the task, a transfer to a gate is the same as the transfer to another code segment.

The gate mechanism allows tasks to execute more privileged procedures in the same manner as they execute procedures at the same privilege level. Because of this, the task of programming is simplified and the programmer need not distinguish between routines based on privilege.

Gates   Privilege protection for control transfers between code segments at different privilege levels is provided by an eight-byte system structure called a *gate descriptor*, or simply a gate. There are four types of gates: call, trap, interrupt, and task gates. The descriptor type (DT) field in a descriptor distinguishes a segment descriptor (DT=1) from a gate descriptor (DT=0).

The formats of the various gate descriptors are shown in Figure 15.4. The type field is interpreted differently than for a segment descriptor. The definitions for each of the 16 possible types values are given in Table 15.2. Note that some values indicate special system segments, not gates.

Task gates are used for task switching. They control transfers between tasks and make use of task state segments. Task gates and the task state segment are discussed in detail later in this chapter. Trap and interrupt gates are used to service interrupts. Both are used when an interrupt is to be handled within the context of the current task and return control via the IRET instruction. Trap and interrupt gates are discussed in Chapter 7.

Call gates are used for protected control transfer. They are used as the target of normal far CALL and JMP instructions in the same manner as a code segment descriptor would be. *The processor automatically recognizes that the destination descriptor refers to a gate descriptor.* A JMP instruction can access a call gate only if the code segment referred to by the gate is at the same privilege level. A CALL instruction can use a gate to access a code segment of the same or greater privilege.

A call gate may reside in either the global descriptor table (GDT) or the local descriptor table (LDT), but not in the interrupt descriptor table (IDT). A call gate defines the entry point of the procedure and specifies the privilege level required to access the procedure.

FIGURE 15.4

Gate descriptor formats

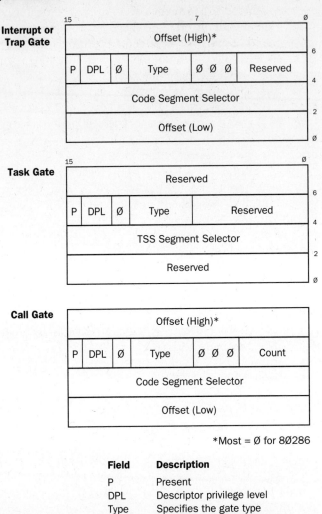

Field	Description
P	Present
DPL	Descriptor privilege level
Type	Specifies the gate type
Count	Number of word (16-bit gate) or dwords (32-bit gate) to be copied to target stack

When an intersegment (far) CALL or JMP instruction selects a call gate, both the gate's privilege and presence will be checked. The gate's DPL (specified in the descriptor's access rights byte) is checked against the privilege of the calling program (the lesser of the caller's CPL or the selector's RPL). If the calling program is less privileged than the gate, the control transfer will not be completed, and a general protection fault (interrupt Dh) is generated by the processor. The error code pushed onto the stack identifies the call gate. If the calling program is at least as privileged as the call gate's DPL, the gate is accessible and the checking process continues.

TABLE 15.2

Type Field Definitions for System Segments

Type Field Value	Bit Settings				Description
0	0	0	0	0	Reserved
1	0	0	0	1	Available 16-bit TSS
2	0	0	1	0	LDT
3	0	0	1	1	Busy 16-bit TSS
4	0	1	0	0	16-bit call gate
5	0	1	0	1	16-bit task gate
6	0	1	1	0	16-bit interrupt gate
7	0	1	1	1	16-bit trap gate
8	1	0	0	0	Reserved
9	1	0	0	1	Available 32-bit TSS
Ah	1	0	1	0	Reserved
Bh	1	0	1	1	Busy 32-bit TSS
Ch	1	1	0	0	32-bit call gate
Dh	1	1	0	1	Reserved
Eh	1	1	1	0	32-bit interrupt gate
Fh	1	1	1	1	32-bit task gate

The presence of the gate is then verified. If the present (P) bit in the gate's descriptor is 0, the target code segment is not present in memory. In this case, the segment not-present fault (interrupt Bh) is generated with an error code that identifies the gate. Presumably, the operating system can then take action to load the required segment into memory and restart the instruction. When P=1, indicating that the segment is present, the transfer is completed. Figure 15.5 illustrates the mechanics of transfer via a call gate.

A call gate transfer is called an *intralevel* transfer if the destination code segment has the same privilege level as the CPL. This condition occurs when the destination segment is nonconforming with DPL = CPL or it is conforming with DPL ≤ CPL. Even if the target location is within the same segment as the control transfer instruction, the full destination address (taken from the gate) is loaded into the CS and IP/EIP registers. The IP value in the gate must be within the segment limit or the processor will generate a general protection fault. If a CALL instruction is used to address the gate, the return address is saved normally.

FIGURE 15.5

Transfer via call gate

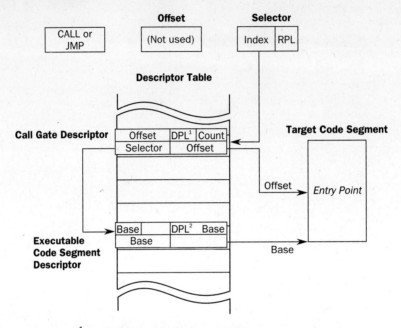

[1] Determines who can access gate

[2] Determines who can access procedure

Jump to nonconforming code segment allowed if:
    Lesser Privilege (CPL, RPL) ≤ gate DPL
    Target segment DPL = CPL

Call or jump to conforming code segment allowed if:
    Lesser Privilege (CPL, RPL) ≤ gate DPL
    Target segment DPL ≤ CPL

The only operational difference from using the call gate is that the address loaded into CS and IP is different from that specified by the call or jump instruction. The gate is completely specified by the segment selector and the offset value is not used. The difference is, however, transparent to the calling program.

If the privilege level of the target code segment of the call gate is different from the CPL, the transfer is called an *interlevel* transfer. If DPL > CPL, however, a general protection fault is generated; the error code identifies the target code segment.

Note that because the CALL instruction automatically saves the return address, and because a jump instruction cannot effect a privilege change, a calling program cannot violate protection by placing an invalid return address on the stack and then jumping to a call gate.

Stack Switching   When a call gate is used to change privilege levels, the CPL is updated, control is transferred to the target code segment, and the stack is switched. One way in which the system ensures integrity is to have each task maintain a separate stack for each privilege level. If this were not so, a less privileged procedure could pass too small a stack to a more privileged called procedure. If the called procedure ran out of stack space, the calling procedure would be responsible—a protection violation. Instead, when a less privileged program transfers control, a new stack is created, any parameters are copied to the new stack, the contents of the processor registers are saved, and execution then proceeds normally. When the called procedure returns control, the saved registers and original stack are restored. A complete description of task switching is presented later in this chapter.

The new stack is selected from the task state segment (TSS). Each task has its own TSS, which is created by the operating system. The TSS contains a stack segment selector and offset value for each of the inner protection rings (0, 1, and 2). The selector and offset are initialized by the operating system and are read-only—the processor does not change them during the life of the task. The DPL of the target code segment is used to select the appropriate stack pointer. The DPL of the new stack segment must equal the new CPL. If not, the processor generates a stack fault (interrupt Ch). No stack pointer is provided for level 3 (least privileged) since there is no less privileged task to call a level 3 procedure.

Parameters to be passed to the called procedure are placed on the stack. When the procedure is invoked through the call gate, the parameters are copied to the new stack. The copied parameters appear on the new stack with the same relative offset to the stack frame as if no stack switch had occurred. The count field of the call gate specifies how many words (for 16-bit call gates) or double-words (for 32-bit call gates) are to be copied.

No parameters are copied if the count is 0. The 5-bit count field allows specifying up to 31 words or doublewords to be copied. If more parameters need to be accessed, the called program must use the SS:SP of the old stack (saved in the TSS) to access the parameters directly. (It can always do so because it is more privileged.) The processor does not check the values passed to the called procedure. Before using any pointers, the called procedure should check each for validity using the ARPL, VERR, VERW, LSL, and LAR instructions as appropriate.

Returning from Procedures   A near return transfers control within the same code segment (and consequently the same privilege level) and is subject only to limit checking. The return address is loaded into the IP/EIP register and checked against the limit of the code segment. If the return address exceeds the limit, the processor generates a general protection fault.

A far return transfers control between code segments, but only if the privilege level of the new code segment is of equal or lesser privilege. The RPL of the CS selector popped off the stack identifies the privilege level of the calling program. If the return instruction discovers that RPL > CPL, an interlevel return occurs.

An interlevel return performs the checks shown in Table 15.3. The code segment that contains the RET instruction is the returning code segment and contains the returning procedure. The stack in effect at the time the RET is executed is termed the returning stack. The code segment to which control is transferred by the RET instruction is called the target code segment and contains the target procedure. The SS and SP values that are loaded from the returning stack define the target stack.

TABLE 15.3

Interlevel Return Protection Checks

Condition to Avoid Exception	Exception	Error Code
SP/ESP of returning procedure must be within the current SS limit	Stack fault	0
SP/ESP+7 of returning procedure must be within the current SS limit	Stack fault	0
SP+n+7 (16-bit return) or ESP+n+15 (32-bit return) of returning procedure must be within current SS limit	Stack fault	Target CS[1]
The RPL of the target CS must be greater than the CPL (of the returning procedure)	General protection	Target CS
The target CS selector must be non-null	General protection	Target CS
The target CS descriptor must be within the descriptor table limit	General protection	Target CS
The target CS descriptor must be a code segment	General protection	Target CS
The target code segment must be present	Segment not present	Target CS
DPL of the target code segment (nonconforming) must be equal to the RPL of the target code segment selector; or the DPL of the target code segment (conforming) must be less than or equal to the RPL of the target code segment selector	General protection	Target CS
Target SS selector on returning stack must be non-null	General protection	CS
Target SS selector on returning stack must be within descriptor table limit	General protection	CS
Target SS descriptor must be a writable data segment	General protection	Target CS
Target stack segment must be present	Stack fault	Target CS
DPL of the target stack segment selector must be equal to the RPL of the target code segment	General protection	Target CS

[1] Error code is 0 on the 80286.

If the return instruction specified a nonzero number of bytes to be removed from the stack, the old values of SS and SP/ESP (taken from the top of the current stack) are adjusted by that value and loaded into the SS and SP/ESP registers. Note that the resultant value of SP/ESP is not checked other than as specified in Table 15.3. If it is not valid, it will not be detected until the first stack operation. The SS and SP/ESP values in use by the returning procedure are not saved. (They are reloaded from the TSS when the procedure is called again.)

The values in the data segment registers are also checked before control is returned. If any of the data segment registers address a segment whose DPL is greater (has less privilege) than the new CPL, that segment register is loaded with a null selector. (This does not apply if the new code segment is conforming.) Any subsequent attempt to address memory using the null selector will cause a general protection fault. This safety measure prevents less privileged code from accessing more privileged data that had been previously addressed by a more privileged procedure.

Page-Level Protection

The memory architecture of the 80386 and 80486 processors allows them to implement a paged memory system. (Paging is described in more detail in Chapter 4.) To provide a secure environment, the protection mechanisms of the processors have been extended to the page level. The page protection available provides for restriction of addressable domain and type checking. The entries that manage protection are located in the two system structures that control paging: the page table and page directory. The format for page table and page directory entries is shown in Figure 15.6. The *user/supervisor* (U/S) bit, *read/write* (R/W) bit, and *supervisor write protect* (WP) bit are used to implement page-level protection.

FIGURE 15.6

Page table and page directory entry format

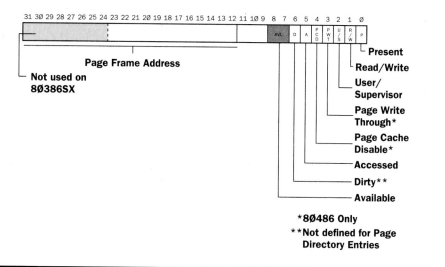

*80486 Only
**Not defined for Page Directory Entries

While segments are classified into four protection levels (0-3), pages have only two levels of privilege. The supervisor level (U/S=0) corresponds to segment privilege levels 0, 1, and 2, and is used for pages that contain the operating system, special system software, and protected system data, such as the page tables. The privilege level of user pages (U/S=1) corresponds to segment privilege level 3. Typically, user pages hold application code and data. When the processor is running at supervisor level all pages in the system are addressable. When the processor is running at user level, only pages at the user level are addressable.

Pages are also marked to allow *read-only* access (R/W=0) or *read/write* access (R/W=1). (Note that read permission implies permission to fetch and subsequently execute instructions.) When the processor is running at supervisor level, all pages are both readable and writable, regardless of the settings of their U/S or R/W bits. If the processor is running at the user level, however, only pages that belong to the user level and are marked for read/write access are writable. Other user pages are readable, but no supervisor pages are readable or writable from user level.

Each entry in a page directory corresponds to a page table. Similarly, each entry in a page table corresponds to a page frame. Protection attributes for a page are a combination (the logical AND) of the corresponding protection attribute bits specified in both the page directory and page table entries. For any one page, the protection attributes in the page table and page directory that describe it may differ. The processor determines the effective protection by checking both entries and combining the attributes, as shown in Table 15.4.

TABLE 15.4

Page Directory and Page Table Protection Combinations

Page Directory Entry		Page Table Entry		Effective Protection	
Privilege	**Access**	**Privilege**	**Access**	**Privilege**	**Access**
Supervisor	R or R/W	Supervisor or User	R or R/W	Supervisor	R/W
User	R or R/W	Supervisor	R or R/W	Supervisor	R/W
User	R	User	R or R/W	User	R
User	R/W	User	R	User	R
User	R/W	User	R/W	User	R/W

Note that the page protection combination information given in all but one of the Intel programmer's reference manuals for the 80386DX, 80386SX, and 80486 is incorrect. The first edition of the 80386 programmer's reference manual (#230985-001) is the only manual that lists the information correctly. The combinations are as shown in Table 15.4.

On the 80486 only, user-level pages may be write-protected against supervisor-level access. Setting the write protect (WP) bit in the processor control register CR0 enables this feature, which is designed to implement the UNIX copy-on-write operation.

Task Switching and the TSS

A *task* is a single, sequential thread of execution. The 80286 and later processors support multitasking, the ability to run more than one task at a time. Each task can be completely isolated from the other. Of course, only one task is actually *executing* at any one time; the CPU simply switches between tasks as directed. A task switch may be initiated by an interrupt or an intertask call, jump, or IRET. Two special system structures, used to define a task and facilitate and control task switching, are the task state segment and the task gate. These structures and their use are explained in this section.

The Task State Segment

The *task state segment* (TSS) is a special system structure that resides in its own memory segment. The information that is stored in the TSS completely defines the task; each task has a single, unique TSS. The definition of a task includes all the information that is needed to start and manage the task. Figure 15.7 shows the format of the TSS for a 16-bit (80286) task. The format for a 32-bit task is shown in Figure 15.8.

FIGURE 15.7

16-bit task state segment

15	0
Task's LDT Selector	2Ah
DS Selector	28h
SS Selector	26h
CS Selector	24h
ES Selector	22h
DI	20h
SI	1Eh
BP	1Ch
SP`	1Ah
BX	18h
DX	16h
CX	14h
AX	12h
FLAGS	1Øh
IP (entry point)	Eh
SS for CPL 2	Ch
SP for CPl 2	Ah
SS for CPL 1	8
SS for CPL 1	6
SS for CPL Ø	4
SP for CPL Ø	2
Backlink Selector	Ø

Note: Shaded areas are static and are not altered after initialization. Other areas are written by each task switch.

The fields of the TSS are classified as either static or dynamic. The static fields are written the first time the task is created and initialized. The processor treats these fields as read-only; they are not modified by the processor after the task is created. The LDT field holds the selector for the task's LDT. The stack fields each hold a segment selector and initial offset for one of the stacks selected when executing at privilege levels 0, 1, and 2.

FIGURE 15.8

32-bit task state segment

31		16	15		1	Ø	
I/O Map Base		ØØØØØØØØØØØØØØØ				T	64h
ØØØØØØØØØØØØØØØØ		Task's LDT Selector					6Øh
ØØØØØØØØØØØØØØØØ		GS					5Ch
ØØØØØØØØØØØØØØØØ		FS					58h
ØØØØØØØØØØØØØØØØ		DS					54h
ØØØØØØØØØØØØØØØØ		SS					5Øh
ØØØØØØØØØØØØØØØØ		CS					4Ch
ØØØØØØØØØØØØØØØØ		ES					48h
EDI							44h
ESI							4Øh
EBP							3Ch
ESP							38h
EBX							34h
EDX							3Øh
ECX							2Ch
EAX							28h
EFLAGS							24h
EIP							2Øh
Reserved							1Ch
ØØØØØØØØØØØØØØØØ		SS for CPL 2					18h
ESP for CPL 2							14h
ØØØØØØØØØØØØØØØØ		SS for CPL 1					1Øh
ESP for CPL 1							Ch
ØØØØØØØØØØØØØØØØ		SS for CPL Ø					8
ESP for CPL Ø							4

Note: Shaded areas are static and are not altered after initialization. Other areas are written by each task switch.

Two fields are unique to the 80386 and 80486. The debug trap (T) bit field, when set, raises a debug exception (interrupt 1) when a task switch to this task occurs. (See Chapter 9 for a discussion of the use of this bit.) The I/O Map Base field contains the starting offset in bytes from the beginning of the TSS where the I/O permission bit map begins. (See Chapter 5 for a discussion of the I/O permission bit map.)

The dynamic fields of the TSS are updated each time a task switch *leaves* the task. The information saved can be thought of as a snapshot of the state of the task. The dynamic fields include the general registers, segment registers, FLAGS/EFLAGS register, and the instruction pointer (IP/EIP).

The selector of the TSS that identifies the previously executing task is saved when the task is given control. This field is called the TSS *backlink* and provides a history of which tasks invoke others. If a new task is loaded to service an interrupt, for example, this field indicates which task is to be restarted when the current task is ended.

The TSS may reside anywhere within the linear address space of the processor. If, however, paging is enabled (80386 and 80486 only) and the TSS spans a page boundary, care must be exercised. If a portion of the TSS data area is located in the higher-addressed page, and that page is not present in memory, the processor generates an exception. It is an unrecoverable error to receive a page fault or general protection exception after the processor has started to read the TSS. This situation can be avoided by aligning the TSS so that it does not cross a page boundary. Alternately, the system can ensure that both pages are present before allowing the task switch.

TSS Descriptor   A system descriptor is used to describe the TSS. A TSS descriptor must be accessible at all times. It must, therefore, be located in the global descriptor table (GDT) and not in a local descriptor table (LDT). The processor identifies a TSS descriptor by the DT and type fields in its descriptor. The descriptor type (DT) will be 0, indicating a system segment. The value in the type field will be either 0001b or 0011b for a 16-bit TSS, or 1001b or 1011b for a 32-bit TSS. The format of a TSS descriptor is given in Figure 15.9.

Like other segment descriptors, the TSS descriptor defines a base address and a limit value. The limit must be large enough to accommodate the minimum TSS size. A 16-bit TSS requires a limit no smaller than 43 (2Bh) bytes and a 32-bit TSS requires a limit no smaller than 103 (67h) bytes. An attempt to switch to a task whose TSS descriptor has too small a limit will cause the processor to generate an invalid TSS exception (interrupt Ah). The use of the granularity (G), present (P), and available (AVL) fields is consistent with their use in data segment descriptors as described in Chapter 4.

The descriptor privilege level (DPL) field restricts access to the TSS descriptor by JUMP or CALL instructions. The DPL is usually set to 0 so that access to the descriptor is restricted to privileged programs. Because the TSS descriptor is a system descriptor, any attempt to load it into a segment register produces a general protection exception. Because the segment cannot be addressed with a register, it cannot be altered improperly.

FIGURE 15.9

The TSS descriptor

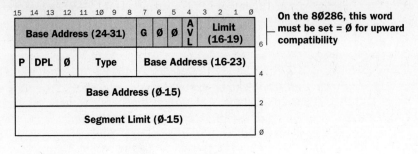

Field	Description
G	Granularity
AVL	Available
P	Present
DPL	Descriptor Privilege Level

TSS descriptors have two states: idle and busy. The second bit of the type field is designated the busy (B) bit and indicates whether the task is idle (Type=xx0x) or busy (Type=xx1x). An attempt to switch to a task that is busy will generate an exception. Tasks are not reentrant.

Task Register   The *task register* (TR) identifies the currently executing task. Like a segment register, the task register has both a program visible and invisible portion. The visible portion contains the selector for a TSS descriptor. The processor uses the invisible portion to cache the base and limit of the TSS as loaded from the TSS descriptor.

The instructions LTR (load task register) and STR (store task register) are provided to access the task register. STR is not a privileged instruction and may be executed at any privilege level. (It may not, however, be executed in real or V86 mode.) LTR is a privileged instruction and may be executed only when the CPL is 0. LTR is typically used during system software initialization to load an initial value into the task register. Once initialized, further changes to TR are made only by task switches.

The Task Gate Descriptor   A task gate provides an indirect, protected method of accessing a task in much the same way as a call gate provides access to a procedure. The task gate is a special form of system descriptor that refers to a TSS descriptor. The format of a task gate was shown previously in Figure 15.4. The selector field must point to a valid TSS descriptor. The RPL in the selector is not used in this application.

When a task gate is used, the DPL of the destination TSS does *not* enter into the protection check. The DPL of the task gate determines access to the TSS descriptor for a task switch. A procedure cannot load the selector for the task gate descriptor unless the selector RPL and the CPL of the procedure are numerically less than or equal to (at least as privileged as) the DPL of the descriptor. A less privileged procedure cannot cause a task switch.

The TSS descriptor is constrained to reside in the GDT. If the DPL of the TSS descriptor is set to allow a lower privileged task to access it, other tasks of equal or more privilege cannot be prevented from accessing it as well. A task gate, however, can reside in a task's LDT. A task that does not have enough privilege to use the TSS descriptor in the GDT (which can have its DPL set to 0) can still call another task through a gate in its LDT. The task gate helps the operating system limit task switching.

Interrupts and exceptions may also need to cause a task switch. Task gates can reside in the interrupt descriptor table (IDT), which allows interrupts to switch tasks. The task gate is placed at the vector for the desired interrupt.

Task Switching

A task switch can be initiated in any one of the following four ways:

- The target selector of a far JMP or CALL instruction selects a TSS descriptor from the GDT. (The offset portion of the target address is ignored.)

- The target selector of a far JMP or CALL instruction selects a task gate from the GDT or LDT. (The offset portion of the target address is ignored.) The selector of the new TSS is located in the gate.

- An interrupt occurs, and the interrupt vector selects a task gate in the IDT. The selector of the new TSS is located in the gate.

- An IRET instruction is executed when the nested task (NT) bit in FLAGS is set (NT=1). The destination task selector is in the backlink field of the task executing the IRET.

No special instructions are required to switch tasks. The normal CALL and JMP instructions and interrupts, for example, become task-switching instructions if they transfer control to a task gate or reference a TSS descriptor. The IRET instruction initiates a task switch only if NT=1.

Note that using a CALL instruction or a hardware or software interrupt to switch tasks implies that a return is expected. Similarly, invoking a task via a JMP or IRET implies that no return is expected. (Which is good, since no return information is saved in those cases.)

The process of switching tasks involves five steps. It's important to be familiar with the steps and the order in which they are performed in case errors occur during the task switch. The five steps are as follows:

1. Check privilege. For JMP or CALL instructions that reference a TSS descriptor or task gate, the greater numeric value (lesser privilege) of the selector's RPL and the CPL must be less than or equal to (at least as privileged as) the descriptor DPL. If not, a general protection exception (interrupt Dh) generated with the error code identifying the descriptor. If the privilege check passes, the current task is designated the *outgoing task*.

2. Check presence and limit. The new task is designated the *incoming task*. The TSS must be present (in memory) and the TSS limit must be a valid value as explained earlier in this section.

Up to this point, all errors are handled in the context of the outgoing task. All errors are restartable and the error handling is generally transparent to the outgoing task.

3. Save outgoing state. The selector of the outgoing TSS is in the TR. The processor updates the dynamic portions of the TSS with their current values. The value of IP/EIP that is saved points to the instruction following the one that invoked the task switch. If execution of the task is resumed, it will start after the instruction that caused the task switch.

4. Load TR. The incoming task selector is loaded into TR. The busy bit in the incoming task's TSS is set (B=1) to indicate that the task is busy. The TS bit in CR0 is set to indicate that a task switch has occurred.

5. Load and execute incoming task. The LDT, AX/EAX, BX/EBX, CX/ECX, DX/EDX, SI/ESI, DI/EDI, BP/EBP, DS, ES, FS, GS, SS, SP/ESP, CS, IP/EIP, and FLAGS/EFLAGS registers are loaded from the incoming TSS. The backlink field is set to point to the outgoing task. If an error occurs, it is handled in the context of the incoming task. If the task is being invoked for the first time, it will appear as if the first instruction has not yet been executed. The second and subsequent task invocations *restore* the state the task had when it returned control. Execution appears to resume at the instruction following the one that invoked the return task switch.

Note that any task switch sets the TS bit in CR0. This bit is used to coordinate use of system resources, such as the math coprocessor, among several tasks. If a task plans to use the NPX, but finds the TS bit set, it should assume that the context of the NPX does not belong to it and must be preserved.

A task switch performs the checks shown in Table 15.5. Note that the order in which the checks are performed is processor-dependent. Intel documentation notes that the order may change in future Intel processors. All conditions must be satisfied if the task switch is to occur without exception. Up to the third check, errors occur in the context of the outgoing task. After the third check, the incoming task is considered valid and errors occur in the context of the incoming task.

Task Linking When the execution of a task is temporarily suspended (by a CALL or interrupt, for example) to execute another task, the tasks are said to be *nested*. The backlink field of the TSS and the NT flag are used to keep track of nested tasks and to implement *task linking* so that the original interrupted task can be restarted.

TABLE 15.5

Interlevel Return Protection Checks

Order (Processor Dependent)

286	386DX	386SX 486	Check Description	Exception	Error Code
1	1	1	Incoming TSS descriptor must be present	Segment not present	Incoming TSS selector
2	2	2	Incoming TSS must be idle (not busy)	General protection	Incoming TSS selector
3	3	3	Incoming TSS limit ≥ 43 (for 16-bit TSS) or limit ≥ 103 (for 32-bit TSS)	Invalid TSS	Incoming TSS selector

Incoming task now valid. All registers and selectors loaded.

286	386DX	386SX 486	Check Description	Exception	Error Code
4	4	4	LDT selector of incoming TSS must be valid	Invalid TSS	Incoming TSS selector
5	5	9	LDT of incoming TSS must be present	Invalid TSS	Incoming TSS selector
6	6	10	Code segment selector must be valid	Invalid TSS	Code segment selector
7	7	11	Code segment must be present	Segment not present	Code segment selector
8	8	5	Code segment DPL must match code selector RPL	Invalid TSS	Code segment selector
9	9	6	Stack segment must be valid	Stack fault	Stack segment selector
10	—	—	Stack segment must be writable data segment	General protection	Stack segment selector
11	10	7	Stack segment is present	Stack fault	Stack segment selector
12	11	8	Stack segment DPL = CPL	Stack fault	Stack segment selector
—	12	12	Stack selector RPL = CPL	General protection	Stack segment selector

TABLE 15.5

(Continued)

286	386DX	386SX 486	Check Description	Exception	Error Code
13	13	13	DS, ES, FS, and GS selectors must be valid	General protection	Segment selector
14	14	14	DS, ES, FS, and GS segments must be readable	General protection	Segment selector
15	15	15	DS, ES, FS, and GS segments must be present	Segment not present	Segment selector
16	16	16	DS, ES, FS, and GS segment DPL ≥ CPL if not conforming segments	General protection	Segment selector

If the NT flag is set (NT=1), it indicates that the current task is nested within the execution of another task. The backlink field of a nested task's TSS is automatically loaded with the selector of the TSS of the interrupted task when the new task is invoked.

When the nested task terminates (via an IRET), the processor interprets the IRET as a task switch request. The processor switches back to the task whose TSS selector is loaded in the backlink field of the terminating task.

Note that although a program will probably not have enough privilege to modify its TSS, a program operating at any privilege level can modify its NT flag. If a task is *not* nested, but the NT bit is set and an IRET is executed, a spurious task switch (and most likely a protection violation) will result. This situation can be avoided by having the operating system initialize the backlink field of all task state segments it creates.

Table 15.6 shows how the fields and flags that are involved in a task switch are affected by a JMP, CALL, or IRET instruction that invokes a task switch. Note that for each case, the incoming task is the task that *will* be executed and the outgoing task is the task that is executing the instruction. In the case of the JMP or CALL, the current task is the one that will be suspended. In the case of the IRET, the current task is the one terminating.

If a task needs to be removed from the linked task chain, trusted (most privileged) software must change the backlink field in the TSS to point to itself, then clear the busy bit of the task. When the removed task executes an IRET, control will then pass back to the trusted software.

The busy bit is used to prevent reentrant task switches. In an interrupt-intensive system, the chain of interrupted tasks may grow quite long. As mentioned earlier, tasks are not reentrant. This is because there is only one TSS for a task, and all state information is saved in the TSS. If the processor allowed a task to be invoked a second time, the saved information would overwrite the state saved during the first invocation and the chain of linked tasks would be corrupted.

TABLE 15.6

Fields and Flags Affected During a Task Switch

Field or Flag	Effect of JMP	Effect of CALL	Effect of IRET
Busy bit of incoming task	Set (must have been 0)	Set (must have been 0)	Unchanged (must have been 1)
Busy bit of outgoing task	Cleared	Unchanged (is 1)	Cleared
NT bit in incoming task FLAGS	Cleared	Set	Unchanged
NT bit in outgoing task FLAGS	Unchanged	Unchanged	Cleared
Backlink in incoming task TSS	Unchanged	Set to TSS selector of outgoing task	Unchanged
Backlink in incoming task TSS	Unchanged	Unchanged	Unchanged

Virtual 8086 Mode

The 80386 and 80486 processors are initialized in real (8086-emulation) mode and, as such, are able to execute 8086 real-mode programs. These processors offer another method of operation, however, in which one or more 8086 real-mode programs can be executed in a protected-mode environment. This mode of operation is called *Virtual-86* mode—V86 mode, for short.

The purpose of the V86 mode is to provide a separate *virtual machine* for an 8086 program running on the processor. A virtual machine is an environment created through a combination of processor capabilities and system software. The result is that a V86 task perceives itself to be the only task executing on an 8086.

A typical virtual machine configuration will provide a set of virtual registers (through its TSS) and a virtual memory space. When software that is executed in the virtual machine attempts to access the external world (through interrupts, exceptions, and I/O) the system software (usually called the virtual machine control program, or *monitor*) can either emulate the action or pass it directly through to the hardware. In effect, a virtual machine is an 8086 hardware interpreter.

A task running in a virtual machine is able to execute all valid 8086 instructions. As mentioned, certain instructions, such as I/O, are executed subject to the approval of the virtual machine monitor. In addition, the full 32-bit register and instruction set of the 80386 and 80486 are available.

V86 Task Structure

A complete V86 task comprises both the 8086 program to be run and the V86 monitor. A V86 task must be defined by a 32-bit TSS; a 16-bit (80286-type) TSS cannot be used to describe a V86 task. The monitor is a protected-mode program and, when it is executing, the processor is running in protected mode. The processor enters V86 mode when control is passed to the V86 task and switches back to protected mode when the monitor regains control.

The monitor always runs at privilege level 0 (most privileged). Typically the monitor initializes the system and installs exception handlers. As with any other protected-mode task, code segment descriptors for the monitor must be located in the GDT or in the task's LDT. The monitor may also need to create data segment descriptors so it can access the V86's interrupt vector table or other portions of the task.

The highest logical address that can be generated by an 8086 program is FFFF:FFFFh. This logical address resolves to 10FFEFh—a 21-bit linear address. On the 8086, the address space wraps at 1Mb and the carry generated into bit 21 would be ignored. On the 80386 and 80486, the carry is not ignored, giving the V86 task access to the linear addresses from 0 to 10FFEFh (1 megabyte plus about 64k). Linear addresses above 10FFEFh are available for the monitor, the operating system, and other system software.

There are two distinct methods for providing 8086 operating system support for the virtual machine. In the first method, the 8086 operating system is run as part of the V86 task—nothing is simulated. For example, a virtual machine is created and a complete copy of MS-DOS is loaded into the machine. Once loaded, other applications are loaded and executed by DOS as desired. As far as DOS and the other applications are concerned, they are executing on an 8086. Access to the keyboard, I/O, hard disk, and so on, is supported through the monitor.

This method is preferable if the applications modify the operating system or depend on undocumented features or structures (as do most DOS applications, for example). In addition, if multiple virtual machines are running (as described later in this section) this method allows a different version of the 8086 operating system to be run in each machine. This ability greatly speeds the process of validating the behavior of an application under different versions of DOS, for example.

The second method requires that the 8086 operating system be simulated by the protected-mode operating system. In a multiple virtual machine environment, using a single, emulated 8086 operating system instead of each machine running a separate copy of the operating system will save some memory, but restricts all machines to the same simulated version of that operating system. In addition, attempts to modify the operating system will have to be trapped and denied or one virtual task may corrupt the others.

Paging   Paging and the virtual machine capability of the 80386 and 80486 can be combined to good advantage. A V86 task, for example, can only generate linear addresses in the first 1Mb of the processor's address space. If it is desired to create more than one V86 task, paging can be used to map different 1Mb physical address spaces to the same 1Mb linear address space.

Recall that 8086 applications may be depending on the 1Mb address wraparound of the 8086 processor. Because the 80386 and 80486 use full 32-bit effective addresses, this wraparound does not occur naturally. If paging is enabled, however, a V86 task can map the 64k linear addresses in the range from 100000h to 110000h (above 1Mb) to the same physical addresses as the first 64k of the address space, 010000h. Paging will also allow the memory space allocated to V86 tasks to be virtualized, allowing more tasks to be run than would fit in the available memory.

If code or data portions of an 8086 operating system or ROM code, for example, are to be shared among multiple V86 tasks, paging will allow these sections of code to be accessed simultaneously. Similarly, I/O to memory-mapped devices can be trapped and redirected if desired.

Protection   In V86 mode, the processor does not interpret values loaded into segment registers as selectors. Instead, the values are interpreted as the high-order 16 bits of a 20-bit linear address, exactly as on the 8086. Because selectors and descriptors are not used, the descriptor protection mechanisms employed by the processor in protected mode are not used. The system, V86 monitor, and other tasks, therefore, must be protected from the actions of the V86 task.

As mentioned previously, a V86 task cannot generate effective addresses beyond 10FFEFh (1Mb plus about 64k). If this area of linear memory is reserved from other tasks, their address spaces will be effectively isolated.

If paging is enabled, the page-level protection mechanism of the processor can be employed. The user/supervisor (U/S) bit of page-table entries belonging to the monitor and other system software should be set to 0 (supervisor-level access only). The V86 task executes in user mode (CPL=3) and cannot access supervisor level pages.

Entering and Leaving V86 Mode

The processor enters V86 mode when the virtual mode (VM) flag in the EFLAGS register is set. A task switch to a 32-bit task, for example, loads the EFLAGS register from the target TSS. (A 16-bit TSS cannot be used since it does not load the high 16 bits of the EFLAGS register where the VM flag is located.) If the VM flag is set in the EFLAGS image, the new task will be executing in V86 mode.

Similarly, an IRET instruction executed in a protected-mode procedure will load an EFLAGS image from the stack. If the new EFLAGS has the VM flag set, the processor will enter virtual mode. Note that the CPL when the IRET is executed must be 0 (most privileged) or the state of the VM flag is not changed, regardless of the value of the VM flag in the EFLAGS image.

A task switch to V86 mode reloads the processor's segment registers from the TSS. When an IRET is used to set the VM flag, however, the segment registers keep the contents they had previously when executing in protected mode. The segment registers should be loaded with values appropriate to 8086 execution.

The processor leaves V86 mode when an interrupt or exception occurs. An interrupt, for example, may invoke a task switch. The task switch loads the image of the EFLAGS register from the target TSS. If the VM flag in the new

EFLAGS image is clear (or if a 16-bit FLAGS image is loaded from an 80286-type TSS), the processor begins executing in protected mode.

If the interrupt or exception handler calls a procedure with a DPL of 0 (most privileged), the processor stores the current value of EFLAGS on the stack, then clears the VM flag. The handler then runs in protected mode. If, however, that handler calls a procedure that is in a conforming code segment or has a DPL other than 0, the processor generates a general protection exception. The error code identifies the selector of the code segment to which the call was made.

APPENDIX A

INSTRUCTION SET REFERENCE

THE 80×86 PROCESSOR INSTRUCTIONS ARE PRESENTED FIRST IN TABULAR FORM.
Table A.1 lists all the instructions described in the reference, the assembler mne-
monic, a short description of the instruction, and the processors that support it.
This table can be used as a quick reference to check a mnemonic or see if the
DAA instruction is valid across the 80×86 family, for example. A second listing
of the instructions, given in Table A.2, groups the instructions by category.

TABLE A.1

Instructions in Alphabetical Order

86/88	286	386	486	Mnemonic	Description
*	*	*	*	AAA	ASCII Adjust AL After Addition
*	*	*	*	AAD	ASCII Adjust AX Before Division
*	*	*	*	AAM	ASCII Adjust AX After Multiply
*	*	*	*	AAS	ASCII Adjust AL After Subtraction
*	*	*	*	ADC	Add Two Operands with Carry
*	*	*	*	ADD	Add Two Operands
*	*	*	*	AND	Perform a Logical AND of Two Operands
	*	*	*	ARPL	Adjust RPL Field of Selector (PM)
	*	*	*	BOUND	Check Array Index Against Bounds
		*	*	BSF	Bit Scan Forward
		*	*	BSR	Bit Scan Reverse
			*	BSWAP	Byte Swap
		*	*	BT	Bit Test
		*	*	BTC	Bit Test and Complement
		*	*	BTR	Bit Test and Reset
		*	*	BTS	Bit Test and Set
*	*	*	*	CALL	Call a Procedure (Subroutine)
*	*	*	*	CBW	Convert Byte in AL to Word in AX
		*	*	CDQ	Convert Doubleword in EAX to Quadword in EDX:EAX
*	*	*	*	CLC	Clear the Carry Flag

TABLE A.1

Instructions in Alphabetical Order (continued)

86/88	286	386	486	Mnemonic	Description
*	*	*	*	CLD	Clear the Direction Flag
*	*	*	*	CLI	Clear the Interrupt Flag
	*	*	*	CLTS	Clear Task Switched Flag
*	*	*	*	CMC	Complement the Carry Flag
*	*	*	*	CMP	Compare Two Operands
*	*	*	*	CMPS	Compare Strings
			*	CMPXCHG	Compare and Exchange
	*	*	*	CTS	Clear Task Switched Flag
*	*	*	*	CWD	Convert Word in AX to Doubleword in DX:AX
		*	*	CWDE	Convert Word in AX to Doubleword in EAX
*	*	*	*	DAA	Decimal Adjust AL After Addition
*	*	*	*	DAS	Decimal Adjust AL After Subtraction
*	*	*	*	DEC	Decrement by 1
*	*	*	*	DIV	Unsigned Division
	*	*	*	ENTER	Make Stack Frame for Procedure
*	*	*	*	ESC	Escape (Access Memory)
*	*	*	*	HLT	Halt the Processor
		*		IBTS	Insert Bit String
*	*	*	*	IDIV	Integer (Signed) Division
	*	*	*	IIMUL	Integer Immediate Multiplication
*	*	*	*	IMUL	Integer (Signed) Multiplication
*	*	*	*	IN	Input Data from I/O Port
*	*	*	*	INC	Increment by 1
	*	*	*	INS	Input String from I/O Port
*	*	*	*	INT	Generate Software Interrupt
*	*	*	*	INTO	Generate Interrupt If Overflow
			*	INVD	Invalidate Cache
			*	INVLPG	Invalidate Page Entry in TLB
*	*	*	*	IRET	Return from Interrupt
		*	*	IRETD	Return from Interrupt Using EIP
*	*	*	*	Jcond	Jump If Condition Met
*	*	*	*	JCXZ	Jump If CX=0

TABLE A.1

Instructions in Alphabetical Order (continued)

86/88	286	386	486	Mnemonic	Description
		*	*	JECXZ	Jump If ECX=0
*	*	*	*	JMP	Unconditional Jump
*	*	*	*	LAHF	Load AH with 8080 Flags
	*	*	*	LAR	Load Access Rights Byte (PM)
*	*	*	*	LDS	Load Register and DS
*	*	*	*	LEA	Load Effective Address (Offset)
	*	*	*	LEAVE	Destroy Stack Frame
*	*	*	*	LES	Load Register and ES
		*	*	LFS	Load Register and FS
	*	*	*	LGDT	Load Global Descriptor Table Register
		*	*	LGS	Load Register and GS
	*	*	*	LIDT	Load Interrupt Descriptor Table Register
	*	*	*	LLDT	Load Local Descriptor Table Register (PM)
	*	*	*	LMSW	Load Machine Status Word
	*	*	*	LOADALL	Load All Processor Registers
*	*	*	*	LOCK	Assert Bus Lock Signal
*	*	*	*	LODS	Load String Operand
*	*	*	*	LOOP	Decrement CX and Loop If Not Zero
*	*	*	*	LOOPE/LOOPZ	Decrement CX and Loop While CX≠0 AND ZF=1
*	*	*	*	LOOPNE/LOOPNZ	Decrement CX and Loop While CX≠0 AND ZF=0
	*	*	*	LSL	Load Segment Limit (PM)
		*	*	LSS	Load Register and SS
	*	*	*	LTR	Load Task Register (PM)
*	*	*	*	MOV	Move Data
*	*	*	*	MOVS	Move String
		*	*	MOVSX	Move with Sign Extension
		*	*	MOVZX	Move with Zero Extension
*	*	*	*	MUL	Unsigned Multiply
*	*	*	*	NEG	Negate (Two's Complement)
*	*	*	*	NOP	No Operation (No-op)

TABLE A.1

Instructions in Alphabetical Order (continued)

86/88	286	386	486	Mnemonic	Description
*	*	*	*	NOT	Logical NOT (One's Complement)
*	*	*	*	OR	Logical (Inclusive) OR
*	*	*	*	OUT	Output Data to I/O Port
	*	*	*	OUTS	Output String to I/O Port
*	*	*	*	POP	Read from the Top of the Stack
	*	*	*	POPA	Pop All General Registers
		*	*	POPAD	Pop All 32-bit General Registers
*	*	*	*	POPF	Load the FLAGS Register from the Stack
		*	*	POPFD	Load the EFLAGS Register from the Stack
*	*	*	*	PUSH	Push Operand onto the Stack
	*	*	*	PUSHA	Push All General Registers
		*	*	PUSHAD	Push All 32-bit General Registers
*	*	*	*	PUSHF	Push the FLAGS Register onto the Stack
		*	*	PUSHFD	Push the EFLAGS Register onto the Stack
*	*	*	*	RCL	Rotate Left Through Carry Flag
*	*	*	*	RCR	Rotate Right Through Carry Flag
*	*	*	*	REP	Repeat the String Instruction Which Follows While CX≠0
				REPC/REPNC	Repeat the String Instruction Which Follows While Testing the Carry Flag
*	*	*	*	REPE/REPZ	Repeat the String Instruction Which Follows CX≠0 and ZF=1
*	*	*	*	REPNE/REPNZ	Repeat the String Instruction Which Follows CX≠0 and ZF=0
*	*	*	*	RET/RETF/RETN	Return from Procedure (Subroutine)
*	*	*	*	ROL	Rotate Left
*	*	*	*	ROR	Rotate Right
*	*	*	*	SAHF	Load AH into 8080 Flags
*	*	*	*	SAL	Shift Arithmetic Left
*	*	*	*	SAR	Shift Arithmetic Right
*	*	*	*	SBB	Subtract with Borrow
*	*	*	*	SCAS	Scan String

TABLE A.1

Instructions in Alphabetical Order (continued)

86/88	286	386	486	Mnemonic	Description
*	*	*	*	SEG	Override Default Segment Register
		*	*	SET*cond*	Set Byte on Condition
	*	*	*	SETALC	Set AL to Carry
	*	*	*	SGDT	Store Global Descriptor Table Register
*	*	*	*	SHL	Shift Logical Left
		*	*	SHLD	Double Precision Shift Logical Left
*	*	*	*	SHR	Shift Logical Right
		*	*	SHRD	Double Precision Shift Logical Right
	*	*	*	SIDT	Store Interrupt Descriptor Table Register
	*	*	*	SLDT	Store Local Descriptor Table Register (PM)
	*	*	*	SMSW	Store Machine Status Word
*	*	*	*	STC	Set the Carry Flag
*	*	*	*	STD	Set the Direction Flag
*	*	*	*	STI	Set the Interrupt Flag
*	*	*	*	STOS	Store String
	*	*	*	STR	Store Task Register (PM)
*	*	*	*	SUB	Subtract
*	*	*	*	TEST	Test (Logical Compare)
	*	*	*	VERR	Verify a Segment for Reading (PM)
	*	*	*	VERW	Verify a Segment for Writing (PM)
*	*	*	*	WAIT	Wait for Asserted Signal
			*	WBINVD	Write-Back and Invalidate Cache
			*	XADD	Exchange and Add
		*		XBTS	Extract Bit String
*	*	*	*	XCHG	Exchange
*	*	*	*	XLAT/XLATB	Translate (Perform Table Lookup)
*	*	*	*	XOR	Logical Exclusive-OR

TABLE A.2

Instruction Summary by Category

General Purpose Data Movement
BSWAP	CMPXCHG	LAHF	LDS	LES	LFS	LGS	LSS
MOV	MOVSX	MOVZX	SAHF	XADD	XCHG	XLAT/XLATB	

Stack Manipulation
POP	POPA	POPAD	POPF	POPFD
PUSH	PUSHA	PUSHAD	PUSHF	PUSHFD

Type Conversion
CBW   CDQ   CWD   CWDE

Input/Output
IN   INS   OUT   OUTS

Arithmetic
ADC	ADD	DEC	DIV	IDIV	IMUL
INC	MUL	NEG	SBB	SUB	XADD

Logical
AND   NOT   OR   XOR

Shift and Rotate
RCL	RCR	ROL	ROR	SAL
SAR	SHL	SHLD	SHR	SHRD

String
INS	LODS	MOVS	OUTS	REP	REPC	REPE	REPNC
REPNE	REPNZ	REPZ	SCAS	STOS			

Test and Comparison
BOUND	BSF	BSR	BT	BTC	BTR
BTS	CMP	CMPS	CMPXCHG	*Jcond*	JCXZ
JECXZ	LOOP	LOOPE	LOOPNE	LOOPNZ	LOOPZ
SET*cond*	TEST	XLAT	XLATB		

Control Transfer
CALL	INT	INTO	IRET	IRETD	*Jcond*
JCXZ	JECXZ	JMP	LOOP	RET	RETF	RETN

Decimal (BCD) Arithmetic
AAA   AAD   AAM   AAS   DAA   DAS

Flag Manipulation and Test
CLC	CLD	CLI	CLTS	CMC	*Jcond*	LAHF	POPF
POPFD	PUSHF	PUSHFD	SAHF	SET*cond*	STC	STD	STI

Address Calculation
LEA   SEG

Processor Control
ESC	HLT	INVD	INVLPG
LOADALL	LOCK	WAIT	WBINVD

Protected-Mode Support
ARPL	CLTS	CTS	LAR	LGDT	LIDT
LLDT	LMSW	LSL	LTR	MOV	SGDT
SID SLDT	SMSW	STR	VERR	VERW	

Miscellaneous
ENTER   LEAVE   NOP

Instruction Encoding

In many instances, symbols are used to represent variable bit fields in the encodings. The instruction forms and most common symbols are presented here in Figures A.1 through A.3 and Tables A.3 through A.9 along with their meanings as used in the encoding descriptions that follow. Symbols that are less common are defined in the encoding entries that use them. For details on encoding instructions, see Chapter 6.

TABLE A.3

Opcode Encoding Symbols

Symbol	Description	Meaning
d	Direction field (1 bit)	0 - The *reg* field specifies the register that is the source operand and the destination is a memory operand as specified by the *mod+r/m* fields. 1 - The destination is a register operand specified by the *reg* field. The source may be a register or memory operand as specified by the *mod+r/m* fields.
w	Word/byte field (1 bit)	0 - Operands are 8-bit. 1 - Operands are 16-bit if the operand size attribute is 16-bit or 32-bit if the operand size attribute is 32-bit.
s	Sign field (1bit)	0 - No action. 1 - The 8-bit immediate data following will be sign-extended to 16 bits if the operand size attribute is 16-bit or sign-extended to 32 bits if the operand size attribute is 32-bit.

FIGURE A.1

The MODEM byte

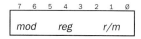

Field	Size	Description
mod	2	mode
reg	3	register
r/m	3	register/memory

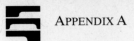

TABLE A.4

Interpretation of the *reg* Field

| reg | w=Ø | w=1 | |
	Both Modes	16-bit Mode	32-bit Mode
ØØØb	AL	AX	EAX
ØØ1b	CL	CX	ECX
Ø1Øb	DL	DX	EDX
Ø11b	BL	BX	EBX
1ØØb	AH	SP	ESP
1Ø1b	CH	BP	EBP
11Øb	DH	SI	ESI
111b	BH	DI	EDI

TABLE A.5

Interpretation of the *mod* and *r/m* Fields in 16-bit Mode

| r/m | mod=ØØb | mod=Ø1b | mod=1Øb | mod=11b | |
				w=Ø	w=1
ØØØb	DS:[BX+SI]	DS:[BX+SI+*disp8*]	DS:[BX+SI+*disp16*]	AL	AX
ØØ1b	DS:[BX+DI]	DS:[BX+DI+*disp8*]	DS:[BX+DI+*disp16*]	CL	CX
Ø1Øb	SS:[BP+SI]	SS:[BP+SI+*disp8*]	SS:[BP+SI+*disp16*]	DL	DX
Ø11b	SS:[BP+DI]	SS:[BP+DI+*disp8*]	SS:[BP+DI+*disp16*]	BL	BX
1ØØb	DS:[SI]	DS:[SI+*disp8*]	DS:[SI+*disp16*]	AH	SP
1Ø1b	DS:[DI]	DS:[DI+*disp8*]	DS:[DI+*disp16*]	CH	BP
11Øb	DS:[*disp16*]	SS:[BP+*disp8*]	SS:[BP+*disp16*]	DH	SI
111b	DS:[BX]	DS:[BX+*disp8*]	DS:[BX+*disp16*]	BH	DI

TABLE A.6

Interpretation of the *mod* and *r/m* Fields in 32-bit Mode

| r/m | mod=ØØb | mod=Ø1b | mod=1Øb | mod=11b | |
				w=Ø	w=1
ØØØb	DS:[EAX]	DS:[EAX+*disp8*]	DS:[EAX+*disp32*]	AL	EAX
ØØ1b	DS:[ECX]	DS:[ECX+*disp8*]	DS:[ECX+*disp32*]	CL	ECX
Ø1Øb	DS:[EDX]	DS:[EDX+*disp8*]	DS:[EDX+*disp32*]	DL	EDX
Ø11b	DS:[EBX]	DS:[EBX+*disp8*]	DS:[EBX+*disp32*]	BL	EBX
1ØØb[1]	[SIB]	[SIB+*disp8*]	[SIB+*disp32*]	AH	ESP
1Ø1b	DS:[*off32*]	DS:[EBP+*disp8*]	DS:[EPB+*disp32*]	CH	EBP
11Øb	DS:[ESI]	DS:[ESI+*disp8*]	DS:[ESI+*disp32*]	DH	ESI
111b	DS:[EDI]	DS:[EDI+*disp8*]	DS:[EDI+*disp32*]	BH	EDI

[1] An r/m value of 1ØØb implies that the SIB byte is present and represents an addressing mode of the form [base + *scale•index*].

FIGURE A.2

The SIB byte

```
7  6   5  4  3   2  1  Ø
+------+------+--------+
| scale| index|  base  |
+------+------+--------+
```

Field	Size	Description
scale	2	scale factor
index	3	index register
base	3	base register

TABLE A.7

Interpretation of the MODRM *mod* and SIB *base* Operand Fields in 32-bit Mode

base	mod=00b	mod=01b	mod=10b
000b	DS:[EAX]	DS:[EAX+*disp8*]	DS:[EAX+*disp32*]
001b	DS:[ECX]	DS:[ECX+*disp8*]	DS:[ECX+*disp32*]
010b	DS:[EDX]	DS:[EDX+*disp8*]	DS:[EDX+*disp32*]
011b	DS:[EBX]	DS:[EBX+*disp8*]	DS:[EBX+*disp32*]
100b	SS:[ESP]	SS:[ESP+*disp8*]	SS:[ESP+*disp32*]
101b	DS:[*off32*]	SS:[EPB+*disp8*]	SS:[EPB+*disp32*]
110b	DS:[ESI]	DS:[ESI+*disp8*]	DS:[ESI+*disp32*]
111b	DS:[EDI]	DS:[EDI+*disp8*]	DS:[EDI+*disp32*]

TABLE A.8

The *scale* Field and Scaling Values for the SIB Byte

scale	Scaling value
00b	1
01b	2
10b	4
11b	8

TABLE A.9

Interpretation of the *Index* Field for the SIB Byte

index	Register Operand
000b	[EAX]
001b	[ECX]
010b	[EDX]
011b	[EBX]
100b	no index
101b	[EBP]
110b	[ESI]
111b	[EDI]

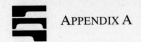

Instruction Timings

The instruction timings are given in clocks and represent the best estimate of actual instruction execution time. The number of clocks an instruction requires to execute can vary depending on the processor mode, number of repetitions, and so on. Execution times also vary significantly among different versions, or steps, of the same processor. The times shown here are for the latest versions of the chips available at the time of publication. The most common symbols used in the timing section of the listings are shown in Table A.10 and the additional clocks required for effective address calculations are shown in Table A.11. Symbols that are used for only one or two instructions are defined in the instruction listing itself.

TABLE A.10

Symbols Used to Represent Execution Timing Variables and Conditions

Timing Symbol	Explanation
n	In bit shift and rotate instructions, the actual number of bits shifted or rotated. Also used for the number of bits that must be scanned in the bit scan instructions.
r	In string instructions, the actual number of times the instruction is repeated.
m	The number of elements in the instruction that is the target of a transfer.
ts	The time required to perform a task switch (protected or virtual mode).
p	The number of parameters used when transferring control via a Call gate.
EA	The clocks required to perform the effective address calculation.
NJ	Indicates the timing when the jump is not taken. The other timing shown is for the case in which the jump is taken.
B	Indicates the timing, when different, for executing the instruction with a byte operand size.
W	Indicates the timing, when different, for executing the instruction with a word operand size.
D	Indicates the timing, when different, for executing the instruction with a doubleword operand size.
PM	Indicates the timing, when different, for executing the instruction in protected mode.
VM	Indicates the timing, when different, for executing the instruction in Virtual-86 mode.
x	The number of memory transfers required by the instruction.
–	Instruction form not available on the indicated processor.

TABLE A.11

Additional Clocks Required for Effective Address Calculations

Effective Address Components		Additional Clocks Required			
		86/88	286	386	486
Displacement	[disp]	6	0	0	0
Base or Index	[BX] [BP] [SI] [DI]	5	0	0	0
Base + disp Index + disp	[BX + disp] [BP + disp] [SI + disp] [DI + disp]	9	0	0	0
Base + Index	[BX + SI] [BP + DI]	7	0	0	0
	[BX + DI] [BP + SI]	8	0	0	0
Base + Index + disp	[BX + SI + disp] [BP + DI + disp]	11	1	0	0
	[BX + DI + disp] [BP + SI + disp]	12	1	0	0
Segment Override	sreg:	2	0	0	1
Base + scale * index (32-bit mode)	[reg32 + scale * reg32]	–	–	1	1[1]

[1] One clock may be added to the 80486 execution time depending on the state of the processor.

Example Instruction Listing

Each entry in the instruction reference follows the same basic format, an example of which is shown in Figure A.3. An explanation of each element in a reference entry is given below.

1. *Title.* Instruction mnemonic and a short description.

2. *Description.* A one or two sentence summary of the basic action of the instruction followed by a more detailed operational description.

3. *Algorithm.* A pseudo-code algorithm that describes how the instruction operates. The functions and control structures used in the pseudo-code algorithms are defined in Table A.12.

4. *Notes.* Any information that is applicable to the instruction including limitations, undocumented uses, and so on.

5. *Flags.* This element shows how the execution of the instruction affects each of the 8086 flags. The symbols used to represent action on the flags are shown in Table A.13.

6. *Encoding and timing.* One block will be present for each unique form of the encoding. The opcode and other bytes are shown along with the timings and number of memory transfers. The number of transfers is useful for calculating the clock penalties for unaligned operands.

FIGURE A.3

BSWAP

Swap Byte Order

DESCRIPTION BSWAP op

BSWAP reverses the order of the bytes in a 32-bit register, leaving the result in the same register.

The 80x86 family of processors uses the "little endian" method of storing data in memory. This means that the least significant byte of a multibyte operand is stored at the lowest addressed byte, and the most significant byte is stored at the highest addressed byte. Processors that store data in the opposite sense are said to use the "big endian" method. The BSWAP instruction offers a convenient method for converting between the two methods. BSWAP is also useful for operating on BCD or ASCII operands that are stored using the big endian method by convention. For example, assume the EAX register contains the value 12345678h. After executing the instruction BSWAP EAX, the register would contain the value 78563412h.

ALGORITHM temp=op
BIT(7-0 of op)=BIT(31-24 of temp)
BIT(15-8 of op)=BIT(23-16 of temp)
BIT(23-16 of op)=BIT(15-8 of temp)
BIT(31-24 of op)=BIT(7-0 of temp)

NOTES 1. When BSWAP is used with a 16-bit register as *op*, the result left in *op* is undefined.

FLAGS

O	D	I	T	S	Z	A	P	C	
									No flags are affected

BSWAP reg32

00001111	11001	r/m

TIMING

Operands	x	88	86	286	386	486
reg32	0	-	-	-	-	1

TABLE A.12

Functions and Control Structures Used in the Pseudocode Algorithms

IF (*cond*) THEN *statement*	If the condition is true, perform the action described by the statement.

IF (*cond*) THEN
  statement$_1$
ELSE
  statement$_2$
ENDIF
	If the condition is true, perform the action described by *statement$_1$*. Otherwise, perform the action described by *statement$_2$*.

IF (*cond$_1$*) THEN
  statement$_1$
ELSEIF (*cond$_2$*) THEN
  statement$_2$
ELSEIF (*cond$_3$*) THEN
     ⋮
ENDIF
	If condition$_n$ is true, perform the action described by the statement$_n$.

WHILE (*cond*)
  statement
ENDWHILE
	If the condition is true, perform the action described by the statement, then repeat.

DO *statement* LOOPWHILE (*cond*)	Perform the action described by the statement, then if the condition is true, repeat.
FOR *var=start* TO *stop* *statement* ENDFOR	Initialize *var* to *start*. Repeatedly perform the statement and increment *var* until *var*>stop.
BIT(*n* of *op*)	Represents the single bit, number *n*, of the specified operand.
SIGN_EXTEND(*op*)	The operand is increased to the required size by duplicating the sign bit to the left.
ZERO_EXTEND(*op*)	The operand is increased to the required size by adding zero bits to the left.
SIZEOF(*op*)	Represents the size of the indicated operand in bytes.
SEGOF(*op*)	Represents the segment of the indicated operand such as might be specified with an override prefix.
dest="EDI"	Quotes are used when an algorithm variable is to literally represent a register or operand.

TABLE A.13

The Symbols Used to Represent the Flag State After an Instruction Execution

Flag Symbol	Explanation
0	Flag is cleared to 0.
1	Flag is set to 1.
*	Flag is set according to the result of the operation.
–	Value of flag is undefined after the operation.

Reference

The reference section which follows lists, alphabetically by mnemonic, all the instructions available on the Intel processors from the 8088 through the 80486. Both real-mode and protected-mode instructions are listed. In addition, where the timings in real mode and protected mode differ, they are shown separately. The floating-point ESC instructions are described separately in Appendix B.

The entry for each instruction includes a description of the operation and use of the instruction, a pseudocode algorithm of its operation, notes on inconsistencies and bugs, the flags affected by instruction execution, and the instruction encoding. The encoding information is shown in binary form. Bits that have fixed values for an instruction are shown as either 0 or 1. Symbols are used when the value for a particular field will vary.

When one mnemonic is used to represent several different forms of an instruction (with different opcodes), all forms will appear under the same heading. The different encodings and timings will be shown as required. An example is the MOV mnemonic, which is used to represent any one of ten different instructions.

The encoding given for most instructions will be the 16-bit encoding and will not show the SIB byte explicitly. The encoding for any instruction that requires the SIB byte can easily be generated by adding that byte directly after the addressing-mode byte as explained in Chapter 6 in the section on 80386 and 80486 encoding.

(no mnemonic)

Address Size Prefix

DESCRIPTION The address size prefix instructs the processor to change the address mode *only* for the instruction that it prefixes.

If the current address mode is 16-bit, the instruction will use 32-bit addressing. Conversely, if the current address mode is 32-bit, the instruction will use 16-bit addressing. The change in address mode affects only the effective address, not the operand size.

Note that the use of SP or ESP in *implicit* stack references in protected mode is determined by the stack address mode specified in the stack segment descriptor and is not affected by this prefix.

ALGORITHM

```
IF (AddressMode=16-bit) THEN
  AddressMode=32-bit   ;Only for instruction that follows
ELSE ;AddressMode=32-bit
  AddressMode=16-bit   ;Only for instruction that follows
ENDIF
```

FLAGS

O	D	I	T	S	Z	A	P	C

No flags are affected

Address Size Prefix

```
01100111
```

TIMING

Operands	x	88	86	286	386	486
(no operands)	0	–	–	–	0	1

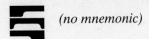

(no mnemonic)

Operand Size Prefix

DESCRIPTION The operand size prefix instructs the processor to change the operand mode *only* for the instruction that it prefixes.

If the current operand mode is 16-bit, the instruction will use 32-bit operands. Conversely, if the current operand mode is 32-bit, the instruction will use 16-bit operands. The change in operand mode affects only the operands, not the size of effective addresses.

ALGORITHM
```
IF (OperandMode=16-bit) THEN
    OperandMode=32-bit  ;Only for instruction that follows
ELSE ;OperandMode=32-bit
    OperandMode=16-bit  ;Only for instruction that follows
ENDIF
```

FLAGS

O	D	I	T	S	Z	A	P	C

No flags are affected

Operand Size Prefix

01100110

TIMING

Operands	x	88	86	286	386	486
(no operands)	0	–	–	–	0	1

AAA

Adjust AL After BCD Addition

DESCRIPTION AAA converts the result of the addition of two valid unpacked BCD digits to a valid 2-digit BCD number and takes the AL register as its implicit operand.

For the previous addition to have had any meaning, each of the two operands of the addition must have had its lower 4 bits contain a number in the range from 0 to 9. The AAA instruction then adjusts AL so that it contains a correct BCD digit. If the addition produced a decimal carry (AF=1), the AH register is incremented and the carry (CF) and auxiliary carry (AF) flags are set to 1. If the addition did not produce a decimal carry, CF and AF are cleared to 0 and AH is not altered. In both cases, the high-order 4 bits of AL are cleared to 0.

Traditionally, this instruction is labeled as ASCII Adjust After Addition. And AAA will adjust the result of the addition of two ASCII characters that were in the range from 30h ("0") to 39h ("9"). This is because the lower 4 bits of those characters fall in the range from 0 to 9. The result of the addition, however, is *not* an ASCII character; it is a BCD digit.

The following example shows how to add BCD numbers then adjust the result:

```
MOV   AH,Ø   ;Clear AH for most significant digit
MOV   AL,6   ;BCD 6 in AL
ADD   AL,5   ;Add BCD 5 to digit in AL
AAA          ;AH=1, AL=1 representing BCD 11.
```

ALGORITHM
```
IF ((AL AND ØFh)>9 OR (AF=1)) THEN
   IF (8Ø86 OR 8Ø88) THEN      ;See note 1
     AL=AL+6
   ELSE ;8Ø286 or later
     AX=AX+6
   ENDIF
   AH=AH+1
   AF=1
   CF=1
ELSE
   AF=Ø
   CF=Ø
ENDIF
AL=AL AND ØFH
```

1. The 8086 and 8088 implement AAA differently than later processors. On the 80286 and later processors, the first addition is performed on AX instead of AL, incrementing the AH register if a carry is generated out of AL. If AX contains 00FFh, executing AAA on an 8088 will leave AX=0105h. On an 80386, the same operation will leave AX=0205h. Despite the different implementation, this instruction does operate as intended for all valid operands.

2. The upper 4 bits of the AL register are always cleared to 0. This is not noted correctly in Intel's documentation for the 80386 and 80486.

FLAGS

O	D	I	T	S	Z	A	P	C
—				—	—	*	—	*

AAA

00110111

TIMING

Operands	x	88	86	286	386	486
(no operands)	0	8	8	3	4	3

AAD

Adjust AX Before BCD Division

DESCRIPTION AAD converts two unpacked BCD digits in the AH and AL registers into a single binary number in the AX register in preparation for a division (DIV) operation.

Before executing AAD, place the most significant BCD digit in the AH register and the least significant BCD digit in the AL register. When AAD is executed, the two BCD digits are combined into a single binary number by setting AL=(AH*10)+AL and clearing AH to 0.

The following example shows how AAD is used to combine two BCD digits:

```
MOV AX,0205h ;The unpacked BCD number 25
AAD ;After AAD, AH=0 and AL=19h (25)
```

ALGORITHM
```
AL=AH*10+AL
AH=0
```

NOTES
1. The AAD instruction generates a 2-byte opcode. The second opcode byte is interpreted by the processor as an 8-bit immediate operand and is the value by which AH will be multiplied before being added to AL. Any 8-bit number, n, may be encoded as immediate data for this instruction yielding the algorithm AX=(AH*n)+AL. For n=8, the instruction would be encoded as follows.

   ```
   DB   0D5h, 08h
   ```

   This opcode variant is not documented or supported. It functions as shown on processors through the 80486, but may not work on future processors.

FLAGS

O	D	I	T	S	Z	A	P	C
—				*	*	—	*	—

AAD

11010101	00001010

TIMING

Operands	x	88	86	286	386	486
(no operands)	0	60	60	14	19	14

AAM

Adjust AX After BCD Multiply

DESCRIPTION   AAM converts the result of the multiplication of two valid unpacked BCD digits into a valid 2-digit unpacked BCD number and takes AX as an implicit operand.

To give a valid result, the digits that have been multiplied must be in the range 0 to 9 and the result should have been placed in the AX register. Because both operands of the multiply are required to be 9 or less, the result must be less than 81 and thus is completely contained in AL. AAM unpacks the result by dividing AX by 10, placing the quotient (the most significant BCD digit) in AH and the remainder (the least significant BCD digit) in AL.

The following example shows how AAM converts the result of a multiplication into BCD digits.

```
MOV  AL,5
MOV  BL,7
MUL  BL        ;Multiply AL by BL, result in AX
AAM            ;After AAM, AX=0305h (BCD 35)
```

ALGORITHM   AH=AL/10
AL=AL MOD 10

NOTES   1. The AAM instruction generates a 2-byte opcode. The second opcode byte is interpreted by the processor as an 8-bit immediate operand and is both the divisor and the modulo with which AX will be operated on. Any 8-bit number, *n*, may be encoded as immediate data for this instruction yielding the algorithm AX=(AH*n)+AL. For *n*=16, the instruction would have the effect of unpacking a hexadecimal number in AL and would be encoded as follows:

```
DB  0D4h, 10h
```

This opcode variant is not documented and therefore not officially supported. It works on processors through the 80486, but may not work on future processors.

FLAGS

O	D	I	T	S	Z	A	P	C
—				*	*	—	*	—

AAM

| 11010100 | 00001010 |

Operands	x	88	86	286	386	486
(no operands)	0	83	83	16	17	15

AAS

Adjust AL After BCD Subtraction

DESCRIPTION AAS converts the result of the subtraction of two valid unpacked BCD digits to a single valid BCD number and takes the AL register as an implicit operand.

For the previous subtraction to have had any meaning, each of the two operands of the subtraction must have had its lower 4 bits contain numbers in the range from 0 to 9. The AAS instruction then adjusts AL so that it contains a correct BCD digit. If the addition produced a decimal borrow (AF=1), the AH register is decremented and the carry (CF) and auxiliary carry (AF) flags are set to 1. If the addition did not produce a decimal carry, CF and AF are cleared to 0 and AH is not altered. In both cases, the high-order 4 bits of AL are cleared to 0.

An example of the use of AAS to adjust a subtraction is shown here:

```
MOV AX,0901h    ;BCD 91
SUB AL,9        ;Minus 9
AAS             ;Gives AX=0802h (BCD 82)
```

ALGORITHM
```
IF ((AL AND 0Fh)>9 OR AF=1) THEN
    AL=(AL-6)
    AH=AH-1
    AF=1
    CF=1
ELSE
    AF=0
    CF=0
ENDIF
AL=AL AND 0Fh
```

NOTES 1. The upper 4 bits of the AL register are always cleared to 0. This is not noted correctly in the Intel Programmer's Reference Manual for the 80386 and 80486.

FLAGS

O	D	I	T	S	Z	A	P	C
—				—	—	*	—	*

AAS

```
00111111
```

TIMING

Operands	x	88	86	286	386	486
(no operands)	0	8	8	3	4	3

ADC

Add Two Operands with Carry

DESCRIPTION   ADC op_1, op_2

ADC performs the addition of op_1, op_2, and the carry flag (CF). The result of the addition is stored in op_1 and is used to set the flags.

The ADC instruction is usually employed as part of an algorithm for multibyte or multiword addition. For example, to add the number 1671h to a 32-bit integer assumed to be in the DX:AX register pair, the following instructions may be used.

```
ADD  AX,1671H
ADC  DX,0
```

The first instruction adds 1671h to the low-order word of the 32-bit integer contained in DX:AX. If the result was greater than FFFFh, this addition will cause a carry out of AX. This carry must be added into bit 16 of the full 32-bit number. In the second instruction, this carry (and an immediate data value of 0) are added to the high-order word in DX.

The ADC instruction can operate on either signed or unsigned operands. The algorithm treats both operands as if they were unsigned, then sets the flags to indicate if a signed overflow has occurred. For example, if the BX register contains 7FFFh and the CF=1, the instruction ADC BX,0 will put the value 8000h in AX and the overflow flag will be set to 1 to indicate an overflow into the sign bit.

ALGORITHM $op_1 = op_1 + op_2 + CF$

FLAGS

O	D	I	T	S	Z	A	P	C
*				*	*	*	*	*

ADC *reg/mem,reg/mem*

000100dw	mod	reg	r/m	disp

d=0, op_1=mod+r/m op_2=reg
 1, op_1=reg op_2=mod+r/m

w=0, operands are 8-bit
 1, operands are 16-bit (16-bit operand mode)
             32-bit (32-bit operand mode)

disp=0- or 2-byte displacement (16-bit address mode)
      0- or 4-byte displacement (32-bit address mode)

TIMING	Operands	*x*	88	86	286	386	486
	reg,reg	0	3	3	2	2	1
	reg,mem	1	B:9+EA W:13+EA	9+EA	7	6	2
	mem,reg	2	B:16+EA W:24+EA	16+EA	7	7	3

ADC *reg/mem,immed*

100000*sw*	*mod* 010 *r/m*	*disp*	*immed*

s=0, immediate data size specified by *w*
  1, sign-extend byte of immediate data

w=0, operands are 8-bit
  1, operands are 16-bit (16-bit operand mode)
      32-bit (32-bit operand mode)

disp=0- or 2-byte displacement (16-bit address mode)
    0- or 4-byte displacement (32-bit address mode)

immed=1- or 2-byte immediate data (16-bit operand mode)
      1- or 4-byte immediate data (32-bit operand mode)

TIMING	Operands	*x*	88	86	286	386	486
	reg,immed	0	4	4	3	2	1
	mem,immed	2	B:17+EA W:25+EA	17+EA	7	7	3

ADC *accum,immed*

0001010*w*	*immed*

w=0, operands are 8-bit
  1, operands are 16-bit (16-bit operand mode)
      32-bit (32-bit operand mode)

immed=1- or 2-byte immediate data (16-bit operand mode)
      1- or 4-byte immediate data (32-bit operand mode)

TIMING	Operands	*x*	88	86	286	386	486
	accum,immed	0	4	4	3	2	1

ADD

Add Two Operands

DESCRIPTION   ADD op_1, op_2

ADD performs the addition of op_1 and op_2. The result of the addition is stored in op_1 and is used to set the flags.

Assume that the AX register contains the value 0004h and that the BX register contains the value F334h. After the instruction ADD AX,BX is executed, AX will contain F338h, the sign flag (SF) will be set to 1 and the zero (ZF), auxiliary carry (AF), parity (PF), carry (CF), and overflow (OF) flags will be cleared to 0. BX will be unchanged.

The ADD instruction can operate on either signed or unsigned operands. The algorithm treats both operands as if they were unsigned, then sets the flags to indicate if a signed overflow has occurred. For example, if AX=7FFFh and the instruction ADD AX,1 is executed, AX will contain 8000h and OF will be set to 1 to indicate an overflow into the sign bit.

ALGORITHM $op_1 = op_1 + op_2$

NOTES   1. The instruction ADD [BX+SI],AL is encoded as 00 00. A block of memory containing zeros unassembles to this instruction.

FLAGS

O	D	I	T	S	Z	A	P	C
*				*	*	*	*	*

ADD *reg/mem,reg/mem*

000000dw	mod	reg	r/m	disp

d=0, op_1=mod+r/m op_2=reg
  1, op_1=reg op_2=mod+r/m

w=0, operands are 8-bit
  1, operands are 16-bit (16-bit operand mode)
          32-bit (32-bit operand mode)

disp=0- or 2-byte displacement (16-bit address mode)
      0- or 4-byte displacement (32-bit address mode)

TIMING

Operands	x	88	86	286	386	486
reg,reg	0	3	3	2	2	1
reg,mem	1	B:9+EA W:13+EA	9+EA	7	6	2
mem,reg	2	B:16+EA W:24+EA	16+EA	7	7	3

ADD *reg/mem,immed*

100000sw	mod	000	r/m	disp		immed

s=0, immediate data size specified by w
  1, sign-extend byte of immediate data

w=0, operands are 8-bit
  1, operands are 16-bit (16-bit operand mode)
           32-bit (32-bit operand mode)

disp=0- or 2-byte displacement (16-bit address mode)
       0- or 4-byte displacement (32-bit address mode)

immed=1- or 2-byte immediate data (16-bit operand mode)
        1- or 4-byte immediate data (32-bit operand mode)

TIMING

Operands	x	88	86	286	386	486
reg,immed	0	4	4	3	2	1
mem,immed	2	B:17+EA W:25+EA	17+EA	7	7	3

ADD *accum,immed*

0000010w	immed

w=0, operands are 8-bit
  1, operands are 16-bit (16-bit operand mode)
           32-bit (32-bit operand mode)

immed=1- or 2-byte immediate data (16-bit operand mode)
        1- or 4-byte immediate data (32-bit operand mode)

TIMING

Operands	x	88	86	286	386	486
accum,immed	0	4	4	3	2	1

AND

Perform a Logical AND of Two Operands

DESCRIPTION AND op_1, op_2

AND performs a bitwise logical AND of op_1 and op_2. The result of the operation is stored in op_1 and is used to set the flags.

To perform a logical AND of the two operands, each bit of the result is set to 1 *if and only if* the corresponding bit in both of the operands is 1; otherwise, the bit in the result is cleared to 0. A truth-table for the bitwise AND operation is shown here:

A	B	A AND B
0	0	0
0	1	0
1	0	0
1	1	1

The AND instruction is often used to clear individual bits in an operand by ANDing the operand with a mask. Each mask bit that is 0 will clear the corresponding bit in the operand.

For example, assume that the CL register contains 56h. After the instruction AND CL,15h is executed, CL will contain 14h, the parity flag (PF) will be set to 1, and the overflow (OF), carry (CF), sign (SF), and zero (ZF) flags will be cleared to 0.

ALGORITHM $op_1=op_1$ AND op_2
OF=Ø
CF=Ø

FLAGS

O	D	I	T	S	Z	A	P	C
0				*	*	—	*	0

AND *reg/mem,reg/mem*

001000dw	mod	reg	r/m	disp

d=0,   op$_1$=mod+r/m   op$_2$=reg
 1,   op$_1$=reg   op$_2$=mod+r/m

w=0, operands are 8-bit
 1, operands are 16-bit (16-bit operand mode)
          32-bit (32-bit operand mode)

disp=0- or 2-byte displacement (16-bit address mode)
    0- or 4-byte displacement (32-bit address mode)

TIMING

Operands	x	88	86	286	386	486
reg,reg	0	3	3	2	2	1
reg,mem	1	B:9+EA W:13+EA	9+EA	7	6	2
mem,reg	2	B:16+EA W:24+EA	16+EA	7	7	3

AND *reg/mem,immed*

| 100000sw | mod | 100 | r/m | disp | immed |

s=0, immediate data size specified by w
 1, sign-extend byte of immediate data

w=0, operands are 8-bit
 1, operands are 16-bit (16-bit operand mode)
          32-bit (32-bit operand mode)

disp=0- or 2-byte displacement (16-bit address mode)
    0- or 4-byte displacement (32-bit address mode)

immed=1- or 2-byte immediate data (16-bit operand mode)
     1- or 4-byte immediate data (32-bit operand mode)

TIMING

Operands	x	88	86	286	386	486
reg,immed	0	4	4	3	2	1
mem,immed	2	B:17+EA W:25+EA	17+EA	7	7	3

AND *accum,immed*

| 0010010w | immed |

w=0, operands are 8-bit
 1, operands are 16-bit (16-bit operand mode)
          32-bit (32-bit operand mode)

immed=1- or 2-byte immediate data (16-bit operand mode)
     1- or 4-byte immediate data (32-bit operand mode)

TIMING

Operands	x	88	86	286	386	486
accum,immed	0	4	4	3	2	1

ARPL

Adjust RPL Field of Selector (PM)

DESCRIPTION ARPL op_1, op_2

ARPL is a protected mode instruction that adjusts the requested privilege level (RPL) of a selector being passed as a parameter to a subroutine so that the selector will not request a higher level of privilege than the task calling the subroutine is allowed. If not done, a protection violation would result.

The ARPL instruction takes two operands. The first is a 16-bit memory or register operand that contains the value of a selector. The second operand must be a register and usually contains the CS selector value of the calling task. If the low-order 2 bits of op_1, the RPL field, are numerically less (more privileged) than the RPL of op_2, ZF is set to 1 and the RPL field of op_1 is set to the RPL of op_2. Otherwise, ZF is cleared to 0.

ALGORITHM
```
IF (BIT(0-1 of op₁)>BIT(0-1 of op₂)) THEN
    BIT(0-1 of op₁)=BIT(0-1 of op₂)
    ZF=1
ELSE
    ZF=0
ENDIF
```

FLAGS

O	D	I	T	S	Z	A	P	C
					*			

ARPL *reg/mem,reg*

01100011	mod	reg	r/m	disp

op_1=mod+r/m, op_2=reg

disp=0- or 2-byte displacement (16-bit address mode)
        0- or 4-byte displacement (32-bit address mode)

TIMING

Operands	x	88	86	286	386	486
reg,reg	0	–	–	10	20	9
mem,reg	2	–	–	11	21	9

BOUND

Check an Array Index Against Bounds

DESCRIPTION BOUND op_1, op_2

BOUND compares a signed array index value in op_1 to an arbitrary upper and lower limit specified for that array and generates an exception if the index is out of bounds.

The index value tested by BOUND is treated as a signed integer number. The lower and upper limits are stored in consecutive locations in memory and pointed to by op_2. If the value in op_1 is greater than or equal to the first bound in memory and less than or equal to the second bound in memory, no action occurs. If, however, the array index exceeds either bound, an interrupt 5 is generated.

The CS:IP saved by the interrupt points to the BOUND instruction that caused the exception, and not to the following instruction.

ALGORITHM IF (op_1<[op_2] OR op_1>[op_2+SIZEOF(op_1)]) THEN Interrupt 5

NOTES
1. Interrupt 5 is used by the IBM PC BIOS to signal a Print-Screen request. If a BOUND exception occurs and no handler has been installed, it will cause the screen to print repeatedly since control is returned to the BOUND instruction which will generate another exception when re-executed. Use of this instruction requires that a new interrupt handler be installed.

FLAGS

O	D	I	T	S	Z	A	P	C

No flags are affected

BOUND reg,mem

01100010	mod	reg	r/m	disp

op_1=reg, op_2=mod+r/m

disp=0- or 2-byte displacement (16-bit address mode)
     0- or 4-byte displacement (32-bit address mode)

TIMING

Operands	x	88	86	286	386	486
reg16,mem32	2	–	–	NJ:13	NJ:10	NJ:7
reg32,mem64	2	–	–	–	NJ:10	NJ:7

Note: Timing shown is for the case when BOUND does *not* generate an interrupt. For the case when an interrupt is generated, see the INT instruction.

BSF

Bit Scan Forward

DESCRIPTION   BSF op_1, op_2

BSF locates the lowest-order bit in op_2 that is set to 1, sets the zero flag (ZF=1) and returns the number of the bit in op_1. If all the bits in op_2 are 0, ZF is cleared and the value of op_1 is undefined.

The BSF instruction can be used to find the lowest-order bit in an operand that is not zero. For example, assume that EBX contains 3B014F0h. After executing the instruction BSF EAX,EBX, the EAX register will contain 4 and ZF will be cleared to 0. BSF might be performed to determine the argument for a subsequent SHR instruction.

ALGORITHM
```
IF (op₂=0) THEN
   ZF=1
   op₁=undefined   ;See note 1
ELSE
   j=0
   WHILE (BIT(j of op₂)=0)
     j=j+1
   ENDWHILE
   op₁=j
   ZF=0
ENDIF
```

NOTES   1. The documentation for the 80386 and 80486 states that if op_2=0, the value of op_1 is undefined. In fact, the 80386 leaves op_1 unchanged in this situation. Early versions of the 80486 actually load an undefined value into op_1. Later versions of the 80486 leave op_1 unchanged. Do not depend on the value of op_1 when op_2=0.

FLAGS

O	D	I	T	S	Z	A	P	C
					*			

BSF *reg,reg/mem*

00001111	10111100	mod	reg	r/m	disp

op_1=reg, op_2=mod+r/m

disp=0- or 2-byte displacement (16-bit address mode)
0- or 4-byte displacement (32-bit address mode)

TIMING

Operands	x	88	86	286	386	486
reg16,reg16	0	–	–	–	11+3n	6-42
reg16,mem16	1	–	–	–	11+3n	7-43
reg32,reg32	0	–	–	–	11+3n	6-42
reg32,mem32	1	–	–	–	11+3n	7-43

n is the number of zero bits that must be scanned in op_2.

BSR

Bit Scan Reverse

DESCRIPTION BSR op_1,op_2

BSR locates the highest-order bit in op_2 that is set to 1, sets the zero flag (ZF=1) and returns the bit number in op_1. If all the bits in op_2 are 0, ZF is cleared and the value of op_1 is undefined.

The BSR instruction can be used to find the highest-order bit in an operand that is not zero. For example, assume that EBX contains 3B014F0h. After executing the instruction BSR EAX,EBX, the EAX register will contain 19h (25) and ZF will be cleared to 0. BSR might be performed to determine the argument for a subsequent SHL instruction such as would be performed when normalizing a binary number.

ALGORITHM
```
IF (op₂=0) THEN
    ZF=1
    op₁=undefined
ELSE
    b=SIZEOF(op₂)*8-1
    WHILE (BIT(b of op₂)=0)
        b=b-1
    ENDWHILE
    op₁=b
    ZF=0
ENDIF
```

FLAGS

O	D	I	T	S	Z	A	P	C
					*			

BSR reg,reg/mem

00001111	10111101	mod	reg	r/m	disp

op_1=reg, op_2=mod+r/m

disp=0- or 2-byte displacement (16-bit address mode)
        0- or 4-byte displacement (32-bit address mode)

TIMING

Operands	x	88	86	286	386	486
reg16,reg16	0	–	–	–	11+3n	6-103
reg16,mem16	1	–	–	–	11+3n	7-104
reg32,reg32	0	–	–	–	11+3n	6-103
reg32,mem32	1	–	–	–	11+3n	7-104

n is the number of zero bits that must be scanned in op_2.

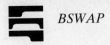

BSWAP

Swap Byte Order

DESCRIPTION   BSWAP *op*

BSWAP reverses the order of the bytes in a 32-bit register, leaving the result in the same register.

The 80x86 family of processors uses the "little endian" method of storing data in memory. This means that the least significant byte of a multibyte operand is stored at the lowest addressed byte, and the most significant byte is stored at the highest addressed byte. Processors that store data in the opposite sense are said to use the "big endian" method. The BSWAP instruction offers a convenient method for converting between the two methods. BSWAP is also useful for operating on BCD or ASCII operands that are stored using the big endian method by convention. For example, assume the EAX register contains the value 12345678h. After executing the instruction BSWAP EAX, the register would contain the value 78563412h.

ALGORITHM
```
temp=op
BIT(7-0 of op)=BIT(31-24 of temp)
BIT(15-8 of op)=BIT(23-16 of temp)
BIT(23-16 of op)=BIT(15-8 of temp)
BIT(31-24 of op)=BIT(7-0 of temp)
```

NOTES   1. When BSWAP is used with a 16-bit register as *op*, the result left in *op* is undefined.

FLAGS

O	D	I	T	S	Z	A	P	C

No flags are affected

BSWAP reg32

00001111	11001	r/m

TIMING

Operands	x	88	86	286	386	486
reg32	0	–	–	–	–	1

BT

Bit Test

DESCRIPTION BT op_1, op_2

BT copies a single bit from op_1 into the carry flag (CF). The number (index) of the bit in op_1 to be copied is specified by op_2.

There are two forms of the BT instruction that, although similar, operate quite differently. In the first form, op_2 is an immediate constant and specifies which bit in op_1 is to be copied to CF. The bit index is given by op_2 modulo the operand size of op_1, allowing any bit in op_1 to be addressed. Or, seen from another point of view, this limits the scope of the instruction to the specified word or doubleword and no further.

For example, assume that the AX register contains 2A45h and the BX register contains 0003h. The instruction BT AX,BX will clear CF to 0 because bit 3 of AX is 0. Conversely, the instruction BT AX,2 will set CF to 1 because bit 2 of AX is 1. In both cases, neither operand is altered.

In the second form, op_1 is a memory reference and op_2 (the index) is specified as a register operand. In this form, op_2 is treated as if it contained two separate fields. The first field is a signed displacement that is added to the effective address specified by op_1. The second field is the unsigned index into the word or doubleword at that address.

The index and displacement are dependent on the size of the operand specified. The displacement is treated as a signed number. So, if 16-bit operands are being used, the displacement can be represented by op_2 SAR 4. If 32-bit operands are being used, the displacement is op_2 SAR 5. The index is calculated by taking the value of op_2 AND 0Fh for 16-bit operands and op_2 AND 1Fh for 32-bit operands.

For example, assume that the EAX register contains 77C85h. The instruction BT DWORD PTR DS:[3C5h],EAX would select bit 5 (77C85h AND 1Fh) of the DWORD at DS:[3FA9h] (3C5h+77C85h SAR 20h).

ALGORITHM
```
b=SIZEOF(op₁)*8      ;operand size in bits
IF (op₂ is immed8) THEN
  IF (op₂>(b-1)) THEN
    CF=undefined
  ELSE
    CF=BIT(op₂ of op₁)
  ENDIF
ELSE   ;op₂ is memory
  i=op₂ AND (b-1)    ;index
  d=op₂ SAR b        ;displacement
  CF=BIT(i of [op₁+d])
ENDIF
```

NOTES 1. When executing this instruction with a memory operand, the processor may access two or four bytes of memory (for 16- and 32-bit operands, respectively) regardless of where the target bit may be in the operand. Avoid using an effective address that would cause the processor to access nonexistent memory. Use of this instruction to reference memory-mapped I/O ports should also be avoided. Instead, use the MOV and TEST instructions.

FLAGS

O	D	I	T	S	Z	A	P	C
								*

BT *reg/mem,reg*

00001111	10100011	mod	reg	r/m	disp

op_1=mod+r/m, op_2=reg

disp=0- or 2-byte displacement (16-bit address mode)
       0- or 4-byte displacement (32-bit address mode)

TIMING

Operands	x	88	86	286	386	486
reg16,reg16	0	–	–	–	3	3
mem16,reg16	1	–	–	–	12	8
reg32,reg32	0	–	–	–	3	3
mem32,reg32	1	–	–	–	12	8

BT *reg/mem, immed*

00001111	10111010	mod	100	r/m	disp	immed8

disp=0- or 2-byte displacement (16-bit address mode)
       0- or 4-byte displacement (32-bit address mode)

immed8=1-byte immediate data

TIMING

Operands	x	88	86	286	386	486
reg16,immed8	0	–	–	–	3	3
mem16,immed8	1	–	–	–	6	3
reg32,immed8	0	–	–	–	3	3
mem32,immed8	1	–	–	–	6	3

BTC

Bit Test and Complement

DESCRIPTION BTC op_1, op_2

BTC copies a single bit from op_1 into the carry flag (CF). The selected bit in op_1 is then complemented. The number of the bit in op_1 to be copied and complemented is specified by op_2.

There are two forms of the BTC instruction that, although similar, operate quite differently. In the first form, op_2 (the index) is an immediate constant and specifies which bit in op_1 will be copied to CF. The bit index is given by op_2 modulo the size of op_1, allowing any bit in op_1 to be addressed. Or, seen from another point of view, this limits the scope of the instruction to the specified word or doubleword and no further.

For example, if the AX register contains 2A45h and the BX register contains 0003h, then the instruction BTC AX,BX will clear CF to 0 and leave the value 2A4Dh in AX. The instruction BTC AX,2 will then set CF to 1 and leave the value 2A49h in AX.

In the second form, op_1 is a memory reference and op_2 (the index) is specified as a register operand. In this form, op_2 is treated as if it contained two separate fields. The first field is a signed displacement that is added to the effective address specified by op_1. The second field is the unsigned index into the word or doubleword at that address.

The index and displacement are dependent on the size of the operand specified. The displacement is treated as a signed number. So, if 16-bit operands are being used, the displacement can be represented by op_2 SAR 4. If 32-bit operands are being used, the displacement is op_2 SAR 5. The index is calculated by taking the value of op_2 AND 0Fh for 16-bit operands and op_2 AND 1Fh for 32-bit operands.

ALGORITHM
```
b=SIZEOF(op₁)*8      ;operand size in bits
IF (op₂ is immed8) THEN
  IF (op₂>(b-1)) THEN
    CF=undefined
  ELSE
    CF=BIT(op₂ of op₁)
  ENDIF
ELSE  ;op₂ is memory
  i=op₂ AND (b-1)    ;index
  d=op₂ SAR b        ;displacement
  CF=BIT(i of [op₁+d])
  BIT(i of [op₁+d])=NOT(BIT(i of op₁+d))
ENDIF
```

NOTES

1. When executing this instruction with a memory operand, the processor may access two or four bytes of memory (for 16- and 32-bit operands, respectively) regardless of where the target bit may be in the operand. Avoid using an effective address that would cause the procesor to access non-existent memory. Use of this instruction to reference memory-mapped I/O ports should also be avoided. Instead, use the MOV and TEST instructions.

FLAGS

O	D	I	T	S	Z	A	P	C
								*

BTC *reg/mem,reg*

00001111	10111011	mod	reg	r/m	disp

op_1=mod+r/m, op_2=reg

disp=0- or 2-byte displacement (16-bit address mode)
      0- or 4-byte displacement (32-bit address mode)

TIMING

Operands	x	88	86	286	386	486
reg16,reg16	0	–	–	–	6	6
mem16,reg16	2	–	–	–	13	13
reg32,reg32	0	–	–	–	6	6
mem32,reg32	2	–	–	–	13	13

BTC *reg/mem,immed*

00001111	10111010	mod	111	r/m	disp	immed8

disp=0- or 2-byte displacement (16-bit address mode)
      0- or 4-byte displacement (32-bit address mode)

immed8=1-byte immediate data

TIMING

Operands	x	88	86	286	386	486
reg16,immed8	0	–	–	–	6	6
mem16,immed8	2	–	–	–	8	8
reg32,immed8	0	–	–	–	6	6
mem32,immed8	2	–	–	–	8	8

BTR

Bit Test and Reset

DESCRIPTION   BTR op_1, op_2

BTR copies a single bit from op_1 into the carry flag (CF). The selected bit in op_1 is then cleared (reset) to 0. The number of the bit in op_1 to be copied and cleared is specified by op_2.

There are two forms of the BTR instruction that, although similar, operate quite differently. In the first form, op_2 (the index) is an immediate constant and specifies which bit in op_1 will be copied to CF. The bit index is given by op_2 modulo the size of op_1, allowing any bit in op_1 to be addressed. Or, seen from another point of view, this limits the scope of the instruction to the specified word or doubleword and no further.

For example, if the AX register contains 2A45h and the BX register contains 0003h, then the instruction BTR AX,BX will clear CF to 0 and leave AX unchanged. The instruction BTR AX,2 will set CF to 1 and leave the value 2A41h in AX.

In the second form, op_1 is a memory reference and op_2, the index, is specified as a register operand. In this form, op_2 is treated as if it contained two separate fields. The first field is a signed displacement that is added to the effective address specified by op_1. The second field is the unsigned index into the word or doubleword at that address.

The index and displacement are dependent on the size of the operand specified. The displacement is treated as a signed number. So, if 16-bit operands are being used, the displacement can be represented by op_2 SAR 4. If 32-bit operands are being used, the displacement is op_2 SAR 5. The index is calculated by taking the value of op_2 AND 0Fh for 16-bit operands and op_2 AND 1Fh for 32-bit operands.

ALGORITHM
```
b=SIZEOF(op₁)*8      ;operand size in bits
IF (op₂ is immed8) THEN
  IF (op₂ >(b-1)) THEN
    CF=undefined
  ELSE
    CF=BIT(op₂ of op₁)
  ENDIF
ELSE   ;op₂ is memory
  i=op₂ AND (b-1)    ;index
  d=op₂ SAR b        ;displacement
  CF=BIT(i of [op₁+d])
  BIT(i of [op₁+d])=0
ENDIF
```

NOTES

1. When executing this instruction with a memory operand, the processor may access two or four bytes of memory (for 16- and 32-bit operands, respectively) regardless of where the target bit may be in the operand. Avoid using an effective address that would cause the processor to access non-existent memory. Use of this instruction to reference memory-mapped I/O ports should also be avoided. Instead, use the MOV and TEST instructions.

FLAGS

O	D	I	T	S	Z	A	P	C
								*

BTR reg/mem,reg

00001111	10110011	mod	reg	r/m	disp

op$_1$=mod+r/m, op$_2$=reg

disp=0- or 2-byte displacement (16-bit address mode)
0- or 4-byte displacement (32-bit address mode)

TIMING

Operands	x	88	86	286	386	486
reg16,reg16	0	–	–	–	6	6
mem16,reg16	2	–	–	–	13	13
reg32,reg32	0	–	–	–	6	6
mem32,reg32	2	–	–	–	13	13

BTR reg/mem,immed

00001111	10111010	mod	110	r/m	disp	immed8

disp=0- or 2-byte displacement (16-bit address mode)
0- or 4-byte displacement (32-bit address mode)

immed8=1-byte immediate data

TIMING

Operands	x	88	86	286	386	486
reg16,immed8	0	–	–	–	6	6
mem16,immed8	2	–	–	–	8	8
reg32,immed8	0	–	–	–	6	6
mem32,immed8	2	–	–	–	8	8

BTS

Bit Test and Set

DESCRIPTION   BTS op_1, op_2

BTS copies a single bit from op_1 into the carry flag (CF). The selected bit in op_1 is then set to 1. The number of the bit in op_1 to be copied and cleared is specified by op_2.

There are two forms of the BTS instruction that, although similar, operate quite differently. In the first form, op_2 (the index) is an immediate constant and specifies which bit in op_1 will be copied to CF. The bit index is given by op_2 modulo the size of op_1, allowing any bit in op_1 to be addressed. Or, seen from another point of view, this limits the scope of the instruction to the specified word or doubleword and no further.

For example, if the AX register contains 2A45h and the BX register contains 0003h, then the instruction BTS AX,BX will clear CF to 0 and leave the value 2A4Dh in AX. The instruction BTS AX,2 will set CF to 1 and leave the value in AX unchanged.

In the second form, op_1 is a memory reference and op_2, the index, is specified as a register operand. In this form, op_2 is treated as if it contained two separate fields. The first field is a signed displacement that is added to the effective address specified by op_1. The second field is the unsigned index into the word or doubleword at that address.

The index and displacement are dependent on the size of the operand specified. The displacement is treated as a signed number. So, if 16-bit operands are being used, the displacement can be represented by op_2 SAR 4. If 32-bit operands are being used, the displacement is op_2 SAR 5. The index is calculated by taking the value of op_2 AND 0Fh for 16-bit operands and op_2 AND 1Fh for 32-bit operands.

ALGORITHM
```
b=SIZEOF(op₁)*8    ;operand size in bits
IF (op₂ is immed8) THEN
  IF (op₂>(b-1)) THEN
    CF=undefined
  ELSE
    CF=BIT(op₂ of op₁)
  ENDIF
ELSE   ;op₂ is memory
  i=op₂ AND (b-1)  ;index
  d=op₂ SAR b        ;displacement
  CF=BIT(i of [op₁+d])
  BIT(i of [op₁+d])=1
ENDIF
```

1. When executing this instruction with a memory operand, the processor may access two or four bytes of memory (for 16- and 32-bit operands, respectively) regardless of where the target bit may be in the operand. Avoid using an effective address that would cause the processor to access non-existent memory. Use of this instruction to reference memory-mapped I/O ports should also be avoided. Instead, use the MOV and TEST instructions.

FLAGS

O	D	I	T	S	Z	A	P	C
								*

BTS *reg/mem,reg*

00001111	10101011	mod	reg	r/m	disp

op_1=mod+r/m, op_2=reg

disp=0- or 2-byte displacement (16-bit address mode)
0- or 4-byte displacement (32-bit address mode)

TIMING

Operands	x	88	86	286	386	486
reg16,reg16	0	–	–	–	6	6
mem16,reg16	2	–	–	–	13	13
reg32,reg32	0	–	–	–	6	6
mem32,reg32	2	–	–	–	13	13

BTS *reg/mem,immed*

00001111	10111010	mod	101	r/m	disp	immed8

disp=0- or 2-byte displacement (16-bit address mode)
0- or 4-byte displacement (32-bit address mode)

immed8=1-byte immediate data

TIMING

Operands	x	88	86	286	386	486
reg16,immed8	0	–	–	–	6	6
mem16,immed8	2	–	–	–	8	8
reg32,immed8	0	–	–	–	6	6
mem32,immed8	2	–	–	–	8	8

CALL

Call a Procedure (Subroutine)

DESCRIPTION   CALL *op*

CALL transfers control to the procedure indicated by its argument. The address of the instruction following the CALL instruction is saved before the transfer occurs.

There are 24 variant forms of the CALL instruction (using four different opcodes), many of which are useful only in protected-mode programs such as operating systems. Which one to use depends on several factors including segment type, operating mode, and target address. The four major forms of CALL used in real-mode programming are described below.

Near direct: This is a transfer to an offset within the same code segment as the CALL. The offset of the following instruction is pushed onto the stack for a return address. The displacement given in the CALL encoding is relative to the address of the following instruction and is added to the IP register.

Near indirect: This is a transfer to an offset within the same code segment as the CALL. The offset of the following instruction is pushed onto the stack for a return address. The value in the specified register or the operand at the specified effective address is loaded into the IP register.

Far direct: This is a transfer to an offset that may be within a different code segment than the CALL. The current code segment and the offset of the following instruction are pushed onto the stack for a return address. Both the new segment and offset are encoded as absolute displacements. The values are read from memory and loaded directly into the CS and IP registers.

Far indirect: This is a transfer to an offset that may be within a different code segment than the CALL. The current code segment and the offset of the following instruction are pushed onto the stack for a return address. The destination segment and offset are stored in memory at the effective address given as the argument to the CALL instruction.

ALGORITHM
```
IF (near direct) THEN
  IF (OperandMode=16-bit) THEN
    PUSH (16-bit EA of next instruction)
    IP=IP+disp16
  ELSE
    PUSH (32-bit EA of next instruction)
    EIP=EIP+disp32
  ENDIF
ELSEIF (near indirect) THEN
  IF (OperandMode=16-bit) THEN
    PUSH (16-bit EA of next instruction)
```

```
        IF (EA=reg) THEN
          IP=reg16
        ELSE
          IP=mem16
        ENDIF
      ELSE
        PUSH (32-bit EA of next instruction)
        IF (EA=reg) THEN
          EIP=reg32
        ELSE
          EIP=mem32
        ENDIF
      ENDIF
    ELSEIF (far direct) THEN
      IF (OperandMode=16-bit) THEN
        PUSH CS   ;16-bit
        PUSH (offset of next instruction) ;16-bit
        IP=disp16   ;in encoding
        CS=disp16   ;in encoding
      ELSEIF ;OperandMode=32-bit
        PUSH CS   ;zero extend to 32 bits
        PUSH (EA of next instruction) ;32-bit
        EIP=disp32
        CS=disp16
      ENDIF
    ELSEIF (far indirect) THEN
      IF (OperandMode=16-bit) THEN
        PUSH CS   ;16-bit
        PUSH (offset of next instruction) ;16-bit
        IP=mem16
        CS=mem16   ;at EA+2
      ELSE  ;OperandMode=32-bit
        PUSH CS   ;padded to 32 bits
        PUSH (offset of next instruction) ;16-bit
        EIP=mem32
        CS=mem16   ;at EA+4
    ENDIF
```

FLAGS	O	D	I	T	S	Z	A	P	C

No flags are affected

CALL *disp* (Near Direct)

| 11101000 | *disp* |

disp=disp16: 2-byte signed relative displacement (16-bit address mode)
      disp32: 4-byte signed relative displacement (32-bit address mode)

TIMING

Operands	*x*	88	86	286	386	486
disp16	1	23	19	7+*m*	7+*m*	3
disp32	1	–	–	–	7+*m*	3

m represents the number of elements in the target instruction.

CALL *reg/mem* (Near Indirect)

| 11111111 | *mod* | 010 | *r/m* |

TIMING

Operands	*x*	88	86	286	386	486
reg16	1	20	16	7+*m*	7+*m*	5
mem16	2	29+EA	21+EA	11+*m*	10+*m*	5
reg32	1	–	–	–	7+*m*	5
mem32	2	–	–	–	10+*m*	5

m represents the number of elements in the target instruction.

CALL *disp16:disp* (Far Direct)

| 10011010 | *disp* | *disp16* |

disp=disp16: 2-byte value to be loaded into the IP register (16-bit address mode)
      disp32: 4-byte value to be loaded into the EIP register (32-bit address mode)

disp16=2-byte value to be loaded into the CS register

TIMING

Operands	x	88	86	286	386	486
disp16:disp16 Real mode	2	36	28	13+m	17+m	18
disp16:disp16 Protected mode, same privilege	–	–	–	PM:26+m	PM:34+m	PM:20
disp16:disp16 Call gate, same privilege	–	–	–	PM:41+m	PM:52+m	PM:35
disp16:disp16 Call gate, more privilege, no parameters	–	–	–	PM:82+m	PM:86+m	PM:69
disp16:disp16 Call gate, more privilege, *p* parameters	–	–	–	PM:86+4p+m	PM:94+4p+m	PM:77+4p
disp16:disp16 Call via Task State Segment	–	–	–	PM:177+m	PM:ts_1	PM:37+ts_3
disp16:disp16 Call via task gate	–	–	–	PM:182+m	PM:ts_2	PM:38+ts_3
disp16:disp32 Real mode	2	–	–	–	17+m	18
disp16:disp32 Protected mode, same privilege	–	–	–	–	PM:34+m	PM:20
disp16:disp32 Call gate, same privilege	–	–	–	–	PM:52+m	PM:35
disp16:disp32 Call gate, more privilege, no parameters	–	–	–	–	PM:86+m	PM:69
disp16:disp32 Call gate, more privilege, *p* parameters	–	–	–	–	PM:94+4p+m	PM:77+4p
disp16:disp32 Call via Task State Segment	–	–	–	–	PM:ts_1	PM:37+ts_3
disp16:disp32 Call via task gate	–	–	–	–	PM:ts_2	PM:38+ts_3

m represents the number of elements in the target instruction.

ts_1, ts_2, and ts_3 represent the time to switch tasks as given in the table at the end of this instruction listing.

CALL *mem16:mem* (Far Indirect)

11111111	mod	011	r/m

mem=mem16: 2-byte value to be loaded into the IP register (16-bit address mode)
  mem32: 4-byte value to be loaded into the EIP register (32-bit address mode)
  mem16=2-byte value to be loaded into the CS register

TIMING

Operands	x	88	86	286	386	486
mem16:mem16 Real mode	4	53+EA	37+EA	16+m	22+m	17
mem16:mem16 Protected mode, same privilege	–	–	–	PM:29+m	PM:38+m	PM:20
mem16:mem16 Call gate, same privilege	–	–	–	PM:44+m	PM:56+m	PM:35
mem16:mem16 Call gate, more privilege, no parameters	–	–	–	PM:83+m	PM:90+m	PM:69
mem16:mem16 Call gate, more privilege, p parameters	–	–	–	PM:90+4p+m	PM:98+4p+m	PM:77+4p
mem16:mem16 Call via Task State Segment	–	–	–	PM:180+m	PM:5+ts_1	PM:37+ts_3
mem16:mem16 Call via task gate	–	–	–	PM:185+m	PM:5+ts_2	PM:38+ts_3
mem16:mem32 Real mode	4	–	–	–	22+m	18
mem16:mem32 Protected mode	–	–	–	–	PM:38+m	PM:20
mem16:mem32 Call gate, same privilege	–	–	–	–	PM:56+m	PM:35
mem16:mem32 Call gate, more privilege, no parameters	–	–	–	–	PM:90+m	PM:69
mem16:mem32 Call gate, more privilege, p parameters	–	–	–	–	PM:98+4p+m	PM:77+4p
mem16:mem32 Call via Task State Segment	–	–	–	–	PM:ts_1	PM:37+ts_3
mem16:mem32 Call via task gate	–	–	–	–	PM:5+ts_2	PM:38+ts_3

m represents the number of elements in the target instruction.

ts_1 indicates the timing required to switch tasks via a Task State Segment (TSS) as shown in the following table.

Old Task	New Task Type (via TSS)		
	386 TSS VM=0	**386 TSS VM=1**	**286 TSS**
386 TSS VM=0	DX:300 SX:392	DX:218 SX:309	DX:273 SX:285
286 TSS	DX:298 SX:310	DX:218 SX:229	DX:273 SX:285

ts_2 indicates the timing required to switch tasks via a task gate as shown in the following table.

Old Task	New Task Type (via task gate)		
	386 TSS VM=0	**386 TSS VM=1**	**286 TSS**
386 TSS VM=0	DX:309 SX:401	DX:226 SX:321	DX:282 SX:294
286 TSS	DX:307 SX:316	DX:226 SX:238	DX:282 SX:294

ts_3 indicates the timing required to switch tasks via a Task State Segment (TSS) or a task gate as shown in the following table.

Old Task	New Task Type (via task gate or TSS)		
	486 TSS	**286 TSS**	**VM TSS**
486 TSS 286 TSS	199	180	177

CBW

Convert Byte in AL to Word in AX

DESCRIPTION CBW converts the 8-bit signed value in the AL register into an equivalent 16-bit signed value in the AX register by duplicating the sign bit to the left.

The CBW instruction sets all of the bits in the AH register to the same value as the sign bit (bit 7) of the AL register. The effect is to create a 16-bit signed result that has the same integer value as the original 8-bit operand.

For example, assume that AX contains 1435h. If the CBW instruction is executed, AX will contain 0035h since bit 7 (the sign bit) of AL was 0 and AH was cleared to 0. Both the original value of AL (35h) and the resulting value of AX (0035h) represent the same signed number.

ALGORITHM
```
IF (BIT(7 of AL)=0) THEN
    AH=00
ELSE
    AH=FFh
ENDIF
```

NOTES
1. The encoding for CBW and CWDE is the same. The mode of operation is dependent on whether the processor is in 16- or 32-bit operand mode.

FLAGS

O	D	I	T	S	Z	A	P	C

No flags are affected

CBW

10011000

TIMING

Operands	x	88	86	286	386	486
(no operands)	0	2	2	2	3	3

CDQ

Convert Doubleword in EAX to Quadword in EDX:EAX

DESCRIPTION CDQ converts the 32-bit signed value in the EAX register into an equivalent 64-bit signed value in the EDX:EAX register pair by duplicating the sign bit to the left.

The CDQ instruction sets all of the bits in the EDX register to the same value as the sign bit (bit 31) of the EAX register. The effect is to create a 64-bit signed result that has the same integer value as the original 32-bit operand. This instruction is often used to prepare the EDX:EAX register pair for division.

For example, assume that EAX contains A04C3A15h. If the CDQ instruction is executed, EAX will still contain A04C3A15h. EDX will be set to FFFFFFFFh since bit 31 (the sign bit) of EAX was 1. Both the original value of EAX (A04C3A15h) and the resulting value of the EDX:EAX register pair (FFFFFFFFA04C3A15h) represent the same signed number.

If, in preparation for an operation, the EDX:EAX register pair is to be cleared to 0:0, the CDQ instruction, a 1-byte opcode, can be used to clear the EDX register as shown below.

```
Encoding    Instruction
2B C0       SUB    EAX,EAX   ;Traditional method takes 4 bytes
2B D2       SUB    EDX,EDX   ;Zeros EAX and EDX separately

2B C0       SUB    EAX,EAX   ;Shortcut takes 3 bytes by copying
99          CDQ              ; sign bit of EAX through EDX
```

ALGORITHM
```
IF (BIT(31 of EAX)=0) THEN
    EDX=0
ELSE
    EDX=FFFFFFFFh
ENDIF
```

NOTES
1. The encoding for CWD and CDQ are the same. The mode of operation is dependent on whether the processor is in 16- or 32-bit operand mode.

FLAGS

O	D	I	T	S	Z	A	P	C

No flags are affected

CDQ

```
10011001
```

TIMING

Operands	x	88	86	286	386	486
(no operands)	0	–	–	–	2	2

CLC

Clear the Carry Flag

DESCRIPTION CLC clears the Carry flag (CF) to 0.

This instruction has no affect on the processor, registers, or other flags. It is often used to clear the CF before returning from a procedure to indicate a successful termination. It is also used to clear the CF during rotate operations involving the CF such as ADC, RCL, and RCR.

ALGORITHM CF=0

FLAGS

O	D	I	T	S	Z	A	P	C
								0

CLC

```
11111000
```

TIMING

Operands	x	88	86	286	386	486
(no operands)	0	2	2	2	2	2

CLD

Clear the Direction Flag

DESCRIPTION CLD clears the Direction flag (DF) to 0.

This instruction has no affect on the registers or other flags. When the direction flag is cleared, however, the processor will auto-increment pointers when using string instructions such as MOVSB and STOSB.

ALGORITHM　　DF=0

FLAGS

O	D	I	T	S	Z	A	P	C
	0							

CLD

11111100

TIMING

Operands	x	88	86	286	386	486
(no operands)	0	2	2	2	2	2

CLI

Clear the Interrupt Flag

DESCRIPTION CLI clears the Interrupt Enable flag (IF) to 0.

This instruction has no affect on the registers or other flags. When IF is cleared, the processor will not recognize maskable interrupts, that is, external interrupt requests that appear on the INTR line of the chip. A nonmaskable interrupt request that appears on the NMI line and all software interrupts, however, are handled normally.

ALGORITHM IF=Ø

FLAGS

O	D	I	T	S	Z	A	P	C
		0						

CLI

11111010

TIMING

Operands	x	88	86	286	386	486
(no operands)	0	2	2	3	8	5

CLTS

Clear Task Switched Flag in CR0/MSW

DESCRIPTION CLTS clears the Task-switched (TS) flag in the CR0 control register (80386 and 80486) or in the machine status word (MSW) of the 80286.

The Task-switched flag is set by the processor each time a task switch occurs, but must be cleared manually. It is used in systems programming to give operating systems an opportunity to save any necessary information (such as the state of the math coprocessor) before allowing a new task to access a system resource.

ALGORITHM
```
IF (80286) THEN
   BIT(3 of MSW)=0
ELSEIF (80386 or 80486)
   BIT(3 of CR0)=0
ENDIF
```

FLAGS

O	D	I	T	S	Z	A	P	C

No flags are affected

CLTS

00001111	00000110

TIMING

Operands	x	88	86	286	386	486
(no operands)	0	–	–	2	6	7

CMC

Complement the Carry Flag

DESCRIPTION CMC complements the Carry flag (CF), setting it to a state opposite its current value. This instruction has no affect on the processor, registers, or other flags.

ALGORITHM
```
IF (CF=0) THEN
    CF=1
ELSE
    CF=0
ENDIF
```

FLAGS

O	D	I	T	S	Z	A	P	C
								*

CMC

11110101

TIMING

Operands	x	88	86	286	386	486
(no operands)	0	2	2	2	2	2

CMP

Compare Two Operands

DESCRIPTION   CMP op_1, op_2

CMP compares two operands by subtracting op_2 from op_1 and using the result to set the flags. The operation is performed in the ALU of the processor but the result is not written to either operand.

The CMP instruction can be used to compare two operands as signed or unsigned quantities. The flags are updated and the relationship between the two arguments can be used by the J*cond* or SET*cond* instructions.

ALGORITHM   temp=op_1-op_2 ;result used to set flags

FLAGS

O	D	I	T	S	Z	A	P	C
*				*	*	*	*	*

CMP *reg/mem,reg/mem*

001110dw	mod	reg	r/m	disp

d=0, op_1=mod+r/m op_2=reg
  1, op_1=reg op_2=mod+r/m

w=0, operands are 8-bit
  1, operands are 16-bit (16-bit operand mode)
            32-bit (32-bit operand mode)

disp=0- or 2-byte displacement (16-bit address mode)
     0- or 4-byte displacement (32-bit address mode)

TIMING

Operands	x	88	86	286	386	486
reg,reg	0	3	3	2	2	1
reg,mem	1	B:9+EA W:13+EA	9+EA	6	5	2
mem,reg	1	B:9+EA W:13+EA	9+EA	7	6	2

CMP *reg/mem,immed*

100000sw	mod	111	r/m	disp	immed

s=0, immediate data size specified by *w*
  1, sign-extend byte of immediate data

w=0, operands are 8-bit
  1, operands are 16-bit (16-bit operand mode)
                   32-bit (32-bit operand mode)

disp=0- or 2-byte displacement (16-bit address mode)
      0- or 4-byte displacement (32-bit address mode)

immed=1- or 2-byte immediate data (16-bit operand mode)
        1- or 4-byte immediate data (32-bit operand mode)

TIMING

Operands	x	88	86	286	386	486
reg,immed	0	4	4	3	2	1
mem,immed	1	B:10+EA W:14+EA	10+EA	6	5	2

CMP *accum,immed*

0011110w	immed

w=0, operands are 8-bit
  1, operands are 16-bit (16-bit operand mode)
                   32-bit (32-bit operand mode)

immed=1- or 2-byte immediate data (16-bit address mode)
        1- or 4-byte immediate data (32-bit address mode)

TIMING

Operands	88	86	286	386	486
accum,immed	4	4	3	2	1

CMPS/CMPSB/ CMPSW/CMPSD

Compare Two Memory String Operands

DESCRIPTION   CMPS op_1, op_2
CMPSB
CMPSW
CMPSD

The CMPS instruction is used to compare data between two memory locations while automatically updating the indexes in preparation for the next comparison.

CMPS compares a memory operand, pointed to by the source index register (SI/ESI), to another location in memory pointed to by the ES segment register and the destination index register (DI/EDI). The comparison is done by subtracting the operand specified by DI/EDI from the operand specified by SI/ESI.

Note that the direction of subtraction for the CMPS instruction is [SI]–[DI] or [ESI–EDI]. The source is specified by op_1 and the destination by op_2. *This is the reverse of the usual Intel operand order convention.*

The source and destination index registers used to form the effective addresses for the comparison are determined by the current address size attribute. If the address size mode is 16-bit, then the SI and DI registers will be used. If 32-bit addressing is in effect, then the ESI and EDI registers will be used.

The options that must be defined when using this instruction are the operand size, the segment register to be used with the effective address of the source index, and whether both indexes will be incremented or decremented after the transfer.

The size of the memory operands may be specified explicitly in the mnemonic or by an operand. In the first method, the transfer size is explicitly declared by using the B, W, or D suffix in combination with the CMPS mnemonic. The resulting instructions (CMPSB, CMPSW, and CMPSD) will transfer a byte, word, or doubleword between memory locations, respectively. The source and destination index registers will then be adjusted by 1, 2, or 4 to point to the next operand to be moved.

The size-explicit forms of the instruction always use the DS segment register when addressing the source operand and the ES segment register when addressing the destination operand. The general form of the instruction (CMPS) takes as arguments two memory operands that define the size of the transfer only. *The effective addresses of the operands are not used as the addresses of the transfer;* the data is always loaded using the source and destination indexes as pointers to memory. A segment override may be specified with op_1 (the source), but not with op_2 (the destination).

For example, the instruction CMPS BYTE PTR [BX],[LIST] would be equivalent to the CMPSB form and would compare the byte at DS:[SI] to the byte at ES:[DI]. The instruction CMPS BYTE PTR CS:[BX],CS:[BX], however, would compare the byte at CS:[SI] to ES:[DI]. In either case, the effective addresses specified by the operands are ignored.

The source and destination index registers will be incremented by the size of the operand if the direction flag (DF) has been cleared to 0 (by the CLD instruction, for example). The registers will be decremented by the size of the operand if DF is set to 1 (by the STD instruction).

For example, assume that the address size attribute is 16-bits and DF is cleared. The instruction CMPSB can be equivalently expressed by the following instructions.

```
CMP  BYTE PTR DS:[SI],BYTE PTR ES:[DI]  ;memory-to-memory
INC  SI
INC  DI
```

All forms of the CMPS instruction may be encoded with the REP prefix. The REP plus CMPS combination is a convenient and frequently used method of comparing two blocks of memory.

ALGORITHM

```
opsize=SIZEOF(operand)    ;Declared by mnemonic or operand
IF (CMPS op₁,op₂) THEN
   seg=SEGMENTOF(op₁)  ;Use override if specified
ELSE
   seg="DS"
ENDIF
IF (AddressMode=16-bit) THEN
   src="SI"
   dest="DI"
ELSE
   src="ESI"
   dest="EDI"
ENDIF
IF (opsize=1) THEN
   temp=BYTE PTR seg:[src]-BYTE PTR ES:[dest] ;Sets FLAGS
ELSEIF (opsize=2) THEN
   temp=WORD PTR seg:[src]-WORD PTR ES:[dest] ;Sets FLAGS
ELSE  ;opsize=4
   temp=DWORD PTR seg:[src]-DWORD PTR ES:[dest] ;Sets FLAGS
ENDIF
IF (DF=0)  ;CLD
   src=src+opsize
   dest=dest+opsize
ELSE  ;STD
   src=src-opsize
   dest=dest-opsize
ENDIF
```

NOTES   1. Early versions of the 80286 incorrectly execute the repeated form of this instruction in protected mode. If, during the execution of this instruction, a segment limit exception or IOPL exception occurs, the value of CX seen by the exception handler will be the value present at the start of the instruction. The SI and DI registers will reflect the iterations performed by the instruction.

FLAGS

O	D	I	T	S	Z	A	P	C
*				*	*	*	*	*

CMPSB/CMPSW/CMPSD

CMPS *reg/mem,reg/mem*

```
1010011w
```

w=0, operands are 8-bit
  1, operands are 16-bit (16-bit operand mode)
                 32-bit (32-bit operand mode)

Note: If present, op_1 and op_2 specify the operand size for the operation and are not included in the encoding. A segment override may also be specified by op_1.

TIMING

Operands	x	88	86	286	386	486
CMPSB CMPSW	2	B:18 W:26	18	8	10	8
CMPSD	2	–	–	–	10	8
REP*cond* CMPSB REP*cond* CMPSW	2r	B:9+17r W:9+25r	9+17r	5+9r	5+9r	7+7r T_0:5
REP*cond* CMPSD	2r	–	–	–	5+9r	7+7r T_0:5

REP*cond* represents one of the following prefix instructions: REP, REPE, REPZ, REPNE, REPNZ.

r represents the number of repetitions when used with a REP*cond* prefix.

T_0 indicates the timing when the number of repetitions is 0.

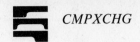

CMPXCHG

Compare and Exchange Two Operands

DESCRIPTION   CMPXCHG op_1, op_2

CMPXCHG compares the accumulator (AL, AX, or EAX register) with the op_1 by internally subtracting op_1 from the accumulator and using the result to set the zero flag (ZF). If the *accum* and op_1 are equal, op_2 is copied into op_1. If the *accum* and op_1 are not equal, then op_1 is loaded into the accumulator.

A typical use for this instruction is to simplify access to shared memory areas in a multiple-processor environment by allowing a flag (in memory) to be tested and set in one operation.

ALGORITHM
```
IF (accum=op₁) THEN
    ZF=1
    op₁=op₂
ELSE
    ZF=0
    accum=op₁
ENDIF
```

NOTES   1. The encoding shown for this instruction was changed beginning with the B-step of the 80486. See the encoding box below.

FLAGS

O	D	I	T	S	Z	A	P	C
					*			

CMPXCHG *reg/mem,reg*

00001111	1011000w	mod	reg	r/m	disp

op_1=mod+r/m, op_2=reg

w=0, operands are 8-bit
  1, operands are 16-bit (16-bit operand mode)
            32-bit (32-bit operand mode)

disp=0- or 2-byte displacement (16-bit address mode)
     0- or 4-byte displacement (32-bit address mode)

Note: On the A-step of the 80486, the CMPXCHG reused the encodings for the XBTS (A6h) and IBTS (A7h) instructions that were included on only the A-B0 steppings of the 80386DX. Because of software conflicts, the encoding was changed beginning with the B-step of the 80486 to that shown above.

Operands	x	88	86	286	386	486
reg,reg	0	–	–	–	–	6
mem,reg	ZR:2 NZ:1	–	–	–	–	ZR:7 NZ:10

NZ indicates the timing and memory transfers when the comparison fails.

ZR indicates the timing memory transfers when the comparison is successful.

CTS

Clear Task Switched Flag

DESCRIPTION CTS is an alternate mnemonic for CLTS. For instruction information see the entry under CLTS.

CWD

Convert Word in AX to Doubleword in DX:AX

DESCRIPTION CDW converts the 16-bit signed value in the AX register into an equivalent 32-bit signed value in the DX:AX register pair by duplicating the sign bit to the left.

The CWD instruction sets all of the bits in the DX register to the same value as the sign bit (bit 15) of the AX register. The effect is to create a 32-bit signed result that has the same integer value as the original 16-bit operand.

For example, assume that AX contains C435h. If the CWD instruction is executed, DX will contain FFFFh since bit 15 (the most significant bit) of AX was 1. Both the original value of AX (C435h) and the resulting value of DX:AX (FFFFC435h) represent the same signed number.

Note the difference between CWD, which sign-extends AX into DX, and CWDE, which sign-extends AX into the EAX register.

ALGORITHM
```
IF (BIT(15 of AX)=0) THEN
    DX=0
ELSE
    DX=FFFFh
ENDIF
```

NOTES
1. The encoding for CWD and CDQ are the same. The mode of operation is dependent on whether the processor is in 16- or 32-bit operand mode.

FLAGS

O	D	I	T	S	Z	A	P	C

No flags are affected

CWD

```
10011001
```

TIMING

Operands	x	88	86	286	386	486
(no operands)	0	5	5	2	2	3

CWDE

Convert Word in AX to Doubleword in EAX

DESCRIPTION CWDE converts the 16-bit signed value in the AX register into an equivalent 32-bit signed value in the EAX register by duplicating the sign bit to the left.

The CWDE instruction simply sets the high-order 16 bits of the EAX register to the same value as the sign bit (bit 15) of the AX register. The effect is to create a 32-bit signed result that has the same integer value as the original 16-bit operand.

For example, assume that AX contains F435h. If the CBW instruction is executed, EAX will contain FFFFF435h since bit 15 (the most significant bit) of AX was 1. Both the original value of AX (F435h) and the resulting value of EAX (FFFFF435h) represent the same signed number.

ALGORITHM
```
IF (BIT(15 of AX)=0) THEN
    EAX=EAX AND 0000FFFFh
ELSE
    EAX=EAX OR FFFF0000h
ENDIF
```

NOTES
1. The encoding for CBW and CWDE is the same. The mode of operation is dependent on whether the processor is in 16- or 32-bit operand mode.

FLAGS

O	D	I	T	S	Z	A	P	C

No flags are affected

CWDE

```
10011000
```

TIMING

Operands	x	88	86	286	386	486
(no operands)	0	–	–	–	3	3

DAA

Decimal Adjust AL After Addition

DESCRIPTION DAA converts the result of the addition of two valid packed BCD operands to a valid packed BCD result and takes the AL register as an implicit operand.

For the previous addition to have had meaning, each of the two byte operands of the addition must have contained a valid BCD digit, ranging from 0 to 9, in both the upper and lower 4 bits. Each operand may contain a packed BCD number ranging from 00 to 99 decimal. The result of the addition must therefore be within the range from 00 to 198 decimal. The DAA instruction adjusts AL so that it contains two valid packed BCD digits.

The DAA instruction is similar to AAA, which operates on the result of the addition of unpacked BCD data.

ALGORITHM
```
IF ((AL AND ØFh)>9 OR (AF=1)) THEN
    AL=AL+6
    AF=1
ENDIF
IF ((AL > 9Fh) OR (CF=1)) THEN
    AL=AL+60h
    CF=1
ENDIF
```

FLAGS

O	D	I	T	S	Z	A	P	C
—				*	*	*	*	*

DAA

```
00100111
```

TIMING

Operands	x	88	86	286	386	486
(no operands)	0	4	4	3	4	2

DAS

Decimal Adjust AL After Subtraction

DESCRIPTION DAS converts the result of the subtraction of two valid packed BCD operands to a valid packed BCD result and takes the AL register as an implicit operand.

For the previous subtraction to have had any meaning, each of the two-byte operands of the subtraction must have had a valid BCD digit, ranging from 0 to 9, in both the upper and lower 4 bits. Each operand may contain a packed BCD number ranging from 00 to 99 decimal. The result of the subtraction must therefore be within the range from -99 to +99 decimal. The DAA instruction adjusts AL so that it contains two valid packed BCD digits. A negative number (n) is represented as 100-n and leaves the CF set to 1 to indicate a decimal borrow.

The DAS instruction is similar to AAS which operates on the result of the addition of unpacked BCD data.

ALGORITHM
```
IF ((AL AND ØFh)>9 OR (AF=1)) THEN
   AL=AL-6
   AF=1
ENDIF
IF ((AL>9Fh) OR (CF=1)) THEN
   AL=AL-6Øh
   CF=1
ENDIF
```

FLAGS

O	D	I	T	S	Z	A	P	C
—				*	*	*	*	*

DAS

00101111

TIMING

Operands	x	88	86	286	386	486
(no operands)	0	4	4	3	4	2

DEC

Decrement Operand by 1

DESCRIPTION   `DEC` *op*

DEC subtracts one from the specified operand and sets the flags according to the result.

For the purpose of the DEC instruction, the operand is treated as an unsigned binary number. For example, if the AX register contains 8000h, the instruction DEC AX will result in 7FFFh being stored into AX.

The DEC instruction requires fewer bytes than the equivalent SUB instruction when subtracting 1 or 2 from an operand as shown below.

```
Encoding     Instruction
83 E8 02     SUB   EAX,2    ;Direct method requires 3 bytes
48           DEC   EAX      ;Shortcut requires only 2 bytes
48           DEC   EAX
```

ALGORITHM   *op=op-1*

FLAGS

O	D	I	T	S	Z	A	P	C
*				*	*	*	*	

DEC *reg/mem*

1111111w	mod	001	r/m	disp

w=0, operands are 8-bit
   1, operands are 16-bit (16-bit operand mode)
                32-bit (32-bit operand mode)

disp=0- or 2-byte displacement (16-bit address mode)
      0- or 4-byte displacement (32-bit address mode)

Note: This encoding is not normally used to decrement a 16- or 32-bit register. The DEC *reg16/reg32* form is provided for that purpose and occupies only a single byte.

TIMING

Operands	x	88	86	286	386	486
reg	0	3	3	2	2	1
mem	2	B:15+EA W:23+EA	15+EA	7	6	3

 *DEC*

DEC *reg16/reg32*

01001	reg

TIMING

Operands	x	88	86	286	386	486
reg16	0	3	3	2	2	1
reg32	0	–	–	–	2	1

DIV

Unsigned Division

DESCRIPTION DIV *op*

DIV performs a division of the accumulator (and its extension if specified) by the source operand, treating both operands as unsigned numbers.

DIV uses the accumulator as an implied operand. The size of the divisor determines which registers are used for the operation as shown in the following table.

Divisor Size	Dividend	Quotient	Remainder
Byte	AX	AL	AH
Word	DX:AX	AX	DX
Doubleword	EDX:EAX	EAX	EDX

If the quotient exceeds the capacity of the destination register (FFh for AL, FFFFh for AX, or FFFFFFFFh for EAX) or division by zero is attempted, the divide error exception (interrupt 0) is generated and both the quotient and remainder are undefined.

For example, assume AX contains 3A2Fh and BL contains 3Bh. After the instruction DIV BL is executed, AL will contain FCh (3A2Fh/3Bh) and AH will contain 1Bh (3A2Fh MOD 3Bh).

The SHR instruction can also be used to perform division by powers of 2 and is generally faster than DIV.

ALGORITHM
```
opsize=SIZEOF(op)
IF (opsize=1) THEN
  dividend=AX
  max=FFh
  quotient=AL
  remainder=AH
ELSEIF (opsize=2) THEN
  dividend=DX:AX
  max=FFFFh
  quotient=AX
  remainder=DX
ELSE  ;opsize=4
  dividend=EDX:EAX
  max=FFFFFFFFh
  quotient=EAX
  remainder=EDX
ENDIF
```

```
IF (op=0) THEN
  INT 0
ELSEIF ((dividend/op)>max) THEN
  quotient=undefined
  remainder=undefined
  INT 0
ELSE
  quotient=dividend/op      ;unsigned division
  remainder=dividend MOD op  ;unsigned modulo
ENDIF
```

FLAGS

O	D	I	T	S	Z	A	P	C
—				—	—	—	—	—

DIV *mem*

1111011w	mod	110	r/m	disp

w=0, operands are 8-bit
  1, operands are 16-bit (16-bit operand mode)
       32-bit (32-bit operand mode)

disp=0- or 2-byte displacement (16-bit address mode)
    0- or 4-byte displacement (32-bit address mode)

TIMING

Operands	x	88	86	286	386	486
reg8	0	80-90	80-90	14	14	16
reg16	0	144-162	144-162	22	22	24
reg32	0	—	—	—	38	40
mem8	1	(86-96)+EA	(86-96)+EA	17	17	16
mem16	1	(158-176)+EA	(154-172)+EA	25	25	24
mem32	1	—	—	—	41	40

ENTER

Make Stack Frame for Procedure

DESCRIPTION   ENTER op_1, op_2

ENTER creates the stack frame and temporary storage required by many high-level block-structured languages.

The ENTER instruction will usually be one of the first instructions to be executed upon entry into the procedure. The number of bytes of local (dynamic) storage that will be allocated on the stack is specified by op_1. This storage is local to the procedure. The lexical nesting level (0 through 31) of the procedure with respect to the high level source code is given by op_2 and determines the number of stack frame pointers that will be copied into the new stack frame from the preceding stack frame. The BP/EBP register is used as the stack frame pointer.

If a 16-bit stack is in use, BP is used as the stack frame pointer and the SP register is used as the stack pointer. If a 32-bit stack is in use, ESP and EBP are used for the stack frame pointer and stack pointer, respectively.

ALGORITHM
```
level=op2 MOD 32
IF (OperandMode=16-bit) THEN
   PUSH BP
   frame_pointer=SP
ELSE
   PUSH EBP
   frame_pointer=ESP
ENDIF
IF (level>0) THEN
   FOR j=1 to level-1
     IF (OperandMode=16-bit) THEN
       BP=BP-2
       PUSH [BP]   ;push memory operand
     ELSE
       EBP=EBP-4
       PUSH [EBP]
     ENDIF
   ENDFOR
   PUSH frame_pointer
ENDIF
IF (operand size mode=16-bit) THEN
  BP=frame_pointer
ELSE
  EBP=frame_pointer
```

```
ENDIF
IF (StackMode=16-bit) THEN
   SP=SP-op₁
ELSE
   ESP=ESP-ZERO_EXTEND(op₁)
ENDIF
```

FLAGS

O	D	I	T	S	Z	A	P	C

No flags are affected

ENTER *immed16,immed8*

11001000	*immed16*	*immed8*

immed16=2-byte immediate data
immed8=1-byte immediate data

TIMING

Operands	*x*	88	86	286	386	486
immed16,0	0	–	–	11	10	14
immed16,1	0	–	–	15	12	17
immed16,*immed8*[1]	0	–	–	16+4(k-1)	15+4(k-1)	17+3k

[1] *immed8*>1

k represents op_2, the level of lexical nesting.

ESC

Escape (Access Memory)

DESCRIPTION ESC op

ESC causes the processor to initiate a memory bus cycle that accesses a memory operand and places its value on the bus.

The ESC instruction is used for interprocessor communication in a multiprocessor environment, such as when a math coprocessor is installed. The ESC instruction causes an effective address to be calculated using the addressing modes of the processor and sent to the bus. The addresses of the instruction and of the memory operand (if any) are saved in the floating-point exception pointers of the processor. No other change to the state of the processor takes place.

This mnemonic form of the instruction is rarely seen as valid ESC encodings may be represented by descriptive mnemonics for 80x87 instructions. The mnemonics begin with the letter F and are recognized by most debuggers and assemblers.

ALGORITHM EA=op
IF (mod≠11) THEN data_bus=(EA)

FLAGS

O	D	I	T	S	Z	A	P	C

No flags are affected

ESC immed,reg/mem

11011	aaa	mod	bbb	r/m

aaa=The high-order 3 bits of the coprocessor opcode

bbb=The low-order 3 bits of the coprocessor opcode

TIMING

Operands	x	88	86	286	386	486
immed,reg	0	2	2	9-20	n/a[1]	n/a[1]
immed,mem	1	B:8+EA W:12+EA	8+EA	9-20	n/a[1]	n/a[1]

[1] No explicit times available. See the encodings for the floating-point instructions.

HLT

Halt the Processor

DESCRIPTION HLT causes the processor to enter the halt state, ceasing all operation until an external interrupt is received.

The processor can be placed in the halt state by executing the HLT instruction. In this state, no further action will be taken by the CPU until an outside event occurs. Events that will return the processor to the active state are activation of the RESET line, a nonmaskable interrupt request on the NMI line, or a maskable interrupt request on INTR if interrupts are enabled.

HLT may be used as an alternative to an endless software loop when waiting for an external event such as a keypress. This technique is more efficient in some preemptive multitasking environments since an endless loop requires constant attention, but a halted process will require only interrupt servicing. An example of this technique is shown in the following example.

```
        STI                     ;Maskable interrupt on
LABEL1:
        HLT                     ;Wait for an interrupt
        IN      AL,60H          ;Check if our key
        CMP     AL,OURKEY
        JNE     LABEL1
```

ALGORITHM None

FLAGS

O	D	I	T	S	Z	A	P	C

No flags are affected

HLT

11110100

TIMING

Operands	x	88	86	286	386	486
(no operands)	0	2	2	2	5	4

IBTS

Insert Bit String

DESCRIPTION IBTS op_1, op_2, op_3, op_4

The IBTS instruction was a short-lived instruction that was introduced on the A-step of the 80386DX processor and removed on the B1-step of the chip. Intel notes that the instruction was removed in order to use the area of the chip previously occupied for other microcircuitry. Beginning with the B1-step 80386DX, executing this opcode will generate an invalid opcode exception. Because some assemblers and debuggers recognize this opcode, it is noted in this reference for completeness. Detailed information on the instruction is not available.

Note that some software products attempted to execute this instruction to identify whether they were being run on a B0-step 80386DX. When the B0-step of the 80486DX was released, it reused this opcode for the CMPXCHG instruction, causing existing software to fail. Because of this conflict, Intel changed the CMPXCHG opcode on the B1-step of the 80486.

The IBTS instruction was designed to insert a bit string from one operand into another operand. If the function performed by the IBTS instruction is required, it can be coded explicitly using the shift double and rotate instructions available on the 80386 and later processors.

IBTS *reg/mem,AX,CL,reg*

00001111	10100111	mod	reg	r/m	disp

disp=0- or 2-byte displacement (16-bit address mode)
0- or 4-byte displacement (32-bit address mode)

TIMING

Operands	x	88	86	286	386	486
reg	0	–	–	–	12	–
mem	2	–	–	–	19	–

IDIV

Integer (Signed) Division

DESCRIPTION IDIV *op*

IDIV performs a signed division of the accumulator (and its extension if specified) by *op*.

DIV uses the accumulator as an implied operand. The size of the divisor determines which registers are used for the operation as shown in the following table.

Divisor	Dividend	Quotient	Remainder
Byte	AX	AL	AH
Word	DX:AX	AX	DX
Doubleword	EDX:EAX	EAX	EDX

If the quotient exceeds the capacity of the destination register or division by zero is attempted, the divide error exception (interrupt 0) is generated and both the quotient and remainder are undefined. The largest positive quotients that may be generated are 7Fh for a byte, 7FFFh for a word, and 7FFFFFFFh for a doubleword. On the 8086 and 8088, the largest negative quotients that may be generated are 81h for a byte and 8001h for a word. On the 80286 and later processors, the IDIV instruction is able to generate the largest negative quotient: 80h for a byte, 8000h for a word, and 80000000h for a doubleword (80386/80486 only).

For example, assume AX contains FC1Eh (-994) and BL contains 56h (86). After the instruction IDIV BL is executed, AL will contain F5h (-11) and AH will contain D0h (-48).

ALGORITHM
```
IF (SIZEOF(op)=1) THEN
    dividend=AX
    maxpos=7Fh
    quotient=AL
    remainder=AH
ELSEIF (SIZEOF(op)=2)) THEN
    dividend=DX:AX
    maxpos=7FFFh
    IF (8088 or 8086) THEN
       maxneg=8001h
    ELSE
       maxneg=8000h
    ENDIF
    quotient=AX
    remainder=DX
```

```
ELSE  ;opsize=4
  dividend=EDX:EAX
  maxpos=7FFFFFFFh
  maxneg=80000000h
  quotient=EAX
  remainder=EDX
ENDIF
IF (op=0) THEN
  INT 0
ELSE
  temp = dividend/op
  IF (temp>maxpos OR temp<maxneg) THEN
    quotient=undefined
    remainder=undefined
    INT 0
  ELSE
    quotient=dividend/op        ;signed division
    remainder=dividend MOD op   ;signed modulo
  ENDIF
ENDIF
```

FLAGS

O	D	I	T	S	Z	A	P	C
—				—	—	—	—	—

IDIV *mem*

1111011w	mod	111	r/m	disp

w=0, operands are 8-bit
  1, operands are 16-bit (16-bit operand mode)
              32-bit (32-bit operand mode)

disp=0- or 2-byte displacement (16-bit address mode)
    0- or 4-byte displacement (32-bit address mode)

TIMING

Operands	x	88	86	286	386	486
reg8	0	101-112	101-112	17	19	19
reg16	0	165-184	165-184	25	27	27
reg32	0	—	—	—	43	43
mem8	1	(107-118)+EA	(107-118)+EA	20	22	20
mem16	1	(175-194)+EA	(171-190)+EA	28	30	28
mem32	1	—	—	—	46	44

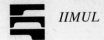

IIMUL

Integer Immediate Multiplication

DESCRIPTION IIMUL is an alternate mnemonic for the IMUL *reg,reg/mem,immed* form of the IMUL instruction. For instruction information, see the listing under that heading.

IMUL

Integer (Signed) Multiplication

DESCRIPTION

```
IMUL op
IMUL op1,op2
IMUL op1,op2,op3
IMUL op1,op3
```

IMUL performs a signed multiplication. Depending on the form used, the number of operands and algorithm used vary.

In the first form of IMUL, the accumulator is the multiplicand and *op* is the multiplier. The size of *op*, which may be a register or memory operand, determines which registers are used as shown in the following table. All operands and results are treated as signed numbers (integers).

Multiplier Size	Multiplicand	Result
8-bit	AL	AX
16-bit	AX	DX:AX
32-bit	EAX	EDX:EAX

The next two forms of IMUL differ only in syntax. In this form, op_1 will always be a register operand and op_2 may be a register or memory operand. The immediate data specified by op_3 may be 8, 16, or 32 bits, depending on the processor. The two operand form, IMUL op_1,op_3, is a shorthand form for IMUL op_1,op_2,op_3 when $op_1=op_2$.

The fourth form of IMUL, available only on the 80386 and 80486, multiplies a register operand (op_1) by a register or memory operand (op_3). This form differs from the previous two forms in that no immediate constant is encoded.

ALGORITHM

```
IF (InstructionForm=op) THEN    ;Form 1
    opsize=SIZEOF(op)
    IF (opsize=1) THEN
      AX=AL*op
      high="AH"
      low="AL"
    ELSEIF (opsize=2) THEN
      DX:AX=AX*op
      high="DX"
      low="AX"
    ELSE  ;opsize=4
      EDX:EAX=EAX*op
      high="EDX"
      low="EAX"
    ENDIF
```

```
      IF (SIGN(low)=0 AND high=0) THEN
        CF=0
        OF=0
      ELSEIF (SIGN(low)=1 AND high=-1) THEN
        CF=1
        OF=1
      ENDIF
    ELSEIF (InstructionForm=op₁,op₂,op₃) THEN
      op₁=op₂*op₃
      IF (result fits in op₁) THEN
        CF=0
        OF=0
      ELSE
        CF=1
        OF=1
      ENDIF
    ELSEIF (InstructionForm=op₁,op₃) THEN
      op₁=op₁*op₃
      IF (result fits in op₁) THEN
        CF=0
        OF=0
      ELSE
        CF=1
        OF=1
      ENDIF
    ELSEIF (InstructionForm=op₁,op₂) THEN
      op₁=op₁*op₂
      IF (result fits in op₁) THEN
        CF=0
        OF=0
      ELSE
        CF=1
        OF=1
      ENDIF
    ENDIF
```

NOTES

1. The 80386 and 80486 use an early-out algorithm to perform the multiply. The time required to perform the multiply depends on the position of the most significant bit in the multiplier. To calculate the actual clock count, use the following formula.

```
IF (multiplier≠0) THEN
  clocks=MAX(3,ceiling(log₂|multiplier|)+6
ELSE
```

```
    clocks=9
ENDIF
IF (multiplier is mem) clocks=clocks+3
```

O	D	I	T	S	Z	A	P	C
*				—	—	—	—	*

IMUL *reg/mem*

1111011*w*	*mod*	101	*r/m*	*disp*

w=0, operands are 8-bit
    1, operands are 16-bit (16-bit operand mode)
               32-bit (32-bit operand mode)

disp=0- or 2-byte displacement (16-bit address mode)
       0- or 4-byte displacement (32-bit address mode)

Operands	x	88	86	286	386	486
reg8	0	80-98	80-98	13	12-17	13-18
reg16	0	128-154	128-154	21	12-25	13-26
reg32	0	–	–	–	12-41	12-42
mem8	1	(86-104)+EA	(86-104)+EA	16	15-20	13-18
mem16	1	(138-164)+EA	(134-160)+EA	24	15-28	13-26
mem32	1	–	–	–	15-44	13-42

IMUL *reg,reg/mem,immed*

IMUL *reg,immed* (alias when *reg* and *reg/mem* specify the same register)

011010*s*1	*mod*	*reg*	*r/m*	*disp*	*immed*

op_1=reg, op_2=mod+r/m

s=0, *immed*=*immed16* (16-bit operand mode)
     immed=*immed32* (32-bit operand mode)
   1, *immed*=*immed8*

disp=0- or 2-byte displacement (16-bit address mode)
       0- or 4-byte displacement (32-bit address mode)

Operands	x	88	86	286	386	486
reg16,reg16,immed8	0	–	–	21	13-26	13-26
reg16,reg16,immed16	0	–	–	21	9-22	13-26
reg16,mem16,immed8	1	–	–	24	14-27	13-26
reg16,mem16,immed16	1	–	–	24	12-25	13-26
reg32,reg32,immed8	0	–	–	–	13-42	13-42
reg32,reg32,immed32	0	–	–	–	9-38	13-42
reg32,mem32,immed8	1	–	–	–	14-43	13-42
reg32,mem32,immed32	1	–	–	–	12-41	13-42

IMUL *reg,reg/mem*

00001111	10101111	mod	reg	r/m	disp

op_1=reg, op_2=mod+r/m

disp=0- or 2-byte displacement (16-bit mode)
0- or 4-byte displacement (32-bit address mode)

Operands	x	88	86	286	386	486
reg16,reg16	0	–	–	–	12-25	13-26
reg16,mem16	1	–	–	–	15-28	13-26
reg32,reg32	0	–	–	–	12-41	13-42
reg32,mem32	1	–	–	–	14-44	13-42

IN

Input Data from I/O Port

DESCRIPTION IN *accum,op*

IN transfers a byte, word, or doubleword from the I/O port specified by *op* to the accumulator.

Two forms of the IN instruction are available. In the first form, the port number is specified by an immediate byte constant, allowing access to ports numbered 0 through 255 (FFh). In the second form, the port number is provided in the DX register. This form allows access to ports 0 through 65535 (FFFFh).

When a word is input from a port, the byte at the port address is transferred to AL and the byte from the port address + 1 is transferred to AH. Similarly, when a doubleword is input, the word at the port address is transferred to AX and the word at the port address + 2 is transferred to the high-order 16-bits of EAX.

ALGORITHM *accum*=I/O-Port

FLAGS

O	D	I	T	S	Z	A	P	C

No flags are affected

IN *accum,immed*

1110010w	immed8

w=0, operands are 8-bit
  1, operands are 16-bit (16-bit operand mode)
         32-bit (32-bit operand mode)

immed8=1-byte immediate data

TIMING

Operands	x	88	86	286	386	486
accum,immed	0	B:10 W:14	10	5	12 PM$_1$:6 PM$_2$:26 VM:26	14 PM$_1$:9 PM$_2$:29 VM:27

PM$_1$ indicates the timing when CPL≤IOPL.

PM$_2$ indicates the timing when CPL>IOPL.

IN *accum*,DX

1110110w

w=0, operands are 8-bit
 1, operands are 16-bit (16-bit operand mode)
            32-bit (32-bit operand mode)

TIMING

Operands	x	88	86	286	386	486
accum,DX	0	B: 8 W: 12	8	5	13 PM_1:7 PM_2:27 VM:27	14 PM_1:8 PM_2:28 VM:27

PM_1 indicates the timing when CPL≤IOPL.

PM_2 indicates the timing when CPL>IOPL.

INC

Increment Operand by 1

DESCRIPTION INC *op*

INC adds one to the operand and sets the flags according to the result.

For the purpose of the INC instruction, the operand is treated as an unsigned binary number. For example, if the AX register contains 7FFFh, the instruction INC AX will result in 8000h being stored into AX.

ALGORITHM *op=op+1*

FLAGS

O	D	I	T	S	Z	A	P	C
*				*	*	*	*	

INC *reg/mem*

1111111w	mod	000	r/m	disp

w=0, operands are 8-bit
   1, operands are 16-bit (16-bit operand mode)
            32-bit (32-bit operand mode)

disp=0- or 2-byte displacement (16-bit address mode)
       0- or 4-byte displacement (32-bit address mode)

Note: This encoding is not normally used to increment a 16- or 32-bit register. The INC *reg16/reg32* form is provided for that purpose and occupies only a single byte.

TIMING

Operands	x	88	86	286	386	486
reg	0	3	2	2	2	1
mem	1	B:15+EA W:23+EA	15+EA	7	6	3

INC *reg16/reg32*

01000	reg

TIMING

Operands	x	88	86	286	386	486
reg16	0	3	3	2	2	1
reg32	0	–	–	–	2	1

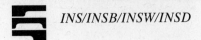

INS/INSB/INSW/INSD

Input String from I/O Port to Memory

DESCRIPTION
```
INS op,DX
INSB
INSW
INSD
```

INS transfers data from the specified I/O port into a memory operand pointed to by the ES segment register and the destination index register (DI/EDI) while updating the index in preparation for the next transfer.

The INS instruction is used to transfer data from an I/O port into memory while automatically updating the effective address in preparation for the next transfer. The ES segment register, in combination with the DI/EDI register, is used to form the effective address for the transfer. The size of the destination index register is determined by the current address mode. If the address mode is 16-bit, then the DI register will be used. If 32-bit addressing is in effect, then the EDI register will be used.

The number of the I/O port to be accessed must be given in the DX register. The INS instruction does not allow the I/O port to be given as immediate data.

The options that must be defined when using this instruction are the operand size and whether the destination index will be incremented or decremented after the transfer.

The size of the transfer (and therefore, the memory operand) may be specified explicitly in the mnemonic or by an operand. In the first method, the transfer size is explicitly declared by using the B, W, or D suffix in combination with the INS mnemonic. The resulting instructions (INSB, INSW, and INSD) will transfer a byte, word, or doubleword from the I/O port, respectively. The destination index register will then be adjusted by 1, 2, or 4 to point to the next operand to be stored.

The destination memory operand must be addressable using the ES segment register. *A segment override cannot be used.* The general form of the instruction (INS) takes a memory argument (*op*) that defines the size of the transfer only. *The effective address of the operand is not used as the address of the transfer;* the data is always stored using the destination index as a pointer to memory. For example, the instruction INS BYTE PTR [BX],DX would be equivalent to the INSB form and would transfer the contents of the I/O port given in the DX register to the byte of memory at ES:[DI]. The effective address of the operand is always ignored.

The destination index register will be incremented by the size of the operand if the direction flag (DF) has been cleared to 0 (by the CLD instruction, for example). The register will be decremented by the size of the operand if DF is set to 1 (by the STD instruction).

For example, assume that the address size attribute is 16-bits and DF is cleared. The instruction INSB will be equivalent to the following instructions.

```
IN    BYTE PTR ES:[DI],DX
INC   DI
```

All forms of the INS instruction may be encoded with the REP prefix to perform a block input of data from an I/O port to memory.

ALGORITHM
```
IF (AddressMode=16-bit) THEN
  dest="DI"
ELSE
  dest="EDI"
ENDIF
opsize=SIZEOF(operand)    ;Declared by mnemonic or operand
IF (opsize=1) THEN
  IN BYTE PTR ES:[dest],DX
ELSEIF (opsize=2) THEN
  IN WORD PTR ES:[dest],DX
ELSE
  IN WORD PTR ES:[dest],DX
ENDIF
IF (DF=0)   ;CLD
  dest=dest+opsize
ELSE   ;STD
  dest=dest-opsize
ENDIF
```

NOTES

1. When used with any REP*cond* instruction prefix, the processor may execute the INS instruction faster than the addressed I/O port is able to supply data.

2. Early versions of the 80286 incorrectly executed this instruction in protected mode. If the ES register contained a null selector or ES:DI pointed past the segment limit when executing the non-repeated INS instruction, the CS:IP value saved by the exception 0Dh handler points to the instruction after the INS instruction instead of to it.

3. Early versions of the 80286 incorrectly execute the repeated form of this instruction in protected mode. If, during the execution of this instruction, a segment limit exception or IOPL exception occurs, the value of CX seen by the exception handler will be the value present at the start of the instruction. The DI register will reflect the iterations performed by the instruction.

4. On some versions of the 80386, the CX/ECX register is not updated properly when any REP*cond* INS instruction is followed by a PUSH, POP, or memory reference instruction. At the conclusion of the repeated instruction, CX/ECX is supposed to be zero. In the case of REP*cond* INS, however, CX/ECX will not be zero, but will be FFFFh/FFFFFFFFh, respectively. The REP*cond* INS instruction is executed the correct number of times and DI/EDI is updated properly. Do not depend on CX/ECX being zero.

5. This instruction is known to malfunction in two cases on some versions of the 80386. The first case occurs when INS or REP INS is followed by an instruction

that uses a different address size. The second case occurs when INS or REP INS is followed by an instruction that implicitly references the stack and the B-bit in the SS descriptor is different than the address size used by the string instruction. In both cases, INS will not update the DI/EDI register properly and REP INS will not update the CX/ECX register properly. The address size used by the instruction is taken from the instruction that *follows* rather than from the string instruction. This can result in the updating of only the lower 16 bits of a 32-bit register or all 32 bits of a register being used as a 16-bit operand.

In programs where 16- and 32-bit code will be mixed or where the stack and code segments may be different sizes, a NOP that uses the same address size as the INS instruction should be explicitly coded as shown below.

```
.386
SEGA    SEGMENT USE16 PARA PUBLIC 'CODE'
        ASSUME  CS:SEGA
        INSW    ;16-bit INS
        NOP     ; followed by 16-bit NOP
        DB 67H  ;32-bit INS
        INSW
        DB 67H  ; followed by 32-bit NOP
        NOP
SEGA    ENDS
SEGB    SEGMENT USE32 PARA PUBLIC 'CODE'
        ASSUME  CS:SEGB
        INSD    ;32-bit INS
        NOP     ; followed by 32-bit NOP
        DB 67H  ;16-bit INS
        INSD
        DB 67H  ; followed by 16-bit NOP
        NOP
SEGB    ENDS
        END
```

6. Early versions of the 80486 processor may hang while executing the INS instruction if the I/O read is split across a doubleword boundary. This is only true for a processor-initiated split, not a BS16# OR BS8# initiated split. To avoid this, all doubleword I/O reads should be aligned.

FLAGS	O	D	I	T	S	Z	A	P	C

No flags are affected

INSB/INSW/INSD

INS *reg/mem,DX*

| 1010101*w* |

w=0, operands are 8-bit
  1, operands are 16-bit (16-bit operand mode)
    32-bit (32-bit operand mode)

Note: If present, the *reg/mem* operand specifies only the operand size and is not included in the encoding.

TIMING

Operands	x	88	86	286	386	486
INSB INSW	1	–	–	5	15 PM_1:9 PM_2:29 VM:29	17 PM_1:10 PM_2:32 VM:30
INSD	1	–	–	–	15 PM_1:9 PM_2:29 VM:29	17 PM_1:10 PM_2:32 VM:30
REP INSB REP INSW	r	–	–	5+4r	14+6r PM_1:8+6r PM_2:28+6r VM:28+6r	16+8r PM_1:10+8r PM_2:30+8r VM:29+8r
REP INSD	r	–	–	–	14+6r PM_1:8+6r PM_2:28+6r VM:28+6r	16+8r PM_1:10+8r PM_2:30+8r VM:29+8r

r represents the number of repetitions executed when used with the REP prefix.

PM_1 indicates the timing when CPL≤IOPL.

PM_2 indicates the timing when CPL>IOPL.

INT

Generate Software Interrupt

DESCRIPTION INT *op*

INT transfers control unconditionally, via software interrupt, to the address stored in the interrupt vector table or interrupt descriptor table corresponding to the interrupt number specified by *op*.

In real mode, the INT instruction works by pushing the FLAGS register and the segment and offset of the instruction following the interrupt on the stack, then transferring control to the address that has been stored in the interrupt vector table corresponding to that interrupt. Each entry in the interrupt vector table is 32 bits and contains a segment and offset. The segmented address for interrupt *n* is stored at memory location 0000:*n**4. In protected mode, the operation of this instruction depends on the current task and the method used to handle the interrupt as explained in Chapter 7.

A short (1-byte) form of this instruction is provided when the interrupt number is 3 to support software debuggers. To use this facility, first point the interrupt vector for INT 3 to an interrupt handler within the debugger. Then, to set a breakpoint at a certain instruction, the byte at the beginning of the target instruction is saved, then replaced with the opcode for INT 3 (CCh). When the INT 3 instruction is executed, the debugger regains control, replaces the CCh with the original byte, and usually displays status to the operator.

Control is usually returned from an interrupt handler to the instruction following the INT instruction by the IRET instruction.

Software interrupts are a convenient method for implementing operating system calls as they do not require the executing program to have any knowledge of the location of the operating system.

ALGORITHM
```
;Real mode algorithm shown
IF (OperandMode=16-bit) THEN
  PUSHF
ELSE
  PUSHFD
ENDIF
IF=0
TF=0
PUSH CS
CS=WORD PTR [0000:(4*n+2)]
IF (AddressMode=16-bit) THEN
  instruction_pointer=IP
ELSE
```

```
    instruction_pointer=EIP
  ENDIF
  IF (OPCODE=CCh) THEN        ;Save offset of next instruction
    PUSH instruction_pointer+1
  ELSE
    PUSH instruction_pointer+2
  ENDIF
  instruction_pointer=ZERO_EXTEND(WORD PTR [0000:(4*n+2)])
```

FLAGS

O	D	I	T	S	Z	A	P	C
		0	0					

INT *immed8*

11001101	*immed8*

immed8=1-byte immediate data specifying interrupt number

TIMING

Operands	x	88	86	286	386	486
immed8 Real mode	5	71	51	23+m	37	30
immed8 Protected mode, same privilege	–	–	–	PM:40+m	PM:59	PM:44
immed8 Protected mode, more privilege	–	–	–	PM:78+m	PM:99	PM:71
immed8 Protected mode, via task gate	–	–	–	PM:167+m	PM:ts_1	PM:37+ts_2
immed8 V86 mode, more privilege	–	–	–	–	VM:119	VM:86
immed8 V86 mode, via task gate	–	–	–	–	VM:ts_1	VM:37+ts_2

m represents the number of elements in the target instruction.

ts_1 and ts_2 represent the time to switch tasks as given in the table at the end of this instruction listing.

INT 3

11001100

Operands	x	88	86	286	386	486
(no operands) Real mode	5	72	52	23+m	33	26
(no operands) Protected mode, same privilege	–	–	–	PM:40+m	PM:59	PM:44
(no operands) Protected mode, more privilege	–	–	–	PM:78+m	PM:99	PM:71
(no operands) Protected mode, via task gate	–	–	–	PM:167+m	PM:ts_1	PM:37+ts_2
(no operands) V86 mode, more privilege	–	–	–	–	VM:119	VM:82
(no operands) V86 mode, via task gate	–	–	–	–	?	VM:37+ts_2

m represents the number of elements in the target instruction.

ts_1 indicates the timing required to switch tasks via a Task State Segment (TSS) as shown in the following table.

Old Task	New Task Type (via TSS)		
	386 TSS VM=0	386 TSS VM=1	286 TSS
386 TSS VM=0	DX:309 SX:467	DX:226 SX:384	DX:282 SX:440
386 TSS VM=1	DX:314 SX:472	DX:231 SX:275	DX:287 SX:445
286 TSS	DX:307 SX:465	DX:224 SX:382	DX:280 SX:438

ts_2 indicates the timing required to switch tasks via a Task State Segment (TSS) as shown in the following table.

Old Task	New Task Type (via task gate or TSS)		
	486 TSS	286 TSS	VM TSS
486 TSS 286 TSS	199	180	177

INTO

Generate Interrupt If Overflow

DESCRIPTION INTO generates a software interrupt (INT 4) if the overflow flag (OF) is set to 1. Otherwise, control proceeds to the following instruction.

The INTO instruction tests the OF and either generates an interrupt 4 or passes control to the instruction that follows. If the interrupt is generated, the effect is the same as if the INT 4 instruction had been executed. (See the description of the INT instruction for details.)

INTO would typically be used in arithmetic or logic algorithms to test for an overflow condition after an operation. If used, an appropriate interrupt handler must be provided and the interrupt vector table changed to direct INT 4 to the new handler.

ALGORITHM   IF (OF=1) THEN INT 4

FLAGS

O	D	I	T	S	Z	A	P	C
		0	0					

Flags affected only if interrupt generated

INTO

```
11001110
```

TIMING

Operands	x	88	86	286	386	486
(no operands) Real mode	5	73 NJ:4	53 NJ:4	24+m NJ:3	35 NJ:3	28 NJ:3
(no operands) Protected mode, same privilege	–	–	–	PM:40+m NJ:3	PM:59 NJ:3	PM:46 NJ:3
(no operands) Protected mode, more privilege	–	–	–	PM:78+m NJ:3	PM:99 NJ:3	PM:73 NJ:3
(no operands) Protected mode, via task gate	–	–	–	PM:167+m NJ:3	PM:ts_1 NJ:3	PM:39+ ts_2 NJ:3
(no operands) V86 mode, more privilege	–	–	–	–	VM:119 NJ:3	VM:84 NJ:3
(no operands) V86 mode, via task gate	–	–	–	–	ts_1	VM:39+ ts_2 NJ:3

m represents the number of elements in the target instruction.

ts_1 indicates the timing required to switch tasks via a Task State Segment (TSS) as shown in the following table.

Old Task	New Task Type (via TSS)		
	386 TSS VM=0	386 TSS VM=1	286 TSS
386 TSS VM=0	DX:309 SX:467	DX:226 SX:384	DX:282 SX:440
386 TSS VM=1	DX:314 SX:472	DX:231 SX:275	DX:287 SX:445
286 TSS	DX:307 SX:465	DX:224 SX:382	DX:280 SX:438

ts_2 indicates the timing required to switch tasks via a Task State Segment (TSS) as shown in the following table.

Old Task	New Task Type (via task gate or TSS)		
	486 TSS	286 TSS	VM TSS
486 TSS 286 TSS	199	180	177

INVD

Invalidate Cache

DESCRIPTION INVD instructs the processor to consider data in both internal and external caches to be invalid.

When this instruction is executed, the internal cache is flushed. In addition, a special bus cycle is issued which indicates that any external caches should also be flushed. Data that is being held in write-back external caches will be discarded.

ALGORITHM None

NOTES
1. On some versions of the 80486, if a cache line fill is in progress when the INVD instruction is executed, the cache line fill buffer is not invalidated. The buffer contents will be moved into the cache, which will contain a valid line when it should have been flushed.

   To work around the problem in software, use the following code to disable the internal cache prior to flushing the cache. Note that the NMI and faults/traps should not occur during this code sequence.

```
        MOV     EAX,CRØ
        OR      EAX,60000000H   ;Set to disable cache
        PUSHFD
        CLI
        MOV     BL,CS:Label
        OUT     port,data       ;Write data to dummy port
        MOV     CRØ,EAX         ;Disable cache
Label:
        INVD                    ;Invalidate cache
        AND     EAX,9FFFFFFFH   ;Enable cache (value may be
        MOV     CRØ,EAX         ; different for no write-thru)
        POPFD
```

FLAGS

O	D	I	T	S	Z	A	P	C

No flags are affected

INVD

00001111	00001000

TIMING

Operands	x	88	86	286	386	486
(no operands)	0	–	–	–	–	4

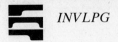

INVLPG

Invalidate Page Entry in TLB

DESCRIPTION INVLPG *op*

INVLPG instructs the processor to invalidate a single entry in the Translation Lookaside Buffer (TLB). If the TLB contains a valid entry which maps the address of the specified memory operand, that TLB entry is marked invalid. The TLB is the cache that is used to manage page table entries.

ALGORITHM None

FLAGS

O	D	I	T	S	Z	A	P	C

No flags are affected

INVD *mem*

00001111	00000001	mod	111	r/m

TIMING

Operands	x	88	86	286	386	486
mem	0	–	–	–	–	H:12 NH:11

H indicates the timing for a hit in the cache.

NH indicates the timing for a miss in the cache.

IRET

Return from Interrupt

DESCRIPTION IRET transfers control to the instruction following an interrupt.

In real mode, the IRET instruction is usually used to exit an interrupt handler and returns control to the calling procedure. The original procedure may have either transferred control by means of a software interrupt or been interrupted by a hardware exception. In protected mode, IRET can also initiate a task switch.

Note that for both interrupts and exceptions, the information on the stack must be valid for this instruction to operate. Misalignment of the stack inside an interrupt handler (by PUSHing more data than is POPed, for example) followed by execution of an IRET will transfer control to an undesired area in memory, usually causing the computer to crash.

ALGORITHM
```
POP IP
POP CS
POPF
```

NOTES 1. The encoding for the IRET and IRETD instructions is identical. The current operand size attribute determines how the opcode is interpreted.

FLAGS

O	D	I	T	S	Z	A	P	C
*	*	*	*	*	*	*	*	*

The FLAGS register is loaded from the stack

IRET

11001111

Operands	x	88	86	286	386	486
(no operands) Real mode	3	44	32	17+m	22	15
(no operands) Protected mode, same privilege	3	–	–	PM:31+m	PM:38	PM:20
(no operands) Protected mode, lesser privilege	3	–	–	PM:55+m	PM:82	PM:36
(no operands) Protected mode, different task	3	–	–	PM:169+m	PM:ts$_1$	PM:32+ts$_2$
(no operands) Protected mode, return to V86 mode	3	–	–	–	PM:60	PM:15

m represents the number of elements in the target instruction.

ts$_1$ indicates the timing required to switch tasks (NT=1) as shown in the following table.

Old Task	New Task		
	386 TSS VM=0	**386 TSS** VM=1	**286 TSS**
386 TSS VM=0	DX:275 SX:328	DX:224 SX:377	DX:271 SX:324
286 TSS	DX:265 SX:318	DX:214 SX:267	DX:232 SX:285

ts$_2$ indicates the timing required to switch tasks (NT=1) as shown in the following table.

Old Task	New Task		
	486 TSS VM=0	**486 TSS** VM=1	**286 TSS**
486 TSS VM=0 or 286 TSS	199	177	180

IRETD

Return from Interrupt Using EIP

DESCRIPTION IRETD transfers control to the instruction following an interrupt.

In real mode, the IRETD instruction is usually used to exit an interrupt handler and returns control to the calling procedure. The original procedure may have either transferred control by means of a software interrupt or been interrupted by a hardware exception. In protected mode, IRETD can also initiate a task switch.

Note that for both interrupts and exceptions, the information on the stack must be valid for this instruction to operate. Misalignment of the stack inside an interrupt handler (by PUSHing more data than is POPed, for example) followed by execution of an IRETD will transfer control to an undesired area in memory, usually causing the computer to crash.

ALGORITHM
```
POP EIP
POP CS
POPFD
```

NOTES
1. The encoding for the IRET and IRETD instructions is identical. The current operand size attribute determines how the opcode is interpreted.

FLAGS

O	D	I	T	S	Z	A	P	C
*	*	*	*	*	*	*	*	*

The EFLAGS register is loaded from the stack

IRETD

11001111

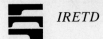
Operands	x	88	86	286	386	486
(no operands) Real mode	3	–	–	–	22	15
(no operands) Protected mode, same privilege	3	–	–	–	PM:38	PM:20
(no operands) Protected mode, lesser privilege	3	–	–	–	PM:82	PM:36
(no operands) Protected mode, different task	3	–	–	–	PM:ts_1	PM:32+ts_2
(no operands) Protected mode, return to V86 mode	3	–	–	–	PM:60	PM:15

m represents the number of elements in the target instruction.

ts_1 indicates the timing required to switch tasks (NT=1) as shown in the following table.

Old Task	New Task		
	386 TSS VM=0	386 TSS VM=1	286 TSS
386 TSS VM=0	DX:275 SX:328	DX:224 SX:377	DX:271 SX:324
286 TSS	DX:265 SX:318	DX:214 SX:267	DX:232 SX:285

ts_2 indicates the timing required to switch tasks (NT=1) as shown in the following table.

Old Task	New Task		
	486 TSS VM=0	486 TSS VM=1	286 TSS
486 TSS VM=0 or 286 TSS	199	177	180

Jcond

Jump Short If Condition Met

DESCRIPTION `Jcond op`

Each of the conditional jump instructions tests one or more of the flags in the FLAGS register and transfers control to the target address specified by *op* if the condition *cond* is met. Otherwise, control passes to the following instruction.

The conditional jump instructions test for predetermined combinations of flags. If the condition is met, the byte of immediate data following the opcode byte is sign-extended to required length and added to the IP/EIP register. A conditional short jump can transfer control to an instruction that is within 127 bytes of the beginning of the instruction following the condition jump. A conditional near jump specifies either a 16-bit signed operand (16-bit address mode) or a 32-bit signed operand (32-bit address mode).

Many of the conditional jump instructions have more than one mnemonic form that assembles to the identical opcode. This aliasing is provided as a convenience for the programmer and has no effect on the object code produced. For example, assume that the contents of the AX register are to be tested and will be deemed valid if in the greater than 1. This criteria can be equivalently expressed since AX must be greater than 1, AX must be 2 or greater, AX must be not less than 2, or AX must be not less than or equal to 1. How the condition is expressed will depend on the programmer and the algorithm.

The following tables give the conditional jump instructions, grouped by application, and the flag conditions that will cause the specified jump to be taken.

Unsigned Comparison

Mnemonic	Description	Flags
JA JNBE	Jump if above Jump if not below or equal	CF=0 and ZF=0
JAE JNB	Jump if above or equal Jump if not below	CF=0
JB JNAE	Jump if below Jump if not above or equal	CF=1
JBE JNA	Jump if below or equal Jump if not above	CF=1 or ZF=1
JE JZ	Jump if equal Jump if zero	ZF=1
JNE JNZ	Jump if not equal Jump if not zero	ZF=0

Signed Comparison

Mnemonic	Description	Condition
JE JZ	Jump if equal Jump if zero	ZF=1
JG JNLE	Jump if greater Jump if not less or equal	ZF=0 or SF=OF
JGE JNL	Jump if greater or equal Jump if not less	SF=OF
JL JNGE	Jump if less Jump if not greater or equal	SF≠OF
JLE JNG	Jump if less or equal Jump if not greater	ZF=1 or SF≠OF
JNE JNZ	Jump if not equal Jump if not zero	ZF=0

Other Conditions

Mnemonic	Description	Condition
JB JC	Jump if borrow Jump if carry	CF=1 CF=1
JNC	Jump if not carry	CF=0
JNO	Jump if not overflow	OF=0
JNP JPO	Jump if not parity Jump if parity odd	PF=0
JNS	Jump if not sign	SF=0
JO	Jump if overflow	OF=1
JP JPE	Jump if parity Jump if parity even	PF=1
JS	Jump if sign	SF=1

ALGORITHM

```
IF (cond) THEN
  IF (AddressMode=16-bit) THEN
    IF (short jump) THEN
      IP=IP+SIGN_EXTEND(disp8)
    ELSE
      IP=IP+disp16
    ENDIF
  ELSE  ;(AddressMode = 32-bit)
    IF (short jump) THEN
      EIP=EIP+SIGN_EXTEND(disp8)
    ELSE
      EIP=EIP+disp32
    ENDIF
  ENDIF
ENDIF
```

FLAGS

O	D	I	T	S	Z	A	P	C

No flags are affected

Jcond (jump short if *cond* met)

0111	*cccc*	*disp8*

disp8=1-byte signed relative displacement

cond	cccc	Opcode	Description
JA	0111	77h	Jump if above (unsigned comparison)
JAE	0011	73h	Jump if above or equal (unsigned comparison)
JB	0010	72h	Jump if below (unsigned comparison)
JBE	0110	76h	Jump if below or equal (unsigned comparison)
JC	0010	72h	Jump if carry
JE	0100	74h	Jump if equal
JG	1111	7Fh	Jump if greater (signed comparison)
JGE	1101	7Dh	Jump if greater or equal (signed comparison)
JL	1100	7Ch	Jump if less (signed comparison)
JLE	1110	7Eh	Jump if less or equal (signed comparison)
JNA	0110	76h	Jump if not above (unsigned comparison)
JNAE	0010	72h	Jump if not above or equal (unsigned comparison)
JNB	0011	73h	Jump if not below (unsigned comparison)
JNBE	0111	77h	Jump if not below or equal (unsigned comparison)
JNC	0011	73h	Jump if not carry
JNE	0101	75h	Jump if not equal
JNG	1110	7Eh	Jump if not greater (unsigned comparison)
JNGE	1100	7Ch	Jump if not greater or equal (unsigned comparison)
JNL	1101	7Dh	Jump if not less (signed comparison)
JNLE	1111	7Fh	Jump if not less or equal (signed comparison)
JNO	0001	71h	Jump if not overflow
JNP	1011	7Bh	Jump if not parity (= parity odd)
JNS	1001	79h	Jump if not sign
JNZ	0101	75h	Jump if not zero
JO	0000	70h	Jump if overflow
JP	1010	7Ah	Jump if parity (=parity even)

JPE	1010	7Ah	Jump if parity even
JPO	1011	7Bh	Jump if parity odd
JS	1000	78h	Jump if sign
JZ	0100	74h	Jump if zero

TIMING

Operands	x	88	86	286	386	486
disp8	0	16 NJ:4	16 NJ:4	7+m NJ:3	7+m NJ:3	3 NJ:1

m represents the number of elements in the target instruction.

Jcond (jump near if *cond* met)

00001111	1000	cccc	disp

disp=2- or 4-byte signed relative displacement

cond	cccc	Opcode	Description
JA	0111	87h	Jump if above (unsigned comparison)
JAE	0011	83h	Jump if above or equal (unsigned comparison)
JB	0010	82h	Jump if below (unsigned comparison)
JBE	0110	86h	Jump if below or equal (unsigned comparison)
JC	0010	82h	Jump if carry
JE	0100	84h	Jump if equal
JG	1111	8Fh	Jump if greater (signed comparison)
JGE	1101	8Dh	Jump if greater or equal (signed comparison)
JL	1100	8Ch	Jump if less (signed comparison)
JLE	1110	8Eh	Jump if less or equal (signed comparison)
JNA	0110	86h	Jump if not above (unsigned comparison)
JNAE	0010	82h	Jump if not above or equal (unsigned comparison)
JNB	0011	83h	Jump if not below (unsigned comparison)
JNBE	0111	87h	Jump if not below or equal (unsigned comparison)
JNC	0011	83h	Jump if not carry
JNE	0101	85h	Jump if not equal
JNG	1110	8Eh	Jump if not greater (unsigned comparison)
JNGE	1100	8Ch	Jump if not greater or equal (unsigned comparison)
JNL	1101	8Dh	Jump if not less (signed comparison)
JNLE	1111	8Fh	Jump if not less or equal (signed comparison)
JNO	0001	81h	Jump if not overflow

JNP	1011	8Bh	Jump if not parity (=parity odd)
JNS	1001	89h	Jump if not sign
JNZ	0101	85h	Jump if not zero
JO	0000	80h	Jump if overflow
JP	1010	8Ah	Jump if parity (= parity even)
JPE	1010	8Ah	Jump if parity even
JPO	1011	8Bh	Jump if parity odd
JS	1000	88h	Jump if sign
JZ	0100	84h	Jump if zero

TIMING

Operands	x	88	86	286	386	486
disp	0	–	–	–	7+m NJ:3	3 NJ:1

m represents the number of elements in the target instruction.

JCXZ

Jump If CX=0

DESCRIPTION　`JCXZ op`

JCXZ tests the contents of the CX register and transfers control to the target address specified by *op* if CX is zero. Otherwise, control passes to the following instruction.

The JCXZ instruction is often used to test CX before executing a loop. Normally, the body of a loop is constructed such that the last statement is the LOOP instruction. Because LOOP decrements CX *before* testing the loop condition, entering a loop with CX=0 will cause the loop to execute 10000h (65536) times. JCXZ can be used to bypass the loop when CX=0.

ALGORITHM　`IF (CX=0) THEN IP=IP+SIGN_EXTEND(disp)`

NOTES

1. The encoding for JCXZ and JECXZ is identical. The interpretation of the encoding depends on the operand size and address-size mode in effect when the opcode is executed.

FLAGS

O	D	I	T	S	Z	A	P	C

No flags are affected

JCXZ

11100011		disp8

disp8=1-byte displacement

TIMING

Operands	x	88	86	286	386	486
disp8	0	18 NJ:6	18 NJ:6	8+m NJ:4	9+m NJ:5	8 NJ:5

m represents the number of elements in the target instruction.

JECXZ

Jump If ECX=0

DESCRIPTION JECXZ *op*

JECXZ tests the contents of the ECX register and transfers control to the target if ECX is zero. Otherwise, control passes to the following instruction.

The JECXZ instruction is often used to test ECX before executing a loop. Normally, the body of a loop is constructed such that the last statement is the LOOP instruction. Because LOOP decrements ECX *before* testing the loop condition, entering a loop with ECX=0 will cause the loop to execute 100000000h (2,147,483,648) times. JECXZ can be used to bypass the loop when ECX=0.

ALGORITHM IF (ECX=0) THEN EIP=EIP+SIGN_EXTEND(*disp*)

NOTES 1. JECXZ uses the same encoding as JCXZ. The interpretation of the encoding depends on the operand size and address-size mode in effect when the opcode is executed.

FLAGS

O	D	I	T	S	Z	A	P	C

No flags are affected

JECXZ

11100011	*disp8*

disp8=1-byte signed relative displacement

TIMING

Operands	x	88	86	286	386	486
JECXZ *disp8*	0	–	–	–	9+m NJ:5	8 NJ:5

m represents the number of elements in the target instruction.

JMP

Jump Unconditionally

DESCRIPTION   JMP *op*

JMP transfers control unconditionally to the target address specified by *op*.

The JMP instruction is used to transfer control to a different location. The new location can be specified as relative to the current location, as a displacement from the beginning of the current code segment, or as a complete address comprising both segment and offset. No flags are affected and, unlike CALL and INT, no information is saved; JMP is a one-way transfer. The forms of JMP used in real mode are described below.

Short direct: The target location is given as a 1-byte signed displacement relative to the beginning of the instruction following the jump. The byte of immediate data following the opcode byte is sign-extended to 16 bits and added to the IP register. Control can be transferred to an instruction that is within 127 bytes of the beginning of the instruction following. On the 80386 and 80486, the displacement is sign-extended to 32 bits and added to the EIP register.

Near direct: The target location is given as a 2-byte signed displacement relative to the beginning of the instruction following the jump. Control can be transferred to an instruction that is within 32768 bytes of the beginning of the instruction following. On the 80386 and 80486, the displacement can be 4 bytes, allowing control to be transferred within a range of 2,147,483,648 bytes.

Near indirect: The target location is given by either a register or memory operand. For a simple register operand, the contents of the specified register are simply loaded into the IP register. When a memory operand is referenced, the word located at the effective address is loaded into the IP register. This form of the JMP instruction is often used when implementing jump tables. On the 80386 and 80486, a 4-byte value can be specified for EIP by referencing either a 32-bit register or a memory operand prefaced with DWORD PTR or FAR PTR.

Far direct: The target location is encoded as immediate data within the instruction. Control is transferred by loading the first two bytes following the opcode into the IP register and loading the following two bytes into the CS register. On the 80386 and 80486, the offset portion of the target address can be 4 bytes and will be loaded into the EIP register.

Far indirect: This jump can take place only through memory; the target location is given by a memory operand. Control is transferred by loading the first two bytes at the effective address into the IP register and the following two bytes into the CS register. On the 80386 and 80486, four bytes at the effective address can be loaded into the EIP register and the following two bytes into the CS register.

ALGORITHM
```
IF (short direct) THEN
   IP=IP+SIGN_EXTEND(disp8)
```

```
  ENDIF
  IF (near direct) THEN
    IP=IP+disp16
  ENDIF
  IF (near indirect) THEN
    IF (op=reg16) THEN
      IP=reg16
    ELSEIF (op=mem16) THEN
      IP=WORD PTR [mem16]
    ENDIF
  ENDIF
  IF (far direct) THEN CS:IP=immed32
  IF (far indirect) THEN
    IP=WORD PTR [mem]
    CS=WORD PTR [mem+2]
  ENDIF
```

NOTES

1. If a segment violation occurs on the target of a short jump and an external interrupt (NMI or INTR) occurs on the same CLK as the GP fault, the A-C0 steps of the 80486 will not correctly handle the GP fault.

FLAGS

O	D	I	T	S	Z	A	P	C

No flags are affected

JMP *disp8* (Short Direct)

11101011	*disp8*

disp8=1-byte signed relative displacement

TIMING

Operands	x	88	86	286	386	486
disp8	0	15	15	7+m	7+m	3

m represents the number of elements in the target instruction.

JMP *disp* (Near Direct)

11101001	*disp*

disp=2-byte displacement (16-bit address mode)
      4-byte displacement (32-bit address mode)

TIMING

Operands	x	88	86	286	386	486
disp16	0	15	15	7+m	7+m	3
disp32	0	–	–	–	7+m	3

m represents the number of elements in the target instruction.

JMP *reg/mem* (Near Indirect)

11111111	mod	100	r/m	disp

TIMING

Operands	x	88	86	286	386	486
reg16	0	11	11	7+m	7+m	5
mem16	0	18+EA	18+EA	11+m	10+m	5
reg32	0	–	–	–	7+m	5
mem32	0	–	–	–	10+m	5

m represents the number of elements in the target instruction.

JMP *disp16:disp* (Far Direct)

11101010	disp	disp16

disp=disp16: 2-byte value to be loaded into the IP register (16-bit address mode)
  disp32: 4-byte value to be loaded into the EIP register (32-bit address mode)

disp16=2-byte value to be loaded into the CS register

TIMING

Operands	x	88	86	286	386	486
disp16:disp16 Real mode	0	15	15	11+m	12+m	17
disp16:disp16 Protected mode	0	–	–	PM:23+m	PM:27+m	PM:19
disp16:disp16 Call gate, same privilege	0	–	–	PM:38+m	PM:45+m	PM:32
disp16:disp16 Call via Task State Segment	0	–	–	PM:175+m	PM:ts_1	PM:42+ts_3
disp16:disp16 Call via task gate	0	–	–	PM:180+m	PM:ts_2	PM:43+ts_3
disp16:disp32 Real mode	0	–	–	–	12+m	17
disp16:disp32 Protected mode	0	–	–	–	PM:27+m	PM:19

disp16:disp32 Call gate, same privilege	0	–	–	–	PM:45+m	PM:32
disp16:disp32 Jump via Task State Segment	0	–	–	–	PM:ts_1	PM:42+ts_3
disp16:disp32 Jump via task gate	0	–	–	–	PM:ts_2	PM:43+ts_3

m represents the number of elements in the target instruction.

ts_1, ts_2, and ts_3 represent the time to switch tasks as given in the table at the end of this instruction listing.

JMP *mem16:mem* (Far Indirect)

11111111	mod	101	r/m

mem=mem16: 2-byte value to be loaded into the IP register (16-bit address mode)
   mem32: 4-byte value to be loaded into the EIP register (32-bit address mode)

   mem16=2-byte value to be loaded into the CS register

TIMING

Operands	x	88	86	286	386	486
mem16:mem16 Real mode	0	24+EA	24+EA	15+m	43+m	13
mem16:mem16 Protected mode	0	–	–	PM:26+m	PM:31+m	PM:18
mem16:mem16 Call gate, same privilege	0	–	–	PM:41+m	PM:49+m	PM:31
mem16:mem16 Jump via Task State Segment	0	–	–	PM:178+m	PM:5+ts_1	PM:41+ts_3
mem16:mem16 Jump via task gate	0	–	–	PM:183+m	PM:5+ts_2	PM:42+ts_3
mem16:mem32 Real mode	0	–	–	–	43+m	13
mem16:mem32 Protected mode	0	–	–	–	PM:31+m	PM:18
mem16:mem32 Call gate, same privilege	0	–	–	–	PM:49+m	PM:31
mem16:mem32 Jump via Task State Segment	0	–	–	–	PM:5+ts_1	PM:41+ts_3
mem16:mem32 Jump via task gate	0	–	–	–	PM:5+ts_2	PM:42+ts_3

m represents the number of elements in the target instruction.

ts_1 indicates the timing required to switch tasks via a Task State Segment (TSS) as shown in the following table.

Old Task	New Task Type (via TSS)		
	386 TSS VM=0	386 TSS VM=1	286 TSS
386 TSS VM=0	DX:300 SX:392	DX:218 SX:309	DX:273 SX:285
286 TSS	DX:298 SX:310	DX:218 SX:229	DX:273 SX:285

ts_2 indicates the timing required to switch tasks via a task gate as shown in the following table.

Old Task	New Task Type (via task gate)		
	386 TSS VM=0	386 TSS VM=1	286 TSS
386 TSS VM=0	DX:309 SX:401	DX:226 SX:321	DX:282 SX:294
286 TSS	DX:307 SX:316	DX:226 SX:238	DX:282 SX:294

ts_3 indicates the timing required to switch tasks via a Task State Segment (TSS) or a task gate as shown in the following table.

Old Task	New Task Type (via task gate or TSS)		
	486 TSS	286 TSS	VM TSS
486 TSS 286 TSS	199	180	177

LAHF

Load AH with 8080 Flags

DESCRIPTION LAHF copies the values of the sign flag (SF), zero flag (ZF), auxiliary carry flag (AF), parity flag (PF), and carry flag (CF) into bits 7, 6, 4, 2, and 0, respectively, of the AH register.

The LAHF instruction was provided to make conversion of assembly languages programs written for the 8080 and 8085 to the 8086 easier. The utility of the command in 80x86 programming is reduced since the four remaining flags are not copied. The bits not copied from the FLAGS register are undefined. If access to all flags is required, use the PUSHF instruction and then POP the image of the flags into a register or memory location.

The LAHF instruction is also used extensively when programming the 80x87 to move the floating-point processor status flags into the 80x86 FLAGS register where they can then be tested using the J*cond* and SET*cond* instructions.

ALGORITHM
```
BIT(0 of AH)=CF
BIT(2 of AH)=PF
BIT(4 of AH)=AF
BIT(6 of AH)=ZF
BIT(7 of AH)=SF
```

FLAGS

O	D	I	T	S	Z	A	P	C

No flags are affected

LAHF

```
10011111
```

TIMING

Operands	x	88	86	286	386	486
(no operands)	0	4	4	2	2	3

LAR

Load Access Rights Byte (PM)

DESCRIPTION LAR op_1, op_2

LAR loads the access-rights byte of a descriptor, specified by the selector in op_2, into op_1 if the descriptor is accessible at the current privilege level (CPL) and at the selector's requestor privilege level (RPL).

ALGORITHM None

NOTES
1. On some versions of the 80386, the LAR does not work correctly if a null selector is specified as op_2. The instruction will operate on the descriptor at entry 0 in the GDT instead of unconditionally clearing the zero flag (ZF).

   To work around this, the descriptor in entry 0 of the GDT should be initialized to all zeros. Any access by LAR to this descriptor will fail, and will be reported with ZF=0, which is the desired behavior.

FLAGS

O	D	I	T	S	Z	A	P	C
					*			

LAR *reg,reg/mem*

00001111	00000010	mod	reg	r/m	disp

op_1=reg, op_2=mod+r/m

disp=0- or 2-byte displacement (16-bit address mode)
     0- or 4-byte displacement (32-bit address mode)

TIMING

Operands	x	88	86	286	386	486
reg16,reg16	0	–	–	PM:14	PM:15	PM:11
reg16,mem16	1	–	–	PM:16	PM:16	PM:11
reg32,reg32	0	–	–	–	PM:15	PM:11
reg32,mem32	1	–	–	–	PM:16	PM:11

LDS

Load Register and DS

DESCRIPTION LDS op_1, op_2

LDS loads a far pointer from the memory address specified by op_2 into the DS segment register and the register by op_1.

The LDS instruction transfers two words (16-bit address mode) or a word and a doubleword (32-bit address mode) from memory into the indicated registers. The word (16-bit address mode) or doubleword (32-bit address mode) at [*mem*] is loaded into *reg*, and the word at [*mem+2*] (16-bit address mode) or [*mem+4*] (32-bit address mode) is loaded into DS.

ALGORITHM
```
IF (OperandMode=16-bit) THEN
    reg16=WORD PTR [mem]
    DS=WORD PTR [mem+2]
ELSE
    reg32=DWORD PTR [mem]
    DS=WORD PTR [mem+4]
ENDIF
```

FLAGS

O	D	I	T	S	Z	A	P	C

No flags are affected

LDS *reg,mem*

11000101	mod	reg	r/m	disp

op_1=reg, op_2=mod+r/m

disp=2-byte displacement (16-bit address mode)
    4-byte displacement (32-bit address mode)

Note: If *mod*=11b, the operation is undefined

TIMING

Operands	x	88	86	286	386	486
reg16,mem32	2	24+EA	16+EA	7 PM:21	7 PM:22 VM:7	6 PM:12 VM:6
reg32,mem48	2	–	–	–	7 PM:22 VM:7	6 PM:12 VM:6

LEA

Load Effective Address (Offset)

DESCRIPTION   LEA op_1,op_2

LEA calculates the effective address of the memory operand specified by op_2 and stores it in the register specified by op_1.

The effective address of a memory operand is automatically calculated by the processor when it performs a memory reference. In some cases, however, the effective address of an operand must be calculated explicitly by a program (to pass to a subroutine, for example). LEA allows the effective address of a memory operand to be calculated at execution time (as opposed to assemble time). For example, assume that the entry point into a portion of code is given by the first word stored at the code header. The offset of the header is in the DI register. The following instructions would point SI to the entry point.

```
MOV BX,[DI]
LEA SI,[DI][BX]
```

Note, however, that the assembler is able to resolve most memory references at assemble time. The result is typically an offset that is encoded into the instruction as immediate data. The same information can also be calculated at execution time using LEA. Using LEA often requires more bytes and more execution time than the equivalent assemble-time address resolution. For example, consider the following two instructions that load the SI register with the offset of a lookup table.

```
MOV SI,OFFSET TABLE      ;size=3 bytes, time=4 clocks
LEA SI,TABLE             ;size=4 bytes, time=8 clocks
```

LEA can also be used to perform simple math among registers. For example, if you wish to load the value BX-30h into the AX register, the instruction LEA AX,[BX-30h] will perform the function handily. Bear in mind that the *r/m* field in the opcode limits the choice of registers that can be used in the memory reference to index and base with an optional displacement. The 80386 and 80486 allow more choices, including scaling to be used.

If the current address-size mode and the size of op_1 match, the offset value is simply loaded into the register. If a 16-bit effective address is loaded into a 32-bit register, the high-order 16-bits of the register will be filled with zeros. If an attempt is made to load a 32-bit address into a 16-bit register, the address is truncated and only the low-order 16 bits are transferred.

ALGORITHM op_1=EA(op_2)

O	D	I	T	S	Z	A	P	C

No flags are affected

LEA *reg,mem*

10001101	mod	reg	r/m	disp

op_1=reg, op_2=mod+r/m

disp=0- or 2-byte displacement (16-bit address mode)
   0- or 4-byte displacement (32-bit address mode)

TIMING

Operands	x	88	86	286	386	486
reg16,mem	0	2+EA	2+EA	3	2	1[1]
reg32,mem	0	–	–	–	2	1[1]

[1] Add one clock if EA includes both a base and index register.

LEAVE

Destroy Stack Frame

DESCRIPTION LEAVE reverses the action of the ENTER instruction, destroying the stack frame and releasing the stack space used by a procedure for local storage.

The LEAVE instruction restores the previous value of BP, the caller's frame pointer. All temporary data stored on the stack is lost.

ALGORITHM
```
IF (StackMode=16-bit) THEN
    SP=BP
ELSE
    ESP=EBP
ENDIF
IF (OperandMode=16-bit) THEN
    POP BP
ELSE
    POP EBP
ENDIF
```

FLAGS

O	D	I	T	S	Z	A	P	C

No flags are affected

LEAVE

11001001

TIMING

Operands	x	88	86	286	386	486
(no operands)	0	–	–	5	4	5

LES

Load Register and ES

DESCRIPTION `LES op₁,op₂`

LES loads a far pointer from the memory address specified by op_2 into the ES segment register and the register by op_1.

The LES instruction transfers two words (16-bit address mode) or a word and a doubleword (32-bit address mode) from memory into the indicated registers. The word (16-bit address mode) or doubleword (32-bit address mode) at [*mem*] is loaded into *reg*, and the word at [*mem*+2] (16-bit address mode) or [*mem*+4] (32-bit address mode) is loaded into ES.

ALGORITHM
```
IF (OperandMode=16 bit) THEN
    reg16=WORD PTR [mem]
    ES=WORD PTR [mem+2]
ELSE
    reg32=DWORD PTR [mem]
    ES=WORD PTR [mem+4]
ENDIF
```

FLAGS

O	D	I	T	S	Z	A	P	C

No flags are affected

LES *reg,mem*

11000100	mod	reg	r/m	disp

op_1=reg, op_2=mod+r/m

disp=2-byte displacement (16-bit address mode)
4-byte displacement (32-bit address mode)

If *mod*=11b, the operation is undefined

TIMING

Operands	x	88	86	286	386	486
reg16,mem32	2	24+EA	16+EA	7 PM:21	7 PM:22 VM:7	6 PM:12 VM:6
reg32,mem48	2	–	–	7 PM:21	7 PM:22 VM:7	6 PM:12 VM:6

LFS

Load Register and FS

DESCRIPTION   LFS op_1, op_2

LFS loads a far pointer from the memory address specified by op_2 into the FS segment register and the register by op_1.

The LFS instruction transfers two words (16-bit address mode) or a word and a doubleword (32-bit address mode) from memory into the indicated registers. The word (16-bit address mode) or doubleword (32-bit address mode) at [*mem*] is loaded into *reg*, and the word at [*mem*+2] (16-bit address mode) or [*mem*+4] (32-bit address mode) is loaded into FS.

ALGORITHM
```
IF (OperandMode=16 bit) THEN
    reg16=WORD PTR [mem]
    FS=WORD PTR [mem+2]
ELSE
    reg32=DWORD PTR [mem]
    FS=WORD PTR [mem+4]
ENDIF
```

FLAGS

O	D	I	T	S	Z	A	P	C

No flags are affected

LFS *reg,mem*

00001111	10110100	mod	reg	r/m	disp

op_1=reg, op_2=mod+r/m

disp=2-byte displacement (16-bit address mode)
       4-byte displacement (32-bit address mode)

If *mod*=11b, the operation is undefined

TIMING

Operands	x	88	86	286	386	486
reg16,mem32	2	–	–	–	7 PM:25 VM:7	6 PM:12 VM:6
reg32,mem48	2	–	–	–	7 PM:25 VM:7	6 PM:12 VM:6

LGDT

Load Global Descriptor Table Register

DESCRIPTION   LGDT *op*

LGDT loads a linear base address and limit value from the 6-byte operand in memory specified by *op* into the global descriptor table register (GDTR).

The LIMIT field of the GDTR is loaded from the first two bytes at the specified effective address. The BASE field is loaded from the subsequent doubleword; the high-order 8 bits are ignored on the 80286.

The LGDT instruction is typically used in operating-system software.

ALGORITHM
```
IF (OperandMode=16-bit) THEN
   GDTR.Limit=mem16
   GDTR.Base=mem32 AND FFFFFFh ;lower 24 bits
ELSE  ;OperandMode=32-bit
   GDTR.Limit=mem16
   GDTR.Base=mem32
ENDIF
```

FLAGS

O	D	I	T	S	Z	A	P	C

No flags are affected

LGDT *mem16:mem32*

00001111	00000001	mod	010	r/m	disp

disp=2-byte displacement (16-bit address mode)
4-byte displacement (32-bit address mode)

If *mod*=11b, the operation is undefined

TIMING

Operands	x	88	86	286	386	486
mem16:mem32	2	–	–	11	11	12

LGS

Load Register and GS

DESCRIPTION LGS op_1, op_2

LGS loads a far pointer from the memory address specified by op_2 into the GS segment register and the register by op_1.

The LGS instruction transfers two words (16-bit address mode) or a word and a doubleword (32-bit mode) from memory into the indicated registers. The word (16-bit address mode) or doubleword (32-bit address mode) at [*mem*] is loaded into *reg*, and the word at [*mem*+2] (16-bit address mode) or [*mem*+4] (32-bit address mode) is loaded into GS.

ALGORITHM
```
IF (OperandMode=16 bit) THEN
    reg16=WORD PTR [mem]
    GS=WORD PTR [mem+2]
ELSE  ;OperandMode=32-bit
    reg32=DWORD PTR [mem]
    GS=WORD PTR [mem+4]
ENDIF
```

FLAGS

O	D	I	T	S	Z	A	P	C

No flags are affected

LGS *reg,mem*

11000101	10110101	mod	reg	r/m	disp

op_1=reg, op_2=mod+r/m

disp=2-byte displacement (16-bit address mode)
    4-byte displacement (32-bit address mode)

If *mod*=11b, the operation is undefined

TIMING

Operands	x	88	86	286	386	486
reg16,mem32	2	–	–	–	7 PM:25	6 PM:12 VM:6
reg32,mem48	2	–	–	–	7 PM:25	6 PM:12 VM:6

LIDT

Load Interrupt Descriptor Table Register

DESCRIPTION LIDT *op*

LIDT loads a linear base address and limit value from the 6-byte operand in memory specified by *op* into the interrupt descriptor table register (IDTR).

The LIMIT field of the IDTR is loaded from the first two bytes at the specified effective address. The BASE field is loaded from the subsequent doubleword; the high-order 8 bits are ignored on the 80286.

The LIDT instruction is typically used in operating-system software.

ALGORITHM
```
IF (OperandMode=16-bit) THEN
    IDTR.Limit=mem16
    IDTR.Base=mem32 AND FFFFFFh ;low-order 24 bits
ELSE  ;OperandMode=32-bit
    IDTR.Limit=mem16
    IDTR.Base=mem32
ENDIF
```

FLAGS

O	D	I	T	S	Z	A	P	C

No flags are affected

LIDT *mem16:mem32*

00001111	00000001	mod	011	r/m	disp

disp=2-byte displacement (16-bit address mode)
4-byte displacement (32-bit address mode)

If *mod*=11b, the operation is undefined

TIMING

Operands	x	88	86	286	386	486
mem16:mem32	2	–	–	12	11	12

LLDT

Load Local Descriptor Table Register (PM)

DESCRIPTION LLDT *op*

LLDT loads a word operand specified by *op* into the Local Descriptor Table Register (LDTR).

The LLDT instruction is typically used in operating-system software.

ALGORITHM LDTR=*op*

FLAGS

O	D	I	T	S	Z	A	P	C

No flags are affected

LLDT *reg16/mem16*

00001111	00000000	mod	010	r/m	disp

disp=0- or 2-byte displacement (16-bit address mode)
        0- or 4-byte displacement (32-bit address mode)

TIMING

Operands	x	88	86	286	386	486
reg16	0	–	–	PM:17	PM:20	PM:11
mem16	1	–	–	PM:19	PM:24	PM:11

LMSW

Load Machine Status Word

DESCRIPTION   LMSW *op*

LMSW loads the Machine Status Word (MSW), an internal register in the processor, from the operand specified by *op*.

The LMSW instruction is used to switch to protected mode on the 80286, but it cannot be used to switch back to real mode. The LMSW instruction is typically used in operating-system software.

On the 80386 and 80486 this instruction is provided for compatibility with 80286 software and programs should use MOV CR0,*op* instead. This instruction does not affect the PG or ET bits, and it cannot be used to clear the PE bit. The Operand-Mode has no affect on this instruction.

ALGORITHM   MSW=*op*

FLAGS

O	D	I	T	S	Z	A	P	C

No flags are affected

LMSW *reg16/mem16*

00001111	00000001	*mod*	110	*r/m*	*disp*

disp=0- or 2-byte displacement (16-bit address mode)
     0- or 4-byte displacement (32-bit address mode)

TIMING

Operands	x	88	86	286	386	486
reg16	0	–	–	3	11	13
mem16	1	–	–	6	14	13

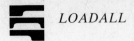
LOADALL

Load All Processor Registers

DESCRIPTION The LOADALL instruction is an undocumented and unsupported instruction that loads the entire state of the processor—the visible registers as well as the internal caches—from real memory. LOADALL was conceived as a way for real-mode programs to run in an 80286 protected-mode multitasking environment with full protection between it and other tasks.

LOADALL is implemented as opcode 0Fh 05h on the 80286 and as 0Fh 07h on the 80386 and 80486. By its nature, this instruction is complex and requires a detailed knowledge of the internal operation of the processors; a tutorial for using this instruction is not presented here. This information is presented only for completeness and to aid your understanding should you encounter the instruction in an application.

The circuit design for the 80286 is stable and is unlikely to be revised. The 80286 version of the LOADALL instruction, therefore, is also relatively stable. Because the designs for the 80386SX and 80486 are still being revised, the chances are good that this instruction will disappear. In either case, *it is recommended that you not use these instructions in your applications.*

80286 LOADALL: The LOADALL instruction reads a 102-byte area of physical memory starting at address 000800h. The entire execution state of the 80286 is defined upon completion of this instruction. The descriptor cache registers for the ES, DS, SS, CS, TR, and LDT are loaded directly from this area. The format of this area is shown below.

Physical Memory Address	Size in Bytes	CPU Register Loaded
800h	6	None
806h	2	MSW
808h	14	None
816h	2	TR
818h	2	FLAGS
81Ah	2	IP
81Ch	2	LDT
81Eh	2	DS
820h	2	SS
822h	2	CS
824h	2	ES
826h	2	DI
828h	2	SI
82Ah	2	BP

82Ch	2	SP
82Eh	2	BX
830h	2	DX
832h	2	CX
834h	2	AX
836h	2	ES descriptor cache
83Ch	2	CS descriptor cache
842h	2	SS descriptor cache
848h	6	DS descriptor cache
84Eh	6	GDTR
854h	6	LDT descriptor cache
85Ah	6	IDTR
860h	6	TSS descriptor cache

The descriptor cache entries have the following format:

Byte	Description
0-2	24-bit physical base address of the segment.
3	Access-rights byte in the format of the access byte in a descriptor. The present bit is redefined as a valid bit. If the valid bit is zero, the descriptor is considered invalid and an attempted memory access using the descriptor will cause exception 0Dh. Simply loading an invalid descriptor will not cause an exception. The DPL fields of the SS and CS descriptor caches determine the CPL.
4-5	16-bit segment limit.

The GDTR and IDTR are in the following format:

Byte	Description
0-2	24-bit physical base address of the segment.
3	Must be 0.
4-5	16-bit segment limit.

No checking is performed between the visible portion of the selector and the invisible portion (the descriptor table entry). No checking of the type or access rights defined by the descriptor is performed. Any new descriptors defined by this instruction will be automatically used by subsequent processor or coprocessor memory references. A subsequent register load will reload the associated descriptor cache register in the normal manner according to the operating mode of the CPU.

80386/80486 LOADALL: The LOADALL instruction reads a 204-byte area of physical memory starting at the memory location pointed to by ES:EDI. The entire execution state of the 80386 and 80486 is defined upon completion of this instruction.

The descriptor cache registers for the ES, DS, SS, CS, TR, and LDT are loaded directly from this area. The format of this area is shown below.

Offset	Size in Bytes	CPU Register Loaded
0h	4	CR0
4h	4	EFLAGS
8h	4	EIP
Ch	4	EDI
10h	4	ESI
14h	4	EBP
18h	4	ESP
1Ch	4	EBX
20h	4	EDX
24h	4	ECX
28h	4	EAX
2Ch	4	DR6
30h	4	DR7
34h	4	TR
38h	4	LDT
3Ch	4	GS (zero extended)
40h	4	FS (zero extended)
44h	4	DS (zero extended)
48h	4	SS (zero extended)
4Ch	4	CS (zero extended)
50h	4	ES (zero extended)
54h	12	TSS descriptor cache
60h	12	IDT descriptor cache
6Ch	12	GDT descriptor cache
78h	12	LDT descriptor cache
84h	12	GS descriptor cache
90h	12	FS descriptor cache
9Ch	12	DS descriptor cache
A8h	12	SS descriptor cache
B4h	12	CS descriptor cache
C0h	12	ES descriptor cache

The descriptor cache entries have the following format:

Byte	Description
0	0
1	Access-rights byte in the format of the access byte in a descriptor. The present bit is redefined as a valid bit. If the valid bit is zero, the descriptor is considered invalid and an attempted memory access using the descriptor will cause exception 0Dh. Simply loading an invalid descriptor will not cause an exception. The DPL fields of the SS and CS descriptor caches determine the CPL.
2–3	0
4–7	32-bit physical base address of the segment.
8–11	32-bit segment limit.

No checking is performed between the visible portion of the selector and invisible portion (the descriptor table entry). No checking of the type or access rights defined by the descriptor is performed. Any new descriptors defined by this instruction will be automatically used by subsequent processor or coprocessor memory references. A subsequent register load will reload the associated descriptor cache register in the normal manner according to the operating mode of the CPU.

ALGORITHM None

FLAGS

O	D	I	T	S	Z	A	P	C
*	*	*	*	*	*	*	*	*

LOADALL

00001111	00000101

TIMING

Operands	x	88	86	286	386	486
(no operands)	51	–	–	195	–	–

LOADALL

00001111	00000111

TIMING

Operands	x	88	86	286	386	486
(no operands)	102	–	–	–	?[1]	?[1]

[1] No timing available. It is, after all, undocumented.

LOCK

Assert Bus Lock Signal

DESCRIPTION LOCK is a 1-byte prefix that asserts the bus LOCK signal while the instruction following executes.

When the processor is working in a multiple-processor environment, it must typically ensure that reads-from or writes-to memory can occur without interference from other processors. The LOCK prefix causes the bus to be locked for the duration of the execution of the following instruction. This prefix is most often used in test-and-set sequences that involve exchanging a register with memory.

The LOCK prefix activates the bus LOCK# signal for the instructions shown below for the processors listed.

8086/8088	All
80286	INS MOVS,OUTS XCHG
80386/80486	BT,BTC,BTR,BTS *mem,reg/immed* ADC,ADD,AND,OR,SBB,SUB,XOR *mem,reg/immed* DEC,INC,NEG,NOT *mem* XCHG *reg,mem* XCHG *mem,reg*
80486	XADD CMPXCHG

ALGORITHM None

NOTES
1. The XCHG instruction causes the 80286 and later processors to automatically generate the LOCK# signal regardless of the presence of the LOCK prefix.

2. Using the LOCK prefix on instructions other than those listed will generate an invalid opcode exception.

FLAGS

O	D	I	T	S	Z	A	P	C

No flags are affected

LOCK

11110000

TIMING

Operands	x	88	86	286	386	486
(no operands)	0	2	2	0	0	1

LODS/LODSB/ LODSW/LODSD

Load String Operand from Memory into Accumulator

DESCRIPTION ````
LODSB

LODSW

LODSD

LODS op
````

LODS copies a memory operand, pointed to by the source index register (SI/ESI), into the accumulator (AL/AX/EAX) while automatically updating the index addresses in preparation for the next transfer.

The LODS instruction is used to transfer data from memory into the accumulator while automatically updating the effective address in preparation for the next transfer. The source index register used to form the effective address for the transfer is determined by the current address-size attribute. If the address-size attribute is 16-bit, then the SI register will be used. If 32-bit addressing is in effect, then the ESI register will be used.

The options that must be defined when using this instruction are the operand size, the segment register to be used with the effective address, and whether the source index will be incremented or decremented after the transfer.

The size of the memory operand (and therefore, the destination register) may be specified explicitly in the mnemonic or by an operand. In the first method, the transfer size is explicitly declared by using the B, W, or D suffix in combination with the LODS mnemonic. The resulting instructions (LODSB, LODSW, and LODSD) will transfer a byte, word, or doubleword to the AL, AX, or EAX register, respectively. The source index register will then be adjusted by 1, 2, or 4 to point to the next operand to be loaded.

The size-explicit forms of the instruction always use the DS register when addressing memory. The general form of the instruction (LODS) takes as an argument a memory operand that defines the size of the transfer only. *The effective address of the operand is not used as the address of the transfer;* the data is always loaded using the source index as a pointer to memory. The use of an operand also provides a syntactically convenient method for specifying a segment override.

For example, the instruction LODS BYTE PTR [BX] would be equivalent to the LODSB form and would transfer the byte at DS:[SI] to AL. The instruction LODS BYTE PTR CS:[BX], however, would transfer the byte at CS:[SI] to AL. In either case, the effective address specified ([BX]) is ignored.

The source index register will be incremented by the size of the operand if the direction flag (DF) has been cleared to 0 (by the CLD instruction, for example).
````

The register will be decremented by the size of the operand if DF is set to 1 (by the STD instruction).

For example, assume that the address-size attribute is 16-bits and DF is cleared. The instruction LODSB will be equivalent to the following instructions.

```
MOV  AL,BYTE PTR DS:[SI]
INC  SI
```

Although all forms of the LODS instruction may be encoded with the REP prefix, this is not normally done. The effect would be to have each load operation overwrite the previous value in the accumulator; all but the last value loaded would be lost.

ALGORITHM

```
opsize=SIZEOF(operand)    ;Declared by mnemonic or operand
IF (LODS op) THEN
  seg=SEGMENTOF(op)
ELSE
  seg="DS"
ENDIF
IF (AddressMode=16-bit) THEN
  source_index="SI"
ELSE   ;AddressMode=32-bit
  source_index="ESI"
ENDIF
IF (opsize=1) THEN
  AL=BYTE PTR seg:[source_index]
ELSEIF (opsize=2) THEN
  AX=WORD PTR seg:[source_index]
ELSE
  EAX=DWORD PTR seg:[source_index]
ENDIF
IF (DF=0)   ;CLD
  source_index=source_index + opsize
ELSE   ;STD
  source_index=source_index - opsize
ENDIF
```

FLAGS

O	D	I	T	S	Z	A	P	C

No flags are affected

LODSB/LODSW/LODSD

LODS *reg/mem*

```
1010110w
```

w=0, operands are 8-bit
  1, operands are 16-bit (16-bit operand mode)
                  32-bit (32-bit operand mode)

Note: If present, the *reg/mem* operand specifies the operand size for the operation and is not included in the encoding. A segment override may also be specified.

TIMING

Operands	x	88	86	286	386	486
LODSB LODSW	1	B:12 W:16	12	5	5	5
LODSD	1	–	–	–	5	5
REP LODSB REP LODSW	r			5+4r	5+6r	7+4r
REP LODSD	r	–	–	–	5+6r	7+4r

r represents the number of repetitions executed when used with the REP prefix.

PM_1 indicates the timing when CPL≤IOPL.

PM_2 indicates the timing when CPL>IOPL.

LOOP

Decrement CX/ECX and Jump If Not Zero

DESCRIPTION LOOP *op*

LOOP decrements CX/ECX by 1 and transfers control to the target operand specified by *op* if CX/ECX is not 0. Otherwise, control passes to the following instruction.

LOOP is a powerful instruction that allows loop logic to be coded compactly. On the more advanced processors, however, LOOP requires more execution time than would the same logic expressed in discrete instructions. For example, the two instructions DEC CX and JZ *label* require $9+m$ clocks on the 80386 compared to $11+m$ for the LOOP instruction.

ALGORITHM
```
IF (AddressMode=16-bit) THEN
   count=CX
ELSE  ;AddressMode=32-bit
   count=ECX
ENDIF
count=count-1
IF (count_0) THEN
   IF (OperandMode=16-bit) THEN
     IP=IP+SIGN_EXTEND(disp8)
   ELSE  ;OperandMode=32-bit
     EIP=EIP+SIGN_EXTEND(disp8)
   ENDIF
ENDIF
```

FLAGS

O	D	I	T	S	Z	A	P	C

No flags are affected

LOOP *disp8*

11100010	*disp8*

disp8=1-byte signed relative displacement

TIMING

Operands	x	88	86	286	386	486
disp8	0	17 NJ:5	17 NJ:5	8+m NJ:4	11+m	7 NJ:6

LOOPE/LOOPZ

Decrement CX and Loop While CX≠0 AND ZF=1

DESCRIPTION
```
LOOPE op
LOOPZ op
```

LOOPE/LOOPZ decrements the CX (ECX) register by 1 and transfers control to the memory address specified by *op* if CX/ECX is not 0 and the zero flag (ZF) is set to 1. Otherwise, control passes to the following instruction.

The LOOPE instruction, and its alias LOOPZ, are typically used in conjunction with the SCAS and CMPS string primitives. The result of these instructions, *not* the adjustment to CX/ECX, is used to set the flags. LOOPE/LOOPZ does not itself change any flags.

ALGORITHM
```
IF (AddressMode=16-bit) THEN
   count=CX
ELSE   ;AddressMode=32-bit
   count=ECX
ENDIF
count=count-1
IF (count≠0 AND ZF=1) THEN
   IF (OperandMode=16-bit) THEN
     IP=IP+SIGN_EXTEND(disp8)
   ELSE   ;OperandMode=32-bit
     EIP=EIP+SIGN_EXTEND(disp8)
   ENDIF
ENDIF
```

FLAGS

O	D	I	T	S	Z	A	P	C

No flags are affected

LOOPE *disp8*

LOOPZ *disp8*

11100001	disp8

disp8=1-byte signed relative displacement

TIMING

Operands	x	88	86	286	386	486
disp8	0	18 NJ:6	18 NJ:6	8+*m* NJ:4	11+*m*	9 NJ:6

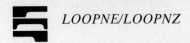

LOOPNE/LOOPNZ

Decrement CX and Loop While CX≠0 AND ZF≠1

DESCRIPTION
```
LOOPNE op
LOOPNZ op
```

LOOPNE/LOOPNZ decrements the CX/ECX register by 1 and transfers control to the target operand if CX/ECX is not 0 and the zero flag (ZF) is cleared to 0. Otherwise, control passes to the following instruction.

The LOOPNE instruction, and its alias LOOPNZ, are typically used in conjunction with the SCAS and CMPS string primitives. The result of these instructions, *not* the adjustment to CX/ECX, is used to set the flags. LOOPNE/LOOPNZ does not itself change any flags.

ALGORITHM
```
IF (AddressMode=16-bit) THEN
   count=CX
ELSE  ;AddressMode=32-bit
   count=ECX
ENDIF
count=count-1
IF (count≠0 AND ZF≠1) THEN
   IF (OperandMode=16-bit) THEN
      IP=IP+SIGN_EXTEND(disp8)
   ELSE  ;OperandMode=32-bit
      EIP=EIP+SIGN_EXTEND(disp8)
   ENDIF
ENDIF
```

FLAGS

O	D	I	T	S	Z	A	P	C

No flags are affected

LOOPNE *disp8*

LOOPNZ *disp8*

11100000	disp8

disp8=1-byte signed relative displacement

TIMING

Operands	x	88	86	286	386	486
disp8	0	19 NJ:5	19 NJ:5	8+m NJ:4	11+m	9 NJ:6

LSL

Load Segment Limit (PM)

DESCRIPTION LSL op_1, op_2

The limit field of a segment descriptor, specified by the selector given by op_2, is loaded into the destination operand specified by op_1, which must be a register.

If the transfer is successful, the zero flag (ZF) is set to 1. Otherwise, ZF is cleared to 0 and the op_1 is unchanged. The LSL instruction is typically used in operating-system software.

ALGORITHM None

NOTES

1. On some versions of the 80386, the LSL does not work correctly if a null selector is specified as op_2. The instruction will operate on the descriptor at entry 0 in the GDT instead of unconditionally clearing the zero flag (ZF).

   To work around this, the descriptor in entry 0 of the GDT should be initialized to all zeros. Any access by LSL to this descriptor will fail, and will be reported with ZF=0, which is the desired behavior.

2. The LSL instruction should not be followed immediately by these instructions that use the stack implicitly: CALL, ENTER, IRET, POP, POPA, POPF, PUSH, PUSHA, PUSHF, and RET. On some versions of the 80386, if the LSL operation succeeded, executing one of these instructions may leave SP/ESP with an incorrect value. Note that stack operations resulting from exceptions or interrupts that follow LSL do update the stack pointer correctly.

FLAGS

O	D	I	T	S	Z	A	P	C
					*			

LSL reg,reg/mem

00001111	00000011	mod	reg	r/m	disp

op_1=reg, op_2=mod+r/m

disp=0- or 2-byte displacement (16-bit address mode)
     0- or 4-byte displacement (32-bit address mode)

Operands	x	88	86	286	386	486
reg16,reg16	0	–	–	PM:14	PM_b:21 PM_p:25	PM:10
reg16,mem16	1	–	–	PM:16	PM_b:22 PM_p:26	PM:10
reg32,reg32	0	–	–	–	PM_b:21 PM_p:25	PM:10
reg32,mem32	1	–	–	–	PM_b:22 PM_p:26	PM:10

PM_b: descriptor has a byte granular segment limit.

PM_p: descriptor has a page granular segment limit.

LSS

Load Register and SS

DESCRIPTION   LSS op_1, op_2

LFS loads a far pointer from the memory address specified by op_2 into the FS segment register and the register by op_1.

The LSS instruction transfers two words (16-bit address mode) or a word and a doubleword (32-bit address mode) from memory into the indicated registers. The word (16-bit address mode) or doubleword (32-bit address mode) at [*mem*] is loaded into *reg* and the word at [*mem+2*] (16-bit address mode) or [*mem+4*] (32-bit address mode) is loaded into SS.

ALGORITHM
```
IF (operand size mode=16 bit) THEN
    reg16=WORD PTR [mem]
    SS=WORD PTR [mem+2]
ELSE
    reg32=DWORD PTR [mem]
    SS=WORD PTR [mem+4]
ENDIF
```

FLAGS

O	D	I	T	S	Z	A	P	C

No flags are affected

LSS reg,mem

00001111	10110010	mod	reg	r/m	disp

op_1=reg, op_2=mod+r/m

disp=2-byte displacement (16-bit address mode)
    4-byte displacement (32-bit address mode)

If *mod*=11b, the operation is undefined

TIMING

Operands	x	88	86	286	386	486
reg16,mem32	2	24+EA	16+EA	7 PM:21	7 PM:22 VM:7	6 PM:12 VM:6
reg32,mem48	2	—	—	7 PM:21	7 PM:22 VM:7	6 PM:12 VM:6

LTR

Load Task Register (PM)

DESCRIPTION   LTR *op*

LTR loads the task register from the operand specified by *op* and marks the loaded Task State Segment (TSS) busy. No task switch is performed.

The LTR instruction is typically used in operating-system software.

ALGORITHM   TR=*op*

FLAGS

O	D	I	T	S	Z	A	P	C

No flags are affected

LTR *reg16/mem16*

00001111	00000000	mod	011	r/m	disp

disp=0- or 2-byte displacement (16-bit address mode)
        0- or 4-byte displacement (32-bit address mode)

TIMING

Operands	x	88	86	286	386	486
reg16	0	–	–	PM:17	PM:23	PM:20
mem16	1	–	–	PM:19	PM:27	PM:20

MOV

Move Data

DESCRIPTION MOV op_1, op_2

MOV transfers a byte, word, or doubleword from op_2 to op_1.

The MOV instruction is the workhorse of the 80x86 family for transferring data between registers and memory. And while all programmers should be familiar with the different instruction forms, the assembler will usually generate the most efficient form for the move.

Note that if the MOV instruction is to be valid, both operands must be the same size. The instruction MOV BX,AL, for example, is both logically and syntactically incorrect.

The CS, IP, and FLAGS registers cannot be accessed with this instruction. Special forms are provided for the special registers available on the advanced processors.

When a 16-bit segment register is specified as the source operand, the MOV instruction behaves differently depending on whether 16- or 32-bit operand size is in effect. If the operand size is 32-bits and the destination (op_1) is a register, the segment register is copied into the low-order 16 bits of the destination register and the high-order 16 bits of the destination register are undefined. If the operand size is 16-bits, the segment register is copied into the low-order 16 bits of the destination register and the high-order 16 bits of the destination register are unchanged. If the destination is a memory operand, the segment register is written to memory as a 16-bit quantity, regardless of the current operand size; bits 16-31 of the destination should be cleared if necessary.

ALGORITHM $op_1 = op_2$

NOTES

1. When the MOV *sreg,reg* form is used on the 8088 and 8086, interrupts will be cleared until the following instruction has executed. This property was designed to allow the stack segment (SS) and stack pointer (SP) registers to be set without an interrupt occurring between the two instructions. If such an interrupt did occur, the SS:SP register pair would most likely point to an invalid stack and cause the system to crash. Early versions of the 8088 and 8086 chips did not implement this function correctly. The 80286 and later processors disable interrupts only when *sreg*=SS.

2. On some versions of the 80386, breakpoints specified by the debug registers DR0-DR3 may produce spurious breakpoints after a MOV from CR3, TR6, or TR7 is executed. The contents of DR0-DR3 are not affected. This condition will persist until the processor executes the next jump instruction. The breakpoint instruction (opcode CCh) and the single-step trap are not affected.

To avoid this situation, before MOVing from CR3, TR6, or TR7, breakpoints should be disabled. After the MOV, a jump should be executed, then breakpoints should be re-enabled.

3. The 80386 executes the MOV to/from special registers (CR*n*, DR*n*, TR*n*) regardless of the setting of the MOD field. The MOD field should be set to 11b, but an early 80386 documentation error indicated that the MOD field value was a don't care. Early versions of the 80486 detect a MOD≠11b as an illegal opcode. This was changed in later versions to ignore the value of MOD. Assemblers that generate MOD≠11b for these instructions will fail on some 80486s.

4. On the 80386, the MOV to/from DR4 and DR5 instructions were aliased to MOV to/from DR6 and DR7, respectively. Early versions of the 80486 generate an invalid opcode for this encoding. Later versions of the 80486 execute the aliased instructions.

5. If a prefetch is pending when a MOV TR5,*reg32* instruction is executed with the control bits (bits 0 and 1) set for a cache read, write, or flush, the A-C0 step of the 80486 processor may hang. To avoid this, use the following code sequence:

```
        JMP     Label       ;Flush the prefetch queue and
                            ; begin the first prefetch at Label
ALIGN 16                    ;Start on a 16-byte boundary
Label:  NOP                 ;Lets 2nd prefetch begin
        IN      AL,port     ;Ensures both prefetches complete
        MOV     TR5,EAX     ;EAX contains the new TR5 value
        NOP                 ;These NOPs ensure no new prefetch
        NOP                 ; started until MOV TR5 completes
```

6. On the A-C0 step of the 80486, if the MOV CR0,*reg32* instruction is used to disable the cache, a line in the cache may be corrupted. Since this instruction is not typically used by applications, this problem should not occur. The code shown below will avoid the problem. Note that the NMI and faults/traps should not occur during this code sequence.

```
        PUSHFD
        CLI
        MOV     BL,CS:Label
        MOV     CRØ,EAX
Label:  POPFD
```

FLAGS	O	D	I	T	S	Z	A	P	C	
										No flags are affected

MOV *reg/mem,reg/mem*

| 100010dw | mod | reg | r/m | disp |

d=0, op_1=mod+r/m op_2=reg
  1, op_1=reg op_2=mod+r/m

w=0 operands are 8-bit
   1 operands are 16-bit (16-bit operand mode)
           32-bit (32-bit operand mode)

disp=0- or 2-byte displacement (16-bit address mode)
       0- or 4-byte displacement (32-bit address mode)

TIMING

Operands	x	88	86	286	386	486
reg,reg	0	2	2	2	2	1
reg,mem	1	B:8+EA W:12+EA	8+EA	3	4	1
mem,reg	1	B:9+EA W:13+EA	9+EA	5	2	1

MOV *reg,immed*

| 1011w | reg | immed |

w=0 operands are 8-bit
   1 operands are 16-bit (16-bit operand mode)
           32-bit (32-bit operand mode)

immed=1- or 2-byte immediate data (16-bit address mode)
         1- or 4-byte immediate data (32-bit address mode)

TIMING

Operands	x	88	86	286	386	486
reg,immed	0	4	4	2	2	1

MOV *reg/mem,immed*

| 1100011w | mod | 000 | r/m | immed |

w=0 operands are 8-bit
   1 operands are 16-bit (16-bit operand mode)
           32-bit (32-bit operand mode)

immed=1- or 2-byte immediate data (16-bit address mode)
         1- or 4-byte immediate data (32-bit address mode)

Note: This encoding is not normally used to move immediate data into a register. The MOV *reg,immed* instruction is provided for this purpose and the opcode occupies only a single byte.

TIMING

Operands	x	88	86	286	386	486
reg,immed	0	10	10	2	2	1
mem,immed	1	B:10+EA W:14+EA	10+EA	3	2	1

MOV *accum,mem*

1010000w	*disp*

w=0 operands are 8-bit
    1 operands are 16-bit (16-bit operand mode)
        32-bit (32-bit operand mode)

disp=2-byte displacement (16-bit address mode)
    4-byte displacement (32-bit address mode)

TIMING

Operands	x	88	86	286	386	486
accum,mem	1	B:10 W:14	10	5	4	1

MOV *mem,accum*

1010001w	*disp*

w=0 operands are 8-bit
    1 operands are 16-bit (16-bit operand mode)
        32-bit (32-bit operand mode)

disp=2-byte displacement (16-bit address mode)
    4-byte displacement (32-bit address mode)

TIMING

Operands	x	88	86	286	386	486
mem,accum	1	B:10 W:14	10	3	2	1

MOV *sreg,reg/mem*

10001110	*mod*	*sreg*	*r/m*	*disp*

op_1=sreg, op_2=mod+r/m

disp=2-byte displacement (16-bit address mode)
    4-byte displacement (32-bit address mode)

TIMING

Operands	x	88	86	286	386	486
sreg,reg16	0	2	2	2 PM:17	2 PM:18 VM:2	3 PM:9 VM:3
sreg,mem16	1	12+EA	8+EA	5 PM:19	5 PM:19 VM:5	3 PM:9 VM:3

MOV *reg/mem,sreg*

10001100	mod	sreg	r/m	disp

op₁=sreg, op₂=mod+r/m

op₁=sreg, op₂=mod+r/m

disp=2-byte displacement (16-bit address mode)
        4 byte displacement (32-bit address mode)

TIMING

Operands	x	88	86	286	386	486
reg16,sreg	0	2	2	2	2	3
mem16,sreg	1	13+EA	9+EA	3	2	3

MOV *reg32/creg,reg32/creg*

00001111	001000d0	11	rrr	r/m

d=0,   op₁=reg32   op₂=creg
  1,   op₁=creg   op₂=reg32

rrr=number of the control register

TIMING

Operands	x	88	86	286	386	486
reg32,creg	0	–	–	–	6	4
creg,reg32	0	–	–	–	CR0:11 CR2:4 CR3:5	CR0:17 CR2:4 CR3:4

MOV *reg32/dreg,reg32/dreg*

00001111	001000d1	11	rrr	r/m

d=0,   op₁=reg32   op₂=dreg
  1,   op₁=dreg   op₂=reg32

rrr=number of the register

Operands	x	88	86	286	386	486
reg32,dreg	0	–	–	–	DR0-3:22 DR6-7:14	9
dreg,reg32	0	–	–	–	DR0-3:22 DR6-7:16	10

MOV *reg32/treg,reg32,treg*

00001111	001001*d*0	11	*rrr*	*r/m*

d=0,   op$_1$=reg32   op$_2$=treg
  1,   op$_1$=treg   op$_2$=reg32

rrr=number of the register

Operands	x	88	86	286	386	486
reg32,treg	0	–	–	–	12	TR3:3 TR4-7:4
treg,reg32	0	–	–	–	12	4

MOVS/MOVSB/ MOVSW/MOVSD

Move String Operand from Memory to Memory

DESCRIPTION

```
MOVSB
MOVSW
MOVSD
MOVS op₁,op₂
```

MOVS copies a memory operand, pointed to by the source index register (SI/ESI), to another location in memory pointed to by the ES segment register and the destination index register (DI/EDI) while automatically updating the indexes in preparation for the next comparison.

The MOVS instruction is used to transfer data from memory to memory while automatically updating the effective addresses in preparation for the next transfer. One execution of the MOVS instruction is equivalent to one execution of the LODS and STOS instructions executed back-to-back.

The source and destination index registers used to form the effective addresses for the transfer are determined by the current address-size attribute. If the address-size attribute is 16-bit, then the SI and DI registers will be used. If 32-bit addressing is in effect, then the ESI and EDI registers will be used.

The options that must be defined when using this instruction are the operand size, the segment register to be used with the effective address of the source index, and whether both indexes will be incremented or decremented after the transfer.

The size of the memory operands may be specified explicitly in the mnemonic or by an operand. In the first method, the transfer size is explicitly declared by using the B, W, or D suffix in combination with the MOVS mnemonic. The resulting instructions (MOVSB, MOVSW, and MOVSD) will transfer a byte, word, or doubleword between memory locations, respectively. The source and destination index registers will then be adjusted by 1, 2, or 4 to point to the next operand to be moved.

The size-explicit forms of the instruction always use the DS segment register when addressing the source operand and the ES segment register when addressing the destination operand. The general form of the instruction (MOVS) takes as arguments two memory operands that define the size of the transfer only. *The effective addresses of the operands are not used as the addresses of the transfer;* the data is always loaded using the source and destination indexes as pointers to memory. A segment override may be specified with op_1, but not with op_2.

For example, the instruction MOVS BYTE PTR [BX],[LIST] would be equivalent to the MOVSB form and would transfer the byte at DS:[SI] to the byte at ES:[DI]. The instruction MOVS BYTE PTR CS:[BX],[BX], however, would transfer the byte at CS:[SI] to ES:[DI]. In either case, the effective addresses specified by the operands are ignored.

The source and destination index registers will be incremented by the size of the operand if the direction flag (DF) has been cleared to 0 (by the CLD instruction, for example). The registers will be decremented by the size of the operand if DF is set to 1 (by the STD instruction).

For example, assume that the address-size attribute is 16-bits and DF is cleared. The instruction MOVSB can be equivalently expressed by the following instructions. (Note that this is one of the few instructions that performs a direct memory-to-memory transfer.)

```
MOV  BYTE PTR ES:[DI],BYTE PTR DS:[SI]  ;memory-to-memory
INC  SI
INC  DI
```

All forms of the MOVS instruction may be encoded with the REP prefix. The REP plus MOVS combination is a convenient and frequently used method of transferring data from one area of memory to another.

ALGORITHM

```
opsize=SIZEOF(operand)    ;Declared by mnemonic or operand
IF (MOVS op1,op2) THEN
   seg=SEGMENTOF(op1)
ELSE
   seg="DS"
ENDIF
IF (AddressMode=16-bit) THEN
   source_index="SI"
   destination_index="DI"
ELSE ;AddressMode=32-bit
   source_index="ESI"
   destination_index="EDI"
ENDIF
IF (opsize=1) THEN
   temp=BYTE PTR seg:[source_index]
   BYTE PTR ES:[destination_index]=temp
ELSEIF (opsize=2) THEN
   temp=WORD PTR seg:[source_index]
   WORD PTR ES:[destination_index]=temp
ELSE  ;opsize=4
   temp=DWORD PTR seg:[source_index]
   DWORD PTR ES:[destination_index]=temp
ENDIF
IF (DF=0)   ;CLD
   source_index=source_index + opsize
   destination_index=destination_index + opsize
```

```
ELSE   ;STD
  source_index=source_index - opsize
  destination_index=destination_index - opsize
ENDIF
```

NOTES

1. Early versions of the 80286 incorrectly executed this instruction in protected mode. If the ES register contained a null selector or ES:DI pointed past the segment limit when executing the non-repeated MOVS instruction, the CS:IP value saved by the exception 0Dh handler points to the instruction after the MOVS instruction instead of to it.

2. Early versions of the 80286 incorrectly executed the repeated form of this instruction in protected mode. If, during the execution of this instruction, a segment limit exception or IOPL exception occurs, the value of CX seen by the exception handler will be the value present at the start of the instruction. The SI and DI registers will reflect the iterations performed by the instruction.

3. This instruction is known to malfunction in two cases on some versions of the 80386. The first case occurs when MOVS or REP*cond* MOVS is followed by an instruction that uses a different address size. The second case occurs when MOVS or REP*cond* MOVS is followed by an instruction that implicitly references the stack and the B-bit in the SS descriptor is different than the address size used by the string instruction. In both cases, MOVS will not update the DI/EDI register properly and REP*cond* MOVS will not update the SI/ESI register properly. The address size used by the instruction is taken from the instruction that *follows* rather than from the string instruction. This can result in the updating of only the lower 16 bits of a 32-bit register or all 32 bits of a register being used as a 16-bit operand.

   In programs where 16- and 32-bit code will be mixed or where the stack and code segments may be different sizes, a NOP that uses the same address size as the MOVS instruction should be explicitly coded as shown below.

```
.386
SEGA    SEGMENT USE16 PARA PUBLIC 'CODE'
        ASSUME  CS:SEGA
        MOVSW   ;16-bit MOVS
        NOP     ; followed by 16-bit NOP
        DB 67H  ;32-bit MOVS
        MOVSW
        DB 67H  ; followed by 32-bit NOP
        NOP
SEGA    ENDS
SEGB    SEGMENT USE32 PARA PUBLIC 'CODE'
        ASSUME  CS:SEGB
        MOVSD   ;32-bit MOVS
        NOP     ; followed by 32-bit NOP
        DB 67H  ;16-bit MOVS
        MOVSD
```

```
          DB 67H  ; followed by 16-bit NOP
          NOP
    SEGB  ENDS
          END
```

FLAGS

O	D	I	T	S	Z	A	P	C

No flags are affected

MOVSB/MOVSW/MOVSD

MOVS op_1,op_2

1010010w

w=0, operands are 8-bit
  1, operands are 16-bit (16-bit operand mode)
          32-bit (32-bit operand mode)

Note: If present, op_1 and op_2 specify the operand size for the operation and are not included in the encoding. A segment override may also be specified by op_2.

TIMING

Operands	x	88	86	286	386	486
MOVSB MOVSW	2	B:18 W:26	18	5	8	7
MOVSD	2	–	–	–	8	7
REP MOVSB REP MOVSW	2r	B:9+17r W:9+25r	9+17r	5+4r	8+4r	12+3r T_0:5 T_1:13
REP MOVSD	2r	–	–	–	8+4r	12+3r T_0:5 T_1:13

r represents the number of repetitions executed when used with the REP prefix.

T_0 indicates the timing when the number of repetitions is 0.

T_1 indicates the timing when the number of repetitions is 1.

MOVSX

Move with Sign Extension

DESCRIPTION   MOVSX op_1, op_2

MOVSX moves the value specified by op_2 into the register or memory operand specified by op_1, sign-extending the value in op_2 to the size required by op_1.

Unlike the MOV instruction, where both operands must be the same size, the MOVSX instruction requires that op_2 always be smaller than op_1.

This instruction provides a faster, shorter, and more versatile replacement for moving and sign-extending an operand than using discrete instructions. It is especially useful for initializing the high part of registers such as in the instruction MOVSX ECX,CL.

ALGORITHM op_1=SIGN_EXTEND(op_2)

FLAGS

O	D	I	T	S	Z	A	P	C

No flags are affected

MOVSX *reg,reg/mem*

00001111	1011111w	mod	reg	r/m	disp

op_1=reg, op_2=mod+r/m

w=0 operands are 8-bit
  1 operands are 16-bit (16-bit operand mode)
    32-bit (32-bit operand mode)

disp=0- or 2-byte displacement (16-bit address mode)
    0- or 4-byte displacement (32-bit address mode)

TIMING

Operands	x	88	86	286	386	486
reg,reg	0	–	–	–	3	3
reg,mem	1	–	–	–	6	3

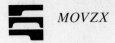

MOVZX

Move with Zero Extension

DESCRIPTION   MOVZX op_1,op_2

MOVZX moves the value specified by op_2 into the register or memory operand specified by op_1, zero-extending the value in op_2 to the size required by op_1.

Unlike the MOV instruction, where both operands must be the same size, the MOVZX instruction requires that op_2 always be smaller than op_1.

This instruction provides a faster, shorter, and more versatile replacement for moving and zero-extending an operand than using discrete instructions. It is especially useful for initializing the high part of registers such as in the instruction MOVZX ESI,SI.

ALGORITHM op_1=ZERO_EXTEND(op_2)

FLAGS

O	D	I	T	S	Z	A	P	C

No flags are affected

MOVZX *reg,reg/mem*

00001111	1011011w	mod	reg	r/m	disp

op_1=reg, op_2=mod+r/m

w=0 operands are 8-bit
   1 operands are 16-bit (16-bit operand mode)
               32-bit (32-bit operand mode)

disp=0- or 2-byte displacement (16-bit address mode)
       0- or 4-byte displacement (32-bit address mode)

TIMING

Operands	x	88	86	286	386	486
reg,reg	0	–	–	–	3	3
reg,mem	1	–	–	–	6	3

MUL

Unsigned Multiply

DESCRIPTION MUL *op*

MUL performs an unsigned multiplication of the accumulator by the operand specified by *op*.

The size of *op*, which may be a register or memory operand, determines which registers are used, as shown in the following table. All operands and results are treated as unsigned numbers.

Multiplier Size	Multiplicand	Result
8-bit	AL	AX
16-bit	AX	DX:AX
32-bit	EAX	EDX:EAX

For example, assume AL contains 21h (33) and BL contains A1h (161). After the instruction MUL BL is executed, AX will contain 14C1h (5313). Since AH≠0, CF and OF will be set to 1.

In cases where the multiplicand is a power of 2, the same result can be achieved in fewer clocks by using the SHL instruction.

ALGORITHM
```
opsize=SIZEOF(op)
IF (opsize=1) THEN
   AX=AL*op
   high="AH"
   low="AL"
ELSEIF (opsize=2) THEN
   DX:AX=AX*op
   high="DX"
   low="AX"
ELSE  ;opsize=4
   EDX:EAX=EAX*op
   high="DX"
   low="AX"
ENDIF
IF (high=0) THEN
   CF=0
   OF=0
ELSE
   CF=1
   OF=1
```

```
            ENDIF
```

NOTES 1. The 80386 and 80486 use an early-out algorithm to perform the multiply. The time required to perform the multiply depends on the position of the most significant bit in the optimizing multiplier. The clock count for these processors is therefore given as a range. To calculate the actual clock count, use the following formula.

```
IF (multiplier≠0) THEN
   clocks=MAX(3,ceiling(log₂|multiplier|)+6
ELSE
   clocks=9
ENDIF
IF (multiplier is mem) clocks=clocks+3
```

FLAGS

O	D	I	T	S	Z	A	P	C
*				—	—	—	—	*

MUL *reg/mem*

1111011w	mod	100	r/m	disp

w=0 operands are 8-bit
  1 operands are 16-bit (16-bit operand mode)
    32-bit (32-bit operand mode)

disp=0- or 2-byte displacement (16-bit address mode)
    0- or 4-byte displacement (32-bit address mode)

TIMING

Operands	x	88	86	286	386	486
reg8	0	70-77	70-77	13	12-17	13-18
reg16	0	113-118	113-118	21	12-25	13-26
reg32	0	—	—	—	12-41	13-42
mem8	1	(76-83)+EA	(76-83)+EA	16	15-20	13-18
mem16	1	(128-143)+EA	(124-139)+EA	24	15-28	13-26
mem32	1	–	–	–	15-44	13-42

NEG

Negate (Two's Complement)

DESCRIPTION NEG *op*

NEG performs a two's-complement subtraction of the operand from zero and sets the flags according to the result.

The 80x86 family uses two's-complement arithmetic for integers. NEG, therefore, reverses the sign of an integer. If the operand is 0, its sign is not changed, since there is no representation for –0 in the two's-complement system.

For example, assume the AX register contains the value 2CBh. After executing the instruction NEG AX, AX will contain FD35h.

ALGORITHM
```
opsize=SIZEOF(op)
IF (opsize=1) THEN
  max_neg=80h
 ELSEIF (opsize=2) THEN
  max_neg=8000h
 ELSEIF (opsize=4) THEN
  max_neg=80000000h
ENDIF
IF (op=0) THEN
  CF=0
ELSE
  IF (op>max_neg) THEN
    NOT op
    INC op  ;Flags set by this instruction
  ELSE
    OF=1
  ENDIF
  CF=1
ENDIF
```

FLAGS

O	D	I	T	S	Z	A	P	C
*				*	*	*	*	*

NEG *reg/mem*

| 1111011w | mod | 011 | r/m | disp |

w=0 operands are 8-bit
  1 operands are 16-bit (16-bit operand mode)
     32-bit (32-bit operand mode)

disp=0- or 2-byte displacement (16-bit address mode)
   0- or 4-byte displacement (32-bit address mode)

TIMING

Operands	x	88	86	286	386	486
reg	0	3	3	2	2	1
mem	2	B:16+EA W:24+EA	16+EA	7	6	3

NOP

No Operation (No-op)

DESCRIPTION NOP causes the CPU to do nothing.

The NOP instruction does nothing and does not change the status of any flags. Because of this property, NOP is a very useful instruction. Its two most common uses are patching out instructions while debugging and padding code for instruction alignment.

Note that the NOP instruction is encoded as XCHG AX,AX.

ALGORITHM
```
IF (OperandMode=16-bit) THEN
        temp=AX
        AX = AX
        AX=temp
ELSE ;OperandMode=32-bit
        temp=EAX
        EAX=EAX
        EAX=temp
ENDIF
```

FLAGS

O	D	I	T	S	Z	A	P	C

No flags are affected

NOP

```
10010000
```

TIMING

Operands	x	88	86	286	386	486
(no operands)	0	3	3	3	3	1[1]

[1] This timing is for the B and later steppings of the 80486. On the A-step, NOP takes 3 clocks to execute.

NOT

Logical NOT (One's Complement)

DESCRIPTION NOT *op*

NOT performs the bitwise complement of *op* and stores the result back into *op*.

The NOT instruction, used on an integer operand, forms the one's complement of the original signed number. Used on an unsigned number, it forms the logical complement. A truthtable for the bitwise NOT operation is shown below.

A	NOT A
0	1
1	0

For example, assume the DX register contains the value F038h. After executing the instruction NOT DX, the DX register will contain the value 0FC7h.

ALGORITHM
```
opsize=SIZEOF(op)
IF (opsize=1) THEN
  pp=FFh-op
 ELSEIF (opsize=2) THEN
  op=FFFFh-op
 ELSE  ;opsize=4
  op=FFFFFFFFh-op
ENDIF
```

FLAGS

O	D	I	T	S	Z	A	P	C

No flags are affected

NOT *reg/mem*

1111011w	mod	010	r/m	disp

w=0, operands are 8-bit
   1, operands are 16-bit (16-bit operand mode)
                32-bit (32-bit operand mode)

disp=0- or 2-byte displacement (16-bit address mode)
     0- or 4-byte displacement (32-bit address mode)

TIMING

Operands	x	88	86	286	386	486
reg	0	3	3	2	2	1
mem	2	B:16+EA W:24+EA	16+EA	7	6	3

OR

Logical (Inclusive) OR

DESCRIPTION   OR op_1, op_2

OR performs a bitwise logical OR of two operands. The result of the operation is stored in op_1 and the flags are set accordingly.

Each bit of the result is cleared to 0 if and only if both corresponding bits in each operand are 0; otherwise, the bit in the result is set to 1. A truth table for the bitwise OR operation is shown below.

A	B	A OR B
0	0	0
0	1	1
1	0	1
1	1	1

Assume the CL register contains 56h. After the instruction OR CL,25h is executed, CL will contain 77h, the parity flag (PF) will be set to 1, and the overflow (OF), carry (CF), sign (SF), and zero (ZF) flags will be cleared to 0.

OR is often used to set bit fields. For example, to set bit 2 in the AL register to 1, the instruction OR AL,04h would be used. In this case, op_2, known as the mask, has the potential to change only bit 2 (04h = 00000100b). Conversely, bit fields can be turned off by ANDing with the one's complement of the mask.

The OR *reg,reg* form of the instruction is often used to check the value of a register in preparation for a conditional jump. The instruction OR AX,AX, for example, will set the flags to reflect the current state of AX.

ALGORITHM $op_1 = op_1$ OR op_2 ;Bitwise OR
CF=0
OF=0

FLAGS

O	D	I	T	S	Z	A	P	C
0				*	*	—	*	0

OR *reg/mem,reg/mem*

000010dw	mod	reg	r/m	disp

$d=0,$ $op_1=mod+r/m$ $op_2=reg$
   $1,$ $op_1=reg$ $op_2=mod+r/m$

$w=0$ operands are 8-bit
    1 operands are 16-bit (16-bit operand mode)
                32-bit (32-bit operand mode)

$disp=0$- or 2-byte displacement (16-bit address mode)
        0- or 4-byte displacement (32-bit address mode)

TIMING

Operands	x	88	86	286	386	486
reg,reg	0	3	3	2	2	1
reg,mem	1	B:9+EA W:13+EA	9+EA	7	6	2
mem,reg	2	B:16+EA W:24+EA	16+EA	7	7	3

OR *reg/mem,immed*

100000sw	mod	001	r/m	disp	immed

$s=0,$ immediate data size specified by w
    1, sign-extend byte of immediate data

$w=0$ operands are 8-bit
    1 operands are 16-bit (16-bit operand mode)
                32-bit (32-bit operand mode)

$disp=0$- or 2-byte displacement (16-bit address mode)
        0- or 4-byte displacement (32-bit address mode)

$immed=1$- or 2-byte immediate data (16-bit operand mode)
            1- or 4-byte immediate data (32-bit operand mode)

TIMING

Operands	x	88	86	286	386	486
reg,immed	0	4	4	3	2	1
mem,immed	2	B:17+EA W:25+EA	17+EA	7	7	3

OR *accum,immed*

| 0000110w | *immed* |

w=0 operands are 8-bit
   1 operands are 16-bit (16-bit operand mode)
               32-bit (32-bit operand mode)

immed=1- or 2-byte immediate data (16-bit operand mode)
            1- or 4-byte immediate data (32-bit operand mode)

TIMING

Operands	x	88	86	286	386	486
accum,immed	0	4	4	3	2	1

OUT

Output Data from Accumulator to I/O Port

DESCRIPTION   OUT *op,accum*

OUT transfers a byte, word, or doubleword from the accumulator to I/O port specified by *op*.

Two forms of the OUT instruction are available. In the first form, the port number is specified by an immediate byte constant, allowing access to ports numbered 0 through 255 (FFh). In the second form, the port number is provided in the DX register. This form allows access to ports numbered 0 through 65535 (FFFFh).

When a word is output to a port, the byte in AL is transferred to the port address and the byte in AH is transferred to the port address + 1. Similarly, when a doubleword is output, the word in AX is transferred to the port address and the high-order 16-bits of EAX are transferred to the word at the port address + 2.

ALGORITHM
```
opsize=SIZEOF(op)
IF (opsize=1) THEN
   I/O-Port=AL
ELSEIF (opsize=2) THEN
   I/O-Port=AX
ELSE  ;opsize=4
   I/O-Port=EAX
ENDIF
```

FLAGS

O	D	I	T	S	Z	A	P	C

No flags are affected

OUT *immed8,accum*

1110011w	immed

w=0, operands are 8-bit
   1, operands are 16-bit (16-bit operand mode)
                 32-bit (32-bit operand mode)

immed=1- or 2-byte immediate data (16-bit address mode)
          1- or 4-byte immediate data (32-bit address mode)

Operands	x	88	86	286	386	486
immed8,accum	0	14	10	3	10 PM_1:4 PM_2:24 VM:24	16 PM_1:11 PM_2:31 VM:29

PM_1 indicates the timing when CPL≤IOPL.

PM_2 indicates the timing when CPL>IOPL.

OUT DX,*accum*

1110111w

w=0, operands are 8-bit
   1, operands are 16-bit (16-bit operand mode)
                  32-bit (32-bit operand mode)

Operands	88	86	286	386	486
DX,*accum*	12	8	3	11 PM_1:5 PM_2:25 VM:25	16 PM_1:10 PM_2:30 VM:29

PM_1 indicates the timing when CPL≤IOPL.

PM_2 indicates the timing when CPL>IOPL.

OUTS/OUTSB/ OUTSW/OUTSD

Output String from Memory to I/O Port

DESCRIPTION
```
OUTSB
OUTSW
OUTSD
OUTS op,DX
```

OUTS transfers data from a memory operand pointed to by the source index register (SI/ESI) to the specified I/O port while updating the source index in preparation for the next transfer.

The OUTS instruction is used to transfer data from memory to an I/O port while automatically updating the effective address in preparation for the next transfer. The DS segment register, which may be overridden, in combination with the source index register are used to form the effective address for the transfer. The size of the source index register is determined by the current address size attribute. If the address size attribute is 16-bits, then the SI register will be used. If 32-bit addressing is in effect, then the ESI register will be used.

The number of the I/O port to be accessed must be given in the DX register. The OUTS instruction does not allow the I/O port to be given as immediate data.

The options that must be defined when using this instruction are the operand size, the segment register to be used with the effective address, and whether the source index will be incremented or decremented after the transfer.

The size of the transfer (and therefore, the memory operand) may be specified explicitly in the mnemonic or by an operand. In the first method, the transfer size is explicitly declared by using the B, W, or D suffix in combination with the OUTS mnemonic. The resulting instructions (OUTSB, OUTSW, and OUTSD) will transfer a byte, word, or doubleword to the I/O port, respectively. The source index register will then be adjusted by 1, 2, or 4 to point to the next operand to be transferred.

The size-explicit forms of the instruction always use the DS register when addressing memory. The general form of the instruction (OUTS) takes a memory argument (op_1) that defines the size of the transfer only. *The effective address of the operand is not used as the address of the transfer;* the data is always stored using the source index as a pointer to memory. The use of an operand also provides a syntactically convenient method for specifying a segment override.

For example, the instruction OUTS BYTE PTR [BX],DX would be equivalent to the OUTSB form and would transfer the byte of memory at DS:[SI] to the I/O port given in the DX register. The effective address of the operand is always ignored.

The source index register will be incremented by the size of the operand if the direction flag (DF) has been cleared to 0 (by the CLD instruction, for example). The register will be decremented by the size of the operand if DF is set to 1 (by the STD instruction).

For example, assume that the address size attribute is 16-bits and DF is cleared. The instruction OUTSB will be equivalent to the following instructions.

```
OUT  BYTE PTR DS:[SI],DX
INC  SI
```

All forms of the OUTS instruction may be encoded with the REP prefix to perform a block input of data from memory to an I/O port.

ALGORITHM

```
opsize=SIZEOF(operand)      ;Declared by mnemonic or operand
IF (OUTS op,DX) THEN
  seg=SEGMENTOF(op)
ELSE
  seg="DS"
ENDIF
IF (AddressMode=16-bit) THEN
  src="SI"
ELSE
  src="ESI"
ENDIF
IF (opsize=1) THEN
  OUT BYTE PTR seg:[src],DX
ELSEIF (opsize=2) THEN
  OUT WORD PTR seg:[src],DX
ELSE  ;opsize=4
  OUT WORD PTR seg:[src],DX
ENDIF
IF (DF=0)   ;CLD
  src=src+opsize
ELSE   ;STD
  src=src-opsize
ENDIF
```

NOTES

1. When used with the REP instruction prefix, the OUTS instruction may be executed faster than the addressed I/O port is able to receive data.

2. Early versions of the 80286 incorrectly execute the repeated form of this instruction in protected mode. If, during the execution of this instruction, a segment limit exception or IOPL exception occurs, the value of CX seen by the exception handler will be the value present at the start of the instruction. The SI register will reflect the iterations performed by the instruction.

FLAGS

O	D	I	T	S	Z	A	P	C

No flags are affected

OUTSB/OUTSW/OUTSD

OUTS reg/mem,DX

```
1010101w
```

w=0, operands are 8-bit
   1, operands are 16-bit (16-bit operand mode)
        32-bit (32-bit operand mode)

Note: If present, the *reg/mem* operand specifies only the operand size and is not included in the encoding. A segment override may also be specified.

TIMING

Operands	x	88	86	286	386	486
OUTSB OUTSW	1	–	–	5	14 PM$_1$:8 PM$_2$:28 VM:28	17 PM$_1$:10 PM$_2$:32 VM:30
OUTSD	1	–	–	–	14 PM$_1$:8 PM$_2$:28 VM:28	17 PM$_1$:10 PM$_2$:32 VM:30
REP OUTSB REP OUTSW	r	–	–	5+4r	12+5r PM$_1$:6+5r PM$_2$:26+5r VM:26+5r	17+5r PM$_1$:11+5r PM$_2$:31+5r VM:30+5r
REP OUTSD	r	–	–	–	12+5r PM$_1$:6+5r PM$_2$:26+5r VM:26+5r	17+5r PM$_1$:11+5r PM$_2$:31+5r VM:30+5r

r represents the number of repetitions executed when used with the REP prefix.

PM$_1$ indicates the timing when CPL≤IOPL.

PM$_2$ indicates the timing when CPL>IOPL.

POP

Read from the Top of the Stack

DESCRIPTION   POP *op*

POP copies the word at the current top of stack to the operand specified by *op* then increments the stack pointer to point to the next stack entry.

The current top of stack is defined by the SS segment register and SP/ESP register. SP/ESP always points to the word at the top of the stack. The POP instruction copies the word at SS:[SP] or SS:[ESP] to *op*, then points SP/ESP to the new top of stack.

The stack may have a size attribute of 16- or 32-bits. The size of the operand that is popped may also be 16- or 32-bits, independent of the stack size attribute.

ALGORITHM
```
IF (StackMode=16-bit) THEN
   IF (SIZEOF(op)=2) THEN
     op=WORD PTR SS:[SP]
     SP=SP+2
   ELSE  ;opsize = 4
     op=DWORD PTR SS:[SP]
     SP=SP+4
   ENDIF
 ELSE   ;stack address size mode=32-bit
   IF (SIZEOF(op)=2) THEN
     op=WORD PTR SS:[ESP]
     ESP=ESP+2
   ELSE ;opsize=4
     op=DWORD PTR SS:[ESP]
     ESP=ESP+4
   ENDIF
 ENDIF
```

FLAGS

O	D	I	T	S	Z	A	P	C

No flags are affected

POP *reg*

01011	reg

TIMING

Operands	x	88	86	286	386	486
reg16	1	12	8	5	4	1
reg32	1	–	–	–	4	1

POP *reg/mem*

10001111	mod	000	r/m	disp

disp=0- or 2-byte displacement (16-bit address mode)
       0- or 4-byte displacement (32-bit address mode)

Note: This encoding is not normally used to pop data into a register. The POP *reg* instruction is provided for this purpose and occupies only 1 byte

TIMING

Operands	x	88	86	286	386	486
reg16	1	12	8	5	5	4
reg32	1	–	–	–	5	4
mem16	2	25+EA	17+EA	5	5	5
mem32	2	–	–	–	5	5

POP *sreg*

00	sreg	111

Note: On the 8086 and 8088, encoding *sreg*=001 for this instruction will generate the instruction POP CS (opcode=0Fh). On the 80286 and later processors, this encoding is used as the first byte of a two-byte opcode sequence. Use this encoding for DS, ES, and SS only.

TIMING

Operands	x	88	86	286	386	486
sreg	1	12	8	5 PM:20	7 PM:21 VM:7	3

POP *sreg*

00001111	10	sreg	001

Note: This form is used for the FS and GS registers of the 80386 and 80486 only.

TIMING

Operands	x	88	86	286	386	486
sreg	1	–	–	–	7 PM:21 VM:7	3

POPA

Pop All General Registers

DESCRIPTION POPA pops the values of seven of the eight general-purpose registers that were saved on the stack by a previous PUSHA instruction, discarding the previous value of SP.

The POPA instruction pops, in order, the DI, SI, BP, SP, BX, DX, CX, and AX registers. The previous value for SP, however, is discarded instead of being copied to the SP register.

ALGORITHM
```
POP  DI
POP  SI
POP  BP
ADD  SP,2 ;discard old SP value
POP  BX
POP  DX
POP  CX
POP  AX
```

NOTES
1. POPA and POPAD have the same encoding. The current operand size attribute determines which instruction is executed.

2. On some versions of the 80386, the POPA instruction corrupts the EAX register, leaving it with an undefined value. This occurs if POPA is immediately followed by an instruction that forms an effective address using a base address register and an additional register other than AX/EAX as an index register as shown here:

```
POPAD
MOV    EBX,DWORD PTR [EDX+EBX*4]
```

Additionally, the processor will hang if the 16-bit POPA instruction is immediately followed by an instruction that forms an effective address using EAX as a base or index register as shown here:

```
POPA
MOV    EBX,DWORD PTR [EAX]
```

Proper operation of the processor cannot be guaranteed until after a RESET occurs. This problem may occur regardless of operating mode. To avoid this situation, a NOP should be encoded after every POPA instruction.

FLAGS

O	D	I	T	S	Z	A	P	C

No flags are affected

POPA

```
01100001
```

Operands	x	88	86	286	386	486
(no operands)	8	–	–	19	24	9

POPAD

Pop All 32-bit General Registers

DESCRIPTION POPAD pops the values of seven of the eight 32-bit general-purpose registers that were saved on the stack by a previous PUSHAD instruction, discarding the previous value of ESP.

The POPAD instruction pops, in order, the EDI, ESI, EBP, ESP, EBX, EDX, ECX, and EAX registers. The previous value for ESP, however, is discarded instead of being copied to the ESP register.

ALGORITHM
```
POP  EDI
POP  ESI
POP  EBP
ADD  ESP,4  ;discard old ESP value
POP  EBX
POP  EDX
POP  ECX
POP  EAX
```

NOTES
1. POPAD and POPA have the same encoding. The current operand size attribute determines which instruction is executed.

2. On some versions of the 80386, the POPAD instruction corrupts the EAX register, leaving it with an undefined value. This occurs if POPA is immediately followed by an instruction that forms an effective address using a base address register and an additional register other than AX/EAX as an index register as shown here:

```
POPAD
MOV   EBX,DWORD PTR [EDX+EBX*4]
```

Additionally, the processor will hang if the 16-bit POPAD instruction is immediately followed by an instruction that forms an effective address using EAX as a base or index register as shown here:

```
POPAD
MOV   EBX,DWORD PTR [EAX]
```

Proper operation of the processor cannot be guaranteed until after a RESET occurs. This problem may occur regardless of operating mode. To avoid this situation, a NOP should be encoded after every POPAD instruction.

FLAGS

O	D	I	T	S	Z	A	P	C

No flags are affected

POPAD

01100001

TIMING

Operands	x	88	86	286	386	486
(no operands)	8	–	–	–	24	9

POPF

Load the FLAGS Register from the Stack

DESCRIPTION POPF copies specific bits from the word at the current top of stack to the FLAGS register then increments the stack pointer register to point to the next stack entry.

The current top of stack is defined by the SS segment register and SP (or ESP) register. SP always points to the word at the top of the stack. The POPF instruction copies selected bits from the word at SS:[SP] to FLAGS, then points to the new top of stack by adding 2 to SP. The new flag bits replace the current values in the FLAGS register.

The POPF and PUSHF instructions allow a procedure to save and then restore the FLAGS register of the calling program. This is almost always the case when writing interrupt handlers, where the state of the processor must be preserved.

POPF is also used to manipulate flags for which there are no direct manipulation instructions. These flags include the various protected mode flags and the trap flag (TF). For example, the following instructions set TF.

```
PUSHF
POP    AX
OR     AX,100h    ;Set bit 8
PUSH   AX
POPF
```

ALGORITHM
```
IF (StackMode=16-bit) THEN
   FLAGS=WORD PTR SS:[SP]    ;selected bits
   SP=SP+2
ELSE ;StackMode=32-bit
   FLAGS=WORD PTR SS:[ESP]    ;selected bits
   ESP=ESP+2
ENDIF
```

NOTES
1. POPF and POPFD have the same encoding. The current operand size attribute determines which instruction is executed.

2. Early versions of the 80286, executing in real mode or in protected mode with CPL≤IOPL, may improperly recognize a pending INTR interrupt after executing POPF, even if interrupts were disabled prior to the POPF and the value popped into the FLAGS register had IF=0. Note that even if improperly recognized, the interrupt is executed correctly.

   To avoid this problem, use the following code sequence shown below in place of a POPF instruction. The JMP transfers control to the PUSH CS instruction which pushes CS onto the stack. The CALL instruction puts the address of the instruction that follows it (the return address) onto the stack, then transfers control to the IRET instruction. IRET then loads CS, IP, and FLAGS from the stack. The effect is that the FLAGS are popped and execution continues at the instruction after the CALL.

```
JMP   $+3   ;Jump over IRET
IRET        ;Pops CS, IP, FLAGS
PUSH CS     ;Removed by IRET
CALL $-2    ;Pushes IP, removed by IRET
```

FLAGS

O	D	I	T	S	Z	A	P	C
*	*	*	*	*	*	*	*	*

POPF

```
10011101
```

TIMING

Operands	x	88	86	286	386	486
(no operands)	1	12	8	5	5	9 PM:6 VM:9

POPFD

Load the EFLAGS Register from the Stack

DESCRIPTION POPFD copies specific bits from the word at the current top of stack to the EFLAGS register then increments the stack pointer register to point to the next stack entry.

The current top of stack is defined by the SS segment register and SP (or ESP) register. SP always points to the word at the top of the stack. The POPF instruction copies selected bits from the word at SS:[SP] to EFLAGS, then points to the new top of stack by adding 4 to SP. The new flag bits replace the current values in the EFLAGS register.

The POPFD and PUSHFD instructions allow a procedure to save and then restore the EFLAGS register of the calling program. This is almost always the case when writing interrupt handlers, where the state of the processor must be preserved.

POPFD is also used to manipulate flags for which there are no direct manipulation instructions. These flags include the various protected mode flags and the trap flag (TF). For example, the following instructions set TF.

```
PUSHFD
POP    EAX
OR     EAX,100h   ;Set bit 8
PUSH   EAX
POPFD
```

ALGORITHM
```
IF (StackMode=16-bit) THEN
   EFLAGS=DWORD PTR SS:[SP]    ;selected bits
   SP=SP+4
ELSE ;StackMode=32-bit
   EFLAGS=DWORD PTR SS:[ESP]    ;selected bits
   ESP=ESP+4
ENDIF
```

NOTES
1. POPFD and POPF have the same encoding. The current operand size attribute determines which instruction is executed.

2. The VM and RF flags are not affected by this instruction.

FLAGS

O	D	I	T	S	Z	A	P	C
*	*	*	*	*	*	*	*	*

POPFD

```
10011101
```

Operands	x	88	86	286	386	486
(no operands)	1	–	–	–	5	9 PM:6 VM:9

PUSH

Push Operand onto the Stack

DESCRIPTION PUSH *op*

PUSH decrements the stack pointer register to make room for a new stack entry. The operand specified by *op* is then copied to the area of memory pointed to by the new stack pointer.

The PUSH instruction is generally used to store data temporarily on the stack. It is also used in most high-level languages to place data on the stack before calling a procedure.

The stack may have a size attribute of 16- or 32-bits. The size of the operand that is popped may also be 16- or 32-bits independent of the stack size attribute.

ALGORITHM
```
IF (StackMode=16-bit) THEN
    IF (SIZEOF(op)=2) THEN
       SP=SP-2
       WORD PTR SS:[SP]=op
    ELSE  ;opsize=4
       SP=SP-4
       DWORD PTR SS:[SP]=op
    ENDIF
  ELSE   ;StackMode=32-bit
    IF (SIZEOF(op)=2) THEN
       ESP=ESP-2
       WORD PTR SS:[ESP]=op
    ELSE  ;opsize=4
       ESP=ESP-4
       DWORD PTR SS:[ESP]=op
    ENDIF
ENDIF
```

NOTES

1. The PUSH instruction operates differently on the 8086 and 8088 than on the 80286 and later members of the 80x86 family. The only time this difference will be evident is when the PUSH SP instruction is executed. On the 8086 and 8088, the value of SP copied to the stack is the value SP will have at the completion of the instruction. On later processors, the value of SP copied to the stack is the value SP has before the instruction is executed. In either case, the pushed data is placed in the correct place on the stack and the SP register has the correct value at the completion of the instruction.

2. On early versions of the 80286, the PUSH *mem* form of this instruction is known to malfunction in protected mode. If the stack limit is violated by the PUSH

mem instruction, the CS:IP value saved by the exception Bh will point after the PUSH instruction instead of to it.

FLAGS

O	D	I	T	S	Z	A	P	C

No flags are affected

PUSH *reg*

01010	reg

TIMING

Operands	x	88	86	286	386	486
reg16	1	15	11	3	2	1
reg32	1	–	–	–	2	1

PUSH *reg/mem*

11111111	mod	110	r/m

Note: This encoding is not normally used to push a register operand. The PUSH *reg* instruction is provided for that purpose and occupies only 1 byte.

TIMING

Operands	x	88	86	286	386	486
reg16	0	15	11	3	5	1
reg32	0	–	–	–	5	1
mem16	1	24+EA	16+EA	5	5	4
mem32	1	–	–	–	5	4

PUSH *sreg*

00	sreg	110

Note: This encoding is used for CS, DS, ES, and SS.

TIMING

Operands	x	88	86	286	386	486
sreg	1	14	10	3	2	3

PUSH *sreg*

| 00001111 | 10 | sreg | 000 |

Note: This encoding is used for FS and GS only.

TIMING

Operands	x	88	86	286	386	486
sreg	1	–	–	–	2	3

PUSH *immed*

| 011010s0 | immed |

s=0, immediate data size specified operand mode
   1, sign-extend byte of immediate data

immed=1- or 2-byte immediate data (16-bit operand mode)
       1- or 4-byte immediate data (32-bit operand mode)

TIMING

Operands	88	86	286	386	486
immed8/immed16	–	–	3	2	1
immed32	–	–	–	2	1

PUSHA

Push All General Registers

DESCRIPTION PUSHA pushes the values of the eight general-purpose registers onto the stack.

The PUSHA instruction pushes, in order, the AX, CX, DX, BX, SP, BP, SI, and DI registers. The value pushed for SP, however, is the value the register had *before* any entries are made to the stack by this instruction.

ALGORITHM
```
temp=SP    ;Save current SP
PUSH  AX
PUSH  CX
PUSH  DX
PUSH  BX
PUSH  temp ;Value of SP before first PUSH
PUSH  BP
PUSH  SI
PUSH  DI
```

NOTES
1. PUSHA and PUSHAD have the same encoding. The current operand size attribute determines which instruction is executed.

FLAGS

O	D	I	T	S	Z	A	P	C

No flags are affected

PUSHA

```
01100000
```

TIMING

Operands	x	88	86	286	386	486
(no operands)	8	–	–	17	18	11

PUSHAD

Push All 32-bit General Registers

DESCRIPTION PUSHAD pushes the values of the eight 32-bit general-purpose registers onto the stack.

The PUSHAD instruction pushes, in order, the EAX, ECX, EDX, EBX, ESP, EBP, ESI, and EDI registers. The value pushed for ESP, however, is the value the register had *before* any entries are made to the stack by this instruction.

ALGORITHM
```
temp=ESP      ;Save current ESP
PUSH  EAX
PUSH  ECX
PUSH  EDX
PUSH  EBX
PUSH  temp    ;Value of ESP before first PUSH
PUSH  EBP
PUSH  ESI
PUSH  EDI
```

NOTES
1. PUSHAD and PUSHA have the same encoding. The current operand size attribute determines which instruction is executed.

FLAGS

O	D	I	T	S	Z	A	P	C

No flags are affected

PUSHAD

01100000

TIMING

Operands	x	88	86	286	386	486
(no operands)	8	–	–	–	18	11

PUSHF

Push the FLAGS Register onto the Stack

DESCRIPTION PUSH decrements the stack pointer register to make room for a new stack entry. The FLAGS register is then copied to the new top of stack.

The PUSHF instruction is generally used to save the state of the FLAGS register so that it can later be restored. Most interrupt handlers will use this instruction in their preamble before executing any instructions that will change the processor state. PUSHF is also used to copy the contents of the FLAGS register before changing individual flags that cannot be accessed directly.

ALGORITHM
```
IF (StackMode=16-bit) THEN
   SP=SP-2
   WORD PTR SS:[SP]=FLAGS
ELSE ;StackMode=32-bit
   ESP=ESP-2
   WORD PTR SS:[ESP]=FLAGS
ENDIF
```

NOTES 1. PUSHF and PUSHFD have the same encoding. The current operand size attribute determines which instruction is executed.

FLAGS

O	D	I	T	S	Z	A	P	C

No flags are affected

PUSHF

10011100

TIMING

Operands	x	88	86	286	386	486
(no operands)	1	14	10	3	4	4 PM:3 VM:4

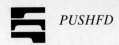

PUSHFD

Push the EFLAGS Register onto the Stack

DESCRIPTION PUSHD decrements the stack pointer register to make room for a new stack entry. The EFLAGS register is then copied to the new top of stack.

The PUSHFD instruction is generally used to save the state of the EFLAGS register so that it can later be restored. Most interrupt handlers will use this instruction in their preamble before executing any instructions that will change the processor state. PUSHFD is also used to copy the contents of the FLAGS register before changing individual flags that cannot be accessed directly.

ALGORITHM
```
IF (StackMode=16-bit) THEN
   SP=SP-4
   DWORD PTR SS:[SP]=EFLAGS
ELSE  ;StackMode=32-bit
   ESP=ESP-4
   DWORD PTR SS:[ESP]=EFLAGS
ENDIF
```

NOTES 1. PUSHF and PUSHFD have the same encoding. The current operand size attribute determines which instruction is executed.

FLAGS

O	D	I	T	S	Z	A	P	C

No flags are affected

PUSHFD

```
10011100
```

TIMING

Operands	x	88	86	286	386	486
(no operands)	1	–	–	–	4	4 PM:3 VM:4

RCL

Rotate Left Through Carry Flag

DESCRIPTION RCL op_1,op_2

RCL rotates the bits in the operand specified by op_1 left by the count specified in op_2. The carry flag (CF) bit in the FLAGS register is treated as if it were the high-order bit of the operand.

The RCL instruction provides a method for performing multielement shifts by allowing the high-order bit of the operand to be stored temporarily in the CF bit. For example, assume that a 32-bit quantity is being stored in the DX:AX register pair. To rotate the entire 32-bit quantity left one bit, two bits must be exchanged between the registers: the current high-order bit of each register must be rotated into the low-order bit of the other register. This can be accomplished with the following instructions.

```
CLC         ;Put Ø in CF
RCL  AX,1   ;Save high-order bit of AX in CF
RCL  DX,1   ;Save high-order bit of DX in CF
ADC  AX,Ø   ;Set low-order bit if needed
```

ALGORITHM
```
h=SIZEOF(op₁)*8-1    ;Number of high-order bit
IF (8086 or 8088) THEN
  count=op₂
ELSE
  count=op₂ MOD 32
ENDIF
WHILE (count≠Ø)
  tempCF=CF
  CF=BIT(h of op₁)
  SHL op₁,1
  BIT(Ø of op₁)=tempCF
  count=count-1
ENDWHILE
IF (op₂=1) THEN
  IF (BIT(h of op₁)≠CF) THEN
    OF=1
  ELSE
    OF=Ø
  ENDIF
ELSE
  OF=undefined
ENDIF
```

NOTES 1. The 80286, 80386, and 80486 do not recognize a rotation count greater than 31. If a rotation count greater than 31 is specified, only the lower 5 bits of the count will be used. The 8086 and 8088 do not limit the rotation count; the 80386 and 80486, when running in Virtual-86 mode, do limit the rotation count.

FLAGS

O	D	I	T	S	Z	A	P	C
*								*

RCL *reg/mem,*1

1101000w	mod	010	r/m	disp

w=0, operands are 8-bit
  1, operands are 16-bit (16-bit operand mode)
         32-bit (32-bit operand mode)

disp=0- or 2-byte displacement (16-bit address mode)
      0- or 4-byte displacement (32-bit address mode)

TIMING

Operands	x	88	86	286	386	486
reg,1	0	2	2	2	9	3
mem,1	2	B:15+EA W:23+EA	15+EA	7	10	4

RCL *reg/mem,*CL

1101001w	mod	010	r/m	disp

w=0, operands are 8-bit
  1, operands are 16-bit (16-bit operand mode)
         32-bit (32-bit operand mode)

disp=0- or 2-byte displacement (16-bit address mode)
      0- or 4-byte displacement (32-bit address mode)

TIMING

Operands	x	88	86	286	386	486
reg,CL	0	8+4n	8+4n	5+n	9	8-30
mem,CL	2	B:20+EA+4n W:28+EA+4n	20+EA+4n	8+n	10	9-31

n represents the number of times the operand is rotated.

RCL *reg/mem,immed8*

1100000w	mod	010	r/m	disp	immed

w=0, operands are 8-bit
   1, operands are 16-bit (16-bit operand mode)
            32-bit (32-bit operand mode)

disp=0- or 2-byte displacement (16-bit address mode)
      0- or 4-byte displacement (32-bit address mode)

immed=1- or 2-byte immediate data (16-bit operand mode)
       1- or 4-byte immediate data (32-bit operand mode)

TIMING

Operands	x	88	86	286	386	486
reg,immed8	0	–	–	5+n	9	8-30
mem,immed8	2	–	–	8+n	10	9-31

n represents the number of times the operand is rotated.

RCR

Rotate Right Through Carry Flag

DESCRIPTION RCR op_1, op_2

RCR rotates the bits in the operand specified by op_1 right by the count specified in op_2. The carry flag (CF) bit in the FLAGS register is treated as if it were the high-order bit of the operand.

ALGORITHM

```
h=SIZEOF(op₁)*8-1   ;Number of high-order bit
IF (8086 or 8088) THEN
    count=op₂
ELSE
    count=op₂ MOD 32
ENDIF
WHILE (temp≠0)
  tempCF=CF
  CF=BIT(h of op₁)
  SHR op₁,1  ;Shifts zero into high bit
  BIT(h of op₁)=tempCF
  count=count-1
ENDWHILE
IF (op₂=1) THEN
  IF (BIT(h of op₁)≠BIT(h-1 of op₁)) THEN
    OF=1
  ELSE
    OF=0
  ENDIF
ELSE
  OF=undefined
ENDIF
```

NOTES 1. The 80286, 80386, and 80486 do not recognize a rotation count greater than 31. If a rotation count greater than 31 is specified, only the lower 5 bits of the count will be used. The 8086 and 8088 do not limit the rotation count; the 80386 and 80486, when running in Virtual-86 mode, do limit the rotation count.

FLAGS

O	D	I	T	S	Z	A	P	C
*								*

RCR *reg/mem,1*

1101000w	mod	011	r/m	disp

w=0, operands are 8-bit
   1, operands are 16-bit (16-bit operand mode)
          32-bit (32-bit operand mode)

disp=0- or 2-byte displacement (16-bit address mode)
     0- or 4-byte displacement (32-bit address mode)

TIMING

Operands	x	88	86	286	386	486
reg,1	0	2	2	2	9	3
mem,1	2	B:15+EA W:23+EA	15+EA	7	10	4

RCR *reg/mem,CL*

1101001w	mod	011	r/m	disp

w=0, operands are 8-bit
   1, operands are 16-bit (16-bit operand mode)
          32-bit (32-bit operand mode)

disp=0- or 2-byte displacement (16-bit address mode)
     0- or 4-byte displacement (32-bit address mode)

TIMING

Operands	x	88	86	286	386	486
reg,CL	0	8+4n	8+4n	5+n	9	8-30
mem,CL	2	B:20+EA+4n W:28+EA+4n	20+EA+4n	8+n	10	9-31

n represents the number of times the operand is rotated.

RCR *reg/mem,immed8*

1100000w	mod	011	r/m	disp	immed

w=0, operands are 8-bit
   1, operands are 16-bit (16-bit operand mode)
          32-bit (32-bit operand mode)

disp=0- or 2-byte displacement (16-bit address mode)
     0- or 4-byte displacement (32-bit address mode)

immed=1- or 2-byte immediate data (16-bit operand mode)
        1- or 4-byte immediate data (32-bit operand mode)

Operands	x	88	86	286	386	486
reg,immed8	0	–	–	5+n	9	8-30
mem,immed8	2	–	–	8+n	10	9-31

n represents the number of times the operand is rotated.

REP

Repeat the String Instruction Which Follows While CX≠0

DESCRIPTION REP directs the processor to repeatedly execute the string instruction that follows. The number of repetitions is specified by the CX (ECX) register.

The REP instruction prefix is used with the string primitive instructions to perform block transfers of data. REP will repeat the instruction the number of times specified in the CX register.

Repeated string instructions can be interrupted if the processor has to handle an external interrupt. When the interrupt processing has completed, execution of the repeated string instruction will continue from where it was interrupted. Note, however, that prefixes other than REP (segment override or LOCK) that were specified as part of the original repeated instruction will *not* be properly restarted on the 8088 and 8086. This will cause improper program execution and, in the case of a missed segment override, possibly crash the system. Interrupts may be disabled before the repeated string operation to prevent this situation. If the CX count is high, however, interrupts may be disabled for an unallowable length of time. In this case, the repeated instruction should be performed in several iterations, with interrupts enabled between them. The code below gives an example of this technique.

```
;Move 32000 bytes from CS:[SI] to ES:[DI]
      MOV   CX,32
LABEL1:
      PUSH  CX
      MOV   CX,1000
      CLI
      REP   MOVS BYTE PTR ES:[DI],BYTE PTR CS:[SI]
      STI
      NOP   ;give interrupts a chance
      POP   CX
      LOOP  LABEL1
```

ALGORITHM
```
WHILE (CX≠0)
   service_pending_interrupts
   string_instruction
   CX=CX-1   ;does not affect flags
ENDWHILE
```

NOTES
1. While the REP prefix itself does not affect the flags, when used with the CMPS and SCAS instructions, the flags will be changed by the string instruction.

2. The timing for each of the string instructions when used with the REP prefix is given in the entry for that instruction.

3. The encoding for the REP prefix is identical to the REPNE/REPNZ prefix.

FLAGS

O	D	I	T	S	Z	A	P	C

No flags are affected

REP

11110010

TIMING

Operands	x	88	86	286	386	486
Not applicable. See individual instructions.	–	–	–	–	–	–

REPcond

Repeat String Instruction While Condition Is True

DESCRIPTION
REPE   (Repeat While Equal)
REPZ   (Repeat While Zero)
REPNE (Repeat While not Equal)
REPNZ (Repeat While not Zero)

REP*cond* directs the processor to repeatedly execute the string instruction which follows as long as the specified condition (*cond*) is true. The maximum number of repetitions is specified by the CX (ECX) register.

The REP*cond* instruction prefix is used with the CMPS and SCAS string primitive instructions to perform block compares and searches of data. REP*cond* will repeat the instruction the number of times specified in the CX register or until the specified condition is no longer true.

The REPZ instruction, and its alias REPE, will perform the indicated operation as long as CX≠0 and the zero flag (ZF) is set to 1. The REPNZ instruction, and its alias REPNE, will perform the indicated operation as long as CX≠0 and the zero flag (ZF) is cleared to 0. In either case, the action of the string instruction sets ZF, not the decrementing of the CX register by the REP*cond* prefix.

Repeated string instructions can be interrupted if the processor has to handle an external interrupt. When the interrupt processing has completed, execution of the repeated string instruction will continue from where it was interrupted. Note, however, that prefixes other than REP (segment override or LOCK) that were specified as part of the original repeated instruction *will not* be properly restarted on the 8088 and 8086. This will cause improper program execution and, in the case of a missed segment override, possibly crash the system. Interrupts may be disabled before the repeated string operation to prevent this situation. If the CX count is high, however, interrupts may be disabled for an unallowable length of time. In this case, the repeated instruction should be performed in several iterations, with interrupts enabled between them.

When used with the REP*cond* prefix, CMPS and SCAS will terminate the repeated instruction if either CX=0 or the condition is no longer true. Distinguish between these two cases by using the JCXZ (JECXZ) instruction to test the count register or the J*cond* instructions to test the flags.

ALGORITHM

```
DO
    service_pending_interrupts
    string_instruction   ;sets the flags
    CX=CX-1   ;does not affect flags
LOOPWHILE (CX≠0 and cond)
```

NOTES

1. While the REP*cond* prefix itself does not affect the flags, when used with the CMPS and SCAS instructions, the flags will be changed by the string instruction.

2. The timing for each of the string instructions when used with the REP*cond* prefix is given in the entry for that instruction.

3. The encoding for the REP prefix is identical to the REPNE/REPNZ prefix.

FLAGS

O	D	I	T	S	Z	A	P	C

No flags are affected

REP*cond*

```
1111001z
```

z=0, repeat while ZF=0 (REPNE/REPNZ)
  1, repeat while ZF=1 (REPE/REPZ)

TIMING

Operands	x	88	86	286	386	486
Not applicable. See individual instructions.	–	–	–	–	–	–

REPC/REPNC

Repeat String Instruction While Testing Carry Flag

DESCRIPTION The REPC (repeat while CF=1) and REPNC (repeat while CF=0) prefixes are available only on the NEC V20 and V30 processors. They direct the processor to repeatedly execute the string instruction that follows as long as the specified condition is true. The maximum number of repetitions is specified by the CX (ECX) register.

Because they are usable only on the NEC V20 and V30, the REPC and REPNC prefixes are not particularly useful, although a small amount of NEC-specific software does use these instructions. It is important to be familiar with them, however, because the opcodes used, which were unused in the 8086 and 8088, have since been assigned by Intel. The REPC opcode (64h) is assigned to the FS prefix and the REPNC opcode (65h) is assigned to the GS prefix.

ALGORITHM
```
;---REPC
DO
  CX=CX-1                    ;does not affect flags
  service_pending_interrupts
  string_instruction         ;sets the flags
LOOPWHILE (CX≠0 and CF=1)
;---REPNC
DO
  CX=CX-1                    ;does not affect flags
  service_pending_interrupts
  string_instruction         ;sets the flags
LOOPWHILE (CX≠0 and CF=0)
```

FLAGS

O	D	I	T	S	Z	A	P	C

No flags are affected

REPC/REPNC

1111001c

c=0, repeat while CF=0 (REPNC)
  1, repeat while CF=1 (REPC)

TIMING

Operands	x	V20	V30
(no operands)	–	?[1]	?[1]

[1]Timing not available.

RET/RETN/RETF

Return from Procedure (Subroutine)

DESCRIPTION
```
RET/RETN/RETF
RET/RETN/RETF op
```

RET transfers control from a procedure back to the address stored on the current top of stack. The return address is usually the instruction following the CALL instruction that transferred control to the procedure. If *op* is present, it specifies the number of bytes to be removed from the stack.

The CALL and RET instructions are used to implement a procedure, or subroutine system. CALL pushes the offset (near call) or segment and offset (far call) of the instruction following it onto the stack. This address is used to set the IP and CS registers, as required, when control is returned. Like CALL, RET can be either intrasegment (near) or intersegment (far). The assembler will generate the form required based on the TYPE attribute of the PROC.

Each of the two types of RET takes an optional 1-byte immediate argument that specifies the number of *bytes* to be removed from the stack. These bytes are removed after the return address. This feature is used when the procedure has the responsibility to discard parameters that have pushed as arguments. This is the type of calling convention used in BASIC and FORTRAN, for example. In C, the calling procedure has the responsibility for removing pushed parameters.

ALGORITHM
```
IF (OperandMode=16-bit) THEN
  POP IP
ELSE  ;OperandMode=32-bit
  POP EIP
ENDIF
IF (RETF) THEN
  POP CS
ENDIF
IF (RET op) THEN
  IF (StackMode=16-bit) THEN
    SP=SP+SIGN_EXTEND(op)
  ELSE  ;StackMode=32-bit
    ESP=ESP+SIGN_EXTEND(op)
  ENDIF
ENDIF
```

NOTES
1. A far return with pop (RET *immed16*) takes one less clock cycle to execute than the far return without pop on the 8088 and 8086.

FLAGS

O	D	I	T	S	Z	A	P	C

No flags are affected

RET (near/intrasegment)

RETN

```
11000011
```

TIMING

Operands	x	88	86	286	386	486
(no operands) Return near, real mode, or same privilege	1	20	16	11+m	10+m	5

m represents the number of elements in the target instruction.

RET *immed16* (near/intrasegment)

RETN *immed16*

```
11000010    immed16
```

immed16=2-byte immediate data

TIMING

Operands	x	88	86	286	386	486
immed16 Return near, real mode, or same privilege	1	24	20	11+m	10+m	5

RET (far/intersegment)

RETF

```
11001011
```

TIMING

Operands	*x*	88	86	286	386	486
(no operands)	2	34	26	15+*m*	18+*m*	13
(no operands) same privilege	2	–	–	PM:25+*m*	PM:32+*m*	PM:17
(no operands) lesser privilege, switch stacks	2			PM:55	PM:68	PM:35

m represents the number of elements in the target instruction.

RET *immed16* (far/intersegment)

11001010	*immed16*

immed16=2-byte immediate data

TIMING

Operands	*x*	88	86	286	386	486
(no operands)	2	33	25	15+*m*	18+*m*	14
(no operands) same privilege	2	–	–	PM:25+*m*	PM:32+*m*	PM:18
(no operands) lesser privilege, switch stacks	2	–	–	PM:55+*m*	PM:68	PM:36

m represents the number of elements in the target instruction.

ROL

Rotate Left

DESCRIPTION   ROL op_1, op_2

ROL rotates the bits in the operand specified by op_1 left by the count specified in op_2.

The ROL moves each bit in the operand to the next-higher bit position. The high-order bit is moved to the low-order position. The last bit rotated is copied to the carry flag.

ALGORITHM
```
h=SIZEOF(op₁)*8-1    ;Number of high-order bit
IF (8086 or 8088) THEN
   count=op₂
ELSE
   count=op₂ MOD 32
ENDIF
WHILE (temp≠0)
   CF=BIT(h of op₁)
   SHL op₁,1   ;Shifts zero into low bit
   ADC op₁,CF
   count=count-1
ENDWHILE
IF (op₂=1) THEN
   IF (BIT(h of op₁)≠CF) THEN
      OF=1
   ELSE
      OF=0
   ENDIF
ELSE
   OF=undefined
ENDIF
```

NOTES   1. The 80286, 80386, and 80486 do not recognize a rotation count greater than 31. If a rotation count greater than 31 is specified, only the lower 5 bits of the count will be used. The 8086 and 8088 do not limit the rotation count; the 80386 and 80486, when running in Virtual-86 mode, do limit the rotation count.

FLAGS

O	D	I	T	S	Z	A	P	C
*								*

ROL *reg/mem*,1

1101000w	mod	000	r/m	disp

w=0, operands are 8-bit
    1, operands are 16-bit (16-bit operand mode)
               32-bit (32-bit operand mode)

disp=0- or 2-byte displacement (16-bit address mode)
       0- or 4-byte displacement (32-bit address mode)

TIMING

Operands	x	88	86	286	386	486
reg,1	0	2	2	2	3	3
mem,1	2	B:15+EA W:23+EA	15+EA	7	7	4

ROL *reg/mem*,CL

1101001w	mod	000	r/m	disp

w=0, operands are 8-bit
    1, operands are 16-bit (16-bit operand mode)
               32-bit (32-bit operand mode)

disp=0- or 2-byte displacement (16-bit address mode)
       0- or 4-byte displacement (32-bit address mode)

TIMING

Operands	x	88	86	286	386	486
reg,CL	0	8+4n	8+4n	5+n	3	3
mem,CL	2	B:20+EA+4n W:28+EA+4n	20+EA-4n	8+n	7	4

n represents the number of times the operand is rotated.

ROL *reg/mem,immed8*

1100000w	mod	000	r/m	disp	immed8

w=0, operands are 8-bit
    1, operands are 16-bit (16-bit operand mode)
               32-bit (32-bit operand mode)

disp=0- or 2-byte displacement (16-bit address mode)
       0- or 4-byte displacement (32-bit address mode)

immed=1-byte immediate data

TIMING

Operands	x	88	86	286	386	486
reg,1	0	–	–	5+n	3	2
mem,1	2	–	–	8+n	7	4

n represents the number of times the operand is rotated.

ROR

Rotate Right

DESCRIPTION   ROR op_1, op_2

ROR rotates the bits in the operand specified by op_1 right by the count specified in op_2.

Bits that are shifted out of the right of the operand are shifted back into the left side of the operand. The last bit rotated is copied to the carry flag.

ALGORITHM
```
h=SIZEOF(op₁)*8-1    ;Number of high-order bit
IF (8086 or 8088) THEN
  count=op₂
ELSE
  count=op₂ MOD 32
ENDIF
WHILE (temp≠0)
  CF=BIT(0 of op₁)
  SHR op₁,1  ;Shifts zero into high bit
  BIT(h of op₁)=CF
  count=count-1
ENDWHILE
IF (op₂=1) THEN
  IF (BIT(h of op₁)≠BIT(h-1 of op₁)) THEN
    OF=1
  ELSE
    OF=0
  ENDIF
ELSE
  OF=undefined
ENDIF
```

NOTES   1. The 80286, 80386, and 80486 do not recognize a rotation count greater than 31. If a rotation count greater than 31 is specified, only the lower 5 bits of the count will be used. The 8086 and 8088 do not limit the rotation count; the 80386 and 80486, when running in Virtual-86 mode, do limit the rotation count.

FLAGS

O	D	I	T	S	Z	A	P	C
*								*

ROR *reg/mem,1*

1101000w	mod	001	r/m	disp

w=0, operands are 8-bit
   1, operands are 16-bit (16-bit operand mode)
      32-bit (32-bit operand mode)

disp=0- or 2-byte displacement (16-bit address mode)
     0- or 4-byte displacement (32-bit address mode)

TIMING

Operands	x	88	86	286	386	486
reg,1	0	2	2	2	3	3
mem,1	2	B:15+EA W:23+EA	15+EA	7	7	4

ROR *reg/mem,CL*

1101001w	mod	001	r/m	disp

w=0, operands are 8-bit
   1, operands are 16-bit (16-bit operand mode)
      32-bit (32-bit operand mode)

disp=0- or 2-byte displacement (16-bit address mode)
     0- or 4-byte displacement (32-bit address mode)

TIMING

Operands	x	88	86	286	386	486
reg,CL	0	8+4n	8+4n	5+n	3	3
mem,CL	2	B:20+EA+4n W:28+EA+4n	20+EA+4n	8+n	7	4

n represents the number of times the operand is rotated.

ROR *reg/mem,immed8*

1100000w	mod	001	r/m	disp	immed8

w=0, operands are 8-bit
   1, operands are 16-bit (16-bit operand mode)
      32-bit (32-bit operand mode)

disp=0- or 2-byte displacement (16-bit address mode)
     0- or 4-byte displacement (32-bit address mode)

immed=1 byte immediate data

Operands	x	88	86	286	386	486
reg,immed8	0	–	–	5+n	3	2
mem,immed8	2	–	–	8+n	7	4

n represents the number of times the operand is rotated.

SAHF

Store AH into 8080 Flags

DESCRIPTION SAHF copies the value of bits 7, 6, 4, 2, and 0 of the AH register into the sign flag (SF), zero flag (ZF), auxiliary carry flag (AF), parity flag (PF), and carry flag (CF), respectively.

The SAHF instruction was provided to make conversion of assembly languages programs written for the 8080 and 8085 to the 8086 easier. The utility of the command in 80x86 programming is reduced since the four remaining flags (overflow flag (OF), direction flag (DF), interrupt enable flag (IF), and trap flag (TF)) are not copied. The flags not copied from AH are unchanged. If access to all flags is required, use the PUSHF/PUSHFD instruction and then POP the image of the flags into a register or memory location.

ALGORITHM
```
CF=BIT(0 of AH)
PF=BIT(2 of AH)
AF=BIT(4 of AH)
ZF=BIT(6 of AH)
SF=BIT(7 of AH)
```

FLAGS

O	D	I	T	S	Z	A	P	C
				*	*	*	*	*

SAHF

10011110

TIMING

Operands	x	88	86	286	386	486
(no operands)	0	4	4	2	3	2

SAL

Shift Arithmetic Left (Same as SHL)

DESCRIPTION   SAL op_1, op_2

SAL shifts the bits in the operand specified by op_1 left by the count specified by op_2.

During the operation of the SAL instruction, each shift causes a zero bit to be shifted in on the right. The high-order bit of the destination before the shift is lost. If it is necessary to preserve this bit, use the RCL instruction.

The SAL instruction can be used to multiply a number by a power of 2. Each 1-bit shift left corresponds to a multiplication by 2. If the sign bit of the destination retains its original value (indicating that only non-significant bits have been lost) the overflow flag (OF) is cleared to 0.

ALGORITHM
```
h=SIZEOF(op₁)*8-1   ;Number of high-order bit
IF (8086 OR 8088) THEN
  count=op₂
ELSE
  count=op₂ MOD 32
ENDIF
WHILE (temp≠0)
  CF=BIT(h of op₁)
  op₁=op₁*2
  count=count-1
ENDWHILE
IF (op₂=1) THEN
  IF (BIT(h of op₁)≠CF) THEN
    OF=1
  ELSE
    OF=0
  ENDIF
ELSE
  OF=undefined
ENDIF
```

NOTES
1. The encoding and operation of this instruction are identical to the SHL instruction.

2. The 80286, 80386, and 80486 do not recognize a shift count greater than 31. If a shift count greater than 31 is specified, only the lower 5 bits of the count will be used. The 8086 and 8088 do not limit the shift count; the 80386 and 80486, when running in Virtual-86 mode, do limit the shift count.

FLAGS

O	D	I	T	S	Z	A	P	C
*				*	*	—	*	*

SAL *reg/mem,1*

1101000w	mod	100	r/m	disp

w=0, operands are 8-bit
   1, operands are 16-bit (16-bit operand mode)
          32-bit (32-bit operand mode)

disp=0- or 2-byte displacement (16-bit address mode)
       0- or 4-byte displacement (32-bit address mode)

TIMING

Operands	x	88	86	286	386	486
reg,1	0	2	2	2	3	3
mem,1	2	B:15+EA W:23+EA	15+EA	7	7	4

SAL *reg/mem,CL*

1101001w	mod	100	r/m	disp

w=0, operands are 8-bit
   1, operands are 16-bit (16-bit operand mode)
          32-bit (32-bit operand mode)

disp=0- or 2-byte displacement (16-bit address mode)
       0- or 4-byte displacement (32-bit address mode)

TIMING

Operands	x	88	86	286	386	486
reg,CL	0	8+4n	8+4n	5+n	3	3
mem,CL	2	B:20+EA+4n W:28+EA+4n	20+EA+4n	8+n	7	4

n represents the number of times the operand is shifted.

SAL *reg/mem,immed8*

1100000w	mod	100	r/m	disp	immed8

w=0, operands are 8-bit
   1, operands are 16-bit (16-bit operand mode)
          32-bit (32-bit operand mode)

disp=0- or 2-byte displacement (16-bit address mode)
       0- or 4-byte displacement (32-bit address mode)

immed=1-byte immediate data

Operands	88	86	286	386	486
reg,1	–	–	5+n	3	2
mem,1	–	–	8+n	7	4

n represents the number of times the operand is shifted.

SAR

Shift Arithmetic Right

DESCRIPTION   SAR op_1, op_2

SAR shifts the bits in the operand specified by op_1 right by the count specified by op_2. Duplicates of the original sign bit of the destination operand are shifted in from the left.

During the operation of the SAR instruction, each shift causes a copy of the original sign bit of the destination operand to be shifted in from the left. The bit that occupied the low-order position of the destination operand before the shift is lost. If it is necessary to preserve this bit, see the RCR instruction.

SAR may be used as an alternative to the IDIV instruction when the destination operand is positive. With both instructions, positive numbers are truncated toward zero. For example, an integer division of 4 by 2 yields 2. Equivalently, shifting 04h right one bit (shifting in the 0 sign bit on the left) yields 02h. When the operand is negative, IDIV still truncates toward 0. SAR, however, truncates toward negative infinity. For example, integer division of -3 by 2 yields -1 while shifting FDh (-3) one bit to the right (shifting in the 1 sign bit on the left) yields FEh (-2).

SAR shifts in duplicates of the sign bit of the original destination operand, preserving the sign. SHR shifts in zeros, treating the destination operand as an unsigned number.

ALGORITHM
```
h=SIZEOF(op₁)*8-1    ;Number of high-order bit
IF (8086 OR 8088) THEN
  count=op₂
ELSE
  count=op₂ MOD 32
ENDIF
WHILE (temp≠0)
  CF=BIT(0 of op₁)
  op₁=op₁/2   ;Signed division, rounding down
  count=count-1
ENDWHILE
IF (op₂=1) THEN
  IF (BIT(h of op₁)≠BIT(h-1 of op₁) THEN
    OF=1
  ELSE
    OF=0
  ENDIF
ELSE
  OF=0
ENDIF
```

NOTES 1. The 80286, 80386, and 80486 do not recognize a shift count greater than 31. If a shift count greater than 31 is specified, only the lower 5 bits of the count will be used. The 8086 and 8088 do not limit the shift count; the 80386 and 80486, when running in Virtual-86 mode, do limit the shift count.

FLAGS

O	D	I	T	S	Z	A	P	C
*				*	*	—	*	*

SAR *reg/mem,1*

1101000w	mod	111	r/m	disp

w=0, operands are 8-bit
   1, operands are 16-bit (16-bit operand mode)
      32-bit (32-bit operand mode)

disp=0- or 2-byte displacement (16-bit address mode)
     0- or 4-byte displacement (32-bit address mode)

TIMING

Operands	x	88	86	286	386	486
reg,1	0	2	2	2	3	3
mem,1	2	B:15+EA W:23+EA	15+EA	7	7	4

SAR *reg/mem,CL*

1101001w	mod	111	r/m	disp

w=0, operands are 8-bit
   1, operands are 16-bit (16-bit operand mode)
      32-bit (32-bit operand mode)

disp=0- or 2-byte displacement (16-bit address mode)
     0- or 4-byte displacement (32-bit address mode)

TIMING

Operands	x	88	86	286	386	486
reg,CL	0	8+4n	8+4n	5+n	3	3
mem,CL	2	B:20+EA+4n W:28+EA+4n	20+EA+4n	8+n	7	4

n represents the number of times the operand is shifted.

SAR *reg/mem,immed8*

1100000w	mod	111	r/m	disp	immed8

w=0, operands are 8-bit
   1, operands are 16-bit (16-bit operand mode)
                    32-bit (32-bit operand mode)

disp=0- or 2-byte displacement (16-bit address mode)
     0- or 4-byte displacement (32-bit address mode)

immed=1-byte immediate data

TIMING

Operands	88	86	286	386	486
reg,1	–	–	5+n	3	2
mem,1	–	–	8+n	7	4

n represents the number of times the operand is shifted.

SBB

Subtract with Borrow

SBB op_1, op_2

SBB subtracts op_2 from op_1, then subtracts 1 from op_1 if the carry flag (CF) is set. The result is stored in op_1 and is used to set the flags.

The SBB is the complement of the ADC instruction and is usually part of an algorithm for multibyte or multiword addition. For example, to subtract the value of the BX register from the 32-bit integer in the DX:AX register pair, you would use the following instructions.

```
SUB    AX,BX
SBB    DX,0
```

The first instruction subtracts BX from the low-order word of the 32-bit integer contained in DX:AX. If BX is greater than AX, however, this will have caused a borrow into AX. This borrow must be subtracted from bit 16 of the full 32-bit number (which is bit 0 of DX). In the second instruction, the possible borrow (and the immediate data of 0) is subtracted from the high-order word in DX to give the correct result.

ALGORITHM $op_1 = (op_1 - op_2) - CF$

FLAGS

O	D	I	T	S	Z	A	P	C
*				*	*	*	*	*

SBB reg/mem,reg/mem

000110dw	mod	reg	r/m	disp

d=0,　　op$_1$=mod+r/m　　op$_2$=reg
　　1,　　op$_1$=reg　　　　op$_2$=mod+r/m

w=0, operands are 8-bit
　　1, operands are 16-bit (16-bit operand mode)
　　　　　32-bit (32-bit operand mode)

disp=0- or 2-byte displacement (16-bit address mode)
　　　0- or 4-byte displacement (32-bit address mode)

TIMING

Operands	x	88	86	286	386	486
reg,reg	0	3	3	2	2	1
reg,mem	1	B:9+EA W:13+EA	9+EA	7	6	2
mem, reg	2	B:16+EA W:24+EA	16+EA	7	7	3

SBB *reg/mem,immed*

100000sw	mod	011	r/m	disp	immed

s=0, immediate data size specified by w
  1, sign-extend byte of immediate data

w=0, operands are 8-bit
  1, operands are 16-bit (16-bit operand mode)
     32-bit (32-bit operand mode)

disp=0- or 2-byte displacement (16-bit address mode)
  0- or 4-byte displacement (32-bit address mode)

immed=1- or 2-byte immediate data (16-bit operand mode)
  1- or 4-byte immediate data (32-bit operand mode)

Note: This instruction is not normally used to subtract immediate data from the accumulator. The SBB *accum,immed* instruction is provided for this purpose and occupies fewer bytes.

TIMING

Operands	x	88	86	286	386	486
reg,immed	0	4	4	3	2	1
mem,immed	2	B:17+EA W:25+EA	17+EA	7	7	3

SBB *accum,immed*

0001110w	immed

w=0, operands are 8-bit
  1, operands are 16-bit (16-bit operand mode)
     32-bit (32-bit operand mode)

immed=1- or 2-byte immediate data (16-bit address mode)
  1- or 4-byte immediate data (32-bit address mode)

TIMING

Operands	x	88	86	286	386	486
accum,immed	0	4	4	3	2	1

SCAS/SCASB/ SCASW/SCASD

Scan Memory String, Compare to Accumulator

DESCRIPTION
```
SCASB
SCASW
SCASD
SCAS op
```

SCAS internally subtracts the memory operand pointed to by the ES segment register and the destination index register (DI/EDI) from the accumulator (AL/AX/ EAX) and uses the result to set the flags. The destination index is updated in preparation for the next comparison.

The SCAS instruction is used to compare data in the accumulator to memory while automatically updating the effective address in preparation for the next comparison. The ES segment register in combination with the destination index register is used to form the effective address for the comparison. The size of the destination index register is determined by the current address-size attribute. If the address-size attribute is 16-bits, then the DI register will be used. If 32-bit addressing is in effect, then the EDI register will be used.

The options that must be defined when using this instruction are the operand size and whether the destination index will be incremented or decremented after the comparison.

The size of the register operand (and therefore, the memory operand) may be specified explicitly in the mnemonic or by an operand. In the first method, the transfer size is explicitly declared by using the B, W, or D suffix in combination with the SCAS mnemonic. The resulting instructions (SCASB, SCASW, and SCASD) will compare the AL, AX or EAX register to a byte, word, or doubleword in memory, respectively. The destination index register will then be adjusted by 1, 2, or 4 to point to the next operand to be compared.

The memory operand must be addressable using the ES segment register. *A segment override cannot be used.* The general form of the instruction (SCAS) takes as an argument a memory operand that defines the size of the transfer only. *The effective address of the operand is not used as the address of the transfer*; the data is always compared using the destination index as a pointer to memory. For example, the instruction SCAS BYTE PTR [BX] would be equivalent to the SCASB form and would compare the contents of the AL register to the byte of memory at ES:[DI]. The effective address of the operand is always ignored.

The destination index register will be incremented by the size of the operand if the direction flag (DF) has been cleared to 0 (by the CLD instruction, for example). The register will be decremented by the size of the operand if DF is set to 1 (by the STD instruction).

For example, assume that the address size attribute is 16-bits and DF is cleared. The instruction SCASB will be equivalent to the following instructions.

```
CMP  AL,BYTE PTR ES:[DI]
INC  DI
```

All forms of the SCAS instruction may be encoded with both the REPE/REPZ and REPNE/REPNZ prefixes. Used with the REPE/REPZ prefix, the SCAS instruction would compare the accumulator to memory as long as the CX (ECX) register was greater than zero and the memory operand was equal to the accumulator. This technique might be used to an array in memory for the first nonzero value, for example. The REPNE/REPNZ prefix with the SCAS instruction can be used to locate a byte in memory, such as during a text search.

ALGORITHM

```
opsize=SIZEOF(operand)    ;Declared by mnemonic or operand
IF (AddressMode=16-bit) THEN
  destination_index="DI"
ELSE
  destination_index="EDI"
ENDIF
IF (opsize=1) THEN
  CMP AL,BYTE PTR ES:[destination_index]
ELSEIF (opsize=2) THEN
  CMP AX,WORD PTR ES:[destination_index]
ELSE  ;opsize=4
  CMP EAX,DWORD PTR ES:[destination_index]
ENDIF
IF (DF=0)   ;CLD
  destination_index=destination_index+opsize
ELSE    ;STD
  destination_index=destination_index-opsize
ENDIF
```

NOTES

1. Early versions of the 80286 incorrectly executed the repeated form of this instruction in protected mode. If, during the execution of this instruction, a segment limit exception or IOPL exception occurs, the value of CX seen by the exception handler will be the value present at the start of the instruction. The DI register will reflect the iterations performed by the instruction.

FLAGS

O	D	I	T	S	Z	A	P	C
*				*	*	*	*	*

SCASB/SCASW/SCASD

SCAS *reg/mem*

```
1010111w
```

w=0, operands are 8-bit
  1, operands are 16-bit (16-bit operand mode)
        32-bit (32-bit operand mode)

Note: If present, the *reg/mem* operand specifies the operand size for the operation and is not included in the encoding.

TIMING

Operands	x	88	86	286	386	486
SCASB SCASW	1	B:15 W:19	15	7	8	6
SCASD	1	–	–	–	8	6
REP*cond* SCASB REP*cond* SCASW	r	B:90+15r W:9+19r	9+15r	5+8r	5+8r	7+5r T_0:5
REP*cond* SCASD	r	–	–	–	5+8r	7+5r T_0:5

r represents the number of repetitions executed when used with a REP*cond* prefix.

REP*cond* represents one of the following instruction prefixes: REPE, REPZ, REPNE, REPNZ.

T_0 indicates the timing when the number of repetitions is 0.

SEG

Override Default Segment Register

DESCRIPTION   SEG *op*

SEG, the segment override prefix instruction, specifies a segment register to be used in place of the default when calculating an effective address.

The implementation of the SEG instruction is assembler dependent. Most assemblers do not use the instruction form, but instead use an equivalent syntactical form. For example, the two code fragments shown below will both store the contents of the AX register into the word memory operand located at SS:[BX].

Explicit override:

```
SEG   CS
MOV   [BX],AX
```

Syntactic override:

```
MOV   CS:[BX],AX
```

Note that the default segment cannot be overridden for all instructions. Specifically, stack operations (which use the SS register) and the destination operand of the string instructions (which uses the ES register) cannot be overridden.

ALGORITHM   None

FLAGS

O	D	I	T	S	Z	A	P	C

No flags are affected

SEG *seg*

001	*seg*	110

seg=00, use ES
    01, use CS
    10, use SS
    11, use DS

TIMING

Operands	*x*	88	86	286	386	486
seg	0	2	2	0	0	1

SEG *seg*

01100	seg

seg=100, use FS
     101, use GS

Operands	x	88	86	286	386	486
seg	0	–	–	–	0	1

SETcond

Set Byte on Condition

DESCRIPTION SET*cond op*

Each of the conditional set instructions tests one or more of the flags in the FLAGS register and stores a byte at the destination specified by *op*. If the specified condition is met, a byte value of 01h is stored. Otherwise, a byte value of 00h is stored.

The conditional set instructions test for predetermined combinations of flags. Many of the conditional set instructions have more than one mnemonic form that assembles to the identical opcode. This aliasing is provided as a convenience for the programmer and has no effect on the object code produced. For example, assume that the contents of the AX register are to be tested and will be deemed valid if greater than 1. This criteria can be equivalently expressed as AX must be greater than 1, AX must be 2 or greater, AX must be not less than 2, or AX must be not less than or equal to 1. How the condition is expressed will depend on the programmer and the algorithm.

The following tables give the conditional set instructions, grouped by application, and the flag conditions that will cause the specified condition to be met.

Unsigned Comparison

Mnemonic	Description	Flags
SETA SETNBE	Set if above Set if not below or equal	CF=0 and ZF=0
SETAE SETNB	Set if above or equal Set if not below	CF=0
SETB SETNAE	Set if below Set if not above or equal	CF=1
SETBE SETNA	Set if below or equal Set if not above	CF=1 or ZF=1
SETE SETZ	Set if equal Set if zero	ZF=1
SETNE SETNZ	Set if not equal Set if not zero	ZF=0

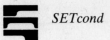

Signed Comparison

Mnemonic	Description	Condition
SETE SETZ	Set if equal Set if zero	ZF=1
SETG SETNLE	Set if greater Set if not less or equal	ZF=0 or SF=OF
SETGE SETNLP	Set if greater or equal Set if not less	SF=OF
SETL SETNGE	Set if less Set if not greater or equal	SF≠OF
SETLE SETNG	Set if less or equal Set if not greater	ZF=1 or SF≠OF
SETNE SETNZ	Set if not equal Set if not zero	ZF=0

Other Conditions

Mnemonic	Description	Condition
SETB SETC	Set if borrow Set if carry	CF=1 CF=1
SETNC	Set if not carry	CF=0
SETNO	Set if not overflow	OF=0
SETNP SETPO	Set if not parity Set if parity odd	PF=0
SETNS	Set if not sign	SF=0
SETO	Set if overflow	OF=1
SETP SETPE	Set if parity Set if parity even	PF=1
SETS	Set if sign	SF=1

ALGORITHM

```
IF (cond=TRUE) THEN
    op=1
ELSE
    op=0
ENDIF
```

NOTES

1. The 80386 executes the SET*cond* instruction regardless of the setting of the REG field. The correct encoding for the REG field is 000b, but the 80386 ignored the field. Early versions of the 80486 detect a REG≠000b as an illegal opcode. This was changed in later versions to ignore the value of REG. Assemblers that generate REG≠000b for these instructions may fail on the earlier 80486s.

FLAGS

O	D	I	T	S	Z	A	P	C

No flags are affected

SET*cond reg8/mem8* (set byte if *cond* met)

00001111	1001*cccc*	mod	000	r/m	disp

disp=0- or 2-byte displacement (16-bit address mode)
0- or 4-byte displacement (32-bit address mode)

cond	cccc	Opcode	Description
SETA	0111	97h	Set if above (unsigned comparison)
SETAE	0011	93h	Set if above or equal (unsigned comparison)
SETB	0010	92h	Set if below (unsigned comparison)
SETBE	0110	96h	Set if below or equal (unsigned comparison)
SETC	0010	92h	Set if carry
SETE	0100	94h	Set if equal
SETG	1111	9Fh	Set if greater (signed comparison)
SETGE	1101	9Dh	Set if greater or equal (signed comparison)
SETL	1100	9Ch	Set if less (signed comparison)
SETLE	1110	9Eh	Set if less or equal (signed comparison)
SETNA	0110	96h	Set if not above (unsigned comparison)
SETNAE	0010	92h	Set if not above or equal (unsigned comparison)
SETNB	0011	93h	Set if not below (unsigned comparison)
SETNBE	0111	97h	Set if not below or equal (unsigned comparison)
SETNC	0011	93h	Set if not carry
SETNE	0101	95h	Set if not equal
SETNG	1110	9Eh	Set if not greater (unsigned comparison)
SETNGE	1100	9Ch	Set if not greater or equal (unsigned comparison)
SETNL	1101	9Dh	Set if not less (signed comparison)
SETNLE	1111	9Fh	Set if not less or equal (signed comparison)
SETNO	0001	91h	Set if not overflow
SETNP	1011	9Bh	Set if not parity (=parity odd)
SETNS	1001	99h	Set if not sign
SETNZ	0101	95h	Set if not zero
SETO	0000	90h	Set if overflow
SETP	1010	9Ah	Set if parity (=parity even)

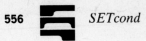

SETPE	1010	9Ah	Set if parity even
SETPO	1011	9Bh	Set if parity odd
SETS	1000	98h	Set if sign
SETZ	0100	94h	Set if zero

TIMING

Operands	x	88	86	286	386	486
reg	0	–	–	–	4	4 NS:3
mem	1	–	–	–	5	3 NS:4

SETALC

Set AL to Carry

DESCRIPTION SETALC is an undocumented opcode that duplicates the value of the carry flag through the AL register.

Although the function is undocumented, the opcode is listed as reserved but undefined in Intel documentation and will not generate the invalid opcode exception if executed. The mnemonic is not supported by most assemblers or debuggers.

Use of this instruction is not recommended as it may cause your code to be incompatible with future Intel products. This information is included only for completeness.

ALGORITHM
```
IF (CF=0) THEN
   AL=0
ELSE
   AL=FFh
ENDIF
```

FLAGS

O	D	I	T	S	Z	A	P	C

No flags are affected

SETALC

11010100

TIMING

Operands	x	88	86	286	386	486
(no operands)	0	–	–	n/a[1]	n/a[1]	n/a[1]

[1] Opcode is undocumented. No timing information available.

SGDT

Store Global Descriptor Table Register

DESCRIPTION   SGDT *op*

SGDT copies the contents of the Global Descriptor Table Register (GDTR) into six bytes of memory at the effective address given by *op*.

The LIMIT field of the GDTR is stored in the first two bytes at the specified effective address. The BASE field is stored into the subsequent doubleword; the high-order 8 bits are written as zeros by the 80386 and 80486 and undefined on the 80286.

The SGDT instruction is typically used in operating-system software.

ALGORITHM   None

FLAGS

O	D	I	T	S	Z	A	P	C

No flags are affected

SGDT *mem*

00001111	00000001	mod	000	r/m	disp

disp=0- or 2-byte displacement (16-bit address mode)
0- or 4-byte displacement (32-bit address mode)

If *mod*=11, the operation is undefined

TIMING

Operands	x	88	86	286	386	486
mem16:mem32	3	–	–	11	9	10

SHL

Shift Logical Left (same as SAL)

DESCRIPTION   SHL op_1, op_2

SHL shifts the bits in the operand specified by op_1 left by the count specified by op_2.

During the operation of the SHL instruction, each shift causes a zero bit to be shifted in on the right. The high-order bit of the destination before the shift is lost. If it is necessary to preserve this bit, use the RCL instruction.

The SHL instruction can be used to multiply a number by a power of 2. Each 1-bit shift left corresponds to a multiplication by 2. If the sign bit of the destination retains its original value (indicating that only non-significant bits have been lost) the overflow flag (OF) is cleared to 0.

ALGORITHM
```
h=SIZEOF(op₁)*8-1    ;Number of high-order bit
IF (8086 OR 8088) THEN
  count=op₂
ELSE
  count=op₂ MOD 32
ENDIF
WHILE (count≠0)
  CF=BIT(h of op₁)
  op₁=op₁*2
  count=count-1
ENDWHILE
IF (op₂=1) THEN
  IF (BIT(h of op₁)≠CF) THEN
    OF=1
  ELSE
    OF=0
  ENDIF
ELSE
  OF=undefined
ENDIF
```

NOTES
1. The encoding and operation of this instruction are identical to the SAL instruction.

2. The 80286, 80386, and 80486 do not recognize a shift count greater than 31. If a shift count greater than 31 is specified, only the lower 5 bits of the count will be used. The 8086 and 8088 do not limit the shift count; the 80386 and 80486, when running in Virtual-86 mode, do limit the shift count.

3. Early versions of the 80486 do not recognize the SHL alias encoding with REG=110b. Later versions of the chip execute this encoding as SHL.

FLAGS

O	D	I	T	S	Z	A	P	C
*				*	*	—	*	*

SHL *reg/mem,1*

1101000w	mod	100	r/m	disp

w=0, operands are 8-bit
   1, operands are 16-bit (16-bit operand mode)
          32-bit (32-bit operand mode)

disp=0- or 2-byte displacement (16-bit address mode)
       0- or 4-byte displacement (32-bit address mode)

TIMING

Operands	x	88	86	286	386	486
reg,1	0	2	2	2	3	3
mem,1	2	B:15+EA W:23+EA	15+EA	7	7	4

SHL *reg/mem,*CL

1101001w	mod	100	r/m	disp

w=0, operands are 8-bit
   1, operands are 16-bit (16-bit operand mode)
          32-bit (32-bit operand mode)

disp=0- or 2-byte displacement (16-bit address mode)
       0- or 4-byte displacement (32-bit address mode)

TIMING

Operands	x	88	86	286	386	486
reg,CL	0	8+4n	8+4n	5+n	3	3
mem,CL	2	B:20+EA+4n W:28+EA+4n	20+EA+4n	8+n	7	4

n represents the number of times the operand is shifted.

SHL *reg/mem,immed8*

1100000w	mod	100	r/m	disp	immed8

w=0, operands are 8-bit
   1, operands are 16-bit (16-bit operand mode)
          32-bit (32-bit operand mode)

disp=0- or 2-byte displacement (16-bit address mode)
  0- or 4-byte displacement (32-bit address mode)

immed=1-byte immediate data

TIMING

Operands	x	88	86	286	386	486
reg,1	0	—	—	5+n	3	2
mem,C1	2	—	—	8+n	7	4

n represents the number of times the operand is shifted.

SHLD

Double Precision Shift Logical Left

DESCRIPTION   SHLD op_1, op_2, op_3

SHLD shifts the operand specified by op_1 to the left by the count specified in op_3. The bits shifted in on the right of op_1 are provided by op_2. Only op_1 is altered.

ALGORITHM
```
h=SIZEOF(op₁)*8-1    ;number of the high-order bit
count=op₃ MOD 32
IF (count>0) THEN
   WHILE (count≠0)
      temp=BIT(h of op₂)
      op₂=op₂*2
      op₁=op₁*2
      op₁=op₁ OR temp
      count=count-1
   ENDWHILE
   CF=temp   ;last bit shifted out
   IF (op₃=1) THEN
      IF (BIT(h of op₁)≠CF) THEN
         OF=1
      ELSE
         OF=0
      ENDIF
   ELSE
      OF=undefined
   ENDIF
ENDIF
```

FLAGS

O	D	I	T	S	Z	A	P	C
*				*	*	—	*	*

SHLD *reg/mem,reg,immed8*

00001111	10100100	mod	reg	r/m	disp	immed8

op_1=mod+r/m, op_2=reg

disp=0- or 2-byte displacement (16-bit address mode)
    0- or 4-byte displacement (32-bit address mode)

immed8=1-byte immediate data.

Operands	x	88	86	286	386	486
reg16,reg16,immed8	0	—	—	—	3	2
reg32,reg32,immed8	0	—	—	—	3	2
mem16,reg16,immed8	2	—	—	—	7	3
mem32,reg32,immed8	2	—	—	—	7	3

SHLD *reg/mem,reg,*CL

00001111	10100101	mod	reg	r/m	disp

op_1=mod+r/m, op_2=reg

disp=0- or 2-byte displacement (16-bit address mode)
0- or 4-byte displacement (32-bit address mode)

Operands	x	88	86	286	386	486
*reg16,reg16,*CL	0	–	–	–	3	3
*reg32,reg32,*CL	0	–	–	–	3	3
*mem16,reg16,*CL	2	–	–	–	7	4
*mem32,reg32,*CL	2	–	–	–	7	4

SHR

Shift Logical Right

DESCRIPTION SHR op_1, op_2

SHR shifts the bits in op_1 to the right the number of times specified by op_2. Zeros are shifted in from the left.

During the operation of the SHR instruction, each shift causes a 0 bit to be shifted in from the left. The bit that occupied the low-order position of the destination operand before the shift is lost. If it is necessary to preserve this bit, see the RCR instruction.

SHR may be used as an alternative to the DIV instruction (or to the IDIV instruction when both operands are positive). With both instructions, positive numbers are truncated toward zero. For example, an integer division of 4 by 2 yields 2. Equivalently, shifting 04h right one bit (shifting in a 0 bit on the left) yields 02h.

SHR shifts in zeros, treating the destination operand as an unsigned number. SHR shifts in duplicates of the sign bit of the original destination operand, preserving the sign.

ALGORITHM
```
h=SIZEOF(op1)*8-1    ;Number of high-order bit
IF (8086 OR 8088) THEN
   count=op2
ELSE
   count=op2 MOD 32
ENDIF
WHILE (count≠0)
   CF=BIT(0 of op1)
   op1=op1/2   ;Unsigned division
   count=count-1
ENDWHILE
IF (op2=1) THEN
   IF (BIT(h of op1)≠BIT(h-1 of op1)) THEN
      OF=1
   ELSE
      OF=0
   ENDIF
ELSE
   OF=0
ENDIF
```

NOTES 1. The 80286, 80386, and 80486 do not recognize a shift count greater than 31. If a shift count greater than 31 is specified, only the lower 5 bits of the count will be used. The 8086 and 8088 do not limit the shift count; the 80386 and 80486, when running in Virtual-86 mode, do limit the shift count.

FLAGS

O	D	I	T	S	Z	A	P	C
*				*	*	—	*	*

SHR *reg/mem*,1

1101000w	mod	101	r/m	disp

w=0, operands are 8-bit
   1, operands are 16-bit (16-bit operand mode)
      32-bit (32-bit operand mode)

disp=0- or 2-byte displacement (16-bit address mode)
     0- or 4-byte displacement (32-bit address mode)

TIMING

Operands	x	88	86	286	386	486
reg,1	0	2	2	2	3	3
mem,1	2	B:15+EA W:23+EA	15+EA	7	7	4

SHR *reg/mem*,CL

1101001w	mod	101	r/m	disp

w=0, operands are 8-bit
   1, operands are 16-bit (16-bit operand mode)
      32-bit (32-bit operand mode)

disp=0- or 2-byte displacement (16-bit address mode)
     0- or 4-byte displacement (32-bit address mode)

TIMING

Operands	x	88	86	286	386	486
reg,CL	0	8+4n	8+4n	5+n	3	3
mem,CL	2	B:20+EA+4n W:28+EA+4n	20+EA+4n	8+n	7	4

n represents the number of times the operand is shifted.

SHR *reg/mem,immed8*

1100000w	mod	101	r/m	disp	immed8

w=0, operands are 8-bit
   1, operands are 16-bit (16-bit operand mode)
          32-bit (32-bit operand mode)

disp=0- or 2-byte displacement (16-bit address mode)
      0- or 4-byte displacement (32-bit address mode)

immed=1-byte immediate data

TIMING

Operands	x	88	86	286	386	486
reg,1	0	–	–	5+n	3	2
mem,1	2	–	–	8+n	7	4

n represents the number of times the operand is shifted.

SHRD

Double Precision Shift Logical Right

DESCRIPTION SHRD op_1, op_2, op_3

SHRD shifts the operand specified by op_1 to the right by the count specified in op_3. The bits shifted in on the left of op_1 are provided by op_2. Only op_1 is altered.

ALGORITHM
```
h=SIZEOF(op₁)*8-1    ;number of the high-order bit
count=op₃ MOD 32
IF (count>Ø) THEN
  WHILE (count≠Ø)
    temp=BIT(Ø of op₁)
    op₁=op₁/2
    op₂=op₂/2
    BIT(h of op₂)=temp
    count=count-1
  ENDWHILE
  CF=temp    ;last bit shifted out
  IF (op₃=1) THEN
    IF (BIT(h of op₁)≠CF) THEN
      OF=1
    ELSE
      OF=Ø
    ENDIF
  ELSE
    OF=undefined
  ENDIF
ENDIF
```

FLAGS

O	D	I	T	S	Z	A	P	C
—				*	*	—	*	*

SHRD *reg/mem,reg,immed8*

00001111	10101100	mod	reg	r/m	disp	immed

op_1=mod+r/m, op_2=reg

disp=0- or 2-byte displacement (16-bit address mode)
0- or 4-byte displacement (32-bit address mode)

immed8=1-byte immediate data

TIMING

Operands	x	88	86	286	386	486
reg16,reg16,immed8	0	–	–	–	3	2
reg32,reg32,immed8	0	–	–	–	3	2
mem16,reg16,immed8	2	–	–	–	7	3
mem32,reg32,immed8	2	–	–	–	7	3

SHRD *reg/mem,reg,CL*

00001111	10101101	mod	reg	r/m	disp

op₁=mod+r/m, op₂=reg

op_1=mod+r/m, op_2=reg

disp=0- or 2-byte displacement (16-bit address mode)
0- or 4-byte displacement (32-bit address mode)

TIMING

Operands	x	88	86	286	386	486
reg16,reg16,CL	0	–	–	–	3	3
reg32,reg32,CL	0	–	–	–	3	3
mem16,reg16,CL	2	–	–	–	7	4
mem32,reg32,CL	2	–	–	–	7	4

SIDT

Store Interrupt Descriptor Table Register

DESCRIPTION   SIDT *op*

SIDT copies the contents of the Interrupt Descriptor Table Register (IDTR) into six bytes of memory at the effective address given by *op*.

The LIMIT field of the IDTR is stored in the first two bytes at the specified effective address. The BASE field is stored into the subsequent doubleword; the high-order 8 bits are written as zeros by the 80386 and 80486 and undefined on the 80286.

The SIDT instruction is typically used in operating-system software.

ALGORITHM   None

FLAGS

O	D	I	T	S	Z	A	P	C

No flags are affected

SIDT *mem*

00001111	00000001	mod	001	r/m	disp

disp=0- or 2-byte displacement (16-bit address mode)
     0- or 4-byte displacement (32-bit address mode)

If *mod*=11, the operation is undefined

TIMING

Operands	x	88	86	286	386	486
mem16:mem32	3	–	–	12	9	10

SLDT

Store Local Descriptor Table Register (PM)

DESCRIPTION SLDT *op*

SLDT stores the Local Descriptor Table Register (LDTR) into the word operand specified by *op*.

The LDTR is a register that points into the Global Descriptor Table. The LDTR instruction is typically used in operating-system software.

ALGORITHM None

FLAGS

O	D	I	T	S	Z	A	P	C

No flags are affected

SLDT reg16/mem16

00001111	00000000	mod	000	r/m	disp

disp=0- or 2-byte displacement (16-bit address mode)
0- or 4-byte displacement (32-bit address mode)

TIMING

Operands	x	88	86	286	386	486
reg16	0	–	–	PM:2	PM:2	PM:2
mem16	1	–	–	PM:3	PM:2	PM:3

SMSW

Store Machine Status Word

DESCRIPTION SMSW *op*

SMSW stores the Machine Status Word (MSW), an internal processor register, to the word operand specified by *op*.

The SMSW instruction is used to switch to protected mode on the 80286, but it cannot be used to switch back to real mode. On the 80386 and 80486 this instruction is provided for compatibility with 80286 software and programs should use MOV *op*,CR0 instead. The SMSW instruction is typically used in operating-system software.

ALGORITHM None

FLAGS

O	D	I	T	S	Z	A	P	C

No flags are affected

SMSW *reg16/mem16*

00001111	00000001	mod	100	r/m	disp

disp=0- or 2-byte displacement (16-bit address mode)
0- or 4-byte displacement (32-bit address mode)

TIMING

Operands	x	88	86	286	386	486
reg16	0	–	–	2	2	2
mem16	1	–	–	3	2	3

STC

Set the Carry Flag

DESCRIPTION STC sets the carry flag (CF) to 1.

This instruction has no affect on the processor, registers, or other flags. It is often used to set the CF before returning from a procedure to indicate an unsuccessful termination. It is also used to set the CF during rotate operations involving the CF such as ADC, RCL, and RCR.

ALGORITHM   CF=1

FLAGS

O	D	I	T	S	Z	A	P	C
								1

STC

```
11111001
```

TIMING

Operands	x	88	86	286	386	486
(no operands)	0	2	2	2	2	2

STD

Set the Direction Flag

DESCRIPTION STD sets the direction flag (DF) to 1.

This instruction has no affect on the registers or other flags. When the direction flag is set, however, the processor will autodecrement pointers when using the string instructions such as MOVSB and STOSB.

ALGORITHM   DF=1

FLAGS

O	D	I	T	S	Z	A	P	C
	1							

STD

```
11111101
```

TIMING

Operands	x	88	86	286	386	486
(no operands)	0	2	2	2	2	2

STI

Set the Interrupt Enable Flag

DESCRIPTION STI sets the interrupt enable flag (IF) to 1.

When IF is set, the 8088 and 8086 recognize maskable interrupts, that is, external interrupt requests that appear on the INTR line of the chip.

When STI is executed, the IF flag will not be set until after the instruction following STI has executed. This feature allows a procedure that operates with interrupts disabled to re-enable interrupts and then execute another statement, such as RET, without being interrupted by a pending interrupt.

ALGORITHM
```
IF=1    ;After execution of following instruction
```

NOTES
1. On some versions of the 80486, interrupts will not be recognized if a single-clock instruction is placed between the STI and CLI instructions. Because the timing for NOP was changed from 3 clocks (in early versions) to 1 clock, the instruction sequence shown here which may have worked on earlier chips should *not* be used.

```
STI
NOP  ;1 clock not long enough to recognize interrupts
CLI
```

FLAGS

O	D	I	T	S	Z	A	P	C
		1						

STI

```
11111011
```

TIMING

Operands	x	88	86	286	386	486
(no operands)	0	2	2	2	8	5

STOS/STOSB/ STOSW/STOSD

Store a String Operand from the Accumulator into Memory

DESCRIPTION
```
STOSB
STOSW
STOSD
STOS op
```

STOS copies the contents of the accumulator (AL/AX/EAX) into a memory operand pointed to by the destination index register (DI/EDI), then updates the destination index in preparation for the next transfer.

The STOS instruction is used to transfer data from the accumulator into memory while automatically updating the effective address in preparation for the next transfer. The ES segment register in combination with the destination index register is used to form the effective address for the transfer. The size of the destination index register is determined by the current address size attribute. If the addressing size attribute is 16-bit, then the DI register will be used. If 32-bit addressing is in effect, then the EDI register will be used.

The options that must be defined when using this instruction are the operand size and whether the destination index will be incremented or decremented after the transfer.

The size of the source register (and therefore, the memory operand) may be specified explicitly in the mnemonic or by an operand. In the first method, the transfer size is explicitly declared by using the B, W, or D suffix in combination with the STOS mnemonic. The resulting instructions (STOSB, STOSW, and STOSD) will transfer a byte, word, or doubleword from the AL, AX, or EAX register, respectively. The destination index register will then be adjusted by 1, 2, or 4 to point to the next operand to be stored.

The destination memory operand must be addressable using the ES segment register. *A segment override cannot be used.* The general form of the instruction (STOS) takes as an argument a memory operand that defines the size of the transfer only. *The effective address of the operand is not used as the address of the transfer;* the data is always stored using the destination index as a pointer to memory. For example, the instruction STOS BYTE PTR [BX] would be equivalent to the STOSB form and would transfer the contents of the AL register to the byte of memory at ES:[DI]. The effective address of the operand is always ignored.

The destination index register will be incremented by the size of the operand if the direction flag (DF) has been cleared to 0 (by the CLD instruction, for example). The register will be decremented by the size of the operand if DF is set to 1 (by the STD instruction).

For example, assume that the address size attribute is 16-bits and DF is cleared. The instruction STOSB will be equivalent to the following instructions.

```
MOV  BYTE PTR ES:[DI],AL
INC  DI
```

All forms of the STOS instruction may be encoded with the REP prefix to perform a block fill of memory with the same value. This technique is often used to initialize areas of memory to some predetermined value. For example, the following instructions will fill a 1k block of memory with zeros.

```
MOV  ES,data_segment    ;must be addressable by ES
CLD                     ;auto-increment DI
MOV  DI,OFFSET BUFFER   ;start fill here
MOV  CX,1024            ;this many bytes
MOV  AL,0               ;fill value
REP  STOSB
```

ALGORITHM
```
opsize=SIZEOF(operand)    ;Declared by mnemonic or operand
IF (AddressMode=16-bit) THEN
  destination_index="DI"
ELSE
  destination_index="EDI"
ENDIF
IF (opsize=1) THEN
  BYTE PTR ES:[destination_index]=AL
ELSEIF (opsize=2) THEN
  WORD PTR ES:[destination_index]=AX
ELSE  ;opsize=4
  WORD PTR ES:[destination_index]=EAX
ENDIF
IF (DF=0)   ;CLD
  destination_index=destination_index+opsize
ELSE   ;STD
  destination_index=destination_index-opsize
ENDIF
```

NOTES

1. Early versions of the 80286 incorrectly executed the repeated form of this instruction in protected mode. If, during the execution of this instruction, a segment limit exception or IOPL exception occurs, the value of CX seen by the exception handler will be the value present at the start of the instruction. The DI register will reflect the iterations performed by the instruction.

2. This instruction is known to malfunction in two cases on some versions of the 80386. The first case occurs when STOS is followed by an instruction that uses a different address size. The second case occurs when STOS is followed by an instruction that implicitly references the stack and the B-bit in the SS descriptor is different than the address size used by the string instruction. In both cases, STOS will not update the DI/EDI register properly. The address size used by the instruction is taken from the instruction that *follows* rather than from the string instruction. This can result in the updating of only the lower 16 bits of a 32-bit register or all 32 bits of a register being used as a 16-bit operand.

In programs where 16- and 32-bit code will be mixed or where the stack and code segments may be different sizes, a NOP that uses the same address size as the STOS instruction should be explicitly coded as shown below.

```
        .386
SEGA    SEGMENT USE16 PARA PUBLIC 'CODE'
        ASSUME  CS:SEGA
        STOSW   ;16-bit STOS
        NOP     ; followed by 16-bit NOP
        DB 67H  ;32-bit STOS
        STOSW
        DB 67H  ; followed by 32-bit NOP
        NOP
SEGA    ENDS
SEGB    SEGMENT USE32 PARA PUBLIC 'CODE'
        ASSUME  CS:SEGB
        STOSD   ;32-bit STOS
        NOP     ; followed by 32-bit NOP
        DB 67H  ;16-bit STOS
        STOSD
        DB 67H  ; followed by 16-bit NOP
        NOP
SEGB    ENDS
        END
```

FLAGS

O	D	I	T	S	Z	A	P	C

No flags are affected

STOSB/STOSW/STOSD

STOS *mem*

```
1010101w
```

w=0, operands are 8-bit
   1, operands are 16-bit (16-bit operand mode)
             32-bit (32-bit operand mode)

TIMING

Operands	x	88	86	286	386	486
STOSB STOSW	1	B:11 W:15	11	3	5	5
STOSD	1	-	-	-	5	5
REP STOSB REP STOSW	r	B:9+10r W:9+14r	9+10r	4+3r	5+5r	7+5r T_0:5
REP STOSD	r	–	–	–	5+5r	7+5r T_0:5

r represents the number of repetitions executed when used with the REP prefix.

T_0 indicates the timing when the number of repetitions is 0.

STR

Store Task Register (PM)

DESCRIPTION   STR *op*

STR stores the Task Register (TR), an internal processor register, to the operand specified by *op*. The STR instruction is typically used in operating-system software.

ALGORITHM   None

FLAGS

O	D	I	T	S	Z	A	P	C

No flags are affected

STR *reg16/mem16*

00001111	00000000	mod	001	r/m	disp

disp=0- or 2-byte displacement (16-bit address mode)
     0- or 4-byte displacement (32-bit address mode)

TIMING

Operands	x	88	86	286	386	486
reg16	0	–	–	PM:2	PM:2	PM:2
mem16	1	–	–	PM:3	PM:2	PM:3

SUB

Subtract Two Operands

DESCRIPTION   SUB op_1, op_2

SUB subtracts the operand specified by op_2 from the operand specified by op_1. The result is stored back into op_1 and is used to set the flags.

ALGORITHM $op_1 = op_1 - op_2$

FLAGS

O	D	I	T	S	Z	A	P	C
*				*	*	*	*	*

SUB *reg/mem,reg/mem*

001010dw	mod	reg	r/m	disp

d=0, op_1=mod+r/m op_2=reg
   1, op_1=reg op_2=mod+r/m

w=0, operands are 8-bit
   1, operands are 16-bit (16-bit operand mode)
        32-bit (32-bit operand mode)

disp=0- or 2-byte displacement (16-bit address mode)
      0- or 4-byte displacement (32-bit address mode)

TIMING

Operands	x	88	86	286	386	486
reg,reg	0	3	3	2	2	1
reg,mem	1	B:9+EA W:13+EA	9+EA	7	6	2
mem,reg	2	B:16+EA W:24+EA	16+EA	7	7	3

SUB *reg/mem,immed*

100000sw	mod	101	r/m	disp	immed

s=0, immediate data size specified by w
   1, sign-extend byte of immediate data

w=0, operands are 8-bit
   1, operands are 16-bit (16-bit operand mode)
        32-bit (32-bit operand mode)

disp=0- or 2-byte displacement (16-bit address mode)
0- or 4-byte displacement (32-bit address mode)

immed=1- or 2-byte immediate data (16-bit operand mode)
1- or 4-byte immediate data (32-bit operand mode)

Note: This instruction is not normally used to subtract immediate data from the accumulator. The SUB *accum,immed* instruction is provided for that purpose and occupies fewer bytes.

TIMING

Operands	x	88	86	286	386	486
reg,immed	0	4	4	3	2	1
mem,immed	1	B:17+EA W:25+EA	17+EA	7	7	3

SUB *accum,immed*

0010110w	immed

w=0, operands are 8-bit
1, operands are 16-bit (16-bit operand mode)
32-bit (32-bit operand mode)

immed=1- or 2-byte immediate data (16-bit address mode)
1- or 4-byte immediate data (32-bit address mode)

TIMING

Operands	x	88	86	286	386	486
accum,immed	0	4	4	3	2	1

TEST

Test (Logical Compare)

DESCRIPTION   TEST op_1, op_2

TEST internally performs the logical AND of op_1 and op_2, using the result to set the flags. Neither operand is altered.

The TEST instruction can be used to determine if a bit in an operand is set where the CMP instruction cannot. For example, assume you wish to determine if bit 5 in the AL register is set to 1. The instruction CMP AL,20h will not accomplish this because the comparison will be true only if bit 5 is the only bit set. If bits 5 and 6 were set (AL=60h), the comparison would fail. The instruction TEST AL,20h will set the zero flag (ZF) to 1 if bit 5 of AL is not set and clear ZF to 0 if bit 5 of AL is set as shown below.

```
TEST  AL,20h   ;Test bit 5
JZ    NotSet
```

ALGORITHM   temp=op_1 AND op_2 ;Result used to set the flags
CF=0
OF=0

NOTES

1. The syntax TEST *mem,reg* cannot be encoded. Most assemblers, however, accept this syntax but generate the instruction TEST *reg,mem*.

2. Early versions of the 80486 do not recognize the alias encoding for the TEST *reg/mem,immed* instruction with REG=001b. Later versions of the chip execute this encoding.

FLAGS

O	D	I	T	S	Z	A	P	C
0				*	*	—	*	0

TEST *reg,reg/mem*

1000010w	mod	reg	r/m	disp

op_1=reg, op_2=mod+r/m

w=0, operands are 8-bit
   1, operands are 16-bit (16-bit operand mode)
              32-bit (32-bit operand mode)

disp=0- or 2-byte displacement (16-bit address mode)
      0- or 4-byte displacement (32-bit address mode)

TIMING

Operands	x	88	86	286	386	486
reg,reg	0	3	3	2	2	1
reg,mem	1	B:9+EA W:13+EA	9+EA	6	5	2

TEST *reg/mem,immed*

1111011w	mod	000	r/m	disp	immed

w=0, operands are 8-bit
    1, operands are 16-bit (16-bit operand mode)
        32-bit (32-bit operand mode)

disp=0- or 2-byte displacement (16-bit address mode)
    0- or 4-byte displacement (32-bit address mode)

immed=1- or 2-byte immediate data (16-bit operand mode)
    1- or 4-byte immediate data (32-bit operand mode)

Note: This encoding of TEST is not normally used to test the accumulator and an immediate operand. The form TEST *accum,immed* is provided for this purpose.

TIMING

Operands	x	88	86	286	386	486
reg,immed	0	5	5	3	2	1
mem,immed	1	11+EA	11+EA	6	5	1

TEST *accum,immed*

1010100w	immed

w=0, operands are 8-bit
    1, operands are 16-bit (16-bit operand mode)
        32-bit (32-bit operand mode)

immed=1- or 2-byte immediate data (16-bit operand mode)
    1- or 4-byte immediate data (32-bit operand mode)

TIMING

Operands	x	88	86	286	386	486
accum,immed	0	4	4	3	2	1

VERR

Verify a Segment for Reading (PM)

DESCRIPTION VERR *op*

VERR determines whether the segment denoted by the selector (*op*) is accessible from the current privilege level (CPL) and whether the segment is readable.

If the segment is accessible, the ZF is set to 1. If not, the ZF is cleared to 0.

ALGORITHM None

NOTES

1. On some versions of the 80386, the VERR does not work correctly if a null selector is specified as op_2. The instruction will operate on the descriptor at entry 0 in the GDT instead of unconditionally clearing the zero flag (ZF).

   To work around this, the descriptor in entry 0 of the GDT should be initialized to all zeros. Any access by VERR to this descriptor will fail, and will be reported with ZF=0, which is the desired behavior.

2. On some versions of the 80386, if the operand of the VERR instruction is not accessible and none of the instructions following VERR in the prefetch queue is a JMP, CALL, or has a memory operand, then the processor will hang after executing the VERR. The processor remains stopped until an INTR, NMI, or RESET occurs. The system timer interrupt will normally unhang the system.

   This condition can be avoided by coding a JMP or J*cond* instruction immediately following the VERR instruction. The last byte of the VERR instruction and the entire jump instruction must be contained in the same aligned doubleword.

FLAGS

O	D	I	T	S	Z	A	P	C
					*			

VERR *reg16/mem16*

00001111	00000000	mod	100	r/m	disp

disp=0- or 2-byte displacement (16-bit address mode)
     0- or 4-byte displacement (32-bit address mode)

TIMING

Operands	x	88	86	286	386	486
reg16	0	–	–	PM:14	PM:10	PM:11
mem16	1	–	–	PM:16	PM:11	PM:11

VERW

Verify a Segment for Writing (PM)

DESCRIPTION   VERW *op*

VERW determines whether the segment denoted by the selector (*op*) is accessible from the current privilege level (CPL) and whether the segment is writable.

If the segment is accessible, the ZF is set to 1. If not, the ZF is cleared to 0.

ALGORITHM None

NOTES
1. On some versions of the 80386, the VERW does not work correctly if a null selector is specified as op_2. The instruction will operate on the descriptor at entry 0 in the GDT instead of unconditionally clearing the zero flag (ZF).

   To work around this, the descriptor in entry 0 of the GDT should be initialized to all zeros. Any access by VERW to this descriptor will fail, and will be reported with ZF=0, which is the desired behavior.

2. On some versions of the 80386, if the operand of the VERW instruction is not accessible and none of the instructions following VERW in the prefetch queue is a JMP, CALL, or has a memory operand, then the processor will hang after executing the VERW. The processor remains stopped until an INTR, NMI, or RESET occurs. The system timer interrupt will normally unhang the system.

   This condition can be avoided by coding a JMP or J*cond* instruction immediately following the VERW instruction. The last byte of the VERW instruction and the entire jump instruction must be contained in the same aligned doubleword.

FLAGS

O	D	I	T	S	Z	A	P	C
					*			

VERW *reg16/mem16*

00001111	00000000	mod	101	r/m	disp

disp=0- or 2-byte displacement (16-bit address mode)
0- or 4-byte displacement (32-bit address mode)

TIMING

Operands	x	88	86	286	386	486
reg16	0	–	–	PM:14	PM:15	PM:11
mem16	1	–	–	PM:16	PM:16	PM:11

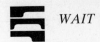

WAIT

Wait for Asserted Signal

DESCRIPTION WAIT causes the processor to enter the wait state until its TEST line becomes active.

The WAIT instruction is used in a multiprocessor environment to synchronize access to memory. Typically, WAIT is used after requesting the math coprocessor chip to write to memory. The WAIT instruction ensures that the coprocessor, which runs asynchronously with the main processor, has finished writing the data before the processor attempts to read it. This use of WAIT, when working with a coprocessor, is required for the 8088 and 8086, but not for later chips.

ALGORITHM None

NOTES
1. If the program may be run on a system that will not have a math coprocessor installed and will be using hardware-based emulation, the ESC instruction FWAIT should be used instead of WAIT.

FLAGS

O	D	I	T	S	Z	A	P	C

No flags are affected

WAIT

10011011

TIMING

Operands	x	88	86	286	386	486
(no operands)	0	3	3	3	6	1-3

WBINVD

Write-Back and Invalidate Cache

DESCRIPTION WBINVD flushes both internal and external caches, directing any external caches to write-back data to main memory before flushing.

ALGORITHM None

NOTES

1. On some versions of the 80486, if a cache line fill is in progress when the WBINVD instruction is executed, the cache line fill buffer is not invalidated. The buffer contents will be moved into the cache, which will contain a valid line when it should have been flushed.

   To work around the problem in software, use the following code to disable the internal cache prior to flushing the cache. Note that the NMI and faults/traps should not occur during this code sequence.

```
        MOV     EAX,CR0
        OR      EAX,60000000H   ;Set to disable cache
        PUSHFD
        CLI
        MOV     BL,CS:Label
        OUT     port,data       ;Write data to dummy port
        MOV     CR0,EAX         ;Disable cache
Label:
        WBINVD                  ;Invalidate cache
        AND     EAX,9FFFFFFFH   ;Enable cache (value may be
        MOV     CR0,EAX         ; different for no write-thru)
        POPFD
```

FLAGS

O	D	I	T	S	Z	A	P	C

No flags are affected

WBINVD

00001111	00001001

TIMING

Operands	x	88	86	286	386	486
(no operands)	0	–	–	–	–	5

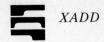

XADD

Exchange and Add

DESCRIPTION   XADD op_1, op_2

XADD transfers the value of op_1 to op_2 and puts the sum of the original values of op_1 and op_2 into op_1.

ALGORITHM   temp=op_1
op_1=temp+op_2
op_2=temp

FLAGS

O	D	I	T	S	Z	A	P	C
*				*	*	*	*	*

XADD *reg/mem,reg*

00001111	1100000w

op_1=mod+r/m, op_2=reg

w=0, operands are 8-bit
    1, operands are 16-bit (16-bit operand mode)
                 32-bit (32-bit operand mode)

disp=0- or 2-byte displacement (16-bit address mode)
         0- or 4-byte displacement (32-bit address mode)

TIMING

Operands	x	88	86	286	386	486
reg,reg	0	–	–	–	–	3
mem,reg	2	–	–	–	–	4

XBTS

Extract Bit String

DESCRIPTION XBTS op_1, op_2, op_3, op_4

The XBTS instruction was a short-lived instruction that was introduced on the A-step of the 80386DX processor and removed on the B1-step of the chip. Intel notes that the instruction was removed in order to use the area of the chip previously occupied for other microcircuitry. Beginning with the B1-step 80386DX, executing this opcode will generate an invalid opcode exception. Because some assemblers and debuggers recognize this opcode, it is noted in this reference for completeness. Detailed information on the instruction is not available.

Note that some software products attempted to execute this instruction to identify if they were being run on a B0-step 80386DX. When the B0-step of the 80486DX was released, it reused this opcode for the CMPXCHG instruction. Because of this conflict, Intel changed the CMPXCHG opcode on the B1-step of the 80486.

The XBTS instruction was designed to extract a bit string from one operand into another operand. If the function performed by the XBTS instruction is required, it can be coded explicitly using the shift double and rotate instructions available on the 80386 and later processors.

XBTS reg,reg/mem,AX,CL

| 00001111 | 10100110 | mod | reg | r/m | disp |

disp=0- or 2-byte displacement (16-bit address mode)
  0- or 4-byte displacement (32-bit address mode)

TIMING

Operands	x	88	86	286	386	486
reg	0	–	–	–	6	–
mem	2	–	–	–	13	–

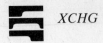

XCHG

Exchange

DESCRIPTION XCHG op_1, op_2

XCHG swaps the contents of the operands specified by op_1 and op_2.

For the XCHG instruction to have meaning, both operands must be the same size and one of the operands must always be a register. Direct memory-to-memory exchanges are not supported.

ALGORITHM
temp=op_1
op_1=op_2
op_2=temp

NOTES
1. The encoding of XCHG *accum,reg*, when the specified register, *reg*, is AX, is 90h, the same opcode as NOP.
2. On the 80286 and later processors, the bus lock signal, LOCK#, is automatically asserted for this instruction.

FLAGS

O	D	I	T	S	Z	A	P	C

No flags are affected

XCHG *reg/mem,reg*

1000011w	mod	reg	r/m	disp

op_1=mod+r/m, op_2=reg

w=0, operands are 8-bit
 1, operands are 16-bit (16-bit operand mode)
      32-bit (32-bit operand mode)

disp=0- or 2-byte displacement (16-bit address mode)
  0- or 4-byte displacement (32-bit address mode)

TIMING

Operands	x	88	86	286	386	486
reg,reg	0	4	4	3	3	3
reg,mem	2	B:17+EA W:25+EA	17+EA	5	5	5

XCHG *accum,reg*

10010	reg

Operands	x	88	86	286	386	486
accum,reg16	0	3	3	3	3	3
accum,reg32	0	–	–	–	3	3

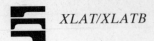

XLAT/XLATB

Translate (Perform Table Lookup)

DESCRIPTION
```
XLAT
XLATB
XLAT op
```

XLAT replaces the current contents of the AL register with a byte from a 256-byte lookup table, using AL as the table index. The BX (EBX) register is assumed to contain the base offset of the table.

The XLAT instruction is used when the offset in BX is known to be relative to the DS segment register. If not, the XLAT *op* form provides a syntax that allows for the encoding of a segment override prefix. The BX (EBX) register is always used for the offset of the table regardless of the specified operand.

The XLAT instruction is normally used to translate between character sets such as ASCII and EBCDIC. The byte value in AL is extended with zeros to a 16-bit value and used as an unsigned displacement from the offset contained in BX.

If the initial value of AL will always fall within a well defined range, the lookup table can be less than 256 bytes. For example, assume possible values for AL are from 10h to 2Fh and from 40h to 5Fh. A 40h-byte lookup table could be constructed and accessed with the following code.

```
            MOV   BX,OFFSET LOOKUP
            SUB   AL,10h    ;Change first legal value to 0.
            CMP   AL,1Fh    ;Use table bytes 0-1Fh
            JBE   DO_LOOKUP
            SUB   AL,10h    ;Value 10h corresponds to table byte 20h
DO_LOOKUP:
            XLAT
```

ALGORITHM
```
EA=BX+ZERO_EXTEND(AL)
AL=BYTE PTR [EA]
```

NOTES
1. Some assemblers accept the alias XLATB for the XLAT instruction.

FLAGS

O	D	I	T	S	Z	A	P	C

No flags are affected

XLAT

| 11010111 |

TIMING

Operands	*x*	88	86	286	386	486
(no operands)	1	11	11	5	5	4

XOR

Logical Exclusive-OR

DESCRIPTION   XOR op_1, op_2

XOR performs a bitwise logical XOR of the operands specified by op_1 and op_2. The result of the operation is stored in op_1 and is used to set the flags.

In the exclusive-or operation, each individual bit of the result is set to 1 if and only if the corresponding bits in each operand have opposite values; otherwise, the bit in the result is cleared to 0. A truth-table for the bitwise XOR operation is shown below.

A	B	A XOR B
0	0	0
0	1	1
1	0	1
1	1	0

XORing two identical operands will always produce a zero result. This property is often used as a small and fast method of initializing a register to 0. For example, to set the AX register to 0, use the instruction XOR AX,AX. On the 8088 and 8086, this instruction requires fewer bytes and clocks than the instruction MOV AX,0.

ALGORITHM $op_1 = op_1$ XOR op_2
CF=0
OF=0

FLAGS

O	D	I	T	S	Z	A	P	C
0				*	*	—	*	0

XOR *reg/mem,reg/mem*

001100dw	mod	reg	r/m	disp

d=0, op_1=mod+r/m op_2=reg
  1, op_1=reg op_2=mod+r/m

w=0, operands are 8-bit
   1, operands are 16-bit (16-bit operand mode)
                32-bit (32-bit operand mode)

disp=0- or 2-byte displacement (16-bit address mode)
      0- or 4-byte displacement (32-bit address mode)

Operands	x	88	86	286	386	486
reg,reg	0	3	3	2	2	1
reg,mem	1	B:9+EA W:13+EA	9+EA	7	6	2
mem,reg	2	B:16+EA W:24+EA	16+EA	7	7	3

XOR *reg/mem,immed*

100000sw	mod	110	r/m	disp	immed

s=0, immediate data size specified by w
  1, sign-extend byte of immediate data

w=0, operands are 8-bit
  1, operands are 16-bit (16-bit operand mode)
      32-bit (32-bit operand mode)

disp=0- or 2-byte displacement (16-bit address mode)
     0- or 4-byte displacement (32-bit address mode)

immed=1- or 2-byte immediate data (16-bit operand mode)
      1- or 4-byte immediate data (32-bit operand mode)

Note: This encoding is not normally used to XOR the accumulator
with immediate data. The XOR *accum,immed* instruction is provided for this purpose.

Operands	x	88	86	286	386	486
reg,immed	0	4	4	3	2	1
mem,immed	1	B:17+EA W:25+EA	17+EA	7	7	3

XOR *accum,immed*

0011010w	immed

immed=1- or 2-byte immediate data (16-bit operand mode)
      1- or 4-byte immediate data (32-bit operand mode)

Operands	x	88	86	286	386	486
accum,immed	0	4	4	3	2	1

APPENDIX B

COPROCESSOR INSTRUCTION REFERENCE

THE INSTRUCTIONS AVAILABLE ON THE 80×87 COPROCESSOR (AND COMPATIBLES) are presented first in tabular form. Table B.1 lists all the instructions described in the reference, their assembler mnemonics, the processors that support them, and a short description of the instructions. This table can be used as a quick reference to check a mnemonic or see if the FCOS instruction is valid across the 80×87 family, for example. A second listing of the instructions, given in Table B.2, groups the instructions by category.

TABLE B.1

Instructions in Alphabetical Order

Instruction	87	287	287XL	387 486 487	Definition
F2XM1	*	*	*	*	2^x-1
F4X4					4x4 Matrix Multiplication Transform[1]
FABS	*	*	*	*	Absolute Value
FADD	*	*	*	*	Add Real
FADDP	*	*	*	*	Add Real and Pop
FBLD	*	*	*	*	Load BCD
FBSTP	*	*	*	*	Store BCD and Pop
FCHS	*	*	*	*	Change Sign
FCLEX	*	*	*	*	Clear Exceptions
FCOM	*	*	*	*	Compare Real
FCOMP	*	*	*	*	Compare Real andRop
FCOMPP	*	*	*	*	Compare Real and Pop Twice
FCOS			*	*	Cosine
FDECSTP	*	*	*	*	Decrement Stack Pointer
FDISI	*	*[2]	*[2]	*[2]	Disable Interrupts
FDIV	*	*	*	*	Divide Real

TABLE B.1

Instructions in Alphabetical Order (continued)

Instruction	87	287	287XL	387 486 487	Definition
FDIVP	*	*	*	*	Divide Real and Pop
FDIVR	*	*	*	*	Reversed Real Divide
FDIVRP	*	*	*	*	Reversed Real Divide and Pop
FENI	*	*[2]	*[2]	*[2]	Enable Interrupts
FFREE	*	*	*	*	Mark Register as Free
FFREEP[3]	*	*	*	*	Mark Register as Free and Pop
FIADD	*	*	*	*	Add Integer
FICOM	*	*	*	*	Compare Integer
FICOMP	*	*	*	*	Compare Integer and Pop
FIDIV	*	*	*	*	Divide Integer
FIDIVR	*	*	*	*	Reversed Integer Divide
FILD	*	*	*	*	Load Integer
FIMUL	*	*	*	*	Multiply Integer
FINCSTP	*	*	*	*	Increment Stack Pointer
FINIT	*	*	*	*	Initialize
FIST	*	*	*	*	Store Integer
FISTP	*	*	*	*	Store Integer and Pop
FISUB	*	*	*	*	Subtract Integer
FISUBR	*	*	*	*	Reverse Integer Subtract
FLD	*	*	*	*	Load Real
FLD1	*	*	*	*	Load Constant: +1.0
FLDCW	*	*	*	*	Load Control Word
FLDENV	*	*	*	*	Load Environment
FLDL2E	*	*	*	*	Load Constant: $\log_2 e$
FLDL2T	*	*	*	*	Load Constant: $\log_2 10$
FLDLG2	*	*	*	*	Load Constant: $\log_{10} 2$
FLDLN2	*	*	*	*	Load Constant: $\log_e 2$
FLDPI	*	*	*	*	Load Constant: π

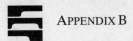

TABLE B.1

Instructions in Alphabetical Order (continued)

Instruction	87	287	287XL	387 486 487	Definition
FLDZ	*	*	*	*	Load Constant: +0.0
FMUL	*	*	*	*	Multiply Real
FMULP	*	*	*	*	Multiply Real and Pop
FNCLEX	*	*	*	*	Clear Exceptions
FNDISI	*	*[2]	*[2]	*[2]	Disable Interrupts
FNENI	*	*[2]	*[2]	*[2]	Enable Interrupts
FNINIT	*	*	*	*	Initialize
FNOP	*	*	*	*	No Operation
FNSAVE	*	*	*	*	Save NPX State
FNSTCW	*	*	*	*	Store Control Word
FNSTENV	*	*	*	*	Store Environment
FNSTSW	*	*	*	*	Store Status Word
FNSTSW AX FNSTSWAX		*	*	*	Store Status Word in AX
FPATAN	*	*	*	*	Partial Arctangent
FPREM	*	*	*	*	Partial Remainder
FPREM1			*	*	Partial Remainder
FPTAN	*	*	*	*	Partial Tangent
FRICHOP					Chop ST to Integer[4]
FRINEAR					Round ST to Nearest or Even[4]
FRINT2					Round ST to Nearest, Halves Away from Zero[4]
FRNDINT	*	*	*	*	Round to Integer
FRSTOR	*	*	*	*	Restore Saved NPX State
FRSTPM			*	[5]	Leave Protected Mode
FSAVE	*	*	*	*	Save NPX State
FSBP0					Select Bank Pointer 0[1]
FSBP1					Select Bank Pointer 1[1]
FSBP2					Select Bank Pointer 2[1]
FSCALE	*	*	*	*	Scale

TABLE B.1

Instructions in Alphabetical Order (continued)

Instruction	87	287	287XL	387 486 487	Definition
FSETPM		*	*	*[2]	Enter Protected Mode
FSIN			*	*	Sine
FSINCOS			*	*	Sine and Cosine
FSQRT	*	*	*	*	Square Root
FST	*	*	*	*	Store Real
FSTCW	*	*	*	*	Store Control Word
FSTENV	*	*	*	*	Store Environment
FSTP	*	*	*	*	Store Real and Pop
FSTSW	*	*	*	*	Store Status Word
FSTSW AX FSTSWAX		*	*	*	Store Status Word in AX
FSUB	*	*	*	*	Subtract Real
FSUBP	*	*	*	*	Subtract Real and Pop
FSUBR	*	*	*	*	Reversed Real Subtract
FSUBRP	*	*	*	*	Reversed Real Subtract and Pop
FTST	*	*	*	*	Test ST Against +0.0
FTSTP[3]	*	*	*	*	Test ST Against +0.0 and Pop
FUCOM			*	*	Unordered Real Compare
FUCOMP			*	*	Unordered Real Compare and Pop
FUCOMPP			*	*	Unordered Real Compare and Pop Twice
FWAIT	*	*	*	*	Wait Until NPX Not Busy
FXAM	*	*	*	*	Examine ST
FXCH	*	*	*	*	Exchange Registers
FXTRACT	*	*	*	*	Extract Exponent and Mantissa
FYL2X	*	*	*	*	$Y*\log_2 X$
FYL2XP1	*	*	*	*	$Y*\log_2(X+1)$

[1] Available on the IIT 2C87, 3C87, and 3C87SX only.
[2] This instruction does not cause an exception, but performs no useful action on the indicated processor.
[3] Undocumented opcode, mnemonic not supported. See opcode map in Appendix C.
[4] Available on the Cyrix EMC87 only.
[5] Generates an invalid opcode exception on these coprocessors.

TABLE B.2

Instruction Summary by Category

Data Transfer

FBLD	FBSTP	FILD	FIST	FISTP
FLD	FST	FSTP	FXCH	

Comparison

FCOM	FCOMP	FCOMPP	FICOM	FICOMP
FTST	FUCOM	FUCOMP	FUCOMPP	FXAM

Constant Load

FLD1	FLDL2E	FLDL2T	FLDLG2	FLDLN2
FLDPI	FLDZ			

Basic Arithmetic

FADD	FADDP	FDIV	FDIVP	FDIVR
FDIVRP	FIADD	FIDIV	FIDIVR	FIMUL
FISUB	FISUBR	FMUL	FMULP	FSUB
FSUBP	FSUBR	FSUBRP		

Advanced Arithmetic

F4X4	FABS	FCHS	FPREM	FPREM1
FRICHOP	FRINEAR	FRINT2	FRNDINT	FSCALE
FSQRT	FXTRACT			

Transcendental

F2XM1	FCOS	FPATAN	FPTAN	FSIN
FSINCOS	FYL2X	FYL2XP1		

Coprocessor Control

FCLEX	FDECSTP	FFREE	FINCSTP	FINIT
FLDCW	FLDENV	FNOP	FRSTOR	FSAVE
FSBP0	FSBP1	FSBP2	FSTCW	FSTENV
FSTSW	FSTSW AX	FSTSWAX	FWAIT	

The following additional instructions, listed in Table B.3, are available only on the indicated non-Intel coprocessors.

TABLE B.3

Proprietary Instructions on Non-Intel Coprocessors

Cyrix Corp.
EMC87 (80387 replacement)

FRICHOP	FRINEAR	FRINT2	FTSTP

Integrated Information Technology Inc.
IIT-2C87 (80287 replacement)
IIT-3C87 (80387 replacement)
IIT-3C87SX (80387SX replacement)

F4X4	FSBP0	FSBP1	FSBP2

Instruction Encoding

The instruction encoding for the NPX is generally simpler than for the CPU. In all cases, the instructions are a minimum of 2 bytes long. The high-order 5 bits of the first opcode byte are always 11011b, which identifies them as ESC (escape) instructions. The instructions take one of five general formats as shown in Table B.4; they may also include an address size, operand size, or segment override prefix.

TABLE B.4

NPX Instruction Encoding Format

Byte 1				Byte 2				Optional Field
11011	OP-A		1	*mod*	1	OP-B	*r/m*	*disp*/SIB
11011	MF		OP-A	*mod*	OP-B		*r/m*	*disp*/SIB
11011	*d*	P	OP-A	11	OP-B		*rrr*	
11011	0	0	1	11	1	OP		
11011	0	1	1	11	1	OP		
76543	2	1	0	76	5	43	210	Bit Position

d   *Destination.* Decoded as:
    0   ST is destination
    1   ST(i) is destination

disp   *Displacement.* 1-, 2-, or 4-byte displacement of memory operand.

MF   *Memory format.* Decoded as:
    00b   32-bit real
    01b   32-bit integer
    10b   64-bit real
    11b   16-bit integer

mod   *Mode field.* Addressed as defined for the processor MOD/RM byte.

OP   *Opcode field.* May be split between the two bytes as OP-A and OP-B.

P   *Pop.* Decoded as:
      0   Do not pop stack.
      1   Pop stack after operation.

r/m   *Register/memory field.* Defined for the processor MOD/RM byte.

rrr   *Register number.* For ST(i) where i=*rrr*b.

SIB   *Scale Index Base.* Byte present for expanded addressing modes.

Instruction Timings

The instruction timings for the floating-point instructions are typically given as a range of clocks representing the best estimate of actual instruction execution time. The number of clocks required to execute an instruction varies depending on the processor mode, type of operands, and so on. Execution times also vary significantly among different versions, or steps, of the same processor. The times shown here are for the latest version of the chips available at time of publication. Unless indicated otherwise, the typical execution time is within 10 percent of the average of the two extremes.

You will find the symbols used in the timing section of the listings in Table B.5. Symbols used for only one or two instructions are defined in the instruction listing itself.

TABLE B.5

Symbols Used to Represent Execution Timing Variables and Conditions

Timing Symbol	Explanation
—	Instruction form not available on the indicated processor.
EA	The clocks required to perform an effective address calculation.
n	In instructions that include a WAIT, *n* is the number of times the CPU examines TEST# line until the NPX lowers BUSY.
x	The number of memory transfers required by the instruction.

Because the processor performs the address decode and setup for the coprocessor, the timing penalties listed for the various memory access modes of the processor also apply to the numeric instructions. (See Chapter 6 for an exhaustive discussion of these penalties.) The penalty clocks assigned to the effective address calculation (EA) are shown in Table B.6.

On the 80486/80487 only, you should add two additional clocks if a reference to a 32-bit memory operand is a cache miss; add three clocks if a reference to a 64-bit memory operand is a cache miss.

TABLE B.6

Additional Clocks Required for Effective Address Calculations

Effective Address Components		Additional Clocks Required			
		86/88	286	386	486
Displacement	[*disp*]	6	0	0	0
Base or index	[BX] [BP] [SI] [DI]	5	0	0	0
Base + *disp* Index + *disp*	[BX + *disp*] [BP + *disp*] [DI + *disp*] [SI + *disp*]	9	0	0	0
Base + index	[BX + SI] [BP + DI]	7	0	0	0
	[BX + DI] [BP + SI]	8	0	0	0
Base + index + *disp*	[BX + SI + *disp*] [BP + DI + *disp*]	11	1	0	0
	[BX + DI + *disp*] [BP + SI + *disp*]	12	1	0	0
Segment override	*sreg*:	2	0	0	1
Base + scale * index (32-bit mode)	[*reg32* + scale * *reg32*]	–	–	1	1[1]

[1]One clock may be added to the 80486 execution time depending on the state of the processor.

Condition Code Bits

On the 8087 and 80287, the condition code bits in the NPX status word should be considered valid only for the comparison instructions (FCOM, FICOM, FTST, and FXAM) and for FPREM. The interpretation of these bits is provided in the entry for those instructions. For all other 8087/80287 instructions, the values of the condition codes should be considered as undefined unless otherwise indicated. A stack fault on the 8087 and 80287 will raise the invalid operation exception. Because the stack fault bit is not defined for the 8087 and 80287, the value shown for this bit in the NPX flags box should be ignored.

On the 80287XL, 80387, and 80486/80487, the condition code bits are set selectively by most instructions. If both the stack flag (SF) and invalid operation exception (IE) bit of the status word are set, indicating a stack exception, bit C_1 indicates whether a stack overflow ($C_1=1$) or underflow ($C_1=0$) has occurred. If the precision exception bit is set, C_1 indicates whether the last rounding in the instruction was upward ($C_1=1$).

Example Instruction Listing

Each entry in the instruction reference follows the same basic format, an example of which is shown in Figure B.1. An explanation of each element in the reference is given below:

1. *Title.* Instruction mnemonic and a short description.

2. *Description.* A one or two sentence summary of the basic action of the instruction followed by a more detailed operational description.

3. *Algorithm.* A pseudocode algorithm that describes how the instruction operates. The functions and control structures used in the pseudo-code algorithms are defined in Table B.7.

4. *Notes.* Any information that is applicable to the instruction including limitations, undocumented uses, and so on.

5. *Flags.* This element shows how the execution of the instruction affects each of the NPX exception flags and condition code bits in the status word. The symbols that are used to represent action on the flags are shown in Table B.8.

6. *Encoding and timing.* One block will be present for each unique form of the encoding. The opcode and other bytes are shown along with the timings and number of memory transfers. The number of word transfers is shown in the column headed x. This is useful for calculating the clock penalties for unaligned operands and cache misses.

Reference

The following reference section lists in mnemonic order all the instructions available on the Intel coprocessors from the 8087 through the 80486/80487, Cyrix coprocessors, and IIT coprocessors.

The timing for the 8087 and 80287 is generally the same, except that the effective address calculation does not increase the execution time for the 80287. The timing shown for the 387 is for the 80387DX. The timing for the 80387SX is typically 50 to 100 percent longer than the time shown for the 80387DX. The instruction execution times for the Cyrix and IIT products are not shown separately. The published execution times indicate that the Cyrix 83D87 (80387DX), 83S87 (80387SX), and EMC87 (80387DX) generally require 50 to 75 percent fewer clocks than the Intel products. IIT does not publish the instruction execution times for their products. More information may be obtained from the manufacturers as indicated in Appendix D.

FIGURE B.1

FSINCOS

Calculate Sine and Cosine of ST

DESCRIPTION FSINCOS calculates both the sine and cosine of ST.

The FSINCOS instruction assumes that the argument in ST is expressed in radians. ST must satisfy the inequality $-2^{63} < ST < +2^{63}$. ST is replaced with sin(ST), and then cos(ST) is pushed onto the stack. Thus after execution, ST(1) contains the sine, and ST contains the cosine of the original operand, which is destroyed.

ALGORITHM
```
IF (ABS(ST)<2^63) THEN
      temp=cos(ST)
      ST=sin(ST)
      DEC TOP
      ST=temp
      C₂=0
ELSE
      C₂=1
ENDIF
```

NOTES 1. The floating-point stack of some versions of the 80486 FPU may be corrupted when an FSINCOS instruction is executed within a particular sequence of code. In addition, this condition is data dependent. There is no indication that the floating-point stack has been corrupted.

NPX FLAGS

S	P	U	O	Z	D	I	C₀	C₁	C₂	C₃
*	*	*			*	*	–	*	*	–

FSINCOS

11011011	11111011

TIMING

Operands	×	87/287	287XL	387	486/487
(no operand)	0	–	201816[*]	150650	243329[*]

[*] Time shown is for arguments in the range $-\pi/4 < x < +\pi/4$. If the time is out of range, up to 76 additional clocks may be required to reduce the operand.
[*] If the time is out of range, add ST/($\pi/4$) clocks.

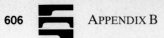

TABLE B.7

Functions and Control Structures Used in the Pseudocode Algorithms

Functions	Control Structures (Description)
IF (*cond*) THEN *statement*	If the condition is true, perform the action described by the statement.

IF (*cond*) THEN
   statement$_1$
ELSE
   statement$_2$
ENDIF
	If the condition is true, perform the action described by statement$_1$. Otherwise, perform the action described by statement$_2$.

IF (*cond$_1$*) THEN
   statement$_1$
ELSEIF (*cond$_2$*) THEN
   statement$_2$
ELSEIF (*cond$_3$*) THEN
   $\vdots$
ENDIF
	If condition$_n$ is true, perform the action described by the statement$_n$.

BIT(*n* of *op*)	Represents the single bit, number *n*, of the specified operand.
NOT(*op*)	Logical NOT of operand.
TAG(i)	Tag value for floating-point register ST(i).
EXPONENT(*op*)	Represents the value of the exponent portion of the operand.
MANTISSA(*op*)	Represents the value of the mantissa portion of the operand.
SIGN(*op*)	Represents the sign of the operand.
ABS(*op*)	Represents the absolute value of the operand.
EXAMINE(*op*)	Indicates that the operand is examined according to the internal logic of the NPX. (This is the function performed by FXAM.)
FPOP	Indicates that the floating-point stack is popped. The tag for the current stack top is marked empty and TOP is incremented.
ROUNDINT(*op*,method)	Represents the value of the operand after being rounded according to the indicated method.
RC	Round according to the current setting of the rounding control (RC) field in the NPX control word.
CHOP	Round by chopping toward zero.
NEAREST	Round to nearest or, if an exact half, to even.
NUMOPS	Represents the number of operands in the form as shown:

FORM	NUMOPS
FADD	0
FADD [*mem*]	1
FADD ST,ST(i)	2

TOP	Represents the current top-of-stack pointer in the NPX status word.

TABLE B.8

Symbols Used to Represent the Flag State after an Instruction Execution

Flag Symbol	Explanation
0	Flag is cleared to 0.
1	Flag is set to 1.
*	Flag is set according to the result of the operation.
–	Value of flag is undefined after the operation.

The entry for each instruction includes a description of the operation and use of the instruction, a pseudocode algorithm of its operation, notes on inconsistencies and bugs, the flags affected by instruction execution, and the instruction encoding. The encoding information is shown in binary form. Bits that have fixed values for an instruction are shown as either 0 or 1. Symbols are used when the value for a particular field will vary.

When one mnemonic is used to represent several different forms of an instruction (with different opcodes), all forms appear under the same heading. The different encodings and timings are shown as required.

The encoding given for all instructions is the 16-bit encoding and doesn't show the SIB byte explicitly. The encoding for any instruction that requires the SIB byte can easily be generated: replace the *disp* byte with the SIB byte and add the subsequent bytes as explained in Chapter 6 in the section on 80386 and 80486 encoding.

 *F2XM1*

F2XM1

Calculate Function 2^X-1

DESCRIPTION   F2XM1 $ST=2^{ST}-1$

F2XM1 (2 to the x minus 1) calculates the function 2^X-1 and returns the result to ST.

On the 8087 and 80287, the value in ST must satisfy the inequality $0 \leq ST \leq 0.5$. On the 80287XL and later coprocessors, the permissible range is greater, and ST must satisfy the inequality $-1 \leq ST \leq 1$. If ST is out of range, the result is undefined, even though no exception is raised. The result is returned in ST, destroying the original operand.

The F2XM1 instruction is designed to provide an accurate result even when x is close to zero. To obtain 2^X, simply add 1.0 to the result returned by F2XM1.

This instruction is useful in performing exponentiation of values other than 2 as shown in the following formulas:

$10^x = 2^{x*log_2 10}$

$e^x = 2^{x*log_2 e}$

$y^x = 2^{x*log_2 y}$

Note that the NPX has dedicated instructions for loading the constants $log_2 10$ and $log_2 e$. The FYL2X instruction may be used to calculate $x*log_2 y$.

See also FYL2X, FLDL2T, FLDL2E.

ALGORITHM $ST=2^{ST}-1$

NPX FLAGS

S	P	U	O	Z	D	I	C_3	C_2	C_1	C_0
*	*	*			*[a]	*[a]	—	—	*	—

[a] Raised only by the 80287XL and later coprocessors.

F2XM1

11011001	11110000

TIMING

Operands	x	87/287	287XL	387	486/487
(no operands)	0	310-630[1]	215-483	167-410	140-279

[1] Typical execution time is 500 clocks.

F4X4

Calculate 4x4 Matrix Multiply Transformation (IIT)

DESCRIPTION F4X4 performs a 4x4 matrix multiply transformation.

The IIT 2C87, 3C87, and 3C87SX coprocessors contain 32 80-bit floating-point registers arranged in four banks of eight registers each. Three of the banks (24 registers) can be addressed directly. The fourth bank is used internally, as by this instruction.

The F4X4 instruction calculates the solution to the following set of simultaneous equations in a single instruction:

$$
\begin{bmatrix} X_n \\ Y_n \\ Z_n \\ W_n \end{bmatrix} = \begin{bmatrix} A_{00} & A_{01} & A_{02} & A_{03} \\ A_{10} & A_{11} & A_{12} & A_{13} \\ A_{20} & A_{21} & A_{22} & A_{23} \\ A_{30} & A_{31} & A_{32} & A_{33} \end{bmatrix} * \begin{bmatrix} X_o \\ Y_o \\ Z_o \\ W_o \end{bmatrix}
$$

The matrix coefficients A_{00}-A_{33} are loaded into the floating-point registers as shown in the input column below, and then the instruction is executed. The results are returned in bank 0 as shown in the output column.

	Input			**Output**
	Floating-Point Register Bank			
Register	**Bank 0**	**Bank 1**	**Bank 2**	**Bank 0**
ST	X_o	A_{33}	A_{31}	X_n
ST(1)	Y_o	A_{23}	A_{21}	Y_n
ST(2)	Z_o	A_{13}	A_{11}	Z_n
ST(3)	W_o	A_{03}	A_{01}	W_n
ST(4)		A_{32}	A_{30}	
ST(5)		A_{22}	A_{20}	
ST(6)		A_{12}	A_{10}	
ST(7)		A_{02}	A_{00}	

See also FSBP0, FSBP1, and FSBP2.

ALGORITHM See equation above.

NPX FLAGS

S	P	U	O	Z	D	I	C_3	C_2	C_1	C_0
*							—	—	—	—

F4X4

| 11011011 | 11110001 |

Operands	x	2C87	3C87SX	3C87
(no operands)	0	242	242	242

FABS

Absolute Value of ST

DESCRIPTION   FABS   :ST=ABS(ST)

The FABS instruction clears the sign bit of ST and leaves the result in ST.

If the original value of ST was positive, it is unchanged by this operation. A negative value will become a positive value with the same magnitude.

The invalid operation exception is raised only on stack underflow, even if the operand is a signaling NaN or unsupported format. C_1 will always be cleared to zero, to indicate either that a stack underflow has occurred (if ST is tagged empty) or that the operation was successful.

ALGORITHM   BIT(sign bit of ST)=0

NPX FLAGS

S	P	U	O	Z	D	I	C_3	C_2	C_1	C_0
*						*	—	—	0	—

FABS

11011001	11100001

TIMING

Operands	x	87/287	287XL	387	486/487
(no operands)	0	10-17	29	14-21	3

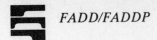

FADD/FADDP

Add Real

DESCRIPTION

```
FADD ST,ST(i)      :ST=ST+ST(i)
FADD ST(i),ST      :ST(i)=ST(i)+ST
FADD ST(i)         :ST(i)=ST(i)+ST
FADD real          :ST=ST+[real]
FADD               :ST(1)=ST(1)+ST, FPOP
FADDP              :ST(1)=ST(1)+ST, FPOP
FADDP ST(i),ST     :ST(i)=ST(i)+ST, FPOP
FADDP ST(i)        :ST(i)=ST(i)+ST, FPOP
```

The FADD and FADDP instructions add the source operand to the destination operand, returning the result to the destination operand.

The source operand may be either a floating-point register or a real memory operand, but the destination is always a floating-point register. The FADDP encoding pops the stack at the conclusion of the operation.

When the FADD or FADDP instructions are coded with no arguments (classical stack form), ST is the source and ST(1) is the destination. The result is returned to ST(1). The floating-point stack is popped at the conclusion of execution, and the result is left in ST. The following instructions have the identical effect:

```
FADD               ;Implied ST(1),ST
FADDP              ;Implied ST(1),ST
FADDP ST(1)        ;Implied ST
FADDP ST(1),ST     ;Explicit operands
```

If the destination is a register operand and is the only operand specified, then ST is automatically implied as the source operand. The instruction FADD ST(5), for example, is equivalent to FADD ST(5),ST. Note that Microsoft's MASM does not support this syntax, although DEBUG does. If, however, a memory operand is referenced, it will be the source and ST will be the destination. FADDP cannot be encoded with a memory operand. If both operands are explicitly coded, ST *must* be one of the operands, although it may be either the source or destination.

Note that the instruction FADD ST,ST(0) will double the operand at the top of the floating-point stack.

ALGORITHM

```
IF (NUMOPS=0) THEN
   ST(1)=ST(1)+ST
   FPOP
ELSEIF (NUMOPS=1) THEN
   IF (real) THEN
      ST=ST+[real]
   ELSE  ;operand is floating-point register
```

```
        ST(i)=ST(i)+ST
      ENDIF
      IF (FADDP) THEN FPOP
    ELSE  ;NUMOPS=2
      dest=dest+src
      IF (FADDP) THEN FPOP
    ENDIF
```

NPX FLAGS

S	P	U	O	Z	D	I	C_3	C_2	C_1	C_0
*	*	*	*		*	*	—	—	*	—

FADD

FADDP

11011110	11000001

TIMING

Operands	x	87/287	287XL	387	486/487
(no operands)	0	70-100	33-41	15-29	8-20

FADD ST,ST(i)

11011000	11000rrr

TIMING

Operands	x	87/287	287XL	387	486/487
ST,ST(i)	0	70-100	30-38	12-26	8-20

FADD ST(i)

FADD ST(i),ST

11011100	11000rrr

TIMING

Operands	x	87/287	287XL	387	486/487
ST(i) ST(i),ST	0	70-100	33-41	15-29	8-20

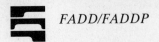

FADD *real32/real64*

11011w00	mod	000	r/m	disp

w = 0, memory operand is *real32*
  1, memory operand is *real64*

TIMING

Operands	x	87/287	287XL	387	486/487
real32	2	(90-120)+EA	40-48	12-29	8-20
real64	4	(95-125)+EA	49-79	15-34	8-20

FADDP ST(i)

FADDP ST(i),ST

11011110	11000rrr

TIMING

Operands	x	87/287	287XL	387	486/487
ST(i) ST(i),ST	0	75-105	33-41	15-29	8-20

FBLD

Load Packed BCD Memory Operand into ST

DESCRIPTION   FBLD *mem*

The FBLD instruction loads a packed BCD operand from memory, converts it to temporary real format, and pushes the resulting value onto the floating-point stack.

The memory operand must be in 80x87 packed BCD format. The sign of the operand is preserved, even when -0 is loaded. The digits are assumed to be in the valid range (0-9). The digits are not verified when loaded, and the result of loading an invalid encoding is undefined.

ALGORITHM   DEC TOP
ST=[*mem*]   ;Packed BCD operand

NPX FLAGS

S	P	U	O	Z	D	I	C_3	C_2	C_1	C_0
*						*	—	—	*	—

FBLD

11011111	mod	100	r/m	disp

TIMING

Operands	x	87/287	287XL	387	486/487
BCD80	5	(290-310)+EA	270-279	45-97	70-103

FBSTP

Store ST to Memory as Packed BCD Operand

DESCRIPTION   FBSTP *mem*

The FBSTP instruction converts ST to an integer value, copies that value to the destination specified by *mem* as a packed BCD operand, and then pops the stack.

For the 8087 and 80287, the value in ST is converted to an integer by adding a value close to 0.5 and then chopping the result. If the rounding must be controlled, use the FRNDINT instruction prior to using the FBSTP instruction. Operation on a denormal operand raises the invalid operation exception. Underflow is not possible.

On the 80287XL and later coprocessors, the value in ST is always rounded according to the current setting of the RC field before being stored. Operation on a denormal is supported and, therefore, an underflow exception can occur.

ALGORITHM
```
IF (8087 OR 80287) THEN
    [mem]=ROUNDINT((ST+0.5),CHOP)
ELSE  ;80287XL and later
    [mem]=ROUNDINT(ST,RC)
ENDIF
FPOP  ;Pop floating-point stack
```

NPX FLAGS

S	P	U	O	Z	D	I	C_3	C_2	C_1	C_0
*						*	—	—	*	—

FBSTP

11011111	mod	110	r/m	disp

TIMING

Operands	x	87/287	287XL	387	486/487
BCD80	5	(520-540)+EA	520-542	112-190	172-176

FCHS

Change Sign of ST

DESCRIPTION FCHS   :ST=-ST

The FCHS instruction complements the sign bit of ST.

If the original value of ST was positive, it is changed to negative by this operation; conversely, a negative value will become a positive value.

The invalid operation exception is raised only on stack underflow, even if the operand is a signaling NaN or unsupported format. C_1 will always be cleared to zero, as a result of either a stack underflow (if ST is tagged empty) or a successful operation.

ALGORITHM BIT(sign bit of ST)=NOT(BIT(sign bit of ST))

NPX FLAGS

S	P	U	O	Z	D	I	C_3	C_2	C_1	C_0
*						*	—	—	0	—

FCHS

11011001	11100000

TIMING

Operands	x	87/287	287XL	387	486/487
(no operands)	0	10-17	31-37	17-24	6

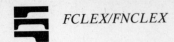

FCLEX/FNCLEX

Clear NPX Exception Flags

DESCRIPTION The FCLEX and FNCLEX instructions clear the NPX exception flags, the IR/ES flag, and the BUSY flag in the status word. The NPX's INT and BUSY lines immediately become inactive. A floating-point exception handler should typically issue this instruction before returning control to the underlying application; otherwise, another interrupt request will be immediately generated.

The FCLEX mnemonic instructs the assembler to generate the opcode for a WAIT instruction prior to the opcode for the FCLEX instruction. If the FNCLEX mnemonic is specified, no WAIT is generated.

ALGORITHM
```
SF=PE=UE=OE=ZE=DI=IE=0
B=0
IR=0;called ES on 287XL and later
```

NPX FLAGS

S	P	U	O	Z	D	I	C_3	C_2	C_1	C_0
0	0	0	0	0	0	0	–	–	–	–

FCLEX

10011011	11011011	11100010

TIMING

Operands	x	87/287	287XL	387	486/487
(no operands)	0	(5-11)+5n	11+5n	17-18	8-10[1]

n is the number of times the CPU examines TEST# line until NPX lowers BUSY.
[1] Add 17 clocks if a numeric exception is pending from a previous instruction.

FNCLEX

11011011	11100010

TIMING

Operands	x	87/287	287XL	387	486/487
(no operands)	0	2-8	8	11	7[1]

[1] Add 17 clocks if a numeric exception is pending from a previous instruction.

FCOM/FCOMP/ FCOMPP

Compare ST to Real

DESCRIPTION

FCOM	:Compare ST to ST(1)
FCOM ST(i)	:Compare ST to ST(i)
FCOM *real*	:Compare ST to [*real*]
FCOMP	:Compare ST to ST(1), FPOP
FCOMP ST(i)	:Compare ST to ST(i), FPOP
FCOMP *real*	:Compare ST to [*real*], FPOP
FCOMPP	:Compare ST to ST(1), FPOP, FPOP

The FCOM, FCOMP, and FCOMPP instructions compare ST to the specified operand (by subtraction), setting the condition codes in the NPX status word to indicate the result.

The operand may be another floating-point register or a short real or long real memory operand. If no operand is coded, ST(1) is used by default.

The condition code bits of the status word are used to report the result of the comparison as shown:

Order	C_3	C_2	C_0	Explanation
ST>op	0	0	0	ST greater than operand
ST<op	0	0	1	ST less than operand
ST=op	1	0	0	ST equal to operand
ST?op	1	1	1	ST not comparable to operand (unordered)

Note that positive and negative forms of zero are treated identically for the purpose of this instruction. NaNs and the projective infinities cannot be compared, so they return $C_3=C_2=C_0=1$ as shown in the table above.

If either or both operands are quiet NaNs, the invalid operation exception will be raised. FUCOM, on the other hand, will not raise this exception.

The FCOMP instruction operates identically to the FCOM instruction, except that the floating-point stack is popped after the comparison.

The FCOMPP instruction operates identically to the FCOM instruction, except that the floating-point stack is popped twice after the comparison. The comparison is always ST to ST(1); no explicit operands may be coded.

See also FICOM, FUCOM, FTST, and FXAM.

ALGORITHM   ConditionCodes=ST compared to operand

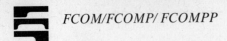
NPX FLAGS	S	P	U	O	Z	D	I	C_3	C_2	C_1	C_0
	*					*	*	*	*	0	*

FCOM

11011000	11010001

TIMING	Operands	x	87/287	287XL	387	486/487
	(no operands)	0	40-50	31	13-21	4

FCOM ST(i)

11011000	11010rrr

TIMING	Operands	x	87/287	287XL	387	486/487
	ST,ST(i)	0	40-50	31	13-21	4

FCOM *real*

11011w00	mod	010	r/m	disp

w = 0, memory operand is *real32*
    1, memory operand is *real64*

TIMING	Operands	x	87/287	287XL	387	486/487
	real32	2	(60-70)+EA	42	13-25	4
	real64	4	(65-75)+EA	51	14-27	4

FCOMP

11011000	11011001

TIMING	Operands	x	87/287	287XL	387	486/487
	(no operands)	0	42-52	33	13-21	4

FCOMP ST(i)

| 11011000 | 11011rrr |

Operands	x	87/287	287XL	387	486/487
ST,ST(i)	0	42-52	33	13-21	4

FCOMP *real*

| 11011w00 | mod | 011 | r/m | disp |

w = 0, memory operand is *real32*
    1, memory operand is *real64*

Operands	x	87/287	287XL	387	486/487
real32	2	(63-73)+EA	42	13-25	4
real64	4	(67-77)+EA	51	14-27	4

FCOMPP

| 11011110 | 11011001 |

Operands	x	87/287	287XL	387	486/487
(no operands)	0	45-55	33	13-21	5

FCOS

Calculate Cosine of ST

DESCRIPTION   FCOS   :ST=cos(ST)

FCOS replaces ST with the cosine of ST.

The FCOS instruction assumes that the argument in ST is expressed in radians. ST must satisfy the inequality $-2^{63} < ST < +2^{63}$.

If the operand is outside the acceptable range, the C_2 flag is set and ST is unchanged. The programmer must reduce the value in ST by an integer multiple of 2π until it is within range.

ALGORITHM
```
IF (ABS(ST)<2^63) THEN
   ST=cos(ST)
   C₂=Ø  ;Reduction complete
ELSE
   C₂=1  ;Reduction incomplete
ENDIF
```

NPX FLAGS

S	P	U	O	Z	D	I	C_3	C_2	C_1	C_0
*	*	*		*	*	—		*	*	—

FCOS

11011001	11111111

TIMING

Operands	x	87/287	287XL	387	486/487
(no operands)	0	–	130-779[1]	122-680[2]	193-279[3]

[1] If out of range, up to 78 additional clocks may be required to reduce the operand.
[2] If out of range, up to 76 additional clocks may be required to reduce the operand.
[3] If out of range, add ST/(π/4) clocks.

FDECSTP

Decrement Top-of-Stack Pointer

DESCRIPTION　FDECSTP subtracts 1 from TOP, the top-of-stack pointer field in the NPX status word.

The subtraction is restricted to the 3-bit field; any borrow out of the field is discarded. No tags or registers are altered. If TOP=0, then executing FDECSTP produces TOP=7.

ALGORITHM
```
IF (TOP=0) THEN
   TOP=7
ELSE
   TOP=TOP-1
ENDIF
```

NPX FLAGS

S	P	U	O	Z	D	I	C_3	C_2	C_1	C_0
							—	—	0	—

FDECSTP

11011001	11110110

TIMING

Operands	x	87/287	287XL	387	486/487
(no operands)	0	6-12	29	22	3

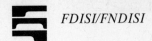
FDISI/FNDISI

Disable NPX Interrupts

DESCRIPTION FDISI sets the interrupt enable mask (IEM) flag in the NPX control word, preventing the NPX from issuing an interrupt request.

The FDISI mnemonic instructs the assembler to generate the opcode for a WAIT instruction prior to the opcode for the FDISI instruction. If the FNDISI mnemonic is specified, no WAIT is generated.

This instruction performs no function on the 80287 and later coprocessors, and does not generate an invalid opcode exception. No registers or internal states are altered.

ALGORITHM IEM=1

NPX FLAGS

S	P	U	O	Z	D	I	C_3	C_2	C_1	C_0
							—	—	—	—

FDISI

10011011	11011011	11100001

TIMING

Operands	x	87/287	287XL	387	486/487
(no operands)	0	$(5\text{-}11)+5n$[1]	–	–	–

n is the number of times the CPU examines TEST# line until NPX lowers BUSY.
[1] This instruction performs no action on the 80287.

FNDISI

11011011	11100001

TIMING

Operands	x	87/287	287XL	387	486/487
(no operands)	0	2-8[1]	–	–	–

[1] This instruction performs no action on the 80287.

FDIV/FDIVP

Divide Real

DESCRIPTION

```
FDIV ST,ST(i)      :ST=ST/ST(i)
FDIV ST(i)         :ST(i)=ST(i)/ST
FDIV ST(i),ST      :ST(i)=ST(i)/ST
FDIV real          :ST=ST/[real]
FDIV               :ST(1)=ST(1)/ST, POP
FDIVP              :ST(1)=ST(1)/ST, POP
FDIVP ST(i)        :ST(i)=ST(i)/ST, POP
FDIVP ST(i),ST     :ST(i)=ST(i)/ST, POP
```

The FDIV and FDIVP instructions divide the destination operand by the source operand and return the result to the destination.

The source operand may be either a floating-point register or a real memory operand, but the destination is always a floating-point register. The FDIVP encoding pops the stack at the conclusion of the operation.

When the FDIV or FDIVP instructions are coded with no arguments (classical stack form), ST is the source and ST(1) is the destination. The result is returned to ST(1). When the floating-point stack is automatically popped at the conclusion of execution, the result is left in ST. The following instructions have the identical effect:

```
FDIV               ;Implied ST(1),ST, FPOP
FDIVP              ;Implied ST(1),ST
FDIVP ST(1)        ;Implied ST
FDIVP ST(1),ST     ;Explicit operands
```

If a register operand is the only operand specified, then it will be the destination and ST is implied as the source operand. The instruction FDIV ST(5), for example, is equivalent to FDIV ST(5),ST. Note that Microsoft's MASM does not support this syntax, although DEBUG does. If, however, a memory operand is specified as the operand, it will be the source and ST will be the destination. FAIVP cannot be encoded with a memory operand. If both operands are explicitly coded, ST *must* be one of the operands, although it may be either the source or destination.

On the 8087 and 80287, operation on a denormal operand raises the invalid operation exception. Underflow is not possible. On the 80287XL and later, operation on a denormal is supported and an underflow exception can occur.

ALGORITHM

```
IF (NUMOPS=0) THEN
   ST(1)=ST(1)/ST
   FPOP
ELSEIF (NUMOPS=1) THEN
   IF (real) THEN
     ST=ST/[real]
```

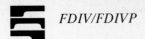

```
        ELSE  ;operand is floating-point register
          ST(i)=ST(i)/ST
        ENDIF
        IF (FDIVP) THEN FPOP
      ELSE  ;NUMOPS=2
        dest=dest/src
        IF (FDIVP) THEN FPOP
      ENDIF
```

NOTES

1. If the divisor is a floating-point stack element tagged as empty with nonzero contents and the next floating-point instruction occurs within 35 NPX CLK counts, some versions of the 80486 FPU will use the empty stack location and produce an invalid result for both the FDIV instruction as well as the following floating-point instruction (due to concurrent execution).

   There is no workaround for this bug other than to avoid the situation. Ensure that a valid divisor is present before executing this instruction. Software that expands the stack using the overflow and underflow exceptions will be affected.

NPX FLAGS

S	P	U	O	Z	D	I	C_3	C_2	C_1	C_0
*	*	*	*	*	*	*	—	—	*	—

FDIV

FDIVP

11011110	11111001

TIMING

Operands	x	87/287	287XL	387	486/487
(no operands)	0	193-203	98	80-83	73[1]

[1] If PC=24-bit, subtract 28 clocks. If PC=53-bit, subtract 11 clocks.

FDIV ST,ST(i)

11011000	11111*rrr*

TIMING

Operands	x	87/287	287XL	387	486/487
ST,ST(i)	0	193-203	95	77-80	73[1]

[1] If PC=24-bit, subtract 28 clocks. If PC=53-bit, subtract 11 clocks.

FDIV ST(i)

FDIV ST(i),ST

11011100	11111*rrr*

TIMING

Operands	x	87/287	287XL	387	486/487
ST(i) ST(i),ST	0	193-203	98	80-83	73[1]

[1] If PC=24-bit, subtract 28 clocks. If PC=53-bit, subtract 11 clocks.

FDIV *real*

11011*w*00	*mod*	110	*r/m*	*disp*

w = 0, memory operand is *real32*
    1, memory operand is *real64*

TIMING

Operands	x	87/287	287XL	387	486/487
real32	2	(215-225)+EA	105	77-85	73[1]
real64	4	(220-230)+EA	114	88-91	73[1]

[1] If PC=24-bit, subtract 28 clocks. If PC=53-bit, subtract 11 clocks.

FDIVP ST(i)

FDIVP ST(i),ST

11011110	11111*rrr*

TIMING

Operands	x	87/287	287XL	387	486/487
ST(i) ST(i),ST	0	197-207	98	80-83	73[1]

[1] If PC=24-bit, subtract 28 clocks. If PC=53-bit, subtract 11 clocks.

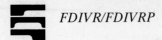

FDIVR/FDIVRP

Reversed Real Divide

DESCRIPTION

```
FDIVR ST,ST(i)      :ST=ST(i)/ST
FDIVR ST(i)         :ST(i)=ST/ST(i)
FDIVR ST(i),ST      :ST(i)=ST/ST(i)
FDIVR real          :ST=[real]/ST
FDIVR               :ST(1)=ST/ST(1), POP
FDIVRP              :ST(1)=ST/ST(1), POP
FDIVRP ST(i)        :ST(i)=ST/ST(i), POP
FDIVRP ST(i),ST     :ST(i)=ST/ST(i), POP
```

The FDIVR and FDIVRP instructions divide the source operand by the destination operand and return the result to the destination.

The reversed divide instructions are provided to allow a division operation to be performed without requiring time-consuming pre-divide and post-divide operand swapping.

The source operand may be either a floating-point register or a real memory operand, but the destination is always a floating-point register. The FDIVRP encoding pops the stack at the conclusion of the operation.

When the FDIVR or FDIVRP instructions are coded with no arguments (classical stack form), ST is the source and ST(1) is the destination. The result is returned to ST(1). When the floating-point stack is automatically popped at the conclusion of execution, the result is left in ST. The following instructions have the identical effect:

```
FDIVR               ;Implied ST(1),ST, FPOP
FDIVRP              ;Implied ST(1),ST
FDIVRP ST(1)        ;Implied ST
FDIVRP ST(1),ST     ;Explicit operands
```

If a register operand is the only operand specified, then it will be the destination and ST is implied as the source operand. The instruction FDIVR ST(5), for example, is equivalent to FDIVR ST(5),ST. Note that Microsoft's MASM does not support this syntax, although DEBUG does. If, however, a memory operand is specified as the operand, it will be the source and ST will be the destination. FDIVRP cannot be encoded with a memory operand. If both operands are explicitly coded, ST *must* be one of the operands, although it may be either the source or destination.

On the 8087 and 80287, operation on a denormal operand raises the invalid operation exception. Underflow is not possible. On the 80287XL and later coprocessors, operation on a denormal is supported and an underflow exception can occur.

ALGORITHM

```
IF (NUMOPS=0) THEN
    ST(1)=ST/ST(1)
    FPOP
ELSEIF (NUMOPS=1) THEN
    IF (real) THEN
        ST=[real]/ST
    ELSE  ;operand is floating-point register
        ST(i)=ST/ST(i)
    ENDIF
    IF (FDIVRP) THEN FPOP
ELSE  ;NUMOPS=2
    dest=src/dest
    IF (FDIVRP) THEN FPOP
ENDIF
```

NOTES

1. If the divisor is a floating-point stack element that is tagged as empty with non-zero contents and the next floating-point instruction occurs within 35 NPX CLK counts, some versions of the 80486 FPU will use the empty stack location, producing an invalid result for both the FDIV instruction as well as the following floating-point instruction (due to concurrent execution).

   There is no workaround for this bug other than to avoid the situation. Ensure that a valid divisor is present before executing this instruction. Software that expands the stack using the overflow and underflow exceptions will be affected.

NPX FLAGS

S	P	U	O	Z	D	I	C_3	C_2	C_1	C_0
*	*	*	*	*	*	*	—	—	*	—

FDIVR

FDIVRP

11011110	11110001

TIMING

Operands	x	87/287	287XL	387	486/487
(no operands)	0	194-204	98	80-83	73[1]

[1] If PC=24-bit, subtract 28 clocks. If PC=53-bit, subtract 11 clocks.

FDIVR ST,ST(i)

11011000	11110rrr

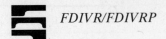

TIMING

Operands	x	87/287	287XL	387	486/487
ST,ST(i)	0	194-204	95	77-80	73[1]

[1] If PC=24-bit, subtract 28 clocks. If PC=53-bit, subtract 11 clocks.

FDIVR ST(i)

FDIVR ST(i),ST

11011100	11110*rrr*

TIMING

Operands	x	87/287	287XL	387	486/487
ST(i) ST(i),ST	0	194-204	98	80-83	73[1]

[1] If PC=24-bit, subtract 28 clocks. If PC=53-bit, subtract 11 clocks.

FDIVR *real*

11011w00	*mod*	111	*r/m*	*disp*

w = 0, memory operand is *real32*
    1, memory operand is *real64*

TIMING

Operands	x	87/287	287XL	387	486/487
real32	2	(216-226)+EA	105	77-85	73[1]
real64	4	(221-231)+EA	114	81-91	73[1]

[1] If PC=24-bit, subtract 28 clocks. If PC=53-bit, subtract 11 clocks.

FDIVRP ST(i)

FDIVRP ST(i),ST

11011110	11110*rrr*

TIMING

Operands	x	87/287	287XL	387	486/487
ST(i) ST(i),ST	0	198-208	98	80-83	73[1]

[1] If PC=24-bit, subtract 28 clocks. If PC=53-bit, subtract 11 clocks.

FENI/FNENI

Enable NPX Interrupts

DESCRIPTION FENI clears the interrupt enable mask (IEM) flag in the NPX control word, allowing the NPX to issue interrupt requests.

The FENI mnemonic instructs the assembler to generate the opcode for a WAIT instruction prior to the opcode for the FENI instruction. If the FNDISI mnemonic is specified, no WAIT is generated.

This instruction performs no function on the 80287 and later coprocessors. If encountered, the instruction is effectively ignored and none of the internal NPX states are affected.

ALGORITHM   IEM=0

NPX FLAGS

S	P	U	O	Z	D	I	C_3	C_2	C_1	C_0
							—	—	—	—

FENI

10011011	11011011	11100000

TIMING

Operands	x	87/287	287XL	387	486/487
(no operands)	0	$(5-11)+5n$[1]	–	–	–

n is the number of times the CPU examines TEST# line until NPX lowers BUSY.
[1] This instruction performs no action on the 80287.

FNENI

11011011	11100000

TIMING

Operands	x	87/287	287XL	387	486/487
(no operands)	0	2-8[1]	–	–	–

[1] This instruction performs no action on the 80287.

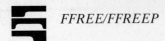

FFREE/FFREEP

Mark Floating-Point Register Free

DESCRIPTION FFREE ST(i)
FFREEP ST(i)

FFREE changes the tag for the specified floating-point register to empty.

The FFREE instruction is used to free a register. Neither the value in the destination register nor TOP is changed by this instruction. The value in the register is, however, unaccessible.

The FFREEP mnemonic, while not supported by assemblers or debuggers, describes the operation of the undocumented form of this instruction. The instruction is a result of the logical design of the NPX circuitry.

FFREEP changes the tag for the specified register to empty and then pops the floating-point stack. The value in the destination register is not changed by this instruction. TOP is changed when the floating-point stack is popped.

ALGORITHM TAG(i)=11b
IF (FFREEP) THEN FPOP

NPX FLAGS

S	P	U	O	Z	D	I	C_3	C_2	C_1	C_0
							—	—	—	—

FFREE

11011101	11000rrr

TIMING

Operands	x	87/287	287XL	387	486/487
ST(i)	0	9-16	25	18	3

FFREEP

11011111	11000rrr

TIMING

Operands	x	87/287	287XL	387	486/487
ST(i)	0	13-20	25	18	3

FIADD

Add Integer

DESCRIPTION FIADD *int*   :ST=ST+[*int*]

The FIADD instruction loads an integer operand from memory, converts it to temporary real format, and adds it to the contents of ST.

The source operand is always an integer memory operand, and the destination is always the stack top.

ALGORITHM ST=ST+[*int*]

NPX FLAGS

S	P	U	O	Z	D	I	C_3	C_2	C_1	C_0
*	*	*a	*		*	*	—	—	*	—

a Raised only by the 80287XL and later coprocessors.

FIADD *int*

11011w10	mod	000	r/m	disp

w = 0, memory operand is *int16*
    1, memory operand is *int32*

TIMING

Operands	x	87/287	287XL	387	486/487
int16	1	(102-137)+EA	71-85	38-64	20-35
int32	2	(108-143)+EA	73-78	34-56	19-32

FICOM/FICOMP

Compare Integer

DESCRIPTION
```
FICOM int      :Compare ST to [int]
FICOMP int     :Compare ST to [int], FPOP
```

The FICOM instruction converts the specified integer memory operand to temporary real and compares ST to it.

The condition code bits of the status word are used to report the result of the comparison as shown:

Order	C_3	C_2	C_0	Explanation
ST>op	0	0	0	ST greater than operand
ST<op	0	0	1	ST less than operand
ST=op	1	0	0	ST equal to operand
ST?op	1	1	1	ST not comparable to operand

Note that positive and negative forms of zero are treated identically for the purpose of this instruction. NaNs and the projective infinities cannot be compared and return $C_3=C_2=C_0=1$, as indicated in the above table.

The FICOMP instruction operates identically to the FICOM instruction, except that the floating-point stack is popped after the comparison.

See also FCOM, FUCOM, FTST, and FXAM.

ALGORITHM
```
ConditionCodes=ST compared to op
```

NPX FLAGS

S	P	U	O	Z	D	I	C_3	C_2	C_1	C_0
*					*	*	*	*	0	*

FICOM int

11011w10	mod	010	r/m	disp

w = 0, memory operand is *int16*
   1, memory operand is *int32*

TIMING

Operands	x	87/287	287XL	387	486/487
int16	1	(72-86)+EA	71-75	39-62	16-20
int32	2	(78-91)+EA	72-79	34-52	15-17

FICOMP int

11011w10	mod	011	r/m	disp

w = 0, memory operand is *int16*
    1, memory operand is *int32*

TIMING

Operands	x	87/287	287XL	387	486/487
int16	1	(74-88)+EA	71-77	39-62	16-20
int32	2	(80-93)+EA	72-79	34-52	15-17

FIDIV

Divide Integer

DESCRIPTION FIDIV *int*

The FIDIV instruction converts the specified integer memory operand to temporary real, divides ST by it, and returns the result to ST.

ALGORITHM ST=ST/[*int*]

NPX FLAGS

S	P	U	O	Z	D	I	C_3	C_2	C_1	C_0
*	*	*	*	*	*	*	—	—	*	—

FIDIV *int*

11011w10	mod	110	r/m	disp

w = 0, memory operand is *int16*
  1, memory operand is *int32*

TIMING

Operands	x	87/287	287XL	387	486/487
int16	1	(224-238)+EA	136-140	105-124	85-89
int32	2	(230-243)+EA	136-143	101-114	84-86

[1] If PC=24-bit, subtract 28 clocks. If PC=53-bit, subtract 11 clocks.

FIDIVR

Reversed Integer Divide

DESCRIPTION   FIDIVR *int*

The FIDIV instruction converts the specified integer memory operand to temporary real, divides ST by it, and returns the result to ST.

ALGORITHM   ST=[*int*]/ST

NPX FLAGS

S	P	U	O	Z	D	I	C_3	C_2	C_1	C_0
*	*	*	*	*	*	*	—	—	*	—

FIDIVR *int*

11011w10	mod	111	r/m	disp

w = 0, memory operand is *int16*
1, memory operand is *int32*

TIMING

Operands	x	87/287	287XL	387	486/487
int16	1	(225-239)+EA	135-141	135-141	85-89[1]
int32	2	(231-245)+EA	137-144	102-115	84-86[1]

[1] If PC=24-bit, subtract 28 clocks. If PC=53-bit, subtract 11 clocks.

FILD

Load Integer Memory Operand onto Stack

DESCRIPTION FILD *int*

The FILD instruction loads an integer operand from memory, converts it to temporary real, and pushes the resulting value onto the floating-point stack.

See also FLD and FBLD.

ALGORITHM DEC TOP
ST=[*mem*]

NPX FLAGS

S	P	U	O	Z	D	I	C_3	C_2	C_1	C_0
*						*	—	—	*	—

FILD *int16/int32*

11011w11	mod	000	r/m	disp

w = 0, memory operand is *int16*
  1, memory operand is *int32*

TIMING

Operands	x	87/287	287XL	387	486/487
int16	1	(46-54)+EA	61-65	42-53	13-16
int32	2	(52-60)+EA	61-68	26-42	9-12

FILD *int64*

11011111	mod	101	r/m	disp

TIMING

Operands	x	87/287	287XL	387	486/487
int64	4	(60-68)+EA	76-87	26-54	10-18

FIMUL

Multiply ST by Integer

DESCRIPTION FIMUL *int*

The FIMUL instruction converts the specified integer memory operand to temporary real, multiplies it by ST, and returns the result to ST.

See also FMUL.

ALGORITHM ST=ST/[*mem*]

NPX FLAGS

S	P	U	O	Z	D	I	C_3	C_2	C_1	C_0
*	*	*[a]	*		*	*	—	—	*	—

[a] Raised only by the 80287XL and later coprocessors.

FIMUL *int*

11011w10	mod	001	r/m	disp

w = 0, memory operand is *int16*
 1, memory operand is *int32*

TIMING

Operands	x	87/287	287XL	387	486/487
int16	1	(124-138)+EA	76-87	46-74	23-27
int32	2	(130-144)+EA	77-88	43-71	22-24

FINCSTP

Increment Top-of-Stack Pointer

DESCRIPTION FINCSTP adds 1 to TOP, the top-of-stack pointer field in the NPX status word.

The addition is restricted to the 3-bit field; any carry out of the field is discarded. No tags or registers are altered. If TOP=7, then executing FINCSTP produces TOP=0.

FINCSTP does not alter the contents of any floating-point registers or tags, nor does it transfer any data. Note that this instruction is not the same as popping the floating-point stack, since it does not set the contents of the previous stack top to empty.

ALGORITHM
```
IF (TOP=7) THEN
   TOP=0
ELSE
   TOP=TOP+1
ENDIF
```

NPX FLAGS

S	P	U	O	Z	D	I	C_3	C_2	C_1	C_0
							—	—	0	—

FINCSTP

11011001	11110111

TIMING

Operands	x	87/287	287XL	387	486/487
(no operands)	0	6-12	28	21	3

FINIT/FNINIT

Initialize NPX

DESCRIPTION The FINIT and FNINIT instructions initialize the NPX to a known state.

On the 8087 and 80287, FINIT performs the functional equivalent of a hardware reset. (The prefetch queue synchronization is not, however, affected.) On the 80387 and later coprocessors, a hardware reset initializes the coprocessor in an error state. A FINIT is required to put the processor in the same condition as an 8087 after reset. See Chapter 13 for details on initialization.

Following FINIT, all error masks are set; the tag word is set to indicate that all registers in the floating-point stack are empty; the stack top (ST) field is reset to 0; and the default rounding, precision, and infinity controls are set. Although infinity control is initialized to 0, the 80287XL and later coprocessors support only affine closure and ignore the setting of this bit. The 80287 and 80287XL are initialized in real mode and may be switched into protected mode using the FSETPM instruction, if desired.

Register	Initial Value	Meaning
Control Word	037Fh	
Infinity control	0	Projective (8087 and 80287)
		Affine (80287XL, 80387, and 80486)
Rounding control	00b	Round to nearest
Precision control	11b	64 bits
Interrupt enable mask	0	Interrupts enabled
Exception masks	111111b	All exceptions masked
Status Word	–	See below
Busy	0	Not busy
Condition code bits	Unchanged	8087 and 80287
	0000b	80287XL, 80387, and 80486
Stack top (ST)	000b	
Interrupt request	0	No interrupt pending
Exception flags	000000b	No exceptions
Tag word	FFFFh	All empty
Registers	Unchanged	
Exception pointers		
Opcode	Unchanged	8087 and 80287
	0	80287XL, 80387, and 80486
Instruction address	Unchanged	8087 and 80287

	0	80287XL, 80387, and 80486
Operand address	Unchanged	8087 and 80287
	0	80287XL, 80387, and 80486

The FINIT mnemonic instructs the assembler to generate the opcode for a WAIT instruction prior to the opcode for the FINIT instruction. If the FNINIT mnemonic is specified, no WAIT is generated.

ALGORITHM

```
ControlWord=37Fh
StatusWord=0
TagWord=FFFFh
```

NOTES

1. In protected mode, if the last byte of a FNINIT instruction falls on the last byte of a segment, some versions of the 80386 will indicate a segment limit fault (interrupt Dh) with the return address on the stack pointing to the FNINIT opcode. The return address should, in fact, point to the next instruction.

   The segment limit exception handler could test for the FNINIT opcode and adjust the return address accordingly. Alternately, the address can be left unchanged and the FNINIT will be executed a second time.

NPX FLAGS

S	P	U	O	Z	D	I	C_3	C_2	C_1	C_0
0	0	0	0	0	0	0	0^a	0^a	0^a	0^a

[a] Unchanged on the 8087 and 80287.

FINIT

10011011	11011011	11100011

TIMING

Operands	x	87/287	287XL	387	486/487
(no operands)	0	(5-11)+5n	28+5n	39-40	18-20[1]

n is the number of times the CPU examines TEST# line until NPX lowers BUSY.
[1] Add 17 clocks if a numeric exception is pending from a previous instruction.

FNINIT

11011011	11100011

TIMING

Operands	x	87/287	287XL	387	486/487
(no operands)	0	2-8	25	33	17[1]

[1] Add 17 clocks if a numeric exception is pending from a previous instruction.

FIST/FISTP

Store ST to Memory as Integer

DESCRIPTION

```
FIST  int
FISTP int
```

The FIST instruction converts ST to an integer value, and then copies that value to the memory operand specified by *int*.

Before being transferred, the value in ST is converted to an integer by rounding according to the setting of the RC field. The destination is always a memory operand and it may be a short (32-bit) or long (64-bit) integer. To convert to an integer result while retaining the result in a floating-point register, see the FRNDINT instruction. Note that negative zero is stored using the same encoding as positive zero.

The FISTP instruction operates identically to the FIST instruction, except that the floating-point stack is popped after ST is stored.

On the 8087 and 80287, operation on a denormal operand raises the invalid operation exception. Underflow is not possible. On the 80287XL and later coprocessors, operation on a denormal is supported and an underflow exception can occur.

ALGORITHM

```
[int]=ST
IF (FISTP) THEN FPOP ;Pop floating-point stack
```

NPX FLAGS

S	P	U	O	Z	D	I	C_3	C_2	C_1	C_0
*	*					*	—	—	*	—

FIST *int*

11011w11	mod	010	r/m	disp

w = 0, memory operand is *int16*
    1, memory operand is *int32*

TIMING

Operands	x	87/287	287XL	387	486/487
int16	1	(80-90)+EA	88-101	58-76	29-34
int32	2	(82-92)+EA	86-100	57-76	28-34

FISTP *int16/int32*

| 11011w11 | mod | 011 | r/m | disp |

w = 0, memory operand is *int16*
    1, memory operand is *int32*

TIMING

Operands	x	87/287	287XL	387	486/487
int16	1	(82-92)+EA	88-101	58-76	29-34
int32	2	(84-94)+EA	86-100	57-76	29-34

FISTP *int64*

| 11011111 | mod | 111 | r/m | disp |

TIMING

Operands	x	87/287	287XL	387	486/487
int64	4	(94-105)+EA	91-108	60-82	29-34

FISUB

Subtract Integer

DESCRIPTION FISUB *int*

The FISUB instruction loads an integer operand from memory, converts it to temporary real format, and subtracts it from the contents of ST.

The source operand is always an integer memory operand, and the destination is the stack top.

See also FISUBR, FSUB, and FSUBR.

ALGORITHM ST=ST-[*int*]

NPX FLAGS

S	P	U	O	Z	D	I	C₃	C₂	C₁	C₀
*	*	*[a]	*		*	*	—	—	*	—

[a] Raised only by the 80287XL and later coprocessors.

FISUB *int*

11011w10	mod	100	r/m	disp

w = 0, memory operand is *int16*
1, memory operand is *int32*

TIMING

Operands	x	87/287	287XL	387	486/487
int16	1	(102-137)+EA	71-83	38-64	20-35
int32	2	(108-143)+EA	73-98	34-56	19-32

FISUBR

Reversed Integer Subtract

DESCRIPTION   FISUBR *int*

The FISUBR instruction loads an integer operand from memory, converts it to temporary real format, and subtracts the contents of ST from it, returning the result to ST.

The source operand is always an integer memory operand and the destination is always the stack top.

The reversed integer subtraction instruction is provided to allow a subtraction operation without requiring time-consuming pre-subtract and post-subtract operand swapping.

See also FISUB, FSUB, and FSUBR.

ALGORITHM   ST=[*int*]-ST

NPX FLAGS

S	P	U	O	Z	D	I	C_3	C_2	C_1	C_0
*	*	*[a]	*		*	*	—	—	*	—

[a] Raised only by the 80287XL and later coprocessors.

FISUBR *int*

11011w10	mod	101	r/m	disp

w = 0, memory operand is *int16*
    1, memory operand is *int32*

TIMING

Operands	x	87/287	287XL	387	486/487
int16	1	(103-139)+EA	72-84	39-65	20-35
int32	2	(109-144)+EA	74-99	35-57	19-32

FLD

Load Real Memory Operand onto Stack

DESCRIPTION

```
FLD ST(i)
FLD int
```

The FLD instruction loads the source operand, converts it to temporary real format (if required), and pushes the resulting value onto the floating-point stack.

The load operation is accomplished by decrementing the top-of-stack pointer (TOP) and copying the source operand to the new stack top. If the source operand is a floating-point register, the index of the register is taken *before* TOP is changed. The source operand may also be a short real, long real, or temporary real memory operand. Short real and long real operands are converted automatically.

Note that coding the instruction FLD ST duplicates the value at the stack top.

On the 8087 and 80287, the FLD *real80* instruction will raise the denormal exception if the memory operand is a denormal. The 80287XL and later coprocessors will not, since the operation is not arithmetic.

On the 8087 and 80287, a denormal will be converted to an unnormal by FLD; on the 80287XL and later coprocessors, the number will be converted to temporary real. If the next instruction is an FXTRACT or FXAM, the 8087/80827 and 80287XL/80387/80486 results will be different.

On the 8087 and 80287, the FLD *real32* and FLD *real64* instructions will not raise an exception when loading a signaling NaN; on the 80287XL and later coprocessors, loading a signaling NaN raises the invalid operation exception.

See also FILD, FBLD, and the constant load instructions.

ALGORITHM

```
DEC TOP
IF (real) THEN
  ST=[real]
ELSE  ;operand is floating-point register
  ST=ST(i)
ENDIF
```

NPX FLAGS

S	P	U	O	Z	D	I	C_3	C_2	C_1	C_0
*					*	*	—	—	*	—

FLD ST(i)

11011001	11000rrr

TIMING

Operands	x	87/287	287XL	387	486/487
ST(i)	0	17-22	21	7-12	4

FLD *real32/real64*

11011w01	mod	000	r/m	disp

w = 0, memory operand is *real32*
    1, memory operand is *real64*

TIMING

Operands	x	87/287	287XL	387	486/487
real32	2	(38-56)+EA	36	9-18	3
real64	4	(40-60)+EA	45	16-23	3

FLD *real80*

11011011	mod	101	r/m	disp

TIMING

Operands	x	87/287	287XL	387	486/487
real80	5	(53-65)+EA	48	12-43	6

FLD1

Load Constant +1.0 onto Stack

DESCRIPTION The FLD1 instruction loads the constant +1.0 from the NPX's constant ROM and pushes the value onto the floating-point stack.

The constant is stored internally in temporary real format and is simply moved to the stack.

See also FLDLG2, FLDLN2, FLDL2E, FLDL2T, FLDPI, and FLD1.

ALGORITHM
```
DEC TOP
  ST=+1.0
```

NPX FLAGS

S	P	U	O	Z	D	I	C_3	C_2	C_1	C_0
*						*	—	—	*	—

FLD1

11011001	11101000

TIMING

Operands	x	87/287	287XL	387	486/487
(no operands)	0	15-21	31	15-22	4

FLDCW

Load Memory Operand into Control Word

DESCRIPTION   FLDCW *mem16*

FLDCW loads the specified 16-bit memory operand into the NPX control word.

The FLDCW instruction is typically used to establish or change the mode of operation of the NPX. If an exception bit in the status word is set and the corresponding mask in the new control word is cleared, an immediate interrupt request is generated before the next instruction is executed when IEM=0. When changing modes, the recommended procedure is to clear any exceptions using the FCLEX instruction.

See also FSTCW, FLDENV, and FRSTOR.

ALGORITHM   ControlWord=[*mem16*]

NPX FLAGS

S	P	U	O	Z	D	I	C_3	C_2	C_1	C_0
							—	—	—	—

FLDCW *mem16*

11011001	mod	101	r/m	disp

TIMING

Operands	x	87/287	287XL	387	486/487
mem16	1	(7-14)+EA	33	19	4

FLDENV

Load Memory Operand into NPX Environment

DESCRIPTION   FLDENV *mem*

FLDENV loads the NPX environment from the memory area specified by the memory operand.

The NPX environment comprises the control, status, and tag words, and the exception pointers. This data will typically have been written by a previous FSTENV instruction. The format of the memory area is dependent on the operating mode of the NPX. The possible formats are listed in the entry for the FSTENV instruction. See also Chapter 10 for a complete description of the possible formats.

Note that if an exception bit in the status word is set and the corresponding mask in the new control word is cleared, an immediate interrupt request is generated before the next instruction is executed. (On the 8087, IEM must also be cleared to 0.)

When the tag word is loaded by this instruction, the 80287XL and later coprocessors interpret the individual tags only as empty (11b) or nonempty (00b, 01b, and 10b). Subsequent operations on a nonempty register always examine the value in the register—not its tag. The 8087 and 80287 examine the tag before each operation. If the tag value disagrees with the register contents, the 8087 and 80287 will honor the tag and won't examine the register.

ALGORITHM   NPX_Environment=[*mem*]

NOTES   1. If either of the two last bytes of memory addressed by FRSTOR is not readable for any reason, the instruction cannot be restarted. This problem will typically arise in demand-paged systems or demand-segmented systems which increase segment size on demand.

To avoid this problem, a dummy value can be read from the last two bytes of the memory operand; alternately, the operand can be aligned on a 128-byte boundary to avoid crossing a segment or page boundary.

NPX FLAGS

S	P	U	O	Z	D	I	C_3	C_2	C_1	C_0
*	*	*	*	*	*	*	*	*	*	*

FLDENV *mem*

11011001	mod	100	r/m	disp

Operands	x	87/287	287XL	387	486/487
mem14byte (real and V86 modes, 16-bit)	7	(35-45)+EA	85	71	44
mem14byte (protected mode, 16-bit)	7	(35-45)+EA[1]	85	71	34
mem28byte (real and V86 modes, 32-bit)	14	–	–	71	44
mem28byte (protected mode, 32-bit)	14	–	–	71	34

[1] 80287 only.

FLDL2E

Load Constant log₂e onto Stack

DESCRIPTION The FLDL2E instruction loads the constant $\log_2 e$ from the NPX's constant ROM and pushes the value onto the floating-point stack.

The constant is stored internally in temporary real format and is simply moved to the stack.

On the 8087 and 80287, rounding control is not in effect for the loading of this constant. On the 80287XL and later coprocessors, rounding control is in effect. If RC is set for chop (round toward 0) or round down (toward $-\infty$), the result is the same as on the 8087 and 80827. If RC is set for round to nearest or even, or round up (toward $+\infty$), the result will differ by one in the least significant bit of the mantissa.

See also FLDLG2, FLDLN2, FLDL2T, FLDPI, FLD1, and FLDZ.

ALGORITHM
```
DEC TOP
ST=log₂e
```

NPX FLAGS

S	P	U	O	Z	D	I	C₃	C₂	C₁	C₀
*						*	—	—	*	—

FLDL2E

11011001	11101010

TIMING

Operands	x	87/287	287XL	387	486/487
(no operands)	0	15-21	47	26-36	8

FLDL2T

Load Constant log$_2$10 onto Stack

DESCRIPTION The FLDL2T instruction loads the constant log$_2$10 from the NPX's constant ROM and pushes the value onto the floating-point stack.

The constant is stored internally in temporary real format and is simply moved to the stack.

On the 8087 and 80287, rounding control is not in effect for the loading of this constant. On the 80287XL and later coprocessors, rounding control is in effect. If RC is set for chop (round toward 0), round down (toward -∞), or round to nearest or even, the result will be the same as on the 8087 and 80287. If RC is set for round up (toward +∞), the result will differ by one in the least significant bit of the mantissa.

See also FLDLG2, FLDLN2, FLDL2E, FLDPI, FLD1, and FLDZ.

ALGORITHM
```
DEC TOP
ST=log₂1Ø
```

NPX FLAGS

S	P	U	O	Z	D	I	C$_3$	C$_2$	C$_1$	C$_0$
*						*	—	—	*	—

FLDL2T

11011001	11101001

TIMING

Operands	x	87/287	287XL	387	486/487
(no operands)	0	16-22	47	26-36	8

FLDLG2

Load Constant $\log_{10}2$ onto Stack

DESCRIPTION The FLDLG2 instruction loads the constant $\log_{10}2$ from the NPX's constant ROM and pushes the value onto the floating-point stack.

The constant is stored internally in temporary real format and is simply moved to the stack.

On the 8087 and 80287, rounding control is not in effect for the loading of this constant. On the 80287XL and later coprocessors, rounding control is in effect. If RC is set for chop (round toward 0) or round down (toward $-\infty$), the result is the same as on the 8087 and 80827. If RC is set for round to nearest or even, or round up (toward $+\infty$), the result will differ by one in the least significant bit of the mantissa.

See also FLDLN2, FLDL2E, FLDL2T, FLDPI, FLD1, and FLDZ.

ALGORITHM
```
DEC TOP
ST=log₁₀2
```

NPX FLAGS

S	P	U	O	Z	D	I	C_3	C_2	C_1	C_0
*						*	—	—	*	—

FLDLG2

11011001	11101100

TIMING

Operands	x	87/287	287XL	387	486/487
(no operands)	0	18-24	48	25-35	8

FLDLN2

Load Constant In 2 onto Stack

DESCRIPTION The FLDLN2 instruction loads the constant ln 2 ($\log_e 2$) from the NPX's constant ROM and pushes the value onto the floating-point stack.

The constant is stored internally in temporary real format and is simply moved to the stack.

On the 8087 and 80287, rounding control is not in effect for the loading of this constant. On the 80287XL and later coprocessors, rounding control is in effect. If RC is set for chop (round toward 0) or round down (toward $-\infty$), the result will be the same as on the 8087 and 80827. If RC is set for round to nearest or even, or round up (toward $+\infty$), the result will differ by one in the least significant bit of the mantissa.

See also FLDLG2, FLDL2E, FLDL2T, FLDPI, FLD1, and FLDZ.

ALGORITHM
```
DEC TOP
ST=1n 2
```

NPX FLAGS

S	P	U	O	Z	D	I	C$_3$	C$_2$	C$_1$	C$_0$
*						*	—	—	*	—

FLDLN2

11011001	11101101

TIMING

Operands	x	87/287	287XL	387	486/487
(no operands)	0	17-23	48	26-38	8

FLDPI

Load Constant Pi (π) onto Stack

DESCRIPTION The FLDPI instruction loads the constant Pi (π) from the NPX's constant ROM and pushes the value onto the floating-point stack.

The constant is stored internally in temporary real format and is simply moved to the stack.

On the 8087 and 80287, rounding control is not in effect for the loading of these constants. On the 80287XL and later coprocessors, rounding control is in effect. If RC is set for chop (round toward 0) or round down (toward -∞), the result is the same as on the 8087 and 80827. If RC is set for round to nearest or even, or round up (toward +∞), the result will differ by one in the least significant bit of the mantissa.

See also FLDLG2, FLDLN2, FLDL2E, FLDL2T, FLD1, and FLDZ.

ALGORITHM
DEC TOP
ST=π

NPX FLAGS

S	P	U	O	Z	D	I	C₃	C₂	C₁	C₀
*						*	—	—	*	—

FLDPI

11011001	11101011

TIMING

Operands	x	87/287	287XL	387	486/487
(no operands)	0	16-22	47	26-36	8

FLDZ

Load Constant +0.0 onto Stack

DESCRIPTION The FLDZ instruction loads the constant +0.0 from the NPX's constant ROM and pushes the value onto the floating-point stack.

The constant is stored internally in temporary real format and is simply moved to the stack.

See also FLDLG2, FLDLN2, FLDL2E, FLDL2T, FLDPI, and FLD1.

ALGORITHM
```
DEC TOP
ST=+0.0
```

NPX FLAGS

S	P	U	O	Z	D	I	C_3	C_2	C_1	C_0
*						*	—	—	*	—

FLDZ

11011001	11101110

TIMING

Operands	x	87/287	287XL	387	486/487
(no operands)	0	11-17	27	10-17	4

FMUL/FMULP

Multiply Real

DESCRIPTION

```
FMUL ST,ST(i)      :ST=ST*ST(i)
FMUL ST(i)         :ST(i)=ST(i)*ST
FMUL ST(i),ST      :ST(i)=ST(i)*ST
FMUL real          :ST=ST*[real]
FMUL               :ST(1)=ST(1)*ST, POP
FMULP              :ST(1)=ST(1)*ST, POP
FMULP ST(i)        :ST(i)=ST(i)*ST, POP
FMULP ST(i),ST     :ST(i)=ST(i)*ST, POP
```

The FMUL and FMULP instructions multiply the destination operand by the source operand and return the result to the destination operand.

The source operand may be either a floating-point register or a real memory operand, but the destination is always a floating-point register. The FMULP encoding pops the stack at the conclusion of the operation.

When the FMUL or FMULP instructions are coded with no arguments (classical stack form), ST is the source and ST(1) is the destination. The result is returned to ST(1). When the floating-point stack is automatically popped at the conclusion of execution, the result is left in ST. The following instructions have the identical effect:

```
FMUL               ;Implied ST(1),ST
FMULP              ;Implied ST(1),ST
FMULP ST(1)        ;Implied ST
FMULP ST(1),ST     ;Explicit operands
```

If the destination is a register operand and is the only operand specified, then ST is automatically implied as the source operand. The instruction FMUL ST(5), for example, is equivalent to FMUL ST(5),ST. Note that Microsoft's MASM does not support this syntax, although DEBUG does. If, however, a memory operand is referenced, it will be the source and ST will be the destination. FMULP cannot be encoded with a memory operand. If both operands are explicitly coded, ST *must* be one of the operands, although it may be either the source or destination.

Note that the instruction FMUL ST,ST(0) will square the operand at the top of the floating-point stack.

ALGORITHM

```
IF (NUMOPS=0) THEN
   ST(1)=ST(1)*ST
   FPOP
ELSEIF (NUMOPS=1) THEN
   IF (real) THEN
     ST=ST*[real]
   ELSE  ;operand is floating-point register
```

```
    ST(i)=ST(i)*ST
  ENDIF
  IF (FMULP) THEN FPOP
ELSE  ;NUMOPS=2
  dest=dest*src
  IF (FMULP) THEN FPOP
ENDIF
```

NPX FLAGS	S	P	U	O	Z	D	I	C₃	C₂	C₁	C₀
	*	*	*	*		*	*	—	—	*	—

FMUL

FMULP

11011110	11001001

Operands	x	87/287	287XL	387	486/487
(no operands)	0	130-145[1]	25-53[2]	17-50	16

[1] If one or both operands has 40 or more trailing zeros in its mantissa, the time is 90-105 clocks.
[2] The typical execution time is 48 clocks.

FMUL ST,ST(i)

11011000	11001rrr

TIMING

Operands	x	87/287	287XL	387	486/487
ST,ST(i)	0	130-145[1]	42-50	46-54	16

[1] If one or both operands has 40 or more trailing zeros in its mantissa, the time is 90-105 clocks.

FMUL ST(i)

FMUL ST(i),ST

11011100	11001rrr

TIMING

Operands	x	87/287	287XL	387	486/487
ST(i) ST(i),ST	0	130-145[1]	25-53[2]	17-50	16

[1] If one or both operands has 40 or more trailing zeros in its mantissa, the time is 90-105 clocks.
[2] The typical execution time is 48 clocks.

FMUL *real*

11011w00	mod	001	r/m	disp

w = 0, memory operand is *real32*
    1, memory operand is *real64*

TIMING

Operands	x	87/287	287XL	387	486/487
real32	2	(110-125)+EA	43-51	19-32	11
real64	4	(154-168)+EA[1]	52-77	23-53	14

[1] If one or both operands has 40 or more trailing zeros in its mantissa, the time is (112-126)+EA clocks.

FMULP ST(i)

FMULP ST(i),ST

11011110	11001rrr

TIMING

Operands	x	87/287	287XL	387	486/487
ST(i) ST(i),ST	0	134-148[1]	25-53[2]	17-50	16

[1] If one or both operands has 40 or more trailing zeros in its mantissa, the time is 94-108 clocks.
[2] The typical execution time is 48 clocks.

FNOP

No Operation

DESCRIPTION FNOP performs no operation.

The FNOP instruction effectively stores the stack top to itself. It is *not*, however, simply an alternate mnemonic for FST ST,ST(0). If ST is tagged as empty, for example, FNOP does not generate a stack exception, while FST ST,ST(0) does.

FNOP updates the exception pointers but does not affect the contents of the floating-point stack and tag word.

ALGORITHM None

NPX FLAGS

S	P	U	O	Z	D	I	C_3	C_2	C_1	C_0
							—	—	—	—

FNOP

11011001	11010000

TIMING

Operands	x	87/287	287XL	387	486/487
(no operands)	0	10-16	19	12	3

FPATAN

Partial Arctangent

DESCRIPTION FPATAN calculates the partial arctangent of ST divided by ST(1).

The FPATAN instruction computes the function

$$\theta = \tan^{-1}\left(\frac{y}{x}\right)$$

where x is taken from ST and y is taken from ST(1). On the 8087 and 80287, the arguments must satisfy the inequality $0 \leq ST(1) < ST < +\infty$. On the 80287XL and later coprocessors, the range of the operands is unrestricted. The result is returned to ST(1), and the stack is popped, destroying both operands and leaving Θ in ST.

See also Chapter 12 for a list of identities for deriving the other trigonometric functions.

See also FPTAN.

ALGORITHM
```
ST(1)=tan⁻¹(ST(1)/ST)
FPOP
```

NPX FLAGS

S	P	U	O	Z	D	I	C_3	C_2	C_1	C_0
*	*	*			*a	*a	—	—	*	—

a Raised only by the 80287XL and later coprocessors.

FPATAN

11011001	11110011

TIMING

Operands	x	87/287	287XL	387	486/487
(no operands)	0	250-800[1]	321-494	250-420	218-303

[1] The typical execution time is 650 clocks.

FPREM

Partial Remainder

DESCRIPTION FPREM performs modulo division of ST by ST(1) and returns the result to ST.

The FPREM instruction is used to reduce the real operand in ST to a value whose magnitude is less than the magnitude of ST(1). FPREM produces an exact result, so the precision exception is never raised and the rounding control has no effect. The sign of the remainder is the same as the sign of the original operand.

The remaindering operation is performed by iterative scaled subtractions and can reduce the exponent of ST by no more than 63 in one execution. If the remainder is less than ST(1) (the modulus), the function is complete and C_2 in the status word is cleared.

If the modulo function is incomplete, C_2 is set to 1, and the result in ST is termed the partial remainder. C_2 can be inspected by storing the status word and reexecuting the instruction until C_2 is clear. Alternately, ST can be compared to ST(1). If ST>ST(1), then FPREM must be executed again. If ST=ST(1), then the remainder is 0.

FPREM is important for reducing arguments to the periodic transcendental functions such as FPTAN. Because FPREM produces an exact result, no roundoff error is introduced into the calculation.

When reduction is complete, the three least-significant bits of the quotient are stored in the condition code bits C_3, C_1, and C_0, respectively. When arguments to the tangent function are reduced by $\pi/4$, this result can be used to identify the octant that contained the original angle.

The FPREM function operates differently than specified by the IEEE 754 standard when rounding the quotient to form a partial remainder. (See the algorithm.) The FPREM1 function is provided for compatibility with that standard.

The FPREM instruction can also be used to normalize ST. If ST is unnormal and ST(1) is greater than ST, FPREM will normalize ST.

On the 8087 and 80287, operation on a denormal operand raises the invalid operation exception. Underflow is not possible. On the 80287XL and later coprocessors, operation on a denormal is supported and an underflow exception can occur.

See also FPREM1.

ALGORITHM
```
t=EXPONENT(ST)-EXPONENT(ST(1))
IF (t<64) THEN
    q=ROUND(ST/ST(1),CHOP)
    ST=ST-(ST(1)*q)
    C₂=0
    C₀=BIT(2 of q)
    C₁=BIT(1 of q)
```

```
        C3=BIT(0 of q)
ELSE
    n=a number between 32 and 63
    q=ROUND((ST/ST(1))/2^(t-n),CHOP)
    ST=ST-(ST(1)*q*2^(t-n))
    C2=1
ENDIF
```

NOTES

1. On the 8087 and 80287, the condition code bits C_3, C_1, and C_0 are incorrect when performing a reduction of 64^n+m, where $n \geq 1$, and m=1 or m=2. A bug fix should be implemented in software.

NPX FLAGS

S	P	U	O	Z	D	I	C_3	C_2	C_1	C_0
*		*			*	*	*	*	*	*

FPREM

11011001	11111000

TIMING

Operands	x	87/287	287XL	387	486/487
(no operands)	0	15-190[1]	81-162	56-140	70-138

[1] The typical execution time is 125 clocks.

FPREM1

Partial Remainder

DESCRIPTION FPREM1 performs modulo division of ST by ST(1) and returns the result to ST.

The FPREM1 instruction is used to reduce the real operand in ST to a value whose magnitude is less than the magnitude of ST(1). FPREM1 produces an exact result, so the precision exception is never raised and the rounding control has no effect. The sign of the remainder is the same as the sign of the original operand.

The remaindering operation is performed by iterative scaled subtractions and can reduce the exponent of ST by no more than 63 in one execution. If the remainder is less than ST(1) (the modulus), the function is complete and C_2 in the status word is cleared.

If the modulo function is incomplete, C_2 is set to 1, resulting in ST being termed the partial remainder. C_2 can be inspected by storing the status word and reexecuting the instruction until C_2 is clear. Alternately, ST can be compared to ST(1). If ST>ST(1), then FPREM1 must be executed again. If ST=ST(1), then the remainder is 0.

FPREM1 is important in reducing arguments in the periodic transcendental functions, such as FPTAN. Because FPREM1 produces an exact result, no round-off error is introduced into the calculation.

When reduction is complete, the three least-significant bits of the quotient are stored in the condition code bits C_3, C_1, and C_0. When arguments to the tangent function are reduced by $\pi/4$, this result can be used to identify the octant that contained the original angle.

The FPREM1 function operates in accordance with the IEEE 754 standard when rounding the quotient to form a partial remainder. (See the algorithm.) The FPREM function is provided for compatibility with earlier coprocessors.

The FPREM1 instruction can also be used to normalize ST. If ST is unnormal and ST(1) is greater than ST, FPREM1 normalizes ST.

See also FPREM.

ALGORITHM
```
t=EXPONENT(ST)-EXPONENT(ST(1))
IF (t<64) THEN
   q=ROUND(ST/ST(1),CHOP)
   ST=ST-(ST(1)*q)
   C₂=0
   C₀=BIT(2 of q)
   C₁=BIT(1 of q)
   C₃=BIT(0 of q)
ELSE
   n=a number between 32 and 63
```

```
q=ROUND((ST/ST(1))/2^(t-n),NEAREST)
ST=ST-(ST(1)*q*2^(t-n))
C₂=1
ENDIF
```

$$q=\text{ROUND}((ST/ST(1))/2^{t-n},\text{NEAREST})$$
$$ST=ST-(ST(1)*q*2^{t-n})$$
$$C_2=1$$

NPX FLAGS

S	P	U	O	Z	D	I	C_3	C_2	C_1	C_0
*		*			*	*	*	*	*	*

FPREM1

11011001	11110101

TIMING

Operands	x	87/287	287XL	387	486/487
(no operands)	0	–	102-192	81-168	72-167

FPTAN

Partial Tangent

DESCRIPTION FPTAN calculates the partial tangent of ST.

The FPTAN instruction computes the function

$$\frac{y}{x} = \tan\theta$$

in which Θ is taken from ST. The result of the operation is a ratio. y replaces Θ on the stack, and x is pushed onto the stack, where it becomes the new ST.

On the 8087 and 80287, the FPTAN function assumes that its argument is valid and inrange. No argument checking is performed. The value of Θ must satisfy the inequality $-\pi/4 \le \Theta \le \pi/4$. In the case of an invalid argument, the result is undefined and no error is signaled.

On the 80287XL and later coprocessors, if value of Θ satisfies the condition $-2^{63} < \Theta < 2^{63}$ it will automatically be reduced to within range. If the operand is outside this range, however, C_2 is set to 1 to indicate that the function is incomplete, and ST is left unchanged.

The 80287XL, 80387, and 80486 always push a value of +1.0 for x. The value of x pushed by the 8087 and 80287 may be any real number. In either case, the ratio is the same. The cotangent can be calculated by executing FDIVR immediately after FPTAN. The following code will leave the 8087 and 80287 in the same state as the later coprocessors:

```
FDIV
FLD1
```

ST(7) must be empty before this instruction is executed to avoid an invalid operation exception. If the invalid operation exception is masked, the 8087 and 80287 leave the original operand unchanged, but push it to ST(1). On the 80287XL and later coprocessors, both ST and ST(1) will contain quiet NaNs.

On the 80287XL and later coprocessors, if condition code bit C_2 is 0 and the precision exception is raised, then $C_1=1$ if the last bit was rounded up. C_1 is undefined for the 8087 and 80287.

See also Chapter 12 for a list of identities for deriving the other trigonometric functions.

See also FPATAN.

NOTES 1. The floating-point stack of some versions of the 80486 FPU may be corrupted when an FPTAN instruction is executed within a particular sequence of code. In addition, this condition is data dependent. There will be no indication that the floating-point stack has been corrupted.

To avoid this, the FPTAN instruction should be followed immediately by one of the following instructions: FCLEX, FINIT, FLDCW, FSTSW, FSTSWAX, FSAVE, or FSTENV. Alternately, the FPTAN can be followed immediately by a WAIT instruction and a non-FPU instruction (such as NOP).

ALGORITHM   `ST(1)=tan(ST)`

NPX FLAGS

S	P	U	O	Z	D	I	C_3	C_2	C_1	C_0
*	*	*[a]			*[a]	*	—	*	*	—

[a] Raised only by the 80287XL and later coprocessors.

FPTAN

11011001	11110010

TIMING

Operands	x	87/287	287XL	387	486/487
(no operands)	0	30-540[1]	198-504[2]	162-430[3]	200-273[4]

[1] The typical execution time is 450 clocks.
[2] If out of range, up to 78 additional clocks may be required to reduce the operand.
[3] If out of range, up to 76 additional clocks may be required to reduce the operand.
[4] If out of range, add $ST/(\pi/4)$ clocks.

FRICHOP

Chop ST to Integer (Cyrix)

DESCRIPTION FRICHOP chops (rounds toward 0) the value in ST to an integer.

This operation is supported only by the Cyrix EMC87 (80387 replacement) coprocessor. It chops ST regardless of the setting of the RC field in the NPX control word.

ALGORITHM ST=ROUND(ST,CHOP)

NPX FLAGS

S	P	U	O	Z	D	I	C_3	C_2	C_1	C_0
*	*				*	*	—	—	*	—

FRICHOP

11011101	11111100

TIMING

Operands	x	EMC87
(no operands)	0	15

FRINEAR

Round ST to Nearest Integer (Cyrix)

DESCRIPTION FRINEAR rounds the value in ST to the nearest integer.

This operation is supported only on the Cyrix EMC87 (80387 replacement) coprocessor. It rounds ST to the nearest integer (or to even if ST is not nearer to either), regardless of the setting of the RC field in the NPX control word.

ALGORITHM

```
ST=ROUND(ST,NEAREST)
```

NPX FLAGS

S	P	U	O	Z	D	I	C_3	C_2	C_1	C_0
*	*				*	*	—	—	*	—

FRICHOP

11011111	11111100

TIMING

Operands	x	EMC87
(no operands)	0	15

FRINT2

Round ST to Integer, Halves Away from 0 (Cyrix)

DESCRIPTION FRINEAR rounds the value in ST to the nearest integer; exact halves are rounded away from zero.

This operation is supported only by the Cyrix EMC87 (80387 replacement) coprocessor. It provides a new rounding mode, which rounds ST to the nearest integer, regardless of the setting of the RC field in the NPX control word. If, however, ST contains an exact half (fractional portion equals 0.5), it is always rounded away from zero (toward the next largest integer in magnitude).

ALGORITHM
```
IF (exact half)
   ST=SIGN(ST)*ROUND(ABS(ST)+.5,NEAREST)
ELSE
   ST=ROUND(ST,NEAREST)
ENDIF
```

NPX FLAGS

S	P	U	O	Z	D	I	C_3	C_2	C_1	C_0
*	*				*	*	—	—	*	—

FRICHOP

11011011	11111100

TIMING

Operands	x	EMC87
(no operands)	0	15

FRNDINT

Round to Integer

DESCRIPTION FRNDINT rounds ST to an integer and returns the result to ST.

The value in ST is rounded depending on the current setting of the RC field in the NPX control word. For example, if ST=6.7, executing FRNDINT leaves 6 in ST if RC is set for chop or round down; it will leave 7 in ST if RC is set for round up or round to nearest or even.

ALGORITHM

```
ST=ROUND(ST,RC)
```

NPX FLAGS

S	P	U	O	Z	D	I	C_3	C_2	C_1	C_0
*	*				*[a]	*	—	—	*	—

[a] Raised only by the 80287XL and later coprocessors.

FRNDINT

11011001	11111100

TIMING

Operands	x	87/287	287XL	387	486/487
(no operands)	0	16-50	73-87	41-62	21-30

FRSTOR

Restore Saved NPX State

DESCRIPTION　FRSTOR *mem*

FRSTOR loads the NPX environment and floating-point stack from the memory area specified by the memory operand.

The NPX state comprises the control, status, and tag words, exception pointers, and floating-point registers. This data will typically have been written by a previous FSAVE instruction. The format of the memory area is dependent on the operating mode of the NPX. Diagrams of the memory image created by the FSAVE instruction are given in the entry for that instruction. See also Chapter 10 for a complete description of the possible formats.

Note that if an exception bit in the status word is set and the corresponding mask in the new control word is cleared, an immediate interrupt request will be generated before the next instruction is executed when IEM=0.

When the tag word is loaded by this instruction, the 80287XL and later coprocessors interpret the individual tags only as empty (11b) or nonempty (00b, 01b, and 10b). Subsequent operations on a nonempty register always examine the value in the register—not its tag. The 8087 and 80287 examine the tag before each operation. If the tag value disagrees with the register contents, the 8087 and 80287 will honor the tag and not examine the register.

See also FSAVE, FSTENV, and FLDENV.

ALGORITHM　NPX_State=[*mem*]

NOTES　1. If either of the two last bytes of memory addressed by FRSTOR is not readable for any reason, the instruction is not restartable. This problem will typically arise in demand-paged systems or demand-segmented systems which increase segment size on demand.

To avoid this problem, a dummy value can be read from the last two bytes of the memory operand. Alternately, the operand can be aligned on a 128-byte boundary to avoid crossing a segment or page boundary.

NPX FLAGS

S	P	U	O	Z	D	I	C_3	C_2	C_1	C_0
*	*	*	*	*	*	*	*	*	*	*

FRSTOR *mem*

11011011	mod	100	r/m	disp

TIMING

Operands	x	87/287	287XL	387	486/487
mem94byte (real and V86 modes, 16-bit)	47	(197-207)+EA	396	308	131
mem94byte (protected mode, 16-bit)	47	197-207[1]	396	308	120
mem108byte (real and V86 modes, 32-bit)	54	–	–	308	131
mem108byte (protected mode, 32-bit)	54	–	–	308	120

[1] 80287 only.

FRSTPM

Leave Protected Mode

DESCRIPTION FRSTPM switches the 80287XL from protected mode to real mode.

The FRSTPM instruction is new on the 80287XL; it is not supported by the original version of the 80287. Although the 80287XL is basically a minor redesign of the 80387 die, the FRSTPM instruction generates an invalid opcode if executed on the 80387 or 80486. This instruction, therefore, was added specifically to the 80287XL circuit design.

Intel documentation notes that this instruction is useful only with CPUs that can also switch back to real mode. The current versions of the 80286 (Intel's or any compatible versions) cannot switch from protected mode to real mode.

Note that the 80386DX, which can be switched from protected to real mode, is compatible with the 80287 if a hardware patch (such as those used on many 80386DX system boards) is employed. It is doubtful that this is the intended platform—software written for 80386 systems will generally mistake an 80287XL for an 80387 and attempts to exchange data over the full 32-bit bus result in a hung computer.

FRSTPM instructs the NPX to use the real mode format for the data written by the FSAVE and FSTENV instructions. Details of the formats are described in the entries for the FSAVE and FSTENV instructions; they are also discussed in Chapter 10.

See also FSETPM.

ALGORITHM None

NPX FLAGS

S	P	U	O	Z	D	I	C_3	C_2	C_1	C_0
0	0	0	0	0	0	0	–	–	–	–

FRSTPM

11011011	11110100

TIMING

Operands	x	87/287	287XL	387	486/487
(no operands)	47	–	12	–[1]	–[1]

[1] Generates an invalid opcode exception.

FSAVE/FNSAVE

Save NPX State

DESCRIPTION   FSAVE *mem*

FSAVE stores the NPX environment and floating-point stack to the memory area specified by the memory operand, then reinitializes the NPX.

The NPX state comprises the control, status, and tag words, exception pointers, and floating-point registers. This data will typically be restored by a later FRSTOR instruction. The format of the memory area is dependent on the operating mode of the NPX. See Chapter 10 for a complete description of the possible formats. The first part of the memory image for each of the formats is the same as that shown for the FSTENV instruction. The eight 80-byte registers are then written out directly following the environment data. ST is written first (lower memory address) and ST(7) is written last (higher memory address).

Note that the floating-point registers are dumped in their stack order. The TOP field in the NPX status word should be used to determine which physical register corresponded to ST at the time the FSAVE instruction was executed.

If an instruction is executing in the NEU when the FNSAVE instruction is decoded, the CPU queues the FNSAVE and will not execute it until the current execution instruction is complete or encounters an unmasked exception. The saved image of the NPX thus reflects the state of the NPX after the completion of any running instruction. The NPX is then initialized as though a FINIT instruction had been executed.

FSAVE is typically used during task switching to save the state of the NPX; alternately, a routine could use the instruction to preserve NPX data before passing control to subroutines that may alter that data. A previously saved environment can be restored using the FRSTOR instruction.

FNSAVE must be executed with CPU interrupts disabled to protect it from other no-wait instructions. For example, if an interrupt handler executed a second FNSAVE, it could destroy the first FNSAVE if it has been queued by the NPX. An FWAIT should be executed after this instruction but *before* the CPU interrupts are enabled or another NPX instruction is executed.

The FSAVE mnemonic instructs the assembler to generate the opcode for a WAIT instruction prior to the opcode for the FSAVE instruction. If the FNSAVE mnemonic is specified, no WAIT is generated.

See also FRSTOR, FSTENV, and FLDENV.

ALGORITHM   NPX_State=[*mem*]

      Initialize   ;Equivalent to FINIT

1. The contents of the data pointer field are undefined if the preceding NPX arithmetic instruction did not use a memory operand.

2. On some versions of the 80386, if the FSAVE/FNSAVE instruction is executed in real or V86 mode, the opcode field stored in memory is incorrect. The linear addresses stored in the instruction pointer field in memory, however, are correct and can be used to read the opcode, if needed. The problem does not occur in protected mode, since no opcode is saved.

   The following code shows how the opcode can be recovered and stored into the save area:

```
FSAVE    [BX]                    ;Save NPX state
MOV      AX,WORD PTR [BX+8]      ;Bits 16-19 of instruction pointer
AND      AX,0F000h               ;Mask unneeded bits
MOV      ES,AX                   ;Use it as segment or selector
MOV      SI,WORD PTR [BX+6]      ;Bits 0-15 of instruction pointer
MOV      AX,WORD PTR ES:[SI]     ;Fetch raw opcode
XCHG     AH,AL                   ;Reverse byte order
AND      AX,7FFh                 ;Mask off top bits
AND      WORD PTR [BX+8],0F800h  ;Erase bad opcode
OR       WORD PTR [BX+8],AX      ;Copy in good opcode
```

3. If either of the two last bytes of memory addressed by FSAVE/FNSAVE is not writeable for any reason, the instruction is not restartable. This problem will typically arise in demand-paged systems or demand-segmented systems that increase segment size on demand.

   To avoid this problem, a dummy value can be written to the last two bytes of the memory operand; alternately, the operand can be aligned on a 128-byte boundary to avoid the crossing of a segment or page boundary.

NPX FLAGS

S	P	U	O	Z	D	I	C_3	C_2	C_1	C_0
							0	0	0	0

FSAVE *mem*

10011011	11011011	mod	110	r/m	disp

TIMING

Operands	x	87/287	287XL	387	486/487
mem94byte (real and V86 modes, 16-bit)	47	(200-216)+EA+5n	524-525+5n	375-376	154[1]
mem94byte (protected mode, 16-bit)	47	200-216+5n[2]	524-525+5n	375-376	143[1]
mem108byte (real and V86 modes, 16-bit)	54	–	–	375-376	154[1]
mem108byte (protected mode, 32-bit)	54	–	–	375-376	143[1]

n is the number of times the CPU examines TEST# line until NPX lowers BUSY.
[1] Add 17 clocks if a numeric exception is pending from a previous instruction.
[2] 80287 only.

FNSAVE *mem*

11011011	mod	110	r/m	disp

TIMING

Operands	x	87/287	287XL	387	486/487
mem94byte (real and V86 modes, 16-bit)	47	(197-213)+EA	521-522	375-376	154[1]
mem94byte (protected mode, 16-bit)	47	197-213[2]	521-522	375-376	143[1]
mem108byte (real and V86 modes, 32-bit)	54	–	–	375-376	154[1]
mem108byte (protected mode, 32-bit)	54	–	–	375-376	143[1]

[1] Add 17 clocks if a numeric exception is pending from a previous instruction.
[2] 80287 only.

FSBP0

Set Bank Pointer to Bank 0 (IIT)

DESCRIPTION FSBP0 selects bank 0 from the four banks of floating-point registers available on the IIT coprocessors.

The FSBP0 instruction is available only on the IIT 2C87, 3C87, and 3C87SX coprocessors. These coprocessors contain 32 80-bit floating-point registers arranged in four banks of eight registers. Three of the banks can be addressed directly. The fourth is used internally for special calculations. At reset, bank 0 is automatically selected.

This instruction is used in combination with the FSBP1, FSBP2, and F4X4 instructions to perform a 4x4 matrix multiply transformation.

See also FSBP1, FSBP2, and F4X4.

ALGORITHM Select bank 0

NPX FLAGS

S	P	U	O	Z	D	I	C_3	C_2	C_1	C_0

FSBP0

11011011	11101000

TIMING

Operands	x	2C87	3C87SX	3C87
(no operands)	0	6	6	6

FSBP1

Set Bank Pointer to Bank 1 (IIT)

DESCRIPTION FSBP1 selects bank 1 from the four banks of floating-point registers available on the IIT coprocessors.

The FSBP1 instruction is available only on the IIT 2C87, 3C87, and 3C87SX coprocessors. These coprocessors contain 32 80-bit floating-point registers arranged in four banks of eight registers. Three of the banks can be addressed directly. The fourth is used internally for special calculations. At reset, bank 0 is automatically selected.

This instruction is used in combination with the FSBP0, FSBP2, and F4X4 instructions to perform a 4x4 matrix multiply transformation.

See also FSBP0, FSBP2, and F4X4.

ALGORITHM   Select bank 1

NPX FLAGS

S	P	U	O	Z	D	I	C_3	C_2	C_1	C_0

FSBP1

11011011	11101011

TIMING

Operands	x	2C87	3C87SX	3C87
(no operands)	0	6	6	6

FSBP2

Set Bank Pointer to Bank 2 (IIT)

DESCRIPTION FSBP2 selects bank 2 from the four banks of floating-point registers available on the IIT coprocessors.

The FSBP2 instruction is available only on the IIT 2C87, 3C87, and 3C87SX coprocessors. These coprocessors contain 32 80-bit floating-point registers arranged in four banks of eight registers. Three of the banks can be addressed directly. The fourth is used internally for special calculations. At reset, bank 0 is automatically selected.

This instruction is used in combination with the FSBP0, FSBP1, and F4X4 instructions to perform a 4x4 matrix multiply transformation.

See also FSBP0, FSBP1, and F4X4.

ALGORITHM Select bank 2

NPX FLAGS

S	P	U	O	Z	D	I	C_3	C_2	C_1	C_0

FSBP2

11011011	11101010

TIMING

Operands	x	2C87	3C87SX	3C87
(no operands)	0	6	6	6

FSCALE

Scale ST by ST(1)

DESCRIPTION FSCALE interprets the value in ST(1) as an integer and adds this number to the exponent of the number in ST.

The FSCALE instruction provides a means of quickly performing multiplication or division by powers of two. This operation is often required when scaling array indexes.

On the 8087 and 80287, FSCALE assumes that the scale factor in ST(1) is an integer that satisfies the inequality $-2^{15} \leq ST(1) < +2^{15}$. If ST(1) is not an integer value, the value is chopped to the next smallest integer in magnitude (chopped toward zero). If the value is out of range or $0 < ST(1) < 1$, FSCALE produces an undefined result and doesn't signal an exception. Typically, the value in ST is unchanged but should not be depended on.

On the 80287XL and later coprocessors, there is no limit on the range of the scale factor in ST(1). The value in ST(1) is still chopped toward zero. If ST(1) is 0, ST is unchanged.

See also FXTRACT.

ALGORITHM
```
t=ROUND(ST(1),CHOP)
IF (8087 or 80287) THEN
  IF (t<-2^15 OR t≥2^15 OR ABS(t<1)) THEN
    ST=undefined
  ELSE
    ST=ST*2^t
  ENDIF
ELSE  ;80287XL or later
  IF (t≠0) THEN ST=ST*2^t
ENDIF
```

NOTES
1. If $-1 < ST(1) < 1$, ST contains a pseudo-denormal or denormal, and the underflow exception is unmasked, some versions of the 80486 FPU produce an incorrect result. The 80486 returns ST as the result.

   There is no workaround for this bug other than to avoid the situation. Fortunately this situation rarely occurs since the 80486 does not produce pseudo-denormals, and most applications run with the underflow exception masked.

NPX FLAGS	S	P	U	O	Z	D	I	C_3	C_2	C_1	C_0
	*	*[a]	*	*		*[a]	*	—	—	*	—

[a] Raised only by the 80287XL and later coprocessors.

FSCALE

11011001	11111101

TIMING	Operands	x	87/287	287XL	387	486/487
	(no operands)	0	32-38	74-93	44-82	30-32

FSETPM

Enter Protected Mode

DESCRIPTION FSETPM sets the operating mode of the 80287 to protected mode.

FSETPM instructs the NPX to use the protected-mode format for the data written by the FSAVE and FSTENV instructions. The details of the formats are described in the entries for the FSAVE and FSTENV instructions; they are also discussed in Chapter 10.

This instruction is ignored on the 80387 and later coprocessors.

See also FRSTPM.

ALGORITHM None

NPX FLAGS

S	P	U	O	Z	D	I	C_3	C_2	C_1	C_0
0	0	0	0	0	0	0	–	–	–	–

FSETPM

11011011	11100100

TIMING

Operands	x	87/287	287XL	387	486/487
(no operands)	0	2-8[1]	12	–	–

[1] This instruction is not available on the 8087.

FSIN

Calculate Sine of ST

DESCRIPTION　FSIN　:ST=sin(ST)

FSIN replaces ST with the sine of ST.

The FSIN instruction assumes that the argument in ST is expressed in radians. ST must satisfy the inequality $-2^{63} < ST < +2^{63}$.

If the operand lies outside the acceptable range, the C_2 flag is set and ST is unchanged. The programmer must reduce the value in ST by an integer multiple of 2π until it is within range.

ALGORITHM
```
IF (ABS(ST)<2^63) THEN
   ST=sin(ST)
   C_2=0
ELSE
   C_2=1
ENDIF
```

NPX FLAGS

S	P	U	O	Z	D	I	C_3	C_2	C_1	C_0
*	*	*		*	*	—	*	*	*	—

FSIN

11011001	11111110

TIMING

Operands	x	87/287	287XL	387	486/487
(no operands)	0	–	129-778[1]	121-680	193-279[2]

[1] Time shown is for arguments in the range $-\pi/4 < x < +\pi/4$. If out of range, up to 78 additional clocks may be required to reduce the operand.
[2] If out of range, add $ST/(\pi/4)$ clocks.

FSINCOS

Calculate Sine and Cosine of ST

DESCRIPTION FSINCOS calculates both the sine and cosine of ST.

The FSINCOS instruction assumes that the argument in ST is expressed in radians. ST must satisfy the inequality $-2^{63} < ST < +2^{63}$. ST is replaced with sin(ST), and then cos(ST) is pushed onto the stack. Thus after execution, ST(1) contains the sine, and ST contains the cosine of the original operand, which is destroyed.

If the operand is outside the acceptable range, the C_2 flag is set and ST is unchanged. The programmer must reduce the value in ST by an integer multiple of 2π until it is within range.

ALGORITHM
```
IF (ABS(ST)<2^63) THEN
    temp=cos(ST)
    ST=sin(ST)
    DEC TOP
    ST=temp
    C₂=0
ELSE
    C₂=1
ENDIF
```

NOTES
1. The floating-point stack of some versions of the 80486 FPU may be corrupted when an FSINCOS instruction is executed within a particular sequence of code. In addition, this condition is data dependent. There is no indication that the floating-point stack has been corrupted.

    To avoid this, the FSINCOS instruction should be followed immediately by one of the following instructions: FCLEX, FINIT, FLDCW, FSTSW, FSTSWAX, FSAVE, or FSTENV. Alternately, the FSINCOS can be followed immediately by a WAIT instruction and a non-FPU instruction (such as NOP).

NPX FLAGS

S	P	U	O	Z	D	I	C_3	C_2	C_1	C_0
*	*	*			*	*	—	*	*	—

FSINCOS

11011011	11111011

TIMING

Operands	x	87/287	287XL	387	486/487
(no operands)	0	–	201-816[1]	150-650	243-329[2]

[1] Time shown is for arguments in the range $-\pi/4 < x < +\pi/4$. If out of range, up to 78 additional clocks may be required to reduce the operand.
[2] If out of range, add $ST/(\pi/4)$ clocks.

FSQRT

Square Root

DESCRIPTION   FSQRT   :ST=√ST

FSQRT calculates the square root of ST and returns the result to ST.

The range of the FSQRT function is $-0.0 \leq ST \leq +\infty$. If ST is not within this range, an invalid operation exception will be generated. The square root of -0.0 is defined to be -0.0.

On the 8087 and 80287, operation on a denormal operand raises the invalid operation exception. Underflow is not possible. On the 80287XL and later coprocessors, operation on a denormal is supported and an underflow exception can occur.

ALGORITHM
```
IF (ST≥+0.0) THEN
    ST=√ST
ELSEIF (ST<-0.0) THEN
    IE=1
ENDIF
```

NPX FLAGS

S	P	U	O	Z	D	I	C_3	C_2	C_1	C_0
*	*			*	*	—	—	—	*	—

FSQRT

11011001	11111010

TIMING

Operands	x	87/287	287XL	387	486/487
(no operands)	0	180-186	129-136	97-111	83-87

Times shown are for the case when the argument is in range.

FST/FSTP

Store ST to Real Memory Operand

DESCRIPTION
```
FST  ST(i)
FST  real
FSTP ST(i)
FSTP real
```

The FST instructions copies the temporary real value in ST to the specified operand, converting format if necessary.

If the destination specified by the operand is a floating-point register or temporary real memory operand, then ST is not altered during the transfer. If the destination is a short real or long real memory operand, however, the mantissa is rounded to the width of the destination according to the setting of the RC field. The exponent is also converted to fit the width and bias of the exponent field of the destination.

Note that if ST is tagged as special (it contains a NaN or a denormal), then the mantissa is not rounded, but is chopped on the right and transferred. The exponent is also chopped on the right and stored without further conversion. This procedure preserves the value's identification as a NaN (exponent all ones) or a denormal (exponent all zeros), so it can later be loaded and tagged appropriately.

The operation of the FSTP instruction is identical to the FST instruction, except that the stack is popped at the conclusion of the operation.

Note that coding FSTP ST(0) is equivalent to popping the floating-point stack with no data transfer (an FPOP).

ALGORITHM
```
IF (real) THEN
  [real]=ST   ;See text if NaN or denormal
ELSE  ;operand is floating-point register
  ST(i)=ST
ENDIF
IF (FSTP) THEN FPOP ;Pop floating-point stack
```

NPX FLAGS

S	P	U	O	Z	D	I	C_3	C_2	C_1	C_0
*	*	*	*		*[a]	*	—	—	*[b]	—

[a] Raised only by the 80287XL and later coprocessors.
[b] For FLD *real80*, if SF=0, then C_1 does not indicate rounding and will be cleared to 0.

FST ST(i)

11011101	11010*rrr*

TIMING

Operands	x	87/287	287XL	387	486/487
ST(i)	0	15-22	18	7-11	3

FST *real*

11011*w*01	*mod*	010	*r/m*	*disp*

w = 0, memory operand is *real32*
　　1, memory operand is *real64*

TIMING

Operands	x	87/287	287XL	387	486/487
real32	2	(84-90)+EA	51	25-43	7[1]
real64	4	(96-104)+EA	56	32-44	8[2]

[1] Execution requires 27 clocks if operand is 0.0.
[2] Execution requires 28 clocks if operand is 0.0.

FSTP ST(i)

11011101	11011*rrr*

TIMING

Operands	x	87/287	287XL	387	486/487
ST(i)	0	17-24	19	7-11	3

FSTP *real32/real64*

11011*w*01	*mod*	011	*r/m*	*disp*

w = 0, memory operand is *real32*
　　1, memory operand is *real64*

TIMING

Operands	x	87/287	287XL	387	486/487
real32	2	(86-92)+EA	51	25-43	7[1]
real64	4	(98-106)+EA	56	32-44	8[2]

[1] Execution requires 27 clocks if operand is 0.0.
[2] Execution requires 28 clocks if operand is 0.0.

FSTP *real80*

11011011	mod	111	r/m	disp

TIMING

Operands	x	87/287	287XL	387	486/487
real80	5	(52-58)+EA	61	46-52	6

FSTCW/FNSTCW

Store Control Word

DESCRIPTION
FSTCW *mem16*
FNSTCW *mem16*

FSTCW and FNSTCW store the NPX control word into the specified 16-bit memory operand.

The FSTCW instruction is typically used to save the mode of operation of the NPX before modifying it.

The FSTCW mnemonic instructs the assembler to generate the opcode for a WAIT instruction prior to the one for the FSTCW instruction. If the FNSTCW mnemonic is specified, no WAIT is generated.

See also FLDCW, FSTENV, FLDENV, FSAVE, and FRSTOR.

ALGORITHM   [*mem16*]=ControlWord

NPX FLAGS

S	P	U	O	Z	D	I	C_3	C_2	C_1	C_0
							—	—	—	—

FSTCW *mem16*

10011011	11011001	mod	111	r/m	disp

TIMING

Operands	x	87/287	287XL	387	486/487
mem16	1	(15-21)+EA+5*n*	21+5*n*	21-22	4-6[1]

n is the number of times the CPU examines TEST# line until NPX lowers BUSY.
[1] Add 17 clocks if a numeric exception is pending from a previous instruction.

FNSTCW *mem16*

11011001	mod	111	r/m	disp

TIMING

Operands	x	87/287	287XL	387	486/487
mem16	1	(12-18)+EA	18	15	3[1]

[1] Add 17 clocks if a numeric exception is pending from a previous instruction.

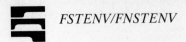

FSTENV/FNSTENV

Store Environment

FSTENV *mem*

FNSTENV *mem*

The FSTENV and FNSTENV instructions store the NPX environment to the memory area specified by the operand.

The NPX environment comprises the control, status, and tag words, and the exception pointers. The format of the memory area is dependent on the operating mode of the NPX. Typically, this data will be reloaded by a subsequent FLDENV instruction. The memory image for each of the formats is shown below in Figures B.6 through B.9. See also Chapter 10 for a complete description of the possible formats. After saving the environment, FSTENV sets the individual exception masks. The IEM bit, however, is not altered.

FIGURE B.6

16-bit real-mode FSTENV memory format

Data Pointer (bits 16-19)	Ø	Ø Ø Ø Ø Ø Ø Ø Ø Ø Ø Ø
Data Pointer (bits Ø-15)		
Instruction Pointer (bits 16-31)	Ø	Opcode (11 bits)
Instruction Pointer (bits Ø-15)		
Tag Word		
Status Word		
Control Word		

If an instruction is executing in the NEU when the FNSTENV instruction is decoded, the CPU queues the FNSTENV and will not execute it until the current execution instruction completes or encounters an unmasked exception. The saved image of the NPX thus reflects the state of the NPX after the completion of any running instruction. The NPX is then initialized as though a FINIT instruction had been executed.

FNSTENV must be executed with CPU interrupts disabled to protect it from other no-wait instructions. For example, if an interrupt handler executed a second FNSTENV, it could destroy the first FNSTENV if it were queued by the NPX. An FWAIT should be executed after this instruction but before CPU interrupts are enabled or another NPX instruction is executed.

Task switchers or exception handlers will typically save the environment to the CPU stack for examination. The handler will then have access to the exception pointers which identify the failed instruction and operand.

See also FLDENV, FSAVE, and FRSTOR.

FIGURE B.7

32-bit real-mode FSTENV memory format

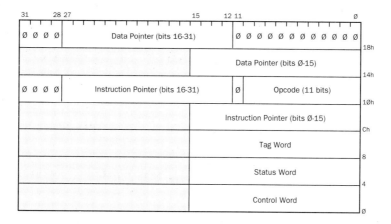

FIGURE B.8

16-bit protected-mode FSTENV memory format

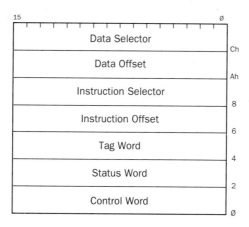

ALGORITHM

```
[mem]=NPX_Environment
PM=UM=OM=ZM=DM=IM=1
```

32-bit protected-mode FSTENV memory format

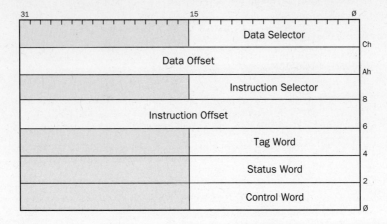

1. The contents of the data pointer field are undefined if the preceding NPX arithmetic instruction did not use a memory operand.

2. On some versions of the 80386, when the FSAVE/FNSAVE instruction is executed in real or V86 mode, the opcode field stored in memory is incorrect. The linear addresses stored in the instruction pointer field in memory, however, is correct and can be used to read the opcode, if necessary. The problem does not occur in protected mode since no opcode is saved.

   The following codes show how the opcode can be recovered and stored into the save area:

```
FSTENV  [BX]                    ;Save NPX environment
MOV     AX,WORD PTR [BX+8]      ;Bits 16-19 of instruction pointer
AND     AX,0F000h               ;Mask unneeded bits
MOV     ES,AX                   ;Use it as segment or selector
MOV     SI,WORD PTR [BX+6]      ;Bits 0-15 of instruction pointer
MOV     AX,WORD PTR ES:[SI]     ;Fetch raw opcode
XCHG    AH,AL                   ;Reverse byte order
AND     AX,7FFh                 ;Mask off top bits
AND     WORD PTR [BX+8],0F800h  ;Erase bad opcode
OR      WORD PTR [BX+8],AX      ;Copy in good opcode
```

3. If either of the two last bytes of memory addressed by FSTENV/FNSTENV is not writeable for any reason, the instruction is not restartable. This problem will typically arise in demand-paged systems or demand-segmented systems that increase segment size on demand.

To avoid this problem, a dummy value can be written to the last two bytes of the memory operand. Alternately, the operand can be aligned on a 128-byte boundary to avoid crossing a segment or page boundary.

NPX FLAGS

S	P	U	O	Z	D	I	C_3	C_2	C_1	C_0
							—	—	—	—

FSTENV *mem*

10011011	11011001	mod	110	r/m	disp

TIMING

Operands	x	87/287	287XL	387	486/487
mem14byte (real and V86 modes, 16-bit)	7	(43-53)+EA+5n	192-193	103-104	67[1]
mem14byte (protected mode, 16-bit)	7	(43-53)+5n[2]	192-193	103-104	56[1]
mem28byte (real and V86 modes, 32-bit)	14	–	–	103-104	67[1]
mem28byte (protected mode, 32-bit)	14	–	–	103-104	56[1]

n is the number of times the CPU examines TEST# line until NPX lowers BUSY.
[1] Add 17 clocks if a numeric exception is pending from a previous instruction.
[2] 80287 only.

FNSTENV *mem*

11011001	mod	110	r/m	disp

TIMING

Operands	x	87/287	287XL	387	486/487
mem14byte (real and V86 modes, 16-bit)	7	(40-50)+EA	192-193	103-104	67[1]
mem14byte (protected mode, 16-bit)	7	(40-50)+EA[2]	192-193	103-104	56[1]
mem28byte (real and V86 modes, 32-bit)	14	–	–	103-104	67[1]
mem28byte (protected mode, 32-bit)	14	–	–	103-104	56[1]

[1] Add 17 clocks if a numeric exception is pending from a previous instruction.
[2] 80287 only.

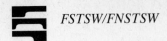

FSTSW/FNSTSW

Store Status Word

DESCRIPTION
FSTSW *mem16*
FNSTSW *mem16*

FSTSW and FNSTSW store the NPX status word into the specified 16-bit memory operand.

The FSTSW instruction is typically used to obtain a copy of the status word to check the operation of the NPX during execution. The status of the condition code bits, for example, is used to implement conditional branching following a comparison or FPREM instruction. The no-wait form, FNSTSW, can be used to poll the NPX to determine if it is busy or not. And by checking the exception flags, exception handlers that do not use interrupts can be implemented.

The following instructions show how to use the FSTSW for condition branching. The specific conditional jumps and the conditions under which they are taken are discussed in the entries for the FCOM, FICOM, FUCOM, FTST, and FXAM instructions.

```
FSTSW  [mem16]
MOV    AX,[mem16]
SAHF
Jcond
```

The FSTSW mnemonic instructs the assembler to generate the opcode for a WAIT instruction prior to the opcode for the FSTSW instruction. If the FNSTSW mnemonic is specified, no WAIT is generated.

See also FSTSWAX, FLDSW, FLDSWAX, FSTENV, FLDENV, FSAVE, and FRSTOR.

ALGORITHM [*mem16*]=StatusWord

NPX FLAGS

S	P	U	O	Z	D	I	C₃	C₂	C₁	C₀
							$-$	$-$	$-$	$-$

FSTSW *mem16*

10011011	11011111	mod	111	r/m	disp

TIMING

Operands	x	87/287	287XL	387	486/487
mem16	1	(15-21)+EA+5n	21+5n	21-22	4-6[1]

n is the number of times the CPU examines TEST# line until NPX lowers BUSY.
[1] Add 18 clocks if a numeric exception is pending from a previous instruction.

FNSTSW *mem16*

11011111	mod	111	r/m	disp

TIMING

Operands	x	87/287	287XL	387	486/487
mem16	1	(12-18)+EA	18	15	3[1]

[1] Add 18 clocks if a numeric exception is pending from a previous instruction.

FSTSW AX/FNSTSW AX

Store Status Word in AX

DESCRIPTION

```
FSTSW AX
FSTSWAX
FNSTSW AX
FNSTSWAX
```

FSTSW AX and FNSTSW AX store the NPX status word into the AX register of the CPU.

The FSTSW instruction is typically used to obtain a copy of the status word to check the operation of the NPX during execution. The status of the condition code bits, for example, is used to implement conditional branching following a comparison or FPREM instruction. The no-wait form, FNSTSW, can be used to poll the NPX to determine if it is busy or not. And by checking the exception flags, exception handlers that do not use interrupts can be implemented.

The following instructions show how to use the FSTSW for condition branching. The specific conditional jumps and the conditions under which they are taken are discussed in the entries for the FCOM, FICOM, FUCOM, FTST, and FXAM instructions.

```
FSTSW AX
SAHF
Jcond
```

The FSTSW mnemonic instructs the assembler to generate the opcode for a WAIT instruction prior to the one for the FSTSW instruction. If the FNSTSW mnemonic is specified, no WAIT is generated.

The encoding of this instruction does not allow registers other than AX to be specified. Because of this, the syntax of some assemblers and debuggers omits the space before AX.

See also FSTSWAX, FLDSW, FLDSWAX, FSTENV, FLDENV, FSAVE, and FRSTOR.

ALGORITHM   [*mem*]=StatusWord

NPX FLAGS

S	P	U	O	Z	D	I	C_3	C_2	C_1	C_0
							—	—	—	—

FSTSW AX

FSTSWAX

| 10011011 | 11011111 | 11100000 |

TIMING

Operands	x	87/287	287XL	387	486/487
AX	1	$13\text{-}19+5n^1$	$21+5n$	19-20	$4\text{-}6^2$

n is the number of times the CPU examines TEST# line until NPX lowers BUSY.
[1] This instruction is not available on the 8087.
[2] Add 18 clocks if a numeric exception is pending from a previous instruction.

FNSTSW AX

FNSTSWAX

| 11011111 | 11100000 |

TIMING

Operands	x	87/287	287XL	387	486/487
AX	1	$10\text{-}16^1$	18	13	3^2

[1] This instruction is not available on the 8087.
[2] Add 18 clocks if a numeric exception is pending from a previous instruction.

FSUB/FSUBP

Subtract Real

DESCRIPTION

```
FSUB ST,ST(i)      :ST=ST-ST(i)
FSUB ST(i)         :ST(i)=ST(i)-ST
FSUB ST(i),ST      :ST(i)=ST(i)-ST
FSUB real          :ST=ST-[real]
FSUB               :ST(1)=ST(1)-ST, POP
FSUBP              :ST(1)=ST(1)-ST, POP
FSUBP ST(i)        :ST(i)=ST(i)-ST, POP
FSUBP ST(i),ST     :ST(i)=ST(i)-ST, POP
```

The FSUB and FSUBP instructions subtract the source operand from the destination operand and return the result to the destination.

The source operand may be either a floating-point register or a real memory operand, but the destination is always a floating-point register. The FSUBP encoding pops the stack at the conclusion of the operation.

When the FSUB or FSUBP instructions are coded with no arguments (classical stack form), ST is the source and ST(1), the destination. The result is returned in ST(1). When the floating-point stack is automatically popped at the conclusion of execution, the result is left in ST. The following instructions have the identical effect:

```
FSUB               ;Implied ST(1),ST
FSUBP              ;Implied ST(1),ST
FSUBP ST(1)        ;Implied ST
FSUBP ST(1),ST     ;Explicit operands
```

If a register operand is the only operand specified, then ST is automatically implied as the source operand and the specified register will be the destination. The instruction FSUB ST(5), for example, is equivalent to FSUB ST(5),ST. Note that Microsoft's MASM does not support this syntax, although DEBUG does. If, however, the operand is a memory operand, it will be the source and ST will be the destination. FSUBP cannot be coded with a memory operand. If both operands are explicitly coded, ST *must* be one of the operands, although it may be either the source or destination.

See also FSUBR, FISUB, and FISUBR.

ALGORITHM

```
IF (NUMOPS=0) THEN
   ST(1)=ST(1)-ST
   FPOP
ELSEIF (NUMOPS=1) THEN
   IF (mem) THEN
      ST=ST-[mem]
   ELSE  ;operand is floating-point register
```

```
        ST(i)=ST(i)-ST
      ENDIF
      IF (FSUBP) THEN FPOP
    ELSE  ;NUMOPS=2
      dest=dest-src
      IF (FSUBP) THEN FPOP
    ENDIF
```

NOTES

1. The description given of the operation of this instruction in the Intel manuals is incorrect. Intel's definition identifies the operation as "destination = ST - the other operand" regardless of which operand is designated as the source or destination. In fact, the correct operation is as described here.

NPX FLAGS

S	P	U	O	Z	D	I	C_3	C_2	C_1	C_0
*	*	*	*		*	*	—	—	*	—

FSUB

FSUBP

11011110	11101001

TIMING

Operands	x	87/287	287XL	387	486/487
(no operands)	0	70-100	33-41	12-26	8-20

FSUB ST,ST(i)

11011000	11101*rrr*

TIMING

Operands	x	87/287	287XL	387	486/487
ST,ST(i)	0	70-100	36-44	15-29	8-20

FSUB ST(i)

FSUB ST(i),ST

| 11011100 | 11101*rrr* |

Operands	x	87/287	287XL	387	486/487
ST(i) ST(i),ST	0	70-100	33-41	12-26	8-20

FSUB *real*

| 11011w00 | mod | 100 | r/m | disp |

w = 0, memory operand is *real32*
    1, memory operand is *real64*

Operands	x	87/287	287XL	387	486/487
real32	2	(90-120)+EA	40-48	12-29	8-20
real64	4	(95-125)+EA	49-77	15-34	8-20

FSUBP ST(i)

FSUBP ST(i),ST

| 11011110 | 11101*rrr* |

Operands	x	87/287	287XL	387	486/487
ST(i) ST(i),ST	0	75-105	33-41	12-26	8-20

FSUBR/FSUBRP

Reversed Real Subtract

DESCRIPTION

```
FSUBR ST,ST(i)        :ST=ST(i)-ST
FSUBR ST(i)           :ST(i)=ST-ST(i)
FSUBR ST(i),ST        :ST(i)=ST-ST(i)
FSUBR real            :ST=[real]-ST
FSUBR                 :ST(1)=ST-ST(1), POP
FSUBRP                :ST(1)=ST-ST(1), POP
FSUBRP ST(i)          :ST(i)=ST-ST(i), POP
FSUBRP ST(i),ST       :ST(i)=ST-ST(i), POP
```

The FSUBR instruction subtracts the destination operand from the source operand and return the result to the destination.

The source operand may be either a floating-point register or a real memory operand, but the destination is always a floating-point register. The FSUBRP encoding pops the stack at the conclusion of the operation.

When the FSUBR or FSUBRP instructions are coded with no arguments (classical stack form), ST is the source and ST(1) is the destination, and the floating-point stack is automatically popped at the conclusion of execution. The following instructions have the identical effect.

```
FSUBR              ;Implied ST(1),ST
FSUBRP             ;Implied ST(1),ST
FSUBRP ST(1)       ;Implied ST
FSUBRP ST(1),ST    ;Explicit operands
```

If a register operand is the only operand specified, then ST is automatically implied as the source operand and the register will be the destination. The instruction FSUBR ST(5), for example, is equivalent to FSUBR ST(5),ST. Note that Microsoft's MASM does not support this syntax, although DEBUG does. If, however, a memory operand is specified, it will be the source and ST will be the destination. FSUBRP cannot be coded with a memory operand. If both operands are explicitly coded, ST *must* be one of the operands, although it may be either the source or destination.

See also FSUB, FISUB, and FISUBR.

ALGORITHM

```
IF (NUMOPS=0) THEN
   ST(1)=ST-ST(1)
   FPOP
ELSEIF (NUMOPS=1) THEN
   IF (real) THEN
     ST=[real]-ST
   ELSE  ;operand is floating-point register
```

```
        ST(i)=ST-ST(i)
      ENDIF
      IF (FSUBRP) THEN FPOP
    ELSE  ;NUMOPS=2
      dest=src-dest
      IF (FSUBRP) THEN FPOP
    ENDIF
```

NOTES

1. The description given of the operation of the instruction in the Intel manuals is incorrect. Intel's definition identifies the operation as "destination = the other operand - ST" regardless of which operand is designated as the source or destination. In fact, the correct operation is as described here.

NPX FLAGS

S	P	U	O	Z	D	I	C_3	C_2	C_1	C_0
*	*	*	*		*	*	—	—	*	—

FSUBR

FSUBRP

11011110	11100001

TIMING

Operands	x	87/287	287XL	387	486/487
(no operands)	0	70-100	33-41	12-26	8-20

FSUBR ST,ST(i)

11011000	11100rrr

TIMING

Operands	x	87/287	287XL	387	486/487
ST,ST(i)	0	70-100	36-44	15-29	8-20

FSUBR ST(i)

FSUBR ST(i),ST

11011100	11100rrr

TIMING

Operands	x	87/287	287XL	387	486/487
ST(i) ST(i),ST	0	70-100	33-41	12-26	8-20

FSUBR *real*

11011w00	mod	101	r/m	disp

w = 0, memory operand is *real32*
   1, memory operand is *real64*

TIMING

Operands	x	87/287	287XL	387	486/487
real32	2	(90-120)+EA	41-49	12-29	8-20
real64	4	(95-125)+EA	50-78	15-34	8-20

FSUBRP ST(i)

FSUBRP ST(i),ST

11011110	11100rrr

TIMING

Operands	x	87/287	287XL	387	486/487
ST(i) ST(i),ST	0	75-105	33-41	12-26	8-20

FTST

Test ST Against +0.0

DESCRIPTION   FTST tests ST by comparing it to +0.0.

The result is posted to the condition codes as shown below. The operation of this instruction is the same as would be produced by the FCOM instruction if ST(1) contained +0.0.

C_3	C_2	C_0	Result
0	0	0	ST is positive and nonzero (ST>+0.0)
0	0	1	ST is negative and nonzero (ST<-0.0)
1	0	0	ST is zero (ST=+0.0 or ST=-0.0)
1	1	1	ST is not comparable (NaN or projective infinity)

The correspondence between the condition code bits and the CPU flag bits is shown below:

NPX	CPU
C_0	CF
C_1	(None)
C_2	PF
C_3	ZF

If the condition code bits are loaded into the CPU FLAGS register, they can be used to direct a conditional jump, as shown in the sample code below:

```
FTST           ;Compare ST to +0.0
FSTSW   [mem16]        ;Write status word to memory
MOV     AX,[mem16]     ; then load into AX
SAHF                   ; and into FLAGS
JP      label          ;ST not comparable (test first)
JA      label          ;ST>0
JAE     label          ;ST≥0
JE      label          ;ST=0
JBE     label          ;ST≤0
JB      label          ;ST<0
```

If it is necessary to distinguish +0.0 from –0.0, use the FXAM instruction.

See also FCOM, FICOM, FUCOM, and FXAM.

ALGORITHM   ConditionCodes=ST compared to +0.0

S	P	U	O	Z	D	I	C_3	C_2	C_1	C_0
*				*	*	*	*	*	0	*

FTST

11011001	11100100

TIMING

Operands	x	87/287	287XL	387	486/487
(no operands)	0	38-48	35	17-25	4

FTSTP

Test ST Against +0.0 and POP (Cyrix)

DESCRIPTION FTSTP tests ST by comparing it to +0.0 and then pops the floating-point stack.

This operation is supported only on the Cyrix EMC87 (80387 replacement) coprocessor. This instruction is identical to the FTST instruction, but pops the floating-point stack at the conclusion of the execution. See the description of the FTST instruction for details on the state of the condition code bits after execution.

ALGORITHM
```
ConditionCodes=ST compared to +0.0
FPOP
```

NPX FLAGS

S	P	U	O	Z	D	I	C_3	C_2	C_1	C_0
*				*	*	*	*	0	*

FTST

11011001	11100110

TIMING

Operands	x	EMC87
(no operands)	0	15

FUCOM/FUCOMP/ FUCOMPP

Unordered Real Compare

DESCRIPTION

```
FUCOM          :Compare ST to ST(1)
FUCOM ST(i)    :Compare ST to ST(i)
FUCOMP         :Compare ST to ST(1), FPOP
FUCOMP ST(i)   :Compare ST to ST(i), FPOP
FUCOMPP        :Compare ST to ST(1), FPOP, FPOP
```

The FUCOM, FUCOMP, and FUCOMPP instructions compare ST to the specified operand and set the condition codes in the NPX status word to indicate the result.

The operand must be another floating-point register. If no operand is coded, ST(1) is used by default.

The condition code bits of the status word are used to report the result of the comparison as shown:

Order	C_3	C_2	C_0	Explanation
ST>op	0	0	0	ST greater than operand
ST<op	0	0	1	ST less than operand
ST=op	1	0	0	ST equal to operand
ST?op	1	1	1	ST not comparable to operand

Note that positive and negative forms of zero are treated identically for the purpose of this instruction. NaNs and the projective infinities cannot be compared; they return $C_3=C_2=C_0=1$ as shown in the table above.

If either operand is a signaling NaN or is in an unsupported format, the invalid operation exception is raised. If a stack fault occurs, the invalid operation exception is also raised. In either case, the condition codes are set to uncomparable.

If either operand is a quiet NaN, the condition bits are set to uncomparable. Unlike FCOM, however, FUCOM does not raise the invalid operation exception when it encounters a quiet NaN.

FUCOMP operates identically to FUCOM except that the floating-point stack is popped after the compare.

FUCOMPP operates identically to FUCOM except that the floating-point stack is popped twice after the compare. The comparison is always ST to ST(1); no explicit operands may be coded.

See also FCOM, FICOM, FTST, and FXAM.

ALGORITHM

```
ConditionCodes=ST compared to operand
```

NPX FLAGS

S	P	U	O	Z	D	I	C_3	C_2	C_1	C_0
*					*	*	*	*	0	*

FUCOM

11011101	11100001

TIMING

Operands	x	87/287	287XL	387	486/487
(no operands)	0	–	31	13-21	4

FUCOM ST(i)

11011101	11100rrr

TIMING

Operands	x	87/287	287XL	387	486/487
ST,ST(i)	0	–	31	13-21	4

FUCOMP

11011101	11101001

TIMING

Operands	x	87/287	287XL	387	486/487
(no operands)	0	–	33	13-21	4

FUCOMP ST(i)

11011101	11101rrr

TIMING

Operands	x	87/287	287XL	387	486/487
ST,ST(i)	0	–	33	13-21	4

FUCOMPP

| 11011010 | 11101001 |

TIMING

Operands	x	87/287	287XL	387	486/487
(no operands)	0	–	33	13-21	5

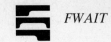

FWAIT

Wait Until NPX Not Busy

DESCRIPTION FWAIT is not actually an NPX instruction, but is an alternate mnemonic for the CPU WAIT instruction described in Appendix A.

You should use the FWAIT mnemonic instead of WAIT for compatibility with floating-point emulators. If you wish to encode explicit WAIT instructions (not those generated automatically by MASM) and your code might be linked with an emulator, they *must* be coded as FWAIT instructions. The FWAIT instruction will be converted into a software interrupt and handled by the emulator. A WAIT instruction will not be changed by the assembler. If a WAIT instruction is executed when no coprocessor is present, the CPU will wait forever. (For more information on emulation, see Chapter 12.)

ALGORITHM None

NPX FLAGS

S	P	U	O	Z	D	I	C_3	C_2	C_1	C_0
							–	–	–	–

FWAIT

```
10011011
```

TIMING

Operands	x	87/287	287XL	387	486/487
(no operands)	0	3+5n	3+5n	6	1-3

n is the number of times the CPU examines TEST# line until NPX lowers BUSY.

FXAM

Examine ST

DESCRIPTION FXAM examines ST and reports on its contents using the condition code bits in the NPX status word.

FXAM is able to classify the sign of ST as positive or negative and its type as NaN, unnormal, denormal, normal, zero, or empty. The result codes generated by FXAM are shown below:

C_3	C_2	C_1	C_0	Type
0	0	0	0	+ Unnormal[1]
0	0	1	0	− Unnormal[1]
0	0	0	1	+ NaN
0	0	1	1	− NaN
0	1	0	0	+ Normal
0	1	1	0	− Normal
0	1	0	1	+ ∞
0	1	1	1	− ∞
1	0	0	0	+ 0.0
1	0	1	0	− 0.0
1	0	0	1	Empty
1	0	1	1	Empty
1	1	0	0	+ Denormal
1	1	1	0	− Denormal
1	1	0	1	Empty[2]
1	1	1	1	Empty[2]

[1] Interpreted as unsupported by the 80287XL and later coprocessors.

[2] These combinations are never generated by the 80287XL and later coprocessors.

Although four different encodings may be returned for an empty register, condition code bits C_3 and C_0 will both be 1 in all cases.

ALGORITHM `ConditionCodes=EXAMINE(ST)`

NPX FLAGS

S	P	U	O	Z	D	I	C_3	C_2	C_1	C_0
							*	*	*	*

FXAM

| 11011001 | 11100101 |

TIMING

Operands	x	87/287	287XL	387	486/487
(no operands)	0	12-23	37-45	24-37	8

FXCH

Exchange Registers

DESCRIPTION   FXCH
                     FXCH ST(i)

FXCH swaps the contents of ST and another floating-point register.

If an operand is not specified, ST(1) is assumed; otherwise, any floating point register may be specified. FXCH cannot be used with memory operands.

Because many NPX instructions will only operate on ST, this instruction provides a method of performing those operations on lower stack elements by first swapping them with ST.

ALGORITHM   temp=ST
                   ST=ST(i)
                   ST(i)=temp

NPX FLAGS

S	P	U	O	Z	D	I	C$_3$	C$_2$	C$_1$	C$_0$
*						*	—	—	0	—

FXCH

11011001	11011001

TIMING

Operands	x	87/287	287XL	387	486/487
(no operands)	0	10-15	25	10-17	4

FXCH ST(i)

11011001	11011*rrr*

TIMING

Operands	x	87/287	287XL	387	486/487
ST(i)	0	10-15	25	10-17	4

FXTRACT

Extract Exponent and Mantissa of ST

DESCRIPTION FXTRACT splits the value encoded in ST into two separate numbers representing the actual value of the mantissa and exponent fields.

The FXTRACT instruction is used to decompose the two fields of the temporary real number in ST. The exponent replaces the value in ST, then the mantissa is pushed onto the stack. When execution is complete, ST contains the original mantissa, expressed as a real number with a true exponent of 0 (3FFFh in biased form). ST(1) contains the value of the original operand's true (unbiased) exponent expressed as a real number.

If ST is 0, the 8087 and 80287 will leave zeros in both ST and ST(1); both zeros will have the same sign as the original operand. If ST is +∞, the invalid operation exception is raised.

On the 80287XL and later coprocessors, if ST is 0, the zero-divide exception is reported and ST(1) is set to -∞. If ST is +∞, no exception is reported.

The FXTRACT instruction may be thought of as the complement to the FSCALE instruction, which combines a separate mantissa and exponent into a single value.

See also FSCALE.

ALGORITHM
```
IF (ST=0) THEN
    DEC TOP
    ST=ST(1)
ELSE
    temp=ST
    ST=EXPONENT(ST)   ;Stored as true exponent
    DEC TOP
    ST=MANTISSA(ST)
ENDIF
```

NPX FLAGS

S	P	U	O	Z	D	I	C_3	C_2	C_1	C_0
*				*[a]	*[a]	*	—	—	*	—

[a] Raised only by the 80287XL and later coprocessors.

FXTRACT

| 11011001 | 11110100 |

TIMING

Operands	x	87/287	287XL	387	486/487
(no operands)	0	27-55[1]	75-83	42-63	16-20

[1] The typical execution time is 50 clocks.

FYL2X

Perform Function y*log₂x

DESCRIPTION FYL2X (y log base 2 of x) calculates the function y*log$_2$x.

X is taken from ST and y is taken from ST(1). The operands must satisfy the inequalities $0 < ST < +\infty$ and $-\infty < ST(1) < +\infty$. FYL2X pops the stack and returns the result to the new ST. Both original operands are destroyed.

The FYL2X function is designed to optimize the calculation of a log to a base other than two. In such a case, the following multiplication is required:

$\log_n x = \log_n 2 * \log_2 x$

See also FYL2XP1.

ALGORITHM
```
ST(1)=ST(1)*log₂(ST)
FPOP
```

NPX FLAGS

S	P	U	O	Z	D	I	C₃	C₂	C₁	C₀
*	*	*[a]	*[a]	*[a]	*[a]	*[a]	—	—	*	—

[a] Raised only by the 80287XL and later coprocessors.

FYL2X

11011001	11110001

TIMING

Operands	x	87/287	287XL	387	486/487
(no operands)	0	900-1100[1]	127-545	99-436	196-329

All times shown assume the arguments are in range.
[1] The typical execution time is 950 clocks.

FYL2XP1

Perform Function y*log₂(x+1)

DESCRIPTION FYL2XP1 (y log base 2 of x plus 1) calculates the function $y*\log_2(x+1)$.

X is taken from ST and y is taken from ST(1). The operands must satisfy the inequalities $-(1-(\sqrt{2}/2)) < ST < (1-(\sqrt{2}/2))$ and $-\infty < ST(1) < +\infty$. FYL2XP1 pops the stack and returns the result to the new ST. Both original operands are destroyed.

The FYL2XP1 function provides greater accuracy than FYL2X in computing the log of a number that is very close to 1. For example, in the argument $x=1+\varepsilon$, where $\varepsilon<<1$, ε providing as the input to the function allows more significant digits to be retained.

FYL2XP1 is typically used when computing compound interest, for example, which requires the calculation of a logarithm of 1.0+n where $0 < n < 0.29$. If 1.0 was added to n, significant digits might be lost. By using FYL2XP1, the result will be as accurate as n to within three units of temporary real precision.

ALGORITHM
$$ST(1)=ST(1)*\log_2(1+ST)$$
FPOP

NPX FLAGS

S	P	U	O	Z	D	I	C₃	C₂	C₁	C₀
*	*	*[a]			*[a]	*[a]	—	—	*	—

[a] Raised only by the 80287XL and later coprocessors.

FYL2XP1

11011001	11111001

TIMING

Operands	x	87/287	287XL	387	486/487
(no operands)	0	700-1000	264-554	210-447	171-326

# APPENDIX C

OPCODE MATRIX

THE OPCODE MATRIX IS A USEFUL TOOL FOR DEBUGGING, DECIPHERING program dumps, or interpreting nonstandard encodings. Three sets of tables are included here for processor one-byte opcodes, two-byte opcodes (where the first byte is 0Fh), and coprocessor opcodes (first byte of D8h-DFh). The following section explains how to use this matrix.

Processor Opcodes

The 8086 and 8088 processors used opcode 0Fh for the POP CS instruction, which was an illegal operation. Beginning with the 80286, this opcode is used as the first byte of a two-byte opcode sequence to access protected mode and advanced instructions. If the first byte of the opcode is 0Fh, use the second byte of the opcode as the key into the two-byte opcode tables. Coprocessor (ESC) instructions begin with opcodes D8h through DFh. Because so many instructions are packed into these opcodes, the instructions are broken out in separate tables. All other opcodes use the one-byte opcode table.

   To look up an opcode, use the first hex digit (high-order 4 bits) of the opcode to select the row of the one-byte opcode matrix. Then use the second hex digit (low-order 4 bits) of the opcode to select the column. If the first byte is 0Fh, use the digits of the second byte as the key into the two-byte opcode matrix. At the intersection of the row and column, you'll find the instruction that corresponds to that opcode. Turn to the instruction references in Appendixes A and B for details of the instruction encodings.

   Some opcodes use the *reg* field of the addressing mode byte as an opcode extension. The entry for these opcodes contains a reference to an instruction group that is broken out in a separate table according to the value of the *reg* field.

   For example, the opcode B4h will be found in the one-byte opcode table as MOV *reg8,immed8* with a register operand of AH. The opcode 0Fh 02h is found in the two-byte opcode table as LAR. The entry for opcode C0h D8h contains a reference to the Group B table. The value of the *reg* field in the second byte (D8h) is 011b, which indicates the RCR instruction. Finally, the opcode D9h E0h is found in the coprocessor tables as FLD1.

These tables contain all documented and undocumented instructions that are provided on Intel, AMD, NEC, Cyrix, and IIT processors and coprocessors. Where appropriate, footnotes to the tables indicate which instructions are valid on particular processors from specific manufacturers. The appearance of an instruction in this matrix does not guarantee that the instruction shown will necessarily be available on future versions or different brands of the processors.

80x86 One-Byte Opcode Map

(first digit = row, second digit = column)

	0	1	2	3	4	5	6	7
0	ADD						PUSH ES	POP ES
1	ADC						PUSH SS	POP SS
2	AND						SEG ES	DAA
3	XOR						SEG SS	AAA
4	INC							
	E/AX	E/CX	E/DX	E/BX	E/SP	E/BP	E/SI	E/DI
5	PUSH							
	E/AX	E/CX	E/DX	E/BX	E/SP	E/BP	E/SI	E/DI
6	PUSHA[2]	POPA[2]	BOUND[2]	ARPL[2]	SEG FS[3] REPNC[11]	SEG GS[3] REPC[11]	Operand Size[3]	Address Size[3]
7	Jcond short							
	JO	JNO	JB JNAE JC	JNB JAE JNC	JZ JE	JNZ JNE	JBE JNA	JNBE JA
8	Arithmetic, Group A				TEST		XCHG	
9	XCHG E/AX with							
	E/AX NOP	E/CX	E/DX	E/BX	E/SP	E/BP	E/SI	E/DI
A	MOV				MOVSB	MOVSW MOVSD	CMPSB	CMPSW CMPSD
B	MOV reg8,immed8							
	AL	CL	DL	BL	AH	CH	DH	BH
C	Shift/Rotate Group B		RETN		LES	LDS	MOV	
D	Shift/Rotate Group B				AAM	AAD	SETALC[2]	XLAT
E	LOOPNE LOOPNZ	LOOPE LOOPZ	LOOP	JCXZ JECXZ[3]	IN		OUT	
F	LOCK		REPNE REPNZ	REP REPE REPZ	HLT	CMC	Unary Group C	

80x86 One-Byte Opcode Map

	8	9	A	B	C	D	E	F
0	OR						PUSH CS	2-Byte opcode[2] POP CS[1]
1	SBB						PUSH DS	POP DS
2	SUB						SEG CS	DAS
3	CMP						SEG DS	AAS
4	DEC							
	E/AX	E/CX	E/DX	E/BX	E/SP	E/BP	E/SI	E/DI
5	POP							
	E/AX	E/CX	E/DX	E/BX	E/SP	E/BP	E/SI	E/DI
6	PUSH[2]	IMUL[2]	PUSH[2]	IMUL[2]	INSB[2]	INSW[2] INSD[3]	OUTSB[2]	OUTSW[2] OUTSD[3]
7	Jcond short							
	JS	JNS	JP JPE	JNP JPO	JL JNGE	JNL JGE	JLE JNG	JNLE JG
8	MOV					LEA	MOV	POP
9	CBW CWDE[3]	CWD CDQ[3]	CALLFAR	WAIT	PUSHF	POPF	SAHF	LAHF
A	TEST		STOSB	STOSW STOSD[3]	LODSB	LODSW LODSD[3]	SCASB	SCASW SCASD[3]
B	MOV							
	E/AX	E/CX	E/DX	E/BX	E/SP	E/BP	E/SI	E/DI
C	ENTER[2]	LEAVE[2]	RETF		INT 3	INT	INTO	IRET
D	ESC (D8h-DFh, see coprocessor opcode matrix)							
E	CALL NEAR	JMP NEAR	JMP FAR	JMP SHORT	IN		OUT	
F	CLC	STC	CLI	STI	CLD	STD	Group D	Group E

80x86 Two-Byte Opcodes

Byte 1 = 0Fh
Byte 2: first digit = row, second digit = column

	0	1	2	3	4	5	6	7
0	Group F	Group G	LAR	LSL		LOADALL[5]	CLTS	LOADALL[3]
1	MOV[9]							
2	MOV[3]						MOV	
3								
4								
5								
6								
7								
8	Jcond near[3]							
	JO	JNO	JB JNAE JG	JNB JAE JNC	JZ JE	JNZ JNE	JBE JNA	JNBE JA
9	SETcond[3]							
	SETO	SETNO	SETB SETNAE SETC	SETNB SETAE SETNC	SETZ SETE	SETNZ SETNE	SETBE SETNA	SETNBE SETA
A	PUSH FS[3]	POP FS[3]		BT[3]	SHLD[3]		CMPXCHG[7]	
							XBTS[6]	IBTS[6]
B	CMPXCHG[8]		LSS[3]	BTR[3]	LFS[3]	LGS[3]	MOVZX[3]	
C	XADD[4]							
D								
E								
F								

80x86 Two-Byte Opcode Map

	8	9	A	B	C	D	E	F
0	INVD[4]	WBINVD[4]						
1								
2								
3								
4								
5								
6								
7								
8	Jcond near[3]							
	JS	JNS	JP JPE	JNP JPO	JL JNGE	JNL JGE	JLE JNG	JNLE JG
9	Setcond[3]							
	SETS	SETNS	SETP SETPE	SETNP SETPO	SETL SETNGE	SETNL SETGE	SETLE SETNG	SETNLE SETG
A	PUSH GS[3]	POP GS[3]		BTS[3]	SHRD[3]			IMUL
B			Group H	BTC[3]	BSF[3]	BSR[3]	MOVSX[3]	
C	BSWAP[4]							
	EAX	ECX	EDX	EBX	ESP	EBP	ESI	EDI
D								
E								
F								

Extended Opcodes Determined by Bits 3–5 of Addressing Mode Byte

mod	bbb	r/m

bbb

Group	000	001	010	011	100	101	110	111
A	ADD	OR	ADC	SBB	AND	SUB	XOR	CMP
B	ROL	ROR	RCL	RCR	SHL SAL	SHR	SAL SHL[10]	SAR
C	TEST	TEST[10]	NOT	NEG	MUL	IMUL	DIV	IDIV
D	INC	DEC						
E	INC	DEC	CALL NEAR	CALL FAR	JMP NEAR	JMP FAR	PUSH	
F	SLDT	STR	LLDT	LTR	VERR	VERW		
G	SGDT	SIDT	LGDT	LIDT	SMSW		LMSW	
H					BT	BTS	BTR	BTC

[1] 8086/8088 only.
[2] NEC V20/V30 and 80286 and later only.
[3] 80386 and later only.
[4] 80486 only.
[5] 80286 only.
[6] 80386DX A-B0 step only.
[7] 80486DX A-step only.
[8] 80486DX B-step and later, all 80486SX.
[9] These opcodes are aliases of one-byte opcodes 88h-8Bh.
[10] Not supported on all 80486DX steps. Use standard opcode.
[11] NEC V20/V30 only.

Coprocessor Opcodes

The coprocessor opcode tables expand the encodings when the first opcode byte is D8h through DFh. To use the tables, turn to the page that indicates the first opcode byte. Use the first hex digit (high-order 4 bits) of the second opcode byte to select the row of the 1-byte opcode matrix. Then use the second hex digit (low-order 4 bits) of the second opcode byte to select the column.

A table entry of ST(i) indicates that the lower 3 bits of the second opcode byte are used as the value for i. The value for i is listed underneath the instruction in the column corresponding to the second digit of the opcode. For example, the opcode D8h D3h corresponds to the instruction FCOM ST(3).

Details on these instructions can be found in the coprocessor instruction reference in Appendix B.

80x87 Opcode Map

Byte 1 = D8h
Byte 2: first digit = row, second digit = column.

	0	1	2	3	4	5	6	7
0,4,8	FADD *real32*							
1,5,9	FCOM *real32*							
2,6,A	FSUB *real32*							
3,7,B	FDIV *real32*							
C	FADD ST(0),ST(i)							
	0	1	2	3	4	5	6	7
D	FCOM ST(i)							
	0	1	2	3	4	5	6	7
E	FSUB ST(0),ST(i)							
	0	1	2	3	4	5	6	7
F	FDIV ST(0),ST(i)							
	0	1	2	3	4	5	6	7

	8	9	A	B	C	D	E	F
0,4,8	FMUL *real32*							
1,5,9	FCOMP *real32*							
2,6,A	FSUBR *real32*							
3,7,B	FDIVR *real32*							
C	FMUL ST(0),ST(i)							
	0	1	2	3	4	5	6	7
D	FCOMP ST(i)							
	0	1	2	3	4	5	6	7
E	FSUBR ST(0),ST(i)							
	0	1	2	3	4	5	6	7
F	FDIVR ST(0),ST(i)							
	0	1	2	3	4	5	6	7

80x87 Opcode Map

Byte 1 = D9h
Byte 2: first digit = row, second digit = column.

	0	1	2	3	4	5	6	7
0,4,8	FLD *real32*							
1,5,9	FST *real32*							
2,6,A	FLDENV							
3,7,B	FSTENV							
C	FLD ST(i)							
	0	1	2	3	4	5	6	7
D	FNOP							
E	FCHS	FABS			FTST	FXAM	FTSTP[1]	
F	F2XM1	FYL2X	FPTAN	FPATAN	FXTRACT	FPREM1[3]	FDECSTP	FINCSTP

	8	9	A	B	C	D	E	F
0,4,8								
1,5,9	FSTP *real32*							
2,6,A	FLDCW							
3,7,B	FSTCW							
C	FXCH ST(i)							
	0	1	2	3	4	5	6	7
D	FSTP[1] ST(i)							
	0	1	2	3	4	5	6	7
E	FLD1	FLDL2T	FLDL2E	FLDPI	FLDLG2	FLDLN2	FLDZ	
F	FPREM	FYL2XP1	FSQRT	FSINCOS[3]	FRNDINT	FSCALE	FSIN[3]	FCOS[3]

Byte 1= DAh
Byte 2: first digit = row, second digit = column.

	0	1	2	3	4	5	6	7
0,4,8	FIADD *int32*							
1,5,9	FICOM *int32*							
2,6,A	FISUB *int32*							
3,7,B	FIDIV *int32*							
C								
D								
E								
F								

	8	9	A	B	C	D	E	F
0,4,8	FIMUL *int32*							
1,5,9	FICOMP *int32*							
2,6,A	FISUBR *int32*							
3,7,B	FIDIVR *int32*							
C								
D								
E		FUCOMPP[3]						
F								

Byte 1 = DBh
Byte 2: first digit = row, second digit = column.

	0	1	2	3	4	5	6	7
0,4,8	FILD int32							
1,5,9	FIST int32							
2,6,A								
3,7,B								
C								
D								
E	FENI[5]	FDISI[5]	FCLEX	FINIT	FSETPM[6]	FRSTPM[4]		
F		F4X4[8]						

	8	9	A	B	C	D	E	F
0,4,8								
1,5,9	FISTP int32							
2,6,A	FLD real80							
3,7,B	FSTP real80							
C								
D								
E	FSBP0[8]		FSBP2[8]	FSBP1[8]	FRINT2[7]			
F								

Byte 1 = DCh
Byte 2: first digit = row, second digit = column.

	0	1	2	3	4	5	6	7
0,4,8	FADD *real64*							
1,5,9	FCOM *real64*							
2,6,A	FSUB *real64*							
3,7,B	FDIV *real64*							
C	FADD ST(i),ST(0)							
D	FCOM[1] ST(i)							
E	FSUBR ST(i),ST(0)							
F	FDIVR ST(i),ST(0)							

	8	9	A	B	C	D	E	F
0,4,8	FMUL *real64*							
1,5,9	FCOMP *real64*							
2,6,A	FSUBR *real64*							
3,7,B	FDIVR *real64*							
C	FMUL ST(i),ST(0)							
D	FCOMP[1] ST(i)							
E	FSUB ST(i),ST(0)							
F	FDIV ST(i),ST(0)							

Byte 1 = DDh
Byte 2: first digit = row, second digit = column.

	0	1	2	3	4	5	6	7
0,4,8	FLD real64							
1,5,9	FST real64							
2,6,A	FRSTOR							
3,7,B	FSAVE							
C	FFREE ST(i)							
	0	1	2	3	4	5	6	7
D	FST ST(i)							
	0	1	2	3	4	5	6	7
E	FUCOM[3] ST(i)							
	0	1	2	3	4	5	6	7
F								

	8	9	A	B	C	D	E	F
0,4,8								
1,5,9	FSTP real64							
2,6,A								
3,7,B	FSTSW							
C	FXCH[1] ST(i)							
	0	1	2	3	4	5	6	7
D	FSTP ST(i)							
	0	1	2	3	4	5	6	7
E	FUCOMP[3] ST(i)							
	0	1	2	3	4	5	6	7
F					FRICHOP[7]			

Byte 1 = DEh
Byte 2: first digit = row, second digit = column.

	0	1	2	3	4	5	6	7
0,4,8	FIADD *int16*							
1,5,9	FICOM *int16*							
2,6,A	FISUB *int16*							
3,7,B	FIDIV *int16*							
C	FADDP ST(i),ST(0)							
	0	1	2	3	4	5	6	7
D	FCOMP[1] ST(i)							
	0	1	2	3	4	5	6	7
E	FSUBRP ST(i),ST(0)							
	0	1	2	3	4	5	6	7
F	FDIVRP ST(i),ST(0)							
	0	1	2	3	4	5	6	7

	8	9	A	B	C	D	E	F
0,4,8	FIMUL *int16*							
1,5,9	FICOMP *int16*							
2,6,A	FISUBR *int16*							
3,7,B	FIDIVR *int16*							
C	FMULP ST(i),ST(0)							
	0	1	2	3	4	5	6	7
D		FCOMPP						
E	FSUBP ST(i),ST(0)							
	0	1	2	3	4	5	6	7
F	FDIVP ST(i),ST(0)							
	0	1	2	3	4	5	6	7

Byte 1 = DFh
Byte 2: first digit = row, second digit = column.

	0	1	2	3	4	5	6	7
0,4,8	FILD *int16*							
1,5,9	FIST *int16*							
2,6,A	FBLD *bcd80*							
3,7,B	FBSTP *bcd80*							
C	FFREEP[1] ST(i)							
	0	1	2	3	4	5	6	7
D	FSTP[1] ST(i)							
	0	1	2	3	4	5	6	7
E	FSTSWAX[2]							
F								

	8	9	A	B	C	D	E	F
0,4,8								
1,5,9	FISTP *int16*							
2,6,A	FILD *int64*							
3,7,B	FST *int64*							
C	FXCH[1] ST(i)							
	0	1	2	3	4	5	6	7
D	FSTP[1] ST(i)							
	0	1	2	3	4	5	6	7
E								
F					FRINEAR[7]			

[1] This encoding is not normally generated by assemblers and compilers.
[2] 80287 only.
[3] 80287XL, 80387 and later.
[4] Recognized on the 80287XL only.
[5] Ignored on 80287 and later.
[6] Ignored on 80387 and later.
[7] Cyrix Fasmath EMC87 only.
[8] IIT coprocessors only.

APPENDIX D
ADDITIONAL PROGRAMMING LITERATURE AND PRODUCTS

THIS APPENDIX PROVIDES RESOURCES FOR MANUALS, DATA SHEETS, LITERATURE, and software and hardware products related to programming.

OEM Literature and Specification Sheets

Intel publishes the following data sheets and reference manuals on their microprocessor products. Inquiries should be directed to:

Intel Corp.
Literature Sales
P.O. Box 58130
Santa Clara, CA 95052-8130
800-548-4725

Order Number	Title
240487	8086/8088 User's Manual, Programmer's and Hardware Reference
210253	80286 High Performance Microprocessor with Memory Management and Protection (Data Sheet)
210498	80286 and 80287 Programmer's Reference Manual
210760	80286 Hardware Reference Manual
210920	80287 80-bit HMOS Numeric Processor Extension (Data Sheet) (No longer in print.)
290376	80287XL/XLT CHMOS III Math Coprocessor (Data Sheet)
231630	386DX Microprocessor, High Performance 32-bit CHMOS Microprocessor with Integrated Memory Management (Data Sheet)
230985	386DX Programmer's Reference Manual
231732	386DX Microprocessor Hardware Reference Manual
240448	387DX Math Coprocessor (Data Sheet)
231917	387DX User's Manual, Programmer's Reference

Order Number	Title
240187	386SX Microprocessor (Data Sheet)
240331	386SX Microprocessor Programmer's Reference Manual
240332	386SX Microprocessor Hardware Reference Manual
240440	i486 Microprocessor (Data Sheet)
240486	i486 Microprocessor Programmer's Reference Manual
240552	i486 Microprocessor Hardware Reference Manual
240950	486SX Microprocessor / 487SX Math Coprocessor (Data Sheet)

Additional Programming Literature

Additional literature on compatible processors and coprocessors may be obtained from the following manufacturers:

Advanced Micro Devices (AMD) Inc.
901 Thompson Place
P.O. Box 3453
Sunnyvale, CA 94088
408-732-2400

Cyrix Corp.
2703 North Central Expressway
Richardson, TX 75080
800-848-2979

Integrated Information Technology (IIT) Inc.
2445 Mission College Blvd.
Santa Clara, CA 95054
800-832-0770

Noteworthy Software and Hardware Products

PDQ and QuickPak Professional Programming Tools
Crescent Software, Inc.
32 Seventy Acres
West Redding, CT 06896
203-438-5300

Lim-Sim Memory Manager
Larsen Computing
1556 Halford Avenue #142
Santa Clara, CA 95051
408-737-0627

Soft-Ice 386/486 Software Debugger
NuMega Technologies, Inc.
P.O. Box 7780
Nashua, NH 03060-7780
603-888-2386

Periscope Hardware and Software Debugging Tools
The Periscope Company, Inc.
1197 Peachtree St.
Plaza Level
Atlanta, GA 30361
404-875-8080

386Max and BlueMax Memory Managers
Qualitas, Inc.
8314 Thoreau Drive
Bethesda, MD 20817
301-907-7420

Sourcer Disassembler
V Communications, Inc.
4320 Stevens Creek Blvd.
Suite 275
San Jose, CA 95129
408-296-4224

≣ INDEX